Praise for Malcolm Byrne's *Iran-Contra*

"At last, the Reagan administration's Iran-Contra affair has a comprehensive history worthy of the scandal which, if the system had worked, should have landed many senior White House officials in the slammer. Byrne has told this complex story in brilliant fashion, from the motives of the President's men, to the follies as the unconstitutional plot was carried out, to the inability of Congress to do the right thing and, finally, to the futility of the independent inquiry whose work ended in a whimper."

—Seymour M. Hersh, author of *Chain of Command: The Road from 9/11 to Abu Ghraib*

"A remarkable book about a remarkable scandal that shook American politics more than a quarter-century ago. Byrne's riveting account is not only good history and an exciting tale of espionage and White House intrigue; it is a warning about the excesses of secrecy and partisanship in American foreign policy."

—Bruce Riedel, author of *The Search for Al Qaeda: Its Leadership, Ideology, and Future*

"A thrilling account of secrecy, connivance, and manipulation in the dark corridors of power in Washington and Tehran. The cast of characters—Casey, Rafsanjani, North, Ghorbanifar, and others—remind one of Sidney Greenstreet and Peter Lorre in *The Maltese Falcon*. By digging into the history of the Iran-Contra affair, Malcolm Byrne shows us how much unchecked powers can damage the security of our nations. A truly fascinating book."

—Maziar Bahari, author of *Then They Came for Me*

"Reopens the vitally important argument over Ronald Reagan's presidency—particularly, as Byrne asserts with his use of many newly available documents, that Reagan was not passive, but 'the driving force' behind that unconstitutional and embarrassing scheme."

—Walter LaFeber, author of *America, Russia, and the Cold War, 1945–2006*

"The Iran-Contra affair transformed U.S. foreign policy in the Persian Gulf. Moreover, it was not a rogue affair by a few misguided members of the National Security Council. As Byrne demonstrates in this meticulously documented reconstruction, it was a presidential initiative with President Reagan engaged at every stage. All other accounts of this tragic episode in American foreign policy must be measured against this authoritative narrative."

—Gary Sick, Columbia University, Member of the National Security Council staff during the presidencies of Ford, Carter and Reagan

"The definitive account of a Washington scandal that was as bizarre as it was important. Byrne has reconstructed events and decisions that led a handful of bureaucrats in the Reagan administration to tie America's fate to jungle fighters in Nicaragua, radical mullahs in Iran, and ambitious geo-strategists in Israel. This book not only traces their twisted paths, but provides as good an answer as we are likely to get to the question, 'What could they possibly have been thinking?'"

—Stephen Kinzer, author of *The Brothers: John Foster Dulles, Allen Dulles, and Their Secret World War*

"An impressive, compelling, and revelatory work. Byrne meticulously lays out the evidence that puts President Reagan at the heart of the decision-making process that led to the scandal and its attempted cover-up. Scholars will appreciate this work's rigor and sophistication; readers of all kinds will be shocked by Byrne's well-told tale of intrigue, covert operations, and an American foreign policy debacle that reverberated around the world."

—David Farber, author of *Taken Hostage: The Iran Hostage Crisis and America's First Encounter with Radical Islam*

"Byrne reaches behind redactions to reveal the most serious usurpation of power imaginable, where officials put political and policy interests ahead of legal and constitutional restraints. His book is a parable for the security scandals of today and should be read by experts and concerned citizens alike."

—John Prados, author of *The Family Jewels, the CIA, Secrecy, and Presidential Power*

"In this outstanding and meticulously researched book, Malcolm Byrne knits together two disastrous foreign policy initiatives of Ronald Reagan's second term. The decision to support the Nicaraguan Contras and to sell arms to Iran to secure the release of U.S. hostages in the Middle East violated U.S. law and every public assurance given to Congress and the U.S. public. These episodes shared an underlying current of ideological zealotry that almost sank the Reagan presidency. As Byrne points out, the failure of the Iran-Contra scandal to lead to greater accountability cleared a path for continuing excesses in the name of national security."

—Cynthia J. Arnson, Director, Latin American Program, Woodrow Wilson International Center for Scholars

"This provocative book should be read as the definitive volume on the Iran-Contra scandal and its impact on the United States, the Middle East and Central America."

—Farideh Farhi, author of *States and Urban-Based Revolutions: Iran and Nicaragua*

Iran-Contra

Iran-Contra
Reagan's Scandal and the Unchecked Abuse of Presidential Power

Malcolm Byrne

Foreword by
Bruce Riedel

 University Press of Kansas

Published by the University Press of Kansas (Lawrence,
Kansas 66045), which was organized by the Kansas
Board of Regents and is operated and funded by
Emporia State University, Fort Hays State University,
Kansas State University, Pittsburg State University, the
University of Kansas, and Wichita State University

Library of Congress Cataloging-in-Publication Data

Byrne, Malcolm.
Iran-Contra : Reagan's scandal and the unchecked
abuse of presidential power / Malcolm Byrne ; foreword
by Bruce Riedel.
pages cm
Includes bibliographical references and index.
ISBN 978-0-7006-1991-7 (hardback : acid-free paper)
1. Iran-Contra Affair, 1985–1990. 2. Reagan, Ronald.
3. Scandals—United States—History—20th century. 4.
Power (Social sciences)—United States—History—20th
century. 5. Executive power—United States—History—
20th century. 6. Political corruption—United States—
History—20th century. 7. United States—Politics and
government—1981–1989. I. Title.
E876.B97 2014
320.97309048—dc23
2014014486

British Library Cataloguing-in-Publication Data is
available.

Printed in the United States of America

10 9 8 7 6 5 4 3 2 1

The paper used in this publication is recycled and
contains 30 percent postconsumer waste. It is acid free
and meets the minimum requirements of the American
National Standard for Permanence of Paper for Printed
Library Materials Z39.48-1992.

For Leila

Contents

Foreword

This is a remarkable book about a remarkable scandal that shook U.S. politics a quarter century ago. The Iran-Contra scandal gravely damaged U.S. national security interests in the late 1980s, but it has been largely forgotten by most U.S. citizens. The intrigues of President Ronald Reagan's spymaster, William Casey, and two of Reagan's national security advisors, Robert McFarlane and John Poindexter, were investigated by a presidential commission, the Congress, and an independent counsel, each of which apportioned blame. A few individuals, most notably Secretary of Defense Caspar Weinberger, were indicted for, convicted of, or pled guilty to misconduct and lying to cover up the scandal. President George H. W. Bush pardoned several of them in the closing days of his administration. Casey died before he could be summoned to testify. Reagan's role in the affair was downplayed, even excused because of his poor health, and gradually forgotten. In time Reagan became an iconic figure, credited by many as one of the great presidents of the twentieth century.

This book is based on years of meticulous research in declassified documents, diaries of senior officials including then Vice President Bush, and interviews. It explores and explains in more depth and texture than ever before the two intelligence operations that created the scandal. Malcolm Byrne has exposed the myths that have endured for decades about the scandal, and he has helped readers understand exactly why Reagan was willing to break the law and sell arms to a deadly enemy of the United States, Iran, just a few years after it held dozens of U.S. diplomats hostage.

This book demonstrates that rather than being on the margin of the intelligence operations in Central America and the Middle East that led to Iran-Contra, Reagan was at their center. He drove the policy process toward a secret opening with Iran because he was obsessed with freeing U.S. hostages taken by Iran's allies in Lebanon. Reagan's decisions, not some rogue operation run by Oliver North, led to the United States selling arms to Iran in return for promises, never entirely fulfilled, to free the hostages. Vice President Bush was also deeply involved in the policy process and kept fully informed on the efforts to free the hostages.

I was a CIA officer serving in the Middle East in the 1980s. The CIA officers killed by Iran's terrorists in Beirut, including Bob Ames and seven of his colleagues, were my friends. The CIA chief in Beirut, William Buckley, who was kidnapped, tortured, and murdered, was also a friend. I still remember the terrible days when Ames was killed and Buckley was taken hostage.

The United States was at war with Iran and its ally, Hezbollah, in the 1980s, at least in a clandestine war. In that war, the idea of trading arms for hostages with your enemy was bizarre from the start. Within the government, the entire project was kept carefully compartmentalized in large part to avoid expert scrutiny, inside the government and outside, of the tortured assumptions underlying the policy. Then it was implemented over the objections of the secretary of state and secretary of defense. Implementation was often done in a "keystone kops," amateurish fashion. Bank accounts were misrecorded, deadlines ignored, and red lines blurred. Byrne's riveting account reveals all the ugly details along with those responsible.

Casey and Reagan believed they had a valuable Iranian partner in a man who failed catastrophically every lie detector test he was administered. Casey's senior advisors all told him the Iranian was a liar; he ignored their judgment and went ahead recklessly. Iran-Contra is a case study in how not to do foreign intelligence operations.

It is also a case study in how not to investigate scandal in the White House. The independent commission headed by Sen. John Tower went out of its way to excuse Reagan from responsibility and to put the blame on an out-of-control National Security Council staff. The congressional investigation produced a more accurate report but also avoided the issue of whether the president's conduct warranted impeachment. The independent counsel took years to bring cases to trial. The redeeming virtue of the investigations, however, was they brought to light the mountains of documents and diaries this book uses to tell the story.

Behind the scenes Reagan had a crucial and enthusiastic partner in Israel. Israeli leaders, including Shimon Peres, desperately wanted to restore the cozy relationship Israel had with Iran before the shah was toppled, when the two states were aligned in a secret entente. Peres and his colleagues refused to believe the ayatollahs would not sooner or later come back to partnering with Israel, even though their professional intelligence officers told them this was a fantasy. Instead Israel became Iran's critical arms supplier in the Iran-Iraq War and enticed the United States into joining it in the madness. U.S. diplomats and spies were told to turn a blind eye to Israeli arms shipments to Iran even before Reagan got into his own arms deals.

The congressional investigation avoided the Israeli angle as much as possible. So did the Tower Report and the independent counsel—it was too hot to handle. Here again this book sets the record straight. Israel helped Ayatollah Khomeini survive the Iran-Iraq War and persuaded Reagan to arm the Iranian regime. How deeply ironic it all seems today when Israel is Iran's foremost enemy.

There are clear lessons to be learned in this book about intelligence operations and scandal. Congressional oversight is a good thing; it can help prevent disaster by exposing misconduct. But it can be undercut by partisan politics all too easily. Disdain for Congress and unquestioning loyalty to the president, an all-too-common feature of many White House staffs, can produce a bunker mentality in which the country's best interests are lost in pursuit of "protecting" the president.

Compartmentalizing delicate and sensitive intelligence operations is also a good thing if done with care. But if compartmentalization becomes a means to keep a bad idea or an illegal program from exposure, then it is a trap that will come to haunt the nation.

The Iran-Contra affair had another legacy. Many of those involved in the 1980s policies or their investigation went on to play a key role in the administration of George W. Bush after 2000. Vice President Dick Cheney, for example, had been one of the members of Congress investigating the scandal in 1987. The abuse of power that lay at the heart of Iran-Contra was for these players only the legitimate use of executive powers. Many of the lies that led to Iran-Contra would be models for the deceptions that led to the misguided U.S. war on Iraq in 2003.

Malcolm Byrne's book is not only good history and an exciting tale of espionage and White House intrigue; it is a warning about the excesses of secrecy and partisanship in U.S. foreign policy. Too often we have been too eager to look forward after scandal breaks, not backward, and consequently have ignored the lessons of past abuses of power. This book offers a rewarding look backward, with lessons for looking forward.

Bruce Riedel

Preface: Settings for the Scandal

The Iran-Contra scandal occurred as the result of a particular—though by no means unique—mix of historical, political, institutional, and personal factors. The personalities—starting with President Ronald Reagan—are critical to the story. But it is equally useful to have a sense of the historical and political context of the affair prior to the Reagan administration entering office in January 1981: the key institutions of the national security establishment, the state of relations between the executive and legislative branches, the tense global environment, and finally Reagan's political outlook upon becoming the country's fortieth president. Each of these elements offers helpful context for understanding the origins, nature, and significance of the affair.

Laying the Institutional Foundations

The cold war established the framework for much of U.S. foreign policy from before the end of World War II at least until the end of the Reagan presidency. The "twilight struggle" particularly affected the development of U.S. national security institutions. Recognizing the emergence of the communist menace, Congress resolved to give the president tools to fend off the new threat. The legislative centerpiece of this concept was the National Security Act of 1947, which created several major entities: a unified military establishment (soon to be the Department of Defense), the Central Intelligence Agency (CIA), and the National Security Council (NSC). Each of these institutions helped shape the U.S. approach to the rest of the world. They also contributed to the bureaucratic and political dynamics that underlay Iran-Contra.

The Defense Department was not originally intended to play the lead in foreign policy, but its influence unsurprisingly swelled wherever U.S. military forces came into play, from the central European theater to regional conflicts such as the Korean and Vietnam Wars. U.S. military advisors were active across the third world, including in Iran during the time of the shah and in Central America for the latter half of the twentieth century. Their influence came directly into play during both the Iran and Contra episodes.

The CIA, an outgrowth of the Office of Strategic Services (OSS), was initially an intelligence-gathering and analysis organization with the core aim of preventing another Pearl Harbor. Within a year, President Harry Truman added to the agency a covert operations capability that could confront the Soviet camp by means that were officially deniable and raised less risk of sparking open superpower conflict. Early CIA operations included planting propaganda and supporting armed resistance groups inside the communist bloc, which usually backfired badly. Soon, agency operatives were orchestrating clandestine political and paramilitary activities in Italy, France, Iran, Guatemala, and other countries. Reagan, like most of his predecessors, believed covert capability offered invaluable flexibility, not least on the domestic political front.

The NSC was envisioned as an advisory body for the president and consisted principally of the president himself, the vice president, and the secretaries of state and defense. Subsequent administrations added advisors, such as the chair of the Joint Chiefs of Staff, and temporary members. The NSC staff at first comprised just two permanent professionals with fewer than two dozen total staff, including clerical support, provisionally assigned from elsewhere.[1] Over time, presidents recognized the bureaucratic efficiencies and political benefits of giving the NSC staff assignments that would normally be within the purview of other agencies—whose personnel might not feel the same undivided loyalty to the president, as opposed to an agency head, that an NSC staffer would.

In 1964, President Lyndon Johnson set a precedent by sending his advisor, McGeorge Bundy, to Vietnam as a personal envoy. President Richard Nixon granted Henry Kissinger a starring role in White House diplomacy with China in the early 1970s, and President Jimmy Carter's advisor, Zbigniew Brzezinski, coveted a similar part. With presidential approval, both Kissinger and Brzezinski used the NSC apparatus to carry out secret initiatives outside normal channels. These precedents—usually occurring at the direct expense of the Department of State as the agency nominally in charge of U.S. foreign policy—opened the way for Reagan to authorize the NSC staff to take on more extensive operational activities, including but not solely during Iran-Contra.

Each of these new institutions grew steadily in size (with DOD and CIA personnel levels reaching into the thousands and budgets in the billions of dollars) as presidents sought expanded analytical and operational capacities along with more policy flexibility—typically in the name of confronting the communist threat. One of the tools of choice the executive branch exploited to impose control over these activities was official secrecy. The system of classifying national security information, of which modern usage in the United States dates to the 1940s, was intended to prevent sensitive data from falling into enemy hands. However, its political value at home was recognized early on. Gen. Leslie Groves, who directed the Manhattan Project during World War II, relied on the classification system to "keep knowledge from those who would interfere directly or indirectly with the progress of the work." Groves's target was not foreign agents but the U.S. government—"Congress and various executive branch offices."[2] The architects of Iran-Contra fully embraced this mind-set, encouraged by the

Reagan administration's full-bore rollback of Carter's secrecy reforms and pronounced resistance to outside scrutiny of its national security policy.

Congress Resurgent

Through the late 1950s, Congress either acquiesced in executive branch expectations for more power and flexibility or was disregarded. Although some members showed concern over the unchecked power of a secret intelligence agency, they were usually swept aside by the majority view that the executive branch should have broad authority to confront the dangers facing U.S. security.[3]

Beginning in the early 1960s, the cold war consensus began to fray. The 1961 Bay of Pigs failure damaged U.S. standing and hurt the reputation of the CIA in the Kennedy White House. In 1965, the Johnson administration committed U.S. troops heavily to the Vietnam War, which within a few years stood as the most divisive social issue in the United States since the Civil War. The subsequent disclosure that in 1964 Johnson had manipulated Congress into passing the Tonkin Gulf Resolution—a major springboard to expanded U.S. involvement in the war—undercut popular confidence in Washington, as did other war-related events such as the Nixon administration's secret bombing of Cambodia.

The 1970s brought more revelations that generated cleavages in public trust in government. The Watergate scandal and exposés of CIA abuses at home and abroad raised alarms about an "imperial presidency," involvement in dubious wars, cozy relations with dictators, and the actions of rogue intelligence agencies. Meanwhile, global changes, such as the widening split between China and the USSR and the Nixon administration's pursuit of better relations with both communist giants, led to a general downgrading of the gravity of the international Marxist threat.

Congress reacted in three ways to these developments, reversing decades of relative passivity: its members launched in-depth investigations into intelligence community and presidential abuses of power, enacted sweeping statutes affecting executive branch independence, and reformed their own institution. In 1975, Sen. Frank Church (D-Idaho) and Rep. Otis Pike (D-N.Y.) opened inquiries into CIA abuses that exposed shocking secrets about Washington's attempts to assassinate foreign leaders, subvert other governments, and spy on U.S. citizens. The Church Committee published fourteen reports with unprecedented detail about the covert side of U.S. policy. The Pike Committee did not publish its final report, but a draft leaked to the media, prompting outrage from the intelligence community.

The public indignation following these revelations helped trigger far-reaching legislation. The War Powers Resolution of 1973 reasserted the role of Congress in setting limits for U.S. engagement in foreign conflicts. In 1974, the Hughes-Ryan Amendment to the Foreign Assistance Act of 1961 required explicit presidential approval of any CIA covert operation and "timely" notification of Congress. A year later, the Clark Amendment barred funding for the CIA's covert action program in Angola, an early assertion of the power of the purse to justify the congressional role in the policy process. In 1976, the Arms Export Control Act (AECA) required congressional approval of weapons shipments abroad and specifically prohibited sales to supporters of terrorism. The first Intelligence Authorization Act, passed in 1978, gave Congress budgetary control over the intelligence community. Three years later, a new version of the act underscored the need to keep the legislative branch "fully and currently informed" about clandestine activities. These were groundbreaking changes that dramatically enhanced the role of lawmakers in limiting and guiding executive branch activities in foreign, military, and intelligence policies.

The reform mood sweeping the electorate did not exempt Congress. Prodded by new members, both chambers overhauled the seniority system, cut back on secret deliberations, and reduced hierarchical committee structures. The number of subcommittees multiplied, staff sizes mushroomed, and the scope and frequency of oversight hearings grew correspondingly. All of these changes brought greater public scrutiny to executive branch activities and raised the public profiles of individual members of Congress. In 1976 and 1977, the Senate and House underscored the priority of greater accountability from the intelligence community by establishing separate permanent select committees for the purpose. Previously the Armed Services Committees had borne the responsibility.

The groundswell to define a more equal congressional role in foreign policy at the expense of traditional presidential control generated significant pushback—from conservatives who saw the changes as part of the liberal post-Vietnam assault on the "mainstream"; from the Republican Party, which charged the principal targets had been GOP occupants of the White House; and from advocates of strong presidential powers. Among the last grouping were most senior officials of the Reagan administration. A revealing incident involved James Baker, Reagan's first chief of staff, who received pointed advice on the subject from then Rep. Richard B. Cheney (R-Wyo.) shortly after the 1980 election. Cheney had held Baker's position under President Gerald Ford. (He would become an influential defender of the president in the aftermath of the Iran-Contra scandal—and eventually vice president of the United States.) Baker took note of Cheney's firm views on the impact of recent congressional activism: "Pres. seriously weakened in recent yrs. Restore power [and] auth to Exec. Branch—Need strong ldrship." In the margin, Baker sketched six stars for emphasis and wrote: "Central theme we ought to push."[4] Another strong advocate of presidential primacy was Attorney General Edwin Meese III, who would promote the concept of the "unitary executive," claiming the presidency to be the sole repository of executive authority and attempts by Congress or the courts to check its exercise by their nature unconstitutional.[5] The idea of unfettered presidential power had great appeal for Reagan as well.

The International Setting

In the late 1970s, global developments presented a series of threats to the United States, according to Reagan and his fellow conservatives. Starting with the collapse of South Vietnam in 1975, a string of nationalist, leftist, or communist takeovers in Cambodia, Chile, the Horn of Africa, Angola, Yemen, and Grenada confirmed for them a dangerous decline of U.S. influence and a corresponding surge in Soviet power across the third world. Their sense of crisis peaked in 1979. In Iran and Nicaragua, revolutions ousted long-standing U.S. allies, substituting regimes assumed to be hostile to the United States. Most ominously, the Soviet invasion of Afghanistan over Christmas seemed irrefutable proof of Moscow's designs to dominate the Persian Gulf.

The upheavals in Iran and Nicaragua were particularly worrisome for the incoming Reagan administration. The United States had thrown its support behind Shah Mohammad Reza Pahlavi since World War II. In 1953, the CIA and Britain's MI-6 jointly organized the ouster of the country's prime minister, Mohammad Mosaddeq, restoring the shah to unchallenged rule. In the early 1970s, the Nixon administration gave the shah carte blanche to stock his arsenals with high-tech U.S. weaponry in return for his commitment to help block Soviet penetration of the petroleum-rich Persian Gulf. Iran's own oil wealth and proximity to the USSR made its protection from Soviet domination a vital U.S. interest. The ability to monitor Soviet missile and arms control developments from U.S. electronic tracking stations in the Alborz Mountains added to Iran's strategic value. Over the years, the shah's authoritarianism incited popular discontent he was ultimately unable to control. On January 16, 1979, he fled the country. Two weeks later, the exiled religious leader Ayatollah Ruhollah Khomeini, a severe critic of the U.S. presence in Iran, returned to take de facto control of the country.

The loss of such a crucial ally represented a major cold war defeat, although many U.S. analysts missed a critical point. The overthrow of the shah and the rise of Khomeini had nothing to do with the U.S.-Soviet conflict. The roots of the Iranian revolution were part of the new phenomenon of political Islam. Policy makers in Washington knew little about Islam and virtually nothing about Iran's clerical establishment, leaving them unprepared to deal with the new regime.[6] This would have repercussions for the Reagan administration's later arms-for-hostages initiative, but in the immediate term the assumption that Washington's loss was Moscow's gain marked a devastating turn for Carter's political standing at home.

A few months later, a further shock to U.S. interests occurred in Nicaragua. Since the mid-nineteenth century, Washington had involved itself directly in the political affairs of the country, reflecting prevailing U.S. presumptions about the region dating to the Monroe Doctrine. U.S. Marines occupied Nicaragua from 1912–1933, after which the United States threw its support behind two generations of right-wing dictators, abetting their control of the country from 1936 until 1979. Members of the ruling Somoza family were valued U.S. clients and enthusiastic collaborators in the cold war, opposing leftists and nationalists in the region and aiding the CIA-orchestrated overthrow of Jacobo Arbenz of Guatemala in 1954 and the Bay of Pigs invasion in 1961. Like Iran under the shah, Nicaragua experienced growing social discontent in the 1970s (brought to a peak by a major 1972 earthquake) that the increasingly corrupt government of Anastasio Somoza Debayle often used force to suppress. By 1979, political opposition had increased to threatening proportions, and Carter administration officials—as they did over the shah—debated whether to back Somoza or accept the inevitability of revolution. After Washington withdrew its support, Somoza fled the country on July 17, two days ahead of the triumphant arrival in the capital of the Sandinista National Liberation Front (FSLN). Few in Washington failed to notice the FSLN had taken its name from the revolutionary Augusto César Sandino, leader of Nicaragua's resistance against U.S. occupation half a century earlier.

Further developments in Iran and Afghanistan in late 1979 raised even deeper concerns for Washington. On November 4, crowds of Iranians, responding to the U.S. decision to admit the ailing shah for medical treatment, overran the U.S. embassy in Tehran, taking its occupants hostage for the next 444 days. The country's clerical leaders had not ordered the assault. A group of students had conceived it, later invoking their fear the United States might attempt another coup as in 1953. However, Khomeini moved quickly to take ownership of the event. The United States accordingly labeled the seizure an act of state terrorism, and the two countries' relations hardened into enmity.

Fewer than eight weeks later, Soviet forces invaded Afghanistan, sending alarms throughout the West over what many feared was an act of naked aggression aimed at seizing control of the Persian Gulf. Revelations from Soviet archives after the collapse of the USSR would show that the Kremlin's aging rulers, locked in their own cold war mind-set, had in fact lashed out reflexively at threats they perceived to Soviet control of Afghanistan, prompted, according to their reasoning, by Washington's need to compensate for its loss of Iran. The mainly defensive nature of the invasion was not at all apparent to most U.S. or Western observers.[7] The Soviets' reckless and panicked move crystalized fears they were preparing to fulfill Russia's historic quest for warm-water ports with only a defenseless Iran in the way.[8]

Carter's final humiliation came in spring 1980. With yellow ribbons symbolizing support for the hostages across the country, he succumbed to the pressure and ordered a highly risky rescue mission in late April. A sandstorm at a rendezvous point in the Iranian desert caused a helicopter and a transport plane to collide, killing eight U.S. service members. Televised images of the wreckage and charred bodies, along with photos of blindfolded hostages from the November 1979 embassy takeover, came to epitomize the image of U.S. impotence in the region.

Each of these crises reinforced in President Reagan a sense of the dangers facing the United States and of his mandate to confront them. He spoke frequently about the obligation to support allies such as the shah and Somoza and rejected Carter's expressed intention to cut U.S. backing to right-wing dictators. Similarly, he felt passionately about standing by "freedom fighters" such as UNITA guerrillas in Angola and condemned previous presidents for abandoning anticommunist forces in the third world, most egregiously South Vietnam. The Iran hostage saga poisoned his views of that country's revolutionary leaders—as it did for virtually all U.S. citizens. The tragedy also brought home to him the full impact of terrorism in both its human—and electoral—dimensions. He resolved never to leave himself vulnerable in the way Carter had.

In the area of domestic politics, Reagan was viscerally opposed to congressional attempts to address the "imperial presidency" in the years just prior to his election. He thought the reforms of the 1970s were an unjustifiable incursion on executive branch prerogatives that would shackle the presidency and endanger the United States in its cold war struggle against the Soviet Union. The perception that those changes reflected liberal post-Vietnam and post-Watergate sensibilities and mostly targeted a previous Republican president added a potent partisan dimension to the contest. As he and his advisors pondered how to advance their controversial objectives in Iran and Nicaragua in the mid-1980s, their methods turned out to matter far less than their results. Despite his reputation as an ideologue, Reagan showed in the course of both covert programs he was fully prepared to follow the most direct path to his goals. Unfortunately, this included a marked readiness to cut political and legal corners, one of the core ingredients of the Iran-Contra affair.

Acknowledgments

When the Iran-Contra scandal broke in November 1986, I was newly employed at the nongovernmental National Security Archive, where my colleagues had already been systematically tracking U.S. activities in Iran and Nicaragua. Therefore, when Ronald Reagan and Edwin Meese disclosed the Iran-Contra connection that same month, we already had a strong foundation of investigative materials to help document what had been taking place in secret for the previous several years. The archive's principal founder and first director, Scott Armstrong, led the efforts to acquire those materials and made the scandal a top priority for the organization, having recognized its historical significance and potential as a tool to explain so many things about our government—how it works and how miserably it can fail. His foresight, creative energy, and encouragement of all of us on staff led to several historiographical breakthroughs. He also was chiefly responsible for encouraging me to pursue this extraordinary story, one of many things for which I am grateful to him.

The archive has been home to several true experts on the Iran-Contra scandal who could easily have written their own books on the subject, if not for competing demands and interests. Over the years, I benefited tremendously from the knowledge, insights, and support of Tom Blanton, Peter Kornbluh, Jim Hershberg, and Jeff Nason, among many others. As I began to focus more intently—if episodically—on this book, I had further help with documents and expertise from other fellow Archivistas, in particular Joyce Battle, Bill Burr, John Prados, Jeff Richelson, and Svetlana Savranskaya. Catherine Nielsen, Gregg Domber, Roger Strother, and Farrah Hassen provided research at various points. Kian Byrne contributed valuable research and editorial assistance. Sue Bechtel, Mary Burroughs, and Mary Curry were of great help in many other ways.

Outside the archive, a very long list of colleagues and friends extended similar backing. Journalist-authors Seymour Hersh, Robert Parry, Patrick Tyler, and Douglas Valentine generously shared documents and research materials with me. I gained a much better understanding of Contra matters from several authorities, including Cindy Arnson, John Dinges, Peter Kornbluh, Robert Pastor, Anthony Quainton, and an unnamed former senior Contra. Iran was a greater challenge because of its relative inaccessibility. Nevertheless, a large number of people offered documents, translations, and general expertise on U.S.-Iranian relations—among them Manuchehr Afzal, Ahmad Ahmadi, Maziar Bahari, Hussein Banai, George Cave, Haleh Esfandiari, Farideh Farhi, Mark Gasiorowski, Nasser Hadian, Mehdi Jedinia, Bijan Khajehpour, Reza Malek-Madani, Hossein

Mousavian, Peyman Pejman, Mahsa Rouhi, Hadi Semati, Gary Sick, Barbara Slavin, and several Iranian officials who made themselves surprisingly available.

My research on Israel's role in the affair was aided significantly by advice and contacts provided by Dmitry Adamsky, Yossi Alpher, Philip Brenner, Zach Levey, and Yoram Peri. Several friends from Central Europe and the former Soviet Union were generous with their help in exploring, through archival research and translations, the cold war backdrop to Iran-Contra: Jordan Baev, Csaba Bekes, Kostadin Grozev, Jamil Hasanli, Wanda Jarzȧbek, Gusztáv Kecskés, Jozsef Litkei, and Oldrich Tůma. Others to thank in this category are Małgorzata Gnoińska, Roland Popp, Bernd Schaefer, and Douglas Selvage. Additional research and translation assistance with German-language materials came from Carolina Dahl.

In recent years, I have spent many hours at the National Archives and Records Administration in College Park, Maryland, and at the Ronald Reagan Presidential Library in Simi Valley, California, where the archivists gave freely of their time and knowledge. A special word of thanks is due to the Freedom of Information Act (FOIA) professionals throughout the U.S. government who work steadily to help uncover our hidden history.

In the course of this project, a very pleasant and informative interlude was my collaboration on a study of the United States and Iran with partners John Tirman, Jim Blight, janet Lang, Hussein Banai, Mahsa Rouhi, and David Weinberg. Our discoveries about the Iran-Iraq War, gained through a series of conferences and discussions with several very candid U.S. and Iranian officials and scholars,[1] contributed directly to this book.

Institutional support came from several quarters. The National Security Archive has been my professional home for many years, and its longtime director, Tom Blanton, has been unfailingly gracious with his flexibility and encouragement. During summer 2006, I was a History and Public Policy Fellow at the Woodrow Wilson International Center for Scholars in Washington, D.C., a paradise for stimulating and stress-free scholarship. I'm grateful to Christian Ostermann as well as to Mike Van Dusen, Haleh Esfandiari, and Sam Wells for the opportunity. The center's staff plays a huge part in making visitors welcome and productive. Lindsay Collins, Lucy Jilka, Mircea Munteanu, Janet Spikes, and Krisztina Terzieva were especially helpful during my time there. Anne Spellmeyer was a dedicated and resourceful research assistant.

For a briefer—but even more idyllic—period, the Brenn Foundation made available the incomparable Musgrove Conference Center for ten days of solitude and intensive writing in January 2012. I am very thankful to Nicole Bagley and her colleagues at the foundation.

It will be hard to repay the kind souls who read part or all of this manuscript in its earlier versions and offered comments: Farideh Farhi, Mark Gasiorowski,

Stephen Kinzer, Chester Pach, John Prados, Bruce Riedel, John Tirman, and most especially Peter Kornbluh and Jim Hershberg. I'm also grateful to Martha Afzal for her many insightful comments and encouragement along the way.

Many thanks to Lisa Thompson for her excellent work on the index.

Mike Briggs of the University Press of Kansas has been a supportive and astute editor. It is a pleasure to work on a book with someone who "gets it" the way Mike does. Larisa Martin and Melanie Stafford were extremely helpful—and patient—throughout the production process. Thanks also to Michael Kehoe, Rebecca Murray, Sara Henderson White, and their colleagues at UPK.

Finally, it is beyond my abilities to convey what I owe to Leila Afzal, my wife, for all she did to help make this book a reality—and has always done to keep me going.

Iran-Contra

Introduction

Shortly after noon on October 5, 1986, a Nicaraguan soldier patrolling the jungle near the Costa Rican border spotted an unidentified prop plane approaching his position. Suspecting a connection to antigovernment guerrillas, he raised his Soviet-made SA-7 missile launcher to his shoulder and fired, managing a rare hit that sent the aged aircraft crashing to earth. Two days later, the Sandinistas paraded the lone survivor, Eugene Hasenfus, from Marinette, Wisconsin, before the international press, where he confirmed his C-123 cargo plane had been on a mission to funnel arms to insurgents. But the forty-five-year-old ex-marine went further, declaring he had been working covertly on behalf of the Central Intelligence Agency (CIA).

One month later, on November 3, an obscure Lebanese newsmagazine published a story alleging earlier in the year a former senior U.S. official had secretly traveled to the Islamic Republic of Iran to strike a deal for the release of U.S. hostages in Beirut. According to the magazine *Ash-Shiraa*, the United States had offered U.S.-made spare parts to sweeten the proposal. Within twenty-four hours Iran's speaker of the Majles (Parliament), Akbar Hashemi Rafsanjani, confirmed the essence of the report in a public speech in Tehran. He identified the head of the secret delegation as Robert McFarlane, former national security advisor to President Ronald Reagan, and added bizarre details of false Irish passports and gifts of pistols, a cake, and a bible.[1]

The two stories generated world headlines and put the Reagan administration in a predicament. The United States had made no secret of its encouragement of the Nicaraguan insurgents, known as the "Contras,"[2] in their bid to overthrow the Marxist-oriented Sandinistas. The president had called them "the moral equal of our founding fathers." But the White House had repeatedly denied providing direct military support because Congress had explicitly forbidden it. U.S. officials immediately insisted there were no government ties to the downed cargo plane, but Hasenfus's confession seemed to catch the administration in a lie.

The allegations of contact with Iran presented an even bigger problem. Ever since Iranians had overthrown the U.S.-backed shah in early 1979, then seized the U.S. embassy several months later, taking its occupants hostage, the two countries had been locked in mutual hostility. President Reagan regularly condemned international terrorists, pledging the United States would never negotiate with them. In January 1984, Washington had singled out Iran as a state sponsor of terrorism. If it turned out the Reagan administration had sent arms to the Islamic Republic as barter for hostages' lives, it would have violated the president's own policy, damaged his credibility on a politically sensitive issue, and possibly broken U.S. law. The president's terse "no comment" responses did little to reassure the public.[3]

Over the month of November 1986, both controversies simmered. On November 13, Reagan tried to stem public skepticism over the Iran allegations by admitting in a nationally televised speech the United States had provided "small amounts of defensive weapons and spare parts" to the Islamic Republic. He denied the shipments amounted to "ransom," however, and insisted, "Our government has a firm policy not to capitulate to terrorist demands. . . . We did not—repeat—did not trade weapons or anything else for hostages, nor will we."[4] Opinion polls showed most U.S. citizens did not believe him.

On November 25, the story became a full-blown scandal. At a White House press conference, just two days before Thanksgiving, a grim-faced Reagan announced he had not been informed about "one of the activities" relating to his Iran policy that raised "serious questions of propriety."[5] Without identifying the activity, he stated that his national security advisor, Vice Adm. John M. Poindexter, had resigned, and that a National Security Council (NSC) staff member named Lt. Col. Oliver L. North had been fired.

After just a four-minute statement, Reagan relinquished the podium to his attorney general, Edwin Meese III, who disclosed not only that the essence of the Hasenfus and Iran allegations was true—the United States had played a role in both operations—but that they had been connected. "In the course of the arms transfers" to Iran, he said, "certain monies which were received . . . were taken and made available to the forces in Central America, which are opposing the Sandinista government there."[6] In other words, profits from arms sales to Iran—between $10–30 million—had been used to support the Contras despite the congressional ban. Meese repeated that the president had not known about the transfer, which quickly became known as the "diversion." But the disclosure of possible criminal wrongdoing by members of the president's staff was enough to create a media sensation. "You could hear people all suck in their breath," said one reporter after the briefing. "It was that kind of story."[7]

For the next year, the Iran-Contra scandal dominated U.S. politics. Congress launched investigations, including three months of televised hearings. A court-appointed independent counsel undertook a high-profile criminal inquiry that lasted more than six years. The president appointed a blue-ribbon commission, headed by former Sen. John Tower (R-Tex.), to study how the NSC process had allegedly broken down. Meanwhile, journalists saturated newspaper and television coverage with daily headlines exploring every conceivable angle of the scandal. At the center of public attention throughout the period was the question of whether Reagan himself had known about the diversion. Was it possible members of his senior staff could engage in something so sensitive without his knowledge? It became the equivalent of Watergate's formulation: What did the president know, and when did he know it?

In fact, the Iran-Contra affair was about much more than that single question. It encompassed highly dubious, and possibly illegal, acts with respect both to strands of policy and to broad-gauged attempts to cover up administration activities following their public disclosure. Far from being the work of a few mid-level "rogue operatives," it involved at various stages an array of senior officials including the president and vice president themselves. But by presenting the diversion to the public in such a dramatic way, the officials managed to marginalize the importance of other critical elements.

A few skeptical observers suspected it was a ploy by the administration. A reporter at the November 25 press conference asked Meese: "What's to prevent an increasingly cynical public from thinking that you went looking for a scapegoat and you came up with this whopper, but it doesn't have a lot to do with the original controversy?"[8] North, who became a household name after the revelation, reached the same conclusion—the diversion itself was a diversion: "This particular detail was so dramatic," he wrote in his memoir, "so sexy, that it might actually—well, *divert* public attention from other, even more important aspects of the story, such as what *else* the President and his top advisers had known about and approved."[9] To a Democratic operative at the time, it looked like a variation on "the old Nixon playbook"—"throw a couple lesser people to the wolves, let out a little information and hope that that will work."[10]

Whether contrived or not, the device served White House interests remarkably well. Meese's presentation was riddled with misstatements and omissions, prompted by a desire to protect the president from political harm, even impeachment, if some of his actions in the early stages of the Iran initiative ever became public knowledge. In fact, this book argues, the driving force behind both sides of the scandal was President Reagan himself. Foot soldiers such as North carried out the operations, often given extraordinary leeway, but the documentary evidence—including White House records released in recent years—supports the view Reagan was a forceful participant in policy discussions, not the cartoon image of utter detachment often portrayed, and provided the primary guidance and direction to his staff on policies close to his heart. The president approved every significant facet of the Iran arms deals, and he encouraged conduct by top aides that had the same aim and outcome as the diversion—to subsidize the Contra war despite the congressional prohibition on U.S. aid.

The accumulated evidence also confirms the president's closest advisors were well informed about key aspects of the secret operations while they were in progress and either actively cooperated with or eventually acquiesced to his wishes.

During the period of the revelations and cover-up in October–November 1986, cabinet-level involvement became more pronounced as the vice president, the secretaries of state and defense, and the chief of staff followed the White House lead in safeguarding the president politically, then withheld evidence (most importantly, their own handwritten notes) from Congress and federal prosecutors—sometimes for years. If that evidence had surfaced earlier, it would have substantially colored public assessments of the scandal and altered the course of key prosecutions. As it was, most of the president's circle of advisors escaped major repercussions.

Although Iran-Contra was the biggest scandal for the extraordinarily popular President Reagan, and it generated enormous press coverage—555 stories in the *Washington Post* and 509 in the *New York Times* alone during the three months after the Iran revelation[11]—the story faded into history without much lasting impact upon the U.S. public. The lack of significant penalty for any of the major players contributed to that outcome. So did the march of world affairs—George H. W. Bush's election as president, the fall of the Berlin Wall, the crackdown in Tiananmen Square, the repeal of apartheid in South Africa, Operation Desert Storm in Iraq, and finally the collapse of the Soviet Union all helped to push the affair well out of the public spotlight. Ironically, even the torrent of media coverage figured as an additional reason, creating a kind of scandal fatigue as allegations surfaced, often in the form of anonymous leaks, and were initially spun by an administration under intense political heat, then dismissed as "old news" when later confirmed by hard evidence.

This book contends the Iran-Contra affair's consignment to historical irrelevance is greatly undeserved. The revelation of wrongdoing had significant effects, almost derailing a presidency that had seemed immune to the political consequences of previous scandals and threatening to alter the domestic electoral picture in both the 1988 and 1992 presidential races. The political struggles surrounding Iran-Contra are of interest because they both exemplified and compounded the escalation of partisanship that marked the Reagan era, manifesting many of the negative effects that would become even more pronounced under subsequent presidents. The affair had significant foreign policy effects as well, undercutting administration objectives overseas and impairing U.S. standing in the world. By placing Iran-Contra in its global historical context, the book offers a depiction of U.S. attempts to make sense of looming shifts in the international arena, as the cold war—unbeknownst to most at the time—neared its denouement, and new threats, notably Islamic fundamentalism and state-sponsored terrorism, were on the rise.

As for the participants, the consequences, as noted, were harsher for some than others. Reexamination in the light of a wider body of evidence than previously available gives a clearer view of the actions of the many individuals who guided, implemented, or simply became caught up in the scandal. After exploring the two covert operations and evaluating the role of participants, the book offers an examination of the immediate aftermath of the scandal. This period featured initial attempts by the president's circle to protect him and his policies. It was followed immediately by the three principal official investigations, under the aegis of Congress, the independent counsel, and a presidential commission, respectively. The formal inquiries are an important part of the story, but previous accounts do not explore them at the level of detail provided here. By presenting them in their proper context, the book builds on the discussion in the first section, then highlights the institutional and other reasons Iran-Contra is still relevant today. These include inherent limits that exist within the U.S. congressional and legal systems that may allow this kind of event to happen again. Thus the book does not just scrutinize the Reagan administration and individual players, it points out structural issues that continue to be a factor in our system of government and makes it clear the scandal was not just an aberration.

Iran-Contra has produced an extraordinary historical record. The 1987 congressional hearings alone yielded more than 30,000 pages of once highly classified files. They include White House emails, NSC meeting minutes, CIA operational cables, transcripts of negotiations with Iran, and dozens of sworn depositions by participants in the affair—from arms dealers to cabinet officers. The files of the independent counsel—gradually becoming open to the public at the National Archives and Records Administration thanks in part to Freedom of Information Act (FOIA) requests by the National Security Archive—add the invaluable personal notes obtained from top presidential aides as well as detailed legal memoranda, Federal Bureau of Investigation (FBI) interviews, and other files that give insights into the roles of key players.

The book also relies on extended independent research at the National Archives, the Reagan presidential library, and the Library of Congress as well as on the results of numerous FOIA requests, many of which were filed by me or my colleagues at the National Security Archive—primarily Peter Kornbluh, Joyce Battle, Tom Blanton, and Scott Armstrong, among others. Particularly enlightening are the minutes of NSC and similar meetings from 1985–1986, only recently available. (Many other presidential, intelligence community, and military records remain classified.) Through the generosity of certain investigators and journalists who covered the scandal, I also had access to selected confidential records from the official inquiries. The most valuable have been unexpurgated transcribed excerpts of North's notebooks[12] and two substantial, annotated chronologies the state of Israel provided to Congress in lieu of subjecting Israeli citizens to formal questioning. Foreign government records are sparse given the restrictive retention policies of most countries, but a sprinkling is available that, along with memoirs, published interviews, and news accounts from Iran, Nicaragua, Israel, Iraq, and even the former Soviet bloc help to provide international perspectives on the affair.

Iran-Contra: Reagan's Scandal and the Unchecked Abuse of Presidential Power is the only book-length treatment of the affair by a nonparticipant that benefits from such an expansive historical record. Most previous studies, several of which are of lasting value for their in-depth coverage and insightful analysis, were published before some of the most crucial materials had become public. Theodore Draper completed his monumental *A Very Thin Line*[13] two years before the appearance of the independent counsel's voluminous three-part final report filled with previously unavailable evidence. In particular, Draper lacked access to the indispensable personal notes of some of Reagan's top advisors. As meticulous as his overall treatment is, he was simply not in a position to produce as categorical a conclusion about the responsibility of these individuals as is now possible in light of those records, and he later felt compelled to supplement his original interpretation with more definitive assessments based on new evidence.[14] Independent Counsel Lawrence Walsh's personal account, *Firewall*,[15] is another essential source. Walsh was intimately familiar with most of the materials just mentioned, because his staff discovered them, but he naturally concentrates on the legal and political aspects of the prosecution, whereas the present volume tries to go beyond questions of culpability and to locate events within their broader historical framework. In addition to these two overarching accounts, several of the affair's participants have written memoirs that have their own value but cannot be considered fully objective. Other useful sources include the biographies of Reagan and historical treatments of Iran and Central America, although of course they do not focus exclusively, or often even in great detail, on Iran-Contra.

Beyond primary documents and secondary sources, this book draws on several dozen interviews with participants in various facets of the scandal and its investigations; U.S. government officials; members of Congress and their staffs; government investigators and attorneys; some of the participants in the covert operations; Iranian, Nicaraguan, Israeli, and ex-Soviet officials; and journalists and academic experts from all of the principal countries drawn into the affair.

Iran-Contra: Reagan's Scandal and the Unchecked Abuse of Presidential Power takes a mostly narrative approach. To reflect the scandal's two intertwining strands, the first twelve chapters alternate between the Contra and Iran operations. Halfway through the volume, Chapter 8 describes the nexus point, in early 1986, where the two operations intersected through the agency of the infamous diversion scheme. The final three chapters explore the aftermath of the scandal's exposure. They describe the administration's initial cover-up attempts starting in October 1986, the joint congressional inquiry of 1987, and the independent counsel's lengthy legal proceedings from 1986–1993. Each of these stages is important to understanding the larger political, legal, and constitutional questions embodied in this unfortunate episode.

1

Raising the Contras

The new foreign policy team that came to Washington under Ronald Reagan in 1981 viewed Central America with alarm, seeing the hand of Moscow as the principal agitator behind the recent growth in indigenous support for leftist political movements in the region. The president soon focused on the Nicaraguan Contras as the keystone of his policy to roll back international communism. After taking care of his top priority—gaining congressional approval of the Republican domestic legislative agenda—he turned to the task of obtaining congressional funds to help the rebels' assault against the ruling Sandinistas. Standing in the way was U.S. public opinion. Most voters simply did not share the sense of dire threat the administration saw emanating from the tiny republics of Central America. Many also feared that the new administration, which made no bones about its support for U.S. intervention in Vietnam, might be tempted to try again closer to the homeland. Congress was split on the issue. In 1981, the Republicans took over the Senate for the first time since 1953, but the Democrats held firm in the House. Although many Democrats endorsed the Contras, and others would waffle under White House pressure, the president was never able to build a consistent base of support in Congress for his aid program.

As this chapter will show, the president made a deliberate decision to turn to clandestine operations as a way to achieve provocative goals with a minimum of controversy. Going covert provided official deniability for U.S. political and paramilitary involvement in the region, which reduced the risk of escalating international tensions and drawing the Soviets into the picture. It also allowed the White House to avoid costly political disputes on Capitol Hill or with the public. As events unfolded, however, efforts to keep a lid on administration activities routinely failed. Thus, a pattern developed that would set the stage for the Contra side of the scandal. As Congress repeatedly uncovered evidence of White House or CIA deception, its members approved more restrictive legislation. In turn, the administration, rather than trying to come to political terms with the Democrat-led opposition, simply took the policy deeper underground.

Defining the Issue

When Reagan entered office on January 20, 1981, he fully subscribed to the age-old Washington view of Latin America as a region of special significance—even privilege—for the United States. "I wasn't the first president concerned about conspiracies and machinations by distant powers in the western hemisphere," Reagan wrote in his memoir. "Since 1823, when our fifth president enunciated the Monroe Doctrine, the United States has stood firmly against interference by European nations in the affairs of the Americas."[1] Reagan's formulation typified his predecessors' impulse to conflate U.S. interests with those of its neighbors. By the early 1980s, the threat was no longer Western European imperialism but Soviet-inspired communism, which the new president defined as the source of many of the world's evils.

Even before entering the White House, Reagan had sounded alarms about Central America and the Caribbean. In early 1979, he warned the Caribbean was "rapidly becoming a Communist lake in what should be an American pond." Yet the United States, he added, "resembles a giant afraid to move."[2] Years later, he would explain why U.S. citizens should have worried more about the crisis he saw in Central America. Aside from "the fact that Americans have always accepted a special responsibility to help others achieve and preserve the democratic freedoms we enjoy," the United States needed to prevent Moscow from creating more satellites like Cuba, which were "a potential jumping off spot for terrorists." If "so-called 'wars of national liberation'" continued, then Soviet subversion "would spread into the continent of South America and North to Mexico." This would threaten the free flow of vital resources and trade through the region and create the prospect of a massive influx of refugees and illegal immigrants into the United States. Left unchecked, the United States itself would be in peril: "As I was told that Lenin once said: 'Once we have Latin America, we won't have to take the United States, the last bastion of capitalism, because it will fall into our outstretched hands like overripe fruit.'"[3]

Evidence from Soviet officials and archives brought to light since the collapse of the USSR indicates that by the 1980s the Kremlin saw Latin America more as an opportunity to distract the United States than as a target of aggression.[4] Nevertheless, so powerful was the image of a "clear and present danger" in Reagan's mind that he maintained it even after he left the White House eight years later, despite the momentous changes that had occurred in the Soviet Union under the "new thinking" of Mikhail Gorbachev. By his own admission, Reagan recalled the Lenin quote in public "often," even though no one has ever located any such statement about Latin America in Lenin's writings.[5]

The first priority of Reagan's policy strategists in 1981 was to fulfill an ambitious domestic agenda—building up the U.S. military, cutting taxes, balancing the budget, and winnowing social programs. Unexpected events during the first year pushed the Central America issue further down the road, among them the end of the Iran hostage crisis on inauguration day, the March assassination attempt against the president, the "Solidarity" crisis in Poland beginning that summer, and the air traffic controllers' strike in August. But before long, the struggle for hearts and minds in the U.S. backyard captured Reagan's attention.

Although Nicaragua became the epicenter of that struggle, El Salvador was where policy makers first turned their sights. As Reagan admonished his advisors, "We can't afford a defeat. El Salvador is the place for a victory."[6] The country's small size, roughly one-fifth the area of Nicaragua, was immaterial. The urgency it represented was as the next apparent target of Soviet/Cuban-backed international communist expansion. A U.S.-supported junta, recently installed, faced an insurgency by leftist guerrillas under the umbrella of the Farabundo Marti National Liberation Front (FMLN). In fall 1980, with President Carter still in office, U.S. intelligence had picked up evidence of Soviet bloc arms shipments entering the country by way of Cuba and Nicaragua. Just ten days before Reagan's inauguration, the guerrillas launched a "final offensive" with evident encouragement from Managua. The assault failed utterly, but Carter decided Nicaragua's conduct required a response—a cutoff in economic aid and a threatened rupture of diplomatic relations. The Sandinistas took steps to curb support for the FMLN, shutting down the rebels' clandestine Radio Liberación, operating from Nicaraguan territory. But by then the Reagan administration had taken office.

Reagan's first secretary of state, the blustery Alexander Haig, wasted little time discrediting Carter's emphasis on human rights and his minimizing of the East-West struggle. Haig had previously served as NATO supreme commander, which heightened his sensitivity to the threat of Soviet power. Immediately upon taking office he declared himself the "vicar" of the president's foreign policy and set out to put his stamp on the administration's new approach. The unbridled growth of the Soviet military, he announced, had posed serious threats from Europe to Afghanistan to Latin America. Of "utmost concern" was the "unprecedented" resort to "risk-taking" by Moscow in the Western Hemisphere—partly through the "Cuban proxy"—which provided significant support for terrorists. "International terrorism," he promised, "will take the place of human rights" in U.S. foreign policy.[7] Fellow hard-liners were happy to support Haig's offensive. Jeane Kirkpatrick, the new UN ambassador, affirmed the Soviet Union was the ultimate threat and stressed that the Western Hemisphere was its most vulnerable target. "Central America," she said, "is the most important place in the world for the United States today."[8]

Haig pressed his views within the administration. At an early NSC meeting, he warned Central America was "in turmoil" but added "these countries could manage if it were not for Cuba. Cuba exploits internal difficulties in these states by exporting arms and subversion." As for Nicaragua, "We probably have enough evidence on hand about Nicaraguan support for El Salvadoran revolutionaries to cut off aid to Nicaragua." The new CIA director, William Casey, backed up Haig's point. "There have been 100 planeloads of arms from Cuba over the past 90 days. The Nicaraguans can't be ignorant of that." Reagan followed the discussion with evident engagement. At a key juncture in the meeting, he posed the questions that would substantially shape the first phase of his administration's policy toward El Salvador and Nicaragua: "How can we intercept these weapons? How can we help?"[9]

That same month, February 1981, the State Department produced a white paper alleging "definitive evidence" of "clandestine military support given by the Soviet Union, Cuba, and their Communist allies" to "Marxist-Leninist guerrillas" in El Salvador. Many of the arms, the report charged, came through Cuba and Nicaragua in a "textbook case of indirect armed aggression by Communist powers through Cuba."[10]

Released by the department's Bureau of Public Affairs, the white paper was the administration's first attempt to sell its plan of attack against "communist subversion" in the region to the U.S. public. The evidence, in some respects, was accurate. Internal State Department records from the time make it clear the United States had discovered a connection through Nicaragua and had made "very strong demarches" to the Sandinista National Liberation Front (FSLN).[11] Newly opened files from the Soviet bloc, particularly the East German Stasi archives, confirm at least small-scale arms and equipment deliveries.[12] The pitch failed, however, and the report itself came under fire for exaggerating Havana's and Moscow's roles and labeling Soviet-backed aggression the root cause of the region's troubles while short-shrifting the problems of economic upheaval and nationalism.

Haig's high-pitched rhetoric generated unease within certain quarters of the administration—turning to outright alarm when he proposed the United States might mount a blockade around Cuba.[13] Some senior officials, including Vice President George H. W. Bush and Secretary of Defense Caspar Weinberger, had absorbed lessons from Vietnam about the consequences of incurring military commitments abroad without clear, attainable goals and broad public support. They preferred quieter alternatives. White House political advisors also rejected Haig's ideas as dangerous distractions from the president's domestic agenda. Both points of view were supported by opinion polls, during the presidential campaign and afterward, that showed military involvement in Central America was a losing issue for the Republicans.[14] Haig's high-stakes campaign was shelved in favor of a less obtrusive approach.

Choosing Weapons

After the White House had achieved most of its first-year legislative goals, attention began to shift to hot spots such as Nicaragua. Nicaragua was "an absolute foreign policy focus of the Reagan Administration," according to diplomat Harry Shlaudeman. "Nothing was more important, except the Soviet Union itself." But beneath the surface sharp disagreements emerged over both the ends of U.S. policy and the means of attaining them. Shlaudeman recalled "great frictions" punctuated by cabinet meetings "where literally people were shouting at one another. The emotions involved were tremendous."[15]

These disputes often reflected the organization of policy making under Reagan. The president put great stock in a "cabinet government" model he defined as follows: "Surround yourself with the best people you can find, delegate authority and don't interfere as long as the overall policy that you've decided upon is being carried out."[16] The catch was Reagan rarely followed through in monitoring whether his aides were properly implementing his orders. He also was reluctant to wade in when senior advisors squabbled. His abrogation of a meaningful management role, particularly in policy areas where he was not deeply engaged, encouraged the strong personalities in his administration to push their own agendas at the expense of cooperation and consensus or risk being outmaneuvered by their colleagues.

In foreign policy, this dynamic became more pronounced just one year into the administration. Reagan's initial plan was to invest primary policy-making authority in his secretaries of state and defense, with the national security advisor assuming a coordinating role. Richard V. Allen, who first occupied the latter post, was not part of the president's inner circle and lasted less than a year before being replaced by Judge William P. Clark, a longtime friend of Reagan's from his years as governor of California. Clark broke the mold of neutral coordinator by trading on his close personal ties and far greater access to the president than either Haig or Weinberger enjoyed. Clark's approach made it easier for his successors, Robert McFarlane and John Poindexter, to be more assertive in defining and implementing policy.

Sharp ideological differences also naturally led to policy disagreements, especially over the Contras. Those officials, usually within the State Department, who sought a broader approach to Central America that included negotiations with the Sandinistas typically confronted skepticism and distrust from hardliners. U.S. diplomats in the field were also split. In Managua "the embassy was quite divided," one former ambassador recalled. "It was [a] very difficult situation actually because there was always tension as we talked about policy choices."[17] The same situation held among NSC staff members, whose rivalry with the State Department for policy control would continue throughout the

Reagan presidency. Shlaudeman described the antagonism as "crazy—the whole business was crazy. You could see some of what later became Iran-Contra in this NSC staff."[18]

A dominant figure in this drama was Casey. Passed over for the job he really wanted—Haig's—Casey became the director of central intelligence (DCI) after Reagan assured him of cabinet rank—highly unusual for the position. As the president's former campaign manager he, too, was an old and trusted ally, adding to his influence. A former Office of Strategic Services (OSS) officer, corporate lawyer, and head of the Securities and Exchange Commission under Nixon, Casey had extensive experience in both government and intelligence. He looked older than his sixty-eight years but had enormous energy and focus and was determined to reinvigorate the CIA after the scandals and operational cutbacks of the 1970s. He was also a resolute cold warrior. Sharing Haig's animosity toward Moscow, he nevertheless understood politics imposed limits on conspicuous activity, and he was perfectly positioned to promote more low-profile ways to advance the administration's agenda in Central America.

By late February, barely five weeks after the inauguration, Casey placed a broad-gauged plan on the president's desk. It called for a "regional effort to expose and counter Marxist and Cuban-sponsored terrorism, insurgency, and subversion in El Salvador, Nicaragua, Guatemala, Honduras, and elsewhere" working either "directly or in cooperation with foreign governments." The NSC met to consider the proposal on February 27. Even Haig inclined toward it after hearing from the department's counselor, McFarlane, that it amounted to a "very worthwhile beginning" the secretary should "welcome and support."[19] Above all, it offered the promise of pushing back the communist tide, as the Reagan presidential campaign had pledged to do. But it also had the advantage of locating the battle below the public radar, both in the region and at home. Reagan understood Washington's allies in Central America would object to overly aggressive measures led by the United States. "I *never* considered sending U.S. troops to fight in Latin America," he insisted. "Hovering over everything, I think, was that old fear of the Great Colossus of the North—the apprehension that we'd try to dictate and dominate Latin American affairs."[20]

As for the home front, White House politicos understood that for most U.S. citizens the anticommunist crusade was a dead letter and would never generate the public support needed to move Congress when the moderate Democratic center strongly favored a negotiated settlement with the Sandinistas, not their overthrow.[21] Going covert also provided significant economic benefits. As Casey explained it, "It is much easier and much less expensive to support an insurgency than it is for us and our friends to resist one. It takes relatively few people and little support to disrupt the internal peace and economic stability of a small country."[22]

After a few hasty revisions, the plan became official policy when Reagan signed a presidential "finding" on March 9 authorizing the CIA to "provide all forms of training, equipment and related assistance to cooperating governments throughout Central America in order to counter foreign-sponsored subversion and terrorism."[23] The requirement to obtain the president's explicit approval was one result of the period of legislative resurgence in Congress in the mid-1970s. The 1974 Hughes-Ryan Amendment to an earlier foreign assistance bill aimed to prevent rogue intelligence operations by making the president personally accountable for them.[24]

One of the chief justifications for the program was to stop Nicaraguan support for leftist rebels in El Salvador, particularly the practice of supplying weapons across the border. Casey's approach managed to avoid political controversy, partly because he couched it as a defensive measure. Few in Congress could criticize a proposal that purported to be aimed at defusing tensions in the region, especially when the Carter administration had initiated something similar.[25]

As noted, however, underlying the decision to go covert was a more practical consideration—the desire to duck congressional and public opposition to an unpopular policy. Congress was identified early on as a potential impediment to the kind of robust policy the new administration, including the president, was eager to pursue. As Reagan's onetime solicitor general wrote later, the general view in the White House was Watergate had taught the wrong lesson—far from requiring tighter constraints on his powers, the "president must be allowed a strong hand in governing the nation and providing leadership."[26]

The objective of building U.S. authority abroad was an additional incentive for action. At an early February 1981 NSC meeting held to discuss the Caribbean Basin, Gen. David Jones, the chair of the Joint Chiefs of Staff, expressed the common sentiment that "American influence has declined," particularly in Latin America. He ascribed the development largely to dramatic drops in numbers of U.S. military advisors and amounts of aid available to allies in the region. "We cannot send more than six advisers into a country without congressional approval," Jones complained. "The law ties our hands."[27] Part of the appeal of this particular covert action was that it targeted not just the enemy in Central America but the U.S. Congress.

The March finding set in motion the concept voiced during the presidential campaign of turning back the communist tide in Central America—what would be dubbed the Reagan Doctrine. It did not take long for the secret war to begin. According to then ambassador to Nicaragua Anthony Quainton, it occurred precisely on March 14, 1982, when the CIA, using Nicaraguan operatives, blew up a bridge between Nicaragua and Honduras. It was the same day Quainton arrived in Managua to assume his duties. Although he was aware the president had just signed a finding, no one had informed him of the impending bridge destruction, leaving him unprepared for the "blaze of klieg lights and microphones" that greeted him at the airport.[28]

But the real jump start for the program to undermine the Sandinistas—and the event that initiated the plunge into secretive policy making—came later in the year. On November 10, the NSC met to discuss further ways to implement U.S. policy in Central America. The freewheeling discussion showed continuing disagreement over whether El Salvador or Nicaragua deserved to be the "principal target" (Kirkpatrick argued for the former, Casey for the latter), but there was unanimous accord on the requirement to act swiftly and forcefully to reverse what was seen as a "deteriorating" political situation in the region. There was also a consensus that virtually every possible approach should be on the table, short of direct U.S. military force—including placing mines in Nicaraguan harbors.

The president himself raised the idea of covert action. Commenting that the press was poised to "accuse us of getting into another Vietnam," he asked, "How can we solve this problem with Congress and public opinion being what they are? We are talking about an impossible option. Are there other things we can do? Can covert actions be traced back to us?" White House Counsel Edwin Meese, who seemed to take control of the discussion even though it was about foreign policy, responded that "political, military, propaganda/covert actions" were in fact possible and "do not require U.S. forces." Reagan wanted to "hear more" about "various alternatives including mining," insisting, "I don't want to back down. I don't want to accept defeat." A few minutes later, he repeated his question: "What other covert actions could be taken that would be truly disabling and not just flea bites?"[29]

The message was clear: the president wanted strong action and gave every sign of understanding it would occur in the face of firm congressional and public opposition. Interestingly, although Meese called for a follow-up meeting two days later to deliberate the options, the president chose not to wait to make the basic decision. The next day, November 17, he signed a national security decision directive (NSDD 17)—a presidential order that did not require the approval of Congress. Planning papers indicated the directive empowered the CIA to carry out a broad array of "political and paramilitary operations against the Cuban presence and the Cuban-Sandinista support infrastructure in Nicaragua," including building "popular support . . . for an opposition front" inside Nicaragua. The NSDD authorized creating a local 500-soldier force, but supporting materials noted U.S. personnel might also "take unilateral paramilitary action."[30]

On December 1, Reagan signed another presidential finding on Central America. Unlike the internal directive, this document, prepared for a congressional audience, obscured the administration's full intentions. Rather than spell out the "political and paramilitary" actions the CIA planned to undertake, the finding's description of the goal was limited to a single paragraph, alluding to "support and conduct [of] . . . paramilitary operations against . . . Nicaragua."[31] In testimony to Congress about the finding shortly after it was signed, neither Casey nor the State Department's top Central America policy maker, Thomas O. Enders, assistant secretary for Western Hemisphere affairs, mentioned the NSDD. The finding, then, rather than serving as the legal record of the president's decision, mainly camouflaged a much broader approach from Congress. Although legislators had no idea about the administration's true intent, it was no secret to the Contras or their Honduran patrons, whom the CIA had already promised to help overthrow the Nicaraguan government. At this early stage, deceiving Congress had already become part of administration strategy.

Raising the Contras

After the overthrow of Nicaraguan dictator Anastasio Somoza Debayle in July 1979, anti-Sandinista conspiracies had sprung up "just about anywhere two Nicaraguans could meet."[32] Small, unorganized, and disparate at first, the FSLN's opponents ranged from the infamous Somoza Guardia Nacional officers to members of the business community to disenchanted ex-Sandinistas to highland peasants. The earliest conflicts with the new regime involved peasants and indigenous people reacting largely to unwelcome economic, agricultural, and social policies thrust on them from Managua. Although these groups were the first and most numerous to resist, they generated virtually no international notice because of their dispersion across remote regions of the country. Other opposition elements, smaller in number but with more connection to the outside world, left Nicaragua to seek foreign help for their cause. The first of these to coalesce to any notable degree were fragments of the Guardia Nacional that had spilled across the borders into Guatemala, Honduras, and Costa Rica. (Many Guardia Nacional leaders emigrated in relative comfort to the United States.)

By December 1979, a cluster of former Guardia Nacional members based in Guatemala had come to the attention of U.S. and Argentine intelligence. Both governments were already exploring opportunities to create problems for the Sandinistas. President Carter's two-track approach of offering financial aid to Managua while simultaneously mounting modest covert operations against the FSLN betrayed his ambivalence on policy and political grounds as well as uncertainty about how to act. Nonintervention and multilateralism were important components of his Latin America policy, but his administration was pulled both by its own inclinations and by powerful outside pressures to counter the widely perceived trend toward communism in Nicaragua and the region.

The military junta in Buenos Aires had much less difficulty identifying its priorities. Still mired in its "dirty war" against leftist forces, the regime had allied itself closely with Somoza in his final years and was appalled at his collapse, which it blamed partially on his abandonment by Carter. Propping up the desperate bands of former Guardia Nacional members was one way to take matters into Argentine hands, further the junta's campaign to eradicate communist influence in the region, and, more specifically, track down and destroy left-wing Montonero guerrillas who had found refuge in the new Nicaragua. With support from the Guatemalan military and local conservative business interests, the Argentines in short order set up a rudimentary paramilitary training program for the Nicaraguans, who soon formed the September 15 Legion, named after the day Central America won its independence from Spain. Some legion members, such as Ricardo "Chino" Lau, had reputations for torture and murder, which may have recommended them to the junta but would rapidly trigger political problems for their U.S. sponsors. One of the legion's leaders, Col. Enrique Bermúdez, Nicaragua's military attaché in Washington, D.C., at the time of the revolution, would play an important and controversial role in the Contra war.

By spring 1980, former Guardia Nacional members, still relatively few in number, were establishing camps along the Honduran border with Nicaragua. The porous frontier made it easy to carry out hit-and-run sprees inside Sandinista territory. The legion complemented these minor strikes with a radio propaganda operation based near the capital city, Tegucigalpa. At the time, Honduras was moving toward civilian governance after years of military rule, with a popular ballot for a constituent assembly set for April 1980 and general elections the following year. Civilian authorities were therefore troubled by the legion's activities, which risked aggravating tensions with neighboring Nicaragua and El Salvador. However, the army was still dominant in Honduras, and the legion was essentially left in peace.

In August 1980, the situation improved further for the anti-Sandinistas when an ardent anticommunist named Col. Gustavo Álvarez Martínez took over the influential post of head of the Honduran Public Security Force. Trained in Honduras and Argentina, and for brief stints in the United States at Fort Benning and Fort Bragg, Álvarez was steeped in the mind-set and tactics that underlay Argentina's dirty war and was intent on making Honduras a spearhead in the regional anticommunist campaign. With his support, Argentine and U.S. training and other forms of assistance for the "Contras," as they came to be called, increased. In spring 1981, Álvarez traveled to Washington, D.C., where he presented to Casey a plan calling for the United States to help consolidate the scattered resistance elements into a unified military force centered in Honduras. Álvarez proposed that the Lilliputian Contra army would then try to prod the Nicaraguan giant into retaliating—for example with a counterstrike into Honduras or Costa Rica—which Washington could use to justify a military intervention into Nicaragua.[33] A shooting war involving U.S. troops was a nonstarter for the Reagan administration, but Álvarez's offer of Honduras as a base of operations had a distinct appeal, and Casey would soon send a senior representative to the country to ramp up the U.S. role in the covert war.

The advent of the Reagan administration was a major turning point for the Contras. Reagan had unapologetically revived the Monroe Doctrine, and his tough anticommunist image was warmly welcomed by conservative governments in Latin America. The United States, Argentina, and Honduras soon formed an informal *tripartita* in the region. In spring 1981, a series of discussions among the three governments cemented their consensus on a broad approach toward Nicaragua: Honduras would provide the territory, Argentina the "front," and the United States the finances.[34] While hundreds of Nicaraguans inside the country fought their own battles against the Sandinistas without significant outside help (or even awareness of the rebels' situation), the war—echoing earlier Latin American history—was about to be taken over by an outside power whose interests did not always coincide with theirs.

Enter Garcia

In early August 1981, the Reagan administration quietly signaled to its partners its readiness to intensify the crusade by dispatching the CIA's freshly appointed operations chief for Latin America, Duane "Dewey" Clarridge, to Tegucigalpa to meet with Álvarez and his colleagues. Like many Reagan-era appointees responsible for Latin America policy, Clarridge had no direct experience in the region and spoke little or no Spanish. But he had other qualities that counted with Casey. At a gathering of CIA station chiefs in Europe earlier in the summer, Clarridge had impressed the director as "a real doer, a real take-charge guy,"[35] willing and able to slash through congressional or bureaucratic roadblocks. Within days Clarridge, who was given to wearing a monocle and Italian silk safari suits,[36] found himself in charge of all CIA covert operations for Central and South America, where his plan, in his words, was "simple": "1. Take the war to Nicaragua. 2. Start killing Cubans."[37]

As he had with Casey, Clarridge made a strong impression on the Hondurans. During this initial visit to Tegucigalpa, he told his audience, "I speak in the name of President Ronald Reagan. We want to support this effort to change the government of Nicaragua." It was the type of unambiguous signal Álvarez and his colleagues wanted to hear. There were just two problems: it exceeded the administration's stated mission in Central America—at least as described to the oversight committees of Congress—and it contradicted the objectives Clarridge's State Department colleagues had for the region.[38]

At about the same time, Clarridge became a member of the Core Group, an interagency body that formulated U.S. policy on Central America. Enders, who chaired the group, supported the Contras but with a different aim. That same month, he traveled to Managua to warn the Sandinista leadership to cut off support for the Salvadoran FMLN or face a hardening of U.S. policy. He was unmoved by assertions of national defense—including from possible U.S. attacks—as the justification for a major military buildup and solicitation of Soviet bloc aid. Returning to Washington, D.C., he continued to push for a two-track approach on El Salvador that prominently featured the threat of military force against Managua—but not to overthrow the regime, only to prod the Sandinistas to the bargaining table. Clarridge, Casey, and other hard-liners, however, maintained the pressure for confrontation, gradually gaining the upper hand. In time, Enders would be pushed out of the department.[39]

Clarridge's foray into the region marked the start of Washington's direct involvement with the rebels. As CIA operatives became more of a presence in and around Contra camps, the rebels took to calling them "Garcia," playing on the last three letters of the name as a wry reference to the U.S. intelligence agency.[40] Over the next year, official U.S. policy held that the Contras were no more than an interdiction force against the flow of Soviet- and Cuban-supplied weapons into Central America. Unofficially, the United States geared up for increasingly aggressive assaults on Nicaraguan military and economic targets. By the beginning of 1982, U.S.-sanctioned training facilities had opened in Florida, California, and Texas, preparing between 800 and 1,200 soldiers for a "war of liberation" in Nicaragua. Despite calls from Congress to shut down the camps—which openly violated the 1794 Neutrality Act[41]—Enders admitted Reagan officials were "winking" at the infractions because the trainees were part of a larger U.S. covert operation.[42]

Meanwhile the conflict began to heat up as exile group attacks against Nicaraguan objectives picked up in frequency and effectiveness. Following the March 14, 1982, bridge attack that coincided with Ambassador Quainton's arrival in Managua, a burst of small-scale assaults took place. "In the 100-day period from 14 March to 21 June," according to U.S. military intelligence, "at least 106 insurgent incidents occurred within Nicaragua." Far from routine interdiction, the "incidents" included sabotage, crop destruction, and the "assassination of minor government officials."[43]

Overt Covert Operations

Try as it might, the Reagan administration could not keep Congress completely out of the picture. Press leaks early in 1982 torpedoed White House attempts to focus public attention on Sandinista gunrunning to Salvadoran leftists; instead, lawmakers zeroed in on U.S. policy toward the region, looking for ways to exert more control over U.S. activities.[44] Efforts to encourage more active negotiations with both Nicaragua and the rebels in El Salvador sputtered because Enders and his colleagues at the State Department were already running low on credibility. The administration had been insisting on "democratization" within Nicaragua as a precondition for better relations, but because that implied a change of government in Managua, the Sandinistas did not treat it seriously. Members of Congress had also welcomed the administration's Caribbean Basin Initiative, at least those parts of the heavily hyped program designed to pump up the region's economy, but the attempt to portray it as altruism was undermined by the deliberate omission of Nicaragua from the list of participants.

By April, the U.S. House Permanent Select Committee on Intelligence (HPSCI) had enough concerns about the U.S. approach to warrant writing the first restrictive language into its authorization bill for future intelligence activities. A secret annex to the Fiscal Year 1983 Intelligence Authorization Act enjoined the administration from using appropriated funds to overthrow the Nicaraguan government, limiting U.S. activities to interdicting arms—a sign the committee still supported the goal the White House publicly proclaimed.[45] Before the end of the year, however, the issue returned to the forefront. The November 8 cover of *Newsweek* featured a photograph of a U.S. military advisor standing over two Honduran soldiers crouched at the open door of a helicopter during a training mission over Honduras. The cover read "America's Secret War, Target: Nicaragua." The story described the U.S. role in guiding and bankrolling Contra operations based in Honduras and quoted anonymous U.S. officials as saying the rebels stood a chance of overthrowing the Sandinistas.[46]

The story did not contain much new information, but it provoked a public backlash against the "secret war." That, in turn, forced Congress to act. Rep. Tom Harkin (D-Iowa) set the pace by proposing to abolish the program outright. HPSCI Chair Edward P. Boland (D-Mass.), who wanted to rein in the program but keep it alive, submitted a variation of the April secret annex as an alternative. The White House could see where events were heading and decided to back Boland's option as the lesser evil.[47] The amendment, which passed the House 411–0 in late December, barred the CIA and Department of Defense (DOD) from supporting military activities that had "the purpose of overthrowing the government of Nicaragua or provoking a military exchange between Nicaragua and Honduras."[48] As the first public set of restrictions on Contra aid, it was a significant step in the back-and-forth between the White House and Congress. But it was also a critical opportunity missed by Congress to close a loophole the administration had already proven willing to exploit—even to the point of violating the law, as it later turned out.

As 1983 got under way, a congressional delegation visited Central America to take a firsthand look at the secret program. U.S. Senate Select Committee on Intelligence (SSCI) member Patrick J. Leahy (D-Vt.), who led the group, met with a number of U.S. and local officials, including Clarridge, who stonewalled about the agency's activities. General Álvarez was less guarded, telling Leahy proudly, "We're going to be in Managua by Christmas." It was the wrong thing to say to a wary group of legislators. The delegation returned to Washington, D.C., and Leahy reported, albeit with careful wording, the Contra operation "was growing beyond that which the Committee had initially understood to be its parameters."[49] Members had been blocked from getting all the answers they wanted but had learned something important nonetheless.

At this point, administration backers of the Contra program decided the time had come to boost their clients' image. Illegal U.S. support was not their only problem. By 1983, questions had surfaced about the rebels themselves. Were they a viable political and military force? What were their goals? How serious was the personal corruption and disregard for human rights? U.S. officials tried a variety of tactics to change appearances on the ground. In late 1982, for example, the CIA engineered the appointment of eight anti-Somoza exiles to a new "directorate" for the Nicaraguan Democratic Force (FDN) in order to turn back accusations the rebel leadership consisted only of former Guardia Nacional members.[50] Clarridge also reportedly urged guerrilla leaders to clamp down on abuses in order to avoid further bad press.

The Hard Sell

Unfortunately for the administration, the facts about the Contras were too plain for cosmetic changes to have real effect. To protect their investment in El Salvador and the Nicaraguan rebels and prolong congressionally funded aid, administration officials launched a major public relations campaign to sell their product to Congress and U.S. citizens. The impetus came from Reagan himself, who continued to view the problem in the context of the global struggle with communism. As he would even more forcefully in subsequent clashes over Contra aid, he put the blame squarely on members of Congress who opposed his program in Central America with a "depth of emotional resistance" he admitted "I never understood." "Well-intentioned or not," he wrote later, "they were in effect furthering Moscow's agenda in Latin America. . . . To me, the seriousness of the problems in Central America was so obvious that we had no choice: Based simply on the difference between right and wrong, it was clear that we should help the people of the region fight the bloodthirsty guerrillas bent on robbing them of freedom."[51]

After a meeting on Central America with Casey and Clark in June 1983, Reagan wrote in his diary: "We're losing if we don't do something soon. . . . We have to take this to the people and make them all see what's going on. If the Soviets win in Central America, we lose in Geneva and every place else."[52] Shortly afterward, on July 1, Clark wrote to the high-level Special Policy Group, "The President has underscored his concern that we must increase our efforts in the public diplomacy field."[53]

But the campaign soon took on a darker cast. Congressional investigators looking into administration tactics later compared it to a classic covert action in a foreign country. A year earlier, in June 1982, Casey had detailed a propaganda expert from the CIA, Walter Raymond Jr., to the NSC staff, where part of his responsibility was to run an extensive interagency program designed, in the words of investigators, to "attempt to manipulate the media, the Congress and public opinion to support the Reagan administration's policies" in Nicaragua.[54] Because the law prohibited CIA officials from domestic lobbying, Casey's ploy of temporarily assigning a CIA employee to another organization was tantamount to dodging the strict letter of the statute.

A key element of the strategy was the creation of the Office of Public Diplomacy for Latin America and the Caribbean (S/LPD), set up at Raymond's suggestion. In effect, S/LPD was a cover. Clark and Secretary of State George P. Shultz (who replaced Haig in July 1982) wanted its director to "be responsible for the development and implementation of a public diplomacy strategy for Central America." They even located the office in the State Department. In actuality—and at President Reagan's request—the director reported to Raymond and the NSC staff, not to officials at the State Department, representing one of several subtle shifts in the control of policy to the White House. In keeping with other aspects of the secret program, this fact also was hidden from Congress.

While S/LPD and its kindred organizations shaped the desired image for U.S. policy, administration officials signed up private firms to take care of the Contras. Rebel leaders and troops had already begun to earn reputations for corruption and disrespect for human rights. In January 1983, Woody Kepner Associates of Miami, a public relations company retained by the CIA, signed a deal with the FDN "to project your organization and its goals in a very positive manner throughout the Caribbean, Central and South America, Europe, and several other specific areas."[55] The initial fee was $300,000. The parties renewed through mid-1985, at which point a much more lucrative Contra public relations campaign was already in full swing.

Military Muscle

In the midst of the CIA's Contra-related operations, the U.S. military added another dimension to the pressure campaign, sometimes in close tandem with the intelligence community.[56] In 1981, military exercises began in and around Honduras, having several purposes. The public explanation centered around protecting Honduras from possible Nicaraguan attack. Unofficially, Washington also wanted to intimidate Managua while putting into place the wherewithal to prosecute the Contra war. In connection with these war games, the Pentagon spent millions building air bases, runways, roads, and other infrastructure and stockpiling tons of supplies, creating a presence so massive U.S. soldiers took to referring to it as the "USS *Honduras*." For critics, it was another sign of the United States imposing its might on the region (earning Honduras the even more unflattering label of Washington's "Central American whore").[57] The scare tactics worked, as Nicaragua's Deputy Foreign Minister Victor Tinoco made plain to U.S. negotiator Shlaudeman over the course of 1984.[58]

Even more alarming to the Sandinistas was the October 25, 1983, U.S. invasion of Grenada. "They were much affected" by it, according to Quainton. "I can still remember the interior minister, Thomas Borge, . . . calling me over to his house and saying, 'Look, we have been watching Grenada and we want to assure you that there will be no provocations here. There will be no American hostages.'"[59]

The Defense Department publicly denied any intent to cooperate with the CIA in its clandestine activities in Nicaragua, but the record shows the opposite. On July 12, 1983, Reagan issued a presidential memorandum directing the Pentagon "to provide maximum possible assistance to the Director of Central Intelligence for improving support to the Nicaraguan resistance forces."[60] That assistance took several forms. According to a 1984 General Accounting Office (GAO) report, for example, the U.S. military built a runway at El Aguacate, thirty-two kilometers from Nicaragua, during a major, eight-month exercise called Big Pine II that began in August 1983. Although a senior Pentagon official testified to Congress the military had no further use for the airstrip, officers at the U.S. Southern Command told the GAO the original idea had been to leave the facility for future CIA operations.

U.S. Air Force and Army units also reportedly performed assignments for the agency. The army's highly classified Intelligence Support Activity, created in the wake of the 1980 Iran hostage rescue mission, was one such entity. Another was a deep-cover aviation unit named Seaspray jointly run by the army's Special Operations Division and the CIA. According to one account, Seaspray helped gather vital signals intelligence, first on internal communications by both leftist and rightist groups in El Salvador, and later on FSLN troop movements, in order to help coordinate Contra attacks and prevent ambushes.[61] Notes taken in fall 1984 by NSC staff member Oliver North (who was by then charged with overseeing the covert war in Nicaragua), offer some corroboration. This early joint venture between the U.S. military and the CIA was apparently never reported to Congress.[62]

A third project, code-named Yellow Fruit, also used U.S. military resources for CIA missions—in ways that presaged North's role as the main foot soldier of Iran-Contra. In addition to detecting arms flows to El Salvador, Yellow Fruit operatives trained Contra soldiers and pilots in Honduras and elsewhere. Moreover, by fall 1983 they were being thought of as a fallback in case Congress decided to cut aid to the rebels. Anticipating that event, the unit reportedly devised a scheme to funnel supplies to the Contras, set up offshore bank accounts, and helped build airstrips in Costa Rica—virtually identical activities to those in which North and his collaborators would soon be engaged. By late 1983, however, the army abruptly shut down the project because of financial irregularities by members of the unit. By the time North and his partners stepped into the picture after the Boland Amendment restrictions had taken effect, the framework set up by Yellow Fruit and other army special operations units was a model for what became known as the "Enterprise" (see Chapter 3).[63]

The Pentagon contributed in other ways as well, each designed to get around restrictions imposed by Congress. In Operation Tipped Kettle, Air Force Maj. Gen. Richard Secord, later North's main contractor on the Contra and Iran arms projects, arranged for tons of captured Palestine Liberation Organization (PLO) weapons to be bought from Israel in May 1983; the following February, Tipped Kettle II yielded more Soviet-built arms from Israel, some of which reached the Contras.[64] Operation Elephant Herd, conceived in mid-1983, provided for the U.S. military to declare certain specially requested equipment "surplus" (having zero dollar value) and transfer it to the CIA for later shipment to the insurgents; in that way the agency could evade the ceilings on aid Congress was contemplating at the time.[65]

The Final Straw

U.S. Representative Boland's attempt to forestall a showdown between Congress and the White House had not put the matter to rest. It was clear the Reagan administration nurtured hopes for continuing to expand the Contra war. Leaks to the press indicated plans to double the rebels' number, vastly increase military aid to the region in the coming year, and mount two large military exercises off the Honduran coast to intimidate the Sandinistas. The exercises were significant in that they marked the culmination of the NSC staff's bureaucratic battle with the State Department over the direction of U.S. policy during this period.[66] In certain respects they helped set the table for North's takeover of the covert war. Meanwhile, throughout 1983, congressional opponents of the war debated how to bring the Contra program back into line. During the spring, U.S. House members pressed for tighter restrictions, and in late July, after what the *Washington Post* described as "one of the most intense, emotional foreign policy debates in

Congress since the end of the Vietnam war," the House voted 228–195 to end all covert aid to the insurgents.[67] Critics of shifting congressional attitudes later pointed out that the sheer magnitude of the Defense Department's known involvement, including prohibitively expensive electronic intelligence gathering on the Sandinistas—all authorized by Capitol Hill—tended to dampen the outrage that followed revelations of North's relatively modest activities.[68]

Three months later, a parallel situation developed. The ongoing antagonism of the House toward the Contra program impelled the administration to begin working more closely with members of the SSCI. The collaboration produced a new presidential finding limiting the scope of the operations Casey had initially envisioned.[69] Nevertheless, the compromise finding, signed by Reagan on September 19, significantly expanded the goals and activities covered by his December 1981 authorization. It included the standard interdiction language but added the political objectives of "bring[ing] the Sandinistas into meaningful negotiations" and "provid[ing] support to opposition leaders and organizations"—all to be accomplished "in cooperation with other governments."[70]

The White House's show of teamwork masked a continuing drive to intensify the military conflict. Behind its ostensible partnership with Capitol Hill, the administration simultaneously escalated its secret attacks on Nicaraguan targets. Even before Reagan signed the new finding, CIA contract agents known as Unilaterally Controlled Latino Assets (UCLAs), under agency guidance, sabotaged Nicaragua's only coastal oil terminal at Puerto Sandino. One month later, on October 10, another assault on an oil storage facility forced the evacuation of the port city of Corinto. For the first time, CIA contractors and even employees took direct part in operations (the Contras took credit but did not participate). Furthermore, the attacks targeted the country's economic infrastructure. Both facts evidently violated agency assurances to legislators.[71]

Despite these breaches, the more conservative Senate held fast to the president's program while the House voted twice, in October and November, to terminate it. In yet another compromise, Congress in early December passed a bill placing a $24 million cap on Contra funding and closing loopholes by prohibiting the CIA from dipping into contingency funds or "reprogrammings" to pad the rebel account. House liberals tried to retain a measure of control by requiring a vote in both chambers on any future appropriations.

By now, however, the White House had effectively changed the rules. During 1983 an ideological shift to the right had taken place within the executive branch. In addition to the leading lights—Casey, Weinberger, Clark, and Kirkpatrick—others began to rise in prominence. At the Defense Department among the key figures were Undersecretary Fred Ikle, Assistant Secretary for International Security Policy Richard Perle, and Deputy Assistant Secretary Nestor Sanchez, a career CIA officer whose responsibility at the Pentagon was Latin America. Their counterparts at the State Department included Assistant Secretary for Human Rights Elliott Abrams, who would soon take over the Latin America portfolio, and Paul Wolfowitz, the former head of policy planning who became assistant secretary for East Asia and the Pacific, another focal point in the confrontation with communism.

In May 1983, hard-liners forced Enders out of the State Department. Enders had been one of the most articulate backers of a two-track policy toward Central America that included a prominent role for negotiations. That approach did not fit with the more confrontational formula preferred by conservatives. In a sign of their growing power, not even the secretary of state could save Enders's job. The new assistant secretary was Langhorne Motley, U.S. ambassador to Brazil, who had the reputation, so valued by the likes of Casey, of someone "willing to play a little rough and dirty."[72] From then on, administration policy took an even more provocative bent—exemplified by the Grenada invasion—that put both moderates in the administration and liberals on Capitol Hill on the defensive.

As the end of 1983 approached, the White House continued to beef up its secret operations. In November, Reagan signed off on a request to "authorize 3,000 additional weapons to be issued to the FDN forces."[73] The administration also approved a boost in the Contras' numbers to 18,000, though without informing lawmakers. Congressional distrust of administration policy, and of Casey in particular, continued to grow in this period. The CIA director, whose testimony to the intelligence committees often left them feeling very much in the dark, evidently revealed his true intentions toward the Sandinistas only to his administration colleagues, once asking an agency Latin America analyst, "What can we do to make the bastards sweat?"[74] It was a throwback to the CIA's 1970 intervention in Chile when President Richard Nixon had instructed then DCI Richard Helms to "make the economy scream."[75]

As the New Year got under way, the CIA implemented plans to "bring the . . . situation to a head."[76] U.S.-run UCLAs began planting mines in Nicaragua's harbors.[77] For the next four months the operations continued, with the CIA crediting the insurgents in order to add to their "credentials" as a paramilitary force.[78] The purpose of the mines, according to a memo North wrote to McFarlane (then the president's national security advisor), was "to severely disrupt the flow of shipping essential to Nicaraguan trade. . . . It is entirely likely that once a ship has been sunk no insurers will cover ships calling in Nicaraguan ports." This, he continued, was only part of "our overall goal of applying stringent economic pressure" on the Sandinistas. Reagan, the record shows, kept abreast of developments during this period through memos from staff and top-level meetings.[79]

On April 6, the *Wall Street Journal* broke the story of the CIA's role in the mining operation and the president's approval of it. Although it was not known publicly at the time, Vice President Bush also played a part—as chair of the Special

Situation Group session that recommended the operation. He had in fact raised the idea himself to the NSC as early as November 1981.[80] On Capitol Hill, reaction to the news was outrage, particularly by members of the SSCI, who claimed they were never told about the scheme. Committee Chair Barry Goldwater (R-Ariz.) wrote Casey a blistering letter: "I've been trying to figure out how I can most easily tell you my feelings about the discovery of the President having approved mining some of the harbors of Central America. It gets down to one, little, simple phrase: I am pissed off!"[81]

One source of Goldwater's anger was the fact that the HPSCI had learned about the operation in January. When a member of the Senate panel charged Reagan had authorized the mining, Goldwater had dutifully denied it. A loyal supporter of the president and defender of Casey, Goldwater was embarrassed. For his part, New York Democrat Daniel Moynihan, the panel's vice chair, was provoked to the point of resigning (temporarily) to protest the CIA's deceptiveness. Not long afterward, both chambers formally condemned the agency for its role in the secret operation. The Sandinistas sued the United States at the World Court, which ultimately ruled in Nicaragua's favor.[82]

For Congress, the issue was not only that the agency had carried out such a provocative and, in the eyes of many, illegal action, but that the administration had flatly deceived the oversight committees about it.[83]

Past as Prologue

Even though the events that constituted the Contra side of the Iran-Contra scandal did not begin to fully roll out until late 1984, when the administration labored to sustain the war by going around the most restrictive Boland Amendment, the groundwork for those controversial activities was already in place. North, ardent promoter of the Contras that he was, did little that was qualitatively different from the actions of several more senior colleagues from whom he took his cue. Atop the list of role models was Reagan. Throughout his first term in the White House, leading up to the harbor mining disclosure, the president had made clear not only his support for the Contras but his view that Congress represented an increasingly unreasonable obstacle to his goals for the insurgency. In early 1984, he conveyed a personal instruction to McFarlane that was broad but emphatic: keep the Contras together "body and soul."[84] As Chapter 3 will show, his subordinates, especially North, took this directive to heart. As they went about their task, usually with the knowledge of their superiors, rarely did they encounter meaningful resistance to their methods.

2

Coping with Iran

For most of Ronald Reagan's presidency, Iran lurked near the top of the foreign policy agenda. The Islamic Republic presented a dilemma. After the hostage saga, which ended on the day of Reagan's inauguration, January 20, 1981, mutual hostility between Tehran and Washington was the order of the day. Yet Iran remained a strategic prize in the rivalry between the United States and the Soviet Union, making it incumbent on the United States to find a way to restore its position of influence with Tehran. Furthermore, Reagan had a personal interest in the country. In 1978, just before the revolution, he had visited briefly and been impressed by the shah. "Iran must receive the worst press of almost any nation," he told a radio audience upon his return home. He especially valued the monarch's role in protecting U.S. cold war interests. "Iran has been [and] is a staunch friend [and] ally of the U.S. It has a clear understanding of the Soviet threat to the free world."[1]

When Reagan took office, the United States faced not one but two major external threats—the recurring menace of Soviet-led communism along with the rise of fundamentalist Islam. U.S. policy makers seemed bereft of good options. It would take events on the ground—led by Iraq's invasion of Iran just prior to the 1980 U.S. elections and a new hostage crisis in Lebanon—to resuscitate a previously disparaged idea of not undermining but making overtures to the clerical regime. The unlikely mover behind this ambitious and controversial concept on the U.S. side was the diffident national security advisor, Robert McFarlane.

No Easy Options

Although the president and his team shared a sense of outrage over Iran's seizure of U.S. hostages, there was by no means unanimity over how to deal in practical terms with the Khomeini regime. Iran was still a multipronged threat to U.S. interests through its ability to choke off Western access to Persian Gulf oil; its intimidation of conservative gulf states such as Saudi Arabia, on which the United States would rely even more after the shah; and the prospect of creating regional instability that the Soviet Union might be able to exploit. Within the Reagan administration there were broad differences over the best approach, depending on which of these interests was emphasized.[2] For example, although Moscow posed a constant threat in many people's minds, not everyone believed it wise to construct a policy toward Iran on that basis alone. Some thought Washington should put more weight on protecting oil and other economic interests, which implied closer ties to the Arab states of the gulf. Others insisted the priority should be protecting Israel. In fact, each of these priorities (among others), was emphasized at one point or another during the Reagan years, leading outside observers to the understandable conclusion the White House had no coherent policy toward Iran.

During Reagan's first term, at least three policy alternatives were seriously considered. In hindsight, each offers important context for how key officials viewed the Islamic Republic. They also indicate what types of actions the administration was willing to take, comparable in their way to arms-for-hostages deals, long before the president decided to ship missiles to Iran.

One approach was, bluntly, to overthrow the Khomeini regime. In spring 1981, CIA Director William Casey, as part of a global strategy to "roll back" Moscow's gains in the third world, proposed a plan to oust the country's clerical ruler. Using "nonlethal" CIA assistance, the program called for setting up a radio station in neighboring Turkey and distributing aid to a royalist group headed by Princess Ashraf, the shah's twin sister, as well as two paramilitary organizations led by former military commanders. The goal was to bring together "moderate" opposition elements to form a new government. Reagan signed a finding authorizing the operation, but it collapsed not long after it got under way.[3] Nevertheless, ideas of this kind surfaced regularly. As late as January 1984, a senior NSC staff expert on the Middle East proposed the United States develop a covert action program against Iran, in the wake of recent terrorist strikes. He noted he was personally in touch with Iranian exiles who wanted to install a pro-Western government with outside support. The Saudi government, he wrote, stood ready to help.[4]

Other proposals to "win back" or undermine the government of Iran appeared at various times. One CIA official estimated in the early 1980s the agency's covert action wing received some "30 to 40 requests per year from Iranians and Iranian exiles to provide us with very fancy intelligence" in return for weapons or other "contraband" items.[5] One of those who approached the agency was Manucher Ghorbanifar, an international arms dealer. Known to U.S. intelligence agencies as a "talented fabricator," Ghorbanifar tried to ingratiate himself with the CIA repeatedly with tales of Iranian hit squads and other stories intelligence officials eventually concluded were mostly fantasy. After the CIA took the significant step in July 1984 of distributing a "fabricator notice" to the intelligence community characterizing him as an unreliable source,[6] Ghorbanifar turned to Israel with a proposal to barter U.S. weapons for hostages. Through the Israelis he was able to find a more receptive ear on the NSC staff (see Chapter 4).

A second method with which Washington chose to deal with Iran was to "contain" it by moving politically closer to neighboring Iraq. The two countries, sharing a long history of mutual enmity, had been at war since September 1980. It was an epochal conflict for both sides. Iraq's dictatorial ruler, Saddam Hussein, had chafed under the terms of the Algiers Accord reached with the shah in 1975. The agreement shifted the two countries' common boundary to Iran's advantage, to the midpoint of the strategically valuable Shatt al-Arab waterway, which led to the Persian Gulf. Hussein argued it had been an imposed agreement, unfair, and more than that, an insult to Iraq.[7] A hodgepodge of historical, political, religious, and cultural grievances underlay the dispute. Sharpening Iraq's motivations were both an expansionist interest in Iran's oil-rich Khuzestan Province and a heightened sense of threat from the new Islamic Republic, whose leadership seemed intent on stirring up Iraq's majority Shiite population against its secular Baathist rulers. When the Iraqis saw how Iran's revolution had impaired its military preparedness, leaving it without its main weapons supplier (the United States) and purging much of its officer corps, Hussein decided to exploit the opportunity and attack.[8]

Washington's official policy was to try to bring the fighting to a halt. But as long as it did not spread across the region and threaten Western access to gulf oil, the war had the undeniable benefit of constraining both hostile powers. In late 1981 and early 1982, however, Iran began to turn the tide, repulsing Iraqi attacks and regaining territory, most importantly in Khuzestan, which Iraq had seized at the beginning of the conflict. Hussein's rash decision to attack had major unanticipated consequences. Above all, it united Iran's population against a common enemy and gave the regime a powerful means to rally support for itself by identifying its survival with that of the nation.

The war also created the conditions for the rise of a new institution, the Islamic Revolutionary Guard Corps (IRGC), which Khomeini had formed as a counterweight to the regular army, seen as generally loyal to the shah. Over the years, the IRGC would become a dominant force in Iranian society, but in the 1980s it was already an important factor in military and political affairs. Just at this critical point in the war, and evidently tied to the coincidental Israeli invasion of Lebanon in June 1982, the IRGC began to build a parallel organization in Lebanon, the Party of God—Hezbollah. Lebanon also had a relatively large Shiite population (the biggest of the nation's seventeen religious sects),[9] and its clerical leadership, or *ulama*, had a long history of close ties to the mullahs of Iran.[10] As such Lebanon was an early objective for true believers in Tehran whose aim was to spread revolutionary Islam across the region. In short order the country, suffering through civil war for years, became a flashpoint between Islamic and non-Islamic forces, drawing in the United States to devastating effect. Hezbollah played an outsized role in the turmoil of the early 1980s, and along with its patron, the IRGC, would be at the center of the secret deals with the United States.

By late June 1982, a shocked Hussein realized his forces were being outmatched. He announced his troops would begin to withdraw and would be out of Iran within ten days. But Tehran would have none of it. Now enjoying the advantage, Iran's forces prepared an all-out offensive some Western analysts thought could lead to a counterinvasion of Iraq. U.S. officials watched with growing alarm. The regime's rhetoric about exporting the Islamic revolution was already troubling, and the prospect of its only serious military rival in the gulf collapsing prompted images of a radical, Shiite-inspired, "Middle Eastern Armageddon."[11]

In May and June, the U.S. national security bureaucracy produced reams of policy papers on ways to avert the "grisly prospect" of an Iranian victory.[12] The high-ranking Senior Interagency Group (SIG) pored over the options but found most of them deficient. Political support would not have any immediate military impact. Arming Iraq further would not answer the regime's more urgent needs for intelligence, strategy, or morale. Stirring up Kurds or Baluchis against Khomeini would need the cooperation of reluctant Turks and Pakistanis and might encourage the Soviets to step up their own tribal activities.[13] Furthermore, exile groups were too sharply divided and their leaders seen as tainted in Iran.

The best option, the group concluded, was to provide badly needed intelligence support.[14] Satellite surveillance had shown Iranian forces were massing near the border with the apparent aim of storming across and cutting off the strategic Basra-Baghdad highway. U.S. officials soon approved a plan to dispatch a CIA official to Baghdad with copies of relevant intelligence to use to warn the Iraqis of the danger, and on July 27, 1982, CIA Near East operations officer Thomas Twetten arrived in the Iraqi capital. In a sign of the complexity of the budding relationship, the Iraqis were initially suspicious enough of U.S. objectives that they almost expelled Twetten from the country, even though the value of what he had brought quickly became clear.[15]

Twetten's briefing for Iraqi intelligence marked a new stage in the development of ties between Washington and Baghdad that culminated in the normalization of relations in November 1984. Through most of the 1980s, U.S. aid took the form of commercial credits, trade in dual-use equipment, tacit approval of direct military support from other Arab states, diplomatic backing, and combat advice, including the provision of targeting data for use against Iranian positions. That support did not extend to direct U.S. weapons supplies, mainly because U.S. experts believed Baghdad had plenty of other sources (primarily France and the Soviet Union but also other Arab countries with tacit U.S. approval) and that the real need was for better leadership and battlefield strategies. Contrary to widespread belief, the United States also did not supply chemical munitions to Iraq, nor was it official U.S. policy to sanction Hussein's infamous use of chemicals against Iranian forces and later his own (Kurdish) citizens. But notwithstanding the efforts of some U.S. military and diplomatic officials to discourage these violations of international norms, the documentary record shows the United States contributed directly to Iraqi military operations knowing they might entail the use of chemical weapons.[16] Policy makers repeatedly chose the perceived lesser evil of acquiescing to Iraqi offenses—for example, privately downplaying to Iraqi officials public U.S. denunciations of chemical weapons use—over possibly ceding any tactical advantage to the Islamic Republic.[17]

The Reagan administration's behavior toward Iraq offers useful context for assessing its clandestine approach to Iran during this period and for recognizing that the Iran operation was not entirely the aberration U.S. officials portrayed it to be after the scandal broke. The relationship with Baghdad showed that, when operating beyond public scrutiny, U.S. officials were hardly squeamish about cozying up to "hostile states" and supporters of international terrorism if they felt it was justified. Presidential envoy Donald Rumsfeld exemplified this attitude during a cordial session with Hussein in Baghdad in December 1983, part of the administration's bid to solidify bilateral ties.[18] Some of the features of U.S. support for Baghdad just noted were arguably as reprehensible as trading arms for hostages, though U.S. officials glossed over this awkward history after Hussein invaded Kuwait in August 1990.[19]

One contact in particular between the Reagan administration and Hussein's government featured close parallels to the arms deals with Iran. In late 1981, the Defense Department tried to arrange a covert arms-for-arms swap that would have provided Iraq with twenty-four 175 mm cannons from U.S. inventories in exchange for highly prized Soviet-made military hardware in Iraq's possession. This included an advanced tank, the T-72, the U.S. military had been hoping to acquire in order to study its capabilities and vulnerabilities.[20] Almost four years before the Iran operation, this deal showed the Reagan administration was not averse to supplying arms to the Iran-Iraq conflict. The Israelis were involved in the arrangement as well; however, after a series of negotiations it fell through.

Before it collapsed, the attempted arms swap raised some of the same legal problems that would apply to shipping missiles to Iran. Searching for a way around the principal statute governing Foreign Military Sales (FMS)—the Arms Export Control Act (AECA)—Attorney General William French Smith found a creative mechanism based on the Economy Act and the National Security Act that he believed would let the president sell weapons abroad without notifying Congress. In a secret letter to Casey in October 1981, Smith proposed a formulation that would be resurrected to authorize the 1986 missile shipments to Iran.[21]

The Reagan administration's third alternative approach to Iran early on was the one that would generate so much controversy—allowing weapons supplies to the Islamic regime. The idea was an outgrowth of the cold war convictions that drove so much of Washington's foreign policy thinking and was at odds with the views of most U.S. government Middle East experts. How much agreement there was within the government about this approach is unclear because of classification restrictions, but also undoubtedly because the underlying premise was so thoroughly disparaged after the scandal that its promoters had no desire to be associated with it. But the record does make plain McFarlane and the handful of his colleagues whose reputations suffered because of their advocacy of this approach were far from alone.

The first evidence of the subject being raised emerged as early as the first half of 1981, when an interagency debate cropped up over whether to keep discouraging U.S. allies from sending arms to Iran. A number of NSC staff members and CIA analysts concluded Iran was in no shape to fight a major war, and if it lost the conflict with Iraq would leave Baghdad, a long-standing Soviet ally, the unchallenged power in the gulf. Because of the perceived benefits to Moscow, that outcome was as worrisome to these officials as an Iranian victory was to many of their colleagues. In July 1981, the SIG sided with this viewpoint, concluding, "U.S. efforts to discourage third country transfers of non-U.S. origin arms [to Iran] would have only a marginal effect on the conduct and outcome of the war, but could increase opportunities for the Soviets to take advantage of Iran's security concerns."[22]

At this early date, a draft national security decision directive (NSDD) had already been prepared suggesting authorization of allied shipments of non-U.S. equipment to Tehran. Some senior Defense Department officials supported the idea, but the Joint Chiefs of Staff (JCS) weighed in against it, arguing at the SIG meeting it would undermine relations with conservative Arab allies and "intensify the war with Iraq." For the time being the administration decided to keep the Carter-imposed weapons embargo in place,[23] but the question would come up again at the State Department and CIA at least once more the following year. These examples make it clear that arming the Islamic Republic was not a novel concept when it resurfaced in 1985 and finally gained presidential approval.[24]

Events Prepare the Way

Aside from the political and policy motivations that guided administration policy toward Iran, events unfolding in the Middle East during Reagan's first term were an important influence on attitudes in Washington. Three factors in particular came into play that laid the immediate groundwork for the Iran arms-for-hostages deals.

Most important was the continuing bloody conflict between Iran and Iraq. In mounting his attack in September 1980, Hussein had calculated correctly that Iran's military, once the most powerful in the gulf, had deteriorated under Khomeini. But he badly underestimated the Iranians' will to fight and their leaders' ability to draw on religious and historical wellsprings to inspire troops to suicidal acts for the sake of Islam and the nation. One of the enduring images of the conflict was the deployment of "human waves" of poorly trained soldiers and children designed to overwhelm entrenched Iraqi positions by providing too many targets to kill. It was an effective tactic but carried an enormous human cost.[25]

As the war dragged on, Iran became increasingly desperate for weapons and spare parts to replenish its once daunting U.S.-made arsenal. A major reason was Operation Staunch, a State Department initiative launched in 1983 to discourage other countries from supplying arms to the Islamic Republic. For the most part, Tehran had to buy its equipment covertly either from other governments or on the international black market. U.S. intelligence estimates put Iran's annual weapons purchases at almost $2 billion from 1980 to 1982. No fewer than thirty countries obliged either directly or through intermediaries.[26] Private dealers also tried to get in on the bonanza. In the 1980s, the Justice Department filed charges against dozens of would-be deal brokers with Iran. Western European governments, such as France and Italy, along with the European Parliament, showed only tepid interest in stopping the flow of weapons to Iran (even less when it came to Iraq), waiting until 1986 to take meaningful action.[27] Some of the deals envisioned were enormous. One press report in 1984 indicated twenty-five U.S. F-5 jets officially intended for Turkey were in fact headed for Iran— with Lloyd's of London allegedly insuring the shipment.[28]

The second factor that paved the way for the arms-for-hostages deals was the role of Israel. The Israelis were early suppliers of weapons to Iran in its war with Iraq, a circumstance that struck some observers as curious. In public, Iran's religious leaders excoriated the "illegal Zionist entity," but the regime's survival was at stake, and Israel was in a position to offer vital supplies. For Israel, the secret arrangement was about far more than just financial opportunity. During the shah's era, extending almost as far back as the creation of the state of Israel, Tel Aviv had cultivated Iran as part of its "periphery" strategy of balancing the threat from Arab states by developing ties to non-Arab regimes in the region such as Turkey, Iran, and Ethiopia. (The shah once told a U.S. ambassador, "Neither Israel nor Iran wants to be alone in a sea of Arabs.")[29] The benefits included cooperative agreements on intelligence and even nuclear issues.[30] No matter who ruled the country, Iran remained important to Israel for strategic reasons.

Tel Aviv also derived other advantages from supporting Iran, including having its bitter enemy, Iraq, waste precious resources in a debilitating war. "The last thing" Israel wanted to see, according to former CIA Iran expert George Cave, was "an Iraqi victory which would strengthen the Arab hand."[31] "Khomeini was not a friend," as a retired Israeli general put it, "but Saddam Hussein was our enemy!"[32] Israel also stood to gain from the covert arms sales both by trying to improve the treatment of 60,000 Jews in Iran (or obtain permission for them to emigrate) and by earning hard currency from potentially lucrative deals.[33]

For all these reasons, Israel pushed hard to secure a military relationship with the Islamic regime from its inception. Former U.S. ambassador Thomas Pickering was "constantly" approached by Defense Minister Yitzhak Rabin and "urged to seek some sort of dialogue with the Iranians."[34] Before Rabin, his predecessor Moshe Arens reportedly made similar entreaties. After the U.S. embassy takeover in late 1979, President Carter considered it unthinkable to trade weapons while U.S. citizens were being held hostage. Even a personal appeal by Prime Minister Menachem Begin during a state visit in April 1980 was dismissed out of hand.[35] Undeterred, Israel went ahead with shipments of weapons and parts to Iran, from mortars to Phantom jet parts, according to a former senior Israeli military officer.[36] One of these deals involved the sale of 250 tires for U.S.-built F-4 fighter jets in October 1980. Until the end of Carter's term, Tel Aviv continued to badger his administration for consent to ship more weapons, playing up the advantages to both Israel and the United States of pursuing such transactions.

With the election of Reagan, Israel hoped the rules would change. In December 1980, Morris Amitay, former executive director of the American-Israel Public Affairs Committee (AIPAC), the most prominent U.S. pro-Israel lobbying organization, arranged a meeting with Richard V. Allen, head of Reagan's transition team and soon to become national security advisor. Amitay asked for the meeting at the request of Gen. Menachem Meron, the military attaché at the Israeli embassy in Washington, D.C., who wanted to know how the incoming administration would view spare parts shipments from Israel to Iran. Amitay said Allen's response, after a moment's pause, was: "Tell your friends I heard what you said." The Israelis took this as tacit approval, although Allen denied it later.[37]

After Reagan took office, Israel picked up more positive signs. Most importantly, the fifty-two U.S. hostages gained their freedom on inauguration day, removing a prominent sticking point to U.S. endorsement of weapons deals with Iran. Two months later, Secretary of State Alexander Haig promised to develop a "strategic consensus" with Tel Aviv, exemplifying the president's warm feelings toward Israel. Exactly one week after the hostages' release, U.S. Ambassador Samuel Lewis received a new request for consent to ship arms to Iran. Again, however, Washington's response was no. Despite raised hopes in Israel, the new administration, still bitter over the hostage saga, objected to military transfers of any kind to Iran and would not approve deliveries of equipment "subject to United States controls."[38] Begin sent Foreign Minister Yitzhak Shamir to meet personally with Haig to press the matter. Afterward, the two publicly disagreed over whether Haig had opposed military sales of any kind to Iran or, as Shamir reported to Begin, he "did not object to Israel shipping its own parts."[39] Whatever Haig said, he evidently stopped short of a blanket rejection. From the Israeli standpoint, he had given an "amber light," and Tel Aviv moved quickly to take advantage.

In mid-July 1981, a significant operation was exposed when an Argentine CL-44 cargo plane crashed over Soviet territory near the Turkish border. According to a CIA report, the aircraft had been carrying arms and equipment, probably including spare parts for Iran's Air Force, under contract with Israel. The aircraft was on the third of twelve planned flights to the Iranian capital aimed at delivering roughly 5,000 tons of weapons and 300,000 tons of medical supplies.[40] Later in the year, Tel Aviv lobbied for approval of a onetime sale of U.S.-made F-4 parts to Iran. Begin and his colleagues offered several reasons it would be in Washington's interest. One of these was the materiel would help improve contacts with "moderate elements" in Iran's military and simultaneously strengthen their standing within the regime by virtue of having managed to secure vital supplies for the war effort. The Israelis also promised to relay to Washington any intelligence they gathered from these contacts. Finally, Tel Aviv argued Iran's military needed bolstering because it was the only barrier to a communist takeover in the country. In December, Haig acquiesced, but the transaction never took place.[41]

With or without explicit Washington approval, the State Department learned, Israel went ahead with sales of U.S.-origin equipment to Iran on its own.[42] By the end of 1981, according to CIA figures, Israel had sold "at least $28 million in equipment to Tehran."[43] Two years later, Tel Aviv was still arranging deals. Even when senior U.S. officials, including Undersecretary of State Lawrence Eagleburger, objected, Israel gave "no firm assurances" it would stop arming the Islamic Republic.[44]

These deals, all hidden from public view at the time, provide important context to the later U.S.-approved arms program. In particular, the planned F-4 deal and the arguments Israel made to justify it closely matched the rationales offered to the Reagan administration in 1985 and 1986. The Israelis pushed the right buttons—raising the specter of communism and promising renewed influence in Iran. Indeed, the plan neatly fit into the framework of the strengthened strategic partnership. In the early 1980s, however, the pieces were not yet in place to induce Washington to go along with Tel Aviv on this controversial policy.

The Hostage Saga Revisited

The third factor that led directly to the Iran arms deals was a new outbreak of hostage seizures by militant Islamic groups in Lebanon beginning in 1984. A mountainous country on the eastern shore of the Mediterranean Sea smaller than the state of Connecticut, Lebanon had been a combat zone for years. Wracked by civil war since 1975, it fell within Syria's de facto zone of influence, had been the home base for the Palestine Liberation Organization (PLO) since its expulsion from Jordan in 1970, and was a target of repeated Israeli incursions. Along with the Persian Gulf, Lebanon became an early focus of Reagan's Middle East policy, which emphasized the establishment of peace there as key to progress in the Arab-Israel conflict.

In June 1982, the likelihood of achieving that objective soon all but evaporated when Israeli forces mounted an invasion of the country. The spiral of violence that followed, including the assassination of the Christian president-elect and the massacre of hundreds of Palestinian refugees at the Sabra and Shatila refugee camps in West Beirut, prompted Reagan to deploy 1,200 marines to Beirut in September as part of a multinational peacekeeping force.[45] Over the next year, as Christian forces regularly found themselves on the defensive, the administration pushed the marines into a more active role on behalf of those forces, undermining the status of the U.S. military contingent as a neutral peacekeeper.

The Israeli invasion and evidently partisan U.S. presence coincided with the birth in Lebanon of Hezbollah. Iran's Islamic regime had decided conditions in Lebanon, primarily the Shiites' plurality status among the country's seventeen religious sects, made it a promising base for spreading Tehran's revolutionary ideology to the Arab world. Since the 1960s, Khomeini and elements of Lebanon's Shiite clergy had developed bonds while studying together in the holy city of Najaf in Iraq. Those relations were critical to the formation and development of Hezbollah. By sometime in 1982, local Lebanese clerics, backed by IRGC units stationed in the Bekaa Valley, east of Beirut, had formed numerous cells of mostly young and poor peasants instilled with the mission of promoting Islam (Shiism in particular) and political activism in the country. Israeli and U.S. actions during late 1982 and early 1983 inflamed resentments that already ran deep and led directly to the first major acts of violence against U.S. targets in Lebanon.[46]

In April 1983, a delivery van packed with explosives detonated in front of the U.S. embassy in Beirut, ripping away the facade of the high-rise building. The explosion killed sixty-three Lebanese and U.S. citizens, including a senior CIA Near East analyst, Robert Ames, and much of the agency's Beirut staff. Members of Hezbollah operating under the nom de guerre Islamic Jihad ("holy war")[47] took "credit" for the blast and threatened more violence if U.S. forces did not leave the country. Six months later, on October 23, the marines became the target as another bomb on wheels, a yellow Mercedes truck, slammed into their barracks next to the Beirut Airport, setting off a blast that lifted the four-story building off its foundations and killed 241 service personnel.[48] The attacks were the most devastating of their kind ever committed against the United States and quickly brought recriminations on the Reagan administration for its handling of Lebanese policy and failure to protect its forces.

Some critics blamed part of the crisis on infighting between the secretaries of state and defense.[49] George Shultz, who had replaced Haig in July 1982, took an aggressive stand on the deployment and use of the military in the region, while Caspar Weinberger was more guarded about committing U.S. forces to action.[50] Although "shattered" by the attack, according to aides, Reagan took a tough public line at first, reiterating the United States had "vital interests" in Lebanon and vowing to maintain a U.S. presence as "central to our credibility on a global scale." Although the president's concern focused largely on the perceived threat of a Soviet takeover of the Middle East, Shultz warned "radical and rejectionist elements" within the region "will have scored a major victory" if the United States were to pull out. Yet within months, Reagan reversed himself, announcing the marines would soon be "redeployed" from Lebanon.

Not only had the United States failed to limit the violence, it had suffered hundreds of dead and wounded. In the process, the pullout taught extremists in Lebanon and beyond a fundamental lesson—the United States, despite its colossal military power, would capitulate if confronted with too high a human cost. This message would soon translate into a fresh wave of smaller-scale but politically devastating assaults on U.S. citizens abroad.[51]

On the morning of February 10, 1984, Frank Regier, a professor at the American University of Beirut on his way to work was struck on the head by two masked men and stuffed into the backseat of a battered black Renault. The timing of the crime was deliberate. The next day, seventeen men were due to go on trial in Kuwait for a string of bombings committed in that country the previous December. Known later as the Dawa prisoners, fourteen of the accused were members of al-Dawa al-Islamiya, an Iraqi Shiite faction headquartered in Tehran.[52] The other three were Lebanese adherents of Hezbollah—one of them the brother-in-law of Imad Mughniyah, a senior figure in the organization sometimes described as head of its intelligence operations. Mughniyah's purpose in kidnapping Regier, followed by two other U.S. citizens—CNN correspondent Jeremy Levin on March 7 and the CIA station chief in Beirut, William Buckley, nine days later—was to pressure the Kuwaitis to release the Dawa suspects, particularly the three Lebanese. Regier was freed shortly afterward by members of a rival Shiite group, but Mughniyah quickly snatched a replacement, the Reverend Benjamin Weir, a Presbyterian missionary who had lived in Lebanon for more than thirty years. Buckley's capture was a particular jolt for the Reagan administration because he was a high-ranking intelligence officer and a friend and colleague to many inside government, including Casey.

At top-level deliberations the president, as he often did on issues that resonated with him, raised the hostage issue frequently and forcefully. At one National Security Planning Group (NSPG) meeting in October 1984, for example, he held forth in detail on ways to strike back against terrorists in Lebanon and on the priority of rescuing the captives. According to meeting notes, the president "stressed pure retaliation (against Hizballah) is not our objective. Preemption is the important consideration since we believe they are planning new attacks." He further "stressed that he did not see an attack as having much impact on the suicide drivers, but asked whether it would affect the thinking of the leadership. Wouldn't an attack slow things down?" Finally, he emphasized again "his overriding interest in securing the release of the hostages."[53]

Reagan was even willing to contemplate military action against Tehran, Hezbollah's main sponsor. In January 1985, after Islamic Jihad threatened to put on "trial" up to five U.S. hostages captured since 1983 and impose on them the "punishment they deserve," he authorized sending "strong demarches" to Iran. At a NSPG meeting on January 18, he approved armed reprisals against the Islamic Republic: "If they harm just one or two of the hostages, we should go with . . . two strikes as planned. Then we could tell Iran to release the remaining hostages or we would close their harbors through mining." Reagan then had this exchange with Vice Admiral John Poindexter, the deputy national security advisor at the time:

> Vice Admiral Poindexter: I believe that covers the agenda. I recommend we adjourn. We've now agreed that if the hostages are harmed (executed), we will conduct the strikes. . .
> President: (snapping fingers) "Like that."
> Vice Admiral Poindexter: Don't you think we should reconvene the NSPG to make the final decision?
> President: Only if it doesn't delay the strikes. In summary then, if any hostage is harmed, we will [four lines excised].[54]

Here, Reagan displayed more than just a readiness to make tough decisions independent of his advisors' opinions. His interaction with Poindexter also revealed a marked impulsiveness, albeit driven by an emotional reaction to a horrific scenario. He preferred to forgo a thorough assessment of the implications of a military strike than to brook a delay of a matter of hours that would allow the NSPG to reconfirm the advisability of the decision. This impatience on an issue of such magnitude provides context for understanding the president's repeated overruling of his most senior aides in the upcoming arms-for-hostages initiative.

Reagan's feelings about the hostages' plight intensified after he began to meet with their families, starting with the relatives of Father Lawrence Jenco in late June 1985. The experience, according to McFarlane, left Reagan "visibly shaken and moved" and convinced him he had a responsibility to help alleviate their condition. "I just can't ignore their suffering," the president insisted.[55] Eventually, according to a senior CIA counterterrorism official, he became "obsessed." At the end of national security meetings, regardless of their subject, he would ask: "Okay, what are we doing to get my hostages?"[56] After one meeting, Casey wrote presciently, "I suspect he would be willing to run the risk and take the heat in the future if this will lead to springing the hostages."[57]

Beyond his humanitarian reaction, Reagan and others in his administration recognized the political ramifications of the crisis. "The real thing that was driving" the Iran arms deals, the CIA's chief of Near East operations said later, was not only pressure from the families but a spate of "articles in the magazines about the forgotten hostages," often repeating the families' sense the "U.S. Government isn't doing anything." The result was "a lot of fear about the yellow ribbons going back up and that this President would have the same problems that the last President had had with the Iranian hostages."[58] Brent Scowcroft, a member of the Tower Commission appointed by Reagan to look into the affair, recalled the Lebanon hostage saga as a "running sore politically."[59]

The Linchpin

Though it was not yet obvious, there would soon be a convergence between events in the Middle East and the campaign inside the Reagan administration to change U.S. policy toward Iran. The person who engineered that convergence was McFarlane. A former marine lieutenant colonel, McFarlane served as executive assistant to Henry Kissinger and Scowcroft in the Nixon and Ford White Houses, then as a senior aide to Sen. John Tower (R-Tex.) on the Senate Armed Services Committee. After working on the Reagan transition team, he landed the job of counselor to the State Department under Haig, before becoming deputy national security advisor under Clark in January 1982 and eventually succeeding him in October 1983.

McFarlane's initial encounter with the Iran hostage issue preceded the 1980 elections. In August, accompanied by two senior foreign policy advisors to the Reagan campaign, he met at a Washington, D.C., hotel with an obscure figure believed at the time to be Iranian who claimed to represent the Khomeini regime and wanted to discuss the hostages. The meeting apparently came to nothing, as all three U.S. officials insist they rejected out of hand the "Iranian's" suggestion to help arrange for Tehran to return the hostages to the Reagan camp, not to the Carter administration. However, their acknowledgement of the contact contributed to wide-ranging allegations that members of the Reagan team bargained with Iran's government to delay the hostages' release and deny Carter a last-minute "October surprise" in the run-up to the November vote.[60] Regardless of whether those charges had validity, it seems reasonable to infer the meeting made an impression on McFarlane that fed his inclination to pursue similar contacts with Iran in the future.

As Clark's deputy, McFarlane got his first taste of the bitter policy and bureaucratic battles it was the national security advisor's job to mediate. He developed a reputation for first-rate staff work and impressed influential figures in the White House, including Nancy Reagan, with his low-key, almost invisible operating style. This unobtrusive quality undoubtedly helped him win Clark's job. The first candidate for the position had been James Baker, the president's relatively moderate chief of staff, who had the backing of Vice President Bush, Secretary of State Shultz, and the first lady. But when hard-liners Weinberger, Casey, and Clark heard the president had agreed to Baker, they pushed back, and Reagan reversed himself. McFarlane, having no objectionable ideological leanings or power base to threaten cabinet members, became the compromise choice.

Despite his promotion, McFarlane soon coveted a more consequential role as a policy innovator. Beyond the friction of dealing with the combative Shultz and Weinberger, who seemed to clash over most issues of the day, he was disturbed by President Reagan's palpable lack of interest in deciding policy priorities. As time went on, his insecurity around Reagan insiders and the cabinet gave way to his ambitions. In a telling article in 1984 on the organization of the NSC, he interpreted his role as "an independent advisor and policy manager for the president" as well as occasionally a "policy initiator." In this conception, he consciously harkened back to the days of Kissinger and Zbigniew Brzezinski.[61]

By the start of Reagan's second term, Iran had become a subject with major appeal for McFarlane. As someone steeped in the cold war, he saw the country as a strategic prize in the superpower rivalry for influence in the Persian Gulf. As early as 1981, he had suggested to Haig the need to study ways to "deny the region to the Soviet Union," but the idea went nowhere at the time.[62] After becoming national security advisor, he tried again, initiating interagency studies during 1984 he hoped would garner attention within the administration. But the analyses found the United States had little hope of influencing events in Iran, at least while Khomeini was still alive. Even NSC staff expert Geoffrey Kemp's earlier call to overthrow Khomeini assumed relations probably would not improve until the spiritual leader had left the scene. The analyses broached the possibility of shipping weapons to the Islamic Republic but rejected the idea. McFarlane still did not give up, but he would have to wait for fresh approaches from both Iran and Israel before persuading the president to adopt a new policy on Tehran.

3

Taking over the Covert War

The clandestine NSC supply network for the Contras came into existence late in President Reagan's first term. To handle the tricky assignment, Robert McFarlane brought in the energetic Oliver North. North quickly put together a team of private operatives who in turn created the principal mechanism for carrying out the president's orders—dubbed the "Enterprise." Several important players entered the scene in this phase, including the Enterprise's main architect, Richard Secord, who was intent on becoming the rebels' chief weapons supplier via whatever source was available, including U.S. cold war adversaries in the communist bloc. Despite congressional curbs on direct U.S. involvement in the Contra war, North oversaw a handful of risky and costly operations carried out by hired mercenaries. He also engaged in quid pro quo arrangements with the Hondurans that would generate serious legal questions down the road. Each of these actions appeared on their face to violate the Boland Amendments. Although the point of inserting the NSC staff was to remove the CIA from the picture, this turned out to be a sham. CIA personnel remained involved, and the agency's director, William Casey, kept fully apprised of North's activities. When a senior field officer discovered this, he warned if the story leaked it would be "worse than Watergate."

Boland Amendment II

The relevant section of the so-called second Boland Amendment, which went into effect on October 12, 1984, and would cause so much controversy, read as follows: "During fiscal year 1985, no funds available to the Central Intelligence Agency, the Department of Defense, or any other agency or entity of the United States involved in intelligence activities may be obligated or expended for the purpose or which would have the effect of supporting, directly or indirectly, military or paramilitary operations in Nicaragua by any nation, group, organization, movement, or individual."[1]

Like so many issues in the Iran-Contra affair, there were deep disagreements over the significance of the second Boland Amendment. Those who believed the NSC staff fell under the provision cited a number of arguments. For one, the amendment's author, U.S. Rep. Edward Boland (D-Mass.), stated explicitly in the debate prior to a vote on the bill that the section's express intent was to prohibit any U.S. government entity from helping the Contras militarily. Several members of the administration contended the language was too vague and did not specifically include the staff of the NSC because it was not an intelligence agency. The counterargument was that the president's own Executive Order (EO) 12333 of December 4, 1981, "United States Intelligence Activities," defined the NSC as "the highest Executive Branch entity that provides review of, guidance for and direction to the conduct of all national foreign intelligence, counterintelligence, and special activities, and attendant policies and programs." Lee Hamilton (D-Ind.), chair of the U.S. House Permanent Select Committee on Intelligence (HPSCI), affirmed later: "We drafted the Boland Amendment broadly for precisely the reason that we wanted to cover the National Security Council . . . because it was involved in intelligence activities. So members of that staff could not do their work without using intelligence."[2]

Delving deeper into the legal weeds, the president's Intelligence Oversight Board (IOB) gave a contrary opinion in 1985 based in part on the contention that EO 12333 did not name the NSC as one of the members of the intelligence community and that the NSC was not involved in implementing covert actions, only in coordinating them. The problem with the IOB's analysis was the attorney who provided it, Bretton Sciaroni, was denied critical information about North's activities. Sciaroni testified to the congressional select committees he interviewed both North and NSC staff attorney Paul Thompson as part of his legal research, but both omitted the crucial fact that North was supplying military aid to the Contras and raising money on their behalf. He termed North's response a "blanket denial" of any military involvement or fund-raising. Sciaroni also read through documentation Thompson provided, but it did not include key records describing what North had been doing. The resulting opinion was therefore "discredited" in the words of the U.S. Office of the Independent Counsel.[3]

More to the point, Robert McFarlane, who was still national security advisor when Boland II passed, testified later he believed the amendment did cover the NSC staff.[4] Tellingly, when questioned by Congress in 1987, then attorney general Edwin Meese (who had been counselor to the president in October 1984) hedged on the question. Declining to give a "definitive legal opinion," he offered instead his personal sense the law did not apply to North and his colleagues, but he allowed it was an issue "on which reasonable minds might differ."[5]

The administration's handling of Boland II, arguably one of the most significant pieces of legislation affecting the president's foreign policy agenda, was a revealing example of an unusually cavalier approach his aides and at times Reagan himself adopted toward important legal questions. In this case, rather than perform due diligence by bringing in the Justice Department to provide a formal legal opinion based on all the facts,[6] the NSC staff opted for a distinctly self-serving—and dishonest—shortcut that in the end created long-term problems for the administration. The White House could have challenged the constitutionality of the amendment, as some officials hoped the president would do. Others pointed out that because the amendment was not a stand-alone bill but was tied to a continuing resolution on defense spending, vetoing it would have had wider repercussions for the economy. The White House chief of staff, Donald Regan, one of those pushing for a confrontation with Capitol Hill, acknowledged, "It was more of a tactical decision I would think than a real strategic political decision. . . . It was felt that after looking at [it], well we can live with it; we don't like it, [but] we can live with it."[7] Columnist George Will expressed a broader sense of Republican frustration with the president for this attitude, writing that Reagan's "contribution" to his administration's problematic relationship with Congress "has been to fail to make a serious argument in defense of his office. . . . The president," he added, "is not constitutionally interested or articulate enough" to deal with the "impertinence" of Congress.[8]

North's explanation to the select committees about his views on Boland II gives added insight into the White House's indifference on a question of such importance. He insisted "there were people [on the NSC staff] who were concerned about" discovering whether the amendment applied to them. But, he claimed, without noting how the omission of key facts contributed to Sciaroni's dubious opinion, "we sought and obtained legal advice to the effect that it [did] not." He went on to disparage the many "so-called 'legal scholars' who provided . . . advice to the media" that the amendment did in fact cover his activities, yet in responding to a question by committee counsel, he cited not a U.S. government lawyer but just such an outside legal scholar with whom he said he discussed the issue "on a number of occasions." This turned out to be untrue. The scholar, John Norton Moore of the University of Virginia, told the press shortly after North's testimony he had never talked about the legalities of Boland II with him, and although he had once written the amendment was "embroiled in a dispute," he never contended it did not apply to the NSC.[9]

Another element of the debate was whether the amendment covered the president personally. Hamilton stated he did not think so, but he "did read it as applying to other entities of the United States Government" associated with the president, including the NSC. As historian Theodore Draper argued, the law may not have named the president ("a point later made as a way of evading it"), but "he clearly could not act alone and would have had to act through governmental agencies specified directly or indirectly in the amendment."[10]

Carrying Out the President's Orders

By the time Congress finally passed the bill, on October 10, 1984, Reagan administration officials had had the better part of a year to prepare alternate strategies. Although internal splits persisted over how to approach Central America, advocates of a hard line prevailed. The CIA chief analyst, Robert M. Gates, gave expression to that view two months after passage of the amendment. "It is time to talk absolutely straight about Nicaragua," he wrote to DCI Casey in December 1984. "Based on all the assessments we have done, the Contras, even with American support, cannot overthrow the Sandinistas." The solution was to "acknowledge openly . . . that the existence of a Marxist-Leninist regime in Nicaragua . . . is unacceptable to the United States and that the United States will do everything in its power short of invasion to put that regime out."[11]

This view eventually carried the day—except the administration chose not to operate in the open, preferring to act covertly instead. Overriding all other concerns was the worry that if Congress discovered what the administration was up to, it would permanently halt U.S. aid to the rebels. As discussed, legal considerations seemed of little interest.

To help meet the president's charge to keep the Contras alive, McFarlane turned to North. North, who had celebrated his forty-first birthday three days before Boland passed Congress, joined the NSC staff in 1981 as a "gofer" during the fight over congressional approval of the sale of AWACS aircraft to Saudi Arabia.[12] He quickly built a reputation straight out of the Marine Corps manual—resourceful, tireless, dedicated to the mission no matter the obstacles. His hours were extraordinary. He was famous for churning out reams of memoranda that kept his superiors minutely informed. A senior CIA official who worked with him on a daily basis said he "excelled in every respect."[13] A fellow military officer described him as "like a one-armed paper hanger . . . you know, he's talking on this phone—he's talking on that phone. He's in, he's out. . . . Rarely did you . . . get a chance to have a conversation that lasted more than about 3 minutes."[14] In 1983, North received his first assignment dealing with Central America—providing staff support to the Kissinger Commission, which was studying policy options for the region. By the time McFarlane became national security advisor in October of that year, the two men, both Naval Academy graduates, marines, and Vietnam veterans, had grown close. North seemed to have a way about him that inspired forbearance from his superiors. When the younger was promoted to lieutenant colonel, the elder gave him the oak leaf pins he had worn.

North was also a true believer in the Reagan "revolution," sharing most of the political, cultural, and moral precepts the president strove to represent. He deeply admired Reagan personally and enthusiastically shared his sense of U.S. exceptionalism. Vietnam "still burned within him," one biographer wrote, as a place where the United States had lost its honor at the hands of self-interested politicians in Washington. "The Congress of the United States left soldiers in the field unsupported and vulnerable to their Communist enemies," he testified after the scandal. He was determined not to allow the Contras to be abandoned the way the South Vietnamese allies had been, especially when, in his view, fundamental strategic and moral consequences were at stake.[15] He was also a born-again Christian, active in a charismatic church and a regular participant at weekly prayer meetings organized for military officers. By his public deportment, he seemed to define himself in terms of faith in God, devotion to family, patriotism, and duty—wrapping himself in the flag, critics would later say. While on the NSC staff, serving the president became his all-consuming objective. These characteristics help explain the almost evangelical fervor with which he carried out his mission against the mullahs and the Sandinistas.

One other characteristic of North's stood out: his pronounced tendency to fabricate. Colleagues and friends later recalled a pattern of needless fibs, half-truths, and outright lies that left associates shaking their heads.[16] These exaggerations and prevarications became a recurring feature in the Iran-Contra affair, as he openly acknowledged to congressional and federal investigators. He seemed prepared to say anything to try to influence decisions or swing events his way or simply to pump dramatic effect into his storytelling. His superiors, McFarlane and Poindexter, were not impervious to his deceptions. Yet they seemed to indulge his behavior and allowed him to go forward, ultimately at a high cost to the president and the causes in which North so passionately believed.

By the time McFarlane instructed him to oversee the operation, North was familiar with the Contras and understood where administration policy was heading. In January 1984, he had helped draft an NSDD on raising financial support for the rebels, an objective at the core of his later assignment. The directive called for "immediate efforts to obtain additional funding of $10–15 million from foreign or domestic sources to make up for the fact that the current $24 million appropriation will sustain operations only through June 1984."[17] At McFarlane's direction, during the spring he began to develop more direct links with the insurgents, becoming more deeply drawn into both the military and political aspects of their activities. By the time the CIA had been ordered out of the picture, he had established himself as "the kingpin to the Central America opposition," as Poindexter put it, the "switching point that made the whole system work."[18]

North's proposed new role suited Casey perfectly, and the two came to be in frequent contact with each other. The CIA director had understood if Congress were to resume official funding for the Contras, he would have to make concessions over his agency's conduct in Nicaragua, including pulling back substantially on the agency's involvement and reshuffling the Latin America division. High on the Democrats' hit list was the head of the division, Duane Clarridge, who had regularly blocked lawmakers' attempts to get to the bottom of agency doings in the region and who had personally engaged in troubling operational activities, such as drafting a 1983 manual for the Contras that called for "neutralizing" selected civilian officials in Nicaragua and working toward the "moment when the overthrow can be achieved." Most recently, he had helped to mastermind the Nicaraguan harbor minings.[19] Even within the agency, Clarridge was seen as a "cowboy" who, in the words of a CIA analyst at the time, fit the mold of a subset of operatives who "reveled in their ability to break the rules."[20] Rather than punish Clarridge, Casey, clearly signaling his disregard for Capitol Hill, put him in charge of the even more important European division.

In the face of growing intrusiveness from critics, Casey saw the advantage of having an eager subordinate at the White House whose involvement could be used as cover for proscribed activities. He therefore instructed Clarridge to initiate North into the CIA's covert program. In May 1984, Clarridge escorted North to Tegucigalpa, Honduras, and introduced him to several Contra leaders. "If something happens in Congress," Clarridge promised the group, "we will have an alternative way, and to assure that, here is Colonel North. You will never be abandoned."[21] Casey also summoned Adolfo Calero, the head of the largest Contra faction—the Nicaraguan Democratic Force (FDN)—to his office so he could bestow his own endorsement on North.[22]

According to North, Casey personally took him under his wing during 1984. When McFarlane needed a bank account set up to receive a foreign government donation for the Contras, "Casey told me what to do."[23] The ex-OSS man, who North described as a "financial genius," gave him a primer on some of the tricks of the spy trade—how to set up a clandestine accounting system for the FDN, for example, which North ran from his office in the Old Executive Office Building, next door to the White House. "I knew nothing about covert operations when I came to the NSC," North wrote later.[24] Although he was later criticized for puffing up his relationship to senior administration officials, including the president, North seems to have worked more closely at times with Casey than with his direct NSC superiors, an arrangement that caused some uneasiness. But McFarlane was fully in favor of North taking over operations for the CIA. When North proposed to meet Calero again in Honduras in August, McFarlane quickly agreed—as long as he could keep the rendezvous quiet. "Exercise absolute 'stealth,'" McFarlane instructed. "No visible meeting. No press awareness of your presence in area."[25] As long as his objectives meshed with Casey's, McFarlane seemed to have no objection to his subordinate reporting to both men.

For North, the assignment was a platform from which he could accomplish big things—helping to roll back communist influence in the hemisphere, for example. It also fed his recognized appetite for attention and melodrama. According to colleagues, North loved to impress with cloak-and-dagger stories of his exploits, so unlike the desk-bound routine of NSC staff work, and bragged about alleged frequent private interactions with the president and other world leaders. Some saw through the pretense but many inside the government and out did not.

North took full advantage of this to push his agenda. But in the process, a number of NSC staffers reported, he displayed a worrisome disregard not only for the truth but for the impact of his actions. Air Force Col. Ronald Sable, who worked on legislative affairs at the NSC, recalled telling North one day, "If we wanted to get on the other side of the wall, you would be there before anyone else, but you might not check to see if there was a door." According to Vincent Cannistraro, a career CIA officer detailed to the NSC staff, "With Colonel North you could never be certain that what he was telling you was true or was fantasy or was being told you deliberately to mislead you." Others were even harsher. Jacqueline Tillman, who shared the Central America portfolio with North for a time, told a colleague, "I've worked here at the NSC for some weeks now with Ollie North, and I've concluded that not only is he a liar, but he's delusional, power hungry, and a danger to the president and the country."[26]

Eyes and Ears

After initial meetings with key Contra figures, North got down to the mind-boggling challenge of taking over a covert program previously the purview of an entire subdivision within the CIA. As the scope of his assignment became clearer over the next year, he recognized the depth of his inexperience in the role but ploughed ahead, motivated by a combination of zeal for the cause and determination to fulfill a mission he knew to be a personal priority of the president.

Simply put, North had a war to fight. To win it, his priority was to make sure his forces had the necessary weapons and equipment, which meant he had to identify both a steady flow of money and dependable sources of supply.

Before tackling those tasks, though, he needed to know what the Contras' exact requirements were. To find out, he enlisted a young, former Capitol Hill staffer and public relations flack named Robert Owen, who had recently worked for Republican senator Dan Quayle of Indiana. By late May 1984, after numerous encounters with Contra leaders and with North, Owen felt sufficiently drawn to the cause to take leave from his job and, using his own money, travel to Costa Rica and Honduras to scout out the rebels' circumstances. It was the start of a close working relationship with North, who regularly sent his protégé to the region and received a stream of vivid reports from the field. The two adopted code names in their correspondence. North was "Steelhammer," "The Hammer," and "BG" ("Blood and Guts"); Owen often signed his memos "The Courier," or simply "TC."

The Beginnings of the "Enterprise"

With a crude intelligence network in place, supplemented by input from CIA operatives, North developed a clearer picture of the Contras' needs. Next, he began to put in place a modest covert procurement operation. Casey provided the name of a retired U.S. Air Force major general, Richard Secord, to help.

A fighter pilot by training, Secord had spent more than twenty years in special operations with the U.S. Air Force and CIA. His varied career included tours in Vietnam; in Laos, where he ran air infiltration/exfiltration missions as a CIA detailee; and in Iran, where he helped the shah's army put down a Kurdish insurrection in the 1960s and advised the Iranians on military affairs. In 1980, he was appointed to help plan a second attempt to rescue the U.S. hostages in Tehran after the first exploded in flames in the Iranian desert. Secord also had long experience in weapons procurement and as a Pentagon advisor to foreign governments interested in the latest U.S. hardware.[27] North already knew Secord slightly from his role in spearheading the administration's campaign to gain congressional approval to sell AWACS aircraft to Saudi Arabia in 1981.

Secord had many of the qualifications North was looking for, including the important advantage of no longer serving in the government. In May 1983, he had quit the military, his career stalled over allegations of involvement with a blacklisted ex-CIA officer named Edwin Wilson.[28] Ignoring the scandal, Casey saw Secord's potential for helping North's operation. He described him to North as a "man of integrity" who "got things done, and who had been poorly treated."[29]

According to North, Casey's vision was nothing less than to set up an extragovernmental operation capable of taking on sensitive covert missions without answering to Congress or relying on official funding—an "off-the-shelf, self-sustaining, stand-alone entity," as North described it.[30] In its basic conception, it was not much different from the intelligence community's standard procedure for running covert operations: the CIA and other agencies commonly used "proprietaries," shell companies or legitimate businesses, to act as fronts for undercover activities. But Casey was taking the idea a major step further, removing the operation virtually entirely from official scrutiny—even by the agency. That might make it easier to run off-the-books operations, but it significantly raised the risk of abuse. In fact, the idea ran diametrically against the spirit and intent of a host of legal restrictions and reporting requirements instituted by Congress expressly for purposes of presidential and CIA accountability.

North first contacted Secord in July 1984 to explain his proposition. He wanted Secord to meet Calero and make an assessment of the rebels' needs. Secord spent an evening driving the Contra leader around Washington, D.C., then stopped by North's office to give his impressions. He confirmed Owen's general description of the sorry state of the FDN's military position. As for Calero, the former Coca-Cola executive from Managua was a "well-meaning plutocrat" but "out of his depth trying to run an army." Nonetheless, Secord agreed to sign on to North's crusade—but with the expectation he would be able to tap into the potential financial bonanza offered by the deal.[31]

Secord's first task was to find a new source of weapons for the FDN. With funding a major concern, Calero and North wanted to get as much for their limited resources as possible. They also worried about faulty equipment; the Contras had already lost too many recruits because of grenades blowing up in their hands and similar accidents. Calero handed a wish list to Secord, who promised to check the international market. Several months passed before he came back with a set of prices. But Calero was pleased with the results.

By November, the first deal had been struck. Secord's contact was a Canadian arms dealer named Emmanuel Weigensberg. Using funds donated to the Contras by the Saudis as a down payment, Weigensberg's Montreal-based company, TransWorld Arms, negotiated through a Portuguese supplier to buy SA-7 surface-to-air missiles and launchers, RPG-7 rockets, M-79 grenades, 7.62 mm cartridges for Soviet-style AK-47 assault rifles, and other equipment from an unlikely source—the People's Republic of China. The price for the weapons was $1.6 million. After Secord and his colleagues tacked on their brokers' fee, the final bill for the FDN came to $2.3 million.[32]

Sharing the commission were Weigensberg and a Washington lawyer, Thomas Green, who had introduced Secord and Weigensberg.[33] Both men received one-third of the fee, or $240,133 apiece. Secord split the final third with Albert Hakim, an Iranian-born businessman then living in the United States. According to CIA records, in August 1976 the agency's associate deputy director for operations, Theodore Shackley, had proposed the CIA help Hakim obtain a contract to provide Iran security systems for military bases by introducing him to Secord, who was then chief of the U.S. Military Assistance Advisory Group in Iran. In return, the Iranian would become a source for the agency. The idea was scotched when another CIA official, apparently working on the ground in Iran, pointed out the "unsavory reputation" Hakim had developed for "unloading . . . unneeded oversophisticated equipment at exorbitant price[s]."[34] Hakim also came under investigation at one point for allegedly bribing Iranian officials on behalf of the Olin Corporation, but he was never prosecuted.

When Secord was reassigned to Washington, D.C., Hakim would visit him at the Pentagon to "pay my respects. . . . I sort of kept track of him," Hakim admitted, because the general's extensive Middle East contacts would make him an attractive partner if he were to leave government. (The two also shared an acquaintance with Wilson.) In 1980, Secord recruited Hakim to help with the planned second Tehran-led hostage rescue attempt, which never took place. After Secord retired from the military in 1983, the two men went into business together; Hakim made Secord president of a new company called Stanford Technology Trading Group International (STTGI) based in California.[35]

The two partners' first experience as arms brokers for the Contras turned out to be a setback. Persistent delays dogged the shipment from China, including difficulties acquiring end-user certificates (EUCs). An essential part of any international arms transaction—even a covert one—EUCs issued by a recipient government certified the country concerned was the final destination for the weapons. Because the FDN was not a recognized government, the legitimacy of the transaction was in doubt, so Weigensberg resorted to forgeries.

The practice was entirely illegal but not uncommon. Governments such as China's or the communist regimes in Eastern Europe regularly sold weapons on the international gray market to build up hard currency reserves. So valuable was the arms trade they were frequently willing to ignore where a shipment was going, even if it was to an unfriendly state. In this case, the Chinese knew exactly what Weigensberg was trying to do—the problem was only how it would appear.

On December 4, North learned from a Chinese official that a representative of Politechnic, the government-owned arms export company, had blundered by accepting Guatemalan EUCs for the shipment when Guatemala and China were on poor diplomatic terms. The official told North the individual in question, a "Mr. Gu," was "young and inexperienced" and "had made an error."[36] The NSC staffer decided to be candid—admit the EUCs were false, and that the arms were in fact going to the Contras.[37] But the Chinese still needed to maintain at least the pretense of propriety. North, by habit, made detailed notes of the situation: "Weigensberg has 2 people in Beijing—reviewing contract," he wrote. "Needs satisfactory export licen[se]." Weigensberg's eventual solution was to switch to Peruvian EUCs. "Polytechnic has already done business in Peru," North noted.[38]

But while the Chinese military attaché in Ottawa counseled forbearance ("be patient—few more days"), North believed the FDN could not wait. "Talked to Adolfo—*down*," he wrote that same day, "badly needs ammo; losing 3000 recruits for lack of equipment."[39] Fortunately for the rebels, Secord stepped in with a stopgap arrangement, organizing a consignment of 90,000 pounds of grenades and AK-47 rounds to be flown to the FDN from Eastern Europe. Bypassing Weigensberg and Green on the deal, Secord relied instead on a comrade in arms from his days in Laos, a career CIA operative named Thomas G. Clines. As with Hakim, the discredited Wilson provided a common link with Clines. Whereas Secord had only been bruised by the connection (no direct tie to Wilson's arms business was ever proven), Clines had owned a 49 percent interest in Wilson's company and had taken a direct hit, paying $110,000 in civil and criminal penalties as a result of the scandal. Secord reportedly underwrote a portion of the fines.[40]

One year later, the two joined forces again, with Secord hoping to use Clines's expertise in the gray arms market as well as his knowledge of Central America, where he had spent much of his CIA career. To help with logistics for the Enterprise, Secord hired another ex-CIA operative, Rafael "Chi Chi" Quintero, an anti-Castro Cuban exile and Bay of Pigs veteran who had worked under Clines on a number of covert missions in the region.[41]

The second shipment of arms to the Contras actually arrived before the first, even though getting EUCs again turned out to be a problem. This time, North canvassed various Central American governments, including El Salvador, for help. In late January 1985, he told Calero about an approach through Salvadoran Air Force Gen. Juan Rafael Bustillo, who would later collaborate with the covert Contra resupply operation. But according to North's notes, Salvadoran president Jóse Napoleón Duarte rejected the request: "Mtg w/Adolfo. . . . Bustillo Re E.U.C. for M-79 Rounds—*Duarte turned down."[42]

The next day, North contacted U.S. Ambassador to Honduras John Negroponte. As the NSC staffer recorded it, the two discussed several "offline," or off-the-record, topics, including "E.U.C.—5000 M-79 Rds" (a reference to end-user certificates for 5,000 rounds of M-79 ammunition), which seemed plainly to relate to the Contras' supply problems.[43] With no results forthcoming, Secord elevated the pressure. "Mtg w Secord," North wrote on February 5. "Needs to get a bunch of EUCs from Guatemala *NOW* for next shipment."[44]

The Guatemalans finally came through (evidently being on better political terms with the East European governments involved), transferring nine EUCs covering surface-to-air missiles, more than 15,000 grenades and launchers, 10,000 pounds of C-4 explosives, and other supplies worth almost $8 million.[45] The EUCs, dated February 14, were addressed to Energy Resources International in suburban Vienna, Virginia, a company Hakim had formed in Panama in 1978. They were signed by a high Guatemalan military official.[46] For the Chinese shipment, meanwhile, Weigensberg settled on Moroccan EUCs. Those arms finally reached the Contras in early April.

As with other aspects of North's covert activities, success came at a cost—often unanticipated. The Guatemalan generals expected compensation for their rather substantial gesture in supplying the EUCs, and North, seemingly unconcerned about the policy implications of such a blatant quid pro quo, was determined to comply. He wrote a memo to McFarlane attaching copies of the falsified documents and recommending McFarlane sign another memo to top administration officials asking—without hinting at what the Guatemalans had done—"for their views on increased U.S. assistance to Guatemala." The full story he confided only to McFarlane: "The real purpose of your memo is to find a way by which we can compensate the Guatemalans for the extraordinary assistance they are providing to the Nicaraguan freedom fighters."[47]

By early 1985, Secord had pulled together the core elements of the Enterprise. Hakim and his Switzerland-based attorney, Willard I. Zucker, established a string of shell companies to provide cover for the operations and to maintain the flow of funds among them. Clines and Quintero monitored the region and set up the arms deals. Secord managed the operation in close collaboration with North, communicating with him a "wild average" of three or four times a week.[48] He and North worked out a series of codes, purportedly to prevent Soviet or Cuban intelligence from eavesdropping and reporting their plans to the Sandinistas. Secord adopted the pseudonym "Richard Copp," which he picked out of a book he was reading at the time. North became William P. Goode and had the CIA concoct a complete set of false documentation—passport, driver's license, and other identification to go along with it.[49]

The question of Secord's motivations—whether he was a patriot or profiteer—hounded him during the Iran-Contra investigations. Although he held that he was mainly doing a "favor for North and the administration," the arrangement represented a major business opportunity. In his memoir, he pointed to other rationales for his involvement. At one point, he insisted his "main motivation . . . was the nagging sense that things were getting screwed up again in our covert operations, and there weren't a lot of guys around who could fix them." At another point, he expressed a certain professional ambition: "The more I worked with Ollie, the clearer I could see the day when I might be offered another high-level government position, perhaps as deputy director of operations for the CIA."[50] Hakim had a more straightforward explanation. When Secord told him about North's operation, Hakim said he promised they would be "going . . . into this as private businessmen." The Iranian thought the idea was "beautiful. . . . I will help out and make money; why not?"[51]

North backed up this impression. "It was always viewed by myself, by Mr. Mc-Farlane, by Director Casey, that these were private commercial ventures"[52] for Secord. The former general built in markups as high as 40 percent on arms sales for himself and his partner. In 1985 and 1986, he took in more than $3 million and Hakim more than $2.5 million in "direct personal benefits" and cash from the Iran and Contra deals, according to investigators.[53]

The War Continues

In 1984, Nicaragua saw a number of important developments. In addition to the harbor mining episode, a bomb exploded at a press conference near the Nicaragua–Costa Rica border. Edén Pastora, a charismatic, independent-minded Contra leader, was seriously wounded. In November, Sandinista leader Daniel Ortega won election to the presidency. Meanwhile, the insurgents continued to fight despite the pessimistic prognosis of Robert Gates of the CIA. Before North had taken over as the Contras' surreptitious coordinator, some of the rebels had shown an eagerness for action. Working with a private entity from the United States, a group of insurgents put together a plan for assaulting a Sandinista military school located in the town of Santa Clara, just south of the Honduran border. The self-described "missionary-mercenaries" from an Alabama-based organization called Civilian Military Assistance (CMA) were then in Honduras providing training and arms to the rebels. The plan called for flying three Cessna O-2 aircraft, acquired the year before from the U.S. Defense Department, and a Hughes 500 helicopter, and firing rockets at the base. The maneuver took place just after noon on September 1, 1984, but it was an utter failure. Damage from the 2.75-inch rockets was limited to a kitchen area. Casualties included four civilian cooks, but no soldiers. Worse, the Hughes helicopter was hit by Sandinista antiaircraft fire, and all three CMA crew members were killed.[54]

U.S. officials reacted with disbelief. North was adamant to McFarlane the United States, specifically the CIA, had played no part in the scheme. He blamed it on "non-official Americans on-scene at the FDN Headquarters" in Las Vegas, Honduras, who "goaded" Enrique Bermúdez's forces into the attack. North insisted Calero, who knew about the plan, had "left instructions that this operation should *not* be conducted until he had talked to us."[55] The fallout was substantial. Not only had half the Contras' helicopter force been destroyed, at a significant cost to their reputation for military effectiveness, the Hondurans began to apply restrictions on FDN use of their airfields. Meanwhile, Congress blamed the CIA, ignoring its pleas of innocence. At least one member of Congress—Jim Leach (D-Iowa)—charged the operation violated the Arms Export Control Act (AECA), presaging a later legal confrontation over the White House's covert Contra program.[56]

North and the CIA tried to turn disaster into advantage. Agency officials worked on Bermúdez to unload his CMA advisors, who were only making things more complicated from their point of view. North, meanwhile, suggested to McFarlane the administration use the episode to press for a bigger U.S. role (not smaller, as some might have argued) in the Contra war. Finally, to put some positive spin on the dismal event and score a few propaganda points, North reported to McFarlane the FDN would hold a press conference to announce—falsely—the casualties had included Cubans.[57]

North even had an idea for replacing the lost equipment. He asked McFarlane for approval to approach a "private donor for the provision of a replacement civilian helicopter for use on the Northern front." McFarlane balked, writing in the margin of North's memo, "I don't think this is legal." The following year retired Gen. John Singlaub, an anticommunist activist and self-appointed Contra fundraiser, persuaded a wealthy Texan named Ellen Garwood to donate $65,000 for a helicopter—promptly dubbed the "Lady Ellen" in her honor.[58]

Helicopters soon became a focus of a different kind for North, who demonstrated his own readiness to take on risky military exploits on behalf of the Contras. When the Kremlin began sending high-tech Soviet-made Hind-D assault aircraft to its allies in Nicaragua, the White House recognized their potential to tilt the balance on the battlefield. (According to Robert Owen, they "could put a bullet in every square inch of a football field in 10 seconds.")[59]

In November 1984, North sent Owen to Calero with a collection of maps and photographs of the airport in Managua and the proposal the Contras mount an airstrike to take out the helicopters while they were still being assembled. But because the Contras' aircraft would run out of fuel before returning to base, Owen recalled, North understood "it would be a suicide mission." Calero took the idea under advisement but "didn't make a commitment one way or another."[60]

In some cases, North's interdiction efforts clearly violated the second Boland Amendment ban on providing military-logistical help to the rebels. His superiors—McFarlane and Poindexter—typically did nothing to discourage him. In early December 1984, for example, North wrote to McFarlane about a meeting with a retired major from Britain's Special Air Services (SAS), David Walker, who was currently in private business providing security services to foreign governments. But Walker was also looking for more action-oriented work for his Jersey Islands–based companies and, according to North, "suggested that he would be interested in establishing an arrangement with the FDN for certain special operations expertise aimed particularly at destroying Hind helicopters." Without hesitating, North got the sabotage operation under way. "Unless otherwise directed, Walker will be introduced to Calero, and efforts will be made to defray the cost of Walker's operations from other than Calero's limited assets."[61]

Although Walker made the case the helicopters were "more easily destroyed on the ground than in the air," he also suggested the Contras try to get British-made Blowpipe surface-to-air missiles from Chile to knock the sophisticated Hinds out of the sky.[62] North dispatched Calero to Santiago to negotiate with Gen. Augusto Pinochet's representatives. Calero came back a few days later with news he had struck a deal. Using the Contra leader's code name, "Barnaby," North recorded the particulars in his notebook: "Call from Barnaby—Returned from Chile—48 Blowpipes—*free*—8 launchers—25K ea. ($200K total)—Have to inform Brits—8–10 pers. for training—starts 2 Jan—Will have to buy some items from Chileans which are somewhat more expensive—Deliver by sea w/trainers by end of Jan—Will deliver thru Guatemala—Chileans will communicate—Will talk to Dick Secord."[63]

The Chileans seemed willing to help; the only catch was the Pinochet regime required approval from its suppliers, the British. North thought it might be possible for President Reagan to quietly obtain Prime Minister Margaret Thatcher's permission during an upcoming visit to Washington, D.C. The British, after all, had indicated earlier in the year they might have funds available to help the Contras. North continued to try through mid-1986, but never managed to get the Chileans to part with their Blowpipes.[64]

Although arms interdiction was authorized under the December 1981 presidential finding, North's efforts to broker weapons deals and pass along military intelligence or advice to the Contras were activities McFarlane understood breached the second Boland Amendment.[65] Still, North did not stop there.

In early February 1985, U.S. intelligence detected a Nicaraguan merchant ship, the *Monimbó*, steaming in Asian waters. It was believed the ship's cargo included weapons bound for the Nicaraguan military. North locked onto the vessel as a potential target, telling McFarlane he saw three options: "The shipment could be seized and the weapons delivered to the FDN; the ship could be sunk; or the shipment . . . could be made public as a means of preventing the delivery."[66]

Calero, he said, could finance the operation, although he did not have enough trained personnel to handle the first option. The NSC aide remembered, however, the South Korean military had previously offered to help the rebels, and suggested they might be approached—even though he acknowledged it would be an act of piracy on the high seas. If that approach did not pan out, he assured McFarlane, Calero could "quickly be provided with the maritime assets required to sink the vessel before it can reach port at Corinto," on Nicaragua's Pacific coast.

Poindexter, who received a copy of the memo, agreed and wrote at the bottom: "We need to take action to make sure ship does not arrive in Nicaragua. JMP."[67] In the end, no action was taken, reportedly because the South Koreans balked. This did not keep North from boasting later, "The ship ended up on its side on the beach."[68]

At least one actual case of sabotage took place in spring 1985 when Walker oversaw an attack on a key Nicaraguan military depot in Managua. Unfortunately, the chief result was to virtually destroy the Alejandro Dávila Bolaños Military Hospital next door.[69] In their attempts to make the Contras appear a viable military force, too often the result was a growing record not only of ineptitude but of brutality for the damage inflicted, deliberately or not, on civilians or noncombat-related facilities.

Worse Than Watergate

Top administration officials, particularly Casey and McFarlane, went to great lengths to remove any visible traces of CIA involvement with the Contras during the Boland ban. On the operational level, passing the ball to North was an act of legerdemain intended to add deniability to administration support for the rebels in the face of strict congressional (and public) opposition to the program. (The Reagan team deliberately downplayed Nicaragua during the 1984 election campaign.) The ploy may have seemed imaginative, even ingenious, at the time, and its authors might have believed they were doing just enough to conform to the legal constraints on the CIA. But the agency never completely withdrew. Casey played a major role in preparing North for his new assignment, both personally and by assigning senior staff officers such as Clarridge to show him the ropes. The CIA director also, of course, worked diligently to find ways around the congressional ban on Contra funding. Beyond that, he saw to it North had as much help as he could get from the agency—as long as the secret of what they were doing could be protected. This concern went beyond the usual imperative of operational security. Casey and his lieutenants knew if Congress found out about the end run on Contra aid, its opponents would make sure the program never got renewed.

Another CIA official who played a key part in the covert program despite the congressional ban was Alan Fiers, a career operative who became head of the Central America Task Force (CATF) within the Directorate of Operations (DO) in September 1984. Fiers later aided in the official cover-up of agency involvement with the Contras but turned state's evidence in return for a guilty plea to a reduced charge. As he prepared to take over his new job as day-to-day coordinator of CIA activities in Central America, the status of the Contra program was, not surprisingly, high on his mind. As the second Boland Amendment was about to pass both houses of Congress and be signed into law, it was Fiers's clear understanding CIA officials could have no part in supporting the rebels after the ban went into effect. So when Clarridge called him into his office soon thereafter, Fiers felt a distinct uneasiness upon discovering the point of the visit was to introduce him to Oliver North. "He's someone you need to know," Clarridge told Fiers. "He's got responsibilities at the NSC for Central America, and you'll be working with him."[70]

Although Clarridge urged Fiers to cooperate, he and Casey also wanted to make sure neither Fiers nor anyone else without a "need to know" learned too much about the NSC staff's clandestine work. A few weeks after first meeting North, Fiers and North had a telephone conversation centering on a sudden visit to Washington, D.C., by Calero who had been anxious about a shipment of Hind helicopters that had just arrived in Managua. Casey found out about the conversation almost immediately and complained to McFarlane the NSC aide was talking too much about "Calero, Guatemala, MIGs, dollars, etc."[71]

Casey's determination to cover up the Contra program manifested itself in a bizarre incident that took place in late 1984. After Clarridge's transfer out of the Latin America division, Fiers approached his replacement as well as Clair George, the head of the DO, to let them know Clarridge had ordered him to do things he feared went "beyond the bounds" of the congressional restriction. Instead of getting support, Fiers found himself being called to the director's office, along with George, Clarridge's successor, and North.

According to Fiers, "The director sort of leaned back in his chair and said, 'Ollie, Alan says you're operating in Central America' or words to that effect. 'Are you operating in Central America?'" Casey then asked Fiers to repeat to North what he had told Clarridge of his concerns about the second Boland Amendment. He then turned back to North and said, "Now Ollie, I don't want you operating in Central America. You understand that?" North replied, "Yes, sir. I understand it."[72]

As Fiers and George walked through the halls of the CIA afterward, both men knew perfectly well North would remain heavily involved in Central America. George made clear that Casey's behavior had been a "charade"—a game the director and others were ready to play to protect the Contra operations. "Alan, you've got to understand what happened in there. What we saw was for our consumption. Sometime in the dark of night Bill Casey has told the President: 'I'll take care of Central America, Mr. President; don't worry about it.' And what you saw was essentially for our consumption." Fiers replied, "Wow, if that's true and if it blows it will be worse than Watergate."[73]

By 1985, Fiers had joined in the game, becoming one of the CIA's chief contacts with North—second only to Casey—and "the CIA headquarters official most heavily involved with efforts to support the Contras."[74] That summer, he took the lead in fomenting a covert deception himself. With Casey's authorization, he arranged for a private corporation with ties to the CIA to bill the agency for expenses it would not normally claim, then send the excess funds to the Catholic Church in Nicaragua, which was actively involved in anti-Marxist activities. It was a blurring of legitimate and off-the-books activities that mirrored the Iran and Contra operations and showed that sidestepping congressional bans on overseas support activities was hardly unheard of in Casey's CIA.[75]

4

TOW Missiles to Tehran

The presidentially approved covert Iran operation fell into place in spring and summer 1985. Some cabinet officers resisted at first, but a determined national security advisor teamed up with an influential backer—the Israeli government—and found a way to obtain presidential approval. The Israelis had joined forces with the disreputable arms dealer Manucher Ghorbanifar, who pledged access to authorities in Tehran. The catch, as some U.S. officials understood, was the Iranians and Israelis did not necessarily share U.S. objectives; each side had its own priorities, but the key for all concerned was to keep the United States engaged because U.S. weapons were the principal currency of the deals. Constant encouragement by Iranian and Israeli middlemen made it easier for the U.S. participants to convince themselves of both the advisability and viability of the operation. The most essential proponent, however, was President Ronald Reagan. Even after the initial missile transfers failed to produce as promised in August and September 1985, he made it plain he wanted the operation to continue.

Events Come Together

Having warmed to his new post as national security advisor, Robert McFarlane was determined to press forward with new policy initiatives. He knew there were certain buttons he could push on the Iran issue. Both the president and his closest advisors, for example, were susceptible to concerns about Soviet incursions into the region. In 1983, Reagan had confirmed the top U.S. priority for the Near East was to prevent Moscow from attaining "hegemony" by "deterring Soviet expansion and by supporting the sovereignty" of local countries.[1] At a National Security Planning Group (NSPG) meeting in September 1984, the president had recalled the shah's role as a buffer for the West prior to the revolution: "Iran used to be the 'cork' in the bottle as far as Soviet expansion was concerned." He then dropped a comment that in hindsight hinted at his bent toward opening communications with Tehran: "Whoever designed the old strategy of cooperating with Iran," he said, "was on the right track." George Shultz concurred, describing Iran as, "in many respects, the most important country in the region" and adding, "We want to prevent Soviet domination" of the country.[2]

Drawing on these cold war tenets, in spring 1985 McFarlane assigned the CIA to put together yet another analysis that would resuscitate the idea of providing arms to Iran. At his behest, Donald Fortier, a highly regarded senior member of the NSC staff, teamed up with the agency's national intelligence officer (NIO) for the Near East, Graham Fuller, and NSC staffer Howard Teicher to work on the document. Fuller was also respected, in addition to being given to unconventional thinking—by no means a flaw in an NIO. Teicher was barely in his thirties but had several years' experience as an analyst on Middle East and political/military issues. The principal selling point of the analysis was the Soviet threat. Summarizing his ideas for William Casey, Fuller presented a stark image: "The US faces a grim situation in developing a new policy toward Iran. Events are moving largely against our interests and we have few palatable alternatives. In bluntest form the Khomeini regime is faltering and may be moving toward a moment of truth; we will soon see a struggle for succession. . . . Iran has obviously concluded that whether they like Russia and Communism or not, the USSR is the country to come to terms with."[3]

The analysis ignored or downplayed significant evidence of the fragility of Moscow's position in Iran. For all its anti-Americanism, the clerical regime was deeply hostile toward communism and suspicious of Soviet intentions. Ayatollah Khomeini's "neither East nor West" philosophy meant the Soviets could not count on filling the void left by the United States.[4] Over time, intelligence reports confirmed that Moscow's attempts to entice Tehran had failed broadly. In 1983, Khomeini crushed the Iranian Communist Party—the Tudeh—arresting dozens of leading members and executing or exiling others. By early 1985, a U.S. State Department study held out only a remote chance the USSR could exert a "determining influence" over Iran through its ties to the "crippled" communists or to indigenous minority groups.[5] Moreover, U.S. officials were aware the Soviets were troubled about influence flowing in the opposite direction—that the Iranian revolution would encourage the spread of Islamic fundamentalism in the USSR's heavily Muslim-populated Central Asian republics.

Despite the evidence, Fuller and his colleagues warned the prospects would be poor for the United States in the wake of Khomeini's death. "The US has almost no cards to play; the USSR has many," Fuller wrote. After ticking off several options for Washington, Fuller proposed the United States allow its allies to sell arms to the regime in order to demonstrate Tehran did not have to rely exclusively on Moscow.[6]

Three days later, the CIA released a formal analysis known as a Special National Intelligence Estimate (SNIE) on the subject of Iran after Khomeini. Focusing on the same threat of creeping Soviet gains, its authors (led by Fuller) suggested U.S. allies act as proxies for Washington. "The United States is unlikely to be able to directly influence Iranian events, given its current lack of contact or presence in Iran. European states and other friendly states—including Turkey, Pakistan, China, Japan, and even Israel—can provide the next most valuable presence or entrée in Iran to help protect Western interests."[7]

The SNIE then implicitly raised the idea of doing away with Operation Staunch, the 1983 State Department program to block weapons shipments to the Islamic Republic. "The degree to which some of these states can fill a military gap for Iran will be a critical measure of the West's ability to blunt Soviet influence."[8] Despite the proposed 180-degree turn in policy, Fuller said later the standard interagency review process found nothing "highly controversial" in the document, although it emerged the deputy director of intelligence at the CIA, Robert Gates, had pressured the State Department's intelligence bureau not to register a dissent against the analysis.[9]

Fortier and Teicher, along with Fuller, soon began reworking the SNIE into a draft NSDD that, if approved, would become de facto administration policy. The bureaucratic wheels McFarlane had set in motion were finally gaining traction. The draft's tone, like its earlier incarnations, was somewhat breathless. "Dynamic political evolution is taking place inside Iran," the paper began. "Instability caused by the pressures of the Iraq-Iran war, economic deterioration and regime infighting create the potential for major changes in Iran. The Soviet Union is better positioned than the U.S. to exploit and benefit from any power struggle that results in changes in the Iranian regime."[10]

Of nine alternative courses of action in the draft NSDD, the first was to "encourage Western allies and friends to help Iran meet its import requirements . . . [including] provision of selected military equipment as determined on a case-by-case basis."[11]

This was essentially a restatement of the idea presented in a similar draft directive four years earlier (see Chapter 2). However, a midlevel interagency meeting to discuss the concept before sending it up to the principals indicated that once again broad approval would be hard to come by. Representatives from the State and Defense Departments were sharply critical. "It was absurd," said a Pentagon participant later. "So many of us were so highly indignant about the idea, we assumed it wasn't going anywhere."[12] But McFarlane had lost patience with standard procedures and simply went over their heads, submitting the draft "on an eyes only basis" directly to Casey, Shultz, and Weinberger.[13]

The CIA director was enthusiastic. "I strongly endorse the thrust of the draft NSDD," Casey wrote, "particularly its emphasis on the need to take concrete and timely steps to enhance U.S. leverage in order to ensure that the USSR is not the primary beneficiary of change and turmoil in this critical country." He saw evidence the Kremlin had recently "rebuffed" the Iranians in various ways as a development that "strengthen[ed] the case made in the NSDD for our Allies filling the vacuum." In a comment on the state of internal Iranian politics and the "evolution of a post-Khomeini regime," he presciently noted the "likely important role of the Revolutionary Guard in a future Iran" and strongly agreed with the need to "open lines of communications to the existing Iranian leadership."[14]

In contrast, both the secretaries of defense and state rejected the policy shift proposed in the NSDD and its underlying analyses. Weinberger was contemptuous, describing the document to his military aide, Maj. Gen. Colin Powell, as "almost too absurd to comment on. . . . It's like asking Qadhafi to Washington for a cozy chat."[15]

In his formal response to McFarlane, Weinberger toned down his language, changing "absurd" to "questionable," for example. Although he "fully support[ed]" the main objective of preventing Moscow from increasing its influence in Iran, he insisted, "under no circumstances . . . should we now ease our restriction on arms sales to Iran." To do so would be "inexplicably inconsistent" and take away "one of the few ways we have to protect our longer-range interests in both Iran and Iraq."[16]

At the same time, he suggested several alternative intelligence, political, and economic approaches, all consistent with current policy, that the United States could undertake "to try to prevent an increase in Soviet influence and to lead toward a more moderate post-Khomeini Iran." He referred repeatedly to the need to find ways of "identifying" and "providing political and/or financial support" to elements in Iran "who may be more favorably disposed to US concerns." Although two years later he disparaged the term in public testimony, at the time he specifically recommended seeking "ways to establish contacts with 'moderates'" in Iran.[17]

Shultz was more diplomatic but equally negative on the matter of sending arms to Iran. The draft "constructively and perceptively addresses a number of the key issues," he wrote. "I disagree, however, with one point in the analysis and one specific recommendation."[18] The document's assessment of "anti-regime sentiment" in Iran was exaggerated, and the view Tehran would likely move closer to the USSR ignored the "inherent limits on the Iranian-Soviet relationship," including Tehran's "deep historical mistrust" of Moscow and the two countries' competing interests in the region. Like Weinberger, Shultz objected to the arms proposal, arguing it would be "contrary to our interests" of "containing Khomeinism" and "ending the excesses" of his regime.

This assault by the nation's two senior cabinet officials ought to have been enough to derail the initiative. But the peculiar lack of presidential control over disputes among senior aides in the Reagan administration helped McFarlane keep going on his own. Also, although Shultz and Weinberger said no to weapons, neither of them specifically closed the door on contacts with Tehran; on the contrary, both encouraged expanding ties—an opening McFarlane would exploit with the backing of Tel Aviv.

The Reemergence of Israel

In spring 1985, Iranian arms dealer Manucher Ghorbanifar and Saudi Arabian billionaire Adnan Khashoggi, two of the many private brokers hoping to cash in on the Iran-Iraq War, joined forces in a scheme to sell weapons to Iran via Israel. Ghorbanifar had access to senior Iranian officials, and Khashoggi, an ostentatious international businessman and arms dealer, had good contacts inside Israel. Under circumstances that are still unclear,[19] the two men arranged to meet in Europe with a pair of well-connected Israelis, Adolph "Al" Schwimmer and Yaacov Nimrodi. Schwimmer was a founder of Israel Aircraft Industries (IAI), Nimrodi a former military attaché to Tehran who had been born and lived in Iran for many years. Schwimmer was especially close to Prime Minister Shimon Peres. Ghorbanifar, who described himself as Iranian premier Mir-Hossein Mousavi's representative on intelligence matters in Europe, soon made it clear to the Israelis he wanted to buy weapons for Iran. According to the official Israeli government account prepared in the wake of the affair, the two Israelis promptly informed Peres, but the prime minister's initial reaction was negative. The Israeli account states that when Ghorbanifar persisted, saying he had in mind deals worth up to $40 million that could be handled as purely commercial transactions—not government to government—Peres agreed to sanction further talks.[20]

Ghorbanifar and an Iranian expatriate, Cyrus Hashemi, arrived in Israel in early April and met with Israeli Ministry of Defense officials to explore Iran's needs. Although these initial contacts were inconclusive, Ghorbanifar returned at the end of the month to present a new proposal that included selling U.S.-made Tube-launched Optically-tracked Wire-guided (TOW) missiles to Iran. Iranian sources confirmed later that the need for heavier missiles became acute during the Iran-Iraq War, when the Iraqis began replacing their T-55 Soviet-made tanks with greater numbers of the more modern T-72 (known as the "Lion of Babylon"). The Iranians soon discovered their shoulder-fired RPG-7 grenades could not penetrate the new tank's armor.[21]

Israel had TOWs in its inventory, but because they were U.S.-made, Peres decided Washington's approval of the sales would be needed. Ghorbanifar understood this, and in order to sweeten the pot for the Reagan administration, he offered an incentive he thought could not be ignored—the release of William Buckley, the CIA station chief in Beirut taken hostage a year earlier. As it happened, Buckley's captors had sent the CIA a videotape of him being tortured. Casey made sure Reagan saw the tape. Beyond humanitarian concerns, the CIA was frantic to secure Buckley's freedom because of the potential for damage to U.S. intelligence operations in the region if he broke under torture.[22] In other conversations, Ghorbanifar and the Israelis discussed how the deal could improve U.S. ties with Iran. Ghorbanifar insisted the arms would go to "moderates" interested in closer relations with the West—particularly the United States—and that the acquisition of these sought-after weapons would strengthen their position politically inside Iran. This was the same enticement Menachem Begin had used with U.S. officials three years earlier.

While these discussions were taking place, a part-time counterterrorism consultant to the NSC named Michael Ledeen had been trying to persuade McFarlane to explore Israeli government expertise in Iran's internal affairs.[23] A former professor, Ledeen was a Washington think tank analyst who had served as a "special advisor" to Secretary of State Alexander Haig. His main responsibility related to the activities of the Socialist International, which brought him into contact with prominent left-oriented politicians such as Israeli Labor Party leader Shimon Peres. Because Ledeen knew Peres, McFarlane permitted him to travel to Israel, and Ledeen set off in early May. Reagan administration officials later claimed they wanted the information simply to help prepare for the aftermath of Khomeini's death, but the official Israeli account indicated the United States had a sharper objective in mind: "to attempt to bring about the overthrow and replacement of the Iranian regime as soon as possible, before Khomeini died of natural causes." The "greatest danger," Ledeen reportedly told an advisor to Peres, would be if the system Khomeini had put in place survived him. An alternative had to be found before the mold was permanently set.[24]

Although Ledeen may have been focusing initially on politics, during the course of his talks with Peres the prime minister specifically raised the subject of arms to Iran. The Israeli leader let it be known he wanted Washington's approval for a deal with Tehran—the same transaction being negotiated between the Israeli middlemen and Ghorbanifar. He asked Ledeen to pass along his request to McFarlane. Ledeen obliged, although he apparently did not know who else was involved in the deal.[25] The timing of Ledeen's visit, coming just after Ghorbanifar's discussions with the Israelis, was a fluke, according to a senior Israeli official: "That was the coincidence that triggered the whole thing."[26]

At this stage, McFarlane wanted to keep the Ledeen trip to Israel secret, including from the State Department. He considered it a confidential channel, no doubt recalling Henry Kissinger's behind-the-scenes contacts prior to the diplomatic breakthrough with China in 1971.[27] Furthermore, the rivalry between the national security advisor and secretary of state had continued from Kissinger's time through the Carter administration and now into the Reagan era. McFarlane had already undercut Shultz at least twice before regarding the Middle East—in mid-1983 when he undertook a wide-ranging trip of his own to the region and in May 1984 when he instructed Teicher to approach Israel to seek aid for the Contras, falsely advising the secretary Teicher had acted independently.[28] In the case of the Ledeen trip, McFarlane once again tried to keep a close hold on his activities. In early June, though, the U.S. ambassador to Tel Aviv found out about it and told Shultz. The secretary called McFarlane on the carpet, demanding to know the nature of the mission. McFarlane again lied, claiming Ledeen had been operating "on his own hook." He promised to shut down the channel, but in reality had no intention of doing so.[29] He did hold off following up with Peres on the proposed intelligence arrangement, however, possibly to convince Shultz he was keeping his promise.

The Israelis, meanwhile, were moving ahead, and Peres—like Reagan—provided the impetus. The prime minister was renowned for acting on his own authority and outside channels. According to a close colleague, "Peres was the kind of person who whenever someone comes with, let's call it, a crazy idea . . . he'll say, 'go ahead,'" because "maybe through this crazy idea we can solve the problem of nuclear Iran today." He was said to be utterly unconcerned about the views of the relevant ministries or senior officials.[30] In this case he even froze out some of his inner circle. Having balked at first with his old friend, Al Schwimmer, Peres now saw ways to make a deal on Iran work that would derive benefits for Israel. As noted, Israel had always kept alive hopes of reestablishing contacts inside the Islamic Republic. Ghorbanifar seemed, at least to some Israelis, to offer that prospect. But it took Ledeen's visit to get Peres motivated, not because of who Ledeen was but because of who he claimed to represent. According to a close advisor to the prime minister, Ledeen cloaked his mission in mystery, refusing to say ahead of time why he was coming but hinting broadly it was at Reagan's behest. However the message was packaged, to Peres it was clear: the United States—very likely the president himself—wanted Israel's help on a matter of considerable sensitivity, and he decided immediately he would oblige.[31]

Peres not only saw important benefits to helping the United States, there was a personal angle—his relationship with Reagan. He believed the president was "no intellectual," according to aide Nimrod Novik, but he was a "mensch" who had "healthy instincts and his heart was in the right place." Shortly after Peres's inauguration as prime minister in 1984, he had described to Reagan the plight of thousands of Ethiopian Falasha Jews at a refugee camp in Sudan and his hope to evacuate them from the country. Reagan was "really moved, almost to tears," Novik said, and immediately made a commitment to help. When he ultimately followed through, supporting the Israeli operation despite sharply negative Sudanese and Arab reactions, "it was a formative moment for Peres." If Ledeen could be taken at his word, the prime minister envisioned a "great opportunity" to do something for the president that was clearly "very important" to him.[32]

But first, Peres wanted to make sure Ledeen was for real.[33] At around the time of the latter's visit, instead of checking with Israeli intelligence—the Mossad—he asked trusted colleague retired Maj. Gen. Shlomo Gazit to look into the matter. Gazit was former head of military intelligence but most recently had been president of Ben Gurion University. His prized attributes were his close ties to Peres and his position outside the government.[34] Gazit met with Ledeen, Nimrodi, and, on his own initiative, various Israeli officials to try to assess Ghorbanifar's offer and credentials. Ministry of Defense and intelligence experts thought the Iranian was unreliable; the former refused to have anything to do with him—a fact the Israelis apparently did not share with the United States.[35] Rather than cut off the contact, though, Gazit recommended to Peres a test: as part of the transaction, ask that all of the U.S. hostages be freed. This would not only verify Ghorbanifar's connections in Iran but also "strengthen the Americans' motivation to enter the affair," according to an official Israeli account.[36]

On July 3, at Peres's behest, Israel's Foreign Ministry director general, David Kimche, met with McFarlane and asked how the United States would view the opportunity to reopen ties with Iran. Kimche said the Iranians whom Israel had contacted wanted to set up a line of communication with Washington and represented a possible alternative to the current leadership. McFarlane recalled Kimche "went to some length" to explain why Israel "had concluded that these people were legitimate" and wanted to move Iran "away from the rather extreme policies of the time to a . . . less violent coexistence with their neighbors." It is not known whether the subject of hostages came up, but Kimche did raise the possibility Iran would need to see some evidence of good faith from the United States and Israel—in the form of a shipment of arms.[37]

The Search for "Moderates"

At about the same time, Khashoggi gave McFarlane a further prod. On July 1, he sent the national security advisor a lengthy analysis of the internal political situation in Iran, drafted mostly by Ghorbanifar, that included a breakdown of political factions he believed would be vying to take over the country after the death of Khomeini. The leadership, according to Ghorbanifar's analysis, broke down into three "lines": "rightists," including officials in the army, police, Parliament—known as the Majles—and Islamic Revolutionary Guard Corps (IRGC); "leftists," including Prime Minister Mir-Hossein Mousavi and President Ali Khamenei; and "balancers," led by Speaker of the Majles (Parliament) Akbar Hashemi Rafsanjani and including many members of the Majles and the supreme court. The first group needed to be supported, the second to be eliminated, and the third absorbed.[38]

The substance of this analysis surfaced first in Ghorbanifar's discussions with the Israelis in early May, then again a week after McFarlane's meeting with Kimche, when the first contact with an Iranian official took place as part of the incipient deals. Although not a polished intelligence report, the document excited the Israeli and U.S. intermediaries. In Ledeen's words, "Ghorbanifar had for the first time given them what they considered to be a really solid picture, in detail, of the internal Iranian situation and the Iranian connection to international terrorism."[39]

One of the final developments that seemed to convince McFarlane to move ahead with the arms deals was a meeting on July 8 in Hamburg involving the Israeli middlemen, including Kimche, Ghorbanifar, Khashoggi, and a second Iranian, Hassan Karoubi. The Israelis had importuned Ghorbanifar to produce a higher-level official from Tehran to bolster his credibility. Ghorbanifar came up with Karoubi, whom he presented as an ayatollah (which some of the Israelis doubted) and as "the brains" of the "Kitchen Cabinet" in Iran. He reportedly had close connections to Khomeini's son and was influential with Speaker Rafsanjani.[40] The Iranians at the session contended Karoubi represented a group interested in cooperating with the United States to stave off the Soviet threat to Iran. He allegedly was prepared to begin detailed discussions on mutual cooperation—through Israel, because it apparently was even more impractical to deal directly with the United States—and would commit to writing a comprehensive proposal.

The main significance of the meeting lay not so much in the details of what Karoubi said as in the fact he was there at all. The presence of an allegedly senior Iranian official impressed most of the Israelis and U.S. delegates that Ghorbanifar indeed had high-level contacts in the Iranian government who were interested in reshaping Iran's political outlook. In his report to McFarlane, Ledeen could hardly contain himself: "The situation has fundamentally changed for the better. . . . This is the real thing and it is just wonderful news."[41] Within days, McFarlane personally brought the "news" to President Reagan, who had only recently undergone polyp surgery and was still recuperating at the hospital.

Not all the Israelis were taken with Karoubi. Gazit thought he was a "scoundrel" who could not be trusted.[42] But for the U.S. side, the eagerness for a breakthrough overwhelmed any skepticism about the intermediaries or the potential pitfalls of working with them. This would become a recurring theme in the Iran initiative: the susceptibility of seasoned officials and policy analysts to become so easily sold on individuals whose identity, background, and motivations were largely a mystery. Part of the explanation for this tendency was a lack of experience in dealing with Iranians. A CIA official who became involved in early 1986 called several of the players—only partly in jest—"a bunch of foreign policy naïfs, some of whom are really demented."[43] Another part of the explanation lay in Iran's growing significance for U.S. policy makers, whether the concern was about Soviet adventurism or terrorism. In the more than five years since Khomeini had cut off contacts with the "Great Satan," Iran had become a cipher. A direct approach by someone seemingly a part of the country's power structure was bound to draw attention. The questions that needed answers included whether he was who he claimed, whether his motives could be trusted, and whether he could deliver as promised. The previous November the State Department had heard about Karoubi from a retired senior CIA operations officer named Theodore Shackley, but had declined to pursue the contact.[44] Yet clearly Karoubi was someone of note, and other officials Ghorbanifar would bring to the table—relative moderates or not—were unquestionably connected to the top rungs of the Iranian government.

Underlying all these issues was the puzzle of what constituted a "moderate." Most observers in hindsight believed there were no moderates in Iran. But this depended on the definition. It was true the revolution had eliminated from political relevance anyone considered a moderate during the shah's reign. Prominent nonclerical nationalists, such as former prime ministers Shapour Bakhtiar or Mehdi Bazargan, had left the scene by the end of 1979. Several had been killed. (Bakhtiar was murdered in Paris in 1981.) But if the question was whether different factions—extreme and less extreme—existed in the context of the postrevolutionary Islamic Republic, that was a different matter. Senior regime representatives widely accepted the tenets of the Islamic state, including the core concept of "government by Islamic jurists" (*velayat-e faqih*) enshrined in the 1979 Constitution, but even among Khomeini's advisors there was a range of opinion over individual policy choices and implementation, whether in foreign relations, the economy, or cultural affairs. These differences extended to whether Iran should have dealings with adversaries such as Great Britain, the Soviet Union, or the United States.[45] However, the prospect Ghorbanifar held out of finding conspirators at the upper levels of the hierarchy intent on deposing Khomeini and changing the fundamental course of Iranian policy was altogether different.

McFarlane Works on His Colleagues

Although McFarlane would take heat for keeping the president and others out of the loop on the Iran initiative, the record shows from the start he reported quite consistently to his colleagues. Shortly after meeting with Kimche on July 3, he told Weinberger about the Israelis' initial proposition.[46] Ten days later, he notified Shultz in a lengthy cable. Asking that he not share the information, McFarlane described a "proposal by an Iranian official endorsed by the Government of Israel. It has a short term and a long term dimension to it. The short term dimension concerns the seven hostages; the long term dimension involves the establishment of [a] private dialogue with Iranian officials on the broader relation[ship]."[47]

In the same message he described receiving a "private emissary"—Schwimmer—who asked him to convey a message from Peres saying Israel had recently unearthed "serious interest among authoritative persons in the Iranian hierarchy in opening a dialogue with the west." Two of these individuals were Karoubi and Ghorbanifar, who McFarlane said had presented an "extremely pessimistic" picture of Iran to the Israelis and "stated emphatically that they sought a dialogue with the United States." The Iranians were confident they could bring about the release of the U.S. hostages in Lebanon. "But in exchange they would need to show some gain. They sought specifically the delivery from Israel of 100 TOW missiles."[48]

McFarlane acknowledged to Shultz the idea "raises a number of imponderable questions." These included how a deal of this sort would jibe with U.S. policy "against negotiating with terrorists," whether the United States would get caught in a situation of having to "up the ante on more and more arms and where that could conceivably lead," and whether Israel's vaunted contacts were "connected to viable, stable parties in Iran" or were "no more than self-serving self-promoters." In closing, he admitted, "George, I cannot judge the equities on this. We need to think about it. But I don't think we should tarry. . . . On balance I tend to favor going ahead."[49]

McFarlane's cable showed he understood the potential hazards of the plan well before it got under way. So did Shultz. In his response, the secretary wrote, "This situation is loaded with imponderables that call for great caution on our part." He emphasized both the "fraud that seems to accompany so many deals involving arms and Iran and the complications arising from our 'blessing' an Israel-Iran relationship where Israel's interests and ours are not necessarily the same."[50]

But after laying out his qualms, the secretary of state gave his blessing: "We should make a tentative show of interest without commitment. I do not think we could justify turning our backs on the prospect of gaining the release of the other seven hostages and perhaps developing an ability to renew ties with Iran under a more sensible regime—especially when presented to us through the prime minister of Israel." Shultz told McFarlane to have his Israeli "emissary" report to the Iranians the United States was "receptive to the idea of a private dialogue involving a sustained discussion of U.S.-Iranian relations." Explicit in McFarlane's cable was the Iranian requirement that 100 TOW missiles be delivered as the first step in such a dialogue. Shultz did not directly address the point, but did not object to it either. Furthermore, he advised McFarlane to take charge of the matter: "I am inclined to think it should be managed by you personally."[51]

McFarlane clearly had gotten his way. Only two weeks earlier, Weinberger and Shultz had tried to shoot down the idea of sending arms to Iran. Now the secretary of state was authorizing communications with Iranians and implicitly accepted the notion of providing weapons.

A recent hostage drama in Lebanon may have helped bring Shultz around. On June 14, two hijackers had commandeered TWA Flight 847 on its way from Athens to Rome, ultimately taking the plane to Beirut. They shot a passenger, U.S. Navy diver Robert Dean Stethem, and as television cameras captured the scene, dumped his body onto the tarmac. After several days a deal emerged—in essence, an exchange of hostages: Israel pledged to free 766 Shiites from southern Lebanon in exchange for the release of the remaining 39 U.S. citizens on the flight.

The prime mover behind the hijacking was Imad Mughniyah, the same man responsible for kidnapping the U.S. citizens in Beirut who would become the focus of the upcoming arms-for-hostages deals. Both Israel and Iran proved key to the resolution of the crisis. Israel showed a willingness to take part in a bargain over hostages, and Rafsanjani personally interceded with Hezbollah leaders to help end the episode. It was an intriguing development for U.S. officials, not only confirming Tehran's influence with Hezbollah but signaling Rafsanjani's readiness to reach out to the United States. McFarlane and Casey were impressed. The CIA director reportedly persuaded the president to send the Iranian a note of appreciation.[52] Coming just weeks before the idea of an opening to Tehran surfaced, the experience also resonated with other key U.S. officials, particularly Shultz, who seemed to soften his tone by declining to implicate Iran in the initial attack.[53]

Shultz later testified he gave his tentative approval to the contact only in order to keep "some kind of control over it, or association with it," believing McFarlane was "probably going to explore this anyway."[54] In light of his well-known frustration with NSC power grabs, it seems unlikely the secretary would simply have acquiesced without a struggle to another White House initiative that would leave the State Department on the sidelines. Instead, it is tempting to see in Shultz's consent a shrewd bureaucratic maneuver—letting McFarlane assume the risk and accountability in case the contacts with Iran went sour. But an approval was an approval, and McFarlane felt confident he was fully licensed to move forward. His next step was to see the president.

The President Gives the Go-Ahead

On July 13, the same day McFarlane cabled Shultz, President Reagan entered the hospital for abdominal surgery. While recuperating, he continued to see important visitors, often subject to the discretion of White House Chief of Staff Donald Regan, who recalled McFarlane "had been asking from day one to get to see the President." Three days after the surgery, with the chief of staff present, McFarlane was able to tell Reagan about the Israeli-Iranian proposal. The president understood one stated purpose of the proposition was to establish ties with "moderate" Iranian officials, but the immediate goal was to get the hostages out. "The truth is," he wrote in his autobiography, "once we had information from Israel that we could trust the people in Iran, I didn't have to think thirty seconds about saying yes to their proposal. . . . I said there was one thing we wanted: The moderate Iranians had to use their influence with the Hizballah and try to get our hostages freed."[55]

Even so, the president did not give his approval right away. He discussed the idea first with top advisors, once on July 23 and again on August 6, 1985. Both meetings took place in the White House residence, where Reagan continued to recover.[56] At the second meeting, he was joined by Shultz, Weinberger, Regan, and McFarlane and heard, according to McFarlane, a "very vivid, forceful, thorough expression of views of his Cabinet officers involved in this."[57] The topics included "the legal ramifications, the political risks, the matter of Congressional oversight, and . . . the probabilities . . . of this having any promise at all." The secretaries of state and defense reprised their arguments against McFarlane's draft NSDD of the previous month. Shultz later recalled remarking the whole thing was a "very bad idea" and warning that "we are just falling into the arms-for-hostages business and we shouldn't do it." Regan and McFarlane were more positive, with the chief of staff contending the Iranian proposal represented "an opening. I thought we should explore it."[58]

The president's views were opaque. When his aides disagreed, he often did not commit himself right away. As a result, each participant left the meeting with his own reading of where things stood. Shultz and Weinberger believed he opposed the idea; McFarlane thought he was inclined to go ahead. The available clues to Reagan's thinking at the time turned out to be misleading. His anti-Tehran rhetoric was at its peak. In early July, he had called the Islamic Republic part of a "confederation of terrorist states . . . a new, international version of Murder Incorporated. . . . Let me make it plain to the assassins in Beirut and their accomplices. . . . America will never make concessions to terrorists."[59] Yet, according to McFarlane, several days after the meeting, Reagan called to give his explicit authorization to proceed. The chief of staff later confirmed that account, acknowledging the president "did authorize McFarlane to explore it further."[60]

The First TOW Shipments

Before McFarlane was able to flash Reagan's green light to his new partners, private intermediaries in Israel were already moving forward, anxious to nail down Ghorbanifar's commitment to free the hostages. For their part, senior Israeli officials needed to sort out what conditions would be acceptable for proceeding with the deal. At the time, the Labor-Likud coalition government had an informal power-sharing agreement that required a general consensus on major decisions. Peres had given the initial go-ahead for the Iran operation, but the other two coalition leaders—Defense Minister Yitzhak Rabin and Foreign Minister Yitzhak Shamir—acquiesced.[61] Rabin had wanted confirmation of President Reagan's approval, which McFarlane finally delivered, plus assurances Shultz was on board. Both Rabin and Shamir further stipulated if Israel had to deplete its missile stocks on behalf of the United States, then Washington would have to agree to replenish them.[62] McFarlane assured Kimche this would be no problem, although the issue of how to accomplish it resurfaced continually in subsequent months.

Despite some loose ends, the Israeli government decided to go ahead with the operation on August 5, several days before Reagan gave his approval to McFarlane.[63] Within two days of Peres's decision, Khashoggi, at Ghorbanifar's request, deposited a "bridge" loan of $1 million into Nimrodi's bank account to help move the transaction forward.[64] His support was crucial at this stage because of the wall of mistrust between Israelis and Iranians. After some argument, it was established Iran would have to pay for the missiles. Simply turning over hostages would not be enough. The problem was neither Iran nor Israel wanted to make the first move: the Ministry of Defense would not agree to deliver the missiles until Iran paid for them, and Iran refused to pay in advance. It was an inauspicious start to the program and might have marked its untimely end if not for Khashoggi.

As it happened, the amount of the loan exactly equaled the amount Ghorbanifar eventually agreed to provide Israel's Ministry of Defense for the 100 TOWs— $10,000 apiece, or $1 million. Ghorbanifar's extended haggling with Nimrodi and Schwimmer had brought the price down from the $13,000–$14,000 per missile originally demanded. Because Ghorbanifar planned to charge the Iranian government $12,000 per unit, this meant a personal profit of $200,000. Meanwhile, Nimrodi and Schwimmer managed to talk down the Ministry of Defense from $12,000 apiece (the price of replacing each missile) to just less than $6,000, arguing they had to factor in "payoffs" of 20–25 percent to "certain Iranians."[65]

In the midst of these negotiations, Schwimmer set to work finding a "neutral," non-Israeli carrier for the missiles in order to add another layer of deniability to the operation. This benefited Israel and Iran by protecting both governments from potential embarrassment if caught dealing with each other. Schwimmer contracted with a Miami-based aircraft company to take care of the logistics, which he supervised down to the level of selecting a flight plan. Ghorbanifar handled arrangements for landing clearances in Iran.[66]

On August 19, Ghorbanifar and the Israelis met one last time at Nimrodi's house. The Iranian had unsettling news: instead of being able to hand over all of the hostages as initially offered, he could not be sure how many would be freed as a result of the upcoming shipment. Furthermore, he said because the Iranians understood the "special value" of CIA Agent Buckley to the United States, his captors would release him last. Even though he was now going back on his word, the Israelis decided not to scrap the mission. They had their own reasons to keep the wheels turning—reestablishing ties with Tehran, counterbalancing Iraq, and taking the opportunity to provide a benefit to the United States—and it is unclear whether they even informed Washington of Ghorbanifar's backtracking.

The same day, Schwimmer's DC-8 aircraft arrived in Israel to pick up a cargo of ninety-six missiles[67]—plus Ghorbanifar. Because of delays on the ground, the flight did not take off until 2:30 the following morning, flying over Turkey and landing in Tehran at 10:00 a.m. local time. Three hours later, it took off again for the return flight to Israel.[68]

But the shipment produced no hostages. According to Ghorbanifar, his plans had gone awry when the wrong group took control of the weapons. When he got to Tehran, Prime Minister Mir-Hossein Mousavi and his deputy were waiting at the airport, as expected. Unfortunately, the commander of the IRGC unexpectedly appeared with a contingent of troops and took custody of the shipment. Along with the missiles went one of the main purported goals of the mission—to give Ghorbanifar's "moderate" faction something to show for its participation. Making the best of an awkward situation, Ghorbanifar invented a cover story: because this group ended up with nothing, they had no obligation to fulfill their side of the bargain by producing any hostages.

The obvious failure of the deal led to stormy meetings in Paris on September 4 and 5 involving Ghorbanifar, Kimche, Nimrodi, Schwimmer, and Ledeen. By this time, Oliver North—already deeply involved with the Contras—had become fully engaged in tracking the operation, although Ledeen continued to have occasional contacts with the Israelis and Ghorbanifar over the summer. Ghorbanifar took the offensive despite his inability to deliver on his initial promise. He insisted on behalf of his sponsors another transaction be set up in which Iran would receive 400 missiles in return for the release of a single hostage. The Iranians were now demanding more for less. According to Nimrodi, Ghorbanifar insisted he was only following orders from Tehran. To prove it, he telephoned Prime Minister Mousavi directly during one of the meetings and let Nimrodi eavesdrop on the conversation.[69]

Eventually, the Israelis and Ledeen agreed to Ghorbanifar's demand. At no time in this early phase did any of the participants appear to pick up on a fundamental contradiction in Ghorbanifar's representations. According to his analysis of Iran's factional divisions, supplied in early July to McFarlane, Mousavi belonged to the "leftist" (in Khashoggi's version the "extremist") line most closely identified with the Islamic revolution and support for terrorism, the group that needed to be eliminated—not the purportedly moderate group whose prestige the arms deals were supposed to advance. This contradiction should have put the lie to Ghorbanifar's "bona fides," in McFarlane's parlance, and should have been enough to convince the United States to shut down the operation altogether, assuming courting "moderates" was truly the objective. Yet a decision was made to pursue the initiative even as the terms worsened. The determination to press forward showed the desperation in Washington and Tel Aviv to gain tangible results after having made the commitment to Ghorbanifar and the operation.

Peres met with Rabin on September 9 and authorized the Israelis to take up Ghorbanifar on his revised offer. As they had with earlier shipments to Iran at the beginning of the first Reagan administration, the Israelis arrogated to themselves the authority to approve the transaction, giving a broad interpretation to McFarlane's okay given in early August. "McFarlane's initial approval," the official Israeli report read, "given to Kimche on behalf of the President of the United States, was understood to constitute overall approval to continue supplying weaponry to Iran." But even by the Israeli account, the president's authorization called for Israel to transfer 100 TOW missiles, not the additional 400 TOWs envisioned in Ghorbanifar's second proposal.[70]

In the end, President Reagan also sanctioned the second shipment. Although it was significant in its own right, however, his consent seems to have had little practical impact on this part of the operation because Israel was already prepared to move ahead. With Peres's authorization, Khashoggi on September 10 set in motion the financial side of the transaction. Having retrieved his initial investment of $1 million from Ghorbanifar at the end of August, he agreed to put up $4 million more to buy the 400 missiles from Israel. His deposit reached Nimrodi's account three days later, and a day after that Ghorbanifar repaid him the full amount.[71]

Once again, Schwimmer prepared the logistics, taking the missiles from Israeli Defense Forces stocks. Faced with the requirement of transporting them in pallets of twelve, he decided to deliver more rather than fewer missiles this time in order to give the Iranians no excuse to raise an objection. On September 14, a chartered aircraft and crew arrived in Israel to load 408 TOWs on board for the flight to Iran. Two changes were made from the original flight plan— Ghorbanifar's assistant accompanied the flight in his place, and the destination was shifted to Tabriz, in northern Iran. Ghorbanifar maintained this would prevent the IRGC from expropriating the shipment a second time. (In fact, Iranian sources indicate that by 1985 the guards had taken over direct supervision of all war-related acquisitions.)[72]

Early in the morning of September 15, the DC-8 landed in Tabriz as planned, unloaded its cargo, and set off again for Israel. That same day, the group holding the Reverend Benjamin Weir since May 8, 1984, released him on the streets outside the U.S. embassy in Beirut. A special contingent of U.S. officials, under the direction of North, met Weir to debrief him and send him home to the United States. The welcome news about Weir was dampened by bitter disappointment over the fact no other hostages were released. Weinberger, who personally oversaw some of the preparations for retrieving whoever might be coming out, indicated in his daily notes on September 11 that more were expected: "Bud McFarlane—says Iranians told Israelis our 7 hostages would be released in 3 groups to Amb. Bartholomew + we will extract them by helicopter."[73]

Especially worrisome was the fact Buckley did not make it out. On the day of Weir's release, Weinberger noted: "Bud McFarlane—says . . . that Buckley would be brought fm Teheran to Cyprus tonight." On the following day, he wrote: "Saw Colin Powell—no news of release of Buckley—he was not delivered to Cyprus on time."[74] In fact, Buckley had died under torture as early as June 3, although his captors kept it a secret so as not to give up a valuable bargaining chip.

McFarlane claimed, as did Weinberger, he was not sure at first whether the arms transfer had actually been the catalyst for Weir's release. This would become central to the administration's cover story after disclosure of the arms deals. It was partly designed to preserve the possibility other hostages would soon be released and partly to keep alive the fiction the White House was not making secret deals with Tehran. McFarlane later acknowledged, though, "You would have to be a fool not to see that, whatever our intentions were, the reality was apparently arms for hostages."[75]

Crossing a Threshold

In the first series of arms shipments the administration crossed a clear line in its policy toward Iran. Although the United States knew the Islamic Republic had been buying arms for some time on the world market, including from Israel, official approval of a deal with Tehran placed the Reagan administration squarely at odds with stated policy, nullified the moral basis of Operation Staunch, threatened relations with Arab allies who supported Iraq in its war with Iran, and arguably prolonged the fighting in the gulf. The operation also put the president in legal jeopardy because the shipments from Israel to Iran were prohibited under U.S. law. The Arms Export Control Act (AECA), which governed sales of U.S. military equipment abroad, specifically barred weapons transfers by the United States or any other country to a third country that engaged in or supported terrorist acts—which the State Department determined Iran had done. Yet, despite these very real concerns, President Reagan went ahead with the program. Of the main institutional players in the foreign policy arena, only Congress was left completely in the dark—another violation of the AECA. "Mr. Casey [had] expressed the view that Congress should not be advised, and the President agreed with him," McFarlane recalled. "I don't recall any dissent from that position at the time."[76]

5

Quid Pro Quos

While Oliver North busied himself keeping the Contras funded, armed, and engaged on the battlefield, senior policy makers also actively sought financial help for the rebels from foreign governments. This controversial approach generated concern U.S. officials were making end runs around congressional restrictions on funding and the approaches to third countries amounted to bribes because of the inevitable implication those governments would be rewarded for their help. Saudi Arabia, Honduras, Guatemala, and several other governments fielded requests from U.S. officials—including the president and vice president—and duly accommodated them. The Reagan administration defended these interactions on various grounds, including citing the president's constitutional prerogative to engage with foreign leaders. Congressional critics countered later that defying legislative intent in this way was "dangerous and improper," especially when Congress was kept in the dark. The record shows the president's most senior advisors understood perfectly where the line of impropriety lay. Yet they continued making not just implied but explicit assurances to foreign counterparts that their contributions would be compensated. Secrecy became the order of the day. Observing the actions of his superiors, it was small wonder North felt free to pursue his own third-country solicitations.

The June 1984 NSPG Meeting and the Issue of Overseas Solicitations

At 2 p.m. on June 25, 1984, President Ronald Reagan convened a meeting of the top-level National Security Planning Group (NSPG) in the Situation Room, located in the basement of the White House. Cramped in the windowless, wood-paneled room were members of the president's senior foreign policy circle—the vice president, the secretaries of state and defense, the director of the CIA, the chair of the Joint Chiefs of Staff (JCS), and the president's national security advisor. A few lower-level aides sat in chairs lining the walls of the room.

The Situation Room was typically where the president and his advisors discussed burgeoning crises around the world. This time, a different kind of predicament was unfolding. The administration had long argued that Nicaragua, backed by Cuba and the Soviet Union, posed a serious threat to U.S. national security. One of the keys to blunting the danger, the White House insisted, was to throw U.S. backing behind Contra rebel groups based in and around Nicaragua. To the president's deep frustration, most members of Congress refused to accept either his bleak portrayal of the problem or the proposition the Contras were the solution.

In December 1983, lawmakers had put a $24 million cap on U.S. support to the rebels. The move was a compromise, ultimately designed to shut down the U.S. aid program but also intended to give the administration one more shot at winning over both the U.S. House and Senate to its cause before funding ran out. By May, the well was almost dry, and after the revelations the CIA had laced Nicaraguan harbors with mines, Congress was in a foul mood. Not even a speech by the president to both chambers in April helped change many points of view.

The question on the table in the Situation Room that June day was what to do about rebel aid. As he often did on topics of deep personal interest, Reagan spoke frequently, in this case to urge his aides to be "more active" and "keep the pressure on Nicaragua" in order to "make sure that . . . our friends know they can rely on us."[1] After National Security Advisor Robert McFarlane ran through the "good news and bad news from Central America," the discussion turned to alternative approaches to funding the insurgents. CIA Director William Casey suggested asking third countries, such as El Salvador, Guatemala, and Honduras, for help. Others around the table endorsed the idea, including UN Ambassador Jeane Kirkpatrick, who summed up the majority view: "If we can't get the money . . . [from Capitol Hill], then we should make the maximum effort to find the money elsewhere."[2]

There was only one problem—the whole proposal would be illegal. Earlier, Casey had suggested, without elaborating, it would be entirely lawful to reach out to foreign governments for resources Congress had denied. But Secretary of State George Shultz objected, injecting a note of warning into the discussion that was like kryptonite in Washington. "I would like to get money for the Contras also, but another lawyer, Jim Baker [the president's chief of staff], said that if we go out and try to get money from third countries, it is an impeachable offense."

Shultz, one of the lone moderates on Nicaragua in the president's inner circle, was already feeling in the minority in the room after pressing for a stronger White House commitment to the multilateral negotiating process in Central America. His arguments had met with scarcely concealed contempt from Secretary of Defense Caspar Weinberger, among others. The two senior cabinet officials were already on poor terms over policy disagreements and personal differences reaching back many years. According to one State Department official, the relationship "lacked even an element of civility."[3] Now Shultz was placing himself even more squarely at odds with his colleagues.

Casey immediately jumped in. "I am entitled to complete the record," he said, contending Baker had balked at requesting foreign government aid only if the administration failed to notify the oversight committees of Congress.[4] When Weinberger sided with Casey, Shultz was forced to punt, calling for a formal opinion from the attorney general. "It would be the prudent thing to do," he said.

Shortly afterward, McFarlane drew the meeting to a close, proposing that "there be no authority for anyone to seek third party support for the anti-Sandinistas until we have the [legal] information we need." Then he added, "I certainly hope none of this discussion will be made public in any way." It was President Reagan who had the final word. "If such a story gets out," he said, "we'll all be hanging by our thumbs in front of the White House until we find out who did it."[5]

Knowledge of Third-Country Aid

This extraordinary meeting showed North was far from alone in resorting to foreign government solicitations for Contra aid. While he played the role of CIA surrogate in coordinating rebel military and paramilitary operations, his superiors, up to and including the president, were seeking ways around congressional prohibitions. This evolved into a major undertaking that entailed demarches to at least two dozen governments by senior officials as well as by the president and the vice president. Edwin Meese, counselor to the president in 1984, later defended these solicitations as falling within the president's constitutional powers as long as the "assistance . . . was not recycled U.S. tax money or a quid pro quo for U.S. government-provided funds."[6]

Yet documentation uncovered by investigators shows quid pro quos were at times precisely what the president and his aides had in mind. What is more, top officials regarded these activities as so sensitive they often went out of their way to keep even their colleagues in the dark about them. The June 25 NSPG meeting was a case in point. Unbeknownst to several of those in the Situation Room that afternoon, McFarlane and Casey had already spent months drumming up exactly the kind of overseas support McFarlane had counseled deferring until the attorney general made a ruling.

As early as March 27, Casey had written an "eyes only" memo to McFarlane laying out their strategy: "In view of possible difficulties in obtaining supplemental appropriations to carry out the Nicaraguan covert action project through the remainder of this year, I am in full agreement that you should explore funding alternatives with the Israelis and perhaps others."[7]

In fact, McFarlane had already contacted the Israelis to ask if they would be interested in offering basic training to the Contras. Under the umbrella of a 1983 agreement on a "strategic partnership" with Tel Aviv (which Tel Aviv had hoped would sway the U.S. on the matter of arming Iran—see Chapter 2), Washington had helped Israel win a variety of contracts, from training security forces to exploiting water resources in Central America and Africa. McFarlane expected this would soften up the Israelis for a reciprocal request. To his annoyance, they had turned him down, claiming unfavorable domestic political circumstances.[8] McFarlane then directed NSC Middle East staff aide Howard Teicher to raise the subject with them again.

McFarlane's instructions to Teicher betrayed his irritation with the Israelis: "Please also let it be known that, in your view, I am a little disappointed in the outcome but we will not raise it further."[9] His importuning failed on this occasion, but Washington and Tel Aviv would find other ways to make a connection. Casey's memo mentioned the United States was sending a "joint CIA/DoD survey team" to Israel "to inspect captured PLO ordnance." In 1983, he noted, a similar operation code-named Tipped Kettle had yielded "$10 million worth [of] . . . machine guns and ammunition."[10] As it happened, the Israelis came through, transferring a second tranche of weapons to the United States the following July. Unbeknownst to Congress, which had been told only that the weapons would be used for "various purposes," the CIA then funneled a sizable arsenal to the Contras.[11]

In his March memo, Casey proposed another alternative source for overseas funding of the Nicaraguan rebels—South Africa. The CIA director wrote that a senior military official "has indicated that he may be able to make some equipment and training available . . . through the Hondurans." Two weeks later, the agency's senior operations officer for Latin America, Duane Clarridge, was on his way to discuss the overture with representatives of the Pretoria government. Because the Contras' public image was always an important concern, not everyone thought it a good idea to have them associated with the apartheid regime. John McMahon, the CIA's deputy director, cabled word to Clarridge there were "second thoughts around town as to wisdom of involving [South Africa] in already complicated Central American equation. Request you hold off on this aspect of your discussions until we can get definitive word to you."[12] Before the deal could be consummated, the Nicaraguan harbor mining disclosure forced Clarridge to cut short his visit. He later cabled his "deep regret" at not being able to follow through on the offer, "at least for the time being."[13]

McFarlane finally found his pot of gold with another Middle Eastern ally— Saudi Arabia. Thanks to the oil boom of the early 1970s, the Saudis' enormous oil reserves had confirmed their status as a "vital interest" of the United States. Riyadh's attraction intensified after the fall of the shah and the Soviet invasion of Afghanistan, which left Saudi Arabia an increasingly isolated pro-Western outpost in the cold war. Both Washington and Riyadh also shared the goal of blunting Iran's fundamentalist Shiite threat to the Persian Gulf, particularly as the Iran-Iraq War dragged on. Like the U.S. relationship with Israel, U.S.-Saudi ties operated on another level, involving a profusion of secret understandings and covert mutual back-scratching. Among other arrangements, the Saudis funneled billions of dollars in military support to the Afghan *mujahideen* and millions more to Jonas Savimbi's anticommunist UNITA guerrillas in Angola.

In that context, McFarlane saw nothing untoward about uniting the two governments in another campaign against the Soviets. At the same time, he knew perfectly well there were ethical restrictions against making an outright solicitation. Therefore, meeting in late May with Riyadh's ambassador, Prince Bandar bin Sultan, in his opulent residence overlooking the Potomac River, he couched his approach with deliberate indirectness. Discussing Reagan's reelection chances, he suggested the president had only one vulnerability—the Contras. If the rebel movement foundered, especially after Reagan had raised the political stakes so high, it could threaten his chances for a second term. "Bandar listened knowingly," McFarlane later recalled, then assured him, "His Majesty, King Fahd, . . . would probably be pleased to help." Bandar asked how much McFarlane thought the Contras would need. He replied about $1 million per month.[14] It took only a few days for word to arrive the Saudis had decided to contribute precisely that amount "as a humanitarian gesture" to sustain the rebels until the end of the year.

McFarlane's next problem was a practical one: how to get the money quietly to the Contras. Because he had no experience in this area, he told North to find out where the money should be deposited. Within twenty-four hours, North informed him the Contras kept an account at the Miami branch of BAC International Bank of the Grand Cayman Islands—account number 541-48. McFarlane arranged another meeting with the Saudi ambassador and handed him a three-by-five-inch index card with the information. Beginning in early July, and over the next eight months, the account, in the name of Esther Morales, wife of a Panamanian lawyer who was a friend of Adolfo Calero, received a total of $8 million. The following February, the Saudis had more good news for the president. In a meeting with Reagan, King Fahd personally declared his intent to double the monthly contributions, which he subsequently did. In all, the royal family gave $32 million to the cause, a sum that went a long way toward helping the Contras survive the congressional cutoff in aid.[15]

This entire series of transactions was shrouded from outside scrutiny. Under questioning by Congress in late 1986, McFarlane at first misrepresented his own involvement: "I did not solicit any country at any time to make contributions to the Contras." He said he had only seen "reports" and "heard that [the Saudis] have contributed," but "the concrete character of that is beyond my ken." Before the joint Iran-Contra committees the following summer, he conceded he had been "trying to use some tortured language, inappropriately, I think," in his earlier testimony. Although there was no "cry for solicitation," he admitted, "in fact it was unmistakeable in his [Bandar's] own mind that . . . a contribution would have been welcome."[16] Indeed an outright request would have seemed clumsy and inappropriate under the circumstances. Diplomatic discourse at that level is often an exercise in indirectness and subtlety, rarely more so than on a matter as sensitive as the covert bankrolling of an insurgency force. Simply by raising the issue, as he well understood, he had given the prince an opening to demonstrate the king's royal generosity.

But the ruse went further. After the money started coming in, McFarlane and his colleagues disguised its source, letting Congress believe the Contras were managing to generate $1 million a month—and later twice that amount—on their own, "ostensibly from private funds," as McFarlane put it. Reagan himself gave orders no one else should be told about the Saudis' largesse.[17] As McFarlane's testimony and that of his colleagues made clear, the deception continued even after the Contra operations became public knowledge.

After striking pay dirt with Prince Bandar in May 1984, McFarlane made sure the right people heard about it. A day or two after his meeting with the prince, he slipped President Reagan a note card during his morning national security briefing. Reagan called him back later to retrieve the card, which now bore a brief message indicating his "satisfaction and pleasure that this had occurred." McFarlane testified the president instructed him not to divulge the contribution, including to Congress, because of the possible harm to relations with the Saudis and because it might make lawmakers less willing to renew U.S. support for the rebels.[18]

At about the same time, McFarlane "also communicated [the news] to the Vice President personally."[19] During a regular weekly breakfast in late May, he let the secretaries of state and defense know the Contras were covered until year's end, although he apparently did not impart the source of the funds. In his memoir he noted both men were "pleased" with the news and "asked what had happened to reverse the contras' fortunes. 'You don't want to know,' I said." In his 1987 congressional testimony he gave a somewhat different account, saying the two cabinet officers did not ask where the money was coming from, implying they preferred not to know anything about it: "Neither gentleman pressed the matter further."[20]

Which version of the story is true is impossible to determine, but either is plausible. During Iran-Contra, the custom of consciously shielding oneself from the facts in order to preserve deniability was as prevalent as the act of hiding information from colleagues in order to protect one's turf.

Still, there is no doubt at least Weinberger found out the source. Gen. John Vessey, chair of the JCS, recalled that after an Oval Office meeting with the president in late May 1984 to discuss a proposed classified arms sale to Saudi Arabia, McFarlane, Weinberger, and he talked about the Saudi aid offer again. Vessey remembered either he or Weinberger had pushed McFarlane to support the proposed sale to Riyadh because of the help the royal family was giving the Contras.[21]

If Shultz and others were indeed in the dark, at a minimum they were in agreement on the need for secrecy President Reagan expressed at the NSPG meeting. On June 20, five days earlier, the president's top foreign policy aides— Shultz, Weinberger, Casey, McFarlane, John Poindexter, and Kirkpatrick, along with others including North—had gathered to talk about "Contra money." Notes taken by Shultz's aide, Charles Hill, reflect the urgency of the discussion. "Don't give up on the congr chance, altho slim," he wrote. "But plan for other sources. Keep US fingerprints off . . . *even* if Congr turns us down, we *must* not let collapse happen."[22]

Lip Service to the Law

The day after the NSPG meeting, Casey and his general counsel met with Attorney General William French Smith to obtain a legal opinion on third-country aid to the Contras—and end the debate once and for all. But the DCI had an additional stake in the matter. The day before, he had told the NSPG, "The legal position is that CIA is authorized to cooperate and seek support from third countries. In fact, the [president's] finding encourages third country participation and support in this entire effort." Technically, this was true; findings are often written to provide the CIA maximum flexibility to define and carry out operations. In this case, the September 19, 1983, finding under which the CIA was backing the Contras said nothing about what sort of support could be contemplated.

Shultz's insistence on an independent review by the attorney general raised the unwelcome prospect for Casey that the scope of the CIA's activities could be constricted even further. It was important, therefore, to come away with a legal opinion that would sanction third-country funding. To that end, Meese had advised the NSPG it was necessary to inform the Justice Department the administration had a particular course of action in mind, and that the department needed to find a way to *make* it legal—not just render an opinion about *whether* it was legal. "You have to give lawyers guidance when asking them a question," the future attorney general said.[23]

Casey's approach incorporated something of that philosophy. Instead of raising the propriety of foreign government solicitations in general terms, he homed in on the narrow question of "other nations in the region providing aid to the Nicaraguan Contras." Smith's opinion, delivered orally, was equally specific. He saw "no legal concern" as long as no U.S. funds were used, and the foreign government "could not look to the United States to repay that commitment in the future." Casey assured Smith if the option were considered, he would notify the oversight committees.[24]

In fact, the discussion on June 25 had anticipated all three points. Casey himself had recognized the need to notify the appropriate committees; Weinberger had assured everyone only foreign financing would be used, not U.S. funds; and Vice President Bush zeroed in on the issue of reciprocity. In his only recorded comment of the meeting, Bush said: "How can anyone object to the US encouraging third parties to provide help to the anti-Sandinistas under the finding? The only problem that might come up is if the United States were to promise to give these third parties something in return so that some people could interpret this as some kind of an exchange."[25]

And yet, over the course of the next two years, the very officials who defined such a clear line between what was legally acceptable and what was not would repeatedly cross that line. The legal question, by all indications, essentially disappeared as a concern for policy makers. Instead, only vague references to the existence of "private funding" appear in declassified meeting notes with no sign of curiosity on the part of the president or his advisors about the precise source or other basic details, despite the importance of the issue for the administration.[26] Throughout that time, members of Congress would continually be kept in the dark.

Reagan's Role

During the period of the Boland Amendment II ban, Reagan had directly communicated to Central American leaders his encouragement of their support for the rebels. As a prosecuting attorney later put it, his messages included "not-very-subtle reminders . . . of the importance of their security and aid relationships with the United States."[27] The president's personal involvement began, as far as is known, the following spring when he took part in a series of secret quid pro quo arrangements with Central American heads of state. This new level of activism likely was due not just to a sense of heightened Contra need but to the perceived reinforcement of a mandate after Reagan's landslide reelection in November 1984.[28]

The most striking case of this deal making involved the government of Honduras. Situated on Nicaragua's northern border, Honduras had been a haven for anti-Sandinista rebels since the 1979 Nicaraguan revolution. But the eagerness of the Honduran generals to help undermine the Sandinistas was tempered by the threat of cross-border reprisals by the far more powerful Sandinista military.

In late January 1985, the Hondurans' fears seemed about to prove true when

U.S. intelligence reported "indications of an attack" by Nicaraguan forces. "The Sandinistas have been sporadically firing into Honduras with their artillery and rockets," North wrote to McFarlane.[29] On February 7, the Crisis Pre-Planning Group (CPPG) met to discuss the problem. The CPPG consisted of deputies to members of the NSPG, whose job was to anticipate emergencies around the world that might affect U.S. interests and recommend actions to avert or resolve them. The day before the meeting, North had already drafted a letter for Reagan to send to President Roberto Suazo Córdova indicating Washington's readiness to contemplate an invasion in order to prevent a Sandinista attack. At the CPPG, the members decided the tone of the letter was "excessive in the present circumstances" but agreed to recommend sending an "oral demarche" offering a boost in economic and security assistance if Tegucigalpa would continue backing the rebels. The meeting began a process that led to Reagan sending a formal letter to Suazo offering a quid pro quo of increased aid in exchange for a Honduran commitment to stand up to Sandinista threats and continue to shore up Contra forces based on their territory.

Four days after the CPPG meeting, North and Raymond Burghardt, a colleague on the NSC staff, drafted a memo for McFarlane to forward to Shultz, Weinberger, Casey, and Vessey asking for their agreement on the language of a Reagan letter to Suazo. Their cover memo specifically mentioned a "strategy for enticing the Hondurans to greater support for the Nicaraguan resistance."[30]

The memo also noted the State Department had proposed changes that "would link the letter to our on-going dialogue with Honduras." Later the administration would claim no quid pro quos had been struck with any foreign governments. But as the cover memo stated, "The Hondurans tend to view all issues in the context of that [U.S.] dialogue." It was assumed Tegucigalpa would implicitly understand any additional support for the Contras would be duly noted and reflected within the framework of the broader U.S. relationship. Moreover, North and Burghardt advised McFarlane they had removed a more direct reference to the linkage between the bilateral security relationship and the Contras and inserted instead an anodyne reference to support for the peoples of Central America.

The CPPG had also agreed on the advisability of including "several other enticements" to the Hondurans. These included a bump in economic support funds (ESF) on a "phased release" so as not to create political waves prior to upcoming Honduran elections, expedited military assistance from the Pentagon, and expanded CIA "covert support to Honduras." (The specifics of the latter have been excised from the declassified document.) North and Burghardt understood the sensitivities. "Obviously," they advised McFarlane, "this part of the message should not be contained in a written document, but rather delivered verbally by a discreet emissary."[31]

McFarlane forwarded his aides' memo the next day to Shultz, Weinberger, Casey, and Vessey. Over the next few days, there was disagreement about whether to send an emissary. The State Department's bureau in charge of the region raised doubts about the plan, arguing the subject of "conditionality"—establishing a quid pro quo—should not be raised with Suazo. Instead of sending a special envoy, the State Department proposed having John Negroponte, the U.S. ambassador to Tegucigalpa, hand a letter to Suazo from Reagan that avoided explicit mention of U.S. expectations. The department also claimed arranging an expedited release of ESF was "probably too hard."[32] Ultimately, McFarlane recommended to Reagan that Negroponte deliver a general letter from the president to Suazo but that a second emissary carry the signed original of the letter and "very privately" spell out the administration's understanding of what was expected in return.[33] Reagan duly approved, and Negroponte delivered the letter, calling on Suazo's government to "continue to do all in its power to support those who struggle for freedom and democracy."[34]

The administration's aversion to being explicit grew out of the fear the secret agreement would leak to Congress. In the weeks prior to the Honduras solicitation, Reagan officials had begun talks with key lawmakers about alternatives to congressional funding. A press report noted one option being discussed was to use other countries or individuals as "conduits."[35] But the White House and State Department were not ready to acknowledge this openly. The day after Reagan signed off on the plan, North and Burghardt told McFarlane, "To date, all Administration officials have been able to state to the Congress that we have not approached any other government to support the resistance. Once the [attached documents] are transmitted we will no longer be able to make such a claim and any of the appropriate committees may place a call for all relevant cables on this matter at any time."[36]

Ambassador Negroponte in particular could expect questions about overtures to the Hondurans since the second Boland Amendment passed. North and Burghardt made clear they understood congressional aims: "Notwithstanding our own interpretations, it is very clear from the colloquy during the debate on the C.R. [continuing resolution] that the legislative intent was to deny any direct or indirect support for military/paramilitary operations in Nicaragua." They urged going ahead with the original idea of a special emissary because to do otherwise would "place both Amb. Negroponte and our hopes with the Hill at increased jeopardy."[37] In other words, they were not worried about violating "legislative intent" or administration commitments not to provide even indirect aid to the Contras. Their only concern was what problems would befall the Central America program if Congress discovered what they were doing.

The person who ultimately delivered the sensitive U.S. message to Suazo was Vice President Bush, notwithstanding his earlier concern about promising third parties inducements. Bush was already scheduled to visit Honduras in mid-March as part of a regional tour. During his meeting with Suazo, he was able to confirm Reagan had expedited a delivery of military equipment to Honduras and inform him further that other critical supplies would be coming directly from U.S. stocks. He also told Suazo blocked economic aid would begin to flow again, and Washington would soon expand a series of ongoing security programs. Before the end of the month the first arms shipments arrived, and the Honduran military oversaw their delivery to the rebels. Honduran officials duly expressed their appreciation. Recipients of this information included the White House, NSC staff, State Department, Defense Intelligence Agency, National Security Agency, U.S. Southern Command in Panama, and ambassadors to Honduras, Panama, Nicaragua, and Costa Rica.[38]

Problems continued to intervene, however. Sandinista military pressure prompted the Hondurans to order the rebels to move their camps to less vulnerable locations. On April 24, the U.S. House of Representatives dealt a further blow by defeating an administration request for more aid. Since February, North had been rolling out a strategy to influence the upcoming vote, including drafting a peace plan that, if the Sandinistas rejected it, would create a pretext for a series of Contra attacks designed to show legislators they were a viable military force that deserved U.S. backing. Reagan had simultaneously elevated the rhetoric, calling the Contras "the moral equal of our Founding Fathers."[39] The House vote stunned rebel supporters—including the Hondurans.

This was another point at which McFarlane stepped in to prompt the president to contact Central American heads of state personally and persuade them of his determination to renew congressional funding. It was particularly important in the case of Honduras, where local military commanders were wavering in their commitment to the rebels. One senior official told Nicaraguan Democratic Force (FDN) leader Alfonso Robelo the vote "finishes Honduran support." The next day, the Honduran military seized a shipment of ammunition headed for the Contra base at Las Vegas, near the Nicaraguan border. The move prompted Reagan to telephone Suazo directly to press him to intercede with the military. The mediation worked. Reagan's notes indicated Suazo "will call his mil commander [and] tell him to deliver the ammunition." But Suazo did not let the opportunity pass to ask for something in return. He told Reagan about a "high-level group" coming to Washington the following week to discuss an aid package. Reagan assured him the group would get high-level attention: "Shultz [and] Weinberger will meet with them."[40] It was more evidence of the virtual impossibility of making requests without raising expectations of a trade-off.

Despite this special consideration, the Hondurans still hesitated to cooperate. In early May, additional Sandinista artillery and ground assaults against Contras based in Honduras led Suazo to order their main base camp moved further away from the Nicaraguan border. Furthermore, the country's presidential election season was getting under way, and the Honduran leader apparently felt vulnerable to domestic political pressures because of his support for the rebels. During his visit to Washington, D.C., in late May Reagan once again entreated him to maintain his commitments. A briefing memorandum for their meeting advised: "Without making the linkage too explicit, it would be useful to remind Suazo that in return for our help—in the form of security assurances as well as aid—we do expect cooperation in pursuit of our mutual objectives."[41]

The Reagan administration also arranged quid pro quo deals with other Central American countries. In early 1985, during negotiations for more end-user certificates (EUCs) Richard Secord needed to buy arms on the gray market, a Guatemalan officer presented U.S. officials a "wish list" of equipment needed "to prosecute their war against the Cuban-supported guerrillas." The list included helicopters, troop vehicles, mortars, M-16 rifles, tactical radar, and ammunition. North was anxious to come through for the Guatemalans and pulled together the necessary paperwork for McFarlane to present to the principal decision makers—Shultz, Weinberger, Casey, and Vessey. The NSC aide couched the approach as a request for "their views on increased U.S. assistance to Guatemala" allegedly discussed during McFarlane's recent visit to the region. But in his cover note to McFarlane, North wrote: "The real purpose of your memo is to find a way by which we can compensate the Guatemalans for the extraordinary assistance they are providing to the Nicaraguan freedom fighters."[42] McFarlane checked the "Approve" box, indicating he would pass on the memo to Shultz and the others.

Costa Rica, on Nicaragua's southern border, became an important base of operations for the Contra war as well as a partner in more quid pro quo arrangements. As early as the June 1984 NSPG meeting, Casey had suggested offering the government of Luis Alberto Monge inducements to back the cause. During summer 1985, Monge agreed to let his country be used to create a southern front against the Sandinistas, among other steps (see Chapter 7), in return for U.S. assistance with certain covert projects designed to counter the threat from Nicaragua. From late 1984 through 1986 at least three secret projects were under way in Costa Rica involving the CIA and the National Security Agency: one aimed at strengthening the country's defense forces, another at setting up a sophisticated communications system for security purposes, and a third at using Nicaraguan nationals living in Costa Rica to help in case of Sandinista aggression.[43] In addition, at least two Costa Rican officials benefited personally from helping the Contras. Minister of Public Security Benjamin Piza, later identified as a CIA asset, got to meet with President Reagan at the White House and have his picture taken in return for allowing the airstrip to be built. More traditional payments went to a civil guard official identified as Colonel Montero for arranging guard services for the strip.[44]

Other Solicitations

Taking his cue from the president and his cabinet, North looked for other ways to help bridge the Contra funding gap, although admonishing the rebels to keep the subject under wraps.[45] In the process, he involved a number of prominent figures both inside and outside the administration.

One of North's ardent allies was retired Maj. Gen. John Singlaub, former chief of staff of U.S. armed forces in South Korea. After President Jimmy Carter fired him for publicly criticizing U.S. policy on Korea, Singlaub undertook a one-man anticommunist crusade that sometimes made North look impassive by comparison. Singlaub's mission soon led him to the Contras. By January 1984, he had already offered to provide FDN leader Calero with retired military advisors as trainers and to raise money from private sources. Although he contacted Calero on his own initiative, Singlaub went to the trouble of notifying U.S. officials, including North, of what he was doing.[46] North sought McFarlane's endorsement of the retired general's efforts, which McFarlane later characterized as constituting disallowed "direct or indirect" support.[47]

Singlaub provided weapons to Calero (see Chapter 7), but his main contribution to North's operation was to help extract money from other governments. Through the U.S. Council on World Freedom, a chapter of the World Anti-Communist League (WACL) he founded, Singlaub had formed close relationships with kindred true believers around the world, particularly among pro–United States governments in Asia. In late 1984, he began to approach some of them on behalf of the Contras.

Toward the end of November 1984, he met in Washington, D.C., with a representative of the South Korean government and a senior official from the Taiwan interests section to talk about what they might be willing to do. With characteristic frankness, he told them the Contras desperately needed "bullets and guns." When they balked at Singlaub's lack of official U.S. government backing, he told them that was precisely the point. As a private citizen, he had a "certain flexibility that the government . . . did not have in view of . . . the Boland Amendment." Although both officials, friends of the general for many years, assured him they wanted to help, they said they would have to check with their superiors.[48]

At 4:15 that afternoon, Singlaub made his way to North's office in the Old Executive Office Building to report on the meetings. According to North's sparse notes, Singlaub emphasized that "USG could *not* come to Taiwanese"—that is, there could be no official contact with Washington. The Koreans and Taiwanese did not want to cross Capitol Hill any more than North and the administration did. They also relied on Congress to approve necessary U.S. aid.[49]

To maintain official deniability, Singlaub suggested he visit Taipei and Seoul in January to bump the request to a higher level, and North quickly gave his "blessing."[50] Singlaub made the trip, meeting with Taiwan's foreign minister, whom he had known from earlier in his career, and with a senior official in the Korean Central Intelligence Agency. He reiterated the urgency of the Contras' needs, proposed to both a $5 million donation, and even suggested how they could make their contributions.[51] The key, he told North, was the U.S. government had to send Taiwan an unequivocal signal that "we would be greatly pleased" with an offer of support.[52] In the end, South Korea decided not to give. Taiwan agreed to cooperate after several solicitations, including two unsuccessful approaches by Calero himself in 1984.

North and his administration colleagues did not limit themselves to U.S. allies. On November 28, 1984, the same day Singlaub was appealing to the Taiwanese, North met with the military attaché from Taipei's adversary, the People's Republic of China (see Chapter 3). Over lunch at the elite Cosmos Club, North put forward a classic carrot and stick. As the enticement, he "advised [the official] that Adolfo Calero, the Head of the FDN, was willing to commit to a recognition of the PRC once the Resistance Forces had succeeded." The "stick" was a not-so-veiled threat to take his business elsewhere—"to re-initiate discussions for a similar delivery via Chile."[53] Singlaub made a similar threat to the Taiwanese. According to North's notes, Singlaub warned them a "new govt. in Managua could cost the ROC [Republic of China] an embassy."[54] In his negotiations with Iran, North would repeatedly make promises in the name of the U.S. government he knew to be either false or not his to make.

Others in the administration were kept apprised of these efforts to get help from foreign governments. For example, NSC Asia specialist Gaston Sigur arranged North's lunch with the Chinese defense attaché and gave him the phone number of a South Korean official to contact, although he claimed to be largely ignorant of the solicitations that followed.[55] Vessey met with the same Chinese official after North's lunch. The JCS chair also knew about the original Saudi donation to the Contras, having been told about it on two occasions by Prince Bandar bin Sultan himself.

By this period, a broad swath of U.S. officials—from the State Department, the CIA, and the Pentagon to members of the NSPG—were familiar with attempts to get foreign governments to donate to the rebels, giving the appearance that circumventing Congress on Contra aid had become virtually an administration-wide pursuit.

6

HAWKS

Between November and December 1985, the Iran initiative reached its nadir. Despite the failure of the Iranian middlemen to obtain freedom for the hostages as promised after the first TOW shipments, Washington and Tel Aviv persuaded themselves they could turn the operation around. However, the next transaction—involving sophisticated antiaircraft missiles—imploded spectacularly after a series of logistical blunders and miscommunications. Worse, overeager U.S. officials crossed lines of operational and legal propriety, leading the CIA, among others, to protect not only itself but the president from charges serious enough to raise the prospect of impeachment. At a closely held White House meeting afterward, Ronald Reagan surprised his most senior aides by vowing to keep the operation alive regardless of the penalty.

How the Deals Survived

Despite the disappointment over the initial TOW transaction, key administration officials viewed the release of even a single hostage as a better result than any previous hostage-recovery effort had produced. From their perspective, the August and September deals represented a breakthrough. Ghorbanifar, therefore, managed to shed his image as the discredited "fabricator," as portrayed by the CIA, and instead came to be seen as a "legitimate channel to the highest levels of the Khomeini regime."[1]

A second reason the Iran initiative persisted was simply that the main operatives—in Iran, Israel, and the United States—had a vested interest in its continuation. For Tehran, the exigencies of the Iran-Iraq War made it imperative to keep seeking reliable weapons sources. After Baghdad considerably strengthened its mostly French- and Soviet-supplied air forces, Iran came under pressure to build up its air defense capabilities, according to Hassan Rouhani, who was chosen to lead the effort.[2] Subsequent Iranian requests heavily emphasized missiles capable of shooting down Iraqi attack aircraft. Top on the wish list was the Homing All the Way Killer (HAWK) missile, a sophisticated weapon the shah had acquired from the United States for his arsenal. Spare parts for the aging Iranian inventory became a particularly urgent need. The arms dealers—Manucher Ghorbanifar,

Yaacov Nimrodi, and Al Schwimmer—remained engaged purely for reasons of profit. For David Kimche of the Israeli Foreign Ministry, the primary focus was the potential benefit to his country's interests. As for Michael Ledeen, who carried Robert McFarlane's portfolio, there was the prospect of a major diplomatic success plus undoubtedly the attraction of being a player in a highly sensitive operation.

McFarlane himself was buffeted by conflicting reactions. He had a good deal to lose if the deals went sour. Just two months earlier, the secretaries of state and defense had dismissed his proposal to send arms to Iran. Having gone ahead, even with the president's approval, he stood to lose stature in the eyes of the cabinet officers he most wanted to impress. Still, he had enough distance from the operation to see the outcome of the TOW deals as a "rather dramatic signal that we were being duped." He was reluctant to go forward, but as he admitted later, he allowed himself to hope he was wrong, that perhaps Ghorbanifar and his Iranian cohorts had been manipulated by higher-ups who had used the process for their own ends. He consoled himself with the adage "matters seldom go the way one thinks they will in the Middle East."[3]

But the most important impetus for staying the course was the president's unflagging desire to find a way out of the hostage crisis. Reagan had been "obviously pleased" even one captive had gotten out in September.[4] He seems not to have worried the stakes for the United States had risen significantly with only the one release to show for it. When presented the next set of proposals he never hesitated, shrugging off the doubts of his two senior foreign policy advisors, George Shultz and Caspar Weinberger. McFarlane may have helped launch the initiative from the U.S. side, but it would not have gotten off the ground—or continued—without the president's backing.

Getting Back on Track

On October 3, Islamic Jihad, the organization that had admitted kidnapping several of the current hostages in Lebanon, sent shudders through the U.S. intelligence community by announcing they would execute William Buckley, the CIA agent McFarlane had hoped would be the first U.S. hostage released under the TOW deal in August. At that time, the Iranians had said Buckley was too ill to be moved. In late September, word had come that Buckley might be released within a few days. Now, just as suddenly, those hopes had come crashing to earth. Oliver North, monitoring the situation at McFarlane's behest, decided it was time to establish once and for all whether Buckley was still alive and whether there was any possibility of freeing him. He instructed Ledeen to gather Ghorbanifar and the two Israeli businessmen, Schwimmer and Nimrodi, for a discussion in Washington, D.C.

North chose an impressive site—the Old Executive Office Building, immediately next door to the White House.[5] The session was originally set for October 7, but that day Palestinian terrorists hijacked an Italian cruise ship, the *Achille Lauro*, off Egypt's Mediterranean coast. As the NSC staff's coordinator for counterterrorism, North was preoccupied with the unfolding crisis.[6] The others waited a day, then met without him.

It was an important meeting for advancing the next phase of the initiative. According to Ledeen, Ghorbanifar "conveyed from his Iranians the promise of more hostages for weapons," then proceeded to talk about "all kinds of weapons . . . everything from Phoenix missiles to Sidewinders to [H]arpoons, Hawks, TOWS, everything known to man."[7] But Ghorbanifar was shrewd enough not to talk only about weapons. Playing on U.S. interest in developing political contacts, he also raised the possibility of introducing a "senior Iranian official" he claimed to represent. From Ghorbanifar's characterization, Ledeen took this to mean someone who wanted not only to cooperate with the United States but to change the government of Iran. With that enticement, Ledeen was able to convince McFarlane to approve the next meeting, set to take place later in the month.

Toward the end of October, in Geneva, Ledeen got to meet the "senior Iranian." He was Hassan Karoubi, the same representative Israeli Foreign Ministry official David Kimche had met in July, whose presence had persuaded key Israelis that Ghorbanifar's Iranian government contacts were significant. According to Nimrodi, Karoubi emphasized Iran continued to have a pressing need for arms, especially HAWKs, which he said were needed to defend Qom, the holy city in central Iran where Khomeini had set up his headquarters. He specifically mentioned a requirement for 150 HAWKS plus 200 Sidewinders and 30–50 highly sophisticated Phoenix missiles. In Nimrodi's version, Ledeen offered substantial U.S. help for Iran, including providing experts and technicians, establishing joint committees, and sharing intelligence in return for the release of all of the U.S. hostages as soon as possible.[8]

Despite Ghorbanifar's attempt to package Karoubi as someone who wanted to advance Iranian-U.S. relations, he proved no more interested in a strategic dialogue than Ghorbanifar. His main purpose at the meeting was essentially cosmetic—to add luster to the arms deals for the benefit of the U.S. participants. After a perfunctory statement on improved relations, he repeated the laundry list Ghorbanifar had presented earlier in the month. The five-step mechanism he proposed called for delivery of one or more hostages to start, followed by a single shipment of arms, followed by more hostages, and so on. A few days later, a skeptical McFarlane picked at the details as Ledeen and North pressed him to give the proposal a chance. McFarlane wondered about the Iranians with whom the United States would be dealing, implying, according to North's notes, there were "very few sensible people in [the] Iranian Army." Ledeen countered he was "willing to deal w/Israelis to bring out credible military and political leaders." The Israelis themselves would clear the idea with their leadership ("Schwimmer will go to Shimon Peres"). Finally, McFarlane came around, although with preconditions: "RCM—Not one single item w/o live Americans," North wrote.[9]

With McFarlane's okay, the intermediaries met several times during the first half of November to continue preparations for the next shipment. The national security advisor had already vetoed sending anything other than HAWK missiles. He told Weinberger, "We might give them—thru Israelis—Hawks but no Phoenix."[10] Two other issues remained, at least in the minds of the Israelis: first, did President Reagan still approve of the operation? Second, if the Israelis had to deplete their own stocks by transferring missiles directly to Iran, could they count on the United States to replace them? McFarlane personally reassured Defense Minister Yitzhak Rabin on both scores in Washington, D.C., on November 15.[11] The requirements for the HAWK deal were falling into place.

In the Loop

As he had during the TOW shipments in August and September, McFarlane made sure to keep the president and his aides up to date about the HAWK transaction. Despite claiming to be out of the loop after the scandal broke, these officials got regular briefings from the national security advisor. On November 9, the day after confirming the deal with Kimche, McFarlane called Weinberger overseas on a secure telephone to tell him about the plan. Weinberger recorded the conversation in his notes: "Bud McFarlane fm Washington—on secure—wants to start 'negot' exploration with Iranians (+ Israelis) to give Iranians weapons for our hostages."[12] The next day, the two spoke again: "Negotiations are with 3 Iranian dissidents who say they want to overthrow government. We'll demand release of all hostages."[13] McFarlane also let Shultz in on the proposal. The secretary immediately briefed his aides, telling Michael Armacost, the undersecretary of state, "In last few days Bud asked Cap how to get 600 Hawks + 200 Phoenix to Iran."[14] The day before giving Rabin the thumbs up, McFarlane also told CIA Director William Casey who filled in his deputy, John McMahon. The latter recorded a note for his files on the "Israeli plan to move arms to certain elements of the Iranian military who are prepared to overthrow the government."[15] Finally, according to McFarlane, he also informed the president and vice president of the planned shipment within a day or two of meeting with Rabin.[16]

Initial reactions to the plan were mixed. Shultz and Weinberger flatly disapproved for policy and legal reasons. In their conversation on November 9, the secretary of defense told McFarlane bluntly he objected to the idea. A few days later, Shultz and Armacost complained the operation was "highly illegal. Cap won't do it I'm sure. . . . Another sign of funny stuff on Iran issue," they grumbled.[17]

But for the time being, the most important voice on the issue—Reagan's—was still in favor. On the eve of the milestone November 1985 U.S.-Soviet summit in Geneva, the first direct encounter between cold war rivals Reagan and Mikhail Gorbachev, McFarlane found time to convey the plan to Reagan, who replied, "Well, cross your fingers or hope for the best, and keep me informed." White House Chief of Staff Donald Regan remembered both he and the president were "hopeful."[18] On the morning of November 19, McFarlane again gathered with Reagan and Regan in the latter's second-floor bedroom at the Villa Palmetta in Geneva to explain the convoluted sequence of weapons pickups and deliveries, secret communications, and monitoring of the operation. McFarlane also described the cover story that would be used—the missiles would be referred to as oil-drilling equipment. Later, Regan said he had never heard anything like the tale McFarlane spun. For his part, the president listened carefully but characteristically asked few questions, with the usual result that each person left the meeting with a different impression of his reaction. McFarlane thought he looked pleased. "Well, I hope it works," he recalled the president saying. Regan was not sure at first whether the president had absorbed the whole story, but later agreed if he had not explicitly said yes to the deal, he had not said no either.[19]

Later in the day, McFarlane visited Shultz in his suite at the Intercontinental Hotel and gave him the same detailed rundown. He assured the secretary none of the HAWKs would be transferred until confirmation of the hostages' release had arrived. Although it was nominally a deal between Israel and Iran, he confirmed Israel expected to buy replacement missiles from the United States. Shultz reiterated his opposition, saying it was a "very bad idea" that would not work. Furthermore, he resented only being informed, not consulted, and he worried the operation "could do a lot of damage to the President." McFarlane responded, "George, you ought to say so, if you think so. Tell the President." But Shultz demurred—"he was not going to interfere," McFarlane later wrote.[20]

Weinberger, who did not take part in the summit, heard from McFarlane around midday, Washington, D.C., time on November 19. By habit, he scribbled down the gist of the call. "Bud McFarlane fm Geneva—update on meetings— all OK so far."[21] But McFarlane also needed information. He wanted to find out whether the Defense Department, which had custody of the weapons, would be able to locate enough missiles from U.S. inventories to restock Israel's supplies. ("[McFarlane] wants us to try to get 500 Hawks for sale to Israel to pass on to Iran fr release of 5 hostages Thurs.," Weinberger wrote.)[22] Replenishment was a fundamental issue for Tel Aviv. Perennial tensions with Arab neighbors made the Israelis loath to lower their state of military readiness even temporarily.

Weinberger sent McFarlane's query down the line to the office that monitored weapons supplies and within hours got a preliminary answer from his military assistant, Maj. Gen. Colin Powell. He jotted down the results: "Colin Powell in office—re data on Hawks—can't be given to Israel or Iran w/o Cong[ressional] Notification—breaking them up into several packages of 28 Hawks to keep each package under $14 million is a clear violation."[23]

This was not good news for the HAWK operation. First, according to Powell's information, McFarlane's scheme would require notification of Congress if the total value of the arms sold to Iran exceeded $14 million. This was one of the key provisions of the Arms Export Control Act (AECA), the legislation that governed transfers of U.S. military equipment abroad, including via an intermediary country (in this case, Israel). Moreover, Henry Gaffney, the Pentagon official who punched up the data on his computer for Powell, had anticipated the possibility of subdividing the weapons and indicated this would be a "clear violation," too. But Gaffney's report was hardly neutral. He said later he got a "clear signal" from Powell to frame his report "as negatively as possible," an order he understood came from Weinberger.[24]

McFarlane took the message in stride. He and Weinberger had been antagonistic for some time, and their personal animus had spilled over into policy disputes over Lebanon and other issues. When the defense secretary had scoffed at McFarlane's draft NSDD a few months earlier, the divide had grown. Now, McFarlane for once seemed to have the inside track: he had the president on his side. When Weinberger picked up the phone to pass along Gaffney's assessment, McFarlane dismissed him with a polite "thanks for the call."[25] The next day, Weinberger made one more pitch: "We shouldn't pay Iranians anything." But McFarlane cut him short again—"President has decided to do it thru Israelis."[26] The deals would go ahead.

"One Hell of an Operation"

North's role in the HAWK operation began when Rabin telephoned him at McFarlane's suggestion on November 17 to explain, "We have a problem" and to ask for his help.[27] The Israelis were already finalizing preparations for the operation. While Nimrodi was in Geneva with Ghorbanifar and his chief Iranian contact, Mohsen Kangarlou, Schwimmer took the lead in arranging logistics. The day after Rabin's call, North contacted Schwimmer for the first time to find out where things stood.[28] The Israelis and Iranians had agreed to ship the first allotment of missiles within two days. Over the course of the next three or four days, all the hostages—code-named "boxes"—were to be delivered.[29] Although a total of up to 600 missiles had been contemplated, the United States and Israel agreed to reduce the number to 120. Prime Minister Peres himself approved shipping 80 missiles in the first installment on condition the United States would ship the remaining 40 units.[30]

North and Schwimmer also discussed methods of payment, agreeing Schwimmer would deposit $1 million into the Enterprise's Lake Resources account in Switzerland.[31] The deposit, which went through on November 20, was meant "to cover the cost of this whole transaction in terms of renting airplanes and warehouse space and the appropriate charges for various people on the ground, those kinds of things," North testified later.[32] Until that point the account had been dedicated to the Contra program. North admitted the bulk of the deposit did in fact go to support the Nicaraguan rebels, with Israel evidently acquiescing. This was the first commingling of Iran- and Contra-related funds, later seen as one of the most serious legal breaches of the entire affair.

Over the next few days, the subject of finances came up repeatedly. North and Schwimmer talked about prices to charge for the missiles, settling on a figure of $225,000 apiece. North also discussed with Israel's purchasing agent in New York, Avraham ben Yousef, how to package the transaction—"Start Buy Orders @ $14M or Less"—reflecting North's desire to avoid notifying Congress by squeezing below the reporting limit. They also worried about keeping the transaction low-key. Normal procedures, such as requesting a letter of offer and acceptance, would "attract attention"; a "cash transfer" would "create severe visibility" problems.[33]

On November 20, North learned the full amount for the weapons had been transferred: "18M Deposited . . . Covers 80H @ 255K," but North's notes show different methods of arranging the exchanges of hostages and arms were also being contemplated. Rabin and North talked about what seemed to be a sequential exchange of two, three, and one hostage (five from the United States and one from France) for each of three shipments of weapons:

One	27—2	5+1 French
	27—3	
	26—1[34]	

If North was actually considering this, it went directly against McFarlane's order not to transfer any weapons before "live Americans" had been freed. Although North generally kept McFarlane, and later John Poindexter, apprised of where things stood in the Iran initiative, he was also willing to make decisions on his own and to decide later how much to tell his superiors.

North was by no means new to the subject of hostages in Lebanon. Most of his time on the NSC staff dealt with counterterrorism activities, which included plumbing every possible lead to Islamic fundamentalists in the environs of Beirut. His notebook entries in the days leading up to Rabin's call show a blur of activity aimed at freeing the hostages: meeting with agents from the Drug Enforcement Administration (DEA) to develop contacts among Lebanon's Christian Phalange and Druze militias; attending sessions of the Terrorist Incident Working Group, where the possible location of the U.S. captives was discussed ("5 of 6 now in Bldg. #18");[35] communicating with the Syrians; and maintaining frequent contact with Terry Waite, the Anglican Church official trying to arrange face-to-face meetings with the captors themselves.

None of these attempts bore fruit. North's experience paralleled the U.S. intelligence community's inability, going back to the Iran hostage crisis of 1979–1981, to unearth "actionable" information on the captives or their captors. That grim track record contributed to the eagerness of the Iran arms deal participants to pursue what often seemed a futile exercise.

The HAWK shipment ran into trouble virtually from the start. Schwimmer, responsible for the air operation on the Israeli side, had no problem obtaining eighty missiles from Israeli military stocks, but he could not find an air charter company to take the cargo from Israel directly to Iran. Given the harshness of Tehran's rhetoric against Tel Aviv, the few commercial concerns willing to consider the highly risky operation demanded enormous financial guarantees against potential losses.[36] Schwimmer's alternative was to ship the weapons to an intermediate country, transfer them to other aircraft, then move them to their destination. That way the point of origin of the weapons could not be traced.

The country the Israelis picked to "launder" the operation was Portugal, a favorite transshipment point for global arms deals. For some reason, however, Schwimmer either was unable to acquire the necessary clearances from the Portuguese or never made the attempt, thinking the United States would do so.[37] It fell to North to "take care of th[e] problem." His first instinct was to turn to Richard Secord, his private-sector partner on the Contra project. "The reason I asked General Secord," he said later, "is he had contacts in [Portugal] . . . because of the other covert operation [the Contras]. He had a lot of experience in the aviation business, fixing aviation problems, particularly covert ones, and he was an expert on Iran."[38] Secord balked at first, claiming to be "up to my ass in alligators" trying to get the Contra supply operation up and running. But North insisted.[39] To lend an official cast to the effort, North gave Secord a letter on White House stationery saying, "Your discreet assistance is again required in support of our national interests." Secord was to go to Portugal and elsewhere "as necessary in order to arrange for the transfer of sensitive materiel being shipped from Israel." He was instructed to "exercise great caution that this activity does not become public knowledge."[40]

Although no one focused on it at the time, the stage was being set for some of the most questionable aspects of the Iran initiative. U.S. officials were beginning to take a direct role in the operation, whereas until then McFarlane had been able to paint it as primarily an Israeli-Iranian activity, despite the need for Washington's approval to go forward. By instructing North to help get third-country transit rights, McFarlane had taken another step toward eventual U.S. control of the operation.

When Secord and his partner, Tom Clines, arrived in Lisbon on November 20, they turned to a Portuguese company named Defex, with which Clines had close ties, in hopes the firm's government contacts would help cut through red tape and obtain the needed landing clearances. But it would not be so simple: permission would have to come directly from the foreign minister. The problem was a new government had just been elected, headed by the Social Democrat Aníbal Cavaco Silva, leaving Defex's high-level connections suddenly out of power.[41] When Portuguese Foreign Ministry officials learned a retired U.S. general was trying to arrange an arms shipment to Iran, they insisted on checking with the U.S. embassy. Because of the cloak of secrecy over the operation, however, embassy officials were unaware of both the operation and Secord, and declined to endorse the request, affirming instead that the United States had an embargo in place against Iran.

With the deadline for a decision on the flight from Tel Aviv fast approaching, Secord made a desperate attempt to reach the Portuguese leadership himself. Learning Cavaco Silva and Foreign Minister Pedro Pires de Miranda were due to return from a trip to Brussels late on November 21, he made his way to the airport in Lisbon, where, claiming to represent the "American administration," he tried to accost them. Unfortunately, he went to the wrong section of the airport and failed to get close to the delegation. Yet, he managed to create enough of a commotion to provoke the foreign minister to protest to the U.S. chargé d'affaires.[42] In a report to Washington, the CIA station chief in Lisbon concluded the airport incident "probably doomed the effort to failure. . . . The Prime Minister reacted strongly and negatively to this approach and viewed all subsequent contacts with suspicion."[43]

At 4:50 the next morning, the station chief called Secord with an offer to help. He had been summoned to his office at 3:00 a.m. by Duane Clarridge at agency headquarters, who by this time had teamed up with North to try to break the Portuguese impasse. True to character, Secord turned down the offer, still expecting to handle the problem on his own. But eight hours later, using his pseudonym, Richard Copp, he called back with an "urgent request for assistance." For the rest of the day, "Copp" and the station chief, working together with the embassy's chargé, tried frantically to reach the Portuguese foreign minister. Although the U.S. ambassador had been left out of the loop, on instructions from the NSC staff, the chargé was brought in after the station chief pointed out that word would eventually leak back to the embassy anyway.[44]

By November 22, McFarlane himself entered the picture. In the midst of a tour of Europe to brief allies on the just-completed U.S.-Soviet summit, he reportedly interrupted a meeting with the pope to place a call to Pires de Miranda. The two eventually spoke late in the evening and, according to the foreign minister, reached an agreement to allow the aircraft to pass through Portugal. All the United States had to do was produce a diplomatic note acknowledging the purpose of the flights, the cargo, and itinerary. But a misunderstanding developed, and the resulting paperwork was inadequate for Portugal's purposes, mainly because it lacked any reference to the hostages. Twenty-four hours later, the issue still had not been resolved; the Portuguese wanted a second note, but Washington refused to spell out the hostage connection on paper.[45]

While Secord, the CIA, and the NSC staff labored to get around the roadblock, Schwimmer in Tel Aviv was still attempting to charter an aircraft. On Friday, November 22, he finally arranged with the Israeli military to use an El Al 747 cargo plane, on which eighty HAWK missiles were loaded for delivery to Portugal. He also leased two aircraft from a European company to ferry the missiles from Lisbon to their destination in Iran. But for financial reasons the leases were only good for a limited amount of time. After that, whether or not the aircraft had been used, they would have to be released.[46]

This time pressure added to the frenetic pace of the efforts to get Portugal to clear the operation. Finally, on November 22, with the deadline almost upon them, the Israelis decided to have the El Al 747 take off for Lisbon, even without landing rights, on the chance they would come through in time. It was a desperate move—one for which neither side wanted to claim responsibility later.[47] By prior arrangement, the plane was to fly to a certain "go/no go" point, where it would be ordered either to continue to Lisbon or to turn back to Tel Aviv. At the critical moment, Portuguese permission had still failed to materialize, and the plane returned to Israel where the missiles were off-loaded.

To make matters worse, Schwimmer also discharged the two other planes he had leased. North and his U.S. colleagues were livid. "Unbelievable as it may seem," North wrote to Poindexter, "I have just talked to Schwimmer, in TA [Tel Aviv,] who advises that they have released their DC-8s in spite of my call to DK [Kimche] instructing that they be put on hold until we could iron out the clearance problems in [Lisbon]. Schwimmer released them to save $ and now does not think that they can be rechartered before Monday. . . . One hell of an operation."[48]

With this latest jolt, Washington decided to explore alternative routes and aircraft. North passed the news to Secord, who suggested using a plane already scheduled to fly a load of ammunition to the Contras as part of the Enterprise's resupply operation. He said the plane could be repainted overnight, in order to disguise it, and put into service by noon the next day. Clarridge came up with a better option, however. In checking with the CIA Air Branch, he learned a proprietary aircraft—one belonging to a company posing as a legitimate business but secretly owned by the CIA—might be available. From his desk at CIA headquarters in Langley, Virginia, Clarridge began sending urgent cables to posts in Turkey and elsewhere to alert them they might be needed.

Meanwhile, the Iranians expected the weapons to be delivered on time and made payments as scheduled. The Iranian government, apparently satisfied with the way the earlier TOW deals had worked, had agreed to pay up front this time around, obviating the need for Adnan Khashoggi's "bridge financing." Thus, while the logistics problems were turning into a "bit of a horror story," in North's words,[49] Ghorbanifar's Swiss accounts grew with deposits of $24.72 million and $20 million intended in part to pay for eighty HAWKS at a cost of roughly $300,000 apiece. Ghorbanifar in turn instructed his bank to arrange transfers of $18 million and $6 million to Nimrodi's account. The first amount was to cover the reduced cost Ghorbanifar had paid for the missiles—$225,000 each. The second figure he asked Nimrodi to keep on account for payments he claimed he would have to make to top-level Iranians, including Prime Minister Mir-Hossein Mousavi, Speaker of the Majles (Parliament) Akbar Hashemi Rafsanjani, and President Ali Khamenei. According to the Israelis, Ghorbanifar also set aside $1 million for himself.[50]

Drawing In the CIA

The withdrawal of Schwimmer's aircraft left a vacuum that drew Washington further into what had until then been primarily an Israeli operation. With Clarridge's help, Secord got in touch with the CIA liaison officer at the proprietary company, St. Lucia Airlines.[51] Now with North and Clarridge involved in helping with the charter, the line between the airline's "legitimate" commercial operations and those ordered by the CIA was becoming blurred. If the agency was to get directly involved in a covert activity of this sort, legal authorizations would be needed, as Clarridge knew, including a presidential finding. Moreover, the finding had to be reported to Congress—something North and his partners were determined to avoid. Instead, Clarridge went only as far as to seek approval from his superior, Edward Juchniewicz, the associate deputy director of operations. Juchniewicz said it was acceptable as long as all the CIA provided was the name of an airline; if they went beyond that, it would be a different story. But although he apparently never told Juchniewicz, Clarridge had already crossed the line by helping to intervene with Portuguese officials. He would cross it again when searching for alternative landing spots for the aircraft.

As the Portugal option disintegrated, Cyprus emerged as the next best laundering site for the missile shipment. From November 22–24, plans were made and discarded involving various aspects of the operation. Whatever course they chose, Clarridge decided the aircraft would have to fly through Turkish airspace as the most direct route. But picking Cyprus simply substituted one problem for another. Because of its ongoing conflict with the Greek government of Cyprus, Turkey had a long-standing policy of refusing transit rights for aircraft that originated there. So although Cyprus would disguise the flight's true point of origin (Israel), it would mean having to get authorization to overfly Turkish territory on the way to Iran.

Clarridge and North decided to take their chances. It required a full twenty-four hours for the St. Lucia Boeing 707 to be cleaned (its last contract had been to fly chickens around Europe) and prepared for hauling missiles. On November 24, it left Tel Aviv with eighteen HAWKs on board. Yet another wrinkle developed, however, when the Israelis neglected to give the pilot the proper documentation for the shipment. When he reached Cyprus, local customs officials demanded to inspect the airplane, but because he had no cargo manifest he simply made one up, somehow managing to satisfy everyone even though the document bore no official stamps or certification of authenticity.

When it came to clearing Turkish air traffic control, the captain again talked his way through, first reporting a fake diplomatic clearance number, then, when that was refused, executing what a colleague called a "filibuster"—shifting altitude and giving fallacious estimates of his position to ground control for an hour and a half until he reached Iranian airspace. Ironically, the last and potentially most hazardous leg of the journey—flying over Iran—turned out to be uneventful, and the 707 landed safely in Tehran early on the morning of November 25. The pilot did not even have to use the code phrase "I am coming for Mustafa" to allow safe entry into Iranian airspace.[52]

Blowback

Unfortunately, the delivery of the eighteen HAWKS did not end the saga. The Iranians were irritated, first, that the flight was three days late. Second, the cargo contained a fraction of the eighty missiles promised. The smaller size of the St. Lucia Boeing 707 versus the original El Al 747 accounted for that. North and his colleagues had planned four more flights over the next several days to handle the remaining items, but a much more serious problem interrupted their plans. The Iranians who met the flight in Tehran found, to their shock, the missiles were not what they had expected. Iran's greatest need at the time was for a weapon that could shoot down high-flying Iraqi aircraft. In their understanding, the most recent version of the missile, the so-called Improved HAWK, or I-HAWK, had that capability, and therefore this was the version they specified. But when they cracked open the crates they believed they had been sent the wrong model. A test of one of the missiles appeared to confirm this.[53] Accounts differ over whether this was the case. Nimrodi is convinced they received an earlier model, and he blames Israeli Ministry of Defense Security Chief Chaim Carmon, who oversaw the loading of the missiles into the aircraft, for switching them without telling Nimrodi or Schwimmer.[54] But the director general of the Ministry of Defense, Menachem Meron, claimed later Israel had indeed delivered I-HAWKs. The problem, he said, was the Iranian military did not understand the improved version did not fly any higher; it only featured updated software that made it more accurate and easier to control. He insisted it was "first-line equipment," the same model Israel and the United States maintained in their inventories. No amount of explanation was enough to placate the Iranians, however. To make matters worse, the weapons still bore the blue Star of David, the insignia of the Israeli Air Force. According to Meron, someone simply forgot to remove them before shipment.[55]

Incensed, the Iranians accused the Israelis of cheating them. When Rafsanjani heard the news he declared the debacle nothing less than a plot to embarrass Iran or possibly even to topple him from power. How else to explain the evidence the missiles came from Israel, Tehran's avowed enemy?[56] According to Nimrodi, Prime Minister Mousavi called the hotel in Geneva in a rage to berate his representative, Mohsen Kangarlou, who had been waiting with Ghorbanifar and Nimrodi for confirmation of the transaction. Mousavi accused Kangarlou of fraud, causing the terrified aide to faint on the spot. Ghorbanifar, too, was shaken and shouted at Nimrodi the Israelis were thieves and cheats. Mousavi threatened to impound the St. Lucia plane, crew, and seventeen remaining missiles until all of the money Iran had just transferred to Ghorbanifar's accounts was returned. In fact, the Iranians allowed the 707 to leave the country the same day but did not return the missiles until the following February.[57]

The HAWK deal produced nothing but problems and disappointments. Most importantly, no hostages were released—an even worse result than the TOW deals had yielded in September. In this instance even North recognized the Iranians had a strong case to argue they had been shortchanged. A related outcome was the spreading of ill will between the Iranians and their Israeli and U.S. counterparts. Far from creating the atmosphere of trust everyone had hoped for, the bungled operation deepened suspicions on all sides. Mousavi specifically blamed the United States and gave Ghorbanifar a message to pass to President Reagan to that effect. The disaster also damaged relations between the U.S. and Israeli participants, eventually leading the U.S. side to take full charge of future transactions.

The Retroactive Finding

In their haste to get the missiles to Iran, North and Clarridge gave only scant attention to the legality of what they were trying to do. When Clarridge cleared with his superior, Juchniewicz, his plan to engage the CIA proprietary airline he offered the barest outline of the facts. "It was a very short conversation," Juchniewicz recalled, from which he concluded "there was no attempt to ask for assistance beyond the naming . . . of a commercial carrier that could be leased by the White House. There was no suggestion that we needed to commit people, money or anything else." Moreover, Clarridge claimed he was only acting "as a friend" of North's, not responding to an official White House request for assistance. Despite this shaky reasoning, Juchniewicz made no objections, electing to view it as a "purely commercial transaction."[58]

Juchniewicz's boss, CIA Deputy Director McMahon, did not buy his interpretation. McMahon first heard about the Portuguese snafu on Saturday, November 23, the day after Clarridge's conversation with Juchniewicz. Although the details were sparse, McMahon was wary enough to leave his subordinate instructions to keep the agency out of it. But when McMahon got to the office the following Monday, Juchniewicz asked him: "Hey, do you know what those guys did?" The deputy director was incensed. He yelled: "Goddammit, I told you not to get involved!" Juchniewicz insisted: "We're not involved. . . . They asked if we knew the name of a secure airline and we gave them the name of our proprietary." McMahon was not satisfied: "For Christ's sake, we can't do that without a Finding." He ordered the CIA general counsel to be briefed immediately and to produce a document for the president to sign. In the meantime, no further CIA activity on the NSC project was to take place.[59]

The finding did not take long to prepare. Stanley Sporkin, the top lawyer at the CIA, gathered briefly with knowledgeable agency operatives and with North.[60] Within a day or two, he handed a draft to McMahon that identified the scope of the operation as "Hostage Rescue—Middle East" and described it as covering "the provision of assistance by the Central Intelligence Agency to private parties in their attempt to obtain the release of Americans held hostage in the Middle East. Such assistance is to include the provision of transportation, communications, and other necessary support. As part of these efforts certain foreign materiel and munitions may be provided to the Government of Iran which is taking steps to facilitate the release of the American hostages."[61] A year later, when investigators discovered Sporkin's finding, which the president signed on December 5, 1985, it raised some of the most serious problems for the Reagan administration. Contradicting White House claims the Iran initiative had centered on a strategic opening to Tehran, the version clearly construed the operation first and foremost as an arms-for-hostages deal. There was no language reflecting a broader political objective.

Legally, the administration ran into trouble in two areas. First, the finding presumed to cover everything carried out before the president's grant of approval. The key phrase read, "All prior actions taken by U.S. Government officials in furtherance of this effort are hereby ratified." McMahon had instructed Sporkin to put in language of this sort as a way to validate—after the fact—CIA activities he knew would be illegal without written authorization. The main difficulty was the law allowed findings to cover only future activities. Another catch arose over an order in the finding to keep Congress in the dark about the operation. Written for the president's signature, the relevant passage read, "Because of the extreme sensitivity of these operations, in the exercise of the President's constitutional authorities, I direct the Director of Central Intelligence not to brief the Congress of the United States, as provided for in Section 501 of the National Security Act of 1947, as amended, until such time as I may direct otherwise."[62] A basic precept of the law governing findings was Congress had to be informed each time the president signed one. That way, lawmakers would not only be made aware of each activity but also be assured the president had accepted accountability for it. Congressional investigators looking back at the HAWK operation saw these provisions in the December 5 finding as attempts to evade the president's responsibility. The White House insisted protecting hostages' lives justified extraordinary secrecy, even though the law provided for exigencies by allowing limited distribution of especially sensitive findings to as few as eight senior members of Congress. This made the risk of leaks extremely low.

Nonetheless, Poindexter, on his first formal day as national security advisor—December 5, the same day Reagan signed the finding—took the controversial document and, without making copies for lawmakers or even the CIA, locked the original in his office safe, where it remained until the scandal broke. He later played down the document as mainly a "CYA" exercise for the CIA, justifying withholding it from Congress on the grounds both of the Iran operation's sensitivity and his fear its disclosure would "embarrass" the president.[63]

"They Can Impeach Me If They Want"

After the arms-for-hostages revelation, the president's defenders blamed his misguided approval of the operation on the lack of a full airing of views from his senior aides. In this interpretation, Reagan himself was a kind of hostage—first to McFarlane and then Poindexter. But the president did have access to opposing arguments from his closest advisors on more than one occasion. On December 7, in the wake of the HAWK fiasco and the contentious finding, he held a particularly significant meeting. Attending were Shultz, Weinberger, Regan, McFarlane, Poindexter, and McMahon. Only Vice President George Bush, who was at the army-navy football game, and Casey, who was also out of town, were absent. By design, the group met in the family quarters of the White House. As Poindexter explained: "If you want to have a . . . free-wheeling discussion, you have it at the residence in a less formal setting where everybody could be comfortable. You only have principals in attendance, not a lot of staff around, and everybody feels free to express their view without it being published in the *Washington Post* the following day."[64]

The president's aides used the occasion to be blunt. After McFarlane reviewed the project from its beginnings and made a recommendation for how to continue, Shultz and Weinberger spoke out sharply against the initiative. In a rare show of agreement, they argued the United States had a long-standing policy of not dealing with terrorists—codified most recently in Operation Staunch—which the arms deals threatened to undermine completely. They added the United States would also create major diplomatic problems for itself with its allies, particularly moderate Arabs. Jordan and Saudi Arabia, for example, would feel even more threatened by Iran than before, and it would be difficult for Washington to explain why it had made weapons available to Tehran but had recently turned down requests to Amman or Riyadh.[65]

McMahon supported these objections. "What the hell are we doing here?" he asked. "Where is the formal authority?" He disputed the assumptions made about the Iranians on the other side: "I pointed out that we had no knowledge of any moderates in Iran, that most of the moderates had been slaughtered when Khomeini took over." He asserted any weapons transferred to Iran "would end up in the front, and that would be to the detriment of the Iran-Iraq balance."[66]

There were also legal issues. Weinberger explained to the president that the AECA prohibited the kinds of transactions that had already occurred. It specifically banned weapons exports to countries supporting terrorism even if they passed through a third country. Furthermore, under the act, the president was supposed to approve all transfers in advance, in writing, and notify Congress to make them legal. Of course, none of these steps had been followed in the Iran deals. Weinberger scribbled a note to himself afterward: "I argued strongly that we have an embargo that makes arms sales to Iran illegal [and the] President couldn't violate it. Furthermore, 'washing' transaction thru Israel wouldn't make it legal. Shultz, Don Regan agreed."[67]

Reagan's response to this formidable show of opposition reflected how important the hostage issue was for him. According to Weinberger, the president said "he could answer charges of illegality but he couldn't answer charge that 'big strong President Reagan passed up a chance to free hostages.'"[68] In other words, he was willing to contemplate breaking the law in order to get the hostages back.

Shultz confirms Weinberger's account. Back at the State Department, he told aides Reagan had said the U.S. public would not understand if four hostages died because "I wouldn't break the law." Reagan then insisted: "They can impeach me if they want," adding, "visiting days are Wednesday." Weinberger, Shultz recalled, retorted: "You will not be alone."[69]

Regan gives reason to believe the president's resolve had more than just a humanitarian motivation. Regan told the Tower Commission the president wanted to keep the arms deals going because "we weren't getting anywhere in getting more hostages out. And we were going to spend another Christmas with hostages there." That would leave him "looking powerless and inept as President because he's unable to do anything to get the hostages out."[70]

One other point of agreement among meeting participants was the president had been a forceful contributor to the discussion. Critics frequently lampooned him as disengaged from the policy process to the point of requiring cue cards. There were grounds for this caricature on issues in which he had no deep interest, but on subjects he felt strongly about, such as the Contras or the hostages, it was inadequate. According to some witnesses, he was at his most impressive during crises such as this. Charles Allen, the CIA national intelligence officer for counterterrorism (whom Casey would draft to keep tabs on Ghorbanifar), described Reagan's demeanor during the recent *Achille Lauro* hijacking as "incredibly strong. . . . The presence he had . . . he ran a very tight meeting. . . . It was very intense. . . . It still stands out in my mind."[71]

As he had been in the summer, Reagan was cryptic with his aides about whether to keep the operation alive. Once again, Shultz and Weinberger thought they had prevailed. "I felt that between Secretary Weinberger and I, we'd made a real dent," Shultz said later. The secretary of defense told his staff at the Pentagon he believed they had "strangled the baby in the cradle."[72] Advocates for pressing ahead on Iran, chiefly McFarlane and Poindexter, left the family quarters thinking the opposite. The president himself saw the situation as a "stalemate." All that appears to have been agreed to initially was McFarlane would travel to London to tell the Iranian and Israeli intermediaries there could be no more weapons deals until progress had been made on the political front. The United States would be pleased to pursue a strategic opening with Iran, he was to tell them, and even work on the release of hostages, but these steps had to come first—arms would be discussed later.[73] At best, the Shultz-Weinberger camp had won a temporary stay.

McFarlane's trip to London was discouraging. A three-hour session with Ghorbanifar had made it clear the Iranian had no interest in a political opening regardless of his superiors' views in Tehran. McFarlane's conclusion for the president, delivered at a special debriefing on December 10 with other senior officials present, was the arms deals should be terminated.[74] The president's diary entry for December 9 indicates he took to heart an alarming threat Ghorbanifar had ascribed to the hostage-takers: "Bud is back from London. . . . His meeting with the Iranians did not achieve it's [sic] purpose which was to persuade them to free our hostages 1st [and] then we'd supply the weapons. Their top man said he believed if he took that proposal to the terrorists they would kill our people."[75]

Yet, Reagan decided to push forward. Casey confirmed this to McMahon after the same top-level session: "I had the idea that the President had not entirely given up on encouraging the Israelis to carry on with the Iranians. I suspect he would be willing to run the risk and take the heat in the future if this will lead to springing the hostages. It appears that Bud has the action."[76]

Within a month, senior foreign policy officials would have another opportunity to "strangle" the initiative, but no one managed to persuade the president to reverse course.

Nicaraguan Sandinista leader Daniel Ortega, the Reagan administration's nemesis in Central America, delivers a speech before an image of onetime rebel leader Augusto Sandino on February 21, 1984. (Claude Urraca/Sygma/Corbis)

Nicaraguan Contra *comandos* at an unspecified location in Central America. (Photographer unknown)

Contra leaders Alfonso Robelo, Arturo Cruz Sr., and Adolfo Calero meet with President Reagan at the White House on April 4, 1985, as the administration prepares to launch another initiative to generate aid for the rebels. At far right is the White House's designated contact with the Contras, Oliver L. North. (Ronald Reagan Presidential Library)

Iranian weapons dealer Manucher Ghorbanifar was a chief instigator of the U.S.-Israel-Iran arms-for-hostages deals, remaining a fixture despite repeated indications he was deceiving all sides. (Ted Thai/Time & Life Pictures/Getty Images)

Ayatollah Ruhollah Khomeini (center), Iran's supreme leader until his death in 1989, poses with several leading Iranian political figures in the late 1980s. From left: Speaker of the Majles (Parliament) Akbar Hashemi Rafsanjani, President Ali Khamenei, Foreign Minister Ali Akbar Velayati, Khomeini, Intelligence Minister Mohammad Reyshahri, head of the judiciary Abdolkarim Mousavi Ardebili, and Prime Minister Mir-Hossein Mousavi. Several of these officials—notably Khomeini, Khamenei, Rafsanjani, and Mousavi—were aware of the arms deals with the United States. (Official website of Hashemi Rafsanjani, http://www .hashemirafsanjani.ir/en/node/134311)

Saudi billionaire Adnan Khashoggi, who provided "bridge financing" to allow the Iranian arms-for-hostages deals to go forward starting in 1985. (Roland Godefroy)

Director of the Central Intelligence Agency William J. Casey (left) and Secretary of State Alexander M. Haig were two of the Reagan administration's most resolute cold warriors. At the time of this photograph in early March 1981, Casey had just submitted a plan to the president for covertly combatting communist forces in Central America. (Ronald Reagan Presidential Library)

President Reagan welcomes Israeli Prime Minister Shimon Peres to the White House on October 17, 1985. Peres was instrumental in encouraging U.S. and Israeli cooperation in the covert initiative with Iran during 1985–1986. (Ronald Reagan Presidential Library)

President Reagan holds an emotional meeting with relatives of U.S. hostages at the White House on October 28, 1985. He is flanked by White House Chief of Staff Donald T. Regan (to his left) and National Security Advisor Robert C. McFarlane (to his right). On the table lies a large yellow ribbon, the symbol of support for U.S. hostages dating from the Carter presidency. (Ronald Reagan Presidential Library)

U.S. Marines fire a tube-launched optically-tracked wire-guided (TOW) antitank missile. The United States sold a version of this missile to Iran in 1985–1986. (U.S. Marine Corps)

A U.S.-made Homing All the Way Killer (HAWK) antiaircraft missile similar to those shipped to Iran via Israel in November 1985. After test firing one of the missiles, the Iranians declared them unacceptable and returned the rest. (Ted Gomes, U.S. Defense Department)

An aerial view of the warehouse at Ilopango, El Salvador, used by the Enterprise for the covert Contra resupply program. Operations coordinator Col. Robert C. Dutton (retired) compiled a photo album about the program shortly before it was exposed, which Oliver North told him he intended to share with President Reagan. (Reproduced as Select Committee Exhibit RCD-11)

An Enterprise flight crew stands next to a C-123K cargo plane used to ferry supplies to the Contras from Ilopango, El Salvador. (Reproduced as Select Committee Exhibit RCD-11)

National Security Advisor Robert C. McFarlane (right) and National Security Council staff member Oliver L. North, two of the principal implementers of the covert Iran and Contra operations, pose at McFarlane's retirement ceremony in December 1985. (Ronald Reagan Presidential Library)

Vice Adm. John M. Poindexter served as President Reagan's national security advisor from December 1985 to November 1986, playing a vital role as a link between the president and the Iran and Contra operations. (U.S. Navy)

Richard V. Secord, a principal figure in the private network known as the Enterprise that carried out operations on behalf of the National Security Council staff. Secord was a retired U.S. Air Force major general with extensive experience in clandestine operations and had served with the U.S. Military Assistance Advisory Group in Iran during the shah's rule. (U.S. Air Force)

Albert Hakim, Iranian expatriate and business partner of Richard Secord, prepares to testify to the congressional select committees on June 3, 1987. Hakim managed the Enterprise's finances, set up dummy companies, served as translator with Iranian officials, and briefly assumed the role of lead U.S. negotiator on the arms-for-hostages deals in October 1986. (Bettmann/CORBIS)

David Kimche, former director general of the Israeli Foreign Ministry, helped initiate the U.S.-Israeli arms-for-hostages deals with Iran in 1985 through his relationship with U.S. National Security Advisor Robert McFarlane. (Malcolm Byrne)

Amiram Nir (left), counterterrorism advisor to Israeli prime minister Shimon Peres (shown with Israeli intelligence official Rafi Eitan) in 1985. Nir combined forces with Oliver North and the Enterprise beginning in December 1985, focusing on the Iran arms deals but collaborating on plans for other joint covert operations as well. (Moshe Shai/FLASH90)

President Reagan discusses Central America with advisors in the Oval Office on March 24, 1986, a few days after the House voted down an administration request for $100 million for the Contras that included military aid. From left are Vice President George H. W. Bush, National Security Advisor John M. Poindexter, Deputy National Security Advisor Donald R. Fortier, White House Chief of Staff Donald T. Regan, Oliver L. North, Deputy Secretary of State John C. Whitehead, Assistant Secretary of State Elliott Abrams, and the president. (Ronald Reagan Presidential Library)

The National Security Planning Group (NSPG) meets in the White House Situation Room to discuss Contra funding on May 16, 1986. That morning, the *New York Times* reported that deep divisions among rebel groups risked a cutoff in U.S. aid. Seated at the table, clockwise from left, are President Reagan, Secretary of State George P. Shultz, Secretary of the Treasury James A. Baker, Director of the CIA William J. Casey, White House Chief of Staff Donald T. Regan, National Security Advisor John M. Poindexter, Director of the Office of Management and Budget James Miller, Army Chief of Staff Gen. John A. Wickham Jr., Secretary of Defense Caspar W. Weinberger, and Vice President George H. W. Bush. Seated against the far wall, from left, are Assistant Secretary of State Elliott Abrams, CIA Chief of the Central American Task Force Alan D. Fiers, Oliver L. North, and two other aides. (Ronald Reagan Presidential Library)

President Reagan greets former national security advisor Robert C. McFarlane in the Oval Office upon McFarlane's return from his covert mission to Tehran on May 29, 1986. White House Chief of Staff Donald T. Regan and Vice President George H. W. Bush look on. McFarlane briefed the group on the mission's failure and recommended aborting the Iran initiative, but Reagan decided to press ahead. (Ronald Reagan Presidential Library)

President Reagan meets with top advisors in the Oval Office on November 25, 1986, just prior to informing the nation of the connection between the Iran and Contra operations. From left: Secretary of Defense Caspar W. Weinberger, Secretary of State George P. Shultz, Attorney General Edwin Meese III, White House Chief of Staff Donald T. Regan, and the president. (Ronald Reagan Presidential Library)

After a terse statement to reporters in the White House Briefing Room about the Iran-Contra connection on November 25, 1986, President Reagan relinquishes the podium to Attorney General Edwin Meese III. White House spokesman Larry Speakes and Secretary of Defense Caspar W. Weinberger (in background) look on. (Ronald Reagan Presidential Library)

Former judge Lawrence E. Walsh speaks with reporters in Washington, D.C., after a special panel of the U.S. Court of Appeals appointed him independent counsel for Iran/Contra matters on December 19, 1986. (Wally McNamee/CORBIS)

U.S. House Select Committee Chair Lee H. Hamilton (D-Ind.) swears in former national security advisor John M. Poindexter before his testimony on July 15, 1987. Poindexter's denial that he informed President Reagan of the funding diversion to the Contras marked the climax of the televised hearings. Seated to Hamilton's right is House Select Committee ranking member Richard B. Cheney (R-Wyo.); to Hamilton's left (in light-colored jacket) is Senate Select Committee Chair Daniel K. Inouye (D-Hawaii). In the front row, at far left of photo, is House Chief Counsel John W. Nields Jr.; seated in front of Hamilton is House Select Committee member Thomas S. Foley (D-Wash.); at far right of photo is Senate Chief Counsel Arthur L. Liman. (Bettmann/CORBIS)

7

Tightening the Reins on the Contras

Ronald Reagan's landslide reelection in November 1984 reinforced the administration's sense of a broad political mandate, and in his second term he felt freer to address overseas priorities such as the Contras. But the elections produced only modest Republican gains in the House, and even the president's determination to use his momentum to pressure Congress to fund the rebels—to "make them feel the heat if they won't see the light"—was not always sufficient. The White House faced several tough battles during the year, from reducing the budget deficit to funding the MX missile, that eroded its standing on Capitol Hill. Few confrontations became more bitter, however, than those affecting the Contras—especially in the military sphere. The U.S. public still did not buy into the administration's alarmist views, and congressional opponents remained suspicious their restrictions on U.S. support were being routinely ignored. This was, in fact, the case. As the president's second term got under way, NSC staff and their private-sector collaborators solidified their control over rebel activities (particularly weapons purchases) and scrambled to build a viable resupply operation that could fly—literally and politically—under the radar. According to one of his closest aides, the president kept himself informed on many of these activities while Oliver North and Robert McFarlane steered congressional Democrats away from the facts.

Staff Changes

In 1985, the White House staff underwent a major reorganization. Edwin Meese left his post as presidential counselor to become attorney general, White House Chief of Staff James Baker exchanged roles with Secretary of the Treasury Donald Regan, and Deputy Chief of Staff Michael Deaver exited the White House to enter private business.[1] The "troika" of Meese, Baker, and Deaver had been the locus of White House power since early in the first term. Their departure, along with the rise to prominence of Regan, with his reputation for high-handedness and pronounced disdain for Congress, left the president without an important buffer against his own unchecked policy impulses. Another key appointment at this time was Patrick Buchanan as communications director. Buchanan was a polarizing figure who relished targeting liberals using language about communist domination that emerged straight out of the 1950s "red scare." Democrats saw his rise as chief shaper of the White House message as yet another sign of a steady shift to a more ideological and confrontational administration line.

On the NSC staff, circumstances were also evolving as McFarlane began to insert himself more aggressively into the policy process. Signs of his "ascendance" were noted in a *New York Times* article in May 1985, including his relocation to a larger office much closer to the president, more frequent quotations in print and appearances on television news shows, and more forceful performances at NSC meetings. He even began signing presidential decision memos "Robert C. McFarlane, for the President."[2] The press attributed this new prominence to a growing self-confidence. By his own account it was also a product of frustration. The bickering between George Shultz and Caspar Weinberger, he told reporters on background, was a serious disruption to the policy process.

Worse, in his view (though he did not state it so openly), was the president's shocking indifference to fundamental duties such as defining administration foreign policy priorities for the second term. On one occasion in late 1984, he gave Reagan a large binder containing an assortment of possible major policy initiatives, asking him to choose two in order to maximize attention on each. When he returned, Reagan's response was a genial, "Let's do them all!"[3] (Baker had gone through a similar experience the year before when he discovered Reagan had chosen to watch *The Sound of Music* on television over preparing for the Williamsburg economic summit the following day.)[4] The ease with which the president abdicated responsibility on issues of such importance was a defining feature of his approach to management. It was also an essential precondition for the excesses of Iran-Contra.

One of the areas of policy for which McFarlane assumed the lead was Nicaragua. In mid-1985, the Democratic chair of the House Ways and Means Committee remarked, "There's only one man from the Administration anyone up here thinks about when it comes to . . . Central America, and that's McFarlane."[5] As early as April—after the resounding defeat of a $14 million Contra aid bill in the House in March—McFarlane turned once again to North to try to bridge the funding gap. As before, North enjoyed broad support from his superiors, including CIA Director William Casey. Mindful of the need for Congress to reinstate its support, these officials maintained a shifting set of cover stories to disguise their activities—whether they involved supplying weapons to the rebels, approaching third countries, or raising money from wealthy private donors.

Tightening the Reins on Contra Weapons Purchases

Central to the NSC staff's thinking about battlefield strategy was the ability to supply the Contras on Nicaragua's southern border. North's ideas about how to keep up a regular flow of arms and equipment developed in tandem with his thinking about this second front. By early 1985, Adolfo Calero found himself in a somewhat enviable position, having a certain amount of cash on hand with which to buy needed supplies and several potential sources in what North described as the "very cut-throat business" of international arms sales from which to choose.[6] Aside from Richard Secord, there was John Singlaub, whom North had encouraged to set up operations with the rebels. Another notable player was a U.S. citizen named Ronald Martin.

After the second Boland Amendment went into effect in late 1984, Martin, who in the past had been investigated by the Bureau of Alcohol, Tobacco, and Firearms (ATF) and had faced charges of illegally supplying weapons to drug dealers, was approached by a retired colonel, James McCoy, who had recently served as U.S. defense attaché in Nicaragua. McCoy and Martin eventually set up an "arms Supermarket" in Honduras, bringing large quantities of weapons into the country, where the Honduran government would take custody and the Nicaraguan Democratic Force (FDN) could buy what its members needed on a regular basis. McCoy's partner, Mario Dellamico, had good contacts in the Honduran military, who agreed to supply end-user certificates (EUCs) for the operation.[7]

North and Secord quickly became aware of the new partnership and the competition it represented for their own evolving plan to run the Contras. On May 1, 1985, North noted: "'Martin' setting up munitions 'supermarket' in Tegu[cigalpa]." It was the first of many references to Martin, McCoy, and their chief Honduran go-between, Col. Héctor Aplicano. Calero was happy with the freedom to choose his supplier. The supermarket had the advantage of speedy delivery, and its prices were generally better than the Enterprise's. So were Singlaub's, thanks to his connection to an Austrian arms broker named Werner Glatt. Based in Switzerland, Glatt dealt directly with the Soviet bloc and was able to get large quantities of AK-47 rifles and other munitions for about half the usual price. Even North had to agree Glatt seemed to be offering, in Singlaub's words, a "very, very good price and a bargain."[8]

The competition rankled North and Secord on two levels. Secord stood to lose substantial profits. By agreement with North, and in contrast to Singlaub, who cared only about the worldwide anticommunist campaign and took no commission, Secord had created the Enterprise on a for-profit basis. His practice of levying 20–30 percent markups, which he maintained were low for the arms industry, wound up hurting his competitiveness. Calero later claimed to be unaware Secord was not selling at cost.[9] Meanwhile, the situation threatened to undermine North's control over Contra operations.

The two men talked about their growing problem in mid-May. North was interested that "Ron Martin [and] Mario Dellamico (Cuban American) [were] wanted in Guatemala for criminal activity."[10] He tried to dig up similar dirt to undercut Glatt. A few days later, he heard from his CIA colleague Duane Clarridge that Glatt "buys weapons for Omanis & South Africans," but otherwise there was "nothing specific."[11] Still, North told Congress later he had been warned by Casey about a "broker who he was concerned had also been involved in reverse technology transfer to the Eastern Bloc, and he told me to do everything possible to discourage further purchases."[12] North tried to get Calero to abort a specific deal he had in the works with Glatt, calling him on the same day in mid-May he talked with Secord. Calero seemed to agree: "Call to Adolfo . . . will stop move w/Glatt," North noted. But three days later, Secord called to say it "sounded like Calero was going to have to go through with Glatt purchase."[13]

As time passed, the competition got more intense. After the embarrassment of the Weigensberg episodes that spring (involving forged documents and a delayed shipment; see Chapter 3), Secord decided to give his friend Tom Clines exclusive responsibility for weapons deliveries. In March and May 1985, Clines successfully managed two shipments of arms—not from China as Weigensberg had, but from Eastern Europe, mainly Poland and Romania, where officials were more swayed by foreign currency than cold war ideology.[14] Clines's intermediary in this case was a notorious Syrian arms broker named Monzer al-Kassar, labeled by international law enforcement as a regular supplier to rogue states and terrorists. U.S. authorities later accused him of criminality ranging from smuggling drugs to murdering rivals. (One of his alleged clients was former Palestine Liberation Front leader Abu Abbas, who hijacked the cruise ship *Achille Lauro* a few months later in 1985.) Al-Kassar's involvement—earning $1.5 million in total from the Enterprise—underscored the squalid side of the covert arms business, which U.S. participants overlooked as a necessary evil and justified by the correctness of the Contra cause. John Poindexter told Congress al-Kassar's association with the White House–run operation had not disturbed him: "When you are buying arms on the Third World market . . . you often have to deal with people that you might not want to go to dinner with."[15]

Even though Clines was delivering needed weapons, Calero continued to scout for options. In early June, CIA field officers reported to Washington the Martin-McCoy operation had resurfaced—with the backing of the Honduran military—and Calero had been in touch with them. The Hondurans were counting on either a share of the profits or a "good deal" on their own purchases through the supermarket.[16] At around this time, Clines literally came to blows with McCoy's partner, Dellamico. Secord had hired a Danish ship, the *Erria*, to bring an arms shipment from Poland and Portugal to Honduras. After it landed at Puerto Cortes, Dellamico decided to scout out his rival, talking his way on board by pretending to be a colleague of Clines and getting the captain to show him the cargo manifest. Clines arrived on the scene and after a loud exchange had Dellamico thrown off the ship.[17] North and Secord realized their privileged position as suppliers to the Contras included no guarantees.

Watershed in Miami

On June 28, 1985, North called a meeting of the two senior political and military leaders of the FDN and key members of the Enterprise for a "program review" of Contra operations. Gathered at an airport hotel in Miami in addition to North were Calero, Enrique Bermúdez, Secord, Clines, and Rafael Quintero. The meeting did not start until 10:00 at night and lasted until dawn. North began "on a pretty hard note," castigating Calero because the "limited funds they had might be getting wasted, squandered or even worse, some people might be lining their pockets."[18] He singled out Calero's brother, Mario, for "procuring non-lethal things in the United States and shipping them down" to Central America. "Unless this was . . . carefully handled it could turn into a real mess for Calero," Secord recalled North saying.[19]

The Contras' image and corruption problems went far beyond the Contra leader's brother. North's private courier, Rob Owen, had raised apprehensions about some of the people Calero had chosen to lead operations in the south. One individual, Fernando "el Negro" Chamorro, Owen wrote in April, "drinks a fair amount and may surround himself with people who are in the war not only to fight, but to make money." Owen listed several others "who are questionable because of past indiscretions" ranging from "drug running" and "sales of goods provided by USG [U.S. government]" to "pocketing certain 'commissions.'" Bermúdez himself was developing a reputation not only for ineptitude as a military commander but also personal corruption and greed, although North appears not to have targeted him at the Miami meeting.[20]

North's harangue of Calero left the group "thunderstruck." Having "all but pistol whipped" the Contra leader, who was said to be offended but did not try to defend himself, North moved the discussion to the main program review, which focused on the rebels' most urgent problem first—the deplorable state of their aerial supply network. After the second Boland Amendment, the CIA had for the most part pulled out, leaving the insurgents a collection of aging aircraft and precious little else in the way of infrastructure. "They were really in desperate straits," Secord recalled. Compounding the outdated equipment and poorly prepared pilots, "there were no trained logistics supply officers, maintenance officers, communications people, very little of . . . the sinews of warfare." Every-one agreed a smoothly functioning resupply operation was the sine qua non for keeping the war going. "There was no way around it," said Secord. Some rebel units were thirty days' march from the nearest supply depot. "You either had to develop an air-drop capability or they were going to be forced from the field."[21]

The other main subject in Miami was the need to open a southern front against the Sandinistas. For most of the Contra war, fighting had been concentrated in northern Nicaragua. Since 1984, the Sandinistas had instituted a major draft that brought their troop levels up to 60,000 regulars plus 150,000 militia and reserve units. The strategy of deploying them close to the Honduran border was making it harder for Contra bands to slip into Nicaragua, carry out raids, and escape without significant casualties.[22] To arm its forces, Managua had turned to the Soviet bloc for everything from AK-47 rifles and heavy artillery to helicopters and high-tech radar scanners.[23] The advantage appeared to be steadily swinging the Sandinistas' way. Soon they were staging strikes inside Honduran territory, which were not only costly for the Contras but made the Honduran government reconsider the hazards of allowing its territory to serve as a base for rebel oper-ations. North and the CIA were determined to open a second front in Costa Rica without any further delay.

The Miami meeting was a turning point in the White House–directed Contra war. It led to a number of important changes in strategies for handling finances, aerial resupply functions, and the conduct of the war itself. For Secord it was a "watershed"[24] that brought the Enterprise into a much more direct role in each of these critical areas. Soon, it would turn into a dominant position. North and Secord moved quickly to define the next steps needed to carry out these new responsibilities. They included expanding the Enterprise's web of financial enti-ties, establishing a full-fledged logistics operation with a main base for running the resupply effort (especially for the southern front), and setting up an emer-gency landing facility.[25]

The Southern Front

Two principal obstacles confronted a viable southern front strategy. One was to get the government of Costa Rica, which formed Nicaragua's entire southern frontier, to agree to let its territory be used for the expanding war. The other was to build up a responsive and aggressive rebel force in the area.

At the time, the main rebel group based in southern Nicaragua was the Revo-lutionary Democratic Alliance (ARDE), the second-largest faction after the FDN. Its leader was Edén ("Commander Zero") Pastora, a former Sandinista who be-came a legend after storming the Nicaraguan Parliament and taking its members hostage in August 1978. After breaking with Managua in 1982, Pastora had been recruited by Clarridge, who hoped to trade on the former's credibility as an anti-Somocista and proven soldier. But Pastora's refusal to align his organization with the FDN disenchanted those in Washington who had been trying to unite the various rebel elements under a single tent. By mid-1984, the administration had cut off his support and was looking for an alternative to lead the fight from the south.[26]

In early spring 1985, North began to focus concretely on forming a new front. He sent his personal emissary, Owen, to Central America to raise the issue with rebel figures, receiving in return a four-page draft plan at the beginning of April after several weeks of discussions. North updated McFarlane on his thinking, reminding him on May 1 that future plans included "opening of a southern front . . . which will distract [Sandinista] units currently committed to the northern front."[27]

In early July, those plans took shape with the appointment of a new U.S. ambassador to Costa Rica, Lewis Tambs. Before leaving for his new post, Tambs met with North, who gave him his instructions. "Before I went [to Costa Rica], Ollie said when you get down there you should open the southern front," Tambs said later. If he had any qualms about taking orders from the NSC staff instead of his superiors at the State Department, Tambs noted in "subsequent meetings and conversations . . . that was confirmed by [Elliott] Abrams," assistant secretary of state for Latin America, and Alan Fiers, head of the CIA Central American Task Force (CATF). "That was sort of our mission," he said."[28]

Tambs's first step was to get Costa Rican president Alberto Monge to agree to the concept of opening a Contra base on his country's territory. Specifically, the Contras required an airstrip for the purpose of resupplying the rebels inside Nicaragua. Monge had an interest in getting rid of the Contra elements currently based within Costa Rican borders. He also had certain needs of his own he believed the United States could supply. Meeting on August 12, the two men quickly came to an agreement, with Monge indicating he would be willing to help in return for assistance with funding a "certain operation" in Costa Rica—a quid pro quo U.S. investigators would later describe as "possibly illegal."[29] Monge also stipulated the airstrip be kept well away from the border to dampen any Sandinista temptations to retaliate. Tambs immediately passed the word to his superiors and to the local CIA chief of station, Joseph Fernandez.

Less than a week later, Fernandez set off with Owen to scout out a property known as Santa Elena in a section called Potrero Grande in northwestern Costa Rica. The location was selected, Fernandez said later, by Benjamin Piza, Monge's minister of public security, because it was "inaccessible from the North and South . . . a series of canyons and mountains." It thus had abundant "natural protection." Owen reported to North the site looked promising and showed him the photographs he had taken from a helicopter Piza had provided for the purpose.[30]

North approved the choice and began to look into buying the property. It turned into an exercise in constructing false identities, each designed to bury ever deeper the true function and ownership of the airstrip. North first tapped an ex-marine friend named William Haskell to front as the buyer. Using the pseudonym Robert Olmsted, Haskell posed as a representative for the Santa Elena Development Corporation, a fabricated company listing William Goode and Richard Copp (aliases for North and Secord) as directors. Haskell told the owner of the property the company wanted to use it to promote tourism. A second false company, Udall Research Corporation, made the actual purchase. In the fall, Piza, who collaborated in other ways with North's operation, helped establish another layer of cover by having Udall backdate a letter "authorizing" the Costa Rican government to hold "Civil Guard training" exercises on the property. That way, the civil guard could provide security for the field without arousing local suspicions. North indicated in his notebook Piza would "seal off area with signs, guards, made to look like gov't installations."[31]

It turned out to be much effort for very little return. Construction on the 6,520-foot dirt runway was delayed repeatedly. It did not begin until January 1986 and was not finished until the following May. By then heavy rains were turning the surface to mud, rendering it virtually unusable. Just one month later, Costa Ricans elected a new president, Óscar Arias Sánchez, a future Nobel Peace Prize winner for his role in helping to craft a regional peace agreement, who proved far less yielding to U.S. entreaties to use the country as an operations base for the Contra war. As soon as he found out about the Santa Elena airstrip, Arias protested. Piza, however, was able to keep it operational for several months, for which North thanked him by arranging a photo opportunity with President Reagan.[32]

Ilopango

A crucial decision made at the time of the June 28 Miami meeting was to have Secord set up an airlift operation to move weapons and supplies to the Contra forces in and around Nicaragua. The Santa Elena airstrip was needed as a backup facility and emergency landing site for aircraft resupplying the southern front. But even more important was the establishment of a primary transshipment point. "Without that, we had nothing," Secord declared.[33] The initial plan was to set up a base in Honduras, where the main body of rebel fighters was located, but the only airstrip available there was in poor condition, and in any event, the Honduran government was not inclined to authorize this new activity.

North and Secord decided instead to turn to neighboring El Salvador. Through a former CIA operative named Felix Rodriguez, they were able to convince senior Salvadoran officials to allow them to set up the secret resupply operation at Ilopango Air Force Base, just outside the capital, San Salvador.

The idea to involve Rodriguez in the Contras' cause apparently came from U.S. Army Col. James Steele, head of the U.S. Military Group (Milgroup) in El Salvador. Steele had met Rodriguez earlier in the year when Rodriguez was helping to develop a counterinsurgency operation for the Salvadoran military. The onetime CIA agent and Bay of Pigs veteran had come with high-level references, conspicuously from Donald Gregg, Vice President George Bush's national security advisor, who had known him from their CIA days in Vietnam and helped place him in El Salvador. Steele was given the task of monitoring Rodriguez's activities by U.S. Ambassador Thomas Pickering, who was not entirely comfortable with Rodriguez's entry onto the scene. But the ex-agent's scheme for fighting insurgents using helicopters turned out to be effective, and his relations with Salvadoran military authorities became close. Steele evidently thought well of him, and when he and North began to discuss Contra operations together in September, it was not long before Rodriguez's name came up.[34]

As part of the deal they eventually agreed to, the Salvadorans provided space for aircraft and a warehouse for supplies—plus security, access to fuel for sale, and even help in locating housing for the crews. Ilopango was already playing host to the Milgroup under Steele and to the CIA, with little attempt to segregate their facilities. A few more personnel and aging aircraft would hardly be noticed.

To manage day-to-day operations at Ilopango, Secord turned to another ex-colleague, Richard Gadd. A recently retired U.S. Air Force lieutenant colonel with experience in special operations, Gadd had worked with Secord on the second Iran hostage rescue operation in 1980 before leaving the Pentagon to join a defense contractor in 1982. In effect, his job at Ilopango was to start up a small air services company and run it—buying several aircraft, hiring air and ground crews, and overseeing their activities. Even for someone with his expertise in comparable Pentagon black operations, it was not an easy assignment. Locating aircraft that could take off and land on short airstrips, carry heavy loads, and fit within the Enterprise's tight budget took months. At one point, Gadd located three C-123 cargo planes owned by the Venezuelan Air Force, but he was never able to satisfy that country's concerns about the intended uses of the aircraft. Not even North's intervention through official channels could change the Venezuelans' minds.[35]

At last, a "bedraggled little air force" (in Secord's words) began to take shape, eventually including two Vietnam-era Fairchild C-123 Providers, two Canadian C-7 Caribous, and a single-engine short-takeoff-or-landing (STOL) aircraft manufactured by Georgia-based Maule Air. The jet-assisted twin-prop C-123 could carry a 24,000-pound payload and had a maximum range of 1,500 miles; the smaller C-7, which also had short takeoff capability, could haul 5,000 pounds on a 900-mile mission.[36] Gadd enlisted into the operation Southern Air Transport (SAT), a former CIA proprietary carrier[37] that acted as a commercial intermediary—and that Secord at the same time was using to ship missiles to Iran. To disguise their activities further, Gadd and SAT jointly acquired a "shell company" called Amalgamated Commercial Enterprises (ACE). Gadd's instructions from Secord included the admonition the operation "should be kept very low key and not be known to the general public. . . . I was told to protect both his name and the White House."[38] It was not until spring 1986 that the Enterprise was finally ready to begin shipping weapons directly to the Contras.

Contras and Drugs

One of the darker secrets of the Contra war was the willingness of U.S. government officials to cooperate with rebels and others suspected—or known—to be in the drug-running business. From the early days of the conflict, U.S. officials had solid evidence members of one of the rebel groups, the September 15th Legion, had decided to go into narcotics dealing to support its paramilitary activities.[39] As early as March 1985, North wrote in his notes: "Pastora revealed as drug dealer."[40] By the previous fall, the CIA already had reports indicating several of Pastora's ARDE lieutenants, including Adolfo "Popo" Chamorro, Carol Prado, and Gerardo Durán, had struck a deal with a known international trafficker as a way to generate resources for ARDE. In return for the use of the alliance's pilots to fly drugs into the United States, the dealer, Jorge Morales, gave cash payments and aircraft to Pastora's organization.[41] "We knew that everybody around Pastora was involved in cocaine," Alan Fiers of the CIA testified later.[42]

By then, the ARDE leader was on the outs with the CIA. Fiers said the narcotics connection underscored the agency's position: "You just can't deal with this man." Yet the stigma of drug ties did not stop the agency from maintaining contact with him, a fact indirectly confirmed by Clarridge.[43] The same frequently applied to the northern front Contras. Over time, reports of drug involvement reached the agency about nine individual guerrillas as well as three companies and more than twenty pilots and others associated with the Contra program.[44] According to U.S. intelligence, out of a total of some fifty people under suspicion during the 1980s, the CIA kept up ties with about two dozen of them without regard to whether the allegations were true.[45]

The Enterprise team also regularly came across suspected drug operators. Owen warned North in April 1985 that Calero's prospective choice of "El Negro"

Chamorro as the FDN's military commander at the southern front would mean bringing in confederates tied to narcotics. Chamorro himself was later accused of drug involvement, according to an internal CIA report.[46] A few months later, North recorded in his notes a meeting with Owen at which the two discussed a "Honduran DC-6 which is being used for runs out of New Orleans [and] is probably being used for drug runs into U.S."[47] According to Fiers, the Costa Rica farm of a CIA "asset" named John Hull, a rancher from Indiana, also may have been used as a "transshipment point for drugs," and Hull "could have been a willing accomplice in using it."[48]

Even though the drug war had been a popular policy objective for every presidential administration since at least Nixon and was formally a part of the CIA's mission, senior officials and field operatives in Central America frequently saw it as a distraction from their main goal. "Narcotics was not something [CIA field personnel] were looking for in the 1980s," said a chief of station from the period. In reality it was no more than a "target of opportunity," according to a future chief of the CATF. To Clarridge, it was simply "not a big deal."[49] More often when the agency did show an interest, it was when the enemy was doing the trafficking. In a major investigative report on Contras and drugs, the CIA inspector general, citing a CATF agent, noted "all of the Central American Stations were seeking information that would link the Sandinistas to drug trafficking. The goal was to diminish the image of the Sandinistas." But in the case of the Contras, "the overriding priority task of their Stations and Bases was to support [them]," according to the inspector general. Regardless of any "derogatory stuff" that showed Pastora and other rebel figures were "scoundrels," the message to field officers was plain, as a former chief of station testified: "We were going to play with these guys. . . . That was made clear by Casey and Clarridge."[50] Not surprisingly, agency officers failed to tell Congress all they knew about the insurgents and their involvement in the drug trade.[51]

As early as 1982, Casey took steps to shield the Contras from legal scrutiny. While drug allegations circulated about the September 15th Legion, the CIA and Justice Department prepared a memorandum of understanding (MOU) about how the intelligence agency should handle reports of criminal activities by its assets in the field. The very act of putting together such an MOU was tacit confirmation the CIA routinely dealt with individuals who might engage in illegalities. The problem was the CIA use of these unsavory characters as intelligence sources or proxy agents—a widely recognized fact of life for intelligence operatives—placed the agency directly at cross-purposes with the Justice Department and the Drug Enforcement Administration (DEA), whose mission was to put those same people out of business.[52] For Casey and his colleagues, the concern was to preserve the freedom of their operatives to associate with anyone they thought could help their operations. As one CIA lawyer put it, his aim for the MOU was to protect agency "equities," which meant keeping CIA operations as free as possible from law-enforcement constraints.[53]

The MOU built on prior arrangements dating from the Carter administration and on Reagan's Executive Order (EO) 12333, governing U.S. intelligence activities.[54] When Casey and Attorney General William French Smith signed the MOU in early 1982, it featured two points relevant to this discussion. First, it applied only to nonemployees. CIA employees were held to relatively high legal standards of conduct, but the requirements for nonemployees were much looser. Unlike the Reagan executive order, however, which described an employee as anyone "acting" for an intelligence agency, the MOU changed the operative definition to a "staff employee or contract employee of the Agency." In other words, private individuals who merely collaborated with the CIA, such as the Contras (with or without pay), were now subject to the far more lax standards of the MOU.

But the agreement did not cover drug crimes; the Carter administration's version had the same omission. A Justice Department lawyer noticed the oversight, but the attorney general decided there was no need to change the MOU. Instead he informed Casey (in a letter codrafted by a CIA attorney) that because federal statute and EO 12333 already contained provisions concerning drug-related intelligence gathering and dissemination, "no formal requirement regarding the reporting of narcotics violations has been included in these procedures." But the statute he cited required only that the agency cooperate "when requested by the Attorney General," and the executive order dealt with routine drug intelligence-gathering activities; neither set of provisions established a clear requirement to initiate reporting if and when agents spotted possible drug violations. The implication that CIA agents had no obligation to report Contra narcotics trafficking to law enforcement could not have been lost on Casey, who pronounced himself "pleased" with the final agreement for striking the "right balance between enforcement of the law and protection of intelligence sources and methods."[55]

The Nicaraguan Humanitarian Assistance Office

In early August 1985, the Contras received an important boost when Congress approved a $27 million aid package. The victory came after steady lobbying from the administration (and was almost certainly helped by Daniel Ortega's high-profile trip to Moscow just before the vote), but there was a crucial limitation—the funds could be used only for "humanitarian" purposes. Still, it was a meaningful development because it represented a renewed willingness by Congress to provide direct support to the rebels. It also offered a significant opportunity for North and his covert activity. If Enterprise operatives could get plugged into the program of shipping humanitarian supplies to the Contras, it would give them ideal official cover for their deliveries of lethal equipment.

Some Democrats on Capitol Hill foresaw this possibility. According to a State Department official, House Foreign Affairs Committee staff members burst into laughter during a briefing on administration plans for the aid. "We see what you are trying to do," he recalled the reaction. "You are going to put that $27 million in Ollie North's shop, [and] he is going to really run with it."[56] This was exactly what happened. The Latin America Bureau of the State Department, headed by Abrams, "went back to the drawing board" to come up with a structure that would get past Democratic concerns, and at the end of August President Reagan authorized the creation of the Nicaraguan Humanitarian Assistance Office (NHAO) within the department to manage the program. Despite continued warnings about "letting Ollie get too close to this,"[57] Congress acquiesced, and the money was approved.

NHAO was officially under the State Department, but as with the Office of Public Diplomacy, the NSC staff exerted significant influence over its operations. At early organizational meetings of the new entity, North put forward the names of Rodriguez, Gadd, and Owen as his recommendations for working with the State Department. NHAO's director, Ambassador Robert Duemling, was disinclined, especially regarding Owen, who North had proposed as a liaison with the FDN. "We don't need a liaison," Duemling retorted. But the pressure was intense: Duemling's own superiors pressed him to go along; shortly afterward, the three main FDN leaders, Alfonso Calero, Robelo, and Arturo Cruz Sr., wrote a letter specifically asking for Owen. Still, Duemling held firm.[58]

Only after the first humanitarian flight created a major embarrassment did North finally prevail. On October 10, the NHAO aircraft had landed in Honduras—but with a television news crew on board. The Honduran government had wanted to keep its role as a staging point in the program secret and was furious at the breach of security, which produced international headlines. The generals promptly prohibited any more flights. Other problems apparently contributed to a buildup of Honduran irritation, including recent U.S. embassy denials of any connection to the rebels, poor coordination with the Honduran military regarding Contra support, and U.S. sluggishness in delivering economic aid to Tegucigalpa. Nevertheless, North took advantage of the opening to press his case, and at the first opportunity scolded Duemling, saying Owen would never have let the incident happen. Duemling finally relented, and North gained an important asset inside the operation.[59]

As an official representative of the humanitarian assistance program, Owen could now travel freely to Central America as North's "eyes and ears" without having to explain himself or his connection to the NSC staff. North could also ease up on his own travel schedule and worry less about curious White House colleagues. After much cajoling, including visits by Poindexter, North, U.S. Ambassador John Ferch, and at least two CIA officials, the Hondurans finally agreed to allow more NHAO deliveries, although they insisted the flights not come directly from the United States.[60] North and his colleagues found a way to deal with this aggravation, too. At the end of December, a delegation representing the Restricted Interagency Group (RIG),[61] which managed Central America policy—North, Fiers, and Elliott Abrams's deputy, William Walker—went to El Salvador seeking permission to use the Ilopango base as a transit station for shipments of humanitarian supplies from the United States to Honduras. They succeeded, thanks to the cooperation of the head of the Salvadoran Air Force, Gen. Juan Rafael Bustillo. But Bustillo, too, had a condition. He would only work through Rodriguez, not the CIA. It seemed like an easy call, and the deal was made. But when the operation picked up again in early 1986, Rodriguez would prove a significant headache.[62]

Smiling and Dialing

As always, a major preoccupation for North was how to keep the money flowing. In late spring 1985, he had written to McFarlane pleading for more approaches to Saudi Arabia. "Efforts should, therefore, be made to have the current donors deliver the remainder of their $25M pledge ($8.5M) and to seek an additional $15–20M" for a needed expansion of Contra forces.[63] While McFarlane and other senior members of the administration, including the president, continued to appeal to foreign governments, North enlisted a group of private fund-raisers who had spent careers raising money for conservative causes by tapping wealthy U.S. citizens. Richard Miller had worked on the 1980 Reagan election campaign and had eventually been appointed head of public affairs for the Agency for International Development (AID). In 1984, he resigned to build a career in public relations, forming a company called International Business Communications (IBC). In September 1984, IBC began to provide services for the Nicaraguan Development Council, an organization closely tied to Calero. That association allowed Miller entrée to all the senior FDN leaders as well as to North.

The first joint effort of Miller and North was almost farcical. In spring 1985, North heard from a contact about a certain Saudi prince interested in making a multimillion-dollar contribution to the Contras. North quickly put him in touch with Miller, then acting as a consultant to the NSC. Despite being unable to confirm the identity of the prince, whose name was given both as Mousalreza Ebrahim Zadeh and Al-Masoudi, Miller went ahead, his appetite whetted by the prince's promise of an extra $1 million for his help in marketing the oil intended to generate the revenues for his contribution. North's own interest in Zadeh intensified when the prince offered to help locate and free the U.S. hostages being held in Lebanon. Over several months, Miller and North buttered up the prince, paying for trips to Europe and other indulgences and enlisting the aid of a U.S. ambassador and at least one DEA agent to get Zadeh out of various jams he caused himself. Miller initially covered these expenses from IBC accounts but got reimbursed with Contra support funds authorized by North. North claimed he had McFarlane's imprimatur for these activities, but McFarlane denied it.

In the end, the "prince" turned out too good to be true. Not only was he not a member of the Saudi royal family, he was not even Saudi; he was Iranian. After bouncing a $250,000 check at a Pennsylvania bank, he came under FBI scrutiny, was arrested, and ultimately pled guilty to bank fraud—but not before North stepped in more than once to try to delay the investigation, still believing the prince might come through with a donation.[64]

Fortunately for the Contras, North's other joint ventures with Miller and his associates were more lucrative. Miller introduced North to Carl "Spitz" Channell, a longtime conservative fund-raiser interested in working on the rebels' cause. Channell and North soon came up with a stratagem to home in on extremely wealthy individuals. Under this approach, either Channell or Miller arranged meetings with potential donors, many of whom had contributed to Channell's activities before. The donors typically flew to Washington, D.C., staying at the opulent Hay-Adams Hotel, just across Lafayette Park from the White House. North would deliver a dramatic presentation on the plight of the Contras, calculated to play on emotions as much as to inform, then discreetly step out of the room to allow Channell to handle the solicitations, which North knew he could not legally do.

North delivered his first pitch on June 27, 1985, the day before the Miami hotel meeting. It took place in the Old Executive Office Building, where North's office was located. Miller and IBC made most of the arrangements. North included a slide show, which quickly became the hallmark of his approach. After a reception and dinner at the Hay-Adams, Channell handed Calero a check for $50,000, describing it as the sum total of the contributions Channell's organization, the National Endowment for the Preservation of Liberty (NEPL), had collected for the rebels thus far.[65] Subsequent appearances would net even more.

Not all of the presentations took place in Washington, D.C. The following September, North flew to Dallas on a plane chartered by Channell to meet with Texas oil magnate Nelson Bunker Hunt. At a small dinner at the Petroleum Club he provided Hunt a list of supplies the Contras needed, including a grenade launcher and several other lethal items. North then exited, and Channell did the rest. Hunt subsequently offered a donation and a loan, together totaling

$475,000. Channell eventually returned the principal on the loan because he could not find anyone to guarantee it, but Hunt later gave NEPL another contribution of $237,000.

North and Channell performed several more of their "one-two punch" operations during 1985 and 1986. In 1986, William O'Boyle, a New York businessman, was told he was one of only a handful of U.S. supporters asked to help the president's policy. He gave $130,000 intended to buy two small aircraft for the Enterprise. Two elderly widows were solicited. Ellen Garwood of Austin, Texas, gave more than $1.6 million in cash and stocks after a tearful North described the Contras' lack of food, clothing, and military equipment. But the list of supplies Channell showed Garwood was not humanitarian; it was strictly lethal and included bullets, hand grenades, and even missiles. One month later, Garwood donated an additional $350,000, and the Enterprise (as noted in Chapter 3) bought and named a helicopter after her, the "Lady Ellen." A second widow, Barbara Newington, of Greenwich, Connecticut, contributed more than $2.8 million in a two-year period, although she denied any of it was intended for military supplies. In all, a dozen major contributors to the North-Channell operation ("smiling and dialing for dollars," as Owen called it) made up more than 90 percent of the funds NEPL brought in during 1985 and 1986.[66]

There were several problems with these solicitations. First, NEPL was licensed as a tax-exempt charitable foundation. As such, it was illegal for the organization to raise money for lethal equipment. Channell and Miller knew this and went to some lengths to cover their tracks—describing weapons on their books as "Toys," calling North by the code name "Green," and setting up an account in the Cayman Islands under the name I.C., Inc. for the funds.[67] In spring 1987, Channell and Miller pleaded guilty to conspiracy to defraud the United States and named North as an unindicted coconspirator. North also violated at least the spirit of the law prohibiting federal officials from seeking donations. He, too, understood the restriction, as he made clear to a number of donors.

Another objection to these tactics raised by critics was they involved unabashedly trading money for access to power. North was often not the only White House official to participate in the briefings. Regan sometimes appeared, as did Buchanan, Abrams, and others. In some cases, potential donors were told explicitly contributions of $300,000 would get them a few quiet minutes with the president himself.[68] There were also reports North provided classified information to contributors about Soviet activities in Central America as part of his pitch.

Finally, there was the question of what happened to all the money North, Channell, and Miller collected. All told, during this period NEPL acquired $10,385,929 in contributions solicited for various causes. Of this, $6,323,020 collected from June 1985 to November 1986 was intended for the Contras. But only half of that, $3,306,882, actually reached the rebels. Calero received $1,080,000.

Another $488,882 went to other Contra support. Meanwhile, $1,738,000 went to a Lake Resources account set up in Switzerland by Secord's Enterprise partners, mainly for weapons purchases, after being "washed" through IBC's I.C. account. North had told Calero at the meeting in Miami that from then on donor funds for the Contras would have to go directly to Secord's Enterprise accounts rather than to Calero himself, who would no longer have the authority to make his own arms-buying decisions.[69]

Many of the funds that did not reach the Contras went to North's partners. According to the Office of the Independent Counsel's (OIC) records, Channell and another business associate received a total of $615,000 during this period. Miller and his partner at IBC garnered roughly $1.7 million, including "commissions" totaling $442,000. Two former White House officials, David Fischer and Martin Artiano, who helped set up meetings with the president and top aides for the donors, received $662,000.[70]

What Did Reagan Know?

Throughout this period, President Reagan was briefed in some detail about Contra military operations in Central America. For instance, in September 1984 the National Security Planning Group (NSPG) discussed a pending shipment from Bulgaria of Soviet-bloc L-39 aircraft to the Sandinistas. The group assessed whether to share intelligence with the Contras to support an attack on the shipment. Reagan spoke up several times, asking how the FDN planned to carry out the strike and actively debating strategies for when and how to publicize the Bulgarian delivery.[71]

In late October 1985, in the midst of an apparent "major military buildup and combat offensive" in Nicaragua, Reagan stepped in again. He authorized overflights of the country by SR-71 and U-2 aircraft to "collect detailed imagery and signals intelligence which will better allow us to assess the full impact of [Soviet bloc] activities in the region." Attached to the authorizing memo was an additional sheet North provided Poindexter that read: "You should also tell the President that we intend to air-drop this intelligence to two Resistance units deployed along the Rio Escondito, along with two Honduran provided 106 mm recoilless rifles which will be used to sink one or both of the arms carriers which show up in photograph at Tab I."[72]

Poindexter, who briefed the president on the memo, could not recall whether they discussed this separate piece of information.[73] However, when he replaced McFarlane as national security advisor and took over regular briefing responsibilities, Poindexter did acknowledge he had "many, many meetings with the President talking to him extensively about the way he thought" about the Contras.[74] Although he considered Reagan "not a man for great detail," he noted these sessions were sometimes quite specific. After Poindexter's first trip to the region in his new post in late 1985, for example, he gave the president a "rather detailed" account of how Costa Rican officials had given Secord's operation access to an airstrip to use in the Contra resupply effort.[75]

This raises the question of how much Reagan knew about North and his illicit operations in Central America. According to Poindexter, Reagan was "clearly aware" North was the "primary staff officer on the NSC for the democratic resistance," and "North would have participated in probably several meetings with the President."[76] In a later interview, the former national security advisor went further. "He knew the NSC staff was running support for the Contras," Poindexter said. "The only thing he didn't know was about the use of excess funds for the Contras. He knew that Secord was running logistics operations, with Ollie's coordination." Asked if the president was aware North's work included coordinating with the rebels on military matters, he answered: "Yes."[77] Reagan himself confirmed the broader point in his testimony at Poindexter's trial in 1990, which showed, despite his failing memory, a surprisingly detailed understanding of the logistics of the resupply operation North oversaw (see Chapter 15).[78]

As for Vice President Bush, an OIC memo in 1991 assessing his criminal liability noted he continued to take part in Contra-related meetings at high levels during the period of the Boland II aid cutoff. The memo lists twelve such sessions but indicates there were more. Bush also served as a diplomatic emissary to Central America on several occasions, on at least one of which there is direct evidence he was asked to help get the Guatemalan president on board with military support for the Contras (see Chapter 9). Moreover, Bush knew something of North's activities with the rebels. The OIC memo continues, "It is quite evident that the Vice President and his staff, like many in the Reagan Administration, shared a general awareness of North's status as the NSC's 'action officer' with respect to the Contras." Bush's staff members were better informed, having a "substantial 'window' into North's resupply operation by virtue of their dealings with Felix Rodriguez." On the "ultimate question" of whether Bush's level of knowledge was "sufficient to implicate him" on a conspiracy charge similar to the one North and others faced, the memo concluded: "Mr. Bush is surrounded by a solid wall of denials on this issue." Although this meant there was "no basis" for pressing criminal charges against him in connection with Contra aid, there is no doubt he was substantially more aware of the issue, and specifically of NSC staff involvement, than he was willing to acknowledge to investigators.[79]

"Cleaning Up the Historical Record"

During summer 1985, news stories began to appear in Miami and the Central America region linking North directly to covert aid to the Contras. The accounts were so specific they prompted the curiosity of the president's Intelligence Oversight Board (IOB), an organization created by President Gerald Ford in 1976 to probe questionable intelligence-related activities. Congressional opponents of Contra aid were also quick to take notice. During a visit to the West Coast with the president in mid-August, McFarlane received at least three letters from Democrats in the House and Senate asking for an answer to the media allegations. This set in motion one of most flagrant attempts by the White House to deceive Congress about its activities in Central America.

The most detailed request for information came from Rep. Michael Barnes, the Democratic chair of the House Subcommittee on Western Hemisphere Affairs, the main body overseeing U.S. policy in Central America. Poindexter, who received the letter for McFarlane while his superior was out of town, assigned five staffers, including North, to respond. In his staffing note, Poindexter wrote that Barnes, a persistent critic of the Contra program, "is really a trouble maker. We have good answers to all of this."[80]

Barnes's request included "all information and documents pertaining to any contact between Lt. Col. North and Nicaraguan rebel leaders as of enactment of the [second] Boland Amendment in October, 1984." But instead of pulling together the relevant files, the principal staffer in charge of maintaining NSC records, Brenda Reger, recommended dramatically limiting the search. "The search should be as narrowly focused as was the request," she wrote to Poindexter. "There is unlikely to be a great deal of documentation such as is described but we should search the files only on that basis." Reger suggested she select particular staff members to carry out the search instead of tasking the NSC secretariat, which was standard practice. She also offered to "brief" staff on "how to conduct the narrowly defined search," which would focus on NSC institutional records and specifically exclude working files and other "convenience files"— even those in North's own office. Noting appointment and telephone logs had "become favorite targets of such inquiries," Reger proposed North first provide a sample of his own logs and calendars to "give us a sense of what they consist of," then "be terribly forthcoming and bury Mr. Barnes" in records with essentially "no substance." Poindexter gave his approval.[81]

Within a week, the NSC staff had pulled roughly fifty documents, of which as many as twenty were deemed worth reviewing and were forwarded to NSC General Counsel Cmdr. Paul Thompson. Thompson, who apparently was aware of the limited search but made no objection, in turn gave the documents to McFarlane, advising he consider invoking executive privilege because six of the items raised potential concerns.[82]

McFarlane went over the "problem documents" with North in detail. Although he testified later he was unaware of many of the specifics of North's actions in Central America, the record shows he knew North was involved not only in raising funds and providing direction to the Contras' military efforts but helping to supply weapons as well. Each of these activities directly violated the second Boland Amendment. In late August and early September 1985, the two discussed how to conceal North's actions. One idea was to alter the documents to remove any sign of illicit activity. For example, a memorandum from April 1985 revealed North's recommendation the Contras' "current donors [the Saudis] be approached to provide $15–20M additional between now and June 1, 1985." North suggested replacing the phrase with "an effort must be made to persuade the Congress to support the Contras."[83] The aim was to erase all evidence third countries were being solicited to help fund the rebels.

McFarlane's justification for altering the record was the documents could be misunderstood. He told North there were a "half-dozen cases" in which "any objective reading . . . would probably" conclude North's actions had been "close to or even beyond the law." McFarlane wanted to go over each of the six problem records and "find out if my reading was the same as his," he later testified to Congress. As he did, North "pointed out where my own interpretation was just not accurate . . . and he just said, you are misreading my intent, and I can make it reflect what I have said if this is ambiguous to you, and I said all right, do that." Subsequent evidence and McFarlane's own testimony showed the untruthfulness of his congressional testimony. He had known in detail about North's activities because he had received regular updates. His intent, like North's, was nothing less than to cover their tracks, and both men were prepared to falsify the record to accomplish that. As North told Fiers, "Bud McFarlane just perjured himself for me—God bless him."[84]

In the end, North did not alter any documents until November 1986, when the affair was about to be exposed. Instead, McFarlane tried to assuage congressional concerns by simply denying any wrongdoing by North in letters to congressional critics. On September 5, he wrote to Lee Hamilton, the influential Democratic chair of the House Permanent Select Committee on Intelligence. Referring to media allegations, he declared, "Like you, I take such charges very seriously and consequently have thoroughly examined the facts and all matters which in any remote fashion could bear upon these charges. From that review I can state with deep personal conviction that at no time did I or any member of the National Security Council staff violate the letter or spirit of the law."[85]

McFarlane went on to insist, "We did not solicit funds or other support for military or paramilitary activities either from Americans or third parties. We did not offer tactical advice for the conduct of their military activities or their organizations." Both statements were demonstrably false. McFarlane wrote much the same thing to Barnes one week later. One difference between the two letters was a postscript McFarlane added to Hamilton's complaining that after a recent article outlined allegations against North, the NSC staffer "suffered a number of intrusions on his family life. Demonstrators at his home pushed down a fence; one of his pets was poisoned and his automobile was damaged." He offered this instance of "harassment" not to "engender sympathy" but as another reason for "bringing this matter to a close."[86]

Neither Hamilton nor Barnes was satisfied with McFarlane's response. During the following month, the national security advisor met with various senators and representatives, repeating his version of events. At the end of September, Barnes asked for a second time to see actual documentation supporting his account. McFarlane finally invited Barnes to the White House to review materials he had pulled together—but he refused to allow him either to take the documents out of his office or to make copies; he could only examine them on the premises. McFarlane later admitted it was an offer he knew Barnes could not accept. Barnes declined, believing McFarlane was not serious and the materials he had gathered were not all the relevant ones. At the end of October, he tried once more, offering to place the documents under the safekeeping of the House Intelligence Committee to allay McFarlane's professed concern for their security. But McFarlane never responded.[87]

In the meantime, Hamilton and other legislators, despite misgivings, chose to take him at his word rather than press the issue. "I basically believed them," Hamilton said years afterward about both McFarlane and North. "They were intent, they were sincere, they looked honest," and "their loyalty to the president came through very strongly."[88] He also complained the deep partisan split over Contra aid undercut the committee's ability to dig further into executive branch activities. The combination of executive privilege and political divisions within the committee hampered the search for documents and restricted the availability of officials such as McFarlane to closed, informal briefings rather than full-blown hearings. It was another case of lawmakers stepping on their own prerogatives, and McFarlane took ample advantage—misleading legislators, confident he could do so without being held to account.

As he hoped it would, the controversy faded for the time being. McFarlane later described his answers to Congress as "too categorical," but denied telling outright lies: "At the time I didn't believe it but at the time I was wrong and I admit that." After years on the White House staff, he said, he had learned in dealing with Congress, "You don't lie. You put your own interpretation on what the truth is."[89]

8

A Neat Idea

U.S. officials soon managed to get the derailed Iran project back on track. Days after the HAWK "horror story," the various intermediaries assembled in Europe to air recriminations but then quickly returned to making bargains. The scale of the recent breakdown failed to lead Washington to question whether it had the capacity to handle such a complex undertaking. Instead, U.S. officials blamed the private Israeli intermediaries. More importantly, Ronald Reagan never faltered in his resolve to use the secret initiative to put an end to the hostage crisis. Israeli officials shuffled their team, bringing in a new player who quickly established a bond with Oliver North. In the meantime, Reagan authorized the U.S. side—led by a new national security advisor—to take direct control of the operation. This forced administration lawyers to confront gaping legal questions largely unheeded until then. This was also the period when Manucher Ghorbanifar and North put into play the infamous idea to divert funds from the Iran operation to the Contras. Linking the two covert programs provided a powerful new incentive to press ahead with the arms-for-hostages deals regardless of the risks.

The Admiral

The elevation of Vice Adm. John Poindexter to the post of national security advisor, replacing the increasingly hesitant McFarlane, gave the initiative further momentum. Known as an archetypal staff officer, Poindexter would make it his mission to fulfill the commander in chief's directives for the duration of the operation.

Poindexter's résumé was remarkable. Top in his class at the U.S. Naval Academy, he served for a time as brigade commander—the highest-ranking midshipman. He earned a doctorate in nuclear physics at the California Institute of Technology before going on to serve under three secretaries of the navy and as executive assistant to the chief of naval operations. He also had tours commanding a guided missile cruiser and a destroyer squadron. Shortly after the assassination attempt on Reagan in March 1981, Poindexter accepted an appointment to the White House, where his assignment was to modernize the computer and communications systems used in crisis management. In 1983, despite no foreign policy experience, he made the transition from high-tech efficiency expert to deputy national security advisor under McFarlane. The hijacking of the *Achille Lauro* cruise ship off the Mediterranean coast of Egypt in October 1985 brought him internal recognition for overseeing the pursuit and capture of the hijackers. When McFarlane stepped down, no one could agree on a replacement, leaving the vice admiral, in Reagan's words, "everyone's second choice."[1]

Along with his other attributes, Poindexter brought to the position unconditional loyalty to the president—and marked political tone deafness. The latter trait was not necessarily a negative to his colleagues. White House patience with Congress and the press was at a low point. Poindexter was unwilling to bow to what he saw as intrusive outside demands on the White House. He believed absolutely in the president's primacy in foreign affairs, and his dedication to fulfilling Reagan's objectives—especially with respect to the Contras—combined with his disparaging opinion of the congressional opposition, led him to take an active, even aggressive, approach compared with the more traditional policy coordinating role of a national security advisor.

Claiming later he had the president's full approval, Poindexter set about providing the NSC staff a greater operational capacity in order to help it accomplish Reagan's goals. He acknowledged, looking back, this was a provocative approach, but justified it by arguing simply, "Sometimes it's the only way to get things done." He pointed to the *Achille Lauro* operation as the type of action that never would have succeeded through "normal" channels. Given congressional opposition, having the NSC staff become operational with the Contras "was the only option we had."[2]

One of the ways he went about his assignment was to apply new technology. During his initial White House tour, he had encouraged IBM to set up a beta test site for its "Professional Office System," or PROFS, an early intranet platform (email) that provided unheard-of speed and convenience users around the world now take for granted. It also created the opportunity to carry on sensitive business without being scrutinized, even by one's colleagues. NSC procedures called for standard communications to be routed through the executive secretariat, where they could be monitored by other staff. The intention was to track PROFS notes in a similar way. Poindexter discovered, however, he could use his workstation to bypass the executive secretariat and contact individual staff members privately. On August 31, 1985, he wrote a message to North instructing him to respond at any time by hitting "Reply" to the same message, thus creating a new note that would reach only Poindexter. The subject line Poindexter chose was "Private Blank Check." Robert McFarlane, who had a PROFS workstation installed at his home, was able to do the same thing.

The IBM platform was part of the almost revolutionary change in information technology Poindexter helped to introduce at the White House. Before long, NSC staff had independent access to data from other federal agencies, such as the Defense Department, as well as the ability to communicate rapidly and directly with U.S. embassies, military posts, and other entities overseas—including foreign governments.[3] These innovations allowed North and his NSC colleagues to operate with unprecedented autonomy, cutting out the State Department and the Pentagon at will and making it far easier to conduct unsupervised activities such as the Iran and Contra operations.

While highly knowledgeable about technology, in hindsight Poindexter's relative inexperience in international affairs and unfamiliarity with these covert operations is keenly apparent. As of early December, he was more sanguine about the Iran initiative than McFarlane. But his knowledge of the Middle East did not compare with his predecessor's, and he was not as steeped in the details of the secret deals. Instead, he drew confidence from the conviction he knew how to read the president, who had been clear in his support for the arms-for-hostages scheme.[4] His optimism also grew out of the steady stream of input he received from North, who was warming to the Iran assignment since being brought in to help with the HAWK transfer, and on whom Poindexter relied heavily for information.

"Polecat"

No sooner had McFarlane announced his resignation than North drafted a four-page, single-spaced options paper, dated December 4, to bring Poindexter up to date on the operation and make a pitch for where it should go next. Reflecting his punishing schedule, North's PROFS terminal stamped the time of the message as 2:02 a.m.

North's thrust was to urge that the deals continue. Blaming the HAWK debacle on the middlemen from each side—Ghorbanifar, Al Schwimmer, and Michael Ledeen—he wrote that the botched transaction had "created an atmosphere of extraordinary distrust on the part of the Iranians." He credited Richard Secord and Israeli official David Kimche with managing to put together a "renewed dialogue which still promises hope for achieving our three objectives." He identified these objectives as building support for a pragmatic faction that could take power in Iran, achieving the return of all U.S. hostages, and obtaining a promise of no more terrorism aimed at the United States. Having built up expectations of progress, North then applied pressure to act. "Based on what we can conclude from intelligence in Beirut, we believe that they [the Iranians] are very concerned that the hostages . . . may be killed . . . time is very short for all parties concerned." At each decision point of the Iran initiative, North would repeat this basic warning in order to justify pressing ahead. In this note alone, he raised the possible deaths of hostages or renewed terrorist strikes three times, even though he had to acknowledge that "the threat to carry out sanctions against us has not, to my knowledge, ever arisen."[5]

The deal North laid out for Poindexter was as follows:

—The total "package" from the Israelis wd consist of 50 I HAWKS w/PIP (product improvement package) and 3300 basic TOWs.
—Deliveries wd commence on or about 12 December as follows:

H-hr:	1 707 w/300 TOWs = 1 AMCIT
H+10hrs:	1 707 (same A/C) w/300 TOWs = 1 AMCIT
H+16hrs:	1 747 w/50 HAWKs & 400 TOWs = 2 AMCITs
H+20hrs:	1 707 w/300 TOWs = 1 AMCIT
H+24hrs:	1 747 w/2000 TOWs = French Hostage

Translated, the plan envisioned the Israelis would ship 3,300 TOWs and 50 Improved HAWKs from their own stocks in five stages within a twenty-four-hour period. After each shipment, one or more U.S. citizens (AMCITS) would be freed. A French hostage would follow the final shipment of 2,000 TOWs. Here again, even when no hostages came out of Lebanon after the HAWK shipment, North was ready to commit the United States, via Israel, to sending still larger shipments. He had to admit this new arrangement did "not meet one of the basic criteria established at the opening of this venture: a single transaction which wd be preceded by a release of [all] the hostages."[6] Attributing the change to the requirement to build confidence with the Iranians, he declared in the same memo, "We all believe that it is about the only way we can get the overall process moving." Stating again the hostages' lives were in the balance, he never considered that the repeated disappointments and heightened stakes might justify turning off the operation instead.

Within forty-eight hours, North had reworked his computer message into a formal memorandum and distributed it, evidently with Poindexter's blessing, up to the top rungs of the administration.[7] It, too, laid out the history of the program, followed by descriptions of what the Iranians were now offering and how continuing with the operation would further U.S. interests. In outlining U.S. goals, North was careful to place the political agenda at the top—noting a "more moderate Iranian government is essential to stability in the Persian Gulf and MidEast." Only after the goals of bringing about a "credible" Iranian military and an end to "Shia fundamentalist terrorism" did he list "return of the American hostages." When the arms-for-hostages scandal broke, the administration insisted the larger geostrategic purpose of the initiative had always come first. Even if that were the case for some, North's memo showed how difficult it was to separate the two aims: "It is unlikely . . . that we can proceed further toward the first three [goals]—and not at all on the hostage release unless we allow the process of delivery to begin."[8]

Finally, North briefly set out the reasons the United States might choose not to accept the latest Iranian proposal, including the fact it would breach official policy on making concessions to terrorists, might constitute a "double cross" by Iran, and would temporarily deplete Israel's missile stockpiles. He acknowledged, "Such an arrangement, bartering for the lives of innocent human beings, is repugnant." But in the end, he stressed, as always, the danger of doing nothing: "After carefully considering the liabilities inherent in this plan, it would appear that we must make one last try or we will risk condemning some or all of the hostages to death and undergoing a renewed wave of Islamic Jihad terrorism. While the risks of proceeding are significant, the risks of not trying are even greater."[9]

North's memo was his best attempt to cajole the administration's top brass into making a quick decision in favor of the next phase of the arms deals. He suggested the entire transaction could take place within ten days, and the intermediaries would meet even sooner—the next day—to decide whether to go ahead (thus underscoring the ever-present sense of urgency). Poindexter used the memo to brief George Shultz. It was the first in-depth discussion between the two since Poindexter had taken over as national security advisor. Shultz was delighted his new colleague seemed more open to sharing information than McFarlane.[10] Nevertheless, he stuck to his opposition to the initiative. His top aides ridiculed it, as they apparently often did when it came to North's ideas. Relatively early in the initiative, Shultz's inner circle began to refer to the NSC staffer and the arms-for-hostages deals as "Polecat." It was a play on the name North, which led to "pole," and from there to "Polecat," which to Charles Hill, Shultz's executive assistant, "was something that kind of smelled."[11] Hill's notes of a conversation with Michael Armacost, the undersecretary of state for political affairs, record how the secretary's aides felt about North's latest scheme, sometimes referred to as "Night Owl": "Ollie told Iranians that as part of *Night Owl* deal—they shd give up [terrorism]—install moderate govt—win war w [Iraq] . . . *ha ha* Ollie is laughable."[12]

Promoting Ghorbanifar

On December 6, North flew to London to confer on the details with the Iranian and Israeli intermediaries. After a meeting the president held with his top aides in the White House family quarters the next day, North learned over the phone the administration's position on the arms deals had suddenly changed. At Reagan's direction, McFarlane arrived the following day to meet with Ghorbanifar and present a fundamentally different proposal than the one North had been trying to nail down. McFarlane's very unwelcome message to the group in London was that from now on the arms-for-hostages deals and the strategic dialogue between the United States and Iran had to be treated separately, and the hostages had to be released by their captors before any further discussion of weapons or long-range ties could take place. The hostages "just spoil the entire issue," McFarlane said later.[13] The response was harsh. Ghorbanifar flatly refused to pass the proposal to Tehran. Banging his fist on a table, he said: "If I take this news back to my colleagues, they will go mad! They might say, 'To hell with the hostages! Let the Hezbollah kill them!'" McFarlane stalked out of the meeting, but North let him know that he, too, was unhappy. As problematic as Ghorbanifar was, he said, "I still think this thing can be made to work."[14] Kimche had already told McFarlane earlier in the day he disagreed with the administration's new tack. Later, Kimche recalled McFarlane and Ghorbanifar had been speaking "in two completely different languages."[15]

Long afterward, McFarlane wondered whether Ghorbanifar and North "did not perhaps collude" in speculating the hostages might be killed if the deals ended. He suggested North "certainly knew that it would have leverage with President Reagan,"[16] and North did indeed raise the issue repeatedly. More plausible is that Ghorbanifar had threatened the possibility before, and North, either out of genuine concern or simply an urge to shock his superiors into action, invariably recycled it in his memos.

North kept up the campaign to retain Ghorbanifar after the London meetings. The day he returned to Washington, D.C., he drafted a summary of the sessions for McFarlane and Poindexter that included a detailed defense of the rationale for keeping the Iranian on board no matter how distasteful that might be. (McFarlane had recently called Ghorbanifar "one of the most despicable characters I have ever met.")[17] "The Israelis believe him to be genuine," North claimed. Furthermore, "Israel believes strongly in using any means to bridge into Iran. . . . Whether we trust Ghorbanifar or not, he is irrefutably the deepest penetration we have yet achieved into the current Iranian Government."[18]

North agreed with Ghorbanifar's proposal to "'deliver something' so that he can retain credibility with the regime in Tehran." But here their logic failed. According to North, Ghorbanifar had "even suggested that the weapons delivered be useful only to the Army or Air Force (not the Revolutionary Guards) and that they be 'technically disabled.'" North was harkening back to the first TOW shipment in August, which the Islamic Revolutionary Guard Corps (IRGC) had appropriated, preempting the group expecting to acquire the missiles.

No one appeared to recall that Ghorbanifar and Adnan Khashoggi's original breakdown of political factions in Iran, which helped constitute the strategic rationale for the arms deals, treated some senior IRGC officers as "moderate"—or at least not extremist. This should have raised the question why the IRGC should be denied some of these weapons. Furthermore, none of the U.S. or Israeli operatives seems to have asked how providing disabled missiles could possibly help build the trust needed for long-term relations—or demonstrate Ghorbanifar's credibility to the regime.[19] Throughout the initiative there was little if any effort to reconcile the conflicting goals of satisfying the regime and supporting elements seeking to overthrow it.

North's memo raised several options for his superiors. They included accepting Ghorbanifar's "game plan," staging a hostage rescue attempt, and doing nothing.[20] A final option, "which has not yet been discussed," broke new conceptual ground—proposing the United States take over direct control of the operation. Instead of relying on the Israelis, North said, "we could, with an appropriate covert action Finding, commence deliveries ourselves, using Secord as our conduit to control Ghorbanifar and delivery operations." North pointed out, "Our greatest liability throughout has been lack of operational control over transactions with Ghorbanifar." This way, any number of advantages could result, including not having to deal with the sensitive matter of replenishing Israeli stocks (see following section). Within a month, the Reagan administration would opt for a very similar approach.

The "Starling"

While President Reagan had Oliver North on his staff, Israeli prime minister Shimon Peres had Amiram Nir. A counterterrorism advisor, Nir was a virtual carbon copy of North: hyperenergetic, ambitious, charismatic, and exhilarated by the idea of working outside channels. Nir's background was in television, not intelligence or antiterrorism. His job had been a plum, a reward for his political work for the Labor Party. None of these facts had endeared him to Israeli intelligence circles—which may have been one of the reasons Peres appointed him. According to some of his associates, Nir also shared North's penchant for deceptiveness toward colleagues and superiors. Kimche claimed he eventually quit the Iran operation in part because of Nir. "It was the fact that Nir was a liar, and that he misled us, and he played a few very, very dirty tricks on Schwimmer and Nimrodi, and I was absolutely disgusted by the way he was behaving on the whole thing."[21]

Nir's first extended contacts with U.S. antiterrorist officials appear to have come in August 1985 when he went on a two-week "get acquainted" tour of Washington, D.C. In June, North made note of their imminent collaboration in his notebook—"Amiram Nir . . . August Mtg—cooperative ventures."[22] The two hit it off immediately. North recalled their teamwork took off during the frantic hours following the hijacking of the *Achille Lauro* cruise ship in October.[23] By the following month, their plans for "cooperative ventures" were taking shape in ways that would parallel their future joint efforts in the Iran arms deals.

According to Nir, he did not become "active" on the Lebanese hostage case until late November, when he forwarded to Peres a suggestion that an ally of Israel, Gen. Antoine Lahad, the Christian head of the Southern Lebanon Army (SLA), be asked to release some of the large number of Shiites he had detained (those "who didn't spill blood") as a way to entice the Shiites holding the U.S. hostages in Beirut to do the same.[24] Earlier in the month, Nir and North had hashed out ideas for using Druze, Phalange, or other allied forces in Lebanon to leverage the hostages' freedom.[25] Nir proposed to Peres he discreetly approach Washington to see how the administration would react to this variation on a theme.

The Lahad idea was not Nir's. It had originated the previous July from an unexpected source—the director of the Episcopal Fund for World Relief, Canon Samir Habiby. A Palestinian by birth, Habiby was a friend of Terry Waite, the archbishop of Canterbury's envoy, who had undertaken his own crusade to mediate an end to the hostage crises in Lebanon. In the late spring, the two church representatives had also traveled to the United States to be introduced to U.S. counterterrorism officials. In the course of their visit, they were referred to North by Vice President George Bush's office. Among the ideas Waite floated to Washington was to influence the emir of Kuwait to commute the death sentences of the Dawa prisoners to life imprisonment. As he explained to Bush's national security advisor, Donald Gregg, under Islamic law if the families of a victim forgive the criminal for his deeds, it is possible for him to be released—often with the payment of "blood money" to the families. Waite theorized some of the relatives of those killed or injured in the December 1983 Kuwait bombings might be persuaded to call for leniency for the Dawa as a first step toward inducing Hezbollah's Imad Mughniyah to reciprocate.

The idea seemed to leave Gregg confused, but North encouraged Waite and Habiby, notwithstanding U.S. policy against making concessions on the Dawa seventeen. Waite's way of blurring this inconsistency was semantic. Instead of a concession, he called it a "humanitarian opening." He believed its chances for success would be boosted if it could coincide with the upcoming Muslim Ramadan holy days. Whatever happened to the plan is unclear, although North's notebooks reflect a number of contacts with Kuwaiti officials, and later the Dawa figured prominently in the arms-for-hostages negotiations with Iran. What is evident is North and Waite kept in close touch throughout the coming months. For North, the Anglican cleric represented his best source of information on the hostages and their captors ("our only access to events in Lebanon," reflecting the continuing problems with U.S. intelligence) as well as a potential cover for his part in the arms deals. For Waite, North was a valuable contact inside the U.S. government, which would probably have to approve any agreement he might reach with the hostage-takers.[26]

During a follow-up meeting with North in London in July, Waite's friend Habiby sketched out a second plan—approaching Lahad.[27] From the available evidence, Nir's presentation of the idea to his prime minister in late November led to his entrée into the Iran initiative. North considered Nir a kindred spirit and a highly desirable alternative to the discredited Nimrodi and Schwimmer. The trick was to convince Peres to bring him on board in place of the prime minister's personal friends.

The ploy did not work right away. A week later in London, North asked Kimche whether Nir already knew about the arms deals. He was told no. On December 12, Nir sent a second note to Peres that fit the North mold perfectly: according to Nir, Israel's longtime nemesis, Yasser Arafat, head of the Palestine Liberation Organization (PLO), had his own plan to cut a deal between Hezbollah and the Kuwaiti government that would free the hostages. He urged Peres to act quickly to prevent Arafat from scoring a propaganda coup and obtaining a "quid pro quo" from the United States that would almost certainly be to Israel's detriment.[28] Within a day, Peres gave Nir permission to join the team.

Nimrodi reacted bitterly to Nir's arrival. "The starling Nir went to the raven North," as he put it, "and told him, in the American phrase, 'Whatever they can do we can do better.'"[29] The only thing wrong with Nimrodi's assumption was Nir was not acting on his own. The raven and the starling were working together and made a powerful team. Peres had to intercede personally with Schwimmer to get him to work past his resentment, but it was only a matter of weeks before the two original Israeli members of the operation found themselves cut out altogether.

Nir Holds Sway

Whether Peres knew it or not, Nir's addition meshed perfectly with Poindexter's plans for inaugurating a new cast of characters. Put off by the sloppiness of the HAWK operation and accepting North's version of events, which centered the blame on the Israelis, he decided it was time to get rid of part of the old crowd. "I wanted people involved that I was, frankly, more comfortable with."[30]

The first formal meeting of the new team happened in Washington, D.C., the day after New Year's, 1986. Nir had been tied up in briefings with Israeli officials, getting brought up to date and elaborating a revised plan for bringing the initiative back on track. The terrorist attacks on the Rome and Vienna Airports on December 27, 1985, which left 16 dead and 117 wounded, added urgency to his efforts.[31] He called North immediately after the attacks to set up a meeting with Poindexter to review his new proposal. On his way, he stopped in London to meet Ghorbanifar and make sure the Iranians would cooperate. There was no time for Ghorbanifar to get final approval from his superiors—Nir was in too much of a hurry—so a number of specifics were left dangling.

In Poindexter's office, Nir laid out a six-point plan that called for the delivery of 4,000 TOW missiles to Iran plus the exchange of Shiite detainees in southern Lebanon in return for the U.S. hostages. He proposed the following sequence:

- Release an agreed number of Lahad's captive Shiites
- Ship 500 unimproved TOWs via an Israeli Boeing 707 to Iran
- Take delivery of all five hostages, while simultaneously handing over additional Shiite captives
- Transfer the remaining 3,500 TOWs
- Release the remainder of the agreed number of Shiites[32]

Nir assured Poindexter and North that Israel would take the lead and make all the arrangements. This would allow Washington to claim no direct involvement—a requirement, Nir pointed out, McFarlane had laid down in London a month earlier. He argued temporarily leaving the United States out of the operation would also give time for the distrust between Washington and Tehran to mend. There were several other features to the plan, including getting a commitment from Iran to forswear any further hostage-taking or other terrorist acts against the United States. Nir even offered to collect and return the HAWK missiles from the previous November.

Nir told his hosts Israel was offering to undertake this mission because the Israelis believed their interests coincided with those of Washington. Tel Aviv simply wanted to help. But two important aspects had to be agreed upon beforehand. First, Israel would be allowed to restock its inventory of TOWs according to a preset timetable and price schedule. After all, he told them, by shipping 4,000 missiles in addition to the 500 the United States already owed from the August–September deals, Israel would be down to two-thirds of its war reserves; this made the Israeli Defense Forces nervous, particularly with the threat from Syria looming. Second, if word of the new deal leaked, the Reagan administration would have to acknowledge it knew about the transaction and had approved it. The Israelis may have wanted to do Washington a favor, but they were not going to publicly shoulder the responsibility alone.

Poindexter and North reacted positively to Nir's ideas. Poindexter quizzed Nir on a variety of related topics, such as the state of play in the Iran-Iraq War, whether these deals did not constitute paying ransom for hostages, and the credibility of Ghorbanifar. Nir responded that as long as neither of the combatants in the war made political moves in Israel's direction, it served Israel's interests to have neither side win. He said Tel Aviv "was not thrilled about trades like this" but argued the actual kidnappers would not be directly involved, only a state that had influence with them; he emphasized the strategic element of the deals and that the release of the hostages should be seen as an "additional benefit" and a "test" of the alleged moderates with whom they would be dealing in Iran. On the last point, Nir said he did not know Ghorbanifar well, having just met him three days earlier, but it seemed he had been responsible for getting Benjamin Weir released, and this showed he had ties to elements within Iran who could come through on the hostages.[33]

Nir had not only come forward at the right time, while the Rome and Vienna attacks were still resonating, but he struck Poindexter as someone who could bring new energy, creativity, and competence to the deals. He found the cover story screening U.S. involvement and the swap with Shiite captives "better [and] more effective," according to his notes. He also appreciated there was "no risk to US if don't get 5" hostages because the plan envisioned holding back on the remaining 3,500 missiles if no captives were released after the first shipment of 500 TOWs. Finally, he was impressed by Nir's rationale for the operation, writing in capital letters: "VIEW AS TEST OF INTENTIONS." When the scandal erupted just eleven months later, the administration would eagerly resurrect the rationalizations Poindexter and North had discussed with Nir at this meeting.

Making It Legal

After the November shipments Poindexter had caricatured CIA Deputy Director John McMahon's fretting over legal problems as no more than a "CYA" exercise. But during the December discussions he had heard Shultz and Caspar Weinberger repeatedly raise objections on the same grounds. "It sounds self-serving," he said later, "but until I took over [as national security advisor] it was a very poorly run operation." It had started out as a "back-of-the-envelope operation, and that's not my style." He blamed McFarlane for keeping senior officials out of the loop about certain aspects, but he also charged that the "National Security Council—not the staff—was delinquent, including the president, the vice president, and the secretaries of state and defense."[34] So after Nir left, Poindexter assigned North to see that an appropriate presidential finding was prepared (he noted the December 1985 version was a "draft") to cover the next phase of the deals and that Attorney General Edwin Meese was brought in to approve it. On the same day, North phoned Stanley Sporkin of the CIA, who earlier had helped paste together the December finding for the HAWKs, and dictated the substance of what he thought ought to go into the document. Over the next three days, the two worked out a sufficiently complete draft to take to the president.

From the start, the versions created in January had a basic difference from the finding Reagan had signed on December 5. Instead of authorizing the "provision of assistance . . . to obtain the release of Americans held hostage in the Middle East," the new versions shied away from the subject of hostages entirely. Poindexter was out of his depth on matters of politics, but he had been sensitized by the secretaries of state and defense to the potential for controversy here. He made sure the new finding focused instead on the more palatable goal of "establishing a more moderate government in Iran."[35]

The first draft Sporkin prepared, based on North's recommendations, provided that the director of central intelligence (DCI) inform the House and Senate Intelligence Committees of the finding as called for by law. But the next day, Sporkin added the option of not informing the committees—claiming the same privilege as in the December 5 finding. By the end of the day on January 3, North had retyped the finding, leaving in the language directing the DCI "to refrain from reporting this Finding to the Congress."[36] This formulation would survive in the final version, but even though the administration argued after the scandal the National Security Act justified keeping information about a covert action secret until it directed otherwise, many members of Congress and the public were skeptical.

Meanwhile, other officials had joined in the drafting process. On January 5, a Sunday, William Casey invited North and Sporkin to his home, where they went over both the finding and a cover document North had prepared for Poindexter to give to the president. Sporkin worried about the absence of any mention of the hostages and won Casey's agreement to insert a reference.[37] North objected, claiming the State Department did not want it there, but without result. (In fact, Shultz's objection had not been to a reference to hostages in the finding, but to the entire arms-for-hostages deal.) Another change was made to the cover memorandum. North had inserted an acknowledgment that the "Israeli sales are technically a violation of our Arms Export Control Act [AECA] embargo for Iran."[38] That phrase disappeared in subsequent versions of the memo. The following day, Meese conveyed his approval of the draft during a brief meeting with North.

Over the next ten days, the president and his chief aides added further refinements, and a flurry of legal opinions combined to change the character of the planned shipments. On January 7, the NSC, including Reagan, Bush, Shultz, Weinberger, Meese, Casey, and Poindexter, met in the Oval Office to hash out once again the pros and cons of the initiative. Shultz and Weinberger revived their objections to the proposed deal, which explicitly included a trade of 4,000 TOWs for five U.S. hostages,[39] but were opposed on all sides.

Beyond a general discussion of whether the operation should go ahead at all, the participants debated whether it was legal for Israel to ship U.S. arms to another country that could not lawfully obtain them directly from the United States. Under the AECA, the mechanism by which Israel had acquired the TOW missiles originally, weapons could not be transferred to a third country if that country faced legal restrictions on receiving military equipment from the United States, which Iran, because of its designation as a supporter of terrorism, clearly did. This was the problem North had highlighted in his earlier draft cover memo. Weinberger also raised the subject during the Oval Office meeting.

A separate puzzle was how to keep the operation a secret from Congress.

Meese Weighs In

Both of these points would become central to the question of whether the administration violated the law with the Iran deals, even those activities covered by the finding Reagan would sign in January 1986. Meese, although he later claimed ignorance about prior phases of the Iran project,[40] put forward opinions for how to deal with both considerations.

First, he told the president that as commander in chief, he had options beyond the AECA. The principal alternative built on the opinion the previous attorney general had formulated in 1981 in connection with a proposed weapons exchange with Iraq (see Chapter 2). The Economy Act, according to that interpretation, allowed the Defense Department to "sell" weapons to another agency, the CIA. Then, through the National Security Act, the president could authorize the shipment from the CIA to Baghdad as part of a "significant intelligence objective."[41] Meese's bottom line at the January 7 NSC meeting was Reagan could rely on the "President's inherent powers as Commander in Chief" and the "President's ability to conduct foreign policy."[42]

Meese and Casey also recommended to the Oval Office group to hold off notifying Congress because of the extreme circumstances, specifically the threat to the hostages' lives. Left unsaid was that Attorney General Smith had counseled in 1981 that the secretary of defense and the CIA director still had to report the activity to the U.S. House and Senate Intelligence Committees. By his own admission, Meese had done no in-depth research into the legality of withholding notification in early 1986, nor had he consulted relevant experts at the Justice Department, but he nevertheless endorsed the step. With the imprimatur of the attorney general, no one present disagreed. The consensus was to hold off informing Capitol Hill at least until the hostages were released—however long that might take.[43]

The United States Takes the Lead

By the end of the discussions, the president and his top advisors had completely changed the nature of Nir's proposal. No longer would Israel assume the lead and see the next transaction through without direct U.S. involvement. The United States would take over instead. The change had less to do with the merits of the Israeli plan than with the legal issues it raised. If the Economy Act and National Security Act were indeed to apply, the United States had to deliver the missiles from its own stocks. (One top official who also had qualms about Israel's central role was the vice president, who warned it might give Tel Aviv too much "leverage" to use with Washington.)[44]

North chose not to inform the Israelis about the change right away. Speaking to Nir by phone after the January 7 meeting (Nir had gone back to Israel), North seems to have misled him about where things stood. Using a code the two had fashioned, North passed on the following secret message:

JOSHUA HAS APPROVED PROCEEDING AS WE HAD HOPED

JOSHUA AND SAMUEL HAVE ALSO AGREED ON METHOD ONE

FOLLOWING ADDITIONAL CONDITIONS APPLY TO ALBERT

RESUPPLY SHOULD BE AS ROUTINE AS POSSIBLE TO PREVENT DISCLOSURE ON
OUR SIDE. MAY TAKE LONGER THAN TWO MONTHS. HOWEVER, ALBERT SAYS IF
CRISIS ARISES JOSHUA PROMISES THAT WE WILL DELIVER ALL REQUIRED BY
GALAXIE IN LESS THAN EIGHTEEN HOURS.

JOSHUA ALSO WANTS BOTH YOUR GOVT AND OURS TO STAY WITH NO COMMENT
IF OPERATION IS DISCLOSED.

IF THESE CONDITIONS ARE ACCEPTABLE TO THE BANANA THEN ORANGES ARE
READY TO PROCEED.[45]

"Joshua" was the president; "Samuel" was Weinberger. "Method one" referred to replenishing Israel's inventory of TOWs through sales.[46] The meaning of "Albert" is unclear, although it does not seem to refer to Hakim.[47] "Galaxie" appears to be a reference to the U.S. military's largest cargo plane, the C-5A Galaxy, which could presumably transfer a large number of missiles to Israel on short notice. "Banana" and "Oranges" were Israel and the United States, respectively.[48] The problem with North's message was it left Nir with the impression his plan from January 2 remained intact. It would be another week before North spelled out the White House intention to take over direct control, shunting Israel to the side.[49]

One more high-level meeting was needed to confirm the new approach. The January 16 session was the last before the president signed the new finding. The final obstacle was to get Weinberger to go along. Shultz had effectively removed himself from the debate by telling Poindexter in so many words he preferred not to be kept fully apprised of the details—a decision for which members of Congress would later sharply criticize him.[50] Shultz did not attend the meeting, citing a previous appointment.

That left Weinberger as the principal opponent of the operation, prompting an impatient reaction from the CIA director. "Casey has called urging that you convene a mtg w/he and Cap ASAP so that we can move on," North wrote to Poindexter. "Casey's view is that Cap will continue to create roadblocks until he is told by you that the President wants this to move NOW and that Cap will have to make it work."[51] In fact, Weinberger was not alone. Among Casey's own subordinates, there were dissenting voices. McMahon was one, having just written to Casey he favored "keeping CIA out of the execution" of the operation, despite Sporkin's assurances on the legalities. Another dissenter was a CIA staff attorney who just the day before the meeting had come under stiff pressure from his superior—and from North—to agree with the idea of having the agency work with an independent "agent" to handle the transactions with Iran and Israel. In a memo for the record, the lawyer wrote, "Despite repeated urgings to concur in variations that would have DoD provide the weapons without other than token CIA involvement, I did not do so."[52]

The CIA lawyer's refusal to back down did not slow the process. Nor, astonishingly, did the CIA's circulation of its third separate "burn notice" on Ghorbanifar—five days after he failed an agency-administered polygraph test.[53] Sporkin and Casey simply ignored these impediments and pressed ahead with their preferred option of having the CIA get the weapons from Defense Department stocks, then deal through a private middleman with the Israelis. The goal of the meeting on January 16 was to bring as much weight as possible to bear on Weinberger. Considerable time had passed, and patience was wearing thin.

The pressure worked. Although Weinberger insisted he wanted Defense Department lawyers to look over the plans, by the next day he had relented, telling Casey his staff had signed off on the arrangement. After recognizing the president was determined to go ahead, he had concluded there was not much left to do. From then on his priority, much like Shultz and McMahon's, became how to minimize his institution's responsibility. Routine transfers of military equipment to the CIA left it up to Casey and his crew to answer for their actions. It was no concern of Weinberger's.[54]

On that same day, January 17, President Reagan signed the finished finding. The document was a watershed in that it provided for the United States to ship arms directly to Iran instead of via Israel. It inserted the CIA into the process as the mechanism for acquiring the weapons from the Defense Department but left the NSC staff as the lead agency. The order also called for assisting "third parties," a phrase understood to refer to Richard Secord and the Enterprise. The avowed goals of the new policy were to establish a "more moderate government in Iran," obtain intelligence on Iran's intentions regarding its neighbors and possible terrorist acts, and "further the release of the American hostages held in Beirut."[55]

At this key juncture, having provided the impetus to proceed, the president appeared to believe his main task was complete. He left it to his subordinates to take care of the mechanics. In hindsight, in light of the extraordinary discord the arms deals generated within his inner circle, his indifference to critical aspects of the operation—making sure it played out as planned, for instance, or anticipating its potential consequences—is remarkable. On January 6, he was so inattentive that he inadvertently signed a draft finding Poindexter had shown him simply in order to get his reaction. He did not read the cover memorandum North, Poindexter, and the others had carefully prepared for the final version in order to describe the legal arguments. Instead, Poindexter summarized the main points for him. "President was briefed verbally from this paper," he wrote in longhand on the last page of the memo. "VP, Don Regan and Don Fortier were present." Reagan did not even initial the memo. Poindexter did it for him: "RR per JMP." That evening the president wrote in his diary, "I gave a go ahead" to sell TOWs to Iran.[56]

Reagan's lack of focus here may have been a reflection of a general disinterest in details, as so many observers have reported. (McFarlane once complained Reagan had the "attention span of a fruit fly.")[57] It might also have been a sign of the early stages of a deteriorating mental condition such as Alzheimer's disease. Ronald Reagan Jr. recalled being painfully aware of his father "flounder[ing]" and "fumbling" through his first presidential candidates' debate with Walter Mondale more than a year before. On another occasion the president himself was upset at not remembering the names of familiar natural landmarks near Los Angeles in August 1986.[58] These and many other reported episodes, although anecdotal, are relevant to any assessment of Reagan's performance while in office. But given his behavior throughout this period it is also likely he considered the finding little more than legal cover for the operation, prompted mainly by the scare surrounding the HAWK authorization. This would fit with his pattern of closely tracking issues about which he was passionate—in this case, the operation itself—while tuning out associated technicalities he believed were the responsibility of his staff.

You Can't Buy Them at Kmart

A few days after the finding was signed, Thomas Twetten, deputy chief of the CIA's Near East division, whom Casey had assigned to the initiative, called a meeting to review logistics and finances.[59] The group included North and two senior CIA officials—Deputy Director for Operations Clair George and General Counsel Sporkin. NSC Counsel Paul Thompson also attended, as did Richard Secord, who did not enjoy a positive reputation in the CIA but who was one of the "third parties" referred to in the finding.[60]

Out of this meeting, the CIA received its marching orders to effect the complex TOW transfer to the agency under the Economy Act. The responsible official at the Defense Department was Weinberger's military assistant, Maj. Gen. Colin Powell. Powell had already begun the process, sending the order down through the ranks to the U.S. Army Missile Command at Redstone Arsenal in Huntsville, Alabama—but never revealing the final destination of the weapons. The plan was to move the missiles to Kelly Air Force Base in San Antonio, Texas, where Secord would arrange to pick them up via nongovernment aircraft for shipment to Israel. From there, another carrier would take them to Iran. Powell later explained to investigators the Defense Department had to be involved in the missile transaction for a simple reason: "You can't buy them at Kmart."[61]

One of North's priorities was to ensure Israel's continued involvement even if it was no longer in the lead. A few days earlier, he had telephoned Nir with the news about the president's decision to sell directly to Iran. Nir did not object strenuously, affecting to be content at not having to deplete Israel's missile stocks. He did protest the decision to let go of Schwimmer and Nimrodi, but accepted North's argument the prices they were asking would have raised legal complications in light of the White House determination to withhold notification of Congress. He dutifully passed the bad news to Schwimmer and Nimrodi, though they did not believe his expressions of regret. Nir's real fear was Israel would be dropped from the initiative altogether. But Washington still needed Nir to be the chief point of contact with Ghorbanifar and, despite the call for a "no comment" response, to help give the administration deniability in case the operation was blown.

As for Ghorbanifar, he managed to remain a part of the equation despite serious questions about his credibility. As early as December 22, Casey had asked Clair George to arrange for a new evaluation of him. Casey, who felt Ghorbanifar offered the best available entrée to the Iranian government, hoped the assessment would show he was basically trustworthy. But the agency's own experts concluded the opposite. A January 11 interview by the chief of the Iran Branch at the home of Ghorbanifar's most ardent U.S. backer, Michael Ledeen, only yielded a recommendation to subject him to a polygraph. The results of the exam shocked CIA officers: Ghorbanifar registered deceptive answers on thirteen of fifteen questions, and the other two—his name and place of birth—were "inconclusive."[62] The Near East division chief drew the obvious conclusions: "Ghorbanifar is a fabricator who has deliberately deceived the U.S. Government concerning his information and activities. . . . It is recommended that the Agency have no dealings whatsoever with Ghorbanifar."[63]

But Casey overruled his subordinates. The CIA director was notorious for following his own instincts even if it meant disregarding his staff experts. (After the scandal broke, he and CIA Deputy Director Robert Gates would come under attack for bypassing the agency's Iran specialists in providing intelligence to the White House.)[64] In this instance, Casey went around both his in-house experts and the reluctant Directorate of Operations, instead instructing counterterrorism chief analyst Charles Allen to "just take another look." Even then Casey did not get the result he wanted. Allen, too, thought the Iranian was a "con man." Nonetheless, Casey, Poindexter, and North chose to allow him to stay on as the linchpin of the initiative, a decision the congressional Iran-Contra report termed "remarkable."[65]

Shortly after the key U.S. players had coordinated their plans, North hurried to London to meet with Ghorbanifar. Secord and Nir had set up the meeting so each side could confirm its understanding of the new methodology. North asked Nir in advance to be the main liaison with Ghorbanifar, thus allowing Washington room to deny it was in direct contact with Iranian officials. Later, North referred to Nir as the Iranian's "case officer." He also asked Nir to pass along the bank account information Ghorbanifar would need to deposit the money for the transaction—again giving the United States a degree of deniability. Nir agreed, and Secord passed him a slip of paper with the number of a Lake Resources account. Nir gave it to Ghorbanifar later that day.[66]

One other matter was discussed at the "premeeting." North informed Nir the United States would be giving Iran samples of military intelligence relating to the war with Iraq. North had agreed to this new requirement from Ghorbanifar in Washington, D.C., the week before. He soon regretted it because it could easily give the Iranians more reason to be dissatisfied. This proved the case because the administration had no intention of providing truly sensitive data. Still, reluctant CIA officers put together a package covering the order of battle on the Iran-Iraq border—including troops, armor, and electronic installations—significant enough to cause McMahon to complain bitterly to Casey, "Everyone here at headquarters advises against this operation." For one thing, Ghorbanifar was a "liar"; for another, the intelligence would aid the "wrong people." McMahon worried it might even give Tehran the "wherewithal" for a successful offensive that could bring "cataclysmic results."[67] Both North and Twetten downplayed the significance of the package, however, saying the material covered territory "where it didn't make any difference." But this only raised the problem North had predicted; as Twetten added: "Of course, the Iranians immediately recognized that we were giving them useless information."[68] The ruse would come back to hurt the program by deepening Iranian mistrust. It also showed once again North's first instinct was often to make a snap decision based on short-term objectives, even when he recognized it might create bigger complications down the road.

At the meeting with Ghorbanifar later in the day, the two sides went over the operation. First, Washington would deliver a sample of intelligence about Iraq's order of battle, then the Iranians would transfer $40 million to the appropriate account. As soon as verification of the deposit was received, Secord would transship, via Israel, the first 1,000 TOWs. Next, the U.S. hostages plus an additional number of Jewish hostages in Lebanon would be released at the same time as the first group of Lahad's Hezbollah prisoners. If all went well, the remaining 3,000 TOWs would be sent to Iran. In the course of the shipments, the unwanted HAWK missiles still languishing in Iran would be reclaimed and Iran's payment returned. The group also talked about the possibility of Iran and the United States combining resources for use against the Soviets, particularly in Afghanistan. North's notes reflect the idea: "Longer term; Iranians willing to move weaps to Afghan Islamic Resistance."[69]

Price Fixing

A crucial part of the proposed deal was the price of the missiles. How much would Iran be willing to pay? The CIA had to pay the U.S. Army the lowest legitimate amount under the requirements of the Economy Act. The CIA then expected to recoup the total from the designated "private" agent, Secord. Secord in turn needed to get the money from the Iranians, although he expected to net a profit for his services. Ghorbanifar was the conduit for the funds from Iran, and he, too, would be sure to build in a sizable fee for his role. But how much would all this amount to? North established in his conversation with Ghorbanifar in Washington, D.C., then confirmed in London, the figure would be an even $10,000 per missile, for a total of $40 million. Because the first stage of the transaction called for the shipment of 1,000 missiles with the remainder held back until a later phase, $10 million would be required for starters. In early February, Ghorbanifar deposited the expected sum into the Lake Resources account.

The agreed-upon amount ended up having a marked impact on the initiative and on the Iran-Contra scandal as a whole. North had already spoken with Nir about what Israel would pay for the TOWs it had sent to Iran in 1985. Nir had quoted between $5,000–$5,500 apiece. North's idea was to use some of the excess paid by Iran to cover the payment for replacement TOWs being shipped to Israel from U.S. arsenals. He soon discovered that through an apparent error the U.S. Army Missile Command would actually be providing the weapons for much less than the real price—$3,469 each instead of $8,435.[70] Part of the confusion, reminiscent of the HAWK problem, had to do with the uncertainty over whether "basic TOWs" were being ordered or "improved TOWs" (I-TOWs). The difference in price between the two was huge, and if Ghorbanifar was willing to pay $10,000 per missile this meant almost $5 million more would be available for other, unchecked uses by the Enterprise and the Israelis.[71]

Genesis of the Diversion

The notion of skimming excess funds from the transaction for other purposes—whether to replenish Israel's stock of TOWs or underwrite other covert activities—was what came to be known as the "diversion." By the time Secord paid the CIA's account $3.7 million for the first 1,000 TOWs (having received $10 million from Ghorbanifar), the transaction had realized a profit of $6.3 million. After the scandal broke, the press and public focused on the act that "put the hyphen in Iran-Contra," as North quipped later—the plan to use the money for the Contra war effort.[72] But that was only one of the intended uses of the surplus revenue. "There was always a concert of opinion that the purposes of the residuals were as follows," North testified: "to sustain the Iranian operation, to support the Nicaraguan resistance, to continue other activities which the Israelis very clearly wanted, and so did we, and to pay for a replacement for the original Israeli TOWs shipped in 1985."[73]

The author of the diversion idea has never been established. The first time it seems to have surfaced was in December 1985, when North himself offhandedly told three Israeli officials that "he was in need of money and that he intended to divert profits from future Iranian transactions to Nicaragua." Secord testified that at around the same time North told him approximately $800,000 remaining from $1 million provided by the Israelis for a series of HAWK shipments was available for other uses. "I assume[d] that they would ask for their money back, but they didn't," Secord testified. "And I discussed this with North also, and later—I believe late December—he told me that they were not going to ask for it back, and we could use it for whatever purpose we wanted. We actually expended it on the Contra project."[74]

In his congressional testimony, North credited both Nir and Ghorbanifar for the diversion concept. "Mr. Nir [was] the first person to suggest that there be a residual and that the residual be applied to the purpose of purchasing replenishments and supporting other activities." Those activities included a series of joint U.S.-Israeli covert operations North and Nir had begun discussing in late 1985 and continued formulating into spring 1986. Ghorbanifar's contribution, according to North, was to specifically suggest helping out the Contras. "Mr. Ghorbanifar by then was aware of my role in support for the Nicaraguan resistance. He had seen my name in the newspapers. He [was] a very well read individual."[75]

This particular conversation, according to North, took place under unusual circumstances. "Mr. Ghorbanifar took me into the bathroom and Mr. Ghorbanifar suggested several incentives to make that February transaction work, and the attractive incentive for me was the one he made that residuals could flow to support the Nicaraguan resistance."[76] Although U.S. intelligence videotaped and recorded the entire meeting, the equipment apparently did not capture that part of the discussion.

However, there was evidently a recording of Ghorbanifar making a very similar proposal to North in the presence of the others: "I think this is now, Ollie, the best chance because we never would have found such a good time, we never get such good money out of this. We do everything. We do hostages free of charge; we do all terrorists free of charge; Central America for you free of charge; American business free of charge; [Karoubi] visit. Everything free."[77] No doubt downplaying his role, North testified he only picked up the ball and ran with it, calling the concept of "using the Ayatollah's money" to help the Contras a "neat idea."[78]

The covert activities North and Nir contemplated included working with Druze militia members in Lebanon to free the hostages. Even though there is no reference to these other operations in the finding, North claimed he had full authorization to pursue them from Poindexter, Casey, and even the president.[79]

More TOWs to Tehran

In late January, North prepared a "Notional Timeline" for Poindexter to send to the president to give him an idea of how the plan was expected to unfold. It incorporated North's usual flare for dramatic detail. Classifying it "top secret" and beginning each page with "PLEASE DESTROY AFTER READING," he laid out a month's worth of anticipated events, beginning with preparations for Secord to take custody of the weapons and arrangements for the CIA to pull together an intelligence sample for Ghorbanifar. On February 9, North envisioned "all U.S. hostages released to U.S./British or Swiss Embassy" followed the next day by "four (4) remaining Lebanese-Jews released by Hizballah." Surprisingly, he inserted the notation under February 11—the anniversary of the Iranian revolution—"Khomeini steps down." That prediction was deemed so far-fetched that when he read the passage to two senior CIA officers, they "laughed aloud."[80] His source for these assurances was Ghorbanifar, and the fact he was willing to put it into a memo for the president—despite the reaction of his CIA colleagues—showed again how fully he had bought into the Iranian's representations.[81]

The phased operation was now ready to get under way. As a first step, funds would be transferred from Iran for 1,000 TOWs. On February 6, North, Secord, and Nir along with the CIA's designated point person, Twetten, traveled again to London to meet Ghorbanifar to finalize the details. Inexplicably, the Iranian failed to materialize. A frustrated North returned to the United States, but Nir stayed in place, and the next day Ghorbanifar arrived with a photocopy of a telex confirming a deposit of $5 million and two additional checks in the amount of $2.5 million apiece. Three days later, Secord's associates wired $1.85 million to a CIA Swiss account, followed by the same amount the next day. The CIA then moved the total of $3.7 million to the Defense Department, thus closing out its obligation under the Economy Act. The schedule was already more than a week behind North's notional timeline, but at least the wheels were turning.[82]

After the money reached the Defense Department account, the army gave authorization to move the weapons out of its storage depot. On February 13, North wrote to Poindexter: "Operation RESCUE is now under way. 1000 items are currently en route from Anniston Alabama." The missiles went first to Kelly Air Force Base, where Secord's flight crew, hired through the former CIA proprietary company Southern Air Transport, took custody for the flights to Israel. Just as with the HAWK shipment, the transfer would be laundered. In Israel, the first tranche of 500 missiles was loaded onto an unmarked Israeli aircraft piloted by a Secord-picked crew and flown to Bandar Abbas, in southern Iran, arriving on February 17. While in Iran, the plane picked up the seventeen HAWK missiles remaining from November and returned them to Israel, as agreed with Ghorbanifar.[83]

The smooth delivery of the first 500 TOWs went a long way toward calming concerns on all sides. Not only were the Iranians and U.S. officials feeling more assured about each other's intentions, the Reagan administration no doubt felt vindicated in taking over the reins of the operation, albeit with the help of its new Israeli colleague, Nir. But there was another wrinkle. The intelligence sample North and the CIA had put together—which North said needed to be "flashy"—turned out to be unsatisfactory to the Iranians. Within a week of receiving it, Ghorbanifar told Nir that Tehran had concluded it was "worthless." He warned all the hostages would be released only if the quality of the next batch was acceptable. Nir thought U.S. officials should insist on speaking directly with Iranian officials in order to straighten things out. He suggested organizing a meeting after the first delivery of 500 TOWs. North agreed, as did Ghorbanifar.[84]

The "Australian" Raises Expectations

The official-to-official meeting was set for Frankfurt on February 19, two days after the first TOW shipment. But when the U.S. delegation arrived, the only Iranian there was a somewhat abashed Ghorbanifar. After telephoning the designated official in Tehran, he told the group the official could join them only after a few days. Once again, North and his colleagues left Europe disappointed. Less than a week later, however, the Iranian appeared, and North, Twetten, Secord, and Hakim, plus Nir, dutifully returned. The Iranian representative was Mohsen Kangarlou, introduced as an assistant to Prime Minister Mir-Hossein Mousavi. The U.S. officials dubbed him the "Australian" because his name sounded like "kangaroo." He turned out to be the same individual Mousavi had violently rebuked after the HAWK deal had fallen apart. It is not clear the U.S. side realized this.[85]

The meeting was understandably tense. It was the first face-to-face intergovernmental contact (outside of the Iran-U.S. Claims Tribunal at the Hague) since the Zbigniew Brzezinski–Ibrahim Yazdi meeting in Algiers in late October 1979, which may have helped precipitate the takeover of the U.S. Embassy in Tehran on November 4. Kangarlou made a lengthy speech about the problems in the U.S.-Iranian relationship. After he remarked that he needed to be sure the U.S. delegation was official, North took out photos of himself with President Reagan, which seemed to have the intended effect. Adding to the tension, Hakim, who had come as a second interpreter (to Ghorbanifar's dismay), saw immediately the two sides were on "different frequencies." Kangarlou seemed interested only in more advanced missiles from the United States, but North spoke mostly about the hostages. Kangarlou complained Iran had lost face after the release of Benjamin Weir the previous September because, he claimed, the Iranians had approved that deal only so they could begin to get "advanced stuff"—specifically Phoenix and Harpoon missiles. He continued that he personally had a stake in the matter, having promised results to his superiors. Iran's interest in Phoenix missiles and other high-tech U.S. equipment had come up several times before. Ghorbanifar had raised it with Secord in Paris immediately after the HAWK operation, and Secord had passed the information to North, who recorded it in his notes as a possible hitch: *"Probs:* Up the Ante. (Phoenix)." For some reason, North professed to never having heard the demand before and advised Kangarlou to drop the subject.[86]

As the meeting stretched into a second day, the agreements reached earlier with Ghorbanifar began to unravel. Kangarlou said the failed HAWK shipment would make it harder to come through with the hostages. Instead of all the U.S. hostages coming out after delivery of the first 1,000 TOWs, he insisted Iran first needed to obtain Phoenix missiles, "then we will start on the hostages. . . . You might not get them all immediately, but we will at least start on it."[87] This new stipulation was in addition to Ghorbanifar's admonition the release of all the hostages would depend on the quality of the next sampling of intelligence (which the U.S. officials had brought to show to experts accompanying Kangarlou). These statements represented a significant retreat from the earlier commitments.

Yet, the U.S. participants went along even after Kangarlou raised a new condition—an additional meeting on Kish Island off Iran's coast in the southern Persian Gulf. When the members of the delegation returned to Washington, D.C., they reported to Casey and Poindexter they fully expected to see at least two hostages freed very shortly. That same day, the second tranche of 500 TOWs arrived in Iran from Israel. In confirming the shipment to North, Secord had further news to report: "I met with [Kangarlou] for about one hour. . . . He emphasized need for quick meeting at Kish and said he would possibly, repeat, possibly surprise us by getting some hostages released before meeting. Suggest you make contingency plan to accommodate early release (i.e., as early as Sunday). So, bottom line is on to Kish ASAP to seize the potential opening now created." In other words, another meeting was now needed before even "some" hostages *might* be released. North's report to McFarlane, who still eagerly followed the operation after his departure from government, showed an awareness the deal might not pan out, but those concerns were drowned out by more wishful thinking: "While all of this could be so much smoke, I believe that we may well be on the verge of a major breakthrough—not only on the hostages/terrorism but on the relationship as a whole."[88]

Although the first and second segments of the TOW transfers of 1986 went off without a hitch, the opening of the second phase of the Iran initiative also produced no hostages. Caught up again in the potential of the undertaking, neither the U.S. team nor Nir managed to maintain their objectivity. No matter how often firm commitments gave way, they persisted in keeping the deals alive.

The U.S. and Israelis' immediate objective was to expand direct, face-to-face contacts with authoritative Iranian officials, among whom they counted Kangarlou. But Kangarlou was neither a new face nor particularly high ranking. More to the point, he was not remotely connected to the so-called moderates Ghorbanifar professed to represent, who presumably held the keys to better relations with the United States. In fact he was listed in Ghorbanifar's breakdown of Iranian factions from mid-1985 as among the extremists who were supposed to be eliminated, not supported.[89] What is more, the U.S. officials learned the TOWs had once again gone to the IRGC, the "true believers" of the Iranian revolution. When the military found out and demanded a share, the U.S. delegation was told, the guards responded that after the arms deals were done they would be happy to sell some of the goods to the military—at a profit.[90] Still, the excitement of the moment, the perception of moving closer to the circles of power in Tehran, and the inexperience of the key operatives led to another extension of the initiative instead of to its termination.

9

Air Contra

By fall 1985, Oliver North's efforts to set up a resupply network for the Contras to replace that of the CIA had literally failed to get off the ground. The Enterprise was having difficulty acquiring aircraft in good working order and organizing a ground crew and facilities. The Hondurans complicated matters by refusing to allow lethal shipments to pass through their territory. North and his cohorts had to adjust by establishing a transit point in El Salvador, at further remove from rebel bases. Crises erupted frequently, including quarrels between Contra groups, instances of reluctance to engage the enemy, and personnel conflicts on the U.S. side. Legal issues abounded but typically were shunted aside in the zeal to achieve operational objectives. The CIA, for example, was still very much in play despite the second Boland Amendment ban. North became more deeply involved, even organizing a resupply flight on his own as Enterprise managers struggled to achieve basic operational capacity. Meanwhile, top U.S. officials kept up their pursuit of legally dubious quid pro quo deals, soliciting the cooperation of the new Honduran president on the very day of his inauguration.

Setting the Agenda

Ronald Reagan remained substantially in the loop concerning the Contras and North's activities on their behalf. In December 1985, after John Poindexter took a whirlwind tour of Central America to encourage local officials to maintain rebel support, he briefed the president in depth. "He knew that Colonel North was . . . the chief [NSC] staff officer . . . with regard to coordination and liaison with the contra leadership," Poindexter testified later. He also "knew that the Contras were receiving arms and that they were receiving them from private parties and third countries."[1] One such case Reagan was "generally familiar" with was North's campaign to get either British Blowpipe or Chinese SA-7 missiles to the rebels.[2] Poindexter's December briefing took the president beyond generalities into specific details. For example, he provided an update on construction of the backup landing site in Costa Rica used by Contra resupply aircraft (see Chapter 7). Reagan later testified he understood those aircraft "weren't officially planes of ours [but] had been helping in the past in deliveries" to the insurgents.[3]

At around the time of Poindexter's trip, the latest congressional authorizations for Nicaragua policy went into effect, a compromise package allowing various intelligence-related activities including provision of communications equipment for the rebels. On January 9, Reagan signed a finding authorizing the CIA to implement these new measures.[4] But the administration saw the congressional concession as hopelessly inadequate because it still barred lethal assistance. The following day, the full NSC met to address Central America for the first time in fifteen months.[5]

One by one, the president's senior advisors spoke, constructing a stark picture of the Contras' predicament, which they viewed squarely in the context of the cold war. Poindexter identified Nicaragua as the "one significant problem area" in the region that demanded success if the United States was to "be able to deal with the Soviets on other regional issues." CIA Director William Casey agreed. "The resistance is the only obstacle, short of direct military intervention, to the consolidation of a Marxist-Leninist regime in Nicaragua."[6]

For the next several minutes Casey spelled out at length the Soviet and Cuban military buildup in the country—a total of $350 million of equipment over the previous five years ranging from "sophisticated tanks and MI-25 attack helicopters" to an "early warning radar capability" to "at least three airfields capable of handling Soviet bear bombers." Major naval bases currently being built would give the Soviets "access to advanced port facilities on both the Pacific and Atlantic coasts." Extensive economic aid, including oil deliveries, from the Soviet bloc as well as Libya and Iran were keeping the Nicaraguan economy afloat. Furthermore, "The Cubans are becoming more directly involved in the fighting." The resistance was holding on, but was "likely to be ground down unless it receives greater help soon."[7]

Following Casey, CIA Central American Task Force Chief Alan Fiers described the situation on the battlefield. "Mr. President, the armed resistance has faced an increasingly difficult challenge from the better-equipped and better-trained Sandinista forces." The Sandinistas, he said, "have constructed helicopter fields and fire support bases at strategic locations. They, also, have developed counterinsurgency battalions which are highly mobile and capable of rapid attack in response to insurgent forces." The Nicaraguan Democratic Force (FDN), for its part, had 8,000 soldiers in Nicaragua and an additional 8,000 in Honduras. But those numbers could become much greater with the proper backing. "If we could have a full program of support, the FDN could grow to 30,000–35,000."[8]

The problem was lack of supplies. "Honduras has refused a resumption of supply flights into Honduras, so it is difficult to resupply the task force in Nicaragua. If they are not resupplied, they will soon be forced to exit, a 45-day march north to Honduras." Resolving the impasse, however, would make it possible to "increase the pressure on the Sandinistas so that they would be facing great difficulty, forced to choose between negotiating with the opposition, collaps[ing], or dealing with the military situation which they could not manage."[9]

Caspar Weinberger declared, "Soviet shipments to Nicaragua have risen dramatically since 1981. There have been a total of 37 deliveries. They continue to pour in tanks, helos, artillery." Unless some dramatic action was taken, "The Sandinistas could undo all the good work which has been done in El Salvador and threaten the other democratic countries in the area."[10] Joint Chiefs of Staff (JCS) Chair Adm. William Crowe agreed. Fresh from a trip to the region, he pointed out the "Nicaraguan insurgency . . . is the largest insurgency in the region . . . [but] it has no strategy and is not well versed in tactics; they spin their wheels a lot."[11]

George Shultz, usually a voice of relative moderation at these gatherings, turned the discussion to possible courses of action. He called on the administration to "make a major push in Congress to have the wraps taken off us on things we can do for UNO [United Nicaraguan Opposition]." He then described how this should be done: "As a strategy with Congress, I would keep the overt program alive (at about $35 million in 1987), but, then, stress the need for a covert program as well." Why? "We need to make it covert in order to go to other countries to ask for support. Elliott [Abrams] already has been out probing. Our present funds end on March 31."[12]

By the end of this litany, the president—the principal target audience at the table—was ready to move forward. Arguments about the Soviet threat played to his own profound fears. He warned Moscow's penchant for subversion (which he traced back to Lenin) could lead to disaster: "We can wake up one day and find ourselves virtually isolated, defeated in the end." There was good news, however. Members of Congress had reassured him about Nicaragua: "They think we have an excellent chance of getting lethal aid now."[13]

Winding down the session, Reagan displayed the decisiveness—and impulsiveness—that characterized his approach to the Contra program. "George, you said I should think it over and decide. Well, I've thought it over. The answer is yes." Speaking about the congressional assistance, he grew impatient. "We should start to go after it now, George, not after the February recess."

At the end of the meeting, an exchange took place that highlighted the NSC interest not only in meaningful action but utter secrecy. Poindexter proposed pulling together a "battle group" led by Abrams and Donald Regan to come up with a strategy for Capitol Hill, but one that included ensuring certain activities remained undisclosed. "It is important that at least part of the funds be covert, and there is no reason to ever talk about the military assistance." Shultz agreed: "We can use the overt program as an asset. We can say that's our assistance." Even the secretary of state was prepared to use overt aid as cover for a lethal program. "There must be no leaks on this meeting," Shultz added. "This must be held tightly." The president replied: "That's right." The exchange evoked Reagan and McFarlane's demand for secrecy at the end of the June 25, 1984, NSPG meeting on Contra funding (see Chapter 5).

Among the staff members seated around the outer fringes of the room was North. His alarm about the Contras' predicament contributed to convening the NSC that day. But the meeting in turn undoubtedly reinforced his conviction that keeping the rebels afloat by any available means would have the strong backing of his superiors. An exchange between Reagan and Crowe must have especially resonated with him. Crowe argued the rebels needed not only weapons but training and advice. "We need some way for our people to get their thoughts to them," he said. "It could be through the Hondurans, or the agency [CIA] people, or we could do it ourselves if the traffic will bear that." But he understood there were legal barriers: "We could have a US military group in Honduras to advise the resistance, but, presently, we are not allowed to do that." Reagan's response was striking: "I understand the difficulty your people have talking with the Contras," he said to Crowe. "There must be some way." "Maybe," he suggested, "they could have barbecues with them."[14]

Though this sounds almost like a tongue-in-cheek remark, it seems likely the president was seriously proposing the U.S. military arrange social encounters with the rebels where unofficial advice—or more—could be provided, as if the informality of a cookout would permit U.S. advisors to sidestep the congressional ban on military guidance. North could not have failed to notice the president's eagerness to find imaginative ways to support the rebels.

Satisfying the Hondurans

A combination of local circumstances and U.S. government intervention eventually solved the Honduras problem. But the process took well into spring 1986. After Poindexter briefed Reagan in December 1985, U.S. officials held several meetings with the Hondurans early in the new year. What they heard were complaints the United States had not taken sufficient care to protect Honduras from being linked publicly with the resupply operation, thus putting the country at risk of attack by the Sandinistas. Local military officers also protested they were not being informed of plans for weapons shipments. (In general, they disparaged the U.S. effort as a "hamburger operation," as Fiers put it.)[15] But North and his U.S. colleagues saw another reason for the logjam: the Hondurans wanted compensation for their troubles.

At first, the main obstacle seemed to be President Roberto Suazo Córdova. Suazo was already angry at Washington's refusal to back his plan to change the Honduran Constitution to allow him to stay in office. He also wanted to boost U.S.

support for Honduras. Earlier in 1985, the Reagan administration had agreed to quid pro quos with Suazo, delivering much-wanted weapons and ammunition in order to keep his government on board (see Chapter 5). But after the awkward experience of the October Nicaraguan Humanitarian Assistance Office (NHAO) flight, the Honduran president reversed his attitude again. "Bobby Suazo just stonewalled everything," Fiers complained. "It wasn't until [he] left office, in late January, that we could even talk to the Hondurans about this thing."[16] The person to talk to then was the new president, José Azcona Hoyo, who won election in November 1985.

Consequently, the parade of U.S. officials visiting Tegucigalpa continued. In addition to officers from the U.S. Southern Command and U.S. Ambassador John Ferch, Deputy Assistant Secretary of State William Walker and Poindexter made the trip from Washington, D.C. In November, Robert Owen, North's deputy, had predicted the new president might also present a challenge because he was seen by his constituents as neither "Honduran or nationalist enough." Azcona had gained far less than a majority at the polls—only 27 percent—and was not even the top vote-getter. He had won because his party garnered the highest totals. To prove his independence, Owen predicted, "he may just decide to give the gringos a hard time with their pet project."[17] U.S. officials understood this, too. Reflecting on the massive U.S. military buildup in Honduras, Weinberger remarked to the NSC on January 10, 1986: "We are concerned that we have focused so much on Honduras as a base, that, now, we face a situation in which the new government there probably will not be as favorable."[18]

Shultz agreed: "We see in Honduras what has happened because of an overt program; they can't stand it." For him, the solution was straightforward: "We need to stand by our friends in Central America, and that means money." An embassy report to Shultz and Abrams the same month made it plain Honduran support for the resistance would hinge on how much military and economic aid was forthcoming from Washington. Because Azcona's inauguration was about to take place, the State Department suggested Vice President George Bush use the occasion to deliver a message that U.S. support for the rebels remained steadfast. Poindexter would simultaneously seek a similar commitment in a separate private meeting with the new president.[19]

Guidance prepared for Bush's meeting was explicit. On a card titled "Special Talking Points—Azcona," the vice president was advised, "Recommend you discuss with him privately." The message for Azcona followed:

> Mr. President, there is one issue I would like to discuss privately with you. Supply of the Democratic Resistance Forces [DRF]. We, President Reagan and I, hope we can work very quietly and discreetly with you. It can be done with deniability. Internal resistance in Nicaragua needs support and

catalyst. Armed resistance and their supply [*sic*]. So we hope in your early days, as soon as possible, you can take a look at supply for the DRF, talk to your military and tell the military to work out ways to assure a supplied front.[20]

The approach to Azcona did not work immediately. The new Honduran leader proved almost as tough a bargainer as Suazo. More visits by Ambassador Ferch, Abrams, and CIA officials finally led to an agreement in late February to allow resupply flights to gear up again—under conditions of strict secrecy. Not long afterward, though, Honduran military officials upped the ante, asking for authority to manage the lethal assistance program—which, after all, was based in their country—and further, to begin receiving the same sophisticated military equipment the United States was giving the rebels.[21]

As was almost always the case when it came to advancing the Contra cause, the administration went along, and by late March Abrams and the head of the U.S. Southern Command, Gen. Jack Galvin, were dispatched to the region, returning with commitments from three Central American leaders to keep up their support for the resistance. It was another straight quid pro quo. The deal Abrams negotiated with Azcona provided for $20 million worth of ground-to-air missiles and other weaponry above and beyond the security assistance already covered under previous agreements. In return, the Hondurans allowed shipments to the rebels to resume, an act Reagan acknowledged in a letter of thanks to Azcona in May along with confirmation the United States would also be releasing the additional economic support funds (ESF) requested.

As Owen had predicted, Azcona was still not satisfied. He notified Reagan later in May Honduran cooperation would depend on a sizable boost of U.S. aid both to the Contras and to Honduras, along with tighter coordination with Tegucigalpa over rebel military operations. He insisted these were conditions previously worked out with senior Reagan administration officials—namely, Deputy Secretary of Defense William H. Taft, Abrams, Poindexter, and Galvin.[22]

All of these arrangements, which provided direct benefits to a foreign government in return for its assistance to the Contras, were expressly prohibited by congressional legislation in effect at the time. Against this background, it would not have been difficult for North to persuade himself he was only emulating his superiors in carrying out his own illicit fund-raising activities—including engineering the "diversion" from Iran.

The Resupply Operation

As 1985 drew to a close, there was good news on the political front. Owen reported several *comandantes* who had previously followed Edén Pastora had gone over to the FDN. This was part of the plan North and his CIA colleagues, mainly Joseph Fernandez, the agency's station chief in Costa Rica, had hoped to implement for some time. The defectors became known as "newly aligned commanders" (NACs). Owen also told North morale was good in the south, in the border area of Costa Rica and Nicaragua. "Yet there is tremendous frustration about the lack of movement of goods from the States," he wrote. Owen was not talking just about guns and ammunition. He was urging deliveries of humanitarian supplies—clothing, medicine to fight mountain leprosy, and other basic goods. The irony, as he pointed out, was that the influx of new *comandantes* and their troops also meant "needs will increase dramatically."[23]

While the U.S. government put diplomatic and political pressure on Central American leaders to support its policy, North tried to figure out how to solve problems on the ground. By most accounts, they were significant but not dire. Owen's typed memos from the field provided regular updates on shortages and the resulting complaints by rebel commanders. The same picture was available to anyone in the U.S. government with access to CIA reports.[24] Even the U.S. media were reporting similar information. Contra military commander Enrique Bermúdez grumbled to the *Washington Post* in January: "We haven't received even a single pair of boot laces."[25]

Although basic supplies were lacking, Contra leaders, like their NSC patrons, mainly fretted over the shortage of military equipment. "We need lethal aid to accelerate the war," Bermúdez demanded. In fact, some munitions had arrived in mid-December through Richard Secord's associate, Tom Clines, who by now was also part of the Iran operation. Because Honduras was temporarily unavailable as a staging area, Clines had arranged for a shipment of Soviet bloc equipment from Portugal to Ilopango Air Base in El Salvador. There to meet the cargo from Defex (the same company he had tried to work with in November regarding the HAWKs) was Rafael Quintero, another CIA veteran at the Miami meeting in June. Quintero had contacted Felix Rodriguez, North's liaison with the Salvadoran Air Force, using the prearranged code name "Mr. Green," to tell him of the impending delivery of "heavy stuff." When the leased Boeing 707 touched down on December 15, Rodriguez personally oversaw the unloading of some 85,000 pounds of ammunition and explosives and, by agreement with his Salvadoran military contacts, arranged for it to be stored for later delivery to the FDN. Over the next six months, about a half-dozen additional Enterprise flights containing a half-million pounds of lethal equipment made their way to Ilopango.

The problem for Bermúdez and his men, therefore, was not the lack of guns and ammunition. The trouble was getting the equipment to the fighters in the field. It was a challenge that proved almost too much for the skeleton crew North had put together.

Taking Shortcuts

Anxious to supply the rebels, North soon crossed another legal barrier. He was already using Owen's humanitarian flights to get intelligence reports on the Contra war. Frustrated at the Enterprise's inability to find working aircraft, he decided to exploit the humanitarian aid operation, even though the law explicitly prohibited any involvement with lethal supplies. His preferred option was still that Secord and his crew create an independent flight capability. That would keep the two activities separate and remove him and the U.S. government one step further from the illicit operations. But it proved far more challenging than anticipated to build a "private" air force, and Richard Gadd, enjoying access to official channels, seemed in a position to move the humanitarian shipments much more expeditiously. The first NHAO shipment, flying on an L-100 leased from Southern Air Transport (SAT), took off for Ilopango on January 10, 1986, almost a month before Gadd was able to acquire the Enterprise's first aircraft.

For North, the temptation to "piggyback," as Fiers put it, onto a ready-made operation was too much to resist. Owen's memos repeatedly warned that without concrete signs of U.S. commitment they would start losing men, particularly the NACs, whose allegiance they had worked hard to win away from Pastora. The opportunity came in late December when the Hondurans finally agreed to open their territory again for resupply activities—as long as the flights did not come directly from the United States. North's idea was simple. He recommended to the Restricted Interagency Group (RIG)—and soon to the Hondurans—the aircraft stop at Ilopango before continuing on to Honduras. Aside from disguising the origin of the flights, the arrangement would make it easier to double dip: the same planes used for humanitarian cargoes could then be filled with lethal supplies.

Fiers's visit to Ilopango at the end of December to meet Salvadoran Air Force Chief of Staff Gen. Juan Rafael Bustillo—a friend of Rodriguez—helped to nail down arrangements with El Salvador.[26] By then, the rebels' supply situation was in disarray. "Incompetence reigns," Owen complained to North. A week before, a group of fighters had gone into Nicaragua and was expecting some 15,000 pounds of deliveries within ten days. "Yet NHAO does not know about it, Joe [Fernandez] does not know what is to be dropped and Negro has never been asked what his people need. . . . These people don't know they are even in a war," Owen wrote in amazement. "They think they're running a business." Then he warned, "If the supplies are not delivered when they are supposed to be, our credibility will once again be zero in the South."[27]

Adding to the mix, a near disaster occurred in early February when Gadd's first C-7 Caribou crash-landed on a Salvadoran highway on its way to Ilopango, the crew desperately pitching out "anything that wasn't alive"[28] to lighten the load. It looked like an operation going nowhere.

North decided he could wait no longer. Calling Gadd at home, he ordered him to start using the aircraft he had leased for NHAO to ferry military supplies—after off-loading the official cargo.

Before long, the two operations—lethal and humanitarian—had become "virtually indistinguishable."[29] At Ilopango, both kinds of cargo were stored side by side in the same Butler buildings. "We didn't differentiate between one and the other," Rodriguez said later. "I was just handling both like the same thing."[30] Owen, meanwhile, formally a consultant to NHAO, started to keep double books, reporting simultaneously to his superiors at the State Department and to his real boss, North.

Reluctance to Fight

For the next few weeks, North's operatives shipped mixed loads into the region. Although the new system took care of the FDN in northern Nicaragua and Honduras, Fernando "El Negro" Chamorro and his men on the southern front still faced serious shortages. This, in turn, threatened the entire two-front strategy: without supplies there was no way to get the southern-based rebels to decamp, march across the border, and fight, "The only way you could get them out of Costa Rica was to assure them that they would have logistical support inside Nicaragua," according to Ambassador Lewis Tambs.[31]

Chamorro had tried to get the FDN to share its supplies and arrange an air-drop for his forces, but without success. In early March, Owen, at North's behest, accompanied a shipment of medical supplies to the region on an NHAO flight. He was then supposed to make sure a fresh payload of military equipment was put on board and fly with it to another location, where it would be repackaged and forwarded to the Contras on the southern front. But the munitions were nowhere to be found. After a frenetic day of communications with the CIA, White House, and FDN, the plan had to be scrapped. The FDN was simply unwilling to part with any equipment under its control. In fact, antagonism between Contra groups ran so deep the insurgents sometimes seemed to forget they were on the same side.[32]

At the end of the month, Owen typed out a trip report that summarized the hitches in the operations, then took the liberty of offering advice to North gleaned from his conversations with fellow operatives—Rodriguez, Quintero, and James Steele, head of the U.S. Military Group (Milgroup) in El Salvador, who remained a frequent presence in Contra operations during the period. Owen addressed the memo to "BG" (Blood and Guts) and signed it "TC" (The Courier). "Both lethal and non-lethal supplies destined for the south should be stockpiled at Cincinnati," the code name for Ilopango. "The FDN cannot be relied on to provide material in a timely manner." Troops needed mortars, light machine guns, and hand grenades not only to stay in the fight but also to maintain morale and unity. Communications also needed improvement, he pointed out, including "between Cinci, Point West and Joe [Fernandez]." Owen added, "Some of the comandantes who said they would side with Negro and UNO/Farn now want to side with Cesar," a rival figure. "To keep this from happening, a drop must go through as quickly as possible. Even now it may be too late."[33]

On the positive side, Gadd had finally started to locate aircraft. After the C-7 crash landing in February, he found a second Caribou as well as a larger C-123 that could take bigger loads on longer hauls. Air drops to the FDN in the north started to follow a routine by late March. Over the next several months Gadd's crews managed to fly some eighty missions to the northern forces. In May alone, the smaller C-7s, which could handle the shorter trip without difficulty, made thirty flights carrying lethal and "soft" cargoes of up to three tons. The south remained a headache.

The obstruction was no longer collaboration as much as incompetence, as Owen had indicated. Pressure on UNO forces in the north had finally garnered their consent to fly a mission on behalf of their erstwhile partners in the south at the beginning of April. But this had to be scrubbed. An exasperating combination of pilot inexperience, mechanical problems, and difficulty in charting a flight path that would not violate Costa Rican airspace (and break a U.S. pledge to the new president, Óscar Arias) convinced a grudging Fernandez to recommend aborting the plan. The experience would help convince North to step in personally.

Also on North's mind was Pastora. The State Department was sending mixed signals about his standing with Washington. Fernandez and his fellows on the ground continued working to induce the NACs to leave the Revolutionary Democratic Alliance (ARDE). But in early March, Shultz met with Pastora, along with Adolfo Calero and Alfonso Robelo, thus giving the controversial ARDE leader a major public relations boost.[34] Shortly afterward, John Singlaub, at the request of Sen. Jesse Helms and—by Singlaub's account—with the consent of Abrams, visited Pastora at his safe house in the Costa Rican capital and signed an agreement to provide "boots . . . food . . . ammunition . . . encrypted communications systems" and other "military needs" in return for Pastora's commitment to move his troops into Nicaragua to engage the Sandinistas.[35] The wording of the deal made it sound like the United States was committing itself to be his supplier—a simple typing error, according to Singlaub.

News of the agreement confused the *comandantes* even further, and some began to question the wisdom of having abandoned Pastora, especially because supplies were still not forthcoming. CIA and other officials who had soured on Pastora tried to reassure the NACs (and Fernandez) Pastora was not being welcomed back into the U.S. fold. Still, pressure for an equipment delivery continued to build. Fiers stressed in a secret cable it was "more crucial than ever that we maintain our commitment to the [NACs] and that the required drop be made at . . . absolutely [the] first possibility." He instructed his operatives to "ensure that [the FDN] understands urgency and assigns proper priority to this mission."[36]

A Blow from Congress

On March 20, the House of Representatives rejected the administration's latest $100 million Contra aid proposal by a vote of 222–210. Administration officials had banked heavily on the new infusion and led the rebels to believe it was a virtual lock. But the debate leading up to the vote had been remarkably acrimonious and featured a heavy dose of scare tactics from the White House. House Democrats generally opposed to Contra aid were specifically targeted by groups such as the National Conservative Political Action Committee (NCPAC) and made to look like nothing more than communist sympathizers. White House Communications Director Patrick Buchanan had declared in the *Washington Post*: "With the vote on contra aid, the Democratic Party will reveal whether it stands with Ronald Reagan and the resistance—or Daniel Ortega and the communists." The president was nearly as shrill, warning Soviet proxies were "just two days driving time from Harlingen, Texas," and "if we don't want to see the map of Central America covered in a sea of red, eventually lapping at our own borders, we must act now."[37]

The new offensive peaked with Reagan's nationwide address on March 16, in which he asked rhetorically, "Will [Congress] provide the assistance the freedom fighters need to deal with Russian tanks and gunships, or will they abandon the democratic resistance to its Communist enemy?" He invoked the bleak period at the dawn of the cold war that had prompted the Truman Doctrine: "It must be our policy, Harry Truman declared, to support peoples struggling to preserve their freedom. . . . We saved freedom in Greece then. And with that same bipartisan spirit, we can save freedom in Nicaragua today. . . . If we fail," he warned, "there will be no evading responsibility—history will hold us accountable."[38]

The confrontational approach—atypical even for discourse on the Contras—reflected growing administration desperation and anger. Throughout the war, the president and his aides had been frustrated by Democratic and public refusal to accept the White House point of view. Three weeks after this speech, GOP pollster Richard Wirthlin reported to Reagan most U.S. citizens continued to oppose Contra aid. "People just don't understand," Reagan wrote in his diary.[39] At a top-level meeting immediately after the vote, White House press spokesman Larry Speakes noted reporters had "asked us if we lost votes because of our rhetoric." Yet Speakes's own response to the questioners had been stiff: "We have issued a presidential statement" that "presented the President's viewpoint." There was no further discussion of the question at the meeting.[40]

But White House pronouncements continued at a high rhetorical pitch. Reagan's depiction of supporters as "those . . . who stood with the forces of freedom" by implication defined opponents as those who did not. He also referred to the bill's defeat as a "dark day for freedom." Unnamed senior White House officials expressed their view the problem had not been taking too hard a line but being too ready to compromise. An earlier agreement—to suspend part of the bill's $70 million in lethal aid for ninety days in order to give negotiations a chance—had been a "fundamental error," a White House operative complained to reporters, because it undercut the strategy to have a "clear definition of the issue" and "not to get things all muddled up."[41]

This was characteristic of senior administration attitudes at the time. Either unable or unwilling to reassess the soundness of their approach, most officials concluded simply that not enough was being done to sell the president's case. In their minds, what was preventing the U.S. public from seeing the light was not so much the existence of legitimate differences over whether the stakes were as high as the president claimed or that fighting a proxy war was the correct response, but a combination of Sandinista propaganda and political manipulation by intransigent members of Congress.

By most accounts, the resort to hard-line tactics led directly to the bill's defeat. Moderate pro-Contra Democrats joined hard-core opponents of the president's policy because they were dismayed by the administration's rhetorical barrage. Even some Republicans thought the attacks were unseemly. Reagan was aware for some on Capitol Hill the vote was meant as a signal. At the March 20 NSC meeting, he stated, "A number of congressmen I called said they would vote 'no' this time but would vote 'yes' on April 15, when Tip will let them vote again." In order to persuade moderate Democrats to oppose the legislation, Speaker of the House Thomas "Tip" O'Neill had made a deal, promising a second vote the following month. Reflecting the well of distrust built up between the president and the speaker, Reagan added: "I don't know what Tip has up his sleeve. . . . We know that promise has been broken before."[42]

The bill's defeat was not fatal—a similar aid package passed the House in late June—but it left an immediate problem: official aid would soon run out. Casey told the NSC after the vote the rebels could hold out for an additional sixty to ninety days "providing they get logistical support." Abrams agreed: "Deliveries will go on into April, May and June even without new money." No one at the meeting appears to have asked how this would be accomplished, but the answer was the Enterprise's makeshift operation would be called upon once more to keep things going.

North at the Helm

After a quick trip to the region by North, Abrams, and Fiers to reassure local leaders following the vote, North continued to try to turn promises into reality. The plan remained to use NHAO-leased aircraft to fly humanitarian aid into the region, then replace it with lethal cargo for direct drops to rebel camps. It was "NHAO by day, private benefactors by night," Fiers commented. Investigators later called it a "rare occasion that a U.S. Government program unwittingly provided cover to a private covert operation."[43] One improvement in the process was the introduction of advanced communications equipment. Poor coordination among the various elements of the program had been a serious deficiency in earlier resupply attempts. Fiers and Fernandez had considered putting a Contra representative at Ilopango to facilitate matters, but so far it had not worked out. A related worry for both the CIA and the super-secretive National Security Agency (NSA) was "COMSEC"—communications security. Enterprise operatives had been using open telephone lines to discuss their highly sensitive activities, a surprising lapse given their fixation with secrecy. The same problem had come up in the Iran initiative. To prevent exposure, NSA officials, reported to be incensed at the breach of security, provided North "encryption support" in early 1986 in the form of portable KL-43 devices.[44]

A KL-43 was a computer terminal that could scramble and unscramble transmissions. Advanced equipment for its time, it was the size of a netbook computer with a keyboard, small LCD screen, and built-in modem. Each day, users entered new encryption keys from the NSA, which provided a fresh set on a monthly basis. With a keystroke, an operator encrypted the text, then dialed the recipient over a standard telephone line. Both users then plugged in telephone couplers, and the sender transmitted the message. At the other end, the press of a "Decrypt" key unscrambled the text.[45] Considering the poor quality of secure phone lines in use at U.S. embassies at the time, the KL-43 was not overly cumbersome for the level of protection it provided. North and his crew used the devices constantly during 1986, occasionally printing out their messages (and unwittingly preserving them for investigators).

Armed with the device, North typed out a hasty, typo-ridden message to Secord laying out a plan for his upcoming shipment. He used prearranged code names for key players: Fiers was "Cliff"; Quintero was "Ralph." With his usual urgent tone, North insisted the troops in the field "cannot wait. . . . Hope we can make this happen the right way this time."[46]

The first stages went relatively smoothly. The L-100 dropped off and picked up its supplies as planned. The CIA provided flight vectors for the second drop zone and "hostile risk" evaluations for the crew, and Steele personally verified the security of the cargo and briefed the SAT pilots on how to evade enemy radar. But all the preparations went for nothing when the crew failed to pinpoint the drop zone. Secord reported to North: "L-100 arrived over DZ on time but never saw inverted L or strobe lite. They remained in area 25 minutes and then aborted." Frustrated and undoubtedly eager to prove the competence of his operation, Secord insisted: "I want to try again tonight." But there were problems. The first was that Steele balked at a second flight. "Steele has informed Ralph that he will not permit another 'half ass' operation. He says we have to establish air/ground radio contact before he will permit op to go forward. This is asinine—no black ops ever use this procedure." Placing the blame for the failed drop on the rebels on the ground rather than his air crew, Secord added: "The answer is to sort out why the troops did not have signals properly displayed."

The second obstacle, as always, was time. "S[AT] wants their bird back," Secord reported. Not long before, Washington had belittled the Israelis for jeopardizing the HAWK shipment to Iran by relying on a private contractor to fly the missiles who insisted on having the aircraft back by a certain time. Now the Enterprise faced the same problem because SAT, officially a commercial carrier, began to pressure Secord to return its plane. It was another reminder of the difficulties of running a covert program without the necessary infrastructure. Still, Secord was ready to move ahead. "I will handle S[AT] if you take care of Steele. This must be done right away or we must return the bird."[47]

North evidently did "take care of Steele" because two nights later Secord tried again. This time the SAT crew managed to unload more than 20,000 pounds of munitions to waiting rebel forces across the border in Nicaragua. The mission was the first successful one of its kind and something of a breakthrough for the motley operation. Not only did it provide a badly needed infusion to the soldiers in the field, it helped on the political level by persuading the uncommitted NACs to move away from Pastora and begin to come to terms with UNO. The drop became a model that could be used for subsequent flights.

Trouble with Felix

Satisfaction over the success soon dissipated, however. Within days, North and Secord found themselves drawn into a simmering conflict that threatened to uncover their secret activities. The conflict now centered on Rodriguez, whom North had placed at Ilopango some months earlier to exploit his close ties to senior Salvadoran military officials. The arrangement had mostly worked fine. Secord said Rodriguez was "very, very helpful" at first, but "over time became more of a problem for us."[48]

By the end of 1985, Rodriguez's stock had risen with the U.S. side when members of the RIG made an unusual visit to Ilopango to help implement the NHAO program. With Rodriguez's help, they managed to persuade the Salvadoran military to allow the program to use the airfield as a way station for aid deliveries. They also elaborated the roles of key team members, including Rodriguez, Steele, and local CIA officials. The agreement was Rodriguez and Steele would gather information about NHAO deliveries and share it with the agency. In early January, Fiers memorialized his instructions to local officers, which included monitoring not just incoming NHAO flights but all cargo leaving Ilopango. The CIA wanted to make sure Pastora's troops received none of these supplies.

Despite the RIG's consensus, coordination on the ground quickly foundered. Fiers began hearing Rodriguez was not providing the necessary information. CIA personnel who apparently had not been told about the RIG's discussions cabled headquarters for clarification: "[A]dditional confusion being introduced into San Salvador scenario by Felix ((Rodriguez)), who . . . [is] insisting that all matters relating to the Ilopango logistics system be channelled through him."[49] At least one flight, they complained, had gone from Guatemala to Honduras on Rodriguez's orders without the CIA being informed. Furthermore, Rodriguez, who went by the code name Max (or Máximo) Gómez, was becoming difficult in other ways. In early January, Steele told North about "probs with Maximo . . . confrontation with Station Chief." The dispute involved "Maximo's girlfriend," described as a "security prob." Later in the month another CIA officer reported Rodriguez had gotten into another "conflict" with two key Contra air force and logistics personnel at Ilopango.[50]

Before long, Fiers had his own run-in with Rodriguez. Not all CIA personnel in the region were in the loop about the resupply operation, but being under orders to monitor Contra air traffic, it was almost inevitable they would stumble across the Enterprise. In early February a field officer notified Fiers a Caribou aircraft had crashed outside San Salvador. It was the plane Gadd had bought for the Enterprise. The CIA operative learned about the incident from the U.S. chargé d'affaires, "who says his source was Felix Rodriguez who apparently has been 'coordinating' all this with Ollie North (one supposes on open phone). . . . What is going on back there?" the officer demanded.[51]

Within four hours, Fiers informed the officer he was on his way to see him—on direct instructions from the CIA deputy director of operations, Clair George. At Ilopango, Fiers filled in the officer on the upcoming weapons shipments and North's role in managing them. It was at this point he crossed paths with Rodriguez. Driving through the airbase with two other agency officers, Fiers was shown a C-130 aircraft taking on supplies—on Rodriguez's orders, he was told—for delivery to the rebels in Honduras. Fiers had just come from Tegucigalpa, where the military had finally agreed to let NHAO flights back into the country, but under strict limitations, including the size of the aircraft. The C-130 was simply too big, Fiers realized, and if it tried to land at Aguacate the Hondurans would be outraged. He headed straight to Rodriguez's headquarters to tell him so. Rodriguez initially resisted, saying he had authorization from North. He challenged Fiers to call North, which Fiers did, persuading North to cancel the flight.

Still, Rodriguez refused to yield. Instead of complying, he went behind North's back, asking Mario Dellamico, rival of Secord and onetime arms supplier to Calero (see Chapter 7), to see the Honduran Army commander about getting clearance for an even larger aircraft, an L-100. The commander equivocated until a CIA official reportedly ordered him to "stand down." The flight never took off, and word quickly got back to an angry Fiers. Within a few days, the CIA took action to rein in Rodriguez (exactly how is not known), and Fiers's field staff could soon report with satisfaction, "The role of the now infamous local 'private American citizen' has been reduced to that of an 'on-looker' at the NHAO/UNO/FDN warehouse at Ilopango." North remarked ruefully to Secord, "Regarding the El Salvador problem, we may have created one of our own with Maximo."[52]

Rodriguez proved North right. Rather than back down, he elevated the dispute to the U.S. vice president's office, a move that carried its own set of risks for the operation. Shortly after the aborted L-100 flight, Rodriguez contacted Bush's secretary to ask for a meeting with him. He had hoped to come to Washington, D.C., within a few days, but could not get an appointment until May 1. In the meantime, North and Secord flew to El Salvador on a chartered executive jet for what Secord called a "summit meeting" with personnel involved in the resupply operation at Ilopango. Contra air force commander Juan Gómez, along with Bermúdez, Bustillo, Rodriguez, Steele, and Quintero, took part in the tense, four-hour session on April 20. Grievances flew from all sides. North chided Bermúdez for not making supplies more available to the southern front. Bermúdez and others criticized the shoddy condition of the Enterprise's meager fleet. (Their low opinion did not keep the Contras from declaring the aircraft belonged to them, not the Enterprise.) The Washington delegation objected. Secord, who viewed the operation largely as a business venture, had no intention of giving away the Enterprise's assets, which were then worth several million dollars.[53]

Afterward, Rodriguez, a trained helicopter pilot, gave some of the group a lift to nearby San Salvador in order to pay a call on the U.S. ambassador, Edwin Corr. The trip was short but harrowing and did not endear Rodriguez to the others. The helicopter had no doors, so the noise was deafening, and Rodriguez, according to Steele, came frighteningly close to "hitting a flagpole . . . and killing everyone aboard."[54] Having narrowly survived, North, Secord, and Steele met with Corr, who was concerned about the impact on local officials of U.S. overt and covert supply operations being run through El Salvador.[55] They discussed the session at Ilopango earlier in the day and the resupply operation in general. Although Rodriguez did not sit in on the meeting, he told the ambassador shortly afterward he probably would be leaving El Salvador because of qualms—"a sixth feeling," as he put it—about the operation. [56]

Rodriguez soon traveled to Washington, D.C., to see Bush. First, he met with Donald Gregg, Bush's national security advisor and Rodriguez's close friend from their CIA days. The scheduling memorandum for the meetings prepared by Gregg's secretary described the purpose as "to brief the Vice President on the status of the war in El Salvador and resupply of the Contras." Gregg later claimed the Contra reference was a mistake, and it might have been meant to read "resupply of the copters," a reference to Rodriguez's helicopter operations in El Salvador. But testimony by Gregg's secretary and his deputy, Col. Samuel J. Watson III, directly contradicted him.[57]

Controversy arose later over whether Bush or his staff knew about the illicit Contra program. The improbability of Gregg's explanation for the scheduling memo affected his credibility on the question, as did his denials he was aware of Rodriguez's support role at Ilopango or that he and the vice president ever focused on the topic of the Contras. Among other evidence, two handwritten notes from Gregg to Bush in February–March 1986 indicated otherwise. One of the notes, recorded in a February 4 memorandum from Watson dealing with logistical problems the Contras were facing, read: "Felix agrees with this." Abrams also recalled he approached Gregg directly in the first half of 1986 to pass on his concern that Rodriguez was talking too much about his connection to the vice president.[58]

None of those in attendance at the May 1 meeting with Bush testified that the Contras were discussed, even though Rodriguez requested the appointment reportedly because of his disaffection with the resupply operation. Instead, they maintained, Rodriguez showed the vice president a photo album of his work relating to the counterinsurgency in El Salvador. As the meeting drew to a close, North suddenly arrived with Ambassador Corr in tow. North had known Rodriguez was going to see Bush and why, because Rodriguez had dropped by his office on the way and mentioned his plans to quit. Unable to change his mind, North tried to stage a preemptive maneuver before Rodriguez could make his feelings known to Bush. On cue, Corr sang Rodriguez's praises to the vice president and expressed the hope he would keep up the good work. The ploy evidently worked. Rodriguez, abashed, decided to return to Ilopango.

The first quarter of 1986 was a transitional phase for the resupply program. Given the sheer scope and nature of North's assignment, it is no surprise as soon as he and the Enterprise crossed one major hurdle, another loomed. Just as the aerial operation was about to become a functioning concern (after a few more tweaks and personnel adjustments), cracks began to appear in the edifice that posed a threat to operational security. The Rodriguez case—which North mistakenly thought he had solved—was one of them. As summer approached, media, congressional, and government inquiries inched closer to the Contra program, forcing North and Secord to spend more time plugging holes in the structure. In the final weeks of its existence they took increasingly extreme—even bizarre—steps not only to keep the Contras afloat but to protect the operation and its prime movers from public and legal scrutiny.

10

Road to Tehran

After the February 1986 meeting with Iranians in Frankfurt, most of the participating U.S. officials favored pressing ahead with the Iran initiative. There still seemed sufficient prospect of breaking through to Iranians at senior levels to justify overlooking the growing list of prior disappointments. Particularly tantalizing was the plan to make a covert visit to the Islamic Republic. Concerns still ran high about the existing intermediaries. One CIA officer believed Manucher Ghorbanifar's performance at Frankfurt proved him every bit the liar the agency had warned. But he managed to stay in the game by deftly playing on the wishful thinking of Reagan advisors and their desire to fulfill the president's wishes regarding the hostages. Oliver North, of course, had the added motivation of knowing the arms sales would generate more unaccountable funds for the Contras and perhaps other off-the-books operations.

Separation Anxiety

Doubts circulated, meanwhile, among the Israelis and Iranians. Amiram Nir suspected the CIA wanted to keep the Israelis away from the planned meeting on Kish Island and even to eliminate them from the initiative altogether. He convinced Prime Minister Shimon Peres to write a personal letter to Ronald Reagan reminding him of the importance Israel attached both to the upcoming meeting and to the related matter of freeing two Israeli soldiers recently kidnapped in Lebanon, possibly by Hezbollah forces. Nir recalled no response from Washington to the letter, but he believed it accomplished its purpose.[1] Ghorbanifar also worried about being cut out of the operation. He would have a busy month struggling to remain indispensable.

Ghorbanifar made his concerns known as early as March 7, when he met with North, Tom Twetten, and Nir in Paris to pass along new demands from Tehran. The Iranian complained to the group about U.S. attempts to go around him and contact other Iranians directly. The U.S. officials promised not to do so. Even North, known for his "Pollyanna optimism," thought it advisable to seek other contacts.[2] Several attempts followed, including a number by Nir, but nothing of substance materialized. In the end, key participants, including Nir and Charles

Allen of the CIA, came to the conclusion that whatever Ghorbanifar's drawbacks, he remained the only direct contact with Iran's leadership and ought to remain part of the operation.

One of the U.S. participants at the session was George Cave, a retired CIA operations officer and Iran expert Twetten had insisted join the team to raise the level of expertise about Iran. Cave's career had taken him undercover throughout the Persian Gulf and South Asia, but he had concentrated on Iran, where he served for a number of years and learned to speak fluent Farsi. Like Twetten and other CIA officers, Cave was unhappy to be brought into the operation—not because he opposed opening contacts with the Islamic Republic but because of Ghorbanifar's role in the operation. He approached CIA Director William Casey personally with his objections in early March but was told simply, "Well, George, do what you can to make it work—the president is obsessed with getting the hostages out."[3] For several months, Cave was a crucial asset for the U.S. side, using his deep familiarity with Iran and his language skills to become familiar with the Iranian representatives and their goals and to provide some authoritative guidance on how to proceed. Cave became convinced the Iranians involved in the arms deals wanted to go beyond weapons to larger strategic goals. Ironically, key U.S. players either did not share that goal or played their hand in ways that undermined the possibility of achieving it.

The Paris meeting in early March raised other issues as well. Ghorbanifar started the discussion off on a down note by reporting that the intelligence Washington had provided in Frankfurt had been extremely poor. He could not guarantee a date for the anticipated meeting on Kish Island, although he set March 20 as a target. Furthermore, he said the currency of the deals would have to change—instead of TOW missiles, the Iranians now wanted spare parts for HAWK missiles. He explained that the Iranian Army had been brought in to establish a clearer picture of the country's needs for U.S. equipment. Up to that point, he said, the army leadership had been frozen out of the secret operation. The U.S. side seemed pleased at this. North chose not to complain about yet another change in Iran's demands. Instead, he told Ghorbanifar this was actually an improvement because it could be argued the requested equipment was more defensive in nature and would therefore be more palatable to the U.S. government.[4] Finally, and possibly of greatest interest to North, Ghorbanifar suggested profits from the deals could be used to aid the rebels in Afghanistan—or in Nicaragua.[5]

Meanwhile, plans for a meeting between U.S. and Iranian officials seemed to move ahead fitfully. In early April, Ghorbanifar came to Washington, D.C., to meet with North along with Twetten, Allen, and Cave. In the days leading up to his visit, Ghorbanifar had once again vented his concerns to Allen that he might soon be removed from the program. North had invited the Iranian in order to reassure him otherwise. He had even promised to let him add as his commission for the upcoming spare parts deal "whatever he thinks right." Feeling more comfortable, Ghorbanifar discussed aspects of the pending deal. The U.S. team did not discourage the request for HAWK parts, asserting only the need to determine what was available from U.S. inventories. They insisted, however, all the hostages be released before any equipment changed hands. In addition to the HAWK spares, the prospect of more TOWs for sale came up, including the notion some of them would go to the Afghan resistance. The group also discussed the factional disputes taking place in Iran and Ghorbanifar's purported efforts to get members of the three political "lines," as spelled out in Adnan Khashoggi's earlier memo, to work together—or at least not to sabotage the effort.[6] He made specific reference to the problem of Prime Minister Mir-Hossein Mousavi, who deeply distrusted Washington but who remained a central figure. Finally, Ghorbanifar noted President Ali Khomeini intended to issue a fatwa against terrorism before the planned U.S. visit to Iran.

All in all, North believed the conversation in Washington, D.C., had gone well. Ghorbanifar seemed assuaged about his continuing role and, encouragingly, appeared prepared to move ahead toward a meeting in Iran—now to be held in Tehran, not Kish. Meanwhile, the two sides had also broached the idea of a preparatory trip to Iran by North and Cave in order to pave the way for a higher-level visit. However, John Poindexter quashed the plan on the grounds it posed too great a physical danger to the U.S. participants, more than would be the case if a higher-ranking figure such as Robert McFarlane were part of the delegation. Casey reportedly supported Poindexter, but most of the team saw it as a significant mistake because it meant the main meeting would take place without adequate planning or a clear understanding by either side of what to expect.[7]

Ramping Up the Diversion

One of the questions now troubling North was Ghorbanifar's ability to obtain the necessary funding for the next planned arms transaction. Both Allen and Cave had gotten signals the Iranian was having financial problems that might affect his ability to make the deposits on time. North pressed Nir to make sure Ghorbanifar came through as quickly as possible. Nir spent much of the rest of April trying to firm up the arrangements.

The financial situation was important for reasons beyond the arms-for-hostages deals. Both Nir and North had other purposes in mind for how to make use of the payments generated from Iran, and both therefore had reason to inflate those payments. North first established a price to be paid to the CIA for the spares. This amounted to $4.337 million, including shipping and handling. (An additional amount of just more than $1 million was to cover the transfer of 508 TOW missiles from U.S. stocks to Israel to replace the missiles sent to Iran earlier.) However, the price for spares North passed to Nir for transmission to Iran was $10,951,035, supplemented shortly afterward by the addition of several previously unavailable parts, leading to a total demanded from Iran of $13,415,876. The two decided simply to round up to an even $15 million, a hike by a factor of more than 3.5.[8]

The principal purpose for North raising the prices so dramatically was to provide continued financing for the Contras. The idea was not new, of course, but Ghorbanifar had been reminding North of it regularly as a way to boost his interest in the arms deals. North formally laid out his plan to divert significant funds to the insurgents in a memo to Poindexter in early April, just after the Washington, D.C., meeting with Ghorbanifar. Known later simply as the "diversion memo," the document suggested allocating the "residual funds" in two ways: to pay $2 million for replacement TOW missiles for Israel because the Israelis had taken missiles out of their own inventories to transfer to Iran in August 1985 and to use $12 million to "purchase critically needed supplies for the Nicaraguan Democratic Resistance Forces. This material is essential . . . to 'bridge' the period between now and when Congressionally-approved lethal assistance . . . can be delivered."[9]

The plan was almost certainly illegal, not to say unconstitutional. It not only blurred the distinctions between a U.S. government–sponsored covert program and a private financial deal—commingling private and government funds in the process—it also appeared to run directly against constitutional prohibitions barring government officials from using funds for purposes specifically disallowed by Congress.[10] To North, however, it was simply a "neat idea."[11] This issue generated the most intense controversy of the entire scandal, although it turned out to be only one of a number of schemes by administration officials to get funds above congressionally approved limits to the Contras.

During their discussions in 1985, North and Nir had come up with plans for a series of covert operations against terrorist targets in the Middle East using off-the-books funds they could control. North made reference to some of these schemes in his notebooks as early as November 1985. The plans involved propaganda, intelligence-gathering, and hostage recovery efforts, but, according to North, they never got any further. North testified he had discussed these and other ideas with Casey and gotten approval to consider them. They fit with the concept he credited to Casey of creating a "self-sustaining operation . . . something you could pull off the shelf" that could get around the need for congressional (i.e., accountable) funding.[12] They created added incentives for North to push ahead with further arms deals with Iran.

In the Loop

After the details were finally in place, the president's aides informed him that within days McFarlane would be traveling to Tehran. The vice president also knew McFarlane's trip was in the offing. At the beginning of April, George Bush made a special request. Knowing the repercussions for the mission if it were discovered, he asked Poindexter whether it would be possible to coordinate the Tehran visit with his own upcoming trip to the Middle East. "If we can manage it," Poindexter wrote to North, "the VP would appreciate it if the Iran trip did not take place until he leaves Saudi Arabia. If that screws up planning too much, then he will understand that we can't do it."[13]

Reagan's two top foreign policy aides also understood what was happening despite their later denials. Secretary of State George Shultz received briefings from Poindexter as well as from his own aides at key moments during spring and early summer 1986. When Ghorbanifar visited Washington, D.C., in April, Shultz spoke to Poindexter, then reported on the conversation to his close advisors: "*Polecat VI* Money man in town w $ to pay for TOWS. If he pays, they'll set the McF mtg. During that mtg our hostg supposed to be released. I [Shultz] sd this all has me horrified. Region petrified that Iran will win + we are helping them. He [Poindexter] said TOWS are defensive wpns. I sd 'so's yr old man.'"[14]

In May, Shultz told the national security advisor, "This is wrong + illegal + Pres is way overexposed."[15] But according to Poindexter, Shultz later reviewed and cleared McFarlane's talking points for the visit.[16] The secretary of state and his aides also had access to highly secret electronic intercepts of Iranian communications conducted by the National Security Agency (NSA). NSA intercepts are considered so sensitive their very existence is treated as classified information, and the word "intercept" is usually blacked out in the public record on Iran-Contra. Although the NSC staff tried to keep Shultz off the distribution list, he and his aides continued to receive reports based on intercepts through Defense Department and other State Department officials.[17]

In early June, Shultz's close aides also received an unusual written warning. The State Department's coordinator for counterterrorism, Robert B. Oakley, took it upon himself to alert Nicholas Platt, the State Department's executive secretary and Shultz's special assistant, about the "latest NSC effort to obtain the release of US hostages." Oakley acknowledged that what he personally knew was "circumstantial" and based on "common sense," but "when put together with other information" acquired over the previous two weeks, including by State Department senior officers Michael Armacost and Arnold Raphel, it left "no doubt" NSC staff activities "during the last ten days in May" were in "direct blatant violation of basic hostage policy" and "equally in violation of both the policy and the law on arms transfers to certain countries." As a result, the

NSC effort carried "explosive domestic political and foreign policy implications." Oakley added, "Too many people strongly suspect or know at least part of what is going on, and are badly upset by it," which made it a high likelihood that ultimately the operation would be leaked.[18]

The State Department was already hearing complaints from a close foreign ally. Oakley wrote his memo after a visit by British prime minister Margaret Thatcher's national security advisor, who traveled to Washington, D.C., specifically to discuss "what we were doing with respect to Iran. . . . They had stuck their necks out to support us and felt let down by what appeared to be a change in our terrorist and Iran policy." Oakley's growing unease about what he knew North was up to regarding Iran—and North and Elliott Abrams with regard to the Contra supply operations—was so great it led him to retire early from the State Department, just weeks before the affair exploded.[19]

As for Secretary of Defense Caspar Weinberger, he too received regular reports on the initiative during 1986. Despite his objections, he followed the president's orders in sending three shipments of arms to Iran. Although McFarlane ordered the NSA to exclude him from the recipients' list for relevant intercepts, the secretary of defense eventually interceded directly with NSA Director Lt. Gen. William Odom. Weinberger's military assistant, Colin Powell, recalls the secretary asked him to "call General Odom and remind him who he works for. . . . We straightened that matter out in a hurry," Powell boasted.[20] Weinberger's notes and the independent counsel's report cite several of these documents, which spell out details of McFarlane's mission, including references to "240 types of spare parts" that "would be available when the delegation arrives" in Tehran.[21] Weinberger continued to pick up important details of the arms-for-hostages deals throughout the year.

Making Plans for Tehran

As the spring wore on, the ups and downs of hammering out the arrangements for the Tehran mission continued. One central element for North and Nir was how much to charge for the HAWK parts. There was no question in their minds they wanted to get as big a profit margin as they could so unaccountable funding would be available for their other projects. North had made mention in his notes of the " need to know residuals" on the transactions, including "how much is left for use by Israelis."[22] To Nir fell the responsibility for haggling with Ghorbanifar, who had his own personal interest in price margins. The two met and talked several times during April and May, finally arriving at a total package of $15 million.

They could not agree, however, on how to coordinate the timing of payments versus release of hostages. As the arms initiative moved into 1986, Poindexter started to insist on getting hostages out before shipping arms to Tehran. "I want several points made clear to them," he wrote to North in mid-April. "There are not to be any parts delivered until all the hostages are free in accordance with the plan that you laid out for me before. None of this half shipment before any are released crap. It is either all or nothing."[23]

The U.S. Customs Sting Operation

In late April, one more bizarre episode occurred. For some time, the U.S. Customs Service had been tracking a group of arms dealers suspected of planning an illegal weapons trade with Iran. A principal figure was Cyrus Hashemi, a well-known wheeler-dealer who had contacted Casey more than once to try to gain his support for backdoor deals with Tehran. Also involved was Samuel Evans, an attorney working for Khashoggi. Several Israeli individuals were part of the web, among them a retired high-ranking general, Avraham Bar-Am. The case involved a plan to sell up to $2.5 billion of embargoed, high-tech Western armaments, including thousands of TOW missiles and some HAWK missile batteries.

As part of the sting operation, Ghorbanifar too was arrested, although Swiss authorities in Geneva released him after only a day. The case underscored Iran's extensive attempts to obtain arms from any available source. It also offered insights into the tight connections between players in the international arms market. North's colleagues reacted to the sting by putting their own operation "on ice" temporarily, but they claimed later not to be surprised Ghorbanifar had other deals in the works. The presumed illegality of those deals did little to sway them against their colleague.[24]

Staying Focused

The U.S. side worked hard to keep the momentum going. North urged Nir to stay on Ghorbanifar's case as far as pricing was concerned. Allen and Cave were also in regular contact with the Iranian, alternately pressing him to move forward and reassuring him his role in the initiative was not in danger. The U.S. officials also tried to impress the Tehran regime itself with warnings, via Ghorbanifar, about the current unsettled world picture. In particular, they warned the Soviet threat that some of the weapons were supposedly intended to counter was growing steadily. But sometimes world events overwhelmed even their own plans. Early on April 15, U.S. warplanes bombed a series of targets in Libya, including Muammar Qaddafi's quarters, in what was billed as a preemptive strike to deter Libyan terrorism. The attack added yet another obstacle to the initiative, in part because Poindexter and North were kept busy with the planning and execution of the raid.[25]

Progress of a kind occurred at meetings in London on May 6–7 between North, Cave, Nir, and Ghorbanifar. The gathering was a compromise on the question of whether to have a preparatory meeting before McFarlane's visit to Tehran. Instead of traveling to Iran, North apparently suggested they simply hook up with Mohsen Kangarlou by telephone from London. Cave was the designated interlocutor with Kangarlou, discussing some of the strategic aspects of the mission as well as logistics. While in London, the U.S. officials also went over prices and availability of spare parts with Ghorbanifar. North's notes reflect a breakdown of HAWK parts, some of which could not be found and others that could not be identified from the Iranians' list; radars; and the amounts to be charged. The total bill for Ghorbanifar and the Iranians was $23,663,911. Whether or not Ghorbanifar knew this was millions of dollars more than the items cost Washington, he went along. (North's proposed charge to the CIA for the equipment was just $12,688,173.)[26]

Cave's conversation with Kangarlou centered on how to coordinate the handover of hostages and equipment. Kangarlou insisted on having all the spare parts arrive at the same time as the U.S. delegation. It is uncertain whether Cave was clear on Poindexter's instructions to North to make sure no parts exchanged hands before all the hostages were released. But he seems to have taken some initiative with the Iranian. When Kangarlou demanded the U.S. group bring all the spares with it, Cave told him, "We can't do that." The Iranian was unmoved. "And [so] we haggled, typical, like you are buying a rug," Cave recalled. Finally, Cave consented to bring a small cargo load, or "what we can carry with us on the one plane, given the fuel, which would be about one pallet." Kangarlou agreed. This of course went directly against Poindexter's orders and represented yet another step back from earlier U.S. demands. What was more, Kangarlou apparently did not even promise all the hostages in return, only that "they would make an effort to release" them after the U.S. officials were in Tehran.[27] This vague understanding raised major complications during the upcoming negotiations.

Mobilizing the Finances

Nevertheless, after the London meeting, North wrote an optimistic note to Poindexter: "I believe we have succeeded. Deposit being made tomorrow (today is a bank holiday in Switzerland). Release of hostages set for 19 May in sequence you have specified. Specific date to be determined by how quickly we can assemble requisite parts. Thank God—he answers prayers. V/R, North."[28]

North's prediction of when deposits would be made turned out to be premature. Ghorbanifar, it seems, was having problems coming up with the finances for the transfer. As before, he turned to Khashoggi, but the Saudi financier was also having "certain liquidity problems." Under pressure from North to speed things up, Nir had joined Khashoggi in trying to get a British businessman named Tiny Rowlands to help underwrite the operation as a commercial venture. They described the deal as part of a much broader undertaking involving many other investors and including not just arms but grain. Moreover, they assured Rowlands the operation had White House approval. Rowlands turned them down, forcing Khashoggi to look elsewhere.[29] Eventually, he found a willing Arab source named Oussama Lababidi and further support from a Cayman Islands–based concern, Vertex International, backed by two Canadian investors, Ernest Walter Miller and Donald Fraser.[30] With $5 million from the former and $10 million from the latter, Ghorbanifar, through Khashoggi, was finally able to make the necessary deposits into Richard Secord's Lake Resources account on May 14 and 16. Not altogether convinced the operation would be a success, Khashoggi reportedly took out a $22 million life insurance policy on Ghorbanifar. He never cashed it in, but his instincts were accurate, because Ghorbanifar was never able to fully repay the bridge loan, leading to major complications for the program when Khashoggi's investors began to demand repayment.

Arriving in Tehran

With the finances finally arranged, the wheels started to turn more quickly. In short order, the spare parts, along with 508 TOW missiles owed to Israel, were moved from a secret U.S. military facility to Kelly Air Force Base in San Antonio, Texas. From there, they were loaded onto two commercial Boeing 707s and flown to Israel, arriving on May 23 and 24. Most of the U.S. delegation—McFarlane, Cave, NSC Middle East expert Howard Teicher,[31] and a CIA communications specialist—set off by chartered executive jet to Ramstein Air Force Base in Germany, then by a CIA proprietary airline, St. Lucia Airways, to a military airfield near Tel Aviv, arriving early on May 23. North and Nir met them there. The group rested for a day before setting off for Tehran.

The delegation traveled under assumed names using false Irish passports—"as if those would fool anyone," Secord noted. McFarlane went as Sean Devlin, Cave as "O'Neil," Teicher as "McGann," and Nir as "Miller." The facts about North are hazy: he went either as "Goode" (his usual nom de guerre) or, as he writes in his memoir, "John Clancy." North also claims Casey gave him a "strip of six white, triangular pills sealed in a plastic wrapper," and told him, "You may need them if things get bad." Cave, the retired CIA operative, did not remember anyone being issued suicide pills, although McFarlane acknowledges he brought with him a bottle of Valium, just in case.[32]

North also came bearing gifts for the Iranians, including six Blackhawk .357 magnum handguns in presentation boxes. While in Tel Aviv, he made a special trip with Nir to a kosher bakery to pick up a cake to deliver in Tehran. North claims in his memoir the cake was for Ghorbanifar's "aging and widowed" mother, but his account is unconvincing. Later reports described the pastry as either in the shape of a key or with a key on top of it—a symbol of the desire to unlock the U.S.-Iranian relationship. Either way, the message was entirely lost on the Iranians. "Nobody knew why they sent a cake," a former Iranian Foreign Ministry official said. "If it came [all the way] from the U.S., it wouldn't be any good anymore!" In the end, members of the Islamic Revolutionary Guard Corps (IRGC) at the airport consumed it.[33]

The delegation finally arrived in Tehran at 8:30 on Sunday morning, May 25, after a flight that took them from Israel south over the Red Sea, around the Arabian Peninsula, and back north over the Persian Gulf. To their surprise, and to McFarlane's indignation, no Iranian officials were on site to meet them. At first the Iranians claimed the delegation had come early and wasn't expected, but McFarlane, already suspicious, was not buying the story. He had been led to believe he might be met by no less a figure than Speaker of the Majles Akbar Hashemi Rafsanjani. Instead, only Ghorbanifar and Kangarlou finally appeared on the scene after the party had spent two hours "cooling our heels."

The delays did not end there. Because they had arrived in the middle of the Muslim fasting month of Ramadan, the visitors were told they would not have their first meeting until evening. In the meantime, they were driven north through the city to the former Hilton Hotel, now known as the *Istiqlal,* or "Independence," where they had the entire top floor set aside for them for security reasons. (Rafsanjani commented later: "We respected them and treated them with hospitality" including putting them up at "our best hotel.")[34] While at the airport, Ghorbanifar had assured them everything was going well, and the Iranians had already sent an envoy to Lebanon to see about the hostages. But at the hotel, he passed on the unsettling news the group might not have their promised meeting with high-ranking Iranians after all.

Opening Round

The first real session took place at 5:15 that afternoon. Along with Kangarlou, two other Iranian officials attended. One was introduced as Ali Samii, who had also taken part in meetings earlier in the year in Germany but whose real name was Fereidun Mehdinejad. "Samii" was either the head or deputy head of intelligence for the IRGC. The other Iranian was presented as First Deputy Prime Minister Mustafavi.[35] Cave believed all the Iranians used cover names (as, of course, did each member of the McFarlane delegation). Samii is referred to in official U.S. accounts as an "intelligence officer," the "Monster"—for his intransigence during the Tehran meetings—and the "Engine" because, in Albert Hakim's words, "he was really the man behind the whole initiative as far as Iran was concerned." Cave learned for the first time that Samii had an intelligence connection when Ghorbanifar told him during a conversation in the hotel corridor.[36]

The meeting began with McFarlane and Mustafavi exchanging general remarks, including about the state of U.S.-Iranian relations. McFarlane tried to assure his hosts of U.S. goodwill: "I'd like to stress something at the beginning. Obviously we've had disagreements over the past eight years. But the U.S. recognizes that Iran is a sovereign power and we should deal on the basis of mutual respect, not intimidation." Although Mustafavi averred this was "not the time to discuss what went wrong over [the] past five years," he could not help commenting, as Cave put it later, the United States "must do more to atone for its sins." The talks quickly degenerated into a testy back-and-forth over the unexpectedly small number of spare parts the group had brought and what Iran was going to do to get the hostages out of Lebanon. Mustafavi admonished McFarlane, "We were told that one-half of the equipment would be brought with McFarlane. You did not bring one-half. This behavior raises doubts about what can be accomplished." McFarlane shot back, "I have come from [the] U.S.A. You are not dealing with Iraq. I did not have to bring anything. We can leave now!" Shortly thereafter, at 7:00 p.m., the conversation ended. Cave later termed the session "hostile." The only agreement reached was the U.S. contingent would prepare an agenda for the next meetings. It was already apparent neither side had done the preparations necessary for serious talks.[37]

Unbeknownst to the visiting group, their hosts briefed their superiors after the session. "We were the guests of the prime minister [Mousavi] at the break of the [Ramadan] fast," Rafsanjani noted in his diary entry for that evening. Kangarlou and an individual named Ahmad Hamidi, identified as director of intelligence for the IRGC, "came over to report on the visiting American delegation. . . . They have brought with them one-fourth of the requested Hawk parts. Mr. McFarlane, special adviser to Reagan, and other top officials are part of the delegation. As official gifts they have brought a Colt [handgun] and some sweets, and have requested a meeting with top officials."[38]

Rafsanjani added, "We decided not to accept the gifts and refuse to meet officially, and instead to keep the negotiations secret" at a somewhat lower level. "It was also agreed to keep the negotiations limited to the issue of American hostages in Lebanon and the exchange of a few Hawk spare parts and other armaments."[39]

For most of the next day—Monday, May 26—the visitors were "left to our own devices." During one of these down periods, while sequestered on the fifteenth floor of their hotel, they engaged in what Cave called playacting. On the assumption their rooms were bugged, they pretended to have a confidential discussion about a "sensitive" briefing they wanted to give the Iranians. The goal was to persuade Tehran the Soviets had a plan to invade the country, a piece of intelligence they hoped would underscore a basic shared interest between Iran and the United States and entice Tehran to be more accommodating toward Washington. The group even made up a fictitious source to lend authority to the story—a Soviet major general North called "Vladimir" who supposedly had taken part in two invasion exercises. Then, for the benefit of Iranian "audio coverage . . . we expressed our concern out loud." It is not known whether the Iranians bought the performance.[40]

After a brief coordinating session on Monday morning, the next meeting with the Iranians took place at about 3:30 in the afternoon. In a more conciliatory mood, Mustafavi reassured his guests he was "at McFarlane's service to solve his problems. I want to remove obstacles. Sorry. I want to solve problems, misunderstandings, so they won't be repeated." He went on to assure the delegation other problems that had arisen after their arrival would also be handled—including the Iranians' insistence on searching the U.S. aircraft, seizing their (false) passports and gifts, and questioning the need for the CIA communications specialist to stay on board the plane instead of accompanying the rest of the group. McFarlane was mollified but raised the self-imposed deadline of the following evening for the conclusion of any further talks. "I must depart tomorrow night," he said. "I would like to meet with your Ministers. But I cannot if preliminary problems have not been solved [the exchange of hostages for spare parts]. I have no more to say." Mustafavi countered with the hopeful promise that "[a]t 4:00 p.m., a gentleman with higher authority will be here." McFarlane wrapped up the session by expressing his "great disappointment" Iran had not yet managed to make the necessary decisions to move the process forward and told Mustafavi from then on he intended to meet only with persons of equal rank to himself. "As I am a Minister, I expect to meet with decision-makers. Otherwise, you can work with my staff."[41]

A Cut Above

The "gentleman" Mustafavi promised was introduced as "Dr. Najafi," a leading figure in Iranian foreign relations. During the evening, the U.S. team contacted Washington to try to establish his true identity. The most likely match was Dr. Ali Hadi Najafabadi, chair of the Majles Foreign Affairs Committee and foreign policy advisor to the speaker of the Majles.[42] In his memoir, Rafsanjani referred to Najafabadi as "Dr. Hadi." During the day, Najafabadi must have spoken with Mustafavi and received word the visitors were grumbling. "I was at home," Rafsanjani wrote later, when "Dr. Hadi . . . came over." He was accompanied by another senior official, Hassan Rouhani. "Dr. Rouhani" was a member of the Supreme Defense Council and head of the national air defense force. Until recently, he had commanded the Khatam-al Anbia garrison, a hub of Iran's arms procurement system, and was therefore presumably well aware of the earlier TOW and HAWK shipments. "At their urging," Rafsanjani continued, "we decided that Dr. Hadi would negotiate with the American delegation." Najafabadi had reported McFarlane was not only unhappy but also "felt insulted higher officials did not meet with them, and that his gift was not accepted." An "incensed" McFarlane, Najafabadi went on, had protested, "If he casually went to Russia simply to buy some wildcat fur, Gorbachev would meet with him at least twice a day!"[43]

Najafabadi's entry onto the scene brightened the atmosphere. A short, bearded man in his early sixties, he was well educated, cultured, self-assured, and spoke excellent English. He struck his counterparts as a serious and well-connected emissary, even if he was, as McFarlane said, still only at "sub-minister level." Cave reported he was "several cuts above the other members of the Iranian side." As promised, McFarlane stayed aloof from the first meeting with the new intermediary, which lasted from 9:30 p.m. until 1:50 a.m. North stepped in to take his place.

Not unlike the earlier meeting with Mustafavi and McFarlane, the two sides dwelled on the history of U.S.-Iranian bilateral ties. "Our relations are dark," Najafabadi said. "They are very bad. Maybe you don't like to hear it, but I must be outspoken." He then recounted a story that gave some insight into the Iranians' reluctance to be seen as too cozy with Washington. "The first revolutionary government fell because of one meeting with Brzezinski"—a reference to a brief contact in Algiers on November 1, 1979, between Jimmy Carter's national security advisor and then prime minister Mehdi Bazargan on the anniversary of Algeria's independence. Their handshake was broadcast on Iranian television, apparently an attempt by hard-liners to embarrass Bazargan and claim he was in league with the United States. "As a government, we don't want to be crushed tomorrow," Najafabadi declared.[44]

North acknowledged, "There is a long history of unfortunate relations which cannot be forgotten in a minute." However, he insisted, "we have a great opportunity to establish a relationship between our countries. . . . Men of good will have a chance to build a bridge of confidence." Yes, certain "obstacles" had to be set aside, namely the "release of the U.S. citizens." He also returned to the fact there had been no top leaders for McFarlane to meet. One of the other Iranians present dismissed the complaint, pointing out the previous plan had been for

North to come to Tehran first in order to set an agenda: "But North did not come. . . . The last phone call did not mention Ministerial meetings. We did not agree to such meetings for McFarlane." Najafabadi stepped in to defuse the issue, saying there must have been a "misunderstanding," and in any event the Iranians were not prepared for such high-level talks. "When we accepted his [McFarlane's] visit, it did not mean a direct dialogue would occur on the spot. It is too early at this stage." Shortly, Najafabadi brought the meeting to a close, agreeing to continue at 10:00 the next morning without any Iranian technical experts. "Let us keep it political," he suggested.[45]

Najafabadi's appearance helped to buck up McFarlane's spirits. After the affronts he felt he had endured, the impression Najafabadi left helped to put things in better perspective. What McFarlane could not be sure of was how closely Iran's leaders were following the discussions. Based on subsequent Iranian evidence, they were thoroughly engaged. According to Rafsanjani's memoirs, as soon as the delegation landed, Kangarlou notified high-ranking officials. Rafsanjani claims he put together a small group to oversee the meetings with the visitors. By Rouhani's account, President Ali Khamenei was another member of the leadership in the know about the arms deals. Rafsanjani writes that Ayatollah Khomeini himself was informed about the impending visit of the McFarlane delegation.[46]

In a coded message to Poindexter written after the meeting with Najafabadi, McFarlane gave a scornful read on the situation: "It may be best for us to try to picture what it would be like if after nuclear attack, a surviving Tatar became Vice President; a recent grad student became Secretary of State; and a bookie became the interlocutor for all discourse with foreign countries. While the principals are a cut above this level of qualification the incompetence of the Iranian government to do business requires a rethinking on our part of why there have been so many frustrating failures to deliver on their part."[47]

He explained the difficulties Iranian leaders faced in dealing with U.S. counterparts, using the Brzezinski-Bazargan meeting as an illustration. However, "today the force of events and self-interest has brought them to the point of realizing that we do have some common interests (vis-à-vis the Russians, Afghanistan and perhaps even against Iraq). But they still cannot overcome their more immediate problem of how to talk to us and stay alive." Although he told Poindexter he was heartened by the "statements, conviction and knowledgeable expression" of Najafabadi, he warned "we cannot, in my judgment, be swooned by serious dialogue without acts." He concluded the message: "We are on the way to something that can become a truly strategic gain for us at the expense of the Soviets. But it is going to be painfully slow. As we proceed we cannot be gulled by promises of what will happen tomorrow—at bottom they really are rug merchants. But little by little we can make progress because it is a matter of self-interest for both of us to do so."[48]

The next morning, May 27, at 10:00, after little sleep, North, Cave, and Teicher met again with Najafabadi and the other Iranians, who brought bad news about the U.S. hostages in Lebanon: "Our messenger in Beirut is in touch with those holding the hostages by special means. They made heavy conditions. They asked for Israel to withdraw from the Golan Heights and South Lebanon. [Antoine] Lahad must return to East Beirut, the prisoners in Kuwait must be freed, and all expenses paid for hostage-taking. They do not want money from the U.S. Iran must pay this money."[49]

Najafabadi vowed they would not agree to the new demands. "We told them these conditions must be reduced. We can't make this work. We are negotiating. We are ready to pay for humanitarian reasons. We are negotiating other conditions. We are hopeful these negotiations will succeed."[50]

At roughly this point, McFarlane, playing out his role as the senior representative, summoned Najafabadi to his suite for private discussions. The others continued to talk about financial and logistical details surrounding both the hostages and the remaining spare parts. For the next three hours, McFarlane and Najafabadi carried on what McFarlane thought was a "useful meeting on the whole." After covering a broad swath of policy issues, the conversation got down to the details of arms-for-hostages deals. Najafabadi repeated the latest demands by the hostage-holders but immediately added the Iranians agreed they were unacceptable and were negotiating over them. (On the captors' demand for expenses, McFarlane wrote to Poindexter: "How's that for chutzpah!!!")[51]

McFarlane then told his host that with the way things had developed, he saw little hope the dialogue would ever fully get off the ground. Again writing to Poindexter, McFarlane said:

I then carefully recounted how in the course of the past year, we had negotiated agreements only to have them altered at the last moment or delays imposed which had led to an extremely high level of frustration on the part of the President and that he had only reluctantly agreed to this meeting under a very clear and precise understanding of the arrangements. I then went over in detail what those arrangements were: 1. The U.S. would send a high level delegation to Tehran. They would bring with them a portion of the items they had requested and paid for (which we had done). 2. Upon our arrival, they had agreed to secure the release of the hostages promptly. 3. Upon release of the hostages to our custody, we would call forward the balance of items that had been paid for and those that had not been paid for would be dispatched as soon as payment had been received.[52]

Making a Connection Too Late

McFarlane's explication to Najafabadi marked a crucial moment. For the first time, key U.S. and Iranian representatives were speaking directly about the arms-for-hostages deals without going through the filter of Ghorbanifar and Kangarlou (or North, for that matter). The gulf between the two sides' understanding of the arrangements was finally becoming distinct: "At this point he became somewhat agitated wanting to know just who had agreed to these terms. (I fingered Gorba and [Kangarlou].) He stated that these were not the terms as he understood them. The basic difference was that they expected all deliveries to occur before any release took place. I stated firmly that while misunderstandings happen, I was confident that it had not been our side for we had two witnesses to the agreement. More importantly, however, regardless of misunderstandings, there was simply no latitude for altering the agreement at this time." McFarlane noted Najafabadi was "obviously concerned over the very real possibility that his people (Gorba and [Kangarlou]) had misled him and asked for a break to confer with his colleagues."[53] According to Cave, the U.S. side confirmed Najafabadi's suspicions when he showed them three letters Ghorbanifar had provided the Iranians along with lists of weapons. "We never agreed to anything like this," Cave told him. "Is Ghorbanifar acting as your agent?" Najafabadi asked. The answer was "No." He was only the go-between. Najafabadi was "pretty much put out," Cave recalled later.[54]

At 5:00 that afternoon, the two parties met again. The Iranians appeared to have had a breakthrough. Najafabadi reported in the intervening few hours they had managed to get the hostage-takers to cut their demands. Neither Israeli withdrawal from Golan and south Lebanon, nor Lahad's transfer to East Beirut, would be required. Furthermore, the Iranians would handle the payments for the hostages' upkeep. "The only remaining problem is Kuwait. We agreed to try to get a promise from you that they [the Dawa prisoners] would be released in the future."[55]

McFarlane acknowledged it was clear the Iranians were trying to resolve the current impasse. "I am grateful," he said. But it was too little, too late. "This spirit, if it had been present in our first encounter, would have made clear we could reach some agreement. Unfortunately, we have reached this point after a year and three efforts where we thought we had an agreement. This has affected the President's view of our ability to reach an agreement."[56] As a result, McFarlane said, the president had given firm instructions "if this fourth try did not achieve results it was pointless to pursue an ineffective dialogue." At most, he was willing to give the Iranians ten hours to come up with the hostages. Otherwise, the delegation would have to leave Tehran.

Desperation for a Deal

Najafabadi struck the U.S. team as desperate to persuade McFarlane to compromise. If he would allow the remaining spare parts to be sent "before tomorrow morning, the hostages will be free by noon." McFarlane countered the hostages should come out first, then the remaining parts would be delivered. Najafabadi, surprisingly, agreed. "OK," he said. But he added Rafsanjani would want the staffs of the two sides to work out an agreement first. McFarlane consented, but admonished any agreement would have to be approved by the leaders of both countries.[57]

For the next several hours, North and his colleagues (excluding McFarlane) feverishly drafted a six-point accord that called in the main for the United States to order the aircraft carrying the spare parts to take off from a "neutral site" at 1:00 in the morning of May 28 to arrive in Tehran at 10:00. In return, the Iranians would agree to have the hostages released by 4:00 that morning. If they failed, the aircraft would be ordered back to its base, and the delegation would immediately leave Tehran. Meeting again at 9:30 in the evening, North presented the draft to the Iranians. "McFarlane is not pleased," he said, "but he gives Iran until 0400 to consider this proposal." According to Teicher's notes, the Iranians were not happy with the proposal either. "Their faces displayed anxiety." Najafabadi asked, "How are we supposed to free the hostages by 0400?" North claimed not to understand the problem. "With McFarlane earlier today you told us they would be free by noon." Najafabadi said that had been earlier. "But it is now late." Shortly afterward, Najafabadi and McFarlane met again privately, but the meeting ended badly. According to Teicher's records, "McFarlane concludes that they're just stringing us along. He gives the order to pack and depart."[58]

Yet even then McFarlane did not completely foreclose the possibility of a deal. A flurry of meetings with the Iranians and secure communications with Washington continued late into the night, as Teicher's notes reflect:

> 12:45 Bud talks to John [Poindexter]. Advises us to hold pending discussion w/RR [Reagan].
> 1:30 JMP calls. RR says launch second plane. If no word on hostage release by 4:00, leave Tehran.
> 2:00 RCM meets [Najafabadi]. They ask for us to delay until 6. They will get answer on hostages. RCM says if they give us a time we will launch A/C [aircraft] from T.A. [Tel Aviv] so that it will land here 2 hours after hostages in U.S. custody.
> 2:20 conveyed to Washington. Maybe they're serious now.[59]

Thus, the president himself was brought into the decision-making process and personally ordered the aircraft with the remaining spare parts to take off for Tehran.[60]

By morning, with no sign of progress on the hostages, McFarlane repeated the order to depart. Shortly before 8:00 a.m., Kangarlou reappeared at the hotel with a final offer at compromise: it might be possible to free two hostages right away, but "joint action" would be needed for the other two. McFarlane's reply was curt: "You are not keeping the agreement. We are leaving." As it happened, there may have been an urgent need to get the delegation out. According to Kangarlou, somehow the visitors' cover had been blown and a mob was reported to be on its way to the hotel. Although there was some skepticism later about this, Kangarlou hurried them to their cars, then personally led the caravan down a series of back streets to the airport, avoiding the main highway through the city. When they arrived, their plane had been moved to the military side of the field, out of public view. On McFarlane's orders, Cave had already seen to it the aircraft was fully refueled.[61] Feeling more secure now, Kangarlou went back to pleading for more time, calling to members of the group even as they climbed aboard the aircraft: "Why are you leaving?" McFarlane, in frustration, admonished him to tell his superiors "this was the fourth time they had failed to honor an agreement. . . . The lack of trust will endure for a long time. An important opportunity was lost." At 8:55 a.m., the plane pulled away from the terminal, and the delegation left Iran empty-handed.[62]

Postmortem

The flight back to Tel Aviv was dispirited. Hopes had been raised to their highest point yet by the drama of the secret mission and the contact with Najafabadi, who, although not the top-rung leader they had expected, plainly had a direct line to the country's ruling circles. During the flight, the group, including Nir, engaged in a postmortem of the mission. First, the lack of a preparatory visit by North and Cave left the door wide open for misunderstandings. "They wanted to reach very big goals in a very short period of time," one of Iran's intermediaries agreed years later. "They were in such a hurry to achieve their operation . . . but they came to us with such speed that the conditions were not yet ripe in Iran for an official meeting."[63] As a result, it fell to President Reagan's personal envoy to discover firsthand how far apart the two sides really were from an agreement. Cave lamented later, "We should not have subjected a senior U.S. official to the indignities he [McFarlane] was forced to endure."[64]

Another problem was the limited amount of time available to reach agreement in Tehran. Some members of the group attributed this decision to McFarlane. On the one hand, there is no doubt about McFarlane's instructions from Poindexter, which ultimately came from the president: no exchange of equipment until all the hostages were freed. At the same time, there is some indication McFarlane felt he had some leeway but chose not to use it. Although he had threatened Najafabadi the delegation would have to leave on the night of May 27, he acknowledged in his message that afternoon to Poindexter: "Actually, I don't have to leave tonight but recognizing that we have been here for three working days and they have not produced I wanted to try to build a little fire under them."[65] McFarlane later wrote that Reagan had given him the authority to decide how to proceed in Tehran. "Bud's the one on the scene," he quotes the president as saying (via Poindexter). "Only he can judge what is best. He should do what he thinks is right."[66] Had he chosen to recommend accepting two of the hostages, or leaving part of the delegation behind to continue hammering out an agreement, as the Iranians had suggested, it seems likely the president would have quickly gone along. It is hard to argue, however, with McFarlane's contention that after so many failed bids to follow through on agreements there was little basis for trusting the Iranians would be able to come through this time, even if they had wanted to.

The group understood Iranian domestic politics were a major factor. Senior officials were locked in their own dynamic. Each presumably hoped to advance his own authority through a successful arms agreement with Washington, yet not one was willing to strike a deal alone with the Great Satan without the political cover of involving the others. The result was—and always had been throughout the initiative—decisions could not be made quickly or firmly. It did not help that the mission took place during Ramadan. Cave said it was clear the religious requirement to forgo all food and drink during daylight hours took a toll on the Iranians: "It's really bad when it's during the hot months. . . . They were pretty frazzled," especially when meetings were held before nightfall. Ghorbanifar alone among the Iranians did not observe the fast.[67]

Cave also speculated later the presence of Nir was a strong constraint on the discussions. He recalled warning that Ghorbanifar would immediately inform the Iranians that Nir was an Israeli, and he believes this was one reason they were reluctant to engage more openly.[68]

Moreover, it was finally driven home to some of the U.S. officials—although the CIA already had strong indications earlier—that the Iranians did not have full control over the hostage-takers. At the beginning of May, Allen had written to Casey that the "White House initiative to secure release of American hostages in Lebanon remains dead in the water. We surmise . . . that [name deleted] is unable to provide the assurances and to make the arrangements demanded by our side. . . . We believe that the Iranian Government has not been able to convince the holders of the hostages to release them to Iranian custody."[69]

This analysis proved correct. The exact relationship between Iran and Hezbollah was hazy to outsiders. Iran had been instrumental in creating the organization in 1982 and providing financial and military support, training, and even spiritual guidance. Iranian authorities retained ample influence through the IRGC, the embassies in Beirut and Damascus, and quasi-religious and charitable organizations such as the Martyrs' Foundation. These institutional ties were built on long-standing personal bonds and faith-based loyalties between clerical figures in both countries. Iranian officials had formal attachments to Hezbollah's main decision-making bodies, and available evidence points to Iran's complicity in some of Hezbollah's most notorious acts, including the 1983 Beirut bombings as well as a handful of hostage-taking episodes. But Hezbollah operatives were also capable of acting without Iran's approval and, according to firsthand Western accounts, bristled at being too closely identified with Tehran.[70] Several violent incidents during this period came about because of Lebanese political conditions, rivalries between local Shiite groups, and even over personal reasons that had no relationship to Iran's strategic objectives for the region. A case in point, although this was not apparent to most observers at the time, was Imad Mughniyah's kidnapping of U.S. hostages to pressure Kuwait to release the Dawa prisoners. Mughniyah appeared to pay little heed to Iran's standpoint on the matter.[71]

The bonds between Tehran and Hezbollah were looser than U.S. officials assumed before they undertook their secret mission.[72] Cave recalled that upon arriving in Tehran, "The first thing that struck me was that they said, 'We've sent people to talk to them.' . . . Why not just use the telephone?" he wondered.[73] Later he was more definitive: "Hezbollah certainly wasn't under Iranian control."[74] As the official Israeli account put it gently, Washington's belief Iran had the power to free the hostages in a matter of hours "may have been excessive. It was possible that the channels of communication and the method of exerting pressure required more time."[75]

Another factor was the unreliability of the intermediaries. The Tehran mission exposed how much harm Ghorbanifar had caused. Until then, doubts about him had always been overcome by his evident access to authoritative circles in Iran. But Najafabadi's pained reaction at the realization Ghorbanifar had strung the Iranians along as well was a clear sign to those open to recognizing it. Asked by a congressional investigator whether he was surprised Ghorbanifar was "telling each side what it wanted to hear," given he "couldn't pass a lie detector test on his own name," North answered: "Not at all. But, the level of deception in this particular case was immense."[76] Long after the initiative had collapsed, McFarlane came to similar conclusions about his own subordinate, North. "In fact," he wrote in his memoir, "the collapse of this entire mission was due to lies and deceptions on the part of both North and Ghorbanifar. At the time, however, I was willing to believe that the perfidy was all on the Iranian's part."[77]

Finally, the mission itself was held hostage to the years of abiding distrust and enmity built up between the United States and Iran. Virtually every conversation in Tehran had included lengthy discourses by the Iranians on U.S. misdeeds before and since the 1979 revolution. The Iranian intermediaries professed surprise the delegation had actually shown up, something they said the leadership had not fully expected. Among the U.S. officials, the ill will directed against either the government or the middlemen made itself apparent in the disparaging banter of the communications traffic—whether in McFarlane's take on the general level of incompetence in the country, his comment "at bottom they really are rug merchants," or even Cave's wisecrack that one of the Iranian official's "breath could curl rhino hide."[78] Adding to the mutual suspicion, of course, was the experience of the previous phases of the arms-for-hostages initiative, in which each side felt abused by the other. At the heart of the frustration from the beginning was the lack of clarity in either camp over what the other's true goals were: did they truly want to improve relations in the long term, or were they mainly interested in the short-term prize of weapons and hostages?

Informing the President

President Reagan had kept himself apprised about the mission, speaking personally to McFarlane at least twice while the delegation was in Tehran. His diary entries depict McFarlane as a tough-talking envoy telling the Iranians "no dice" to their "outrageous demands." The former national security advisor had speculated to the president Tehran was "conscious of the Soviet forces on their border [and] their own lack of competence" and "want a long term relationship with us [and] this could be what's behind their negotiations. Now we wait some more." But on May 28, Reagan learned it was all over. "It seems the rug merchants said the Hisballah would only agree to 2 hostages," he wrote. "Bud told them to shove it, went to the airport [and] left for Tel Aviv."[79]

At 9:30 the next morning, McFarlane briefed the president face-to-face in the Oval Office on the failed mission. Bush, Poindexter, and Donald Regan attended along with North and Teicher. During the ten-minute session, McFarlane's message was mostly, but not entirely, negative. Acknowledging that "we did not succeed in gaining the hostages' release," he recommended shutting down the initiative because of the politically uncertain state of play inside Iran and the lack of a competent government. But he also offered the view that the Iranians had a recognized strategic interest in ties with the United States. He added, "They will be back in touch with us. . . . A lot may be possible. . . . You have begun to open the door to these people."[80]

In the end, the president acknowledged the outcome "was a heartbreaking disappointment for all of us." Characteristically, he gave no outward sign to those in the Oval Office of where he stood on the deals. When he did not visibly react, McFarlane recalled, "I left, and that's the last I heard about it."[81]

11

Meltdown

Spring and summer 1986 were frenetic for the Contra program. Good news came in the form of greater success in ferrying supplies to rebels in the field. Even more importantly, the House passed a $100 million aid package, reversing two years of rejection by that body. By this time, most of the Reagan administration's top officials were intent on finding ways to keep the insurgency viable. Delays in the appropriation of the House package meant resources were still badly needed for the short term. The National Security Planning Group (NSPG) debated increasingly outlandish ideas. State Department officials openly pursued third-country financing (after the enactment of authorizing legislation), but they proved just as bungling as some of Oliver North's antics and in the end managed to cross lines of propriety as well. Notes of high-level meetings show the president, far from being detached and apathetic, was a driving force in proposing more aggressive tactics on the rebels' behalf.

For North, the positive developments could not keep pace with setbacks. Conflicts with Felix Rodriguez, mishaps with Contra supply flights, and a growing number of intrusive outside inquiries created huge pressure on the self-described "slightly confused Marine," who eventually showed signs of buckling. He grew increasingly uncompromising, to the point of ruthlessness, in his dealings with adversaries, from private activists targeting him in a lawsuit to the new Costa Rican president. He confronted a growing number of official inquiries with deception and even contempt, leading his former superior, Robert McFarlane, to worry about his mental state. Finally, he engaged in truly reckless behavior in connection with his personal finances that would come back to hurt him legally.

In the end, all the extraordinary efforts to keep the resupply operation afloat were rendered moot by a fluke shot from a Nicaraguan soldier that brought down the Enterprise's cargo plane and with it the entire off-the-books structure.

The NSPG Discusses Funding

On May 16, the Contadora Group met in Panama to continue its three-year effort to produce a peace treaty acceptable to the countries of Central America. On the same day, Ronald Reagan and his senior foreign policy advisors gathered to review the state of play in Nicaragua, one of the main flashpoints the Contadora members hoped to address.[1] Driving the NSPG discussion was how to find financial aid for the Contras. The Contadora process and the question of U.S. assistance for the rebels were intertwined. Secretary of Defense Caspar Weinberger made this clear, arguing the United States needed to "put some brakes on" Contadora because a treaty might make Congress decide there was no longer a need to fund the Contras. Secretary of State George Shultz argued the opposite—Congress would vote against assistance if members thought the administration was not serious about trying a negotiated solution. "We have to say that there is some agreement we could go along with. . . . I know that this bothers some people." The back-and-forth became heated when Shultz charged he was under attack for advocating diplomacy in Nicaragua. "In this town, there is an assault on . . . me and on the State Department for being involved in these negotiations. . . . Some would just like to see the contras achieve a military victory, but we do not have a majority vote [in Congress] for that." Weinberger was dismissive: "There is no assault going on."[2]

On the urgent need for funds there was solid consensus. In his opening briefing, CIA Director William Casey warned that although there was "positive news"—"the resistance has stepped up its activities"—it could be reversed "abruptly and dramatically in the next few months if new assistance is not available." Less than $2 million out of the $27 million humanitarian aid package remained, which would not last past July. Shultz raised the possibility of asking foreign governments to help. "We have some proposals. . . . Some people want to go to the committees to reprogram some money. My feeling is that it would be better to go to other countries and get it there." Even Weinberger agreed, although he urged going further: "Try everything. We should try every country we can find, the committees, and the people of the United States." Otherwise, the situation looked dire: "If the contras are out of business in July, we will have to fight there ourselves some day."[3]

James Baker, secretary of the U.S. Treasury, whom Shultz had invoked two years earlier in warning that soliciting foreign governments would be an impeachable offense, made the point the situation had changed. "George says we now are in a different position with respect to approaching other countries." North, seated in the circle of chairs ringing the wall, spoke up to confirm the point: "The FY-86 intelligence authorization bill permits the State Department to approach other governments for non-military aid."[4]

At one point, the discussion appeared to come close to acknowledging the tightly held NSC operation. As the group considered the possibility of approaching other countries (Casey noted the "Saudis, Israelis, South Koreans, Taiwanese all have some interest"), Reagan apparently mentioned North by name. The official notes do not reflect this. Instead, they quote the president as asking:

"What about the private groups who pay for ads for the Contras? Have they been contacted? Could they do more than ads?"[5] Alan Fiers of the CIA remembered the moment very differently. In contrast to the note taker's awkward phrasing (which wrongly makes Reagan seem unaware so-called private benefactors were already doing much more than buying advertisements), Fiers said the president asked simply: "Well, what about Ollie's people? Can't they help?" At that point, "someone at the end of the table . . . said very quickly, 'That's being worked on,' and the conversation moved on."[6]

Getting Resupply on Track

Hours after the NSPG meeting, North had good news for Poindexter: "You should be aware that the resistance support organization now has more than $6M available for immediate disbursement." Where had this windfall come from? The Iran arms sales. North himself had gotten word from Richard Secord the day before that $6.5 million, part of a larger set of deposits ($15 million from Adnan Khashoggi and $1.685 million from the Israelis) had been credited to the Enterprise's Lake Resources account.[7]

For North, the main priority was to bring the CIA back into its previous role of coordinating the Contra war. Calling it an "urgent need," he pleaded with Poindexter to push for a legislative package that would get it done. "We can only do this by going forward with the reprogramming proposal and getting the requisite authorities for CIA involvement" from Congress. "Unless we do this, we will run increasing risks of trying to manage this program from here with the attendant physical and political liabilities. . . . The more money there is . . . the more inquisitive will become people like Kerry, Barnes, Harkin, et al. While I care not a whit what they say about me, it could well become a political embarrassment for the President and you." This was standard North—aiming a calculated warning at Poindexter whose priority all along had been to protect Reagan. North also became slightly petulant: "I am not complaining . . . but we have to lift some of this onto the CIA so that I can get more than 2–3 hrs of sleep at night." Repeating his earlier point, he went on: "Much of this risk can be avoided simply by covering it with an authorized CIA program undertaken with the $15M. This is what I was about to say in the meeting today, and a point that I believe Shultz does not understand in his advocacy of Third country solicitation."[8]

In fact, Shultz had dismissed the reprogramming idea out of hand at the NSPG meeting, calling it "breathtaking in improbability." But Shultz knew nothing about the new bonanza from the Iran arms deals and evidently not much about North's covert Contra role. Otherwise, he might have seen why North was not so worried about money yet still anxious to find a way to get the CIA back into the game. As it happened, Shultz was right—the administration did not have the necessary support in Congress to win on reprogramming and therefore turned its attention to winning passage of the $100 million assistance bill.

North wanted to get the CIA back into the operation because it had simply become too much for the Enterprise's ragtag organization to handle. The past few months had been a rude awakening. Even when North had participated personally in an arms delivery, it had not been an easy thing. The fact was this was a slapdash operation, subsisting on a tiny budget and recycling shabby equipment. Something needed to be done to whip things into shape and prevent the NSPG's dire predictions from becoming reality.

One of the conclusions from the previous period had been the Enterprise needed a new flight operations manager. Richard Gadd's inability to find decent aircraft or keep them flight-ready had been a cause of growing frustration. By the end of April, Gadd was gone, replaced by Robert Dutton, a retired colonel and longtime acquaintance of Secord from his U.S. Air Force covert action days. Arriving at Secord's doorstep the day after retiring from the military, Dutton was promised a salary of $5,000 a month and handed the assignment of "basically getting the operation working. . . . When I first joined," he said later, "the aircraft were in very poor condition. . . . Because [they] weren't flying, we weren't making any deliveries."[9]

On Dutton's first day, he and Secord went over the legality of the airlift. "He basically said, 'Here is what we're doing. It's a resupply operation. It's being done at the behest of the White House. And here are some of the rules that we operate by.' . . . We discussed the Neutrality Act, and he subsequently gave me a copy of a legal opinion . . . that said, in effect, if we did not deliver people into . . . combat, if we delivered only goods, even if it was arms, that we were legal as far as the Neutrality Act."[10] Secord advised they were also within the parameters of the Arms Export Control Act (AECA) because "no arms came out of or transited the United States." Whether North's involvement was illicit was not something that occurred to Dutton because "North was operating out of the NSC. And as far as I understood, he was . . . working for the President, and I had no need to question the legality of what we were doing."[11] As for the propriety of profiting from the operation, which became a central element of the charges against Secord and Albert Hakim, there seems to have been little discussion. The assumption apparently was Secord's companies were private concerns generating a legitimate income.

In mid-May, Dutton went down to the region to inspect the Enterprise's assets. He found the planes and equipment in poor shape, as expected. The crew was a brighter story: "I found, to my pleasure, that some very highly experienced people had been hired." The manager, William Cooper, had more than 25,000 hours in the air, mostly with the defunct CIA proprietary Air America. "He had conducted these kinds of operations all his life." The number two pilot, John McRainey, had 19,000 hours of flying time. "I was very glad to have them." The maintenance crews were also a pleasant surprise—"the kinds of guys that could put together an operating aircraft with bailing wire and chewing gum."[12]

Dutton saw his first task as establishing a chain of command. Next came the challenge North and Secord had set for him—getting weapons and other supplies, including mountain leprosy medicine, to the southern front. North claimed as many as 150 recruits were signing up every day. Many of them, as Enterprise operative Rafael Quintero pointed out, were joined by families, which added the problem of feeding and clothing a growing population.[13] From North's viewpoint, money was—at least for the time being—not an issue. Neither were weapons. Between late February and late May, Tom Clines's deals with Defex in Portugal produced three shipments to Central America, putting a cache of armaments worth $1 million at the Enterprise's disposal.[14] The problem—as Joseph Fernandez, CIA station chief, reminded North at the beginning of June—was to get them to the southern forces without further delay.

Dutton was already becoming familiar with the gamut of problems facing the operation. In a memo to Secord he ticked off several deficiencies. The two planned to complain to Amalgamated Commercial Enterprises (ACE), a cutout (intermediary) Southern Air Transport (SAT) had created to provide added deniability to the purchase and maintenance of Enterprise aircraft. The failings Dutton noted included buying planes not fully checked, taking too long for repairs, and providing inadequate guidance to maintenance personnel.[15]

When Dutton got to Ilopango Air Base on the night of June 5, the aircraft seemed in good flying order, and the crew's "attitude and preparation" were "excellent." (The original British crew—hired for deniability reasons—turned out to be mostly helicopter pilots who also got into unspecified trouble with the Salvadoran military and "were asked to leave," according to Dutton.)[16] But as he reported to North two days later, "Wx [weather] and coordination problems with Joe [Fernandez] caused 24 hr slip. Also still did not have anyone at West." The lack of reliable weather reports—crucial for successful missions—was a constant difficulty for the pilots, who pleaded vainly to local CIA and U.S. Military Group (Milgroup) officials. Communications lapses were another hindrance only partly resolved by resorting to KL-43 devices. This very likely also accounted for the failure to have someone stationed at Point West ("West"), the Santa Elena airstrip, in case of emergency.

Just such an emergency cropped up on June 9, when the flight finally took place—after Dutton had returned to the United States. What might be termed structural issues were fundamentally to blame. In an attempt to keep its existence secret, the Enterprise had located the airstrip deep in the forest of western Costa Rica. Unfortunately, it happened to be near a Costa Rican government facility, which meant it was quickly discovered. According to a U.S. Army officer stationed in San José at the time, personnel at the nearby facility "would comment about the number of low level flights . . . buzzing them in the early hours of dawn," and "mysteriously disappearing" behind a hill.[17]

Its remote location also created huge logistical difficulties. Because the strip was not paved but made of packed dirt, seasonal downpours made it all but unusable for days at a time, and it required regular maintenance. Miles from serviceable roads, it took hours to reach by car and no fewer than twenty-seven river crossings, virtually ruling out access during the rainy season, which started in May or June. Crews refused to stay overnight because of bats, snakes, and other wildlife.[18]

When the June 9 flight could not locate the drop zone and ran low on fuel, the pilots decided to put their C-123 down at Santa Elena. But taxiing to the end of the runway, they went too far, and the wheels of the still-loaded aircraft sank into the wet soil. Dutton's report masked his frustration. "9 Jun—West manned, RW (runway) checked OK, security OK, launched A/C in AM. On arrival A/C became stuck in mud on R/W." Secord had to dragoon Quintero to go down and put the plane back in commission. North informed John Poindexter: "One of DEMOCRACY INC.'s airplanes is mired in the mud (it is the rainy season down there) on the secret field in Costa Rica. They hope to have it out by dawn."[19] It took an additional day before Secord could finally relay word: "All aircraft out of mud . . . Half of munitions load also back . . . and remainder will be picked up by Caribou today." Secord tried to deflect the implication that after so much time and effort the Enterprise had failed to build an adequate landing facility. "There was no way to forecast this problem. . . . Fact is the field will have limited utility during heavy rains."[20]

Politics constituted another problem. A month before the incident, Óscar Arias was inaugurated president of Costa Rica. Elliott Abrams attended the ceremony as a sign of U.S. comity, but Arias soon made it plain he did not share his predecessor's desire to accommodate Washington. He specifically disapproved of U.S. use of the airstrip. Just two weeks into his term, he summoned Fernandez to discuss the larger operation being run from Costa Rican territory, telling him, "I'm not going to permit that airstrip to be used." Fernandez replied, "I understand," asking that a civil guard contingent stand watch at the site until fuel drums could be removed. The CIA officer then informed Ambassador Lewis Tambs, who asked him to tell North the bad news. Abrams, who had known about the strip for months, was incensed at Arias, telling Fernandez, "We'll have to 'squeeze his balls . . . get tough with him.'"[21]

After promising Arias the site would be vacated, Fernandez was distressed to hear about the marooned C-123. Dutton had told North he was "holding off informing Joe," so the role of messenger fell to Quintero, who was in San

José. Fernandez recalled: "I was so upset, I was shaking. I could envision being PNGed"—declared persona non grata. "I told him to get that aircraft the hell out of Costa Rica!"[22]

Several more headaches confronted Dutton and the Enterprise as the summer went on. They ran low on money for equipment, and flights missed drop zones because of bad weather or communications or suffered mishaps like losing a wing, as happened in early August.[23] The mud incident put the lone C-123 out of commission, leaving the Enterprise with only two smaller C-7 Caribous that lacked the same cargo or fuel capacity. This meant even less efficiency with arms deliveries and more frequent complaints from Contra leaders Adolfo Calero and Enrique Bermúdez. With North's approval, Dutton arranged to purchase a replacement C-123, working directly with the president of SAT to find "another toad."[24]

Assuming all equipment was functioning properly, the procedure for making drops was a challenge in itself. Dutton described what would often happen:

> We would make arrangements with Joe [Fernandez] to contact the force that we were to drop to, we would get instructions back that they would have three bonfires. In some cases they would even give us a pattern that they were going to be laid out in. We had radio frequencies that we were going to be able to talk to the ground force and if we happen to be a little bit off they could talk us right over their heads. These were all conducted as night missions. We would fly them—these, by the way, are long missions. We are talking 7-hour, 6- and 7-hour missions—get down into the drop zone area, there would be no fires, they would fly all over the area trying to make radio contact, there would be no radio contact and it would have been rather wasteful just to throw the load out into a triple canopy jungle, so we brought the load home.[25]

By the end of June, with some tactical modifications by Dutton, the Enterprise crew managed to pull off a successful mission to the southern front, the first since April. With the lone C-123 back in the United States undergoing repairs and a replacement still forthcoming, a plan had to be prepared that would allow the Caribous to carry a load big enough to "do the people any good." That required a refueling stop, for which Dutton chose the international airport in San José. It was either a bold or desperate move given the usual concern for low profiles, but Fernandez and Col. James Steele, commander of Milgroup, were able to make the unorthodox arrangements. The Enterprise's planes typically had no tail markings and were painted with a yellow base camouflage pattern. Either the C-7s received a new paint job for the mission or Dutton was willing to risk being noticed at the mostly civilian airport. Other necessary steps included handling flight plans and tower clearances, keeping curious officials at a distance, and paying for fuel, which was strictly a cash transaction. ("The guy reached into his pocket, pulled out a wad of bills and started counting them off after we calculated what the conversion was," recalled a U.S. Army officer on the scene.)[26] Even though the scheme worked, it must not have been easy because it only occurred once more over the next two months.

Some improvisations were even more controversial. Steele objected—presciently—to the daytime missions Fernandez ordered because of the risk of enemy fire. "But we'd kind of learned our lesson on night missions," according to Dutton. "We were in a desperate situation . . . we just couldn't find the troops and they couldn't find us." Taking off before dawn to arrive over their targets "just at sun-up" was unworkable because in the rainy season fog covered the forest, producing a "sea of white instead of [a] sea of green." On the other hand, afternoon thunderstorms could reach 50,000 feet. "So we finally said, we just got to go in the daytime and hope we can catch it after the fog and before the thunderstorms build up."[27]

Keeping the Lid On

Meanwhile, the facade surrounding the NSC involvement was in danger of crumbling. Media stories in the spring simultaneously built upon and gave rise to private legal proceedings and official investigations into aspects of the Contras' operations. North and his colleagues attempted to deflect the inquiries, but succeeded mainly in compounding the difficulties by lying repeatedly to U.S. officials and engaging in other troubling acts—all under the guise of operational security, or "OPSEC."

Press accounts about secret administration doings in Central America were nothing new. As early as 1982, a *Newsweek* cover story exposed CIA-related operations, creating a credibility problem for the White House. In August 1985, House Democrats called for hearings and access to documents after similar reports surfaced, but the controversy blew over. By spring 1986, however, evidence of U.S. involvement in the Contra war was virtually impossible to keep under wraps. In April, for example, the Associated Press broke a troubling story about an ongoing investigation by the Miami U.S. attorney's office into alleged gunrunning and drug smuggling by the Contras and their U.S. backers.[28] Abrams tried to put out the fire by producing a three-page paper for Congress conceding some Contras "may have engaged" in drug activity but insisting the rebel leadership was clean.[29]

At the end of April, the *Miami Herald* ran a major story that named North as integral to the distribution of private aid to the Contras. In mid-May Poindexter sent North a PROFS note: "Be Cautious: . . . I am afraid you are letting your operational role become too public." North responded the same day: "Done."[30] Poindexter's immediate concern was North had been talking to fellow NSC staffers about his activities, but the growing number of news reports added to his unease.

At the end of May, two U.S. journalists filed a civil lawsuit against a number of individuals believed to be involved in arms and drug dealing in Central America. The main target of the suit was John Hull, the Indiana rancher and CIA asset living in Costa Rica, but it also included Secord, Clines, John Singlaub, and Calero. The journalists, Anthony Avirgan and Martha Honey, were based in Costa Rica and had been following Contra developments particularly closely since the bombing of the Edén Pastora press conference at La Penca two years earlier. (Avirgan, an ABC cameraman, had been severely wounded in the bombing.)

Soon, the press disclosures started to snowball, prompting interest by federal agencies and Congress, which in turn generated new revelations. In early June, Texas Democrat Ron Coleman introduced in the House a resolution of inquiry into "disturbing new reports that our own government officials may have deliberately violated the law" on Contra aid. The resolution raised questions specifically about whether North had set up a "sham network of intermediaries" to mask his operations. The *Miami Herald* followed with more stories about White House involvement, and CBS on June 25 aired a segment on the investigative program *West 57th Street*[31] that tracked closely with the charges in the Avirgan/ Honey suit. This brought the issues to the attention of the U.S. Customs Service, which opened an inquiry into possible Neutrality Act violations by the Enterprise.[32]

Later that summer, NSC actions came under further congressional scrutiny. Poindexter authorized North to appear before the House Intelligence Committee in early August on the assumption he would say nothing to make the operations vulnerable. "I did not authorize him to make false statements," Poindexter testified later. "I did think that he would withhold information and be evasive, frankly." Poindexter did not believe he needed to spell this out to North. "I did not micromanage him," he said. "There was no discussion then or later as to . . . how he would answer" the questions. "Obviously with hindsight," he continued, "it would have been prudent . . . to provide more detailed guidance, but that was not the manner in which I was managing and directing Colonel North at the time."[33] This extraordinarily loose supervision was part of a pattern within the administration that would only become apparent after the scandal. But Poindexter's comment about prudent conduct carried little meaning in light of his admission he counted on North to do what was necessary to cover for the operation. As with much of what transpired during the affairs, the misconduct of a subordinate official sometimes suited perfectly the objectives of his (or her) superiors—with the added advantage of being deniable. Poindexter saw his relationship with the president in very similar terms.

HARDBALL: CONFRONTING OFFICIAL INVESTIGATIONS

On at least seven occasions, North moved to suppress or mislead official investigations he believed posed the threat of disclosure either of the Contra operation or his role in it. An illuminating example was the case of Gen. José Bueso Rosa, a former Honduran military chief of staff, who had helped U.S. officials set up bases and support for the Contras. In 1984, the general had become involved in a plot to assassinate the Honduran president, Robert Suazo Córdova. Funding for the killing was to come from a $10 million cocaine deal. Indicted with several coconspirators in late 1984 in Miami, where the plan was conceived, Bueso surrendered to U.S. authorities in late 1985. At one point, it appeared North and several other U.S. officials—John Negroponte, ambassador to Honduras; Gen. Paul Gorman, head of the U.S. Southern Command; and Duane Clarridge of the CIA—might be subpoenaed to testify at the trial, which could easily have exposed the Contra program. Bueso reached a plea agreement in June 1986, however, and the subpoenas never materialized.[34]

North still had reason to worry. As he reported to Poindexter in mid-September 1986, the Honduran general had come to expect (North did not explain how) his jail sentence would be dramatically shortened, and he would be able to serve out his time in a minimum-security facility. When North discovered this might not be the case, he launched a campaign with the FBI, Justice Department, State Department, Pentagon, and CIA to try to affect the sentencing. His main concern was to prevent a disillusioned Bueso from "singing songs nobody wants to hear."[35] After several high-level meetings (at which some officials said bluntly Bueso was a terrorist and deserved his sentence), North, with help from fellow Restricted Interagency Group (RIG) member Abrams and others, managed to persuade the Justice Department to intercede and to reassign the general to a different facility.

Another instance of North's intervention in a legal case involved the lawsuit brought by journalists Avirgan and Honey, which also sparked an FBI inquiry. When federal prosecutors from Florida went down to Costa Rica in early April 1986, a shaken Rob Owen reported to North the authorities were "not only looking at possible violation of the [N]eutrality [A]ct, but at possible unauthorized use of government funds. . . . If and when I am contacted by the FBI I will not answer any questions without an attorney present. Even then, I will not answer any questions. It is the only way I can see to stem the tide. Perhaps it is time I retire from this line of work and focus on another part of the world and against another group of Godless communists."[36]

But creating a false paper trail was not enough. Secord hired a former CIA operative named Glenn Robinette, an acquaintance of Clines, to find out who was behind certain "derogatory statements" circulating about him.[37] The presumption was Avirgan, Honey, and their lawyers were working for the enemy—either the Democrats or Daniel Ortega. Owen backed up this notion. The two journalists, he advised, were "nothing more than disinformation experts, and they are after me and you."[38] North also tried to turn the FBI loose on the plaintiffs, letting drop a comment to Oliver Revell, the bureau's executive assistant director in charge of investigations, that "he thought the FBI ought to investigate those people that were bringing the suit because he thought they were probably being funded or supported by the Sandinistas." Revell declined.[39] Two years later, a judge threw out the suit for lack of evidence.[40]

FELIX REDUX

Of the many challenges North and the Enterprise faced in keeping the Contra program intact, one of the toughest remained Rodriguez. The ex-CIA agent, who had created a major nuisance in May by going over their heads to Vice President George Bush, continued to obstruct operations at Ilopango. North viewed him as a loose cannon and a threat to OPSEC; Rodriguez also jealously guarded his relationship with Salvadoran generals on the base.

Shortly after Rodriguez returned from Washington, D.C., difficulties bubbled up again. Dutton had become more familiar with "Max Gomez" as he tried to wrest control of the resupply issue. He wrote to his superiors that although things were mostly going well, "Max is [the] only problem." In addition to sowing seeds of mistrust between the Salvadoran Air Force (SAF) and the Enterprise, he was insinuating himself with key officials of Milgroup at Ilopango:

> · I was informed that Max (now a Lt Col in the SAF) has been made the deputy to Steele, by Steele, for this project. He has Steele's KL-43, a Mil Gp car and State Dep mobile radio. He now wants a $10K emergency fund that he will control. He also wants partial control of our fuel fund ($50K). He has isolated all of our people from Steele and the Gen. [Juan Rafael Bustillo] and wants it clear th[at] he will be the only liaison between our people and the Embassy or the Gen. under any reorganization, that he would not take direction from our project manager and that he would work only with the Gen. and the approval/disapproval of our mission.[41]

Dutton added: "Consideration should be given to his future benefit to Project Hope," as they sometimes called the operation. Much as North agreed with Dutton's critique, he understood Rodriguez's value. Dutton himself acknowledged afterward no one else had Rodriguez's close connections to the Salvadoran military: "If Max went, we went."[42] Still, there were too many sheriffs in town, and North sought a situation he could control.

On the same day as the House vote on Contra aid, North met with Rodriguez again. The situation was particularly sensitive because Rodriguez was in a position to scuttle what had become North's central objective—to get the CIA to take over the Enterprise. Months of frustration in trying to get the resupply program on solid footing had finally started to take its toll on North, especially as the Iran initiative absorbed more and more of his time. A revived CIA presence also made sense for Secord, who had a major financial stake in the operation that could be repaid if the agency bought him out.

Standing in the way was Rodriguez. When Dutton went to Ilopango to talk to him in early June, he described a new organizational structure for the resupply program. Given the growing heat from Congress, the FBI, and the media, the aim was to be able to assert North and Secord were no longer running the operation. (As North put it later: "For a covert operation, there sure were a lot of people who knew about it.")[43] In their ever more anxious state of mind, North and Secord even suspected Rodriguez, who had been making little secret of his distrust of the Enterprise, might be a surreptitious source for the Avirgan/Honey lawsuit.

But Rodriguez was not buying the argument. "Discussed reorganization with Cooper, Ramon and Max," Dutton reported in early June. (Cooper was the onsite operations manager for the Enterprise; Ramon was a pseudonym for Rodriguez's deputy, Luis Posada.)[44] "Max . . . did not get understanding of the concept." Worse, he "presented incorrect picture to Steele, . . . possibly others."[45] The situation called for a face-to-face session with North, who asked Rodriguez to meet him in Washington, D.C., on June 25. The participants traded mutual accusations— North that Rodriguez was violating OPSEC by making calls on open phone lines and Rodriguez that the Enterprise operated shabby equipment, a danger to the crews. When Dutton left the meeting, Rodriguez became more pointed, telling North some disreputable figures such as Clines were associated with the program, and "people are stealing here."[46] North waved off the accusations, insisting everyone was clean. He tried to keep Rodriguez inside the tent by offering him a $3,000 monthly payment to serve as "host liaison officer" at Ilopango.[47]

Rodriguez took the blandishment, but the problems did not go away. A core concern—whether originally his own or that of his local patron, Bustillo—was that the shady individuals who populated the Enterprise would try to sell the aircraft and other equipment Bustillo and Rodriguez believed belonged to the Contras and make off with the profits. In July, Rodriguez's fears led him to dispatch armed guards to surround the aircraft and keep the Enterprise crews away. "We were truly guests on this airbase," Dutton recalled. "And if anything happened that . . . made the commander [Bustillo] . . . unhappy, they would simply lock the gate."[48]

Ironically, it was Rodriguez who commandeered an Enterprise plane against instructions, causing the next crisis in the relationship. In early August, the ailing C-123 was parked in Miami awaiting repairs, but Rodriguez decided to use it to take a cargo of spare parts to Ilopango. As Fiers described the incident in a secure phone conversation with a senior field officer: "Apparently, Felix Rodriguez is . . . getting himself out of control and about to get himself and General Bustillo into . . . trouble. . . . It appears that . . . Bustillo and Felix Rodriguez took off from Miami . . . in a C-123K that did not belong to them. . . . We've got to try to get [Rodriguez] out of the Nicaraguan pot because he is really . . . muddying the waters and is going to cause us big problems just at a time when we don't need them."[49]

North decided to contact the vice president's office—specifically Bush's national security advisor. Donald Gregg had recommended Rodriguez to North as someone who could be useful in Central America. North told him, "You're the only one who can control Felix. Will you call him and find out what the hell is going on?"[50] Gregg telephoned his friend in El Salvador who asked to come to Washington, D.C., to explain the situation in person. On August 8, the two met and, according to Rodriguez, Gregg was shocked to hear about the poor state of the resupply operation, allegations of rampant overcharging, and particularly the involvement of Clines. Gregg had spent his career at the CIA and shared the view of many ex-colleagues that Clines's connection to disgraced former agent Edwin Wilson made him anathema.[51] Gregg's response was to convene a meeting a few days later of representatives from the State Department, CIA, and NSC to convey Rodriguez's concerns. Instead of reining in Rodriguez, North had only generated more negative exposure and undermined the objective of having the CIA buy out the Enterprise.[52]

As late as September 30, Rodriguez continued to direct threats at the Enterprise. North's notes that day include the following vivid description of a flight with weapons Rodriguez took to Miami ("Ralph" was Secord's associate, Quintero): "Max flew to Miami w/KC123. . . . Max told Ralph's wife he had 'trouble' today. Brought weapons in on Proj. Dem. aircraft. House is full of automatic weapons. . . . Ralph held prisoner by Max until bills paid. Ralph heard Max tell (L-26) that Bustillo ordered Salvadorans on A/C to shoot pilots who don't return to Ilo."[53]

Gregg's involvement in turn pointed to higher-level U.S. government knowledge of North's activities. Gregg's subsequent explanations were strained. He insisted Rodriguez's concerns, although serious enough to bring together other agency representatives, were not "Vice Presidential level." He also maintained that even though Rodriguez specifically indicated the Enterprise was dealing in grenades (and Gregg himself presumed other ammunition as well), the implication North was therefore involved with lethal equipment, not just humanitarian aid, did not appear to signal a problem to Gregg. "As long as the funds were private," he told investigators, "the flag of illegality did not arise in my mind at all."[54]

THE PRESSURE ON NORTH

Toward the end of his June 25 meeting with Rodriguez, North reportedly glanced at a television in his office tuned to the congressional debate on the pending Contra aid bill. As Rodriguez recalled the moment, North quipped: "Those people want me but they cannot touch me because the old man loves my ass."[55]

Although he exuded his usual brash confidence, by this point North was under enormous political pressure. Both his current and former bosses took note. McFarlane, who was dealing with North mostly on Iran, broached the subject in the first half of June in an email to Poindexter: "I'm getting very worried in Ollie's behalf. . . . Too many people are talking to reporters from the donor community and within the administration." McFarlane recommended clinical treatment. "I don't [know] what you do about it but in Ollie's interest I would get him transferred or sent to Bethesda for disability review board." There was some history behind the suggestion. "Apparently the Marine Corps has already tried to survey him once," McFarlane noted, although he gave no details.[56] Subsequent news reports disclosed that a dozen years earlier North had been hospitalized at Bethesda Naval Hospital for emotional distress, a fact that raised questions in retrospect about how he received clearance to serve on the NSC staff.[57] *Newsweek* magazine quoted sources saying he had been seen running through his neighborhood waving a .45 handgun and shouting "I'm no good! I'm no good!"[58] Despite the "major loss to the staff and contra effort" that would result, McFarlane thought it was worth removing North from the picture.[59]

Poindexter was inscrutable: "I will think about Ollie" was his only reply.[60] Yet, the subject was already on his mind. That very day he had written to North: "I still want to reduce your visibility." As noted, North had been complaining about lack of sleep and had pleaded for Poindexter to help return CIA control of the operation. The day before, he referred to himself offhandedly as "one slightly confused Marine Lt. Col."[61] By the following month, Poindexter's apprehensions became more evident. On July 15 the *Washington Times* ran an item that described North's position at the NSC as "precarious" and suggested there was concern about his having too high a profile.[62] Congressional investigators suspected Poindexter may have planted the story. A dejected North wrote to him that day, lamenting the recent CBS broadcast and the "appalling" *Washington Times* piece, noting Poindexter's "intention that I extricate myself entirely from the Nicaragua issue. . . . It probably wd be best if I were to move on as quietly, but expeditiously as possible," he wrote.[63] Poindexter was avuncular but impatient with North's melodramatic tone: "Now you are getting emotional again." In the end he relented: "I do not want you to leave and to be honest cannot afford to let you go."[64]

HEWING CLOSE TO THE LINE: NORTH AND CORRUPTION

The Enterprise generated a large supply of unaccountable cash—at least $6 million during 1985–1986. According to criminal investigators, the actual total "will never be known because of a purposeful lack of documentation."[65] North himself kept an "operational fund" in his office that he estimated was between $150,000 and $200,000 in cash and another $100,000 in blank travelers checks given him by Calero.

Questions about his use of that fund generated damaging criticism after the scandal. North said he created the account on Casey's instructions and maintained "meticulous records" in a ledger he subsequently destroyed, also on the director's orders, so as to protect identities.[66] But some of North's expenditures were unmistakably for personal use. Prosecutors identified $4,300 worth of travelers checks he cashed, sometimes under his pseudonym of William P. Goode, at stores ranging from a car tire retailer to a hosiery shop. He also used Calero's checks for a $1,000 wedding gift for Owen and a $60 loan for his secretary, Fawn Hall, to use on a beach vacation.[67] The jury at his trial accepted his explanation he was only reimbursing himself for out-of-pocket expenses, but it was hardly standard NSC practice.

North came under intense criticism for the installation of a security gate at his home in northern Virginia. In April 1986, Palestinian terrorist Abu Nidal had made a public threat against several U.S. citizens, including North, Singlaub, a Georgetown University academic named Edward Luttwak, and even the conservative Heritage Foundation. Most of those involved downplayed the incident. North chose to act on the threat. To be sure, his wife had reported disturbances while her husband was away, such as lights being shined onto their property from the road at night. North had described more peculiar events to local police—finding bomb-like devices in his mailbox, sugar in his gas tank, and the family dog poisoned.

Local police agreed to patrol more frequently, but Poindexter was less sensitive to his concerns, and the FBI told him providing security was not its mission. North therefore turned to Secord, who tapped Robinette—already involved with the surveillance of journalists Avirgan and Honey. Robinette's primary business was as a security consultant. In early June he installed a remote-controlled gate opener at the head of the family's driveway.[68]

The job cost $9,000, but North did not pay for it. Secord did. The questions that arose later were: where did the money come from (the answer was an Enterprise account), and was it an inappropriate use of funds coming from a quasi-governmental operation? North also faced skepticism about the nature of the threats. Aspects of his story were never corroborated. No bombs were retrieved from his mailbox, he failed to turn over to the FBI license plate information he claimed to have written down from suspicious cars driving by his house, and the instances of sugar in the gas tank and the poisoned pet were also never verified. Finally, there was the gate itself, made of wood, which from eyewitness descriptions offered nothing near the protection needed to thwart a determined terrorist. Revell further pointed out if a terrorist truly intended to attack, he was unlikely to advertise it beforehand.[69]

Perhaps most embarrassing for North was the disclosure he had tried to make it appear he had paid for the gate himself. Robinette recalls being surprised to receive a phone call from North after the November 1986 revelations about Iran-Contra. After a short conversation, North said, "By the way, you never sent me a bill," and asked him to do so. Robinette, whose expertise within the CIA technical services division included forging documents, prepared two invoices backdated to July 2 and September 22, 1986. A week later, North sent back two fabricated letters of his own (in the same envelope)—one dated May 18, the other October 1, 1986.

Rather than type the notes at home or print them from a computer, he drove to a retail store and used a typewriter on display. After writing the first note, he physically defaced the typewriter ball, then reused it to draft the second letter. He added a different return address, used less formal language, and signed it "Ollie" rather than his full name, which he had used in the first note. All of this was meant to imply the passage of time, including the development of a friendlier relationship with Robinette. Finally, he wrote by hand at the bottom, "Please forgive the type—I literally dropped the ball." At the congressional hearings in 1987, North owned up to most of the incident, admitting he had "tried to paper over that whole thing" and calling it the "grossest misjudgment" of his life. However, he blamed the government for not protecting him against threats to his family and himself. "I think the Government of the United States should have stepped up to it, and didn't. Whether it's because of laws or regulations, I don't know."[70]

North made equally improbable claims about buying a sport utility vehicle

(SUV) investigators suspected he had paid for with Enterprise funds. At his trial, North said he had received a "substantial" insurance settlement from an automobile accident while a midshipman at the U.S. Naval Academy, a portion of which he kept in a steel box bolted to a closet floor in his home. He said he would add to that any spare change left over in his pocket at the end of each week. Over the course of twenty years, the amount grew to "upwards of $15,000," he testified.[71] Out of that "stash," as the prosecutor called it, North said he took a little more than $8,000 to pay for a used GMC Suburban at a local dealership in early October 1985. The rest of his account was equally implausible. He had no explanation for records showing he received cash infusions from Secord on the very days he made a down payment and final payment for the SUV. He declared at first he brought only enough money to the dealership for a down payment because he had a different car in mind, but the salesman testified North had called him specifically about the Suburban several times before stopping by to see the vehicle the same day.

It also emerged that Secord and Hakim had set up a financial fund for North.[72] According to the independent counsel, the two Enterprise partners saw North was under intense pressure, including from his wife, Betsy, who they believed was unhappy with his extended absences, late hours, and the growing stress of negative media exposure. Determined to find a way to keep North engaged in the operations, they contacted Enterprise lawyer Willard Zucker in February 1986 and arranged for him to reach out to North's wife. Zucker was only to say a "certain person" who admired her husband "wishes to help out with . . . education expenses of the children" and to agree on a meeting between himself (Zucker) and Betsy North. Hakim originally had a figure of $500,000 in mind for the fund, but Secord reduced it to $200,000. The details of what North knew about the arrangement are murky. He insists he had no knowledge of a plan to pay for his children's college, but Zucker and North's wife did meet in Philadelphia in March, and according to the lawyer, they discussed the North children. In April, Zucker opened an account with $200,000 he described to Secord as an "insurance fund." The next month the amount was transferred to an account called "B. Button" (elsewhere identified as "Belly Button"), which investigators determined was a code name for North's wife.

A few months later, Betsy North declined another meeting with Zucker, but she has never explained why she agreed to the first encounter, what she expected to come out of it, or any part of her story. The independent counsel admitted there was no proof North ever received any of these funds, but Hakim testified North must have known the fundamental purpose of the exercise and was at least willing to hear out the offer through his wife. During a deposition congressional lawyers asked Hakim if there was any doubt in his mind "if Zucker contacted Mrs. North that Oliver North would know who was sending Zucker?" He responded, "Eventually, I would have found it impossible for him not to know."[73] Hakim later pleaded guilty to the attempt to supplement a government official's salary.

If North was ever as "meticulous" as he claimed about his finances, by mid-1986 he seems to have felt few restraints on his methods.

Going to Extremes

The May NSPG meeting put in sharp relief the administration's worries about Contra funding. As Shultz lamented, "If we don't get money for the freedom fighters, they will be out of business." The continued inability to find alternate sources of support soon pushed the State Department into the same kinds of bizarre operations the NSC staff and CIA had run—with similar results. Shultz noted at the NSPG meeting there were various proposals for how to raise funds, but he had one particular idea in mind: "My feeling is that it would be better to go to other countries and get it there."[74] This was what North and his colleagues had been doing in secret for two years. But a change in the law the previous December had opened the way for the State Department to do the same thing legally. The caveat was the funds had to be the foreign government's own, and no form of quid pro quo could be part of the deal.[75]

Within a few weeks of the NSPG meeting, Abrams began inquiring into logistics. North noted a call from an NSC colleague to "Elliott Abrams regarding the third country issue. . . . Elliott asked where to send money." Reporting to Poindexter, North wrote, "I told Elliott to do nothing, to send no papers and to talk to no one further about this until he talks to you." He added, "At this point I'm not sure who on our side knows what. Help."[76]

Poindexter welcomed Shultz's interest in pursuing other governments because he was anxious for the NSC staff to "get out of the business." However, he and North had mixed feelings because they did not want the Saudi donations to be discovered inadvertently. "To my knowledge Shultz knows nothing about the prior financing," Poindexter wrote to North not long after the NSPG meeting. "I think it should stay that way."[77]

This raised the question of where the State Department should go to make its solicitations. Abrams came up with the idea of Brunei, a tiny sultanate on the north coast of Borneo ruled for centuries by the same family. Sitting on top of major oil and gas fields and home to one of the world's richest men, the recently independent state fit Shultz's conditions it be neither a right-wing dictatorship nor reliant on U.S. aid. Poindexter approved, too, and pointed Abrams to North for help in providing a suitable bank account for the anticipated deposit.

The original plan had been for Shultz to make the approach during a meeting with the sultan in June, but he was talked out of it by the U.S. ambassador to Brunei, who thought it an inappropriate mission for such a senior official. The job fell to Abrams, who took nearly two months to finalize arrangements. In early August, using a false name, "Mr. Kenilworth," Abrams flew to London, one of Brunei's few overseas diplomatic missions, and met secretly with the foreign minister, Prince Mohammed Bolkiah. During a walk in a park, Abrams explained the Reagan administration's need for a $10 million donation, then discreetly handed the minister a piece of paper with an account number on it.

Unaware U.S. law required there be no compensation for foreign government aid, the minister asked, "What is in it for us?" "Well," Abrams reported responding, "the President will know of this, and you will have the gratitude of the Secretary [of State] and of the President for helping us out in this jam." That did not satisfy the prince. "What concrete do we get out of this?" Abrams replied, "You don't get anything concrete out of it."[78] Whether Abrams was quite so blunt (he was recounting the episode to congressional investigators exploring potential violations of the law), it was at least clear to the prince the favor would be looked upon kindly by the Reagan administration. The deposit was made within two weeks.

But the story did not end well. The $10 million initially failed to appear in the account North had designated. Near panic, Abrams inveigled the U.S. ambassador to Brunei to find out what had happened. It emerged later Fawn Hall, North's secretary, had mistyped the account number on the card Abrams gave to the foreign minister. By transposing the second and third digits of a nine-digit number, she inadvertently caused the funds to be sent to a different account.[79] By the time the error had been straightened out, the scandal had broken, and the Brunei government demanded the funds be returned. The money never reached the Contras.

In fact, the State Department tried to prevent the money from getting to its destination. Within a week of the press conference by Reagan and Edwin Meese on November 25, 1986, disclosing the scandal, the department sent a cable, over Shultz's signature, to the U.S. embassy in the capital city of Bandar Seri Begawan. It read: "We wish to prevent deposit of any funds into designated account. . . . If asked, you may inform the [sultan] that we consider the account in question to be an inappropriate channel in light of recent events."[80]

As the State Department worked to gather foreign government support, North was still banking on the Iran arms deals to generate covert resources for the Contras. Late in the summer, he let Fiers in on the "neat idea." Fiers immediately reported it to his superiors, including Clair George, deputy director of operations at CIA. George, according to Fiers, replied: "Well, Alan, now you're one of a handful of people that know that" and advised him to "keep it under your hat."[81]

Planting the Flag?

In late spring 1986, President Reagan's frustration with Congress over Contra funding bubbled over—at least in the presence of his national security advisor. According to Poindexter, the president began a meeting with him on May 1 with the words: "I am really serious. If we can't move the Contra package before June 9, I want to figure out a way to take action unilaterally to provide assistance."[82] One of the sources of the president's determination to rebuff lawmakers turned out to be Israel's ambassador to the United Nations, future Likud prime minister Benjamin Netanyahu. "He has been reading Netanyahu's book on terrorism," Poindexter wrote to NSC staffer Donald Fortier the next day, "and he was taken with the examples of Presidential actions in the past without Congressional approval."[83] In addition, "The President is recalling the 506A action we took on Honduras"—an emergency authorization of $20 million of military aid and training in March 1986 granted in the wake of a surprise Sandinista incursion into Honduras. The president wanted to consider a similar authorization for the Contras.

Poindexter doubted the statute would apply because the rebels were not a recognized government, but Reagan's resolute tone impressed him, and he wrote—with some excitement—the president was anxious to take on a challenge that had loomed over the Contra issue from the start: "The President is ready to confront the Congress on the Constitutional question of who controls foreign policy," Poindexter enthused. Ever prepared to anticipate Reagan's wishes, Poindexter conveyed an instruction to Fortier: "We need to get Abe Sofaer [of the State Department] and other stalwart lawyers thinking in these terms to see if there is some way we could do this, if all else fails."[84]

This represents a rare instance in the available record of the president's personal intention to oppose Congress openly on the principle of restricting administration aid to the Contras.[85] The Justice Department, under Meese, had begun that spring to undertake theoretical reviews of the question of separation of powers, but there is no indication of a focus on the Contras nor of how far the exercise went. What is of interest, given White House resentment over congressional obstruction of Contra aid, is that it took so long for the president to take under serious advisement an open constitutional fight.[86]

The president's May 1 directive had an almost immediate effect. North received a copy of Poindexter's message to Fortier, and a few days later, on May 6, sent a reply. "I know that many have provided input re this missive, but before I depart for a day and one half, let me try to respond briefly: Notwithstanding some of the historical inaccuracies in Ben's [Netanyahu's] book—and the fact that many legislative constraints have been imposed on the President since Truman and Eisenhower, there are still several things which can—and perhaps should be done." North went on, "When I was in El Salvador two weeks ago, Bustillo again raised the issue of Salvadoran, Guatemalan and Honduran support for a 'liberated zone' in Nicaraguan territory." North professed to be "very reluctant" even to raise the issue "for fear that we will be accused of manipulating the event (a la the Tonkin Gulf accusations)," but he insisted developments were unfolding under their own steam. "It is entirely likely that within the next 6 to 8 weeks, the resistance will make a major effort to capture a principal coastal population center, run up the blue and white Nicaraguan flag, salute it—and scream like hell for help."[87] In other words, there might be a way to fulfill Reagan's hope of providing emergency aid to the rebels by formally recognizing them as a legitimate government, which would overcome the technical obstacle purportedly presented by the law.

As always, North presented the situation as if only one real option existed. The choices he put forward were to act decisively or risk repeating an episode that had come to symbolize presidential humiliation. Continuing his message to Poindexter: "At that point the rest of the world will wait to see what we do—recognize the new territory—and UNO [United Nicaraguan Opposition] as the govt—or evacuate them as in a Bay of Pigs. It will undoubtedly be a major crisis—for us and many others."[88]

North made sure Poindexter understood the ball was in Washington's court. "The important thing to know is that Bermúdez, Chamorro and the Indian military leaders have already talked to Bustillo, the Guatemalans and the [deleted]— and they all said the same thing: it depends on what the Gringos do." He then offered his own perspective on what a U.S. intervention would entail, portraying it as uncomplicated and utterly achievable. As he often did when writing about the Democratic Resistance Forces (DRF), he infused the message with plenty of feeling: "It may be the only way we ever get to help given that [Democratic Speaker of the House Thomas P. "Tip"] O'Neill is working to screw them again and that there seems to be no stopping DRF planning for the scenario described above, anyway. The DRF has finally had it with our empty promises of help tomorrow—and intend to seize the initiative at tremendous risk. They see no other course. There probably isn't any. Warm regards, North."[89]

North was not alone in backing this option. The same day, an exchange of messages among NSC staff including Poindexter tossed about legal and legislative strategies for supporting a Contra seizure of territory. Several staffers seemed to recognize the U.S. role might not be so easy to constrain, but they were determined to explore the concept further.[90]

Just two weeks later, the idea surfaced at the May 16 NSPG meeting. White House Chief of Staff Donald Regan raised it, acknowledging that President Reagan himself had wondered about its viability:

Don Regan: But there is another idea which the President has discussed with me, which I can bring up because he probably is reluctant to do so. If a group in Nicaragua calls itself a government or if there is a group which creates a government in exile, that could also create a way to help them.

Secretary Weinberger: We could then use the emergency provisions, just as we did for the Saudis.

Ollie North: Or for the Hondurans.

President Reagan: Can't I recognize a government like that without action by Congress?

Secretary Shultz: Yes, you can.

At this point, however, the president's special envoy to Central America, Philip Habib, interjected another consideration: "The Nicaraguan resistance themselves have some strong reservations about doing that now without support from the other countries in the area." In other words, Congress was not the only obstacle to unilateral U.S. action. "We would need to think it through," Habib advised, and the meeting soon wound to a close.[91]

In the end, of course, no intervention took place. It is unclear exactly why the idea vanished so quickly given the characteristic eagerness of the president's staff to jump into action whenever he expressed a strong policy preference. Time may have run out before the opportunity presented itself, or perhaps a sufficiently broad range of views surfaced that made clear the infeasibility of the maneuver.

The Noriega Interlude

One of strangest schemes to aid the Contras during 1986 involved Panamanian dictator Gen. Manuel Noriega. Despite his appalling human rights reputation, Noriega had been a paid asset of the U.S. intelligence community for many years. As recently as 1984 and 1985, he had provided direct help to the Contras in the form of a large cash donation and help in destroying a Sandinista arms depot.[92] To many in the administration, this made him an acceptable partner—until it was determined he was no longer needed.

Toward the end of August, Noriega telephoned North and asked him to meet with a trusted emissary. North agreed to the meeting, at which the intermediary laid out a proposal from the Panamanian leader. As North described it to Poindexter, "In exchange for a promise from us to 'help clean up his [Noriega's] image' and a commitment to lift our ban on FMS [military] sales to the Panamanian Defense [Force]," Noriega would "undertake to 'take care of' the Sandinista leadership for us."[93] A few weeks earlier, Noriega had been the subject of two front-page *New York Times* articles by investigative journalist Seymour Hersh for a string of atrocious acts, from drug dealing to arms trafficking to political murders.[94]

When North balked at the idea of assassinations, saying the United States could not legally be involved, the emissary "countered that Noriega had numerous assets in place in Nicaragua that could accomplish many things that wd be essential." He then reminded North, "After all, Noriega had helped US w/the operation last year that resulted in the EPS [Sandinista Army] arsenal explosion and fire in Managua." He then added, "w/o many more of these kinds of actions, a contra victory was out of the question."[95]

North was immediately convinced and recommended to his superior they proceed, particularly because there would be nothing to trace the operation back to the U.S. government. "My sense is that this offer is sincere, that Noriega does indeed have the capabilities proffered and that the cost could be borne by Project Democracy (the figure of $1M was mentioned). . . . I believe we could make the appropriate arrangements w/reasonable OPSEC and deniability."[96]

Like North, Poindexter was not put off by the idea of dealing with the likes of Noriega, despite Hersh's exposé of his offenses. "I have nothing against him other than his illegal activities," he wrote. "I wonder what he means about helping him to clean up his act? If he is really serious about that, we should be willing to do that for nearly nothing." Although assassinations were off the table, "more sabotage would be another story. . . . It would be useful for you to talk to him directly to find out exactly what he has in mind with regards to cleaning up his act."[97]

The next day, North met with Duane Clarridge, the CIA director of European operations, to discuss how to pursue it. "Send word back to Noriega to meet in Europe or Israel," he wrote in his notes. "Tell Abrams that Noriega has asked for mtg w/Goode [North] re cleaning up image." For the meeting itself, they came up with five steps (not enumerated in North's notes) as well as a cover story for the payment: "$1M avail for '. . . const./land reclamation.'"[98]

Before long, Noriega set a time and place for the meeting—London on September 22. Before departing, North again ran the idea by his colleagues. At an RIG meeting, the reception was mixed. Fiers testified later, "There was significant silence at the table. And then I recall I said, 'No. We don't want to do that.'"[99] But Abrams was more enthusiastic. Seeking approval from Shultz, he met with two of the secretary of state's close aides, Nicholas Platt and Charles Hill, and explained the plan, which called not only for Panamanian participation but the use of British mercenaries—the same group that had carried out the bombing of the Managua weapons depot the year before. As Hill recorded the conversation, "Noriega offers to do some sabotage (electric pylons) that we're training contras to do but which they can't do for 18 mos. Wd get us on the map fast—by Oct. Do it via mercenaries who may not know who employers are. Brits. Wd do it for cash (not from USG). Wants our go-ahead. Ollie will meet him w/approval of Pdx."[100]

Shultz gave his approval the same day, and within forty-eight hours—immediately after a marathon session with Iranian intermediary Ali Bahramani—North was in London for his meeting with Noriega. There, the two sketched out a plan, recorded in North's ever-present notebook, involving a "school" with "courses for commandos" that would produce "experts" to fight not only in Nicaragua but Afghanistan. "Booby traps, night operations, raids" would be part of the curriculum. At one point North wrote, "Rabin approves," indicating Israeli involvement in the program.[101] The second part of the plan called for sabotaging key facilities in Nicaragua: "airport, refinery, Puerto Sandino, electric system, telephone system."[102]

North proceeded to keep his side of the bargain. His notes from one week after the London discussion include a reference to Jack Lawn, then administrator of the Drug Enforcement Administration (DEA), followed by the words: "Meeting with Noriega, *How to Clean Up Act*."[103] None of the sabotage or other plans came to fruition, however, because the NSC's Contra program itself lurched to an unexpected halt just two weeks later.

Final Days

The month leading up to the dramatic denouement of the Contra program in early October was a typical roller coaster of hopeful developments and unwelcome setbacks for the Enterprise. On the plus side, Dutton finally began to turn the resupply operation into a going concern with regular flights and an increasing number of successful drops of supplies. But September began with a potentially ruinous surprise.

Since May, Costa Rica's President Arias had been an irritant for the Enterprise because he disapproved of U.S. use of the Santa Elena airstrip to resupply the Contras. The CIA station chief in San José, Fernandez, had heard directly from Arias he would no longer tolerate the situation and pledged to comply. In the Enterprise's favor was the fact the country's minister of security, appointed by previous president Luis Alberto Monge, sympathized with the operation. By early fall, however, things had changed. A new minister of security, Hernán Garrón, had taken over. In the first week of September, Fernandez found out Garrón planned to go public with the charge the airstrip was being used as a Contra camp in violation of Costa Rican law. The minister would name names, including possibly Secord. Because Ambassador Tambs was out of the country, Fernandez contacted North, reaching him at five minutes past midnight on September 6.[104]

The revelation set off a small storm among the Enterprise's overseers. Within three minutes of hearing from Fernandez, North initiated a conference call with Abrams and Tambs, who had been tracked down in North Carolina. The tone reflected anger and alarm over the possibility of being exposed: "Tell Arias: [he will] never set foot in W.H.—never get 5¢ of $80M," North wrote in his notes—referring to a threat to cancel a promised USAID disbursement if the press conference went forward. The three officials discussed warning Arias his upcoming meeting with Reagan would be at risk as well. Within the hour, Tambs had reached the Costa Rican president and, without resorting to threats, persuaded him to call off the event.[105]

In a PROFS note to Poindexter later that day, North made it sound like he had called the Costa Rican president personally. "I recognize that I was well beyond my charter in dealing w/a head of state this way and in making threats/offers that may be impossible to deliver, but under the circumstances—and w/Elliott's concurrence—it seemed like the only thing we could do."[106] During his televised testimony in 1987, he admitted he had never spoken to Arias, but it seems at the time of the incident he allowed the fable to spread. Fiers, for one, said he knew immediately the account was false for the simple reason North did not speak Spanish. "North was full of bombast. . . . Look at the famous call to Arias, I was sure he didn't do that. There were other people that he said that he spoke with from time to time and I always wondered how a non-Spanish speaker got through to Spanish-speaking people only." Fiers added, "I never took anything he said at face value because I knew that he was bombastic and embellished the record, and threw curves, speed balls and spit balls to get what he wanted."[107]

At first, North believed the Santa Elena crisis was over. "Best of all, it seems to have worked," he told Poindexter. But Tambs's intervention only postponed the exposure. A few days later, Quintero sent an urgent KL-43 message to Secord: "Costa Rican security forces raided Plantation yesterday and impounded 77 drums of gas." Quintero feared his identity would be blown and was put on an early flight out of the country before his name could be put on a watch list. He assured Secord the airdrops would continue "regardless of the situation." But he, too, blamed the Costa Rican president for the disruption: "Alert Ollie Pres. Arias will attend Reagan's dinner in New York Sept. 22nd. Boy needs to be straightened out by heavy weights."[108]

The press conference eventually took place on September 24. Garrón announced authorities had seized the 1.25-mile gravel airstrip to prevent its use by either drug runners or anti-Sandinista rebels, in keeping with Arias's calls for strict neutrality in the Nicaraguan conflict. Garrón said the strip had been built by the Udall Research Corp., based in Panama, and represented by a Robert Olmsted. He gave an address, two telephone numbers, and a telex number in Panama City. Reporters calling the numbers reached a law firm in Panama but gained no information about either the company or Olmsted.[109]

North took some glee from this fact. Olmsted of course was a fictitious name for William Haskell, one of Secord's Enterprise associates. Reporting to Poindexter, North wrote: "Damage assessment: Udall Resources, Inc., S.A. is a proprietary of Project Democracy. It will cease to exist by noon today. There are no USG fingerprints on any of the operation and Olmsted is not the name of [Secord's] agent—Olmsted does not exist."[110]

To North, Abrams, and their colleagues, Arias had betrayed the United States and the rebels. "The bottom line is that Arias has now seriously violated the understanding we have had with his administration since shortly after his inaugural," North wrote. Abrams and Shultz wanted to "punish" the Costa Rican leader by canceling his meeting with Reagan. "Arias has screwed us badly—and we should not give him what he so obviously wants." A few hours later, North added that Arias was "just a kid. . . . He's not quite so smart as he thinks he is."[111] The meeting with Reagan never took place.[112]

To complete the cover story, North drafted press guidance the following week. He accompanied it with a cover note to Poindexter seeking approval in the wake of a *New York Times* article on the subject. The cover note was decidedly more discouraging about the press conference than his earlier descriptions had been. "The damage done by this revelation is considerable," he reported. At the same time, his depiction of the rarely used airfield as a "vital element in supporting the resistance" as well as other remarks in the memo were significantly overstated.[113] North's purpose was to justify another rebuke to the Costa Rican president, who was reportedly seeking a new appointment with Reagan. North recommended Arias be required to "demonstrate his goodwill toward the resistance through practical steps *before* he is welcomed in the Oval Office." Poindexter approved the press guidance without questioning or editing the misstatements designed to hide the U.S. government connection to the airstrip.[114]

The Santa Elena revelation was a setback during a period of significant accomplishment for the resupply operation. After months of frustration, Dutton had come up with enough incremental improvements in equipment quality and tactics to register consistent successes. He introduced innovations such as having flight crews and commandos agree beforehand on drop zones instead of trying to communicate with troops in real time using unreliable radio devices. Another change was to fly two aircraft per mission, raising the likelihood of success and providing more security in the face of ramped-up Sandinista ground fire.[115] Also contributing to the upswing were Fernandez and Steele. The latter helped persuade Rodriguez and Bustillo to be more cooperative with the Enterprise, notwithstanding new complaints about two-plane formations. Even Rodriguez gave the operation credit.[116]

By mid-September, virtually daily missions to the south were delivering thousands of pounds of supplies, reaching a point unthinkable only weeks before.

Through Fernandez, Dutton received a message from one of the *comandantes* saying, "Please don't deliver any more, they've got all they can carry." Dutton confessed his secret hope had been to impress the CIA. "We were trying to look good."[117]

North reported the encouraging developments to Poindexter. He also asked Dutton to put together a photo album he implied he wanted to show the president. North even asked Dutton to arrange a quick trip to the region so he could thank everyone involved, but the Noriega meeting in London and the sessions with Iranians interfered with the plan.[118]

So routine had the flights become that Cooper joked one day in late September, "Ho-hum, just another day at the office"—to which Dutton replied in Spanish, "*Cuidado!*" (Watch out!).[119]

Denouement: Crash of the C-123

At 9:50 the morning of October 5, a C-123 carrying three U.S. crewmen and a Contra radio operator took off from Ilopango heading for a drop zone inside Nicaragua. Following the usual route for a delivery into the southern part of the country, the plane, topped off with fuel and carrying a payload of about 10,000 pounds of small arms and ammunition, headed down Nicaragua's Pacific coast. From there it turned east and crossed over the coastline of Costa Rica near the Santa Elena airstrip. Unlike most previous missions, this one was to deliver supplies not to UNO but to the Nicaraguan Democratic Force (FDN), based in northern Nicaragua. The circuitous route was necessary because the "Sandies," as Dutton called them, "had moved some mobile guns into [the] region where we normally run from the north."[120]

As they neared the Costa Rican border, Cooper, for reasons unknown, made a decision to cross into Nicaraguan airspace at a point earlier than planned.[121] It was a critical mistake because it took the C-123 directly over an area protected by Sandinista antiaircraft fire. About thirty-five miles north of the border and ninety miles southeast of Managua,[122] the low-flying plane was hit by a SAM-7 missile fired by a fourteen-year-old soldier. Only Eugene Hasenfus, the cargo "kicker," who happened to be wearing a sport parachute he had borrowed from his brother, survived. The radio operator, Cooper, and copilot Wallace "Buzz" Sawyer did not have parachutes on and perished.[123]

When the flight failed to return to base on time, word spread quickly. Rodriguez was in Miami, but his subordinates at Ilopango were tracking the resupply flights and called him. He immediately contacted a staff member in Bush's office, who passed the news to others. Dutton informed North as soon he heard. His message the following day included blame for Rodriguez. "This type situation precisely why I wanted to fly 2-ship [formation]. . . . VP's office should know our friend Max is prime reason we have had to send A/C in single. He should be taken out of this net."[124]

But North knew the problem was now much bigger than Rodriguez. Before any serious search-and-rescue attempts could be mounted for the missing airplane, Cuban radio announced the Sandinistas had shot down a U.S. C-47 in southwestern Nicaragua. Despite the misidentification, everyone connected to the operations must have known immediately it was the Enterprise plane. Within two days, a disheveled Hasenfus was paraded before television cameras in Managua.

Along with arranging for the remains of Cooper and Sawyer and determining what to do about Hasenfus, U.S. officials struggled with the question of how to maintain the overarching cover story and keep their relationship to the secret resupply operation concealed. At an RIG meeting on October 8, Abrams and his colleagues went over ways to make sure the others involved would go along. "El Salvador will deny any facilitative support to contra flights," a summary of the meeting stated. "[President José Napoleón] Duarte agreed that [his government] would deny everything." As for the Contras, "UNO to be asked to assume responsibility for flight and to assist families of Americans involved. Elliott will follow up with Ollie to facilitate this."[125]

North, in Frankfurt in the midst of negotiations with the Iranians, immediately flew back to Washington, D.C. Secord's operatives in the field also returned to the United States. Left behind were the remaining aircraft and equipment Secord and Hakim had fought to preserve in order to sell them to the CIA. In a final irony, the CIA did ultimately take over the small fleet—not to continue the resupply operation but to destroy any vestige of its existence. North described the "extraordinary operation" as follows: "First they had the little air force flown to a remote airfield. Then an enormous crater was dug with bulldozers. The planes were pushed into the pit, covered with explosives, and blown up. The remaining wreckage was saturated with fuel and then cremated. The fire burned for days."[126]

As the resupply operation—and Secord and Hakim's principal business investment—went up in flames, official Washington prepared for the inevitable political and legal fallout.

12

Blowback

The May 1986 Tehran mission produced deep disappointment on the U.S. side. In their impatience for results, the U.S. participants had cut too many corners. Without accepting a prior face-to-face meeting, they left themselves open to consequences that in hindsight seem predictable. To be sure, much of the blame belonged to Manucher Ghorbanifar, who was just as capable of duping Iranian officials as foreign ones. But members of the Reagan administration, too, especially Oliver North, exhibited their own penchant for costly deceptions. Still, all sides continued to want or need something from the others, and as long as Ronald Reagan remained on board, U.S. officials would stay involved. (Vice President George Bush, too, would reaffirm his support.) During the fall, a promising new channel to Tehran seemed to open. Unfortunately, more poor decisions by U.S. participants placed Washington's larger interests in jeopardy. The next few months would bring the customary mix of peaks and low points before the initiative came to an unexpected end at the hands of Iranian political forces beyond the participants' control.

Signs of Desperation

In the days following Robert McFarlane's briefing of President Reagan, not only did contacts with Ghorbanifar and Mohsen Kangarlou revive, but there was considerable talk, born of sheer frustration, about taking more drastic steps to end the hostage trauma. During the month of June, the president and his advisors hashed out the prospect of a straight-up hostage rescue attempt. The idea had first come up while McFarlane was still in Tehran. Two days after his return, John Poindexter wrote to North: "I am beginning to think that we need to seriously think about a rescue effort for the hostages. Is there any way we can get a spy into the Hayy Assallum area [in Lebanon]? See Charlie's [Allen] weekly report [on hostage locations]. Over a period of time we could probably move covertly some . . . people into Yarze."[1]

North agreed, but raised the specter of earlier failed schemes to spring U.S. citizens currently being held captive:

I fully agree that if the current effort fails to achieve release then such a mission should be considered. You will recall that we have not had much success with this kind of endeavor in the past, however. After CIA took so long to organize and then botched the Kilburn effort, Copp [Richard Secord] undertook to see what could be done thru one of the earlier DEA [Drug Enforcement Administration] developed Druze contacts. Dick has been working with Nir on this and now has three people in Beirut and a 40 man Druze force working "for" us. Dick rates the possibility of success on this operation as 30%, but that's better than nothing.[2]

Peter Kilburn, a librarian at the American University of Beirut, had been taken hostage in December 1984. In April 1986, according to news reports, North helped put together a plan either to lure the kidnappers into the open with a fake ransom offer or to have the ransom money chemically treated so it would disintegrate after several days. When the intermediary failed to close the deal with Kilburn's captors, the plan fell through. The CIA and FBI then began putting into effect a second plan, but that operation was interrupted when U.S. forces bombed Libya late in the month. In the aftermath, Kilburn's kidnappers killed him, reportedly after getting paid by Libyan leader Muammar Qaddafi. North blamed the CIA for dragging its feet.[3]

Bringing in the DEA

Even before the arms-for-hostages deals had formally been hatched, virtually every counterterrorism official in the U.S. government had been nurturing contacts with go-betweens who flooded Washington with tall promises of helping to reach the kidnappers. It was a "brutal, ugly story," according to a high CIA official. "People were selling information, selling hostages, selling their rings, selling their clothes, selling letters from them trying to make money out of the hostage business."[4] Some in the Reagan administration thought there were opportunities too good to pass up. During the first half of 1985, at the request of a White House official who was a personal friend of William Buckley, two DEA agents produced a source in Lebanon they thought could deliver the kidnapped CIA operative. But a superior within the DEA soon developed doubts about the reliability of the source, known to the agency as a drug trafficker and a thief. When the informant refused to deliver a set of CIA test questions to the kidnappers, the DEA official and his CIA colleagues wrote off the lead as "hocus[-]pocus . . . a scam."[5]

The two agents, William Dwyer and Frank Tarallo, persisted, turning to North, whom they saw as "running" the government's hostage-tracking program. North immediately saw an opening. He dismissed CIA distrust of the informant and proposed to McFarlane the two agents be detailed temporarily to the NSC to keep the operation going. McFarlane signed off on the idea and at North's recommendation approached Attorney General Edwin Meese, under whom the DEA operated, for his approval. Meese, too, obliged.[6] North then sought out an anonymous private "donor" for the large sums Dwyer and Tarallo said would be needed to "bribe free" not just Buckley but as many as four or more hostages altogether. The donor was H. Ross Perot, the Texas billionaire, already famous for rescuing U.S. citizens in trouble in the Middle East. In all, Perot put up $1.3 million, but the scheme collapsed in the wake of the hijacking of TWA Flight 847 (see Chapter 4). Of the total proffered, $300,000 went to make "payments" to intermediaries. The remaining $1 million was eventually returned to Perot. Instead of cutting loose Dwyer and Tarallo, however, North held on to them as "useful sources" for the main interagency group seeking to locate the hostages.

A year later, in May 1986, Dwyer and Tarallo developed a new rescue plan they had no trouble selling to North. North turned again to Perot for the hefty sums needed for ransom. In June, an assistant of Perot's appeared in Cyprus carrying $2 million for the first two hostages. They were to be taken to Cyprus from Lebanon on board the Enterprise's ship, *Erria*, while the DEA agents created a prearranged diversion with speedboats rented for the occasion. Again, the attempt failed. The middlemen had insisted on getting hold of the money before turning over the hostages, but unlike their counterparts in the Iran initiative, the DEA agents refused. In the aftermath, North came in for rare criticism—from Perot—who accused him of failing to keep him in the picture. It took a personal letter from President Reagan to smooth over the gaffe.[7]

Secord's prediction of a 30 percent chance of success for the DEA operation proved roughly accurate. At the heart of the problem was the same issue plaguing rescue planners since the Carter administration's disastrous attempt in Iran in April 1980—lack of information on the hostages' location. In early June, North pointed this out to Poindexter as a continuing obstacle to any military mission: "In regard to U.S. military rescue ops, JCS [Joint Chiefs of Staff] has steadfastly refused to go beyond the initial thinking stage unless we can develop some hard intelligence on their whereabouts."[8] Before taking on any such attempt, North told Poindexter there should be a "planning cell" at the CIA to make preparations. Intentionally or not, he was sentencing the project to death by committee. In the end, no military rescue attempt took place.

Off the Tracks

Meanwhile, Israel's point man on the Iran initiative, the indefatigable Amiram Nir, set about to regenerate talks. On June 2, he traveled to Paris to hook up with Ghorbanifar and review what had gone wrong in Tehran. Ghorbanifar, ever unpredictable, was circumspect. Rather than explode at his counterparts for fumbling another opportunity, he blamed factional rivalries inside the Islamic regime. But he also expressed frustration at McFarlane's impatience. The Iranians, he said, were baffled as to why he could not wait just six hours for the first two hostages to be delivered. They took it as proof the United States had never intended to come through with the remaining spare parts as promised.

Nir, who had spoken to North beforehand and indeed had sought his permission to go to Paris in the first place, decided to open up a new level of discussion. He asked Ghorbanifar if he thought other intermediaries might be explored to substitute for Kangarlou, who seemed to do nothing but fret over his personal fate in case of failure. Over the next four months, Ghorbanifar produced at least three people inside the Iranian government for Nir to screen.[9] Meanwhile, Kangarlou stayed in the picture. According to George Cave, he and the prime minister's aide kept up an active dialogue, with the Iranian mainly insisting on greater U.S. flexibility regarding the delivery of spare parts before retrieving any hostages. Cave insisted this was unacceptable, and for a time their dialogue foundered. Then the wheels of the operation nearly fell off altogether.

In June, the Iranian intermediaries got hold of a 1985 price list for HAWK spares that showed they had been vastly overcharged. Inexplicably, Iran had never been removed from the U.S. Army Logistics Command's distribution list for pricing information, which automatically went out every few months.[10] Nir passed along a message from Ghorbanifar to North, whose first reaction was disbelief. He did not think a single price breakdown could exist because the parts had several different manufacturers. Cave, who heard about the microfiche from Kangarlou, was equally doubtful, believing the prices must have come from a much earlier period. North became more suspicious when Ghorbanifar refused to hand over the document for verification. Another theory, propounded by Nir, was the Iranians had somehow obtained a list belonging to a U.S. government procurement agency. Secord thought it might be Raytheon, the manufacturer of the HAWK missile. After first denying the extent of the overcharges, U.S. officials tried to explain away the differences by claiming private commercial deals were more expensive than intergovernmental transactions. Later, Secord pointed out the microfiche listed only internal production costs known as cost of manufacture (COM) data that did not include "overhead, general and administrative expenses, cost of capital, transportation expenses, economic escalation factor, and Raytheon's own profit."[11]

The fact was that at virtually every step the middlemen had built in significant price hikes. Revelation of the subsequent overcharging did even further damage to the already fragile relationship between Tehran and Washington. That both were willing to continue at all was a sign of their ongoing mutual dependence. At the same time, neither did a great deal to win the trust of their opposite number. For his part, North lied repeatedly to his interlocutors and did not hesitate to use any kind of deception regardless of the risk ("I would have promised them a trip to Disneyland," he told Congress).[12] His proposal for dealing with the latest snafu, for example, was to trump the Iranians' microfiche with a false one that would make the higher prices seem legitimate. Despite his claims to the contrary, this was not behavior intended to encourage a long-term relationship.

A Hostage Comes Out

As the operation lurched forward, Nir suffered the next embarrassment. As he described it later, Ghorbanifar contacted him with news a single hostage would be released in time for the July 4 celebrations in the United States. Ghorbanifar had come up with the idea of timing the release as a way to gain leverage with the White House.[13] As soon as Nir got word a hostage would be coming out (in his version of events it was a definitive statement by Ghorbanifar), he gave North the good news. It could not have come at a better time for the Reagan administration, given the current state of the initiative. But within twenty-four hours, the day before the planned release, anticipation once again gave way to disappointment when Ghorbanifar phoned Nir to say the Iranians had not been able to arrange the release after all.

Abashed, Nir blamed the failure on an Iraqi attack on an Iranian satellite relay station that he said cut off Iran's communications with the outside world for several days. North also faced embarrassment. In his excitement, he had not only ordered into action the vast machinery set up to deliver the hostages to freedom but also (so he told Nir) informed the president, the vice president, the secretaries of state and defense, and the head of the CIA that a breakthrough was imminent. He now had to tell them it had been a false alarm. Furious, he refused to talk to Nir for weeks, directing Charles Allen to communicate in his place. Allen told Nir that North was having undefined problems, but Nir saw through the ruse and became "clearly alarmed," redoubling his efforts to generate some positive results.[14]

Fortunately for the increasingly shaky operation, the Iranians managed to come through with a single hostage—Lawrence Jenco—three weeks later. When that operation showed signs of delay, Nir became worried he would lose face again with Washington and abruptly told Ghorbanifar to close it down. But

Ghorbanifar, true to form, never passed the message to Tehran. The risky move bought a few precious hours until the pieces of the Jenco deal could fall into place. At around midnight on July 25, Israeli Defense Forces (IDF) intercepted a cable from the Iranian Revolutionary Guard Corps (IRGC) headquarters to its command center in Syria/Lebanon. The communication was addressed to Mr. Mehdinejad—evidently the IRGC intelligence representative the U.S.-led delegation had met in Tehran. It read, "Act immediately in the matter of ret. box which was given as the deposit of the subject of your mission; report immediately to center on the execution of this order."[15] Later, on July 26, the Catholic priest who had been held since January 8, 1985, was set free in rural Lebanon, taken to a Syrian military checkpoint, and from there transported to Damascus.

Jenco's release brought the operation back to life. After being close to despair, North suddenly jumped back in the game. The same day he put together for Poindexter a ten-page packet of "Compartmented Information" urging that the operation go forward. Sent through the NSC's most sensitive channel, System IV, the materials included a draft memo for the president and a draft paper of support from CIA Director William Casey that North said Allen and Duane Clarridge had prepared but that had North's vintage tone. "It is indisputable that the Iranian connection worked this time," the draft read, before warning of the consequences if the operation were terminated. "Peres and Rabin have put their reputation on the Ghorbanifar/[Kangarlou] connection. . . . There would be a considerable loss of face for Nir and his superiors if the link were broken."[16] The next day (Sunday), North was in Frankfurt meeting with Ghorbanifar and Nir. His summary of the discussions offered a more dire prediction for Poindexter to contemplate: "Bottom line . . . is that if we want to prevent the death of one of the remaining three hostages, we are going to have to do something."[17]

Briefing the Vice President

Syria's success in garnering partial credit for Jenco's release gave both North and Nir pause. Hafez al-Assad, the country's wily leader, was happy to be seen as a player. But participants in the Iran initiative were not pleased to see the status of an archenemy of Israel elevated even though it deflected unwelcome attention from the covert NSC effort. Anxious for senior administration officials to know who was really behind Jenco's freedom, North tried to contact Bush, who he understood hoped to go to Syria to welcome the former hostage.[18] Unable to reach Bush personally, he passed a message to the vice president's chief of staff, Craig Fuller.

North then learned Bush was not heading for Syria but for Israel. He and Nir agreed that Nir, who had met Bush before in connection with the vice president's task force on terrorism, should brief him instead. After both North and Fuller discussed the idea with the vice president, and after Nir received permission from Prime Minister Shimon Peres, the meeting went ahead early on the morning of July 29.

The setting was the vice president's suite at the opulent King David Hotel, overlooking the Old City of Jerusalem. Only Bush, Nir, and Fuller as note taker were present. No one else traveling with the vice president knew about the meeting. For twenty-five minutes, Nir described the broad picture and the latest details. Bush reportedly sat in silence except for an occasional question as Nir laid out the program from its inception, providing specific numbers of weapons and spare parts, a rundown of the problematic Tehran trip, and the lessons learned. The main message was unambiguous: "We are dealing with the most radical elements. . . . We've learned they can deliver and the moderates can't."[19] Whether Bush was aware at the time or not, this flatly contradicted the administration's rationale for the program—to forge ties with moderates who favored relations with the United States. Despite the catalog of difficulties, Nir was upbeat: "We have started to establish contact with some success and now more success is expected." Needed now, he said, were decisions, including whether to agree to sequence deliveries of hostages.

The vice president "made no commitments," according to Fuller's notes, only thanking Nir "for having pursued this effort despite doubts and reservations throughout."[20] But Nir, according to Secord, was elated. "Things couldn't have turned out better," he reported. Bush was "very attentive, very interested in everything," especially the "strategic aspect—development of high-level contacts. . . . I think that interested him most."[21] Whether Bush took Nir's main message— the need to return to sequential releases—back to the White House is not known, but that approach would soon be adopted.

A New Channel

Among the painful lessons from the Tehran mission was that Ghorbanifar, once again, had proven critically unreliable. He and Nir had developed a relationship of mutual reliance over the previous six months, however, and North had not yet stirred himself to sever the connection. No doubt there was considerable wishful thinking on North's part things would work out. For all his deceptiveness and self-promotion, Ghorbanifar's access to decision makers in Iran—via Kangarlou—was undeniable. There was also the question of how to locate an alternative entrée to the Iranian leadership. Nevertheless, conferring on the somber journey from Tehran back to Israel, the U.S. officials and Nir concluded something had to change. Secord proposed Albert Hakim sound out his considerable network of expatriate Iranians. ("Albert, we've got to get off this Ghorbanifar kick and get us a dog that can hunt," as Secord put it.)[22] Nir was already seeking new contacts—his objective was not to cut out Ghorbanifar, but to find a way around the wretched Kangarlou. Even the U.S. officials did not anticipate dropping Ghorbanifar altogether (partly for the sake of Nir and the Israeli government). Their preference at this stage was simply to insulate and distract him while they explored a new avenue into Iran. Their efforts soon bore fruit in a way that excited even the vinegary Secord.[23]

Contrary to many foreigners' impression that Iran was fundamentally isolated from the rest of the world, the regime's outside contacts were surprisingly fluid. Hakim's many associates, for example—including business owners enriching themselves in the West—had little difficulty traveling back and forth to the country. Ghorbanifar also had ample freedom to maneuver. At the same time, a great deal of activity was taking place in relation to hostage-release efforts involving attempts by nongovernmental groups to interact not just with Iran but Syria and Hezbollah. Among these were the Church of England, the United Nations, and even the Palestine Liberation Organization (PLO). (Representatives of the two former groups would later be abducted themselves—Anglican envoy Terry Waite and UN official Giandomenico Picco.) Sometimes Iranian officials dealt directly with other governments. Speaker of the Majles (Parliament) Akbar Hashemi Rafsanjani made use of the Japanese as intermediaries in the mid-1980s, and Foreign Minister Ali Akbar Velayati did the same with the Pakistanis. In summer 1986, Deputy Foreign Minister Mohammad Javad Larijani sent a message via the foreign minister of a third country to Secretary of State George Shultz that Tehran was interested in easing relations. Larijani even went public to make his point, although the State Department evidently did not pick up on it.[24] The Islamic Republic's austere image of ideological rigidity concealed substantial political movement and unpredictability.[25]

By early July, Hakim had made contact with some Iranian expatriates he enticed with promises of lucrative business deals. One named Chengiz Farnejad had worked for him in the past, and Hakim had tried to connect him with the CIA as a source three years earlier. U.S. officials went so far as to subject Farnejad to a polygraph, but the results were inconclusive. He proved a critical link, though, introducing to the operation Kamal Darwish, deputy head of Iran's arms procurement operation in London, who had direct connections to Rafsanjani.[26] In short order, Darwish was able to produce a nephew of Rafsanjani named Ali Bahramani, who became the face of what came to be known as the "Second Channel."

Bahramani was only about twenty-five years old, according to his own account, but was already reportedly a senior member of the IRGC, thanks largely to family ties. According to U.S. records from that time, "He has access to considerable sums of Iranian money, high-level Revolutionary Guards intelligence on Afghanistan, and Soviet materiel captured from Iraq."[27] After Hakim contacted him, he quickly agreed to meet with U.S. intermediaries. "Nephew is prepared to play ball," North's notes read.[28]

Bahramani impressed each of the U.S. players, starting with Secord. After a full day of get-acquainted talks in Brussels, Secord raved to North: "Meetings constituted comprehensive tour de force," revealing a "very sharp, well-educated young man" who is a "well-known favorite of Rafsanjani." He recommended moving forward immediately. "My judgment is that we have opened up new and probably much better channel into Iran. This connection has been effectively re-cruited and he wants to start dealing. Recommend you plan on bringing George [Cave] to next meeting in two weeks or less."[29]

Years later, Bahramani would downplay his own importance. "In effect I was only a university student with no official governmental responsibilities."[30] When he returned to Tehran from Brussels he wrote a report for his uncle about his meetings with Secord, Hakim, and Cave. He urged following up with the contacts. Based partly on the U.S. participants' alarming accounts of the Soviet buildup of Iraq's armories and the threat of more chemical weapons deployments, Bahra-mani believed Iran needed to modernize its arsenals, which required the help of Western governments. Rafsanjani brushed him off, he said, claiming stories that the nephew had been told about talks with the United States were untrue. He specifically denied the McFarlane visit had taken place.

Snubbed but not put off, Bahramani turned to Mohsen Rezaie, commander of the IRGC. The Corps was faring poorly on the battlefield and was "forced to falsely advertise to people that they were being victorious," Bahramani recalled. Unlike Rafsanjani, Rezaie "did not deny anything" but said, "I should not con-cern myself with the details of the story." Meanwhile, Bahramani discovered Rafsanjani had shared his report with other officials. "He didn't want to enter alone into something that didn't have anything to do with him per se, but he still did want things to get done through his own channels," Bahramani told an interviewer later. Eventually, and evidently with his uncle's tacit approval, he took up the role of intermediary, carrying on negotiations until the news of the U.S.-Iranian contact broke in a Lebanese newsmagazine.[31]

Within days of Secord's enthusiastic message, North brought Poindexter into the loop and sought his approval to go ahead with Bahramani. He continued to push the Kangarlou/Ghorbanifar avenue as the "only proven means by which we have been able to effect the release of any of the hostages." But he alleged Bahramani had a "specific mandate" from Tehran. That was an overstatement, although North's next comment was probably closer to the truth. "There is con-siderable evidence that [he] is indeed a bona fide intermediary seeking to estab-lish direct contact with the USG for Rafsanjani's faction within the Government of Iran."[32] For some reason, Poindexter did not reply right away, leading North to complain to McFarlane, who was still floating on the margins of the initiative, "We still have no response fm JMP. . . . Have now undertaken to have Casey raise same w/JMP tomorrow at the weekly mtg. The things one must do to get action."[33] North also talked to Poindexter the next day and discussed the need to go through "Joshua"—the code name for President Reagan.[34]

North's restlessness was not unfounded. As he told McFarlane, "The basic problem, as you know, is that we dither so long on these things that by the time we're ready to go to bat, the rules have changed again."[35] That was in fact what happened when, on September 8, another U.S. citizen, Frank Herbert Reed, the director of the Lebanese International School in West Beirut, became the latest hostage in the crisis. The same day, North had pushed Poindexter, reaffirming Bahramani was ready to step into the negotiations and bolstering this good news with a CIA analysis that Kangarlou had provided Cave with "confirmation that Rafsanjani may be moving to take control of the entire process of the U.S. relationship and the hostages."[36]

North added that the CIA and Army Logistics had located a significant quantity of HAWK parts that "had previously been listed as 'unavailable.'" These would "entice the Iranians to proceed," he assured Poindexter.[37] Moving ahead was vital, North again argued, because the hostages' lives were in jeopardy. To underscore the point, he attached a memo from Allen describing a "growing awareness" by Hezbollah's Imad Mughniyah, the perpetrator of several of the kidnappings, that holding French and U.S. captives was not going to gain the release of the Dawa prisoners. "Consequently, . . . officials allege, he is talking of killing the hostages," Allen warned. "No threat from Mughniyah should be considered idle."[38]

The next day, Poindexter met with Reagan, and to North's relief the president approved going forward with the Bahramani channel despite the Reed abduction. A few days later, on September 12, kidnappers captured Joseph Cicippio, a comptroller at the American University of Beirut, adding to the urgency.

Although North's "guidance" from Poindexter called for removing Ghorbanifar from the picture "if at all possible," obstacles stood in the way. One was money. In Allen's estimation, it would require raising at least $4 million to make up for the amount Ghorbanifar reportedly had in hand. Another hurdle was Israel. Washington may have wanted to shunt the Israelis aside, but political and logistical considerations prevented that, as North understood.[39] Thus, when Nir came to Washington, D.C., the following day, he would be treated to assurances, worked out in advance by North and Poindexter, the "joint" deals would continue as before. The difference was Ghorbanifar would have to take a backseat, at best.

Even Nir understood the problem the Iranian posed for security. Ghorbanifar was deeply invested in the arms sales and stood to lose a great deal of money—even his life—if threats supposedly made against him later were genuine. If he were forced out, he could easily expose the entire operation. But he was also Israel's main entrée to Iran and represented important leverage for keeping Washington working toward Tel Aviv's priorities.

North and Poindexter were not at all reluctant to be as deceptive with Nir as they were with the Iranians. They claimed Secord had accidentally stumbled on the new second channel while investigating a "possible illegal diversion of TOW missiles." They added gratuitously that Sen. Edward Kennedy (D-Mass.) and former secretary of state Alexander Haig had looked into Bahramani as well.[40] Nir accepted his partners' promises to continue the deals on a joint basis with Israel. The United States had another opportunity to make the point during Peres's visit to Washington, D.C., on September 15. Peres had raised the concern about Israel being cut out several weeks earlier, and Nir advised North it would probably be on his list of topics for a private conversation with the president.[41]

At this point, the Iran arms deals crisscrossed again with the Nicaragua resupply operation. In the catalogue of Peres's discussion topics for the president that North passed to Poindexter was an item labeled "Israeli Arms." It read, "On Friday night, Defense Minister Rabin offered a significant quantity of captured Soviet bloc arms for use by the Nicaraguan democratic resistance. These arms will be picked up by a foreign flag vessel this week and delivered to the Nicaraguan resistance. If Peres raises this issue, it would be helpful if the President thanked him since the Israelis hold considerable stores of bloc ordnance compatible with what the Nicaraguan resistance now uses."[42]

The Israelis' official account of the affair indicates the request for weapons came from North. Nir reported he told North to contact Rabin, and on September 12 North did so, whereupon the defense minister made a "gift" of the arms. In the end the shipment was returned, never having reached the Contras.[43]

An Iranian in the Oval Office

Having assuaged Nir, North undertook another audacious move—bringing Bahramani to Washington, D.C., for direct talks. After the confusion in Tehran over whether McFarlane truly represented the top levels of the U.S. government, what better way to erase Iranian doubts than to bring Bahramani to North's office in the Old Executive Office Building, next door to the White House?

Getting a senior Iranian official to the nation's capital without being noticed was no small adventure. Bahramani had to travel to Turkey, where Iranians did not require a visa, and from there to the United States undercover. North needed special dispensation from U.S. immigration authorities to waive the U.S. visa requirement, which he obtained with Casey's help. The CIA was less effective when it came to arranging air travel for "the Nephew," forcing North to turn again to Secord and reaffirming the value of having an off-the-shelf capacity near at hand. With no superiors or congressional committees to answer to, Secord leased a private Lear jet in Geneva and picked up the passengers in Istanbul, transiting through Switzerland, Ireland, and Iceland before landing at Dulles Airport near Washington, D.C. "Why Dick can do something in 5 min. that the CIA cannot do in two days is beyond me—but he does," North told Poindexter.[44]

The two days of meetings that followed confirmed U.S. hopes. Gathering in North's cramped work space, then at Secord's suburban Virginia office, not far from the Sheraton Hotel in Seven Corners where Bahramani stayed, the group touched on every outstanding issue—weapons, hostages, the Dawa prisoners, even the possibility of longer-term talks. The nephew raised no contentious demands, was nonideological in his remarks, and presented none of the unpleasant surprises they had come to expect from Ghorbanifar and Kangarlou. He seemed quite at ease. North in comparison came across as slightly overzealous, feeling the need to persuade the visitor of Reagan's deep religious convictions. One of the Iranians who accompanied the nephew finally told Cave North should ease off.[45]

Bahramani did raise two subjects that moved the discussions in two somewhat new directions. He asked the United States to help oust Saddam Hussein, a basic Iranian objective since the start of the war with Iraq. He also sought Washington's influence to persuade the conservative gulf Arab states to stop supporting the Iraqi dictator. Cave was struck by the earnestness of his desire to bring the war to an end. On the intriguing topic of long-term relations, the Iranian proposed forming a joint commission to promote the idea.[46]

North was so pleased with the first day's results he came up with an astonishing idea—he brought Bahramani to the White House in the evening for an extensive guided tour that included the Oval Office. The Iranian reportedly took a camera with him and had his picture taken as a souvenir. North later downplayed the tour, saying he frequently took friends, relatives, and other visitors through the building. But the nephew of a top leader of the Islamic Republic was hardly an ordinary visitor. North made a point of showing him the portrait of President Theodore Roosevelt, drawing a connection between Roosevelt's Nobel Prize–winning role in ending the Russo-Japanese War of 1904–1905 and the prospect Reagan might make a similar contribution to the Iran-Iraq War. Writing to Poindexter afterward, he asked: "Anybody for RR getting the same prize?"[47]

The nephew's visit buoyed U.S. spirits. Both sides agreed to hold another meeting without delay, and North quickly got Poindexter's approval to go ahead. He then set about making preparations. A critical task was to address Israeli sensitivities, which meant bringing Nir back into the picture, at least to a degree.

North had not informed the Israelis of Bahramani's visit, and after the success of the talks he would ensure they played no more than a "supporting role" in the operation. To cushion the impact, he sent Secord to meet Nir in Israel with a letter from Reagan to Peres specifically thanking the prime minister and praising Nir for their contributions to that stage.

Hakim Negotiates the Nine Points

The next round, a series of meetings on October 6–8 in Frankfurt, Germany, took the discussions to an even deeper level. Joining the group was a familiar figure from Frankfurt in February and from Tehran in May—the head of intelligence for the IRGC, Fereidun Mehdinejad, alias "Samii."[48] The significance of his presence, according to Bahramani, was that it reflected the strengthening of a consensus inside Iran's leadership circles favoring the operation. This was taken as good news on its face but in hindsight should have been a red flag for the U.S. side. But the success of the previous meeting helped the U.S. participants to persuade themselves they had turned a corner in the arms deals. The appearance of an IRGC intelligence officer—even one Secord would describe as "Godzilla to the [Nephew's] Bambi"[49]—could be explained by the nephew's expectation for sophisticated intelligence on Iraq's order of battle. Besides, Bahramani was a member of the IRGC himself, pointing up the difficulty of pigeonholing Iran's political scene.

Bahramani had previously told North he planned to bring a Koran to their meetings, so North went to some lengths to reciprocate. Secord's wife bought a New Testament version of the bible that North asked the president, through Poindexter, to inscribe in his own handwriting with a suitable passage: "And the Scripture, foreseeing that God would justify the Gentiles by faith, preached the gospel beforehand to Abraham, saying, 'All the nations shall be blessed in you.' Galatians 3:8—Ronald Reagan, Oct. 3, 1986."

North chose the passage himself but pretended Reagan had done so after a full weekend of prayer. He claimed the president had said to him about the Iran program, "This is a promise that God gave to Abraham. Who am I to say that we should not do this?"[50] Whether the Iranians believed these inventions is hard to know.

The Frankfurt meetings were significant for producing a defined list of agreed-upon steps to be taken by both sides. North arrived with a seven-point list he claimed the president had personally approved:

1. Iran provides funds for 500 TOWs and remainder of HAWK parts.

2. Within 9 days we deliver [HAWK] parts and TOWs (500) plus medical supplies.
3. All American hostages released.
4. Iran provides funds for 1500 TOWs.
5. Within 9 days we will deliver:
   - 1500 TOWs
   - Technical support for HAWKs
   - Updated intelligence on Iraq
   - Communications team
6. Iran will then:
   - Release [John] Pattis
   - Provide body of [William] Buckley
   - Provide copy of Buckley debrief
7. United States will then:
   - Identify sources for other items on [the relative's arms] list. . . .
   - Iran will then work to release other hostages.

North's role in the discussions was cut short by the stunning news one of the Project Democracy aircraft had been lost over Nicaragua. True to form, he invented an extravagant excuse for cutting short his participation, pretending he had to travel first to Reykjavik, where Reagan and Soviet leader Mikhail Gorbachev were about to hold their historic summit. "I've got to go to Iceland—they're going to meet with the president this afternoon." His follow-up was more accurate—and prophetic: "Then I have to go down south. . . . Big problems. . . . It's going to eat the rest of October for me."[51] Although the Iran talks had not gone smoothly, he had no choice but to fly back to Washington, D.C. Secord and Cave soon also departed, leaving Hakim responsible for hammering out a draft agreement with the Iranians. Allowing a private arms dealer to represent the United States would open up North and his associates to scathing criticism, even ridicule, after the story came out. But it was another example of North's modus operandi—to make snap judgments and to aim for maximum short-term gains without due regard for complications down the road.

The nine-point plan that came to be known as the "Hakim Accords" consisted of the following:

1. Iran provides funds to Mr. Hakim for 500 TOWs and, if willing, Iranians will provide for the HAWK spare parts which remain from the previous agreement.
2. Nine working days from now the 500 TOWs and the HAWK spare parts (if accepted by Iran) and the gifted medicines will be delivered to Iran.

3. Before executing Item 4 below, Albert will provide the plan for the release of the Kuwaitis (17 persons).
4. 1 ½ (1 definitely and the 2nd with all effective possible effort) American hostages in Lebanon, through the effort of Iran, will be released by the Lebanese.
5. Using the Letter of Credit method . . . (three to four days after delivery of shipment stipulated in Item 2) additional 500 TOWs (together with a maximum of 100 launchers), within four days after the execution of Item 4 above, will be delivered to Iran. The method of Letter of Credit will be reviewed between Albert and [Excised] by tomorrow night. Iran will pay the funds for 1500 TOWs (the 500 TOWs mentioned above plus an additional 1000 TOWs) and the 1000 TOWs will be delivered to Iran within nine days.[52]
6. The United States will start with the technical support of the HAWKs (material and know-how), update of the military intelligence and maps, establishment and commissioning of the special communication link, and will prepare the chart related to the items (provided by Mr. [Excised]) indicating price and delivery to Iran.
7. Before the return of Mr. [Excised] to Tehran, the subject of the Moslem prisoners (Shia) in Lebanon and the manner of their release by the involved parties will be reviewed by Mr. Secord.[53]
8. Iran will continue its effort for creating the grounds for the release of the rest of the hostages.
9. The steps for delivery of items referred to in the second part of Item 6 above will start.[54]

A comparison of North's and Hakim's lists shows the Iranians came out well ahead. The main U.S. concession was to revert to sequential deliveries of arms and hostages. Moreover, the United States would have to deliver 500 TOWs before even the first hostage came out, and Iran guaranteed to produce only a single captive, not all three of those taken prior to 1986. Hakim committed the United States to work toward the release of some of the Dawa prisoners, yet neglected to include the late CIA officer, Buckley, and postponed consideration of the other U.S. citizens taken during 1986. He even cut the cost of the missiles the United States would sell to Iran.

Still, North not only accepted Hakim's draft, he took credit for it, boasting to Poindexter his "donkey act . . . had quite an effect." Drawing Poindexter a rosy picture, he described Bahramani as desperate for expedited U.S. support: "[The nephew] told Dick that if he returned home without the hope of further help that he 'would be sent back to the front.'" He reported Bahramani wanted to meet even sooner than the follow-up date of November 3 North had proposed.[55]

North, too, was plainly anxious to move forward despite the imbalance in the agreed terms. He flatly misled Poindexter about the results from Frankfurt in order to ensure his approval to proceed. His description of several of the points in the agreement differed substantially from Hakim's version, and he greatly underplayed the friction that had flared up, almost leading to a rupture in the talks.

The gambit worked. Poindexter soon gave the go-ahead to begin implementing the "agreement." The first step was to initiate another shipment of TOW missiles. Meeting in Geneva with an Israeli official and Secord, North made a potentially significant decision. He agreed to allow Israel to unload 500 of the missiles it had received in May but rejected as not up to IDF standards. The United States would replenish those missiles from its stocks. The delivery to Iran, on October 28, went off without difficulty, but North's willingness to risk a further row with the Iranians about the quality of the munitions was another sign that building a foundation for future cooperation was not his real purpose.

Implosion

The day after the TOW shipment, the last major bilateral meeting took place in Mainz, Germany. The atmosphere was edgy because North and Secord betrayed frustration at the lack of definitive action by the Iranians to free the hostages. The promises thrown about on both sides tended toward hyperbole. If the United States would send the technicians sought by Rafsanjani to work on Phoenix missiles, Bahramani pledged, "I will personally get the third guy out."[56] Secord groused that with his expertise in having already built Iran's "goddamn air force" under the shah, he could help the Iranians discover a "billion dollars' worth of stuff they don't know they've got—in two weeks." North added that if only the hostages were freed, Iran would get a "million" TOWs.[57]

The Iranians made two disclosures that shook U.S. confidence further. One was that the members of the proposed Iranian joint commission to develop future relations with the United States included Mehdinejad, Najafabadi (the main Iranian representative at the Tehran meetings), and Kangarlou in addition to another Majles member. (Cave later recalled Hassan Rouhani, then commander of Iran's air defenses, was to be part of the commission.)[58] This was proof the arms deals would not bolster moderates within the regime, as U.S. officials had contended. Instead, the commission comprised a range of political viewpoints, including the hard-line IRGC. Moreover, Kangarlou's presence meant the U.S. side had never managed to rid themselves of the first channel after all. Worse, Bahramani accused Kangarlou of being behind the recent kidnapping of Reed. Becoming aware of the true makeup of the Iranian negotiating team and comprehending its significance "really blew our minds," Cave said later.[59]

Bahramani's second revelation concerned the eruption of a political dispute inside Iran that threatened to expose the initiative. The clash centered on a hard-line figure named Mehdi Hashemi, who was tied by marriage to Ayatollah Ali Montazeri, then Ayatollah Khomeini's designated successor. Hashemi headed the Islamic Liberation Movement, whose mission included spreading the Iranian revolution abroad by supporting extremists intent on expunging Western influence. Mehdinejad later told Hakim that Hashemi, who had recently been arrested, had been involved in a coup attempt in Bahrain and in smuggling arms and explosives to Saudi Arabia during the Hajj, among other offenses.[60] These were the kinds of actions that continued to earn Iran the label of leading state sponsor of terrorism and were at the core of a growing public division in the country over the proper direction for national policy.

Hashemi and his followers believed Rafsanjani had been turning against the war and exerting undue pressure on Hezbollah to free hostages. Aware McFarlane had been in Tehran, they decided to expose the clandestine visit as a way to discredit those policies and avenge Hashemi's imprisonment.[61] (Hashemi was later executed for "corruption on earth.") Bahramani reported that as many as 5 million pamphlets had been printed in mid-October revealing the McFarlane mission.[62] At the same time, a radical group within Lebanese Hezbollah had just printed a story about the ongoing U.S.-Iranian talks. Within days, the disclosure found its way to a bigger news outlet—the magazine *Ash-Shiraa*—and from there exploded into world headlines.

Meanwhile, other unfolding developments had promised serious trouble for the initiative. In mid-October, a lawyer and friend of Casey's named Roy Furmark approached him complaining that associates who had put up financing for the arms sales in hopes of substantial profits were impatient to get their money back. Casey asked Allen and Cave to find out the details. Allen produced a report laying out deep concerns about the initiative and warning of the danger of exposure. "We face a disaster of major proportions," he predicted. "Too many know too much."[63]

Thus, the seeds of the operation's demise had already taken root by the time of the Mainz meeting. After the disclosure in *Ash-Shiraa* on November 3, Cave met a few more times with Mehdinejad, confirming both sides favored moving forward with the dialogue. But in the scandal's aftermath, Shultz finally succeeded in reasserting State Department control over Iran policy, displacing the department's rivals on the NSC staff. Shultz sent a career officer, Ambassador Charles Dunbar, to meet with Mehdinejad, but according to Cave the new envoy did little more than read from a prepared paper and demonstrated no interest in continuing talks on the same terms. The Iranian recognized the change as a "return to zero."[64] By late December, the initiative was finally dead, and Washington had entered full scandal mode.

13

The Early Cover-Up

The shoot-down of the Enterprise's C-123 on October 5, 1986, prompted Ronald Reagan's administration to initiate a significant cover-up of its clandestine support for the Contras. A month later, the *Ash-Shiraa* revelation out of Lebanon touched off a new round of political scrambling on the even more controversial Iran arms deals. Although there were attempts at coordination, especially at the White House, the process had a chaotic, almost knee-jerk quality as agencies and individuals scurried to safeguard their various interests. Some sought to protect the president, the standing of the administration, and the viability of its policies; others to preserve the public approval levels of the Republican Party (especially with presidential elections coming in 1988); still others worked to keep their agencies out of the spotlight; and many naturally focused on limiting their personal exposure. These efforts continued throughout the congressional investigations of 1986–1987 and the legal proceedings that lasted for several years afterward. Here, the inevitable comparisons to the Watergate scandal were apt: the cover-up was in some respects more serious than the underlying acts.

October 5–November 3: Cleanup in Central America

Within hours of the C-123 going down, Felix Rodriguez telephoned George Bush's deputy national security advisor, Sam Watson, at home to deliver the news. CIA Costa Rica Station Chief Joseph Fernandez warned Richard Secord's associate, Robert Dutton, via KL-43: "Situation requires we do necessary damage control." Asking if the aircraft had a tail number, he went on, "If so, we will have to try to cover quickly as record of tail number could lead to very serious implication."[1] In short order, the rest of the Enterprise fleet was destroyed—taken to an isolated location, blown up with explosives, and buried in what Oliver North called the "ultimate cover-up."[2]

A "great plague of amnesia" was how North described the sweeping denials by CIA, Pentagon, and State Department officials in October regarding any connection to Eugene Hasenfus.[3] Congressional leaders were skeptical but unwilling to make direct accusations. "I don't think the intelligence community has ever lied to us," said David Durenberger (R-Minn.), chair of the Senate Select

Committee on Intelligence (SSCI). "The problem is what they don't tell us." The ranking Democrat, Patrick Leahy (D-Vt.), was more prescient: "It will bother me if this turns out to be connected with adjunct soldiers of fortune sent out there with a wink and nod or a shrug as a way of getting around our foreign policy or the law."[4] After the Nicaraguans found evidence of the plane's ties to the CIA, the secretary of state and the president himself began facing questions. Reagan assured reporters the government's hands were clean. Asked who the crew had been working for, he replied: "Not us."[5]

Assistant Secretary of State Elliott Abrams became the administration's front man on the issue. His initial public reaction was only that "some very brave people" have been involved in ferrying supplies to the Contras, "as seems to be the case with this flight. . . . God bless them . . . they are heroes."[6] Appearing on the CNN *Evans & Novak* show and other broadcasts, his denials of official involvement were unqualified. Asked for "categorical assurance that Hasenfus was not under the control, the guidance, the direction, or what have you, of anybody connected with the American government," he replied, "Absolutely. That would be illegal. We are barred from doing that, and we are not doing it." Following up, Novak asked if Abrams was "playing word games that are so common in Washington. You're not talking about the [NSC] or something else?" Abrams insisted, "I am not playing games. . . . No government agencies, none."[7]

Within five days of the shoot-down, Abrams appeared before the Senate Foreign Relations Committee (SFRC), where he acknowledged awareness of a Contra support operation but insisted that "it is not our supply system. . . . We do not encourage people to do this. . . . We don't tell them to do this, we don't ask them to do it. . . . I think it is quite clear . . . the attitude of the administration is that these people are doing a very good thing. . . . But that is without any encouragement and coordination from us, other than a public speech by the president."[8]

Abrams repeated these denials in other settings. Four days later he testified to the House Permanent Select Committee on Intelligence (HPSCI) in closed session. Chair Lee Hamilton (D-Ind.) asked, "Just to be clear, the United States Government has not done anything to facilitate the activities of the private groups, is that a fair statement? We have not furnished money. We have not furnished arms. We have not furnished advice. We have not furnished logistics." When another witness declined to speak for the entire government, Abrams was asked whether he could. "Yes, to the extent of my knowledge that I feel to be complete, other than the general public encouragement that we like this kind of activity."[9]

Abrams also faced questions about "Max Gómez" (Rodriguez's pseudonym), whom Hasenfus had named as part of the resupply operation and whom news accounts had connected to Bush's office. During his October 10 SFRC testimony, the assistant secretary denied knowing anything about whether Rodriguez reported to the vice president ("I have never heard any suggestion of that"), and at his HPSCI appearance four days later, he expanded on the assertion. Two months afterward, before the House Foreign Affairs Committee (HFAC), he declared prior to the Iran-Contra revelations, "I don't think I ever heard of Felix Rodriguez."[10]

In the coming weeks, members of Congress queried Abrams about foreign government assistance to the Contras. Despite his personal attempts to solicit funds from Brunei for the rebels, he denied any knowledge of such support, calling related news reports "false." To the SFRC, he stated: "I think I can say that while I have been Assistant Secretary, which is about 15 months, we have not received a dime from a foreign government, not a dime, from any foreign government." To the SSCI, he declared, "We're not—you know, we're not in the fund[-]raising business."[11]

Abrams was by no means alone in concealing administration involvement. Senior CIA officers Clair George and Alan Fiers, both well informed about the operations (and in Fiers's case an active participant), attended some of the same hearings. Neither contradicted Abrams, and both actively obstructed the inquiries themselves. As George told the HPSCI on October 14, "First I would like to state categorically that the Central Intelligence Agency was not involved directly or indirectly in arranging, directing or facilitating resupply missions conducted by private individuals in support of the Nicaraguan democratic resistance."[12]

George later apologized for this statement, acknowledging it was "wrong." He also regretted not correcting Abrams's "categorical" declarations to the committees. "I didn't have the guts to do it," he said, explaining he had been "overly taken with trying to protect the Central Intelligence Agency." Fiers admitted he "could have been more forthcoming," and there had not been "any doubt" in his mind as to who had been behind the Hasenfus flight.[13] Abrams also apologized for his misleading statements.[14]

November 3–21: Haunted by the HAWK Deal

In the aftermath of the crash, Abrams and U.S. Ambassador to El Salvador Edwin Corr discussed whether the upcoming Reagan-Gorbachev summit in Reykjavik on October 11–12 would sweep the incident off the front pages. It did not, but ironically the November 3 revelation of Robert McFarlane's mission to Tehran did. Although the C-123 shoot-down was a serious political blow and threatened congressional support for a cherished presidential objective, the administration's reaction mainly occupied the energies of midlevel officials because there was no evident tie to senior policy makers. The McFarlane disclosure was a different matter—connecting top-ranking officials directly to a highly contentious and arguably illegal policy.

For the next three weeks, press attention shifted heavily to the Iran story, while behind closed doors at the White House, the State and Defense Departments, CIA, president and cabinet labored to limit their vulnerability. National Security Advisor John Poindexter took the lead, stressing the need daily at his morning briefing to hold off on public comment. Reagan insisted to the press there was "no foundation" to the Lebanese report. "We will never pay off terrorists," he declared, "because that only encourages more of it."[15] Bush noted in his diary, "There is a lot of flak and misinformation out there. It is not a subject we can talk about."[16]

One reason for withholding information was the president had no intention of shutting down the initiative. He fully believed he had done nothing wrong, that somehow dealing directly with Iran was not the same as associating with the hostage-takers themselves. Members of his staff continued to be optimistic about the prospects, despite the publicity. Howard Teicher, who had traveled to Tehran with McFarlane, saw in Iranian public statements the "clearest possible signals . . . that the succession struggle is under[ ]way."[17] He pleaded to keep the initiative alive in hopes of influencing that process. Secretary of State George Shultz and Secretary of Defense Caspar Weinberger remained opposed but differed on how to handle the revelations.

Shultz alone proposed to engage the U.S. public rather than keep a tight hold on information, although he mainly saw it as a way to protect the administration rather than a worthwhile end in itself. In a cable to the national security advisor, he argued that "giving the essential facts to the public" offered the best way to "control the story." But the president, vice president, CIA Director William Casey, and White House Chief of Staff Donald Regan favored staying silent. So did McFarlane, who wrote to North, "I hope to daylights that someone has been purging the NSA's files on this episode."[18] Weinberger, too, "strongly objected" to the secretary of state's preference for "telling all."[19]

Shultz was pessimistic about the direction of events. "It's amateur hour over there [at the White House]," an aide remarked, reflecting the view of the State Department leadership—"a bunch of kids working w/Ollie." Shultz repeatedly criticized the arms-for-hostages policy in discussions with his advisors: "The hostgs keep growing in number. This encourages that." Moreover, the political fallout was likely to be serious. "This cd be the kind of thing where somebody has to resign [and] take the rap." As a member of Nixon's cabinet during Watergate, he recalled individuals "get in [and] can't get out [and] so stonewall [and] get in deeper."[20] One of those he had in mind was the vice president: "What concerns me," he told a friend several days after the Iran revelation, "is Bush on TV" saying it was "ridiculous to even consider selling arms to Iran." The fact was, Shultz asserted, the "VP was part of it . . . in that mtg." Now he risked "getting drawn into web of lies. . . . Shd be v careful how he plays the loyal lieutenant role now."[21] The next day, according to Shultz, he met with the vice president and delivered the same message. Bush assured him, "I'm v[ery] careful what I say," but Shultz rejoined, "You can't be tech[nically] right, you have to be *right*. I told him he was there [and] approved it. He knew and supported it. I sd that's where you are." Assessing how Bush and other backers of the initiative were reacting to the mounting scandal, Shultz concluded ruefully, "They are now lying to themselves."[22]

Shultz's stance understandably raised tensions within the administration. Several of his peers suspected he was looking out for himself more than for the president or his colleagues. (He believed Bush "sees me as a threat.")[23] His detractors tried to undermine his standing with Reagan, but he had support from an unlikely source—hard-line conservatives. Bush noted in his diary, "All in all, a troubling weekend. People running for cover, blaming. . . . The right wing, who is normally on Shultz's case, rallying behind him because of the trading arms for hostages policy."[24]

THE NOVEMBER 10 MEETING

Public pressure soon dictated the need for a formal White House reaction to the Iran revelation. On November 10, the president met with his top advisors to establish a unified version of events and to make sure he could rely on his aides' public support for the policy. Reagan began the discussion by insisting on the need to issue a statement "as result of media, etc.," according to Donald Regan's notes.[25] The president clung to his conviction: "We have not dealt directly w/ terrorists, no bargaining, no ransom." Virtually no one in the room shared this view, but no one immediately challenged him.

Poindexter followed with a recitation of the Iran program filled with deliberate inaccuracies. The "main objective," he declared, had been a "long-term" policy of establishing contacts with "more moderate elements" in Iran "looking to the future." The second aim had been to "stop Iran['s] export of terrorism. . . . Hostage release" was the third. Poindexter then disclosed the existence of the January 1986 presidential finding authorizing the deals, following with a description of Israel's involvement, which he falsely claimed U.S. officials had "stumbled on" while "tracking down its shipments to Iran." The first delivery of arms to Iran in summer 1985, he said, had been "shipped by Israelis," not by the United States; Washington had been informed only "after the fact." Subsequent shipments had been "OKd in advance," but these purportedly consisted only of defensive weapons in "miniscule amts."[26]

Much of Poindexter's account—not to mention the president's—was untrue. Reagan's main goal for the operation was the release of the U.S. hostages, not a long-term relationship with Iranian moderates. The United States did not inadvertently discover a rogue Israeli arms operation, nor had Washington learned only afterward of the first TOW shipment. Both countries had coordinated with each other from the beginning, and Reagan himself had authorized the August 1985 delivery. The total missile count was double the figure Poindexter reported. Furthermore, the account omitted any reference to the November 1985 HAWK debacle and failed to mention the December 5 and January 6 presidential findings.

The legally problematic HAWK operation was deeply troubling to several of the president's aides. In late November, Attorney General Edwin Meese acknowledged his concerns to Shultz (who quoted him in debriefing his aide, Charles Hill): "Certain things cd be violation of a law. P[resident] didn't know about Hawk in Nov [1985]. If it happened [and] P didn't report to Congress, it's a violation."[27] Of course, notwithstanding Meese's contention, Reagan had not only been fully aware of the activity in November 1985, he had approved it—and, indeed, no one had informed Capitol Hill, as required by law. Yet there is no indication any of Reagan's advisors who knew about the shipment and who attended the National Security Planning Group (NSPG) meeting on November 10—including Shultz, Weinberger, Regan, Casey, Poindexter, and the president himself—raised the matter before the group.

Although the purpose of the November 10 session was to coordinate the administration's public stance, it widened the divisions within the NSPG. Weinberger expressed surprise at how many missiles had been traded. Shultz claimed never to have heard about the January finding. He questioned the wisdom of the initiative and according to notes of the discussion engaged in a testy exchange with both the president and Poindexter, asking: "In this context of [hostage] releases how can you say it [TOW sales] not linked? P [President]: It *not linked*! Pdx: How else will we get hostg out? I [Shultz] sd when we cross line, Isr[ael] gets clear field—[and] they supply stuff that really matters." He called for the deals to be shut down once and for all. Returning to the State Department, the secretary complained the others were "distorting the record," "trying to get me to lie," and "taking the president down the drain. . . . It's Watergate all over."[28]

At the meeting Reagan had argued the need to "say something because I'm being held out to dry."[29] Casey had already prepared a statement declaring "unanimous support for the president's decisions" on Iran. Shultz balked, however, suggesting they delete the final word in the quote so that it would reflect backing for the president, but not the policy. His alternative eventually carried the day, although it took another sharp exchange with Poindexter after the session to finalize the change.[30] The incident rankled several of his colleagues, who began to advocate for his removal as secretary of state. Reagan, too, was upset but did not blame Shultz at first. Instead, he told the vice president in a private meeting he was "very suspicious" the "State Department bureaucracy" might be "playing games and trying to undermine the policy."[31]

SHULTZ'S MOTIVATIONS

In hindsight, Shultz's objectives were more complicated than simply protecting the president or disclosing the truth about the Iran initiative. His accounts to Congress contained enough inaccuracies about his own knowledge to raise the question whether they were deliberate. In late 1986, he told lawmakers that from the start of the affair through November 1985 he had been aware of internal discussions about possible arms sales but was never informed any deals had been struck. From December 1985 to May 1986, he said, he understood certain administration officials supported a dialogue with Tehran, but at the time he did not believe arms were part of the operation. After May 1986, he claimed, he heard nothing about weapons deliveries.[32]

The independent counsel, Lawrence Walsh, tracked the secretary's reactions to the unfolding Iran revelations largely through the meticulous contemporaneous notes of Shultz's aides, Hill and Nicholas Platt. According to prosecutors, a few days after the *Ash-Shiraa* story, the secretary began to reconstruct his actions and recollections. Working mainly from memory, he divided his evolving awareness of the operation into the three time periods noted above. But his aides' notes repeatedly contradict the account he gave Congress.

In fall 1985, the record shows McFarlane notified Shultz about the state of talks regarding Iran and specifically about the release of hostage the Reverend Benjamin Weir. Using the code name Shultz and his advisors had coined for North and the covert program, Platt wrote: "Polecat beginning to pay off. Weir has been released . . . other things could happen." Hill noted, "McF & Ollie are getting us into deal where we will have to pay off ISR [Israel]." As for the November 1985 HAWK shipment, Shultz claimed to the HFAC in January 1987 that although he had heard about plans to deliver the missiles, when no hostages emerged, he assumed the deal had not been "consummated."

Regarding the second phase, between December 1985 and May 1986, notes by both of his close aides and by Weinberger reveal several clear-cut instances in which Shultz learned from the president, Poindexter, Weinberger, or assorted State Department officials that in fact the United States had been shipping weapons to Tehran. After a January 7, 1986, meeting with Reagan and other advisors, a dejected Shultz reported to Hill he had been unable to dissuade the president (referred to as "P" in the notes) from continuing the initiative: "P decided to go ahead. Only Cap and I opposed. I won't deb[rie]f anybody about it. (TOWs for hostages.)"[33] On at least four occasions between January and April 1986—at private weekly lunches Shultz attended with Weinberger and Casey—the secretary of state learned Iran deals were continuing; TOW and HAWK missiles were explicitly mentioned, and in at least one case Weinberger showed Shultz highly classified electronic intercepts confirming an active operation. Repeatedly during this period, Shultz lamented to his inner circle the deals were "wrong" and "illegal," and the president was "way overexposed. . . . We will get crucified," he warned.[34]

As for the third phase, Shultz claimed he had heard nothing after early May 1986 about arms going to Iran. The independent counsel's staff found compelling evidence, however, in the form of electronic intercepts, memos from State Department officials, and handwritten notes, confirming the secretary had understood on several occasions through July that weapons continued to be a part of the operation.

Regarding Shultz having "streamlined the evidence," the independent counsel ascribes the secretary's decision to a "Washington practice" of appearing unequivocal as a way to fend off questions and accusations. Shultz's ultimate purpose, prosecutors concluded, was either to avoid divulging his "harsh private criticism of President Reagan" and his circle or to "accommodate the administration's unyielding position of nondisclosure."[35]

Shultz's motivations were probably more self-serving than Walsh concluded. The secretary's opposition to the arms deals (which the independent counsel called "heroic")[36] was a matter of principle, important enough to him that he rebuffed the president's appeal for a public show of support for the policy. But Shultz must have sensed his ethical standing would be diminished if the public learned he had been privy to hard evidence for much of 1986 that the deals were continuing yet chose to walk away from the issue early in the year, instructing his staff, "Let's stay out. . . . Just keep informed."[37] In 1992, when pressed by prosecutors less sympathetic than the congressional questioners who admired his handling of the affair, his testimony occasionally took on an artfulness reminiscent of his controversial subordinate, Abrams.[38] Shultz recalled late 1986 as a "very traumatic period for me."[39]

LOSING CONTROL OF THE STORY

At the CIA in early November, the effort to paper over the Iran operation also began to unravel. The month before, Charles Allen had detected the intermingling of the Iran and Contra programs and concluded a diversion of funds had taken place. By promptly informing his superiors, he created a paper trail that made it harder to claim ignorance (as Casey's deputy, Robert Gates, would do). Soon, the CIA inspector general uncovered similar evidence and demanded more information. This prompted Casey and Gates to contact Poindexter to discuss the ramifications.

Simultaneously at the Justice Department, Meese had become concerned about a possible legal breach in connection with the arms deals. A few days earlier he had quietly instructed a young assistant attorney general named Charles Cooper to look into the matter. Meese's uneasiness undoubtedly grew after White House spokesman Larry Speakes, attempting to provide cover for Reagan, told reporters the president had been "guided by the Attorney General all along in all of this." Meese instructed the Justice Department spokesman to reply that the attorney general had been unaware of the Iran operation until Reagan had signed the January 17, 1986, finding.[40] Poindexter had taken a similar tack on behalf of the president, identifying Shultz and Weinberger as well as Meese as having helped put together that finding. The State Department quickly responded Shultz had not been "directly involved."[41]

Meanwhile, senior attorneys from a number of agencies reached different conclusions about the legal soundness of the Iran deals. Cooper asserted in his report to Meese, completed on November 13, the president's actions had been covered by the National Security Act. White House Counsel Peter Wallison expressed qualms that the Justice Department "had not even begun to research the question in any depth," and Cooper acknowledged to him he had in fact been working on his review only "for about a day."[42] Wallison's concerns led him to call meetings of attorneys from other agencies and even to contact Meese. The State Department counselor, Abraham Sofaer, also voiced serious doubts.[43]

What particularly troubled several of the attorneys who met on November 12—the group included representatives from the Defense Department and the CIA—was their sense the NSC lawyer, Paul Thompson, was "stiffing everybody" on the facts. Thompson had been privy to conversations with North and others directly involved in the affair but seemed unwilling to talk about the details (reminiscent of North's and Poindexter's rebuff of outside agencies snooping into their activities).[44] The split carried more serious implications for the president's political protectors, including Meese, because significant disagreements among the administration's top attorneys would be impossible to disregard if they became public.

Also on November 12, the president and Poindexter briefed congressional leaders at the White House, having concluded that continued official silence was not going to ease outside pressures for disclosure. Reagan insisted the United States had not paid any ransom for hostages. On Meese's advice (even though he had not yet received the legal analysis he had just commissioned), the president declared no laws had been violated.[45] Poindexter repeated the falsehoods he had conveyed to the NSPG two days earlier. The congressional visitors had no alternative sources, so there was little basis to question the account. But the session did not answer all of their concerns. Bush's diary for the day reads: "We had Dole, Cheney, Sen. Byrd and Jim Wright down there. . . . Cheney was very supportive in a lot of ways but not in every way. Dole somewhat noncommittal."[46]

The administration's ongoing disarray fed a sense of urgency to take more aggressive action. A frustrated Reagan pushed for making a statement. "This whole irresponsible press bilge about hostages [and] Iran has gotten totally out of hand," he wrote in his diary on November 12. "The media looks like it's trying to create another Watergate. I laid down the law in the morning meetings—I want to go public personally [and] tell the people the truth. We're trying to arrange it for tomorrow."[47]

THE NOVEMBER 13 SPEECH

The president's speech the next day was his first major address on the Iran affair. The atmosphere inside the White House was taut. According to Bush, the "President show[ed] great tension for the first time. . . . There's tension between the various players." The scene offered an unpleasant reminder: "I remember Watergate. I remember the way things oozed out. . . . It really is hemorrhaging and the President now is going with his speech."[48] The drafting process for Reagan's remarks involved a "hectic struggle."[49] Notwithstanding his expressed intention to tell the truth, the result was an amalgam of misleading and untruthful statements. "I authorized the transfer of small amounts of defensive weapons and spare parts for defensive systems to Iran," he said. "These modest deliveries, taken together, could easily fit into a single cargo plane. They could not, taken together, affect the outcome of the . . . war . . . nor . . . the military balance." He assured the nation "all appropriate Cabinet Officers were fully consulted," and "the actions I authorized were and continue to be in full compliance with federal law." Finally, he asserted, "We did not—repeat—did not trade weapons or anything else for hostages—nor will we."[50]

The instinct to communicate to the nation had been on target, but the dubious assertions—particularly that no arms-for-hostages trade had taken place—left most viewers feeling there was much more to the story. The search for ways to stanch the "hemorrhaging" continued. Regan and Poindexter gave a total of eight interviews on television the next day, but these only added to the confusion. On the one hand, they left the impression the president had approved a request by a "third country" to sell weapons, then a few days later reverted to the original story: Reagan had authorized the shipment in question only after the fact. The two also contradicted each other on which government initiated the idea for the program—Iran or Israel.[51]

Shultz continued to press the White House to publicly disavow further arms deals with Tehran. He made the plea directly in a meeting with the president as well as in a memo to Regan. Raising the stakes, he advised the president he planned to step down as secretary of state. "I told him it's time for me to go," he recalled to aides immediately afterward. But the president, known to be awkward with difficult personnel matters, fended him off: "I don't want you to go. I want y[ou] to stay. I want to talk later about it."[52] Shultz's underlying intent was not to resign—he had threatened to do so at least three times before for lesser reasons[53]—it was to pressure Reagan not only to step back from the initiative but to ratify the State Department's primacy over the NSC staff on Iran policy. The ploy did not immediately produce the result he wanted. If anything it created more resentment among his colleagues, including the White House chief of staff. The next day, Bush noted in his diary, "Don Regan whispered to me that we're having real problems with Shultz. That Shultz was not on board at all."[54]

The gulf between the secretary of state and the rest of the cabinet widened when he appeared a few days later on the CBS Sunday news show *Face the Nation*. Characterizing his awareness of the arms deals as "fragmentary at best," he pointed the finger at Poindexter as the "designated hitter." Asked whether there would be any more weapons deliveries to Tehran, his initial answer was: "It's certainly against our policy." Program host Leslie Stahl persisted: "That's not an answer. Why don't you answer the question directly? I'll ask it again. Will there be any more arms shipments to Iran?" Shultz equivocated once more: "I would certainly say, as far as I'm concerned, no." When Stahl asked, "Do you have the authority to speak for the entire Administration?" Shultz responded frankly, "No."[55]

By his own account, Shultz worried he might get fired for this startling display of candor on national television. The chief of staff complained to Bush that Shultz's insistence on shutting down the Iran program "makes the President look like he's 'wrong.'" Weinberger grumbled that the secretary of state had "distanced himself" further from the others.[56] To Shultz's surprise, in the midst of these reproaches, the president took the opposite view, providing him the statement of support he had been after. What he had been unable to win in private he managed to obtain by going public.[57]

FALSE CHRONOLOGY

As the political fallout continued, congressional leaders made it clear they planned to investigate. Speaker of the House Jim Wright (D-Tex.) accused Reagan's team of violating as many as three separate laws. With polls reflecting ongoing disenchantment with the president's handling of the issue, Poindexter decided to put together a consistent story of what had happened. At his instruction, the NSC staff prepared a lengthy chronology, the true purpose of which was to defend the president, his aides, and the operation itself. The document went through several drafts before its final version appeared on November 20.

On November 17, Assistant Attorney General Cooper obtained a version of the chronology and immediately realized it could dramatically alter his conclusion that the operations had been legal. One revelation was the statement, "On August 22, 1985, the U.S. . . . . acquiesced in an Israeli delivery of military supplies (508 TOWs) to Tehran."[58] Another surprise was the Israelis had shipped HAWK missiles to Iran in November 1985. Cooper had not known about either of these transactions, which predated the January 17, 1986, finding he had stated gave the president adequate legal cover. His concerns at first were not so much about the deliveries themselves, which would be "Israel's problem" if they violated the Arms Export Control Act (AECA). He was more worried about the related AECA requirement the United States "immediately" report such breaches to Congress. Informing Meese immediately about the 1985 shipments, he had the impression the attorney general shared his "surprise and concern."[59] Cooper also "probably" contacted Thompson about the new development, which was about to become a major political crisis.

At the White House the next day, November 18, Wallison convened another meeting of his counterparts from other agencies—the same group that had met the day before Reagan's speech. His aim was to discover as much as possible about the arms deals, having been shut out by the White House staff (and indeed by his chief client, the president). Wallison, Cooper, and Sofaer pleaded with Thompson, who knew far more about the operations, to tell them what had happened. At a minimum, they wanted to know what the White House staff planned to report to the congressional intelligence committees. Thompson refused, saying he was bound by Poindexter's instructions to limit information to those with a need to know. According to Sofaer, the CIA counsel was equally unhelpful. Thompson did reveal one pertinent fact: Reagan had held two meetings about the Iran operation with both Shultz and Weinberger present. He said Reagan had listened to everyone's views and had decided to go ahead with the initiative. Sofaer thought Thompson's refusal to share details was "shocking," and he rushed to report on this "very disturbing" development to the secretary of state.[60]

Either through Meese or Thompson, the word spread internally that legal problems with the pre-1986 Israeli deliveries had surfaced. The following day, North's notes record anxious calls from Poindexter and Assistant Secretary of Defense Richard Armitage. Poindexter's call came at 5:30 p.m. In the midst of discussing the Iran-related events of 1985, North's notation records the comment: "Big issue then was legality." Half an hour later, Armitage called, and North wrote: *"Lawyers*—Israeli shipments in 1985—Did we know about it?"[61]

That evening, Poindexter asked McFarlane, who had been centrally involved in the deals as national security advisor and after his retirement, to look over the chronology. This proved another turning point in the cover-up. McFarlane made several changes plainly designed to protect the president or his staff. One of the main fallacies he put forward in a lengthy PROFS message to Poindexter was the assertion the president had not given prior approval to the first weapons sales by Israel in summer 1985.[62] Even Secord balked when he read this. He asked North about the claim but was told without elaboration that McFarlane had inserted the entry. Secord understood this to mean it was not subject to debate, at which point, by his account, he turned and left the office.[63]

McFarlane made another crucial alteration—deleting direct mention of the HAWK episode. He proposed referring only to "other transfers of equipment . . . between Israel and Iran" that occurred "later in the fall."[64] Both of his modifications were incorporated virtually unchanged into the document.

THE NOVEMBER 19 PRESS CONFERENCE

On November 19, Reagan responded to persistent public frustration by holding a press conference. However, he had no intention of altering his version of events, much less acknowledging error. "The President is going to try to not be conciliatory," Bush noted in his diary. Instead, he planned to say, "'Look, I can understand from everything we've been reading why people are concerned, but here are the facts.'"[65] Reagan followed the plan. "I don't think a mistake was made," he declared to reporters, "and I don't see that it has been a fiasco or a great failure of any kind." Denying he had engaged in an arms-for-hostages swap, he nonetheless pointed to the return of three hostages (and establishing "contacts" with Iranian officials) as evidence "we still have made some ground. . . . I think that what we did was right, and we're going to continue on this path."[66]

The president's remarks contained several important misstatements. He insisted that no third country had taken part in the operations; that the United States became involved in missile shipments only after the January 17, 1986, finding; that the Iranians bought only 1,000 TOWs (not the true figure of 2,004); that those weapons could fit inside a single cargo plane with "plenty of room left over"; and that no arms-for-hostages trade had occurred. His obstinacy hurt his public standing. Twenty minutes after the press conference, the White House was forced to issue a statement confirming the role of a "third country."[67]

Administration officials reacted with disappointment and heightened concern. Only the vice president believed Reagan "did very well," lamenting that "the minute it was over, people jumped all over him, accusing him of misstating."[68] Shultz told the president he had done "well under pressure," but there had been "a gr[ea]t many factual errors." He offered to explain where the inaccuracies were, and a "shaken" Reagan agreed to meet.[69]

THE CIA AND NSC CIRCLE THEIR WAGONS (SEPARATELY)

Behind the scenes, confusion persisted over what had actually happened in 1985, further eroding White House ability to control the story. Legal counsel from the agencies entangled in the arms deals dug deeper into the case in order to try to protect their clients. Sofaer, Wallison, and Cooper became gravely concerned when they discovered some of the president's closest advisors were about to spread more fictions to Congress.

The CIA generated the most serious misgivings. A few days earlier, the intelligence committees of both chambers had requested top-level briefings about the Iran program after Casey's meetings with congressional leaders had failed to allay their concerns. Clair George then briefed Senate Intelligence Committee staff, but his comments included several false statements, among them his denial the CIA had been part of any arms shipments before 1986.[70] The committees wanted to hear from Casey directly.

That prospect produced "pandemonium" at the CIA.[71] At the core of Casey's testimony would be two chronologies—the one the NSC staff was drafting and a separate document being prepared at the CIA. Each contained demonstrably untrue assertions, the most worrisome relating to the HAWK shipment. Officials within the CIA's Directorate of Operations (DO), which had been involved with that shipment, chose to omit any reference to the DO role. Putting the lie to this representation was yet another chronology the chief of the CIA Iran Branch had drafted immediately after the *Ash-Shiraa* story. He had distributed his timeline to his superiors—Thomas Twetten, Bert Dunn, and Casey—as well as to North. Also contradicting the DO was former CIA general counsel Stanley Sporkin, who had recently provided confirmation to agency attorneys both that the shipment had contained weapons and that a retroactive presidential finding had covered it.

The current CIA general counsel, David Doherty, grew troubled enough to request a meeting in Gates's office with George and others. On November 18, a day after hearing Sporkin's account, Doherty had attended the White House session with Wallison, Sofaer, Cooper, and Thompson and had witnessed the NSC counsel imply the CIA had played a bigger role in the operation than had the

NSC staff. Doherty's priority immediately became to amass evidence to defend his agency against NSC attempts to shift the blame.[72]

On November 20, the day before Casey's congressional testimony, Poindexter held a meeting in his office at which the discussion focused on the contradictory accounts about the HAWKs. Casey, Meese, Gates, Thompson, Cooper, and North had gathered to prepare the director's testimony. Casey's initial draft flatly misrepresented the agency's role, declaring: "We in CIA did not find out that our airline had hauled Hawk missiles into Iran until mid-January when we were told by the Iranians." Several of those in the room knew this was false, yet no one protested when North proposed broadening the statement to cover everyone involved (particularly the NSC staff). Instead of "We in CIA," he wrote in by hand, "No one in the USG."[73]

The group also discussed another fabrication: U.S. officials had believed the HAWK cargo was oil-drilling equipment. This was the cover story North and the Israelis had agreed to in 1985 in case the operation was blown.[74] Meese later attributed the statement at the meeting to North but added, "I don't remember anyone dissenting" from it.[75]

The same day, Sofaer obtained a copy of Casey's planned remarks and immediately sounded an alarm. First, the use of Southern Air Transport (SAT) for the HAWK shipment raised a "red flag" because of its possible tie-in to the covert Central America operation. Second, he knew the oil-drilling statement was untrue because he had just learned from Hill that McFarlane had explicitly discussed HAWKs with Shultz the year before. "The whole thing smelled to me like the kind of thing you see in a trial," he said later—"in a narcotics case, for example, where they refer to the drugs as 'shirts' or something like that."[76] He notified Shultz's aides he was "very afraid" of a cover-up, then telephoned Wallison and Deputy Attorney General Arnold Burns to convey his concerns. He also spoke several times to Cooper. Burns offered unconvincing assurances that Meese was already aware of "certain facts" that would resolve any concerns.[77] But Wallison was "shocked" to learn about the oil equipment cover story, and Cooper agreed with Sofaer that if the testimony did not change they would both resign. By the end of the day, Cooper informed Sofaer he had reached Meese and had received instructions to make sure Casey's testimony made no such false claims. The attorney general was cutting short a trip and heading back to Washington, D.C.[78]

In spite of these attempts to straighten out the facts, several erroneous and deceptive statements made their way back into both Casey's and Poindexter's congressional statements on November 21. These included denying a U.S. government role in the HAWK transaction, concealing the existence of the retroactive finding, and misrepresenting CIA knowledge of the actual cargo. Too many people with competing interests—hoping to protect themselves, their superiors, or their agencies—were in a position to impose their views, thus creating additional layers of conflict that risked spinning out of control. The potential for damage to the president led Meese—his closest political protector—to decide to take personal control of crisis management.

November 21–24: An "Informal" Inquiry

When Meese returned to Washington, D.C., on November 21, he gathered his trusted deputies—Burns; Cooper; William Bradford Reynolds, in charge of the Civil Rights Division; and John Richardson, his chief of staff. He told them he was about to recommend to the president an investigation into what exactly was known about the Iran initiative within the administration.

Meese's choice of an investigative team struck some officials as odd. Assistant Attorney General William Weld, head of the Criminal Division, objected "with some feeling" to the fact his office—and the FBI—were left out. At a staff meeting on November 21, he complained, "It didn't make sense for very high-ranking officials" not "intimately familiar" with other Iran-related criminal cases under way to be involved.[79] For several reasons, the attorney general's handling of the entire inquiry over the next four days prompted severe criticism, even from some Republicans.

Early on, the question of "legal problems" arose, specifically over whether there were "other facts" to discover "that would raise crim[inal] problems."[80] Meese initially denied legal issues were at stake. But according to his aides, criminality was the dominant concern. "The big problem for us," Richardson said, "was what laws might have been kicked into focus or violated by the Administration by shipping these arms in '85, before there was a Finding in '86." Meese knew about the earlier shipments from having attended the November 10 meeting run by Reagan and Poindexter. Although he denied being made aware until more than a week afterward, his notes from the session read in part: "508 [TOWs] shipped by Israel—[United States] told after the fact. . . . Results: . . . 3 hostages ret'd: Weir, Jenko, Jacobsen. . . . The entire focus," Richardson noted, was "whether the U.S. Government knew about it and authorized it."[81]

At the White House, Meese told the president, "We really didn't have a coherent picture . . . of what had taken place" in the Iran operation. "We had a lot of people with different parts of the puzzle," but "it was necessary to get an overview" for the president's sake.[82] Reagan agreed, and a deadline of the following Monday was set for a report to the NSPG. Meese returned to the Justice Department, where he and his aides began planning their investigation.

A DESTROYED "FINDING"

Over the weekend, the attorney general's team met or spoke on the telephone with several key players, but a number of those conversations raised serious questions about the inquiry. Meese first telephoned Poindexter on Friday to ask him to pull together relevant documents. Poindexter agreed, then contacted Thompson and North to pass along Meese's request. Poindexter knew Meese was acting on the president's orders because he had attended the attorney general's meeting with the president earlier that day.

Yet, instead of safeguarding the integrity of NSC files, the national security advisor proceeded to destroy one of the key pieces of the official record on the arms deals—the December 1985 retroactive finding. He justified that extraordinary act by claiming the CIA had prepared it merely as a "CYA" measure, drafting it "in a very narrow way" that made the initiative look like strictly an arms-for-hostages deal. "We were being put about the head and shoulders [sic] in the press" for allegedly engaging in a hostage trade, he told investigators. "I decided that it would be politically embarrassing to the President at this point because it would substantiate what was being alleged . . . and so I decided to destroy it." He did so by simply tearing up the document and throwing it into a wastebasket.[83]

Poindexter also had a conversation with North that Friday afternoon. North related the content of his notes about the HAWK shipment, which showed several NSC staff knew about it at the time. "I had the distinct impression that [North] was going to destroy that spiral notebook when he left the office," Poindexter acknowledged. "I didn't tell him to destroy it, but I also didn't tell him not to destroy it." North's notes, and the many PROFS messages they exchanged, were not "something that we had to retain. At this point, we frankly viewed the issues as a political issue,"[84] not as a legal matter requiring the preservation of vital evidence.

FOCUS ON HAWKS

That same Friday, Meese and Cooper spoke to McFarlane. The former national security advisor's portrayal of events was littered with falsehoods. He said he had learned about the HAWK shipment only in May 1986; he implied North had been the central figure, when McFarlane himself had put him into play; he claimed that in November 1985 he thought the cargo was oil equipment; and he professed not to recall discussing the operation with Shultz at the time.[85] Afterward Meese stayed behind for a few moments, and McFarlane told him he was assuming much of the responsibility for the operation himself, but the president had approved the deals.[86]

After the interview, McFarlane wrote a PROFS note to Poindexter reporting, "I spent a couple hours with Ed Meese today going over the record with him." After claiming the "only blind spot" in his recollection was a "shipment in November '85 which still doesn't ring a bell with me," he made a curious assertion that the problem surrounding the lack of notification about the shipment could "be covered if the President made a 'mental finding' before the transfers took place." McFarlane made a similar comment to North after the interview. An entry in North's notebook reads: "RR said he wd support 'Mental Finding.'"[87] Although Meese denied suggesting to McFarlane the president could be covered legally in this way, McFarlane recalled the attorney general mentioning the phrase— outside of Cooper's presence—and "it seemed to stand out in my mind as important."[88]

On Friday evening, Meese telephoned Weinberger but decided after only a short conversation the defense secretary had little to add. How he reached that conclusion so soon is not apparent—Weinberger clearly knew a great deal, particularly about the Iran operation, and, as was later discovered, had a large collection of notes that would have shed critically important light on the president's state of awareness.

On Saturday morning, November 22, Meese and Cooper met first with Shultz, accompanied by his inveterate note taker, Hill. Meese declared that the "key," according to Hill's record, "revolves around Nov 85." At Meese's request, Shultz gave a detailed rundown of his conversation with McFarlane at Geneva. He next told Meese, "You shd know I went to P[resident] Thurs. night," the day after Reagan's disastrous press conference, and in the course of their discussion—with Regan present—he had mentioned to the president the same information about McFarlane's briefing. Shultz said Reagan replied: "I knew about that." (Prior to the Meese interview, Shultz had briefed Hill on his meeting with Reagan, noting the same exchange: "I told P Thursday of what Bud told me about Nov 85. He sd he knew it." He also predicted, "When dug into—will be shown that P pushed these people.")[89] Meese's reaction was to comment the president "didn't make notes" and "had trouble remembering mtgs." He then asked, "As to Nov talk w/ Bud, no contact y[ou] know of that Bud had w/P then?" Shultz answered: "Not to my knowledge—tho I don't know."[90]

Meese's stated interest was in what the president knew about the HAWKs. Yet even though he asked Shultz whether McFarlane had spoken directly to Reagan on the subject, he did not pose the question to McFarlane himself. (He told Shultz simply, "Bud remembers very little.")[91] He dismissed the secretary of state's contention that Reagan had just acknowledged his awareness of the operation, asserting that the president's memory could not be trusted. After further discussion, in which the attorney general displayed a detailed knowledge of the Iran initiative, he told Shultz, "Certain things cd be violation of a law." He declared flatly, "P didn't know about HAWK in Nov.," then concluded that "if it happened and P didn't report to Congress, it's a violation."[92]

Shultz declined to speculate later whether he thought Meese was trying to get him to change his recollection. Hill was more forthright. During the meeting, he said, Meese had stood over Shultz in a "back on your heels" way and posed "leading" questions to the secretary.[93]

DISCOVERY OF THE DIVERSION MEMO

Later that morning, Reynolds and Richardson went to the Old Executive Office Building to look for documents in North's office. Their objective, according to Richardson, was to find evidence on the Iran-related events of 1985. Reynolds described this "fact-gathering task" as a "monumental one . . . about [as] important an endeavor [as] had been undertaken by the Department."[94] Yet for such a sensitive inquiry, their methods reflected little concern the individuals they were investigating might not be fully forthcoming. Instead of personally inspecting the file cabinets, for example, they asked North's assistant, Robert Earl, to locate and bring materials to them. They had no way to be sure what other relevant files might exist.

The situation turned out to be much worse. The Justice Department attorneys were unaware that ever since the C-123 shoot-down North had been culling his files and shredding large numbers of incriminating records. Earl later described this as the final phase in a "damage control operation" that amounted to "termination of the compartment." That meant getting rid of all "sensitive" documents, "all the inner boxes, not the total box, that had already been briefed to the Congress, but the sensitive material within the box within the box within the box, however far it went."[95]

As the two attorneys sorted through piles of records, setting aside items to photocopy, Reynolds came upon a manila folder with the letters "W.H." in red ink across the flap. Among other documents inside was a memorandum entitled "Release of American Hostages in Beirut," a six-page summary of the Iran operation written in early April 1986. On the fifth page was a section that began, "The residual funds from this transaction are allocated as follows . . . $12 million will be used to purchase critically needed supplies for the Nicaraguan Democratic Resistance Forces."[96]

Reynolds's reaction was a low "utterance"—"holy cow" or something a "little more graphic."[97] He kicked Richardson under the table and shoved the memo across to him. Richardson's reaction was the same. This was an entirely new development—evidence of the commingling of the Iran and Contra operations. (That same day, by coincidence, Shultz had told Meese he feared a connection between the two programs might exist.) Trying to avoid drawing attention to the document—which would soon become the most infamous piece of the Iran-Contra record—Reynolds put it back in its folder for later photocopying.

Shortly afterward, the two left for lunch with Meese. Although the memo was the most dramatic item that had caught their eye, they did not immediately mention it. When they did, the attorney general's response was similar to their own: "Oh, shit." As Richardson recalled, "Meese expressed great surprise. . . . [He] sort of squinted his eyes and that sort of thing."[98] After lunch, Meese sent the two lawyers back to North's office to obtain a copy of the document and continue searching. They did so, encountering North, who seemed particularly relaxed and talkative. Although he expected to be questioned then and there, North was told he would have to meet Meese the next day for his interview.

The discovery of the diversion memo radically changed the nature of the inquiry by exposing a new, potentially even more damaging aspect to the scandal. The channeling of arms profits to the Nicaraguan rebels not only brought the Contra controversy back to the forefront but raised serious legal questions about the misappropriation of funds (which should have gone to the U.S. Treasury, not into private hands) and the conduct of covert activities without a finding. If the activity could be traced to Reagan, it would significantly escalate the political risks to his presidency.

The HAWK shipment remained a source of political concern for Meese. While his aides sought more evidence on the diversion, he continued to dig into the November 1985 events, interviewing Sporkin, who also made him aware for the first time of the December finding (which Poindexter had just destroyed). In the evening, Meese had one more interview—with Casey, who initiated the meeting, ostensibly to discuss the implications of fresh reports Ghorbanifar might be about to blow the whistle on the operation.

Unlike the other interviews up to that time, Cooper did not accompany the attorney general to meet with Casey, and Meese took no notes. Surprisingly, he treated the meeting as "just a casual visit" instead of considering the CIA director a crucial witness likely to be knowledgeable about all of the areas Meese was investigating, including the diversion.[99]

NORTH'S INTERVIEW

The next morning, Sunday, Meese's assistants continued to explore leads at the CIA (where Duane Clarridge maintained the false cover story about the HAWKs) and to review documents in North's office. In the afternoon, Meese interviewed North at the Justice Department along with his three principal aides, all of whom took notes. The meeting ran from 2:00–5:45, although Meese left after two hours. He began by telling North his purpose was to "get all the facts from everyone involved" and insisted, according to notes, that the "worst thing [that] can happen is if someone tr[ies] to conceal something to protect selves, RR, put good spin on it. Want nothing anyone can call a cover[-]up."[100]

The first part of the session homed in on the arms deals, including the HAWK operation; the second part took up the diversion angle. North offered a wealth of detail beginning with the role of Michael Ledeen and McFarlane's insertion of North into the operation after the HAWK flight ran into trouble, when Israeli Defense Minister Yitzhak Rabin contacted the national security advisor for help. North made several false statements about his own and Poindexter's initial ignorance of key facts about the November 1985 missile delivery. However, he also made it plain the president himself had known about and approved the shipment: "N *believes* RR authorized it himself b/c M [McFarlane] wouldn't go off on own."[101]

At one point, the attorney general stepped out of his fact-finding mode to dispute North's assessment of Reagan's motives. According to Richardson's rendition, North remarked, "W/RR it always came back to hostages. Drawn to linkage. Terrible mistake to say RR wanted the strategic relationship b/c RR wanted the hostages."[102] But Meese disagreed, "He (RR) talked about *both*—if just relationship, [he would] not agree [to] arms."[103]

When the attorney general raised the diversion, pointing to the key phrase in the memo, North was "visibly surprised . . . you could see him sort of . . . recline back in the chair," Richardson recalled.[104] North asked if they had found a cover memo, too. Reynolds answered in the negative.[105] In contrast with his handling of the HAWKs issue, Meese pressed North on whether the president had approved the use of Iran arms residuals for the Contras and, if so, whether there would be a written record. "If RR approved it . . . you'd have it?" Meese asked. "Other files there it could be in?" North did not know the answer but offered to check.[106]

Shortly before Meese left the interview, North reminded him the HAWK operation was still a political land mine. Referring to the diversion, he said: "If this doesn't come out, only other [problem] is the Nov. Hawks deal. Think someone ought to step up and say this was authorized in Nov."[107]

HOW TO DEAL WITH THE DIVERSION?

After the interview, the Justice Department team convened to discuss where matters stood. According to Cooper, they concluded the president would have to announce the discovery of the diversion. "The Boland Amendment, obviously, was uppermost in our minds," he testified. Even though it was not a criminal statute, there were "associated and general statutes of various kinds that might well be applicable." At the heart of the matter was the question: "Was this United States money?"[108]

Later, Meese claimed the opposite. He insisted the Justice Department lawyers had no concerns about illegalities at that point. He also downplayed the significance of his own inquiry, testifying at North's trial it was not a formal investigation and agreeing with North's attorney it was merely an effort to "try to gather information to protect the president as best you could." Under those circumstances, Meese claimed, North had "no obligation" to tell the truth.[109]

Another concern was that information about the diversion might soon leak. This was not a matter of criminality, but politics. As Cooper testified, "I think I can remember a lot of discussion about the fact that if this information is made public by anyone other than the President, that it would not be possible to convince anybody that the President had every intention of making it public, and so it was of utmost importance that these facts be revealed to the American people by the President."[110]

Recognizing that Meese saw his role not as the nation's chief law enforcement officer but as the president's most trusted political confidant helps explain the attorney general's behavior over the next forty-eight hours. His objective was not to conduct a thorough investigation of potential lawbreaking—something he claimed to find little evidence of, though several of his own subordinates believed it should be a high priority. His goal was to safeguard the president and the administration from the political fallout of this ominous new development.

SHREDDING PARTY

While the Justice Department officials strategized, North made his own plans to prevent further disaster to the covert programs. At 11:00 that evening, he returned to his office, where he spent almost five hours reviewing and shredding documents. The fact he was able to do so—his offices had not been sealed to preserve crucial evidence—produced some of the harshest criticism of Meese. He acknowledged that the possibility of "criminal implications" came up in his interview with North,[111] but his nonchalance about protecting the integrity of the documentary record struck many as inexplicable.

During the 1987 congressional hearings, Sen. George Mitchell (D-Maine) engaged in a revealing exchange with Meese. Mitchell remarked, "A reasonable case can be made that the time at which preservation of documents should occur is the time when inspection of documents occurs, that is, if it is important enough to look at documents, it ought to be important enough to think about preserving them." Meese responded that "it did not occur" to anyone that any such steps were called for at the time.[112]

First, Meese asserted, "we already had examined all the documents"—a considerable exaggeration that glossed over the fact his aides had seen only what North and Earl had chosen to show them. Second, he suggested, North's shredding had been immaterial. "Well, we don't know whether those were relevant documents, irrelevant documents, or what they were," he declared. Stunned, Mitchell replied, "Do you think Colonel North spent from 11:00 in the evening until 4:15 the next morning destroying irrelevant documents?" "I think he probably did," Meese answered, adding that North likely got rid of "a lot of documents" that "had no relationship" to either the Iran or Contra actions. When Mitchell asked his basis for this conclusion, Meese answered, "That is just a guess, as much speculation as yours that there were relevant documents."[113]

Days before this exchange, North had confirmed to the congressional committees he had been "shredding in earnest" since shortly after the shoot-down of the Enterprise plane, and the files covered both the Iran and Contra operations. On the Friday before his interview with Meese, North had told McFarlane there was going to be a "shredding party" that weekend. Earl, Fawn Hall, and others made it clear the shredding had continued even while Meese was conducting his inquiry, culminating in the late-night binge of document destruction following North's interview.

North and Hall had done more than just shred. Some of the more worrisome documents were part of the NSC System IV channel, a tightly restricted filing system reserved for covert activities and other highly sensitive material. System IV documents bore individual identifying numbers and were kept in a secure area near North's office. Staff was required to sign out individual records, then sign them back in after each use. Destroying them would only have left gaps in the files that could easily be discovered. Instead, North ordered Hall to type fresh versions of several memoranda, removing sensitive language and substituting innocuous text. He then instructed her to replace the originals with the altered copies. But Hall never finished the task—apparently because she decided to help North at the shredder—and left some of the originals and altered copies together in the files.[114]

Only after the president's press conference on November 25 did Hall realize what she had done. With help from North, Earl, and an attorney named Tom Green (who later represented Secord), she stuffed the incriminating files into her blouse and boots and carried them out of the Old Executive Office Building past NSC security guards. After getting into Green's car, she turned them over to North.[115]

The November 24 NSPG Meeting

On November 24, the NSPG met from 2:00 until 3:45 in the afternoon to discuss the attorney general's inquiry and other developments. At no point did Meese mention the diversion memorandum. After a detailed summary of the Iran program by George Cave of the CIA, the principals discussed whether and how to "keep channels open." Reagan's views had not budged since the disclosure of the initiative three weeks earlier. According to Weinberger's notes, "RR—definitely feels what we were doing to establish bond is right thing. If Khomeini died we could be charged . . . [with] lost opportunity (not that I give a damn about history)."[116] Shultz, who left the meeting early, told aides the president was "defiant" about going forward. He was "v[ery] hot under the collar . . . frustrated and mad, self-righteous." He had an "understand me and get off my back kind of view." The experience left Shultz bewildered: "Maybe *we* are crazy?" he asked his aides.[117]

Remarkably, the discussion indicated several of those in the room still clung to some of the false positions they had held at the time of the high-level meeting on November 10. When Regan asked, "Did we object to Israelis sending HAWK . . . missiles to Iran?" Poindexter deflected the question by putting the responsibility on McFarlane, conveniently no longer with the government (nor at the meeting): "From July '85 to Dec 7 McFarlane handled this all alone—no documentation."[118]

Meese followed with additional details, largely reflecting information from his recent interviews. He identified the true nature of the cargo and the reason for Iran's return of the HAWKs in early 1986. He also revealed his view the operation itself had been unlawful: it was "not legal because no finding." But his next statement—"President *not* informed"—was patently false, as several individuals in the room were well aware.[119] Shultz had reported to Meese just three days before that the president had advised the secretary of state of his familiarity with the shipment. McFarlane had also told Meese about Reagan's approval, and North had provided similar information the evening before. What is more, by his own testimony, Meese never asked the president about the HAWK operation, which calls into question his grounds for disregarding his colleagues' statements.

Just as surprising as Meese's assertion of Reagan's ignorance was the fact no one challenged it. As the independent counsel's final report noted, "Virtually everyone else present at the senior advisers meeting knew or should have known that Meese's claim . . . was false, but no one corrected [him]. Meese concluded the meeting by asking, 'anyone know anything else that hasn't been revealed?' Again, no one had anything to add."[120]

Meese, with the tacit acquiescence of other top officials, had laid out a version of events all were expected to uphold. Regan later admitted to a grand jury he knew Meese's assertion was false. Shultz's message to his advisors immediately after the meeting was much the same: "They [are] rearranging the record."[121]

The meeting wound down shortly afterward but not before an agitated President Reagan warned once more against leaks. "RR—All of us tell everyone in our shops to shut up," Weinberger recorded the president saying. "Stay off air [and] say nothing. Don't answer questions."[122]

Regan spelled out the president's orders in a memorandum, setting out a strategy and assigning fault for the scandal along lines virtually identical to what the administration ultimately adopted: "Tough as it seems, blame must be put at NSC's door—rogue operation, going on without President's knowledge or sanction. When suspicions arose he took charge, ordered investigation, had meeting of top advisors to get at facts, and find out who knew what. Try to make the best of a sensational story. Anticipate charges of 'out of control,' 'President doesn't know what's going on,' 'Who's in charge,' 'State Department is right in its suspicions of NSC,' 'secret dealing with nefarious characters,' 'Should break off any contacts with: a) Iranians, b) Contras.'"[123]

The NSPG meeting defined the official line on the HAWK deal, but it did not address the funding diversion. Meese's rationale for holding on to that information was that he needed to confirm more details before sharing his findings with colleagues. During the rest of the day on November 24, he tracked down who else may have known about it and whether anyone had told the president. He spoke to Reagan, Bush, Regan, McFarlane, Poindexter, and perhaps others. He met with Casey the next morning. As usual, he kept no record. These meetings were no more than "casual conversations" that did not require notes, he insisted, not "what you might call interviews" intended to "elicit a great deal of information." His failure to follow basic investigative procedure on such a legally and politically significant issue led to further public disapproval, including expressions of "unanimous anger" from Congress.[124]

After his "interviews," Meese met with President Reagan. Also attending was Regan, who told investigators the president had been "crestfallen" at hearing about the diversion. He described his own reaction dramatically as "horror, horror, sheer horror."[125] All reportedly agreed on the need to disclose the matter the following day.

On the morning of November 25, Regan advised Poindexter to be prepared to step down as national security advisor. Meese assigned Cooper to work with Wallison to draft the president's statement for use at the noon press conference. At 10:15 a.m., Reagan met with his senior advisors and accepted Poindexter's resignation. Only then did most of those present hear about the diversion. The president, Shultz, Meese, and Casey proceeded to brief congressional leaders.

That morning, just before the press conference, Secord called Poindexter and pleaded with him not to resign. He urged him to "force the president to step up to the plate and take responsibility for his actions." Poindexter was impassive: "You don't understand," he said. "It's too late. They're building a wall around him."[126]

14

Congress Steps In

The investigative phase of the Iran-Contra scandal—covered in this and the following chapter—provided one last, dramatic setting for confrontation between the executive branch and its two traditional contenders for constitutional power, the legislative and judicial branches. Congress was first to take the public stage. After months of preparation, the Senate and House formed a pair of select committees, one from each chamber, with the stated aim of exploring the facts in the affair in order to draw appropriate policy, political, and constitutional lessons. Over the next eleven weeks, they conducted nationally televised hearings that produced a trove of evidence and a far more detailed picture than available before.

The November 1986 revelations inevitably invoked images of a Watergate-style confrontation between the two branches, particularly because the Democrats had recaptured the Senate in the midterm elections and would take control of both houses in the 100th Congress convening on January 20, 1987. But the comparisons to the earlier scandal were mostly inapt. When the Senate Watergate committee formed in 1973, it was already widely believed Richard Nixon had engaged in or authorized serious misconduct, including a cover-up, for corrupt political purposes. What the public knew about Ronald Reagan's personal actions in summer 1987 was more ambiguous and seemed to involve mostly deplorable policy choices rather than criminal behavior. Also, Reagan was much more popular personally than Nixon, the political landscape had changed substantially as a result of declining economic conditions and a complex international environment, and Congress had largely shed its reformist posture of the 1970s.

Instead, the select Iran-Contra committees were deeply split. A vocal minority of Republicans was determined to avoid the beating its party had sustained in the early 1970s and unabashedly set out to protect the president, minimizing administration misconduct and shifting much of the blame onto congressional Democrats. Democratic leaders played into this strategy, concluding Reagan's popularity made it a high risk to appear to be going after him while he was vulnerable. The investigation was also hampered by confrontational witnesses and the unavailability of evidence that would not surface until long after the proceedings (see Chapter 15). Just as important, the committees marred their own efforts by making procedural decisions based purely on political considerations. In the process, they also severely undercut the work of the independent counsel.

In the end, the experience produced both positive and negative results, making it a highly useful case study of the strengths and weaknesses Congress brings to investigations of government conduct.

Forming the Select Committees

By the nature of the institution, the congressional investigation was steeped in partisan politics. After six years without achieving much of a dent in the president's standing, many Democrats were keen to exploit this gift-wrapped opportunity. Republicans rightly worried about their party's chances in the upcoming 1988 presidential elections, in which Vice President George Bush was the presumed GOP front-runner. White House Communications Director Patrick Buchanan warned Democrats were plotting a "media scavenger hunt" against the president. They were not "after the truth, they're after Ronald Reagan."[1] In fact, the Democratic leadership took a far more cautious approach. Among other compromises, its members agreed to end the hearings in early August and to submit a final report by November, well before the presidential campaign got into full swing.

By January 1987, both chambers had decided on the committees' memberships. On the Democratic side, Senate Majority Leader Robert Byrd (D-W.Va.) and Speaker of the House Jim Wright (D-Tex.) bowed to seniority and the turf concerns of permanent committees, in addition to the dictates of moderation. Daniel Inouye of Hawaii chaired the Senate committee, joined by five other Democrats, including several former or current standing committee chairs: David Boren of Oklahoma, Howell Heflin of Alabama, George Mitchell of Maine, Sam Nunn of Georgia, and Paul Sarbanes of Maryland. Half of the membership had supported Contra aid at some point. "You couldn't have had more of an all-star cast," one Democratic staff member commented.[2]

Sen. Robert Dole (R-Kans.), the outgoing majority leader, picked the GOP membership for the upper chamber, choosing a mix of conservatives and moderates: William Cohen of Maine, Orrin Hatch of Utah, James McClure of Idaho, Warren Rudman of New Hampshire, and Paul Trible of Virginia. Rudman professed to be unenthusiastic, predicting it could be a "nasty, partisan affair." Recalling Watergate, he said: "If you were a Republican and were committed to the truth, you might wind up at odds with your party and your president."[3]

On the House side, Chair Lee Hamilton of Indiana lived up to his reputation for fair-mindedness, picking a few liberals but mostly moderates: Les Aspin of Wisconsin, Edward Boland of Massachusetts, Jack Brooks of Texas, Dante Fascell of Florida, Tom Foley of Washington, Ed Jenkins of Georgia, Peter Rodino of New Jersey, and Louis Stokes of Ohio. Seniority again was a key criterion. Foley had just become House majority leader, and six of the remaining eight were committee chairs.

Minority Leader Robert Michel's (R-Ill.) selections were less restrained: William Broomfield of Michigan, Dick Cheney of Wyoming, Jim Courter of New Jersey, Michael DeWine of Ohio, Henry Hyde of Illinois, and Bill McCollum of Florida. According to a Republican staffer, the GOP members were "specially chosen . . . for their allegiance to the president and the party's policies" as well as for "their willingness to engage in principled combat." As Cheney put it later, the GOP "reached down into the ranks" to select junior legislators Courter, DeWine, and McCollum in the hope they might "put more into it."[4] Democratic staffers were more blunt, one calling the latter "hit men" whose "only objective was to discredit, limit, delay, and confuse the probe any way they could." Some complained the majority should have picked a "bomb thrower" or two to establish balance.[5]

Again with an eye toward moderation—and recalling his Watergate experience—Inouye appointed Rudman as vice chair and created a unified staff, steps that would give the GOP a much more substantial role but that Inouye believed would lend credibility to the proceedings. According to John Nields, the House committee's lead attorney, "With the exception of Lee, [Rudman] was the most important member of the committees. He made a difference, because of the sheer force of his personality and energy."[6] By contrast, Hamilton declined to name Cheney vice chair, and the House committee established two separate staffs, foreshadowing a "bitterly divided" process.[7]

The key staff appointments included the committees' chief counsels, who, along with the chairs, would determine the direction and flow of the investigation. Senate Democrats chose Arthur Liman, a highly regarded attorney from New York whose most celebrated case had been the Attica Prison riot of 1971. Liman had no experience with national security affairs, but his outside-the-beltway status was touted as signaling the absence of a political axe to grind. Each senator was allotted one nomination for a lawyer to join the staff who would be under Liman's supervision.[8]

On the House side, the Democrats selected Nields, who, unlike Liman, had experience with foreign policy scandals on Capitol Hill, including Koreagate, on which he worked under Hamilton. Additional legal staff mainly came either from members' personal staffs or from standing committees such as Judiciary, Government Operations, and Foreign Affairs. These staffers typically had handled federal investigations before, but many lacked specific expertise in key areas of committee focus, and few had any familiarity with intelligence operations.

Early Hurdles

In the crush of an abbreviated schedule and wrestling with sensitive policy and political issues, the committees faced formidable obstacles. One of the most vexing related to classified documentation. The intelligence community, recalling the battles with the Church and Pike Committees a decade earlier, resisted granting access to a large number of members and staff. The clearance process in some cases took until early March, two months after the probe had begun.[9] Despite establishing special, secure facilities on Capitol Hill, the agencies sometimes refused to allow document copies to go to the committees. In some instances, only members could have access and were not always allowed to take notes.[10]

Document acquisition in general created periodic headaches for the committees. House Democrats complained, "Despite its repeated public assurances, the White House did not provide the Select Committees with all the documents and information requested," which "has deprived us of material that quite possibly could resolve a number of key issues."[11] One case involved seven documents about administration quid pro quo deals with Latin American governments that surfaced at the North trial almost two years after the end of the congressional investigation, but that the committees never saw. The records showed Reagan and Bush, among others, had played a substantially greater role in those secret arrangements than Congress had been led to believe. The Senate Select Committee on Intelligence (SSCI) concluded "chaos"—not a cover-up—explained the incident but added that its finding was not definitive: "The committee has simply come to the point of exhausting what appear at this juncture to be productive leads." Hamilton remarked, "It really strains credulity" that the FBI, which conducted the initial White House searches, could have missed such crucial evidence.[12]

An impediment of a related kind may have cropped up in connection with the many depositions committee lawyers conducted. In the view of some Democratic aides and attorneys, the fact that agency and White House counsel were able to accompany witnesses during testimony created a conflict of interest and at times raised questions about the candor of witnesses. As one staff member argued, agency lawyers represent the government, not the individuals being interrogated. That not only created uncertainty as to whether the witness's best interests were always being served, but in given instances could have allowed other agency officials, whose departments (or they themselves) were also under scrutiny, access to confidential information relevant to their case. Committee staff also wondered whether some witnesses might have been subtly swayed by the presence of agency counsel or been coached by them. At a minimum, the administration's practice of sending attorneys to depositions allowed senior officials to keep close tabs on areas of congressional focus and on the substance of the information being conveyed to the committees.[13]

Critical Decisions

Probably the most fateful choice committee leaders made was to set a tight deadline for the proceedings. Compromising with Republican calls for just a three-month investigation, Inouye and Hamilton settled on ten months—the end of October. The decision affected committee activities in a variety of ways, but mostly it placed members under enormous time pressure to pore through vast numbers of documents and examine more than 200 witnesses. The decision also narrowed the window available for the televised hearings, curtailing both the number of witnesses and the length of their testimony. This was a particular handicap when it came to Oliver North's appearance.

A second critical judgment was whether to consider impeachment of Reagan. Rank-and-file Democrats were eager for a robust inquiry that did not shy away from the president. Speaker Wright described a "hot volcanic lava of anger . . . boiling inside the Congress" in reaction to the administration's "flagrant . . . flouting" of the law. First appearing as "whispers," he said, "the audible demands for impeachment proceedings growled in private conversations wherever Democratic Members met."[14]

Not all Democrats shared this attitude. Notably, the two chief counsels, Liman and Nields, opposed seeking Reagan's impeachment. For one thing, it would have required an "extraordinarily high standard of proof," Liman contended, "credible, direct, and conclusive evidence of guilt."[15] For another, the committees were determined not to "establish a precedent that could leave the threat of impeachment hanging over the head of every future president."[16] Nields recalled being "all in favor of impeaching Nixon but I didn't appreciate the collateral damage that it could cause." Furthermore, he "never thought anything Reagan did warranted that. Maybe I have the wrong idea about how engaged he was."[17]

The final decision on whether to pursue impeachment belonged to the Democratic Party leadership. Politics was an unavoidable factor in their thinking. As indicated, Reagan's popularity, despite suffering a decline since the revelations, was still a potent weapon for Republicans.[18] Timing was another reason cited later for forgoing the impeachment route. Just two years remained in Reagan's term. By the time the process had gotten fully under way, they argued, he would soon be out of the White House anyway, mooting a major point of the exercise. A further consideration was Reagan's state of mind (see the Tower Commission section below). Journalist Seymour Hersh quoted a participant at a Senate committee caucus in January 1987 as saying the "President did not have the mental ability to fully understand what happened."[19]

Democratic leaders also expressed worries about the impact of an impeachment on U.S. international standing and the budding relationship between Reagan and Mikhail Gorbachev.[20] Inouye harkened back to earlier instances of Soviet "adventurism"—the 1962 Cuban missile crisis, Soviet gains in the third world in the 1970s, and the invasion of Afghanistan—as examples of the Kremlin's temptation to take advantage of perceived weaknesses in U.S. presidents.[21] Liman played on a similar point after the hearings: "We were all very mindful of the fact that there was an opportunity for the [arms] negotiations with the Soviet Union. We were mindful that if an impeachment process was started, that opportunity would be lost. We were mindful that this country would've been paralyzed."[22]

Wright pointed to the impact of domestic concerns as well. One was the "explosive potential" of a full-blown political battle over impeachment. The shock to the U.S. political system, he and other senior Democrats insisted, would have been too great so soon after the Nixon ordeal. "I had agonized through the long weeks in 1973 that led to the impeachment hearing on President Nixon," Wright recalled. "I wanted no repeat of that scenario. The country could ill afford it."[23] Before the Iran-Contra committees had even been formed, Sen. Daniel Patrick Moynihan (D-N.Y.) voiced the same view: "This nation does not want and does not need another destroyed presidency."[24]

Despite these concerns, senior Democrats, including Iran-Contra committee leaders, claimed they would have seriously contemplated impeachment if they had found direct evidence of grave wrongdoing by Reagan. Rudman told Hersh if there had been proof of an act of commission, the reaction would have been "we have no choice." But "if it's nonfeasance and negligence, there's too much at risk."[25]

The Tower Commission

On February 26, 1987, in the midst of congressional preparations, the President's Special Review Board, or Tower Commission, released its report. Established the previous December in the wake of the scandal, the commission consisted of two former senators—Chair John Tower of Texas and Edmund Muskie of Maine—and a former national security advisor, retired U.S. Air Force Gen. Brent Scowcroft. Muskie was the lone Democrat. All three had generally moderate reputations.

Throughout the investigative period, the White House had taken pains to appear cooperative and open to scrutiny, but along the way indications arose that at a minimum the administration was working to shape and limit its accessibility. The board's formal mission was an example. "The Board shall conduct a comprehensive study of the future role and procedures of the National Security Council (NSC) staff," Executive Order 12575 stated, and "review the NSC staff's proper role in operational activities, especially extremely sensitive . . . missions." In other words, the objective was not to examine the specific events that had precipitated the scandal, only to suggest what the NSC staff should do and what its "future role and procedures" ought to be.[26] Furthermore, the commission's sixty-day deadline precluded an in-depth probe, and its lack of subpoena power virtually guaranteed key witnesses such as former national security advisor John Poindexter, North, and Richard Secord would not cooperate.

Still, the inquiry produced a few surprising results. Late in the process the FBI discovered Poindexter had deleted thousands of White House emails to keep them from investigators. Enterprising agents, however, managed to recover them from backup tapes. The board became absorbed by the richness of the documentary record, and its interviews turned out far more expansive and troubling than expected, particularly about the private Contra aid network.[27] The board's unexpected discoveries necessitated two time extensions to process the evidence. In its final report, the authors reprinted dozens of emails and memos, providing a remarkable opening into the scandal as well as into the internal workings of the White House.

Even though its mandate had not been to "assess individual culpability or be the final arbiter of the facts," the board's report went some distance down that road. It found a "flawed process" and a "failure of responsibility" throughout the affair, for which it castigated several top officials, starting with White House Chief of Staff Donald Regan. "As much as anyone," he "should have insisted that an orderly process be observed. . . . He must bear primary responsibility for the chaos that descended upon the White House" after revelation of the affair. Poindexter, according to the authors, "failed grievously" in connection with the diversion and "may have . . . actively misled" other officials while he and North ran the two operations in an "amateurish" way. Secretary of State George Shultz and Secretary of Defense Caspar Weinberger did not escape blame. The report found they "distanced themselves from the march of events," and instead of offering unqualified advice to the president, "they protected the record as to their own positions on this issue."[28]

As for President Reagan, the board concluded he too shared responsibility. He "did not seem aware" of what his aides were doing, largely because he "did not force his policy to undergo the most critical review" and never "insist[ed] upon accountability and performance review. . . . The NSC system will not work unless the President makes it work," the report concluded.[29] At the televised presentation of its findings, Reagan appeared visibly uncomfortable at what were clearly unexpectedly severe criticisms.

Yet, in emphasizing Reagan's lax "management style" rather than his policy choices, the report tended to cast him more as a victim of inept or unscrupulous aides than a guiding force behind the affair. Subsequent evidence would show this was an understatement of his role. Still, the assessments confirmed an important contributing factor in the scandal—Reagan's aversion for fundamental details of policy. "My sense of Ronald Reagan," Scowcroft said later, "was that he had a few big principles and he pushed hard on those, but he wasn't interested in managing." When it came to judging the appropriateness of the arms-for-hostages deals, for example, Scowcroft believes "he never even thought about it." The president's implied approval was enough to encourage his aides to assume responsibility for the details of these sensitive policies themselves. Scowcroft speculates the real idea man behind the two covert operations was Reagan's trusted friend, CIA Director William Casey: "I can just imagine Bill Casey saying, 'You know, we think, Mr. President, we've figured out a way to get the hostages out and get money to the Contras.' And I can imagine Reagan saying, 'Well, Bill, that would be wonderful.' Without any introspection."[30]

The Tower Commission inquiry spotlighted another important facet of Reagan at the time—his diminished mental acuity. At his first interview with the board, in late January, the president told the committees he had approved Israel's TOW shipment to Iran in August 1985. Just two weeks later, he contradicted that statement, professing to be "surprised" to learn about the Israeli delivery. When Tower asked him about the discrepancy, he picked up a note card the White House counsel had prepared and read it aloud word for word, including the sentence: "If the question comes up at the Tower Board meeting, you might want to say that you were surprised." According to a presidential aide, "Tower's jaw went slack, the faces of Scowcroft and Muskie drained." Scowcroft, who sat immediately to Reagan's right, already understood what was happening. "I could read the index cards," he recalled. "He was reading them" during the interview, not giving independent answers.[31]

"Horrified," Reagan's aides pleaded with Tower afterward to accept a handwritten addendum from the president they hoped would soften the board's expected reaction to the gaffe. Tower agreed to print an excerpt. On the matter of whether he authorized the Israeli shipment, it read, "The simple truth is, 'I don't remember—period.'"[32]

Ascertaining Reagan's State of Mind

Reagan's mental lapses were an acute concern for the White House. David Abshire, a former NATO ambassador and presidential advisor brought in as a "special counselor" to manage the Iran-Contra fallout in early 1987, acknowledges "all of the president's interlocutors were becoming exasperated with Reagan's lack of or confused memory and that he was indifferent about trying to figure it all out."[33] Poindexter believed "by the end of 1986 . . . Alzheimer's had really begun to be a factor."[34] Poindexter was also impressed by Reagan's ability to mask his mood and thoughts—perhaps not surprising for a professional actor. Describing him as unquestionably an introvert, Poindexter recalls he was almost always quiet and reserved whenever he was alone or with close staff. But "when he would pass through the door of the Oval Office, it was like going through a curtain and on stage."[35] This ability undoubtedly helped to dampen persistent rumors about his memory difficulties.

Behind closed doors, reports about the president's condition in spring 1987 were troubling enough that former senator Howard Baker, who would soon replace Regan as chief of staff, brought in an outside consultant to assess the situation. James Cannon, a former advisor to President Ford, arrived the day after the Tower report was released. The "chaos" and disorder he found in the White House shook him, as did the multitude of staff descriptions of Reagan as "inattentive . . . inept . . . lazy [and not] interested in the job." In a confidential memo to Baker he suggested consideration be given to invoking "section four of the 25th amendment"—the U.S. Constitution provision for removing the president for incompetence.[36]

Abshire rejected the notion, insisting Reagan was not incapacitated. Shortly afterward, when Baker and Cannon had an occasion to observe Reagan again, they were amazed to find he seemed "genial" and "charming" and looked "just dandy."[37] The idea of invoking the Twenty-fifth Amendment vanished. In light of the stream of alarming accounts Baker, Cannon, and Abshire had been hearing from White House staff (on top of their own interactions with the president), the question arises how a single vignette could nullify so much direct evidence. In hindsight it seems likely the ramifications of pronouncing the president incompetent were so upsetting—as the implications of impeachment were for Democratic leaders—that his advisors decided it was worth the risk simply to try to ensure he finished his term without further incident.

The observations of Iran-Contra investigators (lacking any ties to the president) strongly supported the sense Reagan was in a weakened state. When Liman made his first visit to 1600 Pennsylvania Avenue, at the time of Reagan's miscue before the Tower Commission, he described a "smell of death around the White House." The president seemed to be "almost a bystander in the whole investigation." It was an "absolutely amazing spectacle," he reported, to witness his wavering over the question of whether he had authorized arms sales to Iran.[38] Nor did the picture improve after Reagan's speech on March 4 and his press conference on March 19. Administration officials were relieved—even elated ("The speech came off beautifully!!" Bush exulted), and his approval ratings received a bump.[39] But committee members and staff were still reeling over what they were witnessing, particularly the gap between the true nature of the Iran arms deals and the picture the White House was presenting of them. Whereas Bush celebrated the president's public comments as "vintage Reagan . . . beautifully delivered," Rudman saw a very different kind of "classic Reagan": "poignant, disarming and more than a little mind-boggling. . . . He truly did inhabit a world of his own."[40]

It may be impossible to judge conclusively from among the conflicting accounts of Reagan's mental state, but the evidence of his frailty cannot be easily discounted when assessing his actions at this stage of his presidency.

Congress versus the Independent Counsel

Members of the congressional committees gained from the Tower Commission's experiences. The latter's document discoveries were a major boost, and the chance to observe key players such as former national security advisor Robert McFarlane, who turned out to be under serious mental stress, helped prepare the committees for what to expect in their own proceedings. The committees also drew lessons from North's and Poindexter's assertions of their Fifth Amendment rights, which raised the question of how to get a full picture of the affair—and sustain public interest—without the testimony of the operations' main actors.

At this juncture the committees were still scrambling to build the foundations for the upcoming hearings. "We had no real evidence or witnesses lined up until two weeks before the hearings began," Nields remembered. The desire to go beyond what previous inquiries had produced created major pressure to deliver North and Poindexter.[41] But this also posed other challenges: it gave North's attorneys leverage to define the terms of his appearance, and it erected a serious obstacle to the independent counsel's attempts to build criminal cases against key targets.

"The tensions between the roles of the independent counsel and the Committee became evident almost immediately," two committee members wrote later.[42] At issue was whether to grant witnesses a form of "limited" immunity from prosecution, a legal provision designed to allow a prosecutor to develop a case against a defendant who had obtained an immunity grant to testify in another forum. The catch was that the immunized testimony itself could not be used against the defendant. This presented a special challenge in the Iran-Contra affair because the witnesses would be appearing on national television, creating a huge burden for prosecutors to prove a later trial would not be tainted.

Rudman tried to persuade Independent Counsel Lawrence Walsh to charge North on the narrower count of destroying evidence, but Walsh's staff was opposed. Ultimately, the committees decided their mission to inform the nation was at least as important as Walsh's mandate to locate legal responsibility. They also understood the vagaries of the legal system meant there was no guarantee when or even if the public would get to hear crucial testimony. What if prosecutors decided to strike a deal and not go to trial? In Liman's view, the committees "had no choice. . . . How could we possibly proceed" without those contributions to the story? he wrote later. Rudman agreed: "Our priority must be to give America the truth."[43]

As a gesture, the committees deferred the most essential witnesses so Walsh could question them first and not "freeze" their testimony. This provided only limited breathing space for prosecutors, though, because of the committees' tight schedule. "The mandate of the committee was constrained by time but not by subject matter," Senators Cohen and Mitchell acknowledged, whereas Walsh's constraints were the opposite. In the end, Liman wrote, granting immunity to North and Poindexter required "swallowing our sense of morality."[44]

In Search of a Strategy

In early March, Liman and two colleagues proposed a hearing strategy to the committee leadership. They recommended following a theme, "just like a trial": whether constitutional processes aimed at preventing the misuse of power had been circumvented.[45] "By examining how foreign policy was made in this case," Liman wrote in a memo, "the hearings will address issues of historic dimensions—the appropriate balance between the Executive Branch and Congress in foreign policy, and the right of oversight and public debate versus secrecy in the formulation and carrying out of policy."[46]

According to the lawyers' interpretation, in the Iran and Contra operations the key players felt stymied by Congress and even other parts of the executive branch. They therefore chose to use "irregular channels" consisting of the "NSC and an elaborate private network." The result was a secret policy that coexisted with the public one and that required its architects to "bypass and mislead not just the Congress, but Cabinet members." In Liman's view, "Iran-Contra wasn't just a series of improper actions, it was a mentality" that "made it patriotic to lie to Congress, to circumvent checks and balances through covert actions, and to create the Enterprise to do what the CIA was not permitted to do." It was "axiomatic" to many of those involved in the operations that "to be effective, you had to go outside the system, and this, more than anything, we wanted to bring out."[47] That became the essential prism through which the committees' majority—though not their minority—viewed the affair.

The Hearings Begin

The televised spectacle began on May 5, 1987, with a sense of expectation not felt since the 1974 Watergate hearings. Almost simultaneously, the independent counsel obtained his first guilty plea—from Carl "Spitz" Channell, the Contra fund-raiser working with the NSC staff (North was named as a coconspirator)—which helped to stimulate the atmosphere of inquiry.

The committees' leadership had decided the proceedings would be held jointly, which required elaborate preparations, including erecting a dais large enough to accommodate all twenty-six members plus lawyers and staff. Worse, two daises would be needed, one for the Senate and one for the House, because the two committees would alternate in presiding over the event.

More intricate arrangements were needed to handle questioning of witnesses, particularly with television cameras rolling. The implications of allowing live TV coverage are difficult to overstate. The leadership recognized how unwieldy it would be to have so many interrogators, but the lure of national media exposure was too much for most members to resist, and few were prepared to sacrifice time on camera for the sake of efficiency.

To accommodate, the leaders established a system of "designated hitters" from both parties to spearhead the interrogations. Other members would follow with additional questions. For "major" witnesses, the lead examiner would be allotted one hour, the others ten to fifteen minutes each. "Minor" witnesses would field fifteen minutes of questions from a principal examiner followed by five minutes from each additional interviewer. To the annoyance of some members, the leaders decided the attorneys would handle the bulk of the interrogations. With such complex issues and voluminous evidence, busy senators and representatives would not be able to spare the many hours required for preparation.

The committees also had to contend with appearances—seemingly trivial but critical in the world of television, as members would soon learn. For example, Hollywood director Steven Spielberg pointed out to Liman—long after the hearings—that the elevated position of the questioners was well known in film as the "villain's angle," whereas witnesses, looking upward at their interrogators, had the "hero's angle."[48] North in particular would make the most of this and other advantages of the televised forum.

Next came a dispute over opening remarks. Originally, the committee leaders—Inouye and Hamilton for the Democrats, Rudman and Cheney for the Republicans—each planned to make twenty-minute statements. But Republicans charged Rudman was not a reliable defender of the White House and should not be counted among the other Republican speakers. They insisted instead on being given five minutes each to speak, unmoved by the reality that more than two dozen members of Congress delivering speeches instead of questioning witnesses would be seen as a waste of airtime and play terribly with the public.

All of these decisions had an impact on popular perceptions of the hearings and on whom viewers saw as the heroes and the villains. The situation recalled the first televised U.S. presidential candidates' debate between John F. Kennedy and Nixon on September 26, 1960. As a later *Time* article put it: "Nixon, pale and underweight from a recent hospitalization, appeared sickly and sweaty, while Kennedy appeared calm and confident." Afterward, most radio listeners polled believed Nixon had won, but the far larger television audience gave Kennedy the win and by most accounts turned the tide in the campaign.[49]

Opening Witnesses

On May 5, 1987, Richard Secord took the stand. He had surprised everyone by volunteering to testify first and agreeing to forgo immunity.[50] The committees quickly approved because he was a major player who they believed would drive early public interest.[51] Secord benefited from being allowed to frame his own case before other witnesses testified—notably his partner, Albert Hakim, to whom the committees had recently granted immunity.[52]

Secord revealed that only $3.5 million of the proceeds the Enterprise accrued had gone to the Contras. He waffled over whether the remainder of the profits belonged to him and Hakim, having at one point foresworn personal gain. Unmasking the seamier side of his activities undermined his claim to be motivated mainly by patriotic duty. Nevertheless, members' constituent mail showed Secord gained broad public sympathy with his pugnacious self-defense and his refusal to tolerate disparaging comments about his role.

McFarlane testified next. He, too, refused immunity but, like Secord, was not an easy witness. "A tortured man,"[53] according to Liman, the dour ex-marine was still wrestling with conflicts between his loyalty to the president and his need to unburden himself of responsibility for much of the scandal. Testifying just weeks after attempting suicide, he was treated with extreme care by the committees.

Still, McFarlane conveyed crucial information. He clarified the scope of Reagan's involvement in the hostage deals, including the president's personal approval of the operation, and confirmed his overriding objective had not been strategic but the short-term aim of freeing the hostages. This challenged the Tower Commission's conclusion Reagan had merely been manipulated by aides. McFarlane said he had assumed the Boland Amendment of October 1984 applied to the NSC staff and had told his colleagues so. This directly contradicted claims by North and others they had acted legally in running the Contra program.

The committees' goal with the next few witnesses was to flesh out the details of North's Contra operations and to bring to light the solicitations for private donations he had made with the help of Channell and others. The cast called to testify included former NSC staff member Gaston Sigur, North's lieutenant in the field Robert Owen, Contra leader Adolfo Calero, self-appointed anticommunist campaigner retired Gen. John Singlaub, and a trio of North's wealthy donors—Ellen Garwood, William O'Boyle, and Joseph Coors.

Sigur, whose specialty at the White House was East Asia, testified about North's attempts to bypass Congress and persuade foreign governments—Taiwan, South Korea, and Singapore—to contribute secretly to the Contras. Asked if he understood he was, "in fact, helping to solicit assistance for the Contras," he replied: "I never particularly thought of it one way or the other, but I guess that's right."[54]

Owen provided stark details about the covert operations in Central America and about the helter-skelter nature of North's activities. "The Courier," as he used to call himself, described trips to a Chinese grocery store in lower Manhattan, where he used the password "Mooey" to pick up wads of cash intended for the rebels. Drawing on Owen's memos to North in 1985, the committee's majority hoped to convey to the public an image of the Contras not as storied freedom fighters but as corrupt and inept. "This war has become a business to many of them," Owen once reported to North. He readily confirmed CIA involvement in supplying the rebels with aid—lethal as well as food—after the Boland Amendments were signed into law. He also conceded that keeping the Contra program covert was probably intended to deceive the U.S. public as much as any foreign U.S. adversary.

However, Owen was also one of several witnesses who used the opportunity to express ardent support for North, contributing to outbursts of "Olliemania" across the country. As his final statement, Owen read into the record a 420-word "poem." His outright adulation of North astounded the committees. "Today on the fertile plains of Central America, cattle graze peacefully. . . . In this far corner of the Third World, we have known darkness and despair that at times seems almost too much to bear. . . . Yet, in our darkest hours, we have three things that help sustain us: Our faith in God Almighty, the love and support of our families, the knowledge that on this troubled earth there still walk men like Ollie North."[55]

Calero expressed a similar ardor for North, even as he put on the record some of the most damaging testimony about the NSC staffer, including his personal use of traveler's checks provided by Calero for the Contras. The committees prepared large white poster boards for TV audiences listing the Washington-area stores where North had cashed checks—National Tire Wholesalers, Farragut Valet, Sugarland Texaco, and Parklane Hosiery, among others. Out of $90,000 in unsigned checks Calero said he gave North, the committees could not account for $30,000.[56] A *Washington Post* headline read "Across the 'Hero' Image of Oliver North, a Shadow Starts to Fall."[57]

The wealthy donors who followed Calero cast more clouds over the purported private Contra fund-raising campaign, confirming North had not acted alone but with the involvement of other administration officials, including the president. The witnesses—a Texas widow, a New York oil executive, and a Colorado beer baron—told of briefings in the Old Executive Office Building and promises of personal meetings with Reagan in return for donations of $300,000 or more. They testified that North and occasionally others would lead the substantive discussions about the rebels' plight, then remove themselves before Channell made the pitch for funds. Rudman called it the "old one-two punch." Their testimony also brought out the fact donors had not known as much as 35 percent of their contributions had gone to cover Channell's expenses.[58]

The next set of witnesses continued the Contra theme. Secord's on-the-ground manager in Central America, retired Col. Robert Dutton, supplied details about the resupply operation, including difficulties with weather, logistics, and coordination. He reconfirmed the sustained involvement of the CIA and Defense Department with the insurgents and gave hints about Reagan's direct interest in the operation, including that Dutton had prepared a special photo album North promised to take to the "top boss." The committees and the media chose to highlight a quote from a message Dutton had once sent to Secord in which he pined for North's secretary: "PPS. Send Fawn—can't continue on milk and cookies."[59]

A potentially explosive witness followed Dutton—Felix Rodriguez, the former CIA agent who sometimes used the pseudonym Max Gómez. Rodriguez poked holes in Secord's image as a patriotic businessman and described his mistrust of the entire "Enterprise." His most anticipated testimony related to his ties to Bush's office. Rodriguez was in a position to place Bush much closer to the center of the Contra operation than was previously known. The vice president noted in his dictated diary at the time he occasionally "thrashed around" at night because of news articles questioning his involvement.[60] In the end, Rodriguez supported Bush's account, prompting the vice president to write wistfully: "I'd like to see banner headlines: BUSH HAS BEEN TELLING THE TRUTH ALL ALONG."[61] Rodriguez dented North's image by recounting the latter's boast the year before he would survive any official inquiries into the Contras because he had the president's backing: "'Those people want me,'" Rodriguez quoted North, "'but they cannot touch me because the old man loves my ass'" (see Chapter 11).[62]

With the next three witnesses, the committees spotlighted State Department and CIA cooperation with North on Contra operations. Former ambassador to Costa Rica Lewis Tambs testified he had followed instructions from the NSC staff to open the southern front in Nicaragua despite congressional restrictions, insisting he thought he was entirely authorized. In closed session, the committees heard from Joseph Fernandez, the CIA station chief in Costa Rica, who admitted supplying the rebels a variety of intelligence, weather data, CIA flight plans, and other information after the Boland Amendments were in effect. Like Tambs, Fernandez, whose identity was protected under the pseudonym Tomas Castillo, said he believed he was acting legally, although he also acknowledged misleading the Tower Commission and CIA investigators about his activities.

Elliott Abrams followed and, as usual, produced sparks. Two previous witnesses had testified he had known about the Point West airstrip in Costa Rica and other protected details about the Contra program. Abrams denied it, claiming ignorance about any of North's illicit activities. Representative Brooks echoed earlier congressional skepticism: "I can only conclude after this that you are either extremely incompetent, or that you are still . . . deceiving us with semantics."[63] Senior Democrats tacitly threatened to pull support for Contra aid if Abrams did not step down from his post at the State Department. Hamilton used Abrams's appearance to highlight the underlying battle between the two branches epitomized by the scandal: "I hope you recognize that the Congress cannot play its constitutional role if it cannot trust the testimony of representatives of the President as truthful and fully informed. The President cannot sustain his policy if he tries to carry that policy out secretly, and his representatives mislead the Congress and the American people."[64]

Hakim returned the hearings' focus to Iran. He too contradicted Secord's assertions of altruistic motives, noting his use of profits to buy extravagances such as a Porsche and an airplane. More troubling was Hakim's depiction of the cavalier handling of negotiations with the Iranians by North and his Enterprise colleagues, who had ostensibly committed the United States to defend Iran against Soviet attack and free the seventeen Dawa prisoners in exchange for the U.S. hostages in Lebanon. Hakim generated headlines with his revelation about trying to create a $200,000 account for North and his family out of arms sales profits (see Chapter 11). He claimed he had done it out of "love" for North despite having met him only once.

The purpose of Glenn Robinette's testimony was to introduce more facts about North's deceitful personal conduct. The former CIA operative discussed the security gate he had installed at North's northern Virginia home at no cost to North and the former NSC aide's elaborate fabrication of correspondence designed to make it look like he had intended to pay for the system (see Chapter 11).

With these firsthand accounts, the committees' majority attempted to demonstrate a pattern of routine ethical indifference by an array of government officials and private intermediaries in the course of the Iran and Contra operations. The goal was also to show they engaged in acts of sweeping dishonesty toward administration colleagues as well as Congress and were prepared to twist and even break the law in the name of "higher" causes.

North's secretary, Hall, provided some of the most eye-opening testimony on the theme of misguided loyalties. To audible gasps, she explained her rationale for shredding, altering, and removing classified materials in November 1986: "I believed in Colonel North and there was a very solid and very valid reason that he must have been doing this and sometimes you have to go above the written law, I believe."[65]

A trio of administration lawyers also testified. Bretton Sciaroni, staff attorney for the President's Intelligence Oversight Board, had rendered a legal opinion to North that the Boland Amendments did not apply to the NSC staff—a view Liman later called "dumb . . . nothing more or less." Put on the defensive by a series of condescending questions from committee members and counsel, Sciaroni reluctantly agreed North had not given him accurate information about the nature of his Contra support operations. His examiners also compelled Sciaroni to admit he had failed the bar exam three times before passing. After weeks of defiant and uncooperative witnesses, the committees behaved as if they had finally found someone on whom to take out their frustrations. "By the time we'd finished with him," according to Liman, "he was destroyed—not just as a witness but as a person."[66]

Charles Cooper, the assistant attorney general Edwin Meese had assigned to his investigating team in late November 1986, fared better, although he was clearly not keen to provide evidence against his superiors. He acknowledged he had been troubled by the falsified NSC staff chronology on the Iran arms deals and by Casey's misleading congressional testimony. He declared he would not believe North even if he were under oath because of North's record of dishonesty in the affair.

Former CIA general counsel Stanley Sporkin, who helped draft the findings Reagan signed on the Iran arms deals in December 1985 and January 1986, contributed to the hearings mainly by providing his blunt view that the operation had been about retrieving hostages, not creating a strategic opening to Tehran.

Game Changer: North Takes the Stand

North's testimony provided the dramatic climax to the hearings. The charismatic marine was already a folk hero to many even though he had absorbed several blows to his credibility from other witnesses. In the weeks beforehand, he and his attorneys had battled relentlessly with the committees behind the scenes. Counting on his star value, they pushed for concessions: insisting he appear early in the hearings, submitting no private deposition in advance, and limiting his testimony to three days total (ten hours a day) with no possibility for recall. They further demanded he be allowed until just a few days before taking the stand to reply to a subpoena for records; that the documents cover only the period January 1, 1984, to November 26, 1986; and that the committees accept his word he had complied fully with the subpoena.

North's extraordinary ultimatums threatened to handcuff the committees. Several members expressed outrage at the idea of allowing a witness to set terms so baldly, especially when they created impossible conditions, such as providing three days to process thousands of pages of evidence. Others warned North's attorneys could force a crippling delay in the hearings by going to court to challenge the requirement for his testimony. Intent on building a bipartisan consensus, the committee leadership gave in on several of the demands and reached a compromise on others. As two senators admitted later, "Oliver North and the Committee had gone eyeball to eyeball and the Committee had blinked." They went on to note this was just the "prologue of what was to come."[67]

North took control of the hearings the moment he entered the room. Dressed in his marine uniform, replete with service decorations, he presented a deliberate contrast with his questioners, who came across as "corpulent and powerful Roman potentates."[68] Many service members reportedly were offended that he invoked the Fifth Amendment while in uniform, but the ploy helped put the committees on the defensive. Inouye, who had lost an arm in combat, took to wearing his Distinguished Service Cross, but to little detectable effect.

North's lead attorney, Brendan Sullivan, continued to keep the committees on their heels. Counsel for a witness at congressional hearings rarely has the opportunity to be heard, but Sullivan made a point of objecting frequently, loudly condemning the process as unfair to his client. He called the hearings the "most extraordinary proceeding, I think, Mr. Chairman, in our 200 years."[69]

When North's testimony got under way, Nields responded with an aggressive tack, described by the *New York Times* as "designed to antagonize." At one point Nields equated North's penchant for secrecy with the practices of "certain Communist countries," adding pointedly: "But that's not the way we do things in America, is it?"[70] From the majority's standpoint, the initial sessions were productive and appeared to support Liman's view they could pry loose important testimony without a comprehensive prior deposition. North acknowledged potentially damaging facts: he had helped set up the Enterprise, diverted funds from the Iran arms sales to the Contras, prepared memos for the president about the diversion, informed other U.S. officials including Abrams about his Contra activities, lied to Congress about those operations, and altered memos and falsified chronologies to cover up the government's (and the president's) role. "I had rarely, if ever, seen a cooperating witness in a criminal case who admitted more than North did," Liman wrote later.[71]

But North had no intention of playing the fall guy. Although he conceded an astonishing degree of deceptiveness, he labored to shift accountability to his higher-ups. He even boasted about his behavior. "I did a lot of things, and I want to stand up and say that I'm proud of them," he declared, but added, "I have never carried out a single act, not one, in which I did not have authority from my superiors." Even after Poindexter "deemed it not to be necessary to ask the president" to approve the diversion, North said he never hesitated to do what he was told: "I saluted smartly and charged up the hill. That's what lieutenant colonels are supposed to do."[72] His justification, as he explained it, was that serving the president constituted a higher responsibility than to be truthful to Congress—or anyone else.

North's testimony often became emotional. To his critics, his tone sounded artificial and self-righteous, but it was extremely effective. One commentator likened him to a young Ronald Reagan "playing in real life parts Reagan only got in movies": "The old master could not teach the new daytime star anything about television. North has taken the box by storm. He has the same kind of voice as the Gipper, a light tenor with a little break in it for emotional moments, like when he says the whole Cabinet was with him in the mess or that he has been faithful to his wife 'since the day I married her.' His neck is as scrawny as a boy's, and he plays the vulnerable scamp."[73]

North's dramatic delivery was in evidence when Liman asked why Reagan had fired him if the diversion had been such a creditable idea:

> Let me just make one thing very clear, counsel. This lieutenant colonel is not going to challenge a decision of the Commander in Chief for whom I still work, and I am proud to work for that Commander in Chief, and if the Commander in Chief tells this lieutenant colonel to go stand in the corner and sit on his head, I will do so. And if the Commander in Chief decides to dismiss me from the NSC staff, this lieutenant colonel will proudly salute and say 'thank you for the opportunity to have served,' and go, and I am not going to criticize his decision no matter how he relieves me, sir.[74]

At times, North managed to put off even some of his defenders. Republican members criticized his "irreverent" and "flip" tone, and the witness himself later conceded he was "far too insolent."[75] However, his audacious rebukes of Congress and the hearings, along with his appeals to patriotism and higher causes, had a powerful impact on segments of the public. His military bearing particularly stood out against Nields's collar-length hair and "hippie look."[76] After his first day of testimony, crowds began to troop daily to Capitol Hill reveling in Olliemania, and tens of thousands of supporters sent pro-North telegrams and made phone calls to committee members.

Stunned by the outpouring (epitomized by Capitol Hill police lining up for photos with North during breaks in his testimony) the leadership hurried to steer the hearings in a safer direction. Some members separated themselves from the committees' counsel.[77] Senator Boren complained "a very serious mistake was made in the tone," and called Nields overly "prosecutorial."[78] One opinion writer noticed "how quickly the Congressmen who had called him a 'criminal,' 'liar' and 'misfit' changed their tune. All of a sudden, that fickle, vacillating and unpredictable Congress had nothing but compliments and fatherly advice for America's new hero."[79] In the midst of the investigation, the committees diverted precious staff resources to answering the torrent of public criticism coming in via constituent mail.[80]

Liman took over North's questioning on the afternoon of the second day. He adopted a more congenial manner—electing, for example, not to pursue North's dubious personal finances. The committees even allowed North to present his celebrated fund-raising pitch for the Contras—albeit without the slides— yielding to minority demands and public pressure.[81] Sullivan, meanwhile, continued his interventions. In a single day, he made the following interjections:

[To Liman]: "That is none of your business. . . . You just ask him the question. . . . Get off his back!"
[To North]: "Don't answer the question. Next question, Mr. Chairman. It won't be answered!"
[To Liman]: "Get on with the questioning. . . . If the witness wants to look at his notes . . . he'll do so."
[To Inouye]: "I'm not a potted plant. I'm here as a lawyer. That's my job."[82]

Some members became livid at Sullivan's tactics and were irritated at Inouye's reluctance to gavel him into silence, reminding the public that congressional rules do not give attorneys the same leeway they have in court.[83] Rep. Jack Brooks was reportedly ready to call the sergeant at arms to arrest Sullivan for contempt. The snag for most Democrats was "none of them wanted to look like the heavy," according to a committee lawyer.[84]

By every measure, North had dominated the committees. When his testimony finally ended, the course of the hearings had shifted radically. An *ABC News* poll a few days after his appearance showed a swing in opinion about his handling of the affair from two-to-one against to majority approval within the space of a week. Other polls continued to reflect substantial public disapproval of North's role, but the power of his performance and raucous support from his backers cowed the committees.[85] "North was the turning point," Senate investigator Thomas Polgar declared. "After that fiasco, there was a panic element. Everybody was anxious to get it wrapped up. We were not about to look for trouble."[86]

Show Stopper: Poindexter (Mostly) Ends the Speculation

North provided the theatrical high points of the hearings, but on the core issues of presidential conduct and constitutional import the decisive witness was Poindexter. Rudman had let it be known the former national security advisor was key to the question that had driven every investigation into the scandal—had the president known about the diversion? After all, Poindexter, not North, had met daily with the president and had been in a position to report to him on the progress of the Iran and Contra operations.

Rudman's comments raised anticipation over whether Poindexter would pin responsibility for the diversion on the president. What the public did not know was Poindexter had already answered the question. Immediately prior to the hearings, he had given a top-secret deposition inside a secure bubble in the Hart Senate Office Building that only Liman and Nields attended from the committees. Not even the chairs participated. Pressed by Liman, Poindexter flatly denied telling Reagan about the diversion, thus ending all prospect of the committees recommending the president's impeachment.[87]

This critical evidence would not surface until Poindexter took his place at the witness table in mid-July and repeated his claims before television cameras. "After working with the President for five-and-a-half years, the last [three] of which were very close, probably closer than any other officer in the White House except the Chief of Staff," he testified, "I was convinced that I understood the President's thinking on this." On Nicaragua, "the policy was very clear, and that was to support the Contras." Therefore, the diversion was not in itself a "secret foreign policy," simply a means of "implementation of" an existing policy that "had not changed since 1981."[88]

In that light, the decision to withhold the details from the president was not an arrogation of authority to himself, Poindexter claimed. "I was convinced that . . . if I had taken it to him that he would have approved it." At the same time, knowing how controversial it would be, "I made a very deliberate decision not to ask the President so that I could insulate him from the decision and provide some future deniability for the President if it ever leaked out. . . . On this whole issue," he concluded, "the buck stops here with me."[89]

In the end, Poindexter proved more loyal to the president than North had been, yet he was seen as the less credible witness. Despite his confession of misleading and withholding information from Congress (because "I simply didn't want any outside interference"),[90] several committee members believed his story did not hold up. His spotless fitness reports dating back to the U.S. Naval Academy described a stickler for the chain of command who never acted without the consent of his superiors. Liman tried to find a crack in his story—arguing the term "plausible deniability" the admiral had invoked implied the person being protected knew what was happening but needed to make it appear he did not. Poindexter refused to budge.[91]

The two Senate committee leaders also had grave doubts about the president's ignorance of the diversion. Outside of the hearings, Inouye and Rudman confronted NSC Staff Counsel Paul Thompson to ask him what he knew. It was an act of "frustration," Rudman wrote, "as we sought the truth in a situation where documents had been destroyed and those involved told stories that often seemed incredible."[92] Senator Nunn told a reporter, "There is a tremendous amount of circumstantial evidence that [Reagan] knew, but there is no direct evidence."[93] At the end of the day, the committees could not dislodge Poindexter's account. Energized Republicans began to argue "insistently" for shutting down the hearings, according to two other members. The rest of the committee, "already exhausted by the punishing pace of the investigation, offered little resistance. . . . The hearings had crested and now began to recede."[94]

Wrapping Up: The President's Top Advisors

Although the committees cut back on the witness list after North's intimidating performance, they decided to close by hearing from four senior Reagan administration officials whose roles in the affair had raised questions.[95] "We . . . know much about what happened but not nearly enough about why and how," one columnist noted. The testimony of key cabinet members and presidential advisors was partly designed to find out.[96]

The first to testify was Shultz, who had made it clear through the media he had been victimized by his colleagues during the course of the secret programs. Shultz spoke positively about the president but maintained his own blamelessness. The NSC staff and Casey, he said, had repeatedly cut him out of the decision-making process on Iran and the Contras. He had warned Reagan the secret program was a terrible idea and had even offered to resign. After the scandal was exposed, he became engaged in a "battle royal" with the president himself to try to get him to face reality and acknowledge his actions to the U.S. public. At that point, he testified, the backstabbing escalated. Casey, for one, wanted Reagan to fire him—telling the president he "needed a new pitcher." Representative Aspin called Shultz's account of administration in-fighting the "most amazing thing I've heard in 17 years in the House."[97]

Discussing the president, Shultz offered praise for his instincts and independent judgment: "I have come to have a profound respect for his capacity to make good decisions and to be decisive. He is not a trimmer. He looks at something and he decides." He dismissed the cartoon image of Reagan as asleep at the controls. "This idea that the President just sits around not paying attention, I don't know where anybody gets that idea. He is a very strong and decisive person."[98]

Shultz conceded Reagan had been a driving force behind the Iran deals and had pushed for them despite objections from his most senior advisors, including at the extraordinary December 7, 1985, White House meeting, at which he had remarked: "The American people will never forgive me if I fail to get these hostages out over this legal question" (see Chapter 6). But he dismissed any notion that Reagan in making that comment "was advocating violating the law." Rather, it was "the kind of statement that I'm sure we all make sometimes when we're frustrated."[99] The committees accepted this characterization without comment. The secretary also confirmed Reagan had personal knowledge of the controversial HAWK shipment at the time, directly contradicting the president's (and Meese's) version of events.

Shultz went on to acknowledge the importance of Congress and the need for forthright relations among the branches of government. He said he had been guided throughout his career by the adage "Trust is the coin of the realm." Afterward, committee praise for Shultz and his forthrightness was often effusive. Republican Senator Trible called his "eloquent soliloquy on democratic values in government . . . the highlight of my 11 years in Congress."[100]

Conservatives were unmoved, however. They appreciated Shultz's opposition to the Iran deals, but few had fully trusted his stance on the Contras, and many were unhappy because they believed he tended to put his public image ahead of Reagan's. Senator Hatch asked whether, as Poindexter had suggested, Shultz had not deliberately shielded himself from unwelcome information about the arms deals. Shultz called the assertion "ridiculous" and insisted again he had been repeatedly misled about the operation. Only when the Office of the Independent Counsel obtained the full notes of Shultz's closest aides several years later, in 1992, did it become apparent that in fact he had significantly shaded his account to Congress of the Iran events (see Chapters 13 and 15).

Meese, who followed Shultz to the stand, got off less easily. The committees' majority sharply criticized his inquiry in late November 1986 in which, among other faults, he failed to safeguard evidence, which North and others subsequently shredded. Rudman called his performance "at best incompetent."[101] Meese defended himself and his investigation with his usual aggressiveness. "At the time, there was nothing that gave [a] hint" the Justice Department was being misled by anyone, he said. Therefore there was no need to take special measures such as locking down North's offices. He stuck to this position even while acknowledging that shortly into his investigation he recognized his colleagues' discoveries might have "criminal implications." Meese also took heat for not bringing the Criminal Division into the process sooner. He claimed no one from that division had asked to be a part of it, but Representative Rodino produced a sworn deposition from Assistant Attorney General William Weld indicating otherwise. Senator Mitchell pressed Meese on his reasons for taking no notes at crucial meetings with Reagan, Bush, Casey, Regan, and Poindexter. The attorney general was also forced to admit he had posed "almost no direct questions" of Poindexter throughout his inquiry. He insisted in the end he had succeeded in unearthing the "essential facts."[102]

Regan testified next. As chief of staff he had a reputation as an intimidator who demanded control over most aspects of White House business. The Tower Commission had pinned much of the blame on him for failing to ensure the president had been fully informed and protected against his aides. Most committee members gave him a respectful reception, however. His main contribution to the hearings was to reconfirm he and the president had known about the HAWK shipment in November 1985 and about the cover story regarding oil-drilling equipment. These admissions contradicted the president's testimony to the Tower Commission.[103] He also disclosed Reagan had held meetings in December 1986 to discuss whether to pardon North and Poindexter. The president decided firmly against it, Regan said, because it was premature and would have implied the two had committed crimes, which Reagan did not believe.[104] In his own defense, Regan claimed he was never directly involved in or even aware of much of what had transpired in the affair itself, certainly not at the level of "operational details." He added he had not exercised close control over Poindexter, who, he said, dealt more or less independently with the president.

The final witness at the public hearings was the combative Weinberger. The committees extended to him much the same deference they had to Shultz, as one of the few senior officials who had tried to put a stop to the Iran arms deals. As Weinberger put it, "I believe[d] this baby had been strangled in its cradle."[105] Instead, he described repeated efforts by White House operatives, mainly Poindexter, to undercut his opposition—from denying him access to electronic intercepts to misleading the president. The entire enterprise, he insisted, had been premised on false assumptions, most notably the presence of moderates in Iran, which he had doubted from the beginning.

Weinberger's rendition of events met with general approval. The committees were still anxious to remind the public of the senselessness of the secret operations, and his account helped emphasize the point. His testimony about being kept in the dark prompted Senators Sarbanes and Nunn to describe the existence of a "junta" in the White House, consisting of lower-level staff who they believed had hijacked U.S. policy and hidden their activities from more sensible officials.

At the time, the committees did not know the secretary of defense had misled them about his awareness of key events—the Saudi donations to the Contras, the November 1985 HAWK shipment, and the issue of replenishing missiles to Israel. Beyond that, he had denied to congressional investigators he kept regular notes of his activities—the discovery of which, years afterward, opened up a far more detailed picture of his knowledge of the scandal and that of the president.

The Final Report

Having run out the clock they themselves set, the committees' concluding task was to compile a record of the proceedings and propose remedies. Totaling 690 pages, the final report contained three main parts: the principal narrative, signed by a majority of members; the minority report, prepared by Republicans who disagreed with the main document; and supplemental views contributed by various members. Separately, the inquiry produced some three dozen lengthy appendixes of hearing testimony, depositions, exhibits, and chronologies.

The majority's narrative took a deeply critical view of the affair: "The common ingredients of the Iran and Contra policies were secrecy, deception, and disdain for the law." Believing "they alone knew what was right," a "small group of senior officials" engaged in a pattern of "pervasive dishonesty," resorting to end runs around Congress and the "privatization" of policy, which undermined the checks and balances of the U.S. Constitution. "When the[ir] goals and the law collided, the law gave way."[106]

The majority also submitted twenty-seven recommendations for improving the policy process. They proposed several ways to tighten executive branch adherence to presidential findings, means for covering the conduct of covert operations and arms sales, and approaches for reaffirming and expanding the rules for congressional notification. At bottom, however, the committees believed the affair was primarily the result of individuals failing to follow existing law, not shortcomings in the law itself. They asserted that under any circumstances, "Congress cannot legislate good judgment, honesty, or fidelity to law."

Eight of the eleven GOP committee members (Senators Rudman, Cohen, and Trible excepted) split with the majority and prepared their own minority report, which was a straightforward defense of the administration, albeit with certain criticisms of choices made. "President Reagan and his staff made mistakes in the Iran-Contra Affair," they acknowledged, but these were "mistakes in judgment, and nothing more." Flatly disagreeing with the majority, they insisted "there was no constitutional crisis, no systematic disrespect for 'the rule of law,' no grand conspiracy, and no Administration-wide dishonesty or coverup." They called the majority's conclusions "hysterical."[107]

Not only did the minority reject the idea that the Iran-Contra operations threatened the ability of Congress to perform its constitutional functions, they complained the authority of the executive branch had been undermined and accused Congress of intruding on presidential turf through the Boland Amendments and other legislation. But they also criticized Reagan for ceding too much to the legislative branch. Although they did not question the Boland Amendments' constitutionality, they believed the president should have vetoed it in 1984 instead of signing it (even though a minority staff member pointed out "this would have been tough given the election timing").[108] They said further the president should have asserted executive privilege during the congressional inquiry instead of putting up a "less-than-robust defense of his office's constitutional powers."[109]

In the minority's view, the Iran deals were no more than an honest attempt at a "strategic opening" that suffered from flawed implementation—essentially identical to the administration's stance. For allowing the deals to fail, they singled out Poindexter, Regan, and Shultz for blame. On the Contra side, the authors concluded "virtually all of the NSC staff's activities were legal, with the possible exception of the diversion." They asserted any deception by the administration was not used to hide illegality but to avoid possible "political reprisals" by Congress, mainly through tighter restrictions on Contra aid. The authors acknowledged, however, it was "self-defeating" to try to sustain the covert program by "deceiving" Capitol Hill, adding, "Whether technically illegal or not, it was politically foolish and counterproductive to mislead Congress, even if misleading took the form of artful evasion or silence instead of overt misstatement."[110]

Again taking the opposite tack from the majority, they made an impassioned defense of the president's powers in foreign policy, then advanced just five recommendations, none of which targeted executive branch prerogatives. Instead the proposals called for steps to limit the reach of Congress, punish legislators for disclosing secrets, and expand the president's flexibility in dealing with "continuing resolutions" such as the Boland Amendments and other legislative conventions.

Rudman was indignant, dismissing the report as "pathetic" and a "disgrace."[111] But it was not a document taken lightly. In later years, Cheney, while serving as vice president in the George W. Bush administration, cited the report as a blueprint for his thinking on presidential power. Calling it an "obscure text," he praised it as "very good in laying out a robust view of the president's prerogatives with respect to the conduct of especially foreign policy and national security matters."[112]

Committee Report Card

Few who were involved with the hearings came away fully satisfied with the results. The goal had been to inform the U.S. public of what had happened during the Iran-Contra affair and to help restore public confidence in "this Nation's Constitutional system of Government."[113] By the time Senator Inouye gaveled the public proceedings to a close on August 3, 1987, the evidence of their success was mixed at best.[114] Even Rudman, who was asked whether the committees had uncovered all the White House's secrets, acknowledged: "I have my doubts."[115]

The public undoubtedly learned a great deal about the operations and the individuals involved. For those inclined to acknowledge the failings of hero figures such as North and Reagan, there was plenty to ponder. The committees did an impressive service by producing a 30,000-page record of exhibits and deposition testimony that went well beyond what had been possible to show television audiences.

On a deeper level, the hearings raised important questions of governance, especially in foreign policy, at the heart of the affair. Constitutional issues surrounding the proper roles of the president and Congress permeated the process. The quality of the rhetoric of the likes of Hamilton, Mitchell, and Inouye, which pointed out the dangers posed by Reagan administration assumptions and actions, was widely remarked upon at the time.

At the same time, the committees fell short in important respects and for a variety of reasons. Unavoidably, politics was a pervasive obstacle. Investigating a sitting president proved a highly charged undertaking, particularly in the case of a popular figure like Reagan. Hyperpartisan behavior was therefore to be expected, especially with presidential elections looming. The Democrats generally erred on the side of restraint and caution—or timidity, in the view of some critics—either to try to preserve bipartisanship or to stave off charges of unfairness by vocal defenders of Reagan and North. At one point during the hearings, a *Washington Post* editorial slammed the committees' "obsequious" and "mawkish" behavior[116] toward North. It is arguable the effort did not pay off because eight Republicans still refused to sign on to the majority report, and the committees still failed utterly against North.

For its part, the minority devoted much of its energy to blocking the majority's attempts to expose administration activities. Rudman slammed his GOP colleagues, "particularly those from the House, who were there not as fact-finders but as unashamed defenders of the president."[117] But Cheney, echoing the views of others, saw his role as straightforward—to protect Reagan from "extreme charges made by his critics."[118] The differences in perceived mission pointed to a broader weakness of congressional investigations. "Very often," a Democratic staffer noted, "one party is involved in investigating and the other party is involved in trying to help the witness." The result is a "round of . . . tough questioning" followed by the equivalent of slow-pitch softball: "'Well, just how much do you like apple pie?'"[119]

The committees' biggest reason for coming up short was their self-imposed deadline. Nields called it the "crushing burden on all of us."[120] Based largely on political considerations, the compressed time frame made it difficult if not impossible to explore more deeply the roots of Reagan administration policies, which could have provided needed context and grist for debates over governance. Still another barrier—institutional in this case—was the determination to create select committees with precise and limited missions. The alternatives may have been just as unpalatable, but turf concerns on the part of powerful standing committees undoubtedly kept Iran-Contra investigators from exploring contentious issues with links to the scandal.[121] Among the topics that for various reasons escaped fuller scrutiny were the following: the Contras themselves, the Israeli angle, sensitive quid pro quo arrangements with the likes of Panama's dictator Manuel Noriega, Bush's role, the conduct of the intelligence community, and the appropriate place for covert action in a democratic society. Even if time had not been an issue, powerful interests would have opposed scrutinizing each of these sensitive areas. The intelligence community would undoubtedly have stepped in, for example, as would Israel's backers—not to mention Republicans with an eye on the 1988 elections.

The committees—at least their majority—reached some strong conclusions about the nature and causes of the scandal. Unlike the Tower Commission—which reproached Reagan only for his "hands-off management style," not for the delinquencies of an "NSC rogue staff"—the majority held Reagan personally liable for actions on his watch. "The ultimate responsibility for the events in the Iran-Contra Affair must rest with the President," said the final report. "It was the President's policy—not an isolated decision by North or Poindexter—to sell arms secretly to Iran and to maintain the Contras 'body and soul.'"[122] According to opinion polls, most U.S. citizens agreed.

Yet, the majority failed to follow its own rhetoric (dismissed by Cheney as "apocalyptic") to its logical conclusion. Wrapping up the hearings, Inouye called the affair a "chilling story—a story of deceit and duplicity and the arrogant disregard of the rule of law."[123] But his criticisms of Reagan's staff for riding "roughshod over the Constitutional restraints built into our form of government" implicitly let the president himself off the hook. The committees had direct evidence—in the form of documents and testimony—Reagan had been prepared to sidestep the law in order to make sure he obtained the hostages' release. Instead of probing further, as the independent counsel did, they chose to gloss over his actions and disregard their constitutional implications. In the long run, that decision, based on reasons both of perceived national interest and political self-protection, arguably undermined the impact of the congressional investigation and the majority's goal of restoring public confidence in the political system.

15

The Independent Counsel

The Office of the Independent Counsel (OIC) investigation was the last official chapter of the Iran-Contra story. Charged with determining whether crimes had been committed and prosecuting the perpetrators, Lawrence Walsh launched what stretched into almost a seven-year inquiry. Complicated legal challenges and remarkably bitter political opposition almost overwhelmed the process, but the OIC managed to win convictions against several of the main participants (though some were vacated on appeal). Late in the investigation, Walsh's staff achieved a string of investigative breakthroughs, uncovering crucial evidence pointing to the culpability of senior officials. The nature of that material, the obstacles the OIC encountered in obtaining and using it at trial, and the political uproar the prosecutions sparked all raised questions about whether top administration officials had obstructed justice. Ultimately, the OIC's mixed results revealed serious impediments to the ability of the U.S. legal system to expose and remedy official wrongdoing in the national security sphere.

First Steps

On December 4, 1986, fewer than ten days after the president's November 25 press conference, Attorney General Edwin Meese made a formal request for a special counsel. After initially excluding his own Criminal Division and the FBI from his team, he now declared there were grounds for investigating criminal conduct. The administration had grasped one of the cardinal lessons of Watergate—to avoid even the appearance of a cover-up.

On December 19, the Special Division of the U.S. Court of Appeals for the District of Columbia named former judge Walsh "Independent Counsel for Iran/Contra Matters." After an early career as a prosecutor and state government attorney in New York, Walsh had been named to the federal bench by President Dwight Eisenhower in 1954. Three years later, Eisenhower appointed him deputy attorney general and during the 1960 presidential campaign reportedly advised Richard Nixon to consider Walsh for the top Justice Department job if he won the race. After John F. Kennedy's victory, Walsh reentered private practice.

Although some Democrats were uncertain about Walsh's impartiality because of his decades-long Republican allegiance, the three-judge selection panel was unconcerned. What mattered most, according to the chief judge, was that he had the experience and stature for a case that could lead to the Oval Office. "I recognized from the very beginning that there was a very strong potential that this thing might balloon into an impeachment investigation," Judge George E. MacKinnon explained. "This was no ordinary choice." As for Walsh's age (one month shy of seventy-five), MacKinnon invited him for an interview to "make sure he was as sharp as I remembered him. . . . We got over that hurdle fast."[1]

The courts gave the OIC a broad mandate to investigate the transfer of arms to Iran beginning roughly in 1984, the role of any intermediaries, the diversion of proceeds to any other person or entity (not just in Nicaragua), and the provision of aid to the Contras. Walsh had urged the appointments panel to grant as much authority as possible because "you never know where a break might come in a case." He also recognized even though the independent counsel would be overseeing criminal prosecutions, the "core of the scandal was political, and politicians—rather than lawyers—would decide what direction events would take."[2]

Walsh assumed the assignment would be "comfortably limited" because the case seemed to revolve around a simple "rogue operation. . . . The natural course," therefore, "was to follow the trail that was already open"—a trail that led first to Oliver North and John Poindexter. Walsh initially thought a team of ten associate counsels would be enough. He chose mainly lawyers with experience prosecuting corruption, organized crime, and "complex litigation in other fields." But he also picked John Keker, a criminal litigator who had been a decorated marine platoon leader in Vietnam—"the perfect man to put up against North if a case ever came to trial." Walsh anticipated a fairly straightforward process that would largely rely on "criminal procedures to develop testimony against higher-ups from unwilling witnesses."[3] In other words, it would involve threats of prison time to get lower-level officials to turn against their superiors.

Before long, Walsh realized he had miscalculated. Many of the issues under scrutiny were new to him, and unlike his corporate defense work, in which he could rely on clients for strong backing and expertise, here he would have virtually no institutional support. "I would have to start from scratch," he wrote later.[4] Speed was also critical because Congress might decide to grant immunity to witnesses essential to his prosecutions. By February he had doubled the staff, which continued to grow until it reached twenty-eight attorneys and ninety support personnel.[5]

The Operational Conspiracy

Midway through February, the OIC staff had sifted through a small mountain of evidence and come up with a basic "blueprint" for the prosecution. One option was to file simple obstruction of justice charges against North and his associates for destroying documents. Another was to pursue illegal Contra fund-raising. Evidence already existed for these counts, and going to trial before Congress extended immunity would avoid having to deal with "tainted" testimony. But the OIC decided there was insufficient time to mount a trial before the two star suspects, North and Poindexter, appeared before the committees, and confronting both Congress and hostile defendants would present greater challenges than handling the question of taint.

Instead, the independent counsel's top deputy, Guy Struve, proposed going after a far more extensive web of criminality. As Walsh described the idea, "The most likely charges were for crimes arising out of the unauthorized conduct of covert hostilities in Nicaragua, the use of a tax-exempt foundation to fund covert hostilities in Nicaragua, and the diversion of proceeds from the Iranian arms sales." The goal would be to "prove a conspiracy to use CIA and other government personnel and assets to carry out illegal covert hostilities in Nicaragua at a time when these activities were prohibited by the Boland Amendments."[6]

A major consideration was that one of the principal laws Reagan officials had allegedly violated—the second Boland Amendment—was a civil statute that carried no criminal penalties. Struve's concept offered a way around this. "The deceitful misuse of government personnel and funds could support a charge of conspiracy to defraud the government," Walsh explained later. The charge in question referred to a concise but extremely wide-ranging section of the U.S. Code (18 U.S.C. 371) that makes it a crime for two or more individuals to conspire to defraud the United States "in any manner" or "for any purpose."[7] Based in part on a 1924 Supreme Court ruling, the definition of defrauding could encompass any action either to "cheat the Government out of property or money," or "to interfere with or obstruct one of its lawful governmental functions by deceit, craft or trickery, or at least by means that are dishonest."[8]

Struve contemplated a variety of other possible charges: spending unappropriated funds, theft of government property (the Iran arms profits), mail fraud, personal enrichment, and obstruction—destroying records and providing false testimony. Because the independent counsel assumed the president had approved the arms-for-hostages deals, the Iran side of the affair (other than the diversion) did not fit easily within the definition of defrauding the government.[9]

The OIC's eventual decision to pursue broad conspiracy and theft charges was by no means unanimous. Several senior attorneys argued it was too difficult to prosecute. Conspiracy cases are typically related to more narrowly focused crimes, not to the kind of vague, all-encompassing phrasing featured in Section 371. The lead FBI agent attached to the office, along with other staff, favored the traditional investigative tack of following the money.[10] Keker, the lead prosecutor on the North trial, believed "we had all the evidence we needed six months into the investigation."[11] But there was a lingering sense that to push for a trial before Congress began calling key witnesses was a risk. A considerable amount of information about events in Iran and Nicaragua, but particularly about the money trail, was still unavailable. Several lawyers thought they could afford to wait until Congress had finished the hearings.[12] In the end, Walsh's view was the conspiracy angle had the overriding advantage of supplying a coherent theory of the crime that tied together disparate parts of the case and provided a reasonable explanation for what had happened. It also offered legal grounds for prosecution of conduct most of the staff fully believed had been illicit, even if the laws in question were nebulous.

On March 16, 1988, the OIC filed a joint indictment against Poindexter, North, Richard Secord, and Albert Hakim. According to the charge, the "conspirators" had performed "three separate but intertwined activities": supporting the Contra war in violation of a congressional ban; using funds from the Iran arms sales for their own purposes instead of turning them over to the U.S. Treasury; and jeopardizing legitimate hostage rescue efforts. According to the 101-page indictment, the first act constituted an "unauthorized covert program" about which the group had "deceived Congress." In the second act, North and Poindexter "deceitfully" used their government positions to "create a hidden slush fund" to generate both profits for the "conspirators" and resources North controlled without proper accountability. The third act jeopardized the government's ongoing attempts to free U.S. hostages in Lebanon because it "outraged" the Iranians by overpricing the weapons.[13]

Obstacles to Prosecutions

A series of barriers confronted the OIC, many of them erected by defendants, appeals courts, and—not least—Ronald Reagan's administration. At every turn, U.S. officials produced delays that risked extending the prosecutions past the expiration of the statute of limitations. The delays in turn increased costs, which fueled opposition to the investigations.

One of the earliest hurdles was a challenge to the Ethics in Government Act, which governed the appointment of independent counsels. North's attorneys filed suit in federal district court in late February 1987 on the grounds the entire institution of independent prosecutors, established in the wake of Watergate, violated the U.S. Constitution separation of powers provisions. Other special counsel probes were facing similar tests. Therefore, the move was not a surprise, and Walsh had a fallback plan: he asked for a parallel appointment from the attorney general to give him legal standing while the constitutional question was under deliberation. Meese complied, and the investigation continued. A year later, the Supreme Court ruled the ethics statute constitutional.

As expected, the congressional immunity grant to three out of the four defendants (Secord declined the offer) threatened to cripple the conspiracy and theft case. From the start, Walsh had seen Congress as a "rival operation" that could "undo my work before it produced any results."[14] Each of the defendants argued to the court that immunity would rule out using the protected testimony of his codefendants, even if it proved his innocence.[15] This would violate their right to a fair trial. U.S. District Judge Gerhard Gesell agreed, and on June 8 he severed the prosecutions, adding significantly to the preparation time because there would now be four separate cases. "No adverse factor shaped or constricted Independent Counsel's criminal investigation more than the congressional immunity grants made to North, Poindexter and Hakim," the independent counsel noted.[16]

Another critical impediment was the need to use classified information at trial. Walsh called the dependence on government secrets "our greatest vulnerability."[17] Criminal trials are largely public proceedings, but in cases involving national security a vital question is how to introduce sensitive evidence in an open setting. Defendants are fully aware if the government refuses to release material they claim is necessary for their defense, a judge may simply dismiss the charges. In his memoir, Walsh wrote scathingly about his two main defendants: "Never before had such a scheme been directed by such ruthless and skilled experts as Poindexter . . . and North."[18]

In 1980, Congress passed the Classified Information Procedures Act (CIPA) to deal with cases of so-called gray mail. Normally, the search for a balance between competing societal interests—protecting legitimate secrets and prosecuting criminal acts—pitted government departments against each other—that is, the intelligence community and the Justice Department. In the Iran-Contra scandal the independent counsel found his investigation at odds with both institutions. In several of the trials, the intelligence agencies and the attorney general cooperated to keep classified information from being introduced. During North's proceeding, Attorney General Richard Thornburgh's denial of access to a range of restricted material forced the independent counsel to drop the two main conspiracy counts.[19] In the trial of former CIA official Joseph Fernandez, the judge dismissed all charges for the same reason.

Although CIPA had been designed to prevent executive branch interference in criminal trials,[20] Thornburgh asserted he was simply "fulfill[ing] the responsibility imposed upon me by the Congress to protect the national security interests of the United States." But the OIC staff was "outraged," suspecting he was putting administration interests above that of the nation. Walsh accused Thornburgh of trying to take control of the trial and condemned the administration's reflexive support for the intelligence agencies as a "stunning disavowal of the president's publicly professed desire for full disclosure."[21] An OIC source described the Justice Department's actions as "tantamount to firing the independent prosecutor."[22]

Other federal departments inhibited the criminal investigations, OIC lawyers charged. "Walsh has gotten the minimum of cooperation from many government agencies," former associate counsel Michael Bromwich declared as the prosecution wound down in 1993. "He basically has had no positive cooperation . . . for six years."[23] According to Walsh, "By February [1987], the CIA had produced a mere handful of records." Only when faced with subpoenas did agency officials become more accommodating. Sometimes even under threat of court order the response seemed designed to hinder. "Production alternated between withholding and flooding with key documents not produced until after months of delay." The White House, too, became less cooperative as time went on—"withholding many of the documents we needed." In mid-1988, for example, only after North gained access to his former office files did the White House produce some 15,000 pages of "new" evidence "that should have been turned over to us" months earlier, Walsh said.[24]

David Abshire, the president's special advisor on Iran-Contra matters, who helped coordinate the White House response to investigators, did not contradict these charges and specifically acknowledged the "CIA was very slow" when it came to the trials, although he blamed the "difficulty [in] evaluating the documents."[25] He unwittingly highlighted the ingrained temptation across government to withhold information for political reasons when he conceded there was a "scary dimension" to turning over so many documents to investigators: "Conceivably, any one of them might contain a smoking gun—something incriminating of the president."[26] Walsh acknowledged he had "asked for heavy sacrifices from the intelligence agencies,"[27] but not surprisingly he was far more acerbic than Abshire about executive branch behavior. "Confronted with giving up information they prefer not to acknowledge, the agencies have nothing to lose by exhausting every possible procedural alternative. . . . In the end, the agencies' indifference to the costs of such a strategy endangers the success of the prosecution."[28]

Sometimes agency demands seemed utterly unjustified. The intelligence community denied access to certain material in the public domain because it had been inadvertently disclosed, not officially released, arguing the distinction mattered to some foreign governments.[29] At the North trial, Judge Gesell became exasperated to discover that the name of Costa Rican official Benjamin

Piza, which the administration had declared secret and unusable in court, had been released a year earlier in a civil lawsuit. The judge expressed "bafflement" at the "ex post facto" classification decision. "I don't know what the rules are anymore," he remarked.[30] OIC attorneys took to calling these pieces of information "fictional secrets."[31]

Before the North trial got under way, Thornburgh intervened in another highly unusual way. As the trial date approached, North's attorneys moved to have the conspiracy and theft charges dropped. Unexpectedly, the Justice Department filed an amicus curiae (friend of the court) brief that agreed the charges were deficient. The prosecutors had made the assumption—widely accepted—that Congress was a coequal branch of government and that the executive branch was obliged to respect its will, as expressed in statutes. By evading the Boland Amendments, the OIC charged, North (and his fellow defendants) had committed crimes. The Justice Department argued this interpretation was "incorrect" because only the "President has plenary authority to represent the United States," and "Congress cannot . . . invade any sphere of constitutional authority granted exclusively to the President." That sphere, the Justice Department stated, included "covert diplomacy that seeks support (including financial contributions) for the foreign policy [the president] articulates on behalf of the Nation."[32]

In short, the administration contended the charges were improper because the legislative branch had no constitutional standing in the foreign policy arena. (This broad interpretation was shared by several Republican members of the congressional select committees.) Judge Gesell forcefully disagreed with the brief, calling it "unprecedented," especially its assertion that even the courts had no authority to review the president's management of foreign policy.[33]

Not all the obstacles the OIC faced were government-driven. Public protests against the prosecutions, largely from partisan defenders of Reagan, George Bush, or the Republican Party, were a constant distraction. As the process dragged on, politicians such as Sen. Robert Dole and conservative columnists questioned everything from the OIC's politics to its spiraling expenses.[34] A common accusation, also emanating from the White House, was that the prosecutions were simply criminalizing legitimate policy differences. Walsh's opponents accused him of harboring a personal vendetta against Reagan (and Bush) and of being motivated either by political bias or careerism. After being reminded of his lifelong Republican ties, including a political appointment in the Eisenhower administration and blue chip professional credentials, critics shifted focus to his subordinates, whom Dole called "highly paid assassins."[35] Harsh rhetoric also came from the subjects of OIC interest. Railing against prosecution tactics, Assistant Secretary of State Elliott Abrams called Walsh worse than Saddam Hussein or Muammar Qaddafi, and former NSC consultant Michael Ledeen compared him to Torquemada, the grand inquisitor. Rep. Dan Burton (R-Ind.) approvingly entered an op-ed into the *Congressional Record* that equated the OIC process with "legal terrorism."[36] Walsh, acutely sensitive to these attacks, became more combative himself, expending considerable time and energy responding in the press (when he was not blocked by court rules) and filing four separate interim reports to present his side of the issues.[37] As the investigation continued, pressures from political opponents mounted.

Back to Basics

Deprived of his original strategy, Walsh turned to prosecuting more traditional charges starting with the trials of North and Poindexter. Over the next several months, the OIC won a number of guilty verdicts and plea agreements. Each case produced important new information about the scandal and the subsequent cover-up as well as grounds to pursue cases against higher-up figures, although not to the extent the prosecution had hoped. Late in this stage of the investigation, however, critical new evidence would surface that spotlighted the possibility of misconduct by the administration's most senior ranks.

PLAN B FOR NORTH

After dropping the conspiracy and theft charges against North, the OIC proceeded with twelve remaining counts in January 1989. Each pointed to suspected deception or minor corruption by the former NSC staffer. Eight charges related to obstruction of official investigations in the form of false statements to congressional panels in 1985 and 1986 and to a presidential inquiry (Meese's November 1986 probe). One count alleged the removal or destruction of official documents in late November 1986. Another charged North with receipt of an illegal gratuity—the security gate at his home. The last two counts alleged his misuse of $4,300 in traveler's checks from Adolfo Calero for personal expenditures and conspiracy to defraud the United States through illegal use of the National Endowment for the Preservation of Liberty (NEPL) to fund-raise for the Contras.

Most of the facts in the case, as the independent counsel pointed out, were "not truly in dispute."[38] Instead, North's attorneys argued his actions had not been illegal, unauthorized, or even unjustified.[39] "I felt like a pawn in a chess game being played by giants," North testified, maintaining he had primarily complied with instructions from superiors.[40] Acknowledging his previous lies to Congress, he told the court, "I knew it wasn't right not to tell the truth on those things but I didn't think it was unlawful." "Head bowed and voice choking with emotion," as the media described it, his demeanor contrasted sharply with the defiance he had shown on national television when he made the same admissions to Congress.[41] As for the charges of acting for personal gain, North repeated he had behaved lawfully, but on these counts he was much more vulnerable (see Chapter 11).

The trial featured several personality clashes involving Judge Gesell, North, defense attorney Brendan Sullivan, and lead prosecutor Keker. Keker later acknowledged he joined the OIC in part because he viewed the tendency of Reagan administration officials to "completely ignore one branch of government because they felt strongly about something" a threat "to the idea behind American democracy." He also admitted being "rankled" by North's behavior at trial, citing as examples the "use of his Christianity," including having a bible "ostentatiously displayed" on the defense counsel's table each day.[42] In his memoir, North wrote at length about the trial but never mentioned Keker by name, referring to him only as the "chief prosecutor" or, occasionally, "my antagonist."[43] The prosecution's case was complicated by the phenomenon of having to call to the stand witnesses who openly admired the defendant.

The trial did have the significant effect of advancing the public record on the Iran-Contra operations. North was forced to turn over his handwritten daily notes—twenty-two spiral-bound notebooks totaling 2,617 pages covering the period from late December 1983 to late November 1986. The notes detail high-level meetings and hundreds of discussions of events at the heart of the scandal. As part of the effort to show broad-ranging authorization for his actions, North's attorneys produced a number of exhibits describing quid pro quo arrangements between White House officials and foreign leaders. These included an extraordinary forty-two-page "stipulation" of facts revealing outreach efforts to governments from Saudi Arabia to South Korea to Israel—and even the regime of Panamanian dictator Manuel Noriega.

On May 4, 1989, the jury found North guilty of three counts—preparing a false chronology and altering and destroying documents relating to Iran in November 1986; removing, falsifying, and/or destroying additional documents on the covert programs from November 21–25, 1986; and accepting the security gate at his home, which constituted an illegal gratuity. In a controversial ruling, Judge Gesell did not send North to prison, sentencing him instead to two years of probation, fines totaling $150,000, and 1,200 hours of community service. Gesell's sentencing statement placed North in the middle of a "very complex power play developed by higher-ups," albeit one in which North took part "willingly and sometimes even excessively." He called the affair a "scheme that reflected a total distrust in some constitutional values" and a "tragic breach of the public trust."[44]

The OIC had argued for a jail term, as had the *New York Times* and other newspaper editorial boards. "I thought North should have known the feeling of the door shutting behind him," a senior attorney said later.[45] The OIC final report maintained that the absence of jail time gave North "little incentive for cooperating" with prosecutors in future trials, and Gesell's decision became a "contributing factor" in the assignment of lighter sentences in subsequent cases.[46]

In July 1990, in an even more damaging blow to the independent counsel, a U.S. Court of Appeals panel vacated North's convictions on the grounds his congressionally immunized testimony *may* have been tainted. The three-judge panel voted two to one along party lines that the trial judge had not gone far enough to ensure none of the witnesses for the prosecution had used North's testimony during the televised hearings. The majority opinion did not fault the independent counsel's case or the handling of evidence, but it required every trial and grand jury witness to be questioned "if necessary . . . line-by-line and item by item" about the substance and sources of their information. The OIC sought a rehearing by the full appeals court, which was rejected, then petitioned the Supreme Court but was denied a hearing. Walsh then initiated a review of all necessary testimony, but when former national security advisor Robert McFarlane declared his statements had been "colored" by North's congressional appearance, the OIC dropped the case permanently.[47]

POINDEXTER

Poindexter's case was far less complicated—and less colorful—than North's. The same issues that came up in the previous case concerning congressional testimony, classified documents, and severing the initial trial applied to Poindexter's prosecution as well. Walsh quickly dropped the original conspiracy and theft charges to focus on obstruction-related allegations. The five remaining charges included false statements to Congress and removing and destroying documents.

Poindexter's defense team was not nearly as sweeping in its demands for classified documents as North's had been, and all outstanding issues were resolved without great difficulty. The independent counsel went to significant lengths to prove prosecution witnesses would testify on the basis of information obtained entirely outside the protected congressional hearings. (The U.S. Court of Appeals panel would not decide on the North case until after the Poindexter trial.)

The main procedural entanglement in the Poindexter trial was whether President Reagan would be compelled to testify. By the time the case went to court on March 5, 1990, the former president had been a private citizen for more than a year. Judge Harold Greene ruled that new President Bush would not have to appear, but after dismissing objections by Reagan's attorneys and the U.S. National Archives (on privacy grounds), Greene ordered that relevant presidential diaries be produced, then that the former president give a deposition. Reagan and the Bush administration eventually claimed executive privilege against releasing even those pages of diaries selected by the judge. But Reagan did not object to being deposed, and in mid-February, before the trial had technically started, he sat for questioning before the judge, attorneys for both sides, and a video camera.

The deposition proved one of the more bizarre moments of the entire OIC process. It marked the first time a former U.S. president had testified in a criminal trial about his own activities in office. But it will be remembered more for the former president's mental lapses, specifically his inability to recall well-known events and individuals. Reagan had trouble identifying Eugene Hasenfus and Calero, had no memory of the HAWK episode—much less of signing a finding to legalize it—and could not describe some of the key conclusions of his own Tower Commission. Startlingly, he downplayed the significance of the diversion to the Contras, claiming he had never seen any proof it occurred.[48]

Reagan replied "I don't recall" or "I can't remember" eighty-eight times during the deposition.[49] Curiously, he could recollect certain facts with great specificity, such as the total cost of weapons sold to Iran—$12.2 million—and details about the use of the clandestine airstrip in Costa Rica for rebel resupply operations. He also forcefully insisted he regularly told his aides to be sure not to violate the law with regard to the Contras.[50]

Reagan's appearance was a mixed blessing for Poindexter. The former president clearly intended to show support for his onetime aide, and he could be seen winking and smiling at the defendant. His testimony helped by describing their close official relationship, characterized by frequent meetings, and showing he "depended on him" for information about the Contras. But prosecutor Daniel Webb was able to get Reagan to concede he would not have approved the destruction of documents nor the provision of false information to Congress—the essence of the charges against Poindexter.[51]

On April 7, 1990, the jury returned guilty verdicts on all five counts against Poindexter. He received concurrent terms of six months in prison for each charge. It was a major victory for the prosecution. The former national security advisor became the first Iran-Contra defendant condemned to incarceration and the highest-ranking White House official since Watergate to receive a prison term for acts committed while in office. The judgment was also a setback for the growing number of independent counsel critics who excoriated Walsh for trying to criminalize policy differences and insisted no senior official had committed crimes during the affair. Even though the judge could have sentenced Poindexter to twenty-seven months, he clearly intended to send a signal to other government officials about lying to Congress: "If the court were not to impose such a penalty here, . . . its action would be tantamount to a statement that a scheme to lie and to obstruct Congress was of no great moment."[52]

Once again, however, an appeals court would undo the verdict. On November 15, 1991, a three-judge panel ruled two to one the trial had been tainted by immunized testimony before Congress and vacated all five felony verdicts. The decision rested mainly on statements by North during the trial that he could not distinguish between his own recollections and Poindexter's protected testimony to Congress. Judge Greene had concluded North lied, but the panel went further than the judges in the North case, ruling that any additional hearings on the subject of taint would be "pointless." The majority also determined that language in two of the counts charging Poindexter with "corruptly" obstructing a congressional probe was unconstitutionally vague. "'Corruptly influencing' a congressional inquiry does not at all clearly encompass lying to Congress," Judge Douglas Ginsberg wrote for the majority. Abner Mikva, chief judge of the appeals court and the only Democratic appointee on the three-person panel, disagreed with both of these points. On the first, he declared future witnesses needed only a "well-timed case of amnesia" to escape punishment. On the second, he rejected Ginsberg's definition of "corruptly," calling Poindexter's congressional testimony a "clear violation . . . of his oath to Congress and his duty not to lie."[53] The Supreme Court again refused to review the case on appeal by the independent counsel.

FERNANDEZ

While the North trial was under way in the District of Columbia, another proceeding began in the nearby Eastern District of Virginia against CIA Station Chief Fernandez. The case was noteworthy for its attempt to prosecute a CIA officer for crimes allegedly committed in the course of his duties. It was also remarkable for the active attempts by the U.S. attorney general to intercede against the prosecution.

On April 24, 1989, Fernandez was charged with four counts of making false and misleading statements to the CIA inspector general and to the Tower Commission. The former CIA agent tried several times to have the charges dismissed but without success. (An earlier indictment in the District of Columbia Circuit had been dismissed for improper venue.) His next tack was to file notices under CIPA of his need to use classified information about CIA activities and facilities in Central America. In one instance, he wanted to identify two agency stations and one facility in Latin America, information deemed admissible in the North trial. In another, he wanted to name three specific agency projects active in Costa Rica. The OIC suggested several substitutions designed to gain intelligence community approval, but the judge rejected them along with an OIC proposal to narrow the indictment.

At this point, the CIA asked the attorney general to file an affidavit under CIPA blocking the release of the information in the first category—even though the agency had previously approved its release for North. The OIC objected based on the fact the information was already available in the media and in some cases had even been confirmed by U.S. officials. The next several months brought extensive discussions among the Justice Department, CIA, OIC, and the court, including an attempt by the attorney general to appeal the court's CIPA ruling. An appeals court rejected the bid on the grounds the attorney general had no standing to do so in a case brought by an independent counsel. Ultimately, the Justice Department chose another route—to file the affidavit the CIA had requested but to bar both categories of information from use at trial. This was reportedly the first time such an affidavit had been filed since the enactment of CIPA. According to Walsh, his team made one last attempt to propose ways to proceed to trial, but the court rejected them and subsequently dismissed the case with prejudice on November 24, 1989. The OIC appealed, but the ruling was upheld in September 1990.[54]

Walsh's reaction to these setbacks was unusually sharp. In an interim report to Congress at the end of 1989, he described in detail the issues and the potential stakes involved in the Fernandez case. Deriding the attorney general's decision to accommodate the CIA without reservation, even though the information under review was in the public domain, the report called the determination and methods of the Justice Department "almost comic" "but for the gravity of the consequences." The report criticized the "flawed decision-making process at work," the inadequate sourcing of information on which the decision was based, and the "far-reaching and speculative" conclusions of those intelligence agencies that had produced supporting affidavits in the case. Warning that the attorney general's policies and views, along with those of the intelligence community, "could jeopardize any prosecution of other government officers heavily involved with classified information," Walsh charged that the agencies' actions "have created an unacceptable enclave that is free from the rule of law."[55]

Climbing the Ladder

In summer 1990, investigators made the first of several major evidentiary breakthroughs when they discovered Secretary of State George Shultz's aide, Charles Hill, had turned over only a small fraction of his voluminous notes to Congress three years earlier. Hill's notes totaled some 12,000 pages and gave an uncommonly clear picture of the thinking—and state of awareness—of senior State Department officials. They also provided entrée to deliberations inside the White House. Hill's notes revealed, among other things, Shultz had known much more about the Iran deals than he had let on in public accounts. Subsequent discoveries of notes of other State Department officials expanded the record. Nicholas Platt, executive secretary of the department, turned over substantial new information, including evidence Abrams was likely more aware of North's Contra support activities than he acknowledged.

The discovery of three other sets of notes added extensively to the OIC's understanding of senior Reagan administration officials' actions. The most significant were those of Secretary of Defense Caspar Weinberger. The secretary had initially told investigators he did not keep diaries or similar records, but in October 1990 prosecutors came across a line in Hill's notes that read, "Cap takes notes but never referred to them so never had to cough them up."[56] It was not until late 1991 that Walsh's staff finally found some 7,000 pages of Weinberger's handwritten materials. (They were among his records donated to the Library of Congress, but an OIC staff member initially checked only Weinberger's classified files, unaware the notes were among his unclassified records.) Not only did the new evidence refute Weinberger's assertions about his lack of knowledge of both sides of the affair, it opened up critical insights into President Reagan's attitude toward the arms deals—for example, his statements at the pivotal December 7, 1985, White House meeting (see Chapter 6).

In 1992, Walsh's team located handwritten records kept by former White House chief of staff Donald Regan. He, too, had repeatedly denied having anything of the sort until his aides advised investigators he had taken voluminous notes he planned to use to write a book.[57] He eventually turned over copies in response to an independent counsel subpoena, insisting he had not intentionally withheld them. Regan's record of administration actions in November 1986 after the Iran arms sales revelations is of particular value.

Finally, the OIC discovered Bush had dictated a diary beginning on November 4, 1986. It was intended to track his thoughts in connection with his upcoming campaign for president, but because this was exactly the period in which the Iran-Contra revelations played out, it contained a wealth of information about his own state of knowledge, perspectives on administration handling of the scandal, and details about President Reagan's thinking as well as that of his cabinet.

WEINBERGER

On June 16, 1992, the OIC indicted Weinberger on five counts of obstruction, perjury, and false statements during the course of the congressional and OIC probes. The specific allegations included withholding relevant notes and making false statements about his note taking, falsely denying knowledge of Saudi funding of the Contras, and claiming he was unaware of both the HAWK shipment to Iran and the question of replenishing Israel's missile stocks. Prosecutors based their case not only on the existence of his voluminous handwritten records but also on the substantive information taken from them. The case was momentous because of Weinberger's cabinet rank, but it took on added significance for the OIC as well. After the judge dismissed an obstruction count earlier in 1992 (based on a technical distinction between lying and obstruction), the OIC filed a new charge on October 30—four days before the presidential elections in which Bush was running for a second term. The recriminations were immediate, mainly because Walsh's office released as part of the indictment a page of Weinberger's notes that contradicted Bush's claims of ignorance about the Iran arms deals. The president's Democratic opponents jumped on the story, with vice presidential candidate Al Gore declaring: "This is the smoking gun."[58] Walsh was accused of being out for the "scalp of the President of the United States" and of being "Inspector Javert Reincarnate."[59] Even some Democrats were baffled by what they saw as the independent counsel's poor judgment in taking such a politically charged step so close to the elections.[60]

Another reason for the case's magnitude was it had the potential to lead prosecutors even higher up the Reagan administration ladder—to Reagan and Bush themselves. Bush might have been called to testify, and it was possible Weinberger or other witnesses would have revealed new information about their superiors. But the question became moot when President Bush surprisingly pardoned Weinberger and five other Iran-Contra participants on December 24, 1992. Political supporters of the president cheered the move, but Walsh, in one of many heated characterizations of the decision, denounced the pardons as a sign of "arrogant disdain for the law" and "the last card in the cover-up."[61] In point of fact, the pardons effectively shut down the investigation and ensured there would be no further formal examination of the former president and vice president.

PRESIDENT REAGAN

Convinced President Reagan had been central to the Iran-Contra affair, the OIC seriously considered indicting him. The president, Walsh concluded, had "created the conditions which made possible the crimes committed by others." Yet, he ultimately decided Reagan's conduct "fell well short of criminality which could be successfully prosecuted" on the grounds "it could not be proved beyond a reasonable doubt that President Reagan knew of the underlying facts of Iran/Contra that were criminal or that he made criminal misrepresentations regarding them."[62]

A detailed legal memorandum prepared for Walsh by OIC attorney Christian Mixter in 1991, "Criminal Liability of Former President Reagan," offers solid supplementary detail and useful prosecution perspective on Reagan's role in each of the principal dimensions of the affair, even though it does not always jibe with the final conclusions of the OIC. Although the memo concludes Reagan should not be prosecuted on any grounds, the information it provides helps flesh out what the president knew (and apparently did not know) about these two covert operations.

On the Iran operation, Mixter noted, "the record is quite clear that President Reagan was briefed, in advance, on each group of weapons sold to Iran." Although he noted "this subject involves a number of close legal calls" as to whether Reagan himself or the arms deals in general violated any criminal statutes, Mixter concluded they did not.[63] He also maintained Reagan did not contravene the law by not reporting the operation to Congress immediately because he had received explicit legal advice from Meese indicating he did not have to do so.

Mixter mostly exonerates Reagan from criminal culpability, but he could not resist critiquing Meese's guidance for the president. "Whether the Attorney General's advice, even though supportable, was appropriate as a matter of interbranch relations under civil law lies outside the scope of this memorandum." He characterized Meese's view that the National Security Act authorized deferring reports to Capitol Hill as "steering the entire congressional notification process into a blind alley" and described Meese's interpretation as "considerably more aggressive than any of the authorities that support it." After explaining his reasons for this conclusion, he added, "Finally, it is rather obvious that the 1985 addition to the Intelligence Authorization Act was intended to ensure that at least the intelligence committees would receive prior notice of covert arms transactions, and not to enshrine a mechanism by which no one in Congress would learn of such a transfer until well after it was completed."[64]

More than once Mixter commented on Reagan's evident disinterest in the legal aspects of the operations. For example: "There is no indication that the President paid the slightest heed during 1985 to the limitations on retransfers of weapons pursuant to the arms export statutes." He concluded Reagan "simply never focused on" the laws in question.[65]

Regarding the 1985 Israeli arms sales to Iran, executed with Reagan's approval, Mixter's memo points out that their legal foundation was much shakier than that of the 1986 U.S. arms sales. Even Poindexter believed they had "legal problems," according to the memo. "Yet," Mixter goes on, "that is precisely how the Iran Initiative was structured during much of 1985—with no consultation with legal counsel, no written Finding, and an unwritten Presidential determination that Congress would not be notified." There was no way, the memo continues, any of the 1985 sales "can be reconciled with . . . arms export statutes" such as the Arms Export Control Act (AECA). Mixter writes that, furthermore, attempts by the Justice Department Office of Legal Counsel (OLC) to justify the 1985 TOW deals under the National Security Act were based on three separate, incorrect assumptions about the facts of the case and were therefore "not a particularly persuasive gloss on how the civil law ought to operate." Not even Meese would give "unequivocal support" to the OLC's conclusions in his congressional testimony.[66]

Regarding the NSC staff's Contra activities, the memo states "a coherent portrait of the President's knowledge . . . is quite difficult to assemble." Some of this uncertainty is ascribed to the president's staff deliberately withholding information from him. There is no question Reagan wanted to see the Contras supported "body and soul," the memo notes, and "his views on the importance of Contra assistance remained constant" throughout the period.[67] The president was aware of Secord's and Hakim's operations in support of the Contras (and made a point of stating at the Poindexter trial they were active only "when it was legal to provide such aid"). But the memo concludes Poindexter's view of Reagan's level of awareness was probably on target—"He knew the job was getting done. The exact way we were getting it done was something that would not have been particularly relevant to him."[68]

Reagan also indisputably approved and participated in quid pro quo discussions with foreign governments. The OIC memo points out Reagan probably did not know some of the funds raised in that way went (or were meant to go) to the Enterprise instead of directly to the Contras, but he certainly believed these approaches were crucial to the survival of the rebel campaign. Despite the overarching statutory injunction against any expectation of reciprocity, Reagan made it plain during trial testimony in 1990 that a tit-for-tat was exactly what he expected from countries such as Honduras.

Mixter also felt confident Reagan did not know about the diversion, although by the time the OIC final report was drafted the latter's conclusion was much more equivocal. Conceding no "direct evidence" could be found of Reagan's awareness of North's scheme, the final report termed it "doubtful" the president would have put up with "successive Iranian affronts during 1986 unless he knew" the arms sales were helping fund the Nicaraguan rebels.[69]

As for Reagan's role in the postexposure cover-up, or at least his responses to official inquiries, Mixter repeatedly cites "highly incomplete awareness" or similar descriptions of the president's state of knowledge. He points out when it came to specific false statements Reagan made at press conferences or in public speeches, "there is no basis in the law" for charging misconduct because the statute applies only to false statements made to a "department or agency of the United States."[70] Even so, the contradictory remarks Reagan made before his own Tower Commission, he states, did not merit criminal prosecution because of the "lack of concrete evidence of the President's state of mind." In other words there was no proof of intent to deceive. The OIC final report agreed, citing the "absence of proof beyond a reasonable doubt" Reagan knowingly made false statements or knew his subordinates were obstructing formal investigations.[71] Walsh himself held out the belief that truthful testimony by Poindexter and North—which the prospect of prison time might have induced—would have implicated Reagan. But after a final interview he conducted with the former president in July 1992, he decided Reagan by then had become "partially disabled" by Alzheimer's disease and would not be able to stand trial.[72]

VICE PRESIDENT BUSH

The vice president also came under scrutiny by the OIC, although prosecutors were able to develop far less information about his Iran-Contra activities than about President Reagan's role. The OIC called the investigation of Bush "regrettably incomplete." In fact, it was not until the late discovery (from 1990 to 1992) of the handwritten notes by Weinberger, Regan, Hill, and Platt, along with Bush's dictated diary, that serious questions arose about his actual knowledge of the affair and his candor about it.

Here again, Mixter authored a memo that provides valuable detail on what Bush knew in connection with the affair (see Chapter 7). He notes the vice president's familiarity with the Iran initiative was "coterminous with that of President Reagan," and the two attended many of the same meetings on both sets of operations. He states Bush took part in at least a dozen meetings on Contra aid for which notes showed a detailed involvement in activities such as the quid pro quo arrangements with Central American governments. Still, because of the lack of information as well as Bush's status as a "secondary officer" to the president— himself ruled out for prosecution—Mixter recommended not pursuing a case against the vice president.[73]

However, Mixter's memo was written more than two years before the OIC's investigations came to an end and even before Bush's dictated diary surfaced in late 1992, after Bush had lost the presidency to Democrat Bill Clinton. This led to a fresh review into the circumstances surrounding Bush's failure to produce the diary until then.

In March 1987, the independent counsel had circulated an omnibus document request to the White House requesting notes, diaries, and other records. Bush said later he did not recall seeing the request. The OIC obtained evidence this was not the case.[74] In June 1992, the OIC submitted another document specifically seeking diaries Bush had prepared from May 1985 to December 1987. In September 1992 an administrative assistant to Bush found typed transcripts of the dictated notes and notified him they contained Iran-Contra-related information. Bush's official counsel, C. Boyden Gray, reviewed the materials but decided to delay handing them over to investigators until after the November 1992 elections. Bush's private counsel (and Jimmy Carter's former attorney general), Griffin Bell, concluded in a report that Gray had put off acting on the diaries partly because of the "crush of the campaign."[75] Bell also attributed the delay to "overly broad" requests by the OIC, "widespread confusion" over what was supposed to be produced, and other problems.[76] A more candid account came from former associate White House counsel Lee Liberman, who acknowledged in a deposition the diaries "would have been impossible to deal with in the election campaign because of all the political ramifications, especially since the President's polling numbers were low."[77]

When Bush's notes became public, they revealed another motivation for withholding them—a fundamental aversion to sharing such materials with investigators. During the 1987 select committee hearings, for example, he expressed shock at learning Shultz had given Congress access to notes kept by his aides:

> Howard Baker, in the presence of the President, told me today that George
> Shultz had kept 700 pages of personal notes, dictated to his staff. . . .
> Notes on personal meetings he had with the President. I found this almost
> inconceivable. Not only that he kept the notes, but that he'd turned them
> all over to Congress. And, there will be one embarrassing one, where the
> President talked about impeachment, and saying that visiting hours are 2
> to 4 in Leavenworth or at the jail. I don't understand Shultz's doing this. It's
> part of the reason we have these problems. Congress has the right to know,
> but it doesn't have the right to have access to the innermost working[s] of
> this nature. I would never do it. I would never surrender such documents
> and I wouldn't keep such detailed notes.[78]

The independent counsel planned to question Bush after the 1992 elections, but according to the OIC final report, the president refused to be interviewed (despite previously agreeing) unless the scope was limited to his failure to produce his notes and diary. Walsh declined so as not to preclude other investigative areas and because he did not want to "give the misleading impression of cooperation where there was none." What is more, by the end of 1992 "the statute of limitations had passed on most of the relevant acts and statements of Bush."[79]

On Christmas Eve 1992, President Bush took the unprecedented step of pardoning several key Iran-Contra participants—Weinberger, McFarlane, and Abrams along with Clair George, Alan Fiers, and Duane Clarridge of the CIA. Whereas Reagan had chosen not to use the prerogative on the grounds it would leave those individuals "under a shadow of guilt,"[80] Bush went ahead even though two of those pardoned had not yet been put on trial. His explanations were that the six had been motivated by patriotism, that the legal cases against them had amounted to criminalized policy differences on which adjudication belonged "in the voting booth, not the courtroom," and that the pardons were in line with the "healing tradition" set by past presidents.[81] Walsh vehemently disagreed, arguing Bush's action was a "misuse" of his power that "diverge[d] sharply and inappropriately" from previous presidential practice and "did a grave disservice to the citizens of this country."[82]

In a speech two years later, Walsh was still incensed: "President Bush's pardon not only prevented punishment [for "flagrant crimes"], but it prevented a trial which would have exposed more of the truth about Iran-Contra."[83] He made it plain he believed Bush had acted largely out of self-interest. Reporting to Congress, he wrote, "President Bush cannot escape the appearance that he wished to avoid the public airing of facts about Iran/Contra that would have occurred at trial."[84] To *Newsweek*, he said: "It's hard to find an adjective strong enough to characterize a president who has such contempt for honesty."[85] Immediately after the pardon announcement, he declared: "The Iran-Contra cover-up, which has continued for more than six years, has now been completed with the pardon of Caspar Weinberger."[86]

OTHER NOTABLE CASES

From December 1986 to December 1992, Walsh's office brought charges against fourteen individuals, gaining eleven convictions or guilty pleas. Fernandez's case was dismissed, and Weinberger and Clarridge had not yet gone to trial when President Bush pardoned them. North and Poindexter won reversals of their convictions on appeal. Along the way, the OIC declined to pursue prosecutions of several other individuals, some of them of cabinet rank. These decisions reflected a range of considerations, from insufficient evidence to an expired statute of limitations. In some instances (such as Bush), Walsh and his staff decided there was little of value to be gained. Several cases are worth noting for what they show about the challenges facing prosecutors of alleged crimes in the national security sphere and the OIC's approaches to dealing with them.

At the State Department, the independent counsel homed in on three senior officials but decided not to charge them: Shultz, Hill, and Platt. The OIC made the point Shultz had testified "to great effect" about the department's stalwart attempts to block the Iran arms-for-hostages operation even as top diplomats were kept substantially in the dark about North's activities. However, after the independent counsel's office had the chance to review in detail the handwritten notes of Shultz's two aides (in 1990 and 1991), a far less flattering picture emerged, namely that State Department officials, including Shultz, had been far more informed about the details of the operation than they had acknowledged.

The OIC decided not to prosecute for several reasons. Shultz's congressional testimony, although "incorrect," could not be proven "willfully false." Hill, according to the independent counsel, unquestionably withheld relevant notes from investigators but would have invoked an "oral waiver" from having to produce all of his records, which he had received at one point from the department's legal counsel. Because Shultz, the person who had given the inaccurate testimony in question, was not going to be charged, the OIC decided it would "not be appropriate" to target his subordinate. In Platt's case, Walsh's staff found his withholding of certain notes "troubling" and tried to determine whether he and Hill had colluded in the act, but because Platt's notes were less important and he left his position in spring 1987, several weeks before Shultz's questionable testimony, the OIC chose not to bring him up on charges.[87]

Meese was high on the OIC list of potential defendants. (Walsh chose to view him from the perspective of his personal relationship as friend and advisor to the president rather than in his official role as attorney general.) The OIC probed a number of areas in which Meese was vulnerable, from his attempts to protect the president on the question of his knowledge of the HAWK shipment to the attorney general's awareness of North's Contra-related operation to the legal advice he provided on the Iran program and the Boland Amendments. Although the OIC found troubling evidence of his culpability in various of these activities, including his notable assertions of faulty memory—more than 350 times in his congressional deposition alone[88]—a combination of reasons led Walsh to forgo legal charges. Among the most important was the "sheer passage of time," which mainly resulted from the delayed disclosure of key evidence by Meese's cabinet colleagues.[89]

Regan was a subject of interest on several counts. The OIC looked into his conduct as White House chief of staff with respect to protecting the president from the fallout of the 1985 Iran arms shipments, obstructing the Tower Commission in connection with Reagan's shifting testimony, and withholding his notes from investigators. On the first two matters, the OIC reported finding neither "direct" nor "usable" evidence, but on the third he was indeed primarily at fault. However, Regan became candid and cooperative under questioning, which helped him avoid going to trial.[90]

At the CIA, the figure of greatest interest was Director William Casey, who was diagnosed with a brain tumor just as the independent counsel's investigation got under way and died after a few months. Nevertheless, the OIC final report devotes twenty pages to his activities as a cabinet-level promoter of North's Contra support operations and the Iran arms deals, his possible knowledge of the diversion, and his statements to Congress in late 1986. An abundance of evidence already pointed to Casey backing the two secret programs. The report leans toward the view that he knew about the diversion. Not finding enough evidence of criminality, the OIC nevertheless concluded that by his attitude and behavior he compromised the "objectivity, professionalism, and integrity" of his agency.[91]

Robert Gates was also a "subject" of interest for the independent counsel, although the OIC eventually decided the available evidence did not justify an indictment. Walsh and his staff found Gates's assertion he could not recall being told about a possible diversion by senior CIA colleagues "disquieting" and his claims to being unaware of North's operational role with the Contras difficult to believe. His statements "often seemed scripted and less than candid" but might have left a reasonable doubt with a jury as to whether he deliberately lied at any given point.[92]

Gates's CIA colleague, George, did not manage to escape indictment. The trial of the former deputy director for operations, focusing mostly on the cover-up, was long and complicated, involving a number of dropped charges and a mistrial. But on December 9, 1992, George was found guilty on two counts of making false statements and committing perjury before Congress in connection with Felix Rodriguez's role in the Contra program and North's and Secord's involvement in the Iran operation.

Walsh was especially proud of this successful prosecution of the third-ranking CIA officer, which he saw as proof of the OIC's ability to reach high into the circles of power—although that message was substantially diminished when President Bush pardoned George. Speaking more broadly about the prosecutions, Walsh concluded "the whole series of incidents was so complex and so full of secrecy, there was a real question about whether it could be grasped, and we proved it could. We showed that neither the subtlety of the operation nor the shield of secrecy and intelligence classification could prevent the law from coming home."[93]

Assessments

Looking back at the independent counsel's tenure, historian Theodore Draper gave a bleak review: "Walsh's record as independent counsel has been one of frustration and disappointment. His victories have been minor, his failures major. . . . He largely failed to live up to his own prosecutorial objectives. He obtained light punishment for some of the 'more peripheral players' and entirely missed 'the central figures.'"[94] Others who had served in positions similar to Walsh showed greater sympathy. Sam Dash, former chief counsel to the Senate Watergate committee, praised Walsh for an "exhaustive, professionally conducted investigation that uncovered, to the extent possible, the story of the notorious Reagan-era scandal and that secured sufficient evidence to convict the principal offenders."[95] Leon Silverman, independent counsel in the 1981 inquiry into Secretary of Labor Raymond Donovan, called the challenges he faced "child's play" in comparison to what Iran-Contra presented.[96]

Walsh undoubtedly accomplished far less than he had hoped, and some of the reasons were probably of his own making. He frankly admits he fell short in several respects—"my initial underestimation of the scope of my job; my consistent understaffing; my reliance on document requests rather than subpoenas; and my drastic narrowing of our early investigation in an unsuccessful effort to escape the consequences of the congressional grants of immunity to Poindexter and North."[97] Walsh was slow to appreciate the magnitude of the substantive, legal, and political challenges he faced. The policy questions were highly complex, and fully grasping the workings of the national security sphere from the outside was difficult. For the first time in their careers, OIC attorneys found themselves far less in command of the facts than the individuals they were investigating. Choosing a staff with greater balance between experts in these areas and litigators might at least have made for a speedier process and relieved some of the suffocating political pressure on the office.[98]

On the level of legal strategy, Walsh's decision to pursue the overarching conspiracy charge was probably his most scrutinized miscalculation. Strictly from a legal standpoint, it presented risks, according to former State Department counselor Harold Koh, because it lacked a specific statute on which to base the charge.[99] Instead, it required fitting a tangle of complicated policy and operational actions—governed by civil legislation—under the umbrella of a broad and vague criminal statute. Some of Walsh's colleagues believed the larger conspiracy count was "untriable" because of the virtual certainty that the intelligence community—backed, as it turned out, by the Justice Department—would block the introduction of classified evidence sought by the defense.[100] Similarly, Walsh sometimes puzzled his subordinates by plowing ahead with cases that seemed to offer only marginal results.[101]

Politically, Walsh unwittingly hampered his own cause. At times he seemed tone-deaf to the realities of Washington, D.C. Members of the administration and Congress whose cooperation he would need saw him as high-handed in assuming his priorities as a prosecutor should take precedence over their institutional and political interests.[102] His penchant for staying at the Watergate Hotel and flying first class to his home in Oklahoma on weekends at taxpayers' expense handed his opponents a weapon that could not be neutralized by testimonials from supporters about his punishing work schedule and otherwise ascetic routine.[103] Perhaps the final straw for detractors was the OIC's decision to go forward with the superseding charge against Weinberger and the release of evidence implicating Bush just days before the 1992 elections. Even though there appear to have been contributing procedural reasons, the move made him an easy target for charges of political bias.

But a review of the OIC's experiences makes clear that whatever self-imposed difficulties there may have been, they were slight compared to the external obstacles. Under the circumstances, Walsh's office accomplished some notable successes. These include, as he observes, helping at least to a degree to dispel the "illusion about the escapability of prosecution in this type of operation." How seriously government officials will take that lesson in the future remains to be seen. Like the congressional investigations, the OIC's findings contributed in another way—greatly expanding public understanding of government by uncovering, under conditions of conspicuous resistance, essential information about U.S. policy, the political process, and of course high-level misconduct. Walsh's doggedness in the face of endless legal barriers, undisguised administration hostility, and corrosive partisan opposition was remarkable. From the evidence, it owed much more to his reaction to persistent administration truculence than to his office's political bias or prosecutorial zealotry, as many critics charged. Ultimately, his experience stands as a case study of the potentially debilitating impact of secrecy constraints and partisan politics on the pursuit of official accountability in national security affairs.

Conclusion

President George H. W. Bush's pardons ended all prospects that the independent counsel's investigation would uncover further high-level misconduct in the Iran-Contra affair. By that time, most of the public was disengaged. What had begun as Watergate-style political drama had been reduced to legal wrangling with little hope of a satisfactory resolution. Amid the welter of accusations from all sides and the partisan spin control, it was impossible to find a public consensus even on who the rogues and the white knights were. The story line itself was not always apparent. There were too many moving parts, too much unfamiliar about the countries and issues involved. Pundits longed for the "shapely narrative" of Watergate with its "heroes and villains," its "dramatic unities," its "*deus ex machina* in the Oval Office taping system."[1] But these plot elements eluded Iran-Contra, which, for all of its Shakespearean potential, played out like an episode of Washington reality TV.

Despite the confusion and ambiguity, Iran-Contra was a significant historical and political event. Its conception was perhaps bizarre, its characters eccentric, and its execution often incompetent, but it added up to a serious episode with meaningful consequences. The affair also has value as a window into the era and the people who defined it, as described in the preceding chapters. Finally, Iran-Contra was important because of its legacies—resonating to the present day—which have taken the form of fresh abuses of presidential power at the expense of Congress and the courts and have come at high cost to the interests of U.S. foreign policy.

How Serious Was Iran-Contra?

Defenders and critics of President Ronald Reagan disagree fundamentally over whether the scandal produced grave misconduct—crimes and even constitutional violations—or whether it represented merely mistakes in judgment and was at heart a political, not a criminal, affair. Bush, for example, justified his Christmas Eve 1992 pardons of six Iran-Contra players on the grounds the prosecutions embodied the "criminalization of policy differences." The evidence points strongly to the former conclusion. The two covert programs were poorly conceived, based on skewed readings of the international environment, inadequately staffed, and deliberately concealed from the proper authorities. The entire business was characterized by pervasive dishonesty as officials duped not only the public and formal investigators but each other. By their actions, Oliver North and his operational colleagues—in the Enterprise as well as the CIA, Defense Department, and State Department—raised a host of policy, ethical, and legal concerns. So did their superiors at the White House and in the cabinet. Difficulties arose over everything from bumbling efforts to consummate arms deals and financial transactions to providing a legal basis for shipping missiles to Tehran. Events reached a low point when Reagan told his advisors he was prepared to break the law in order to free the hostages.

One troubling aspect of the administration's attitude was its pronounced disregard for congressional attempts to impose restrictions on its activities. Signs of this disdain appeared throughout the 1984 to 1986 period and at all levels of the executive branch. From the Nicaraguan harbor mining, to the solicitation of foreign governments, to the early 1986 presidential finding authorizing direct weapons deliveries to declared terrorist sponsor Iran, senior officials up to the president either knowingly contravened congressional bans on such activities or deliberately withheld notification of their actions, contrary to the law. When it came to Contra aid, administration attitudes were manifestly hostile. In Elliott Abrams's words, "We were at war, we and the Democrats in Congress." Congressional hearings on Central America were a "form of combat. Questions were weapons, and answers were shields."[2] On the Iran arms initiative, the objective from the president on down was to exclude the legislature—ostensibly for only a brief period on the grounds of protecting hostages' lives.

Even when it could be argued the failure to notify Congress was inadvertent, the best interpretation, based on the available record, is administration officials simply did not take their legal obligations seriously. But there are enough instances in which the participants were clearly aware of the implications—for example, in June 1984 when Secretary of State George Shultz raised the prospect of impeachment—to conclude high-level conduct in this regard was often deliberate. Here again, Reagan likely served as a role model to certain subordinates, worrying only that word of their plans would leak, not whether their activities were legal (see Chapter 5).

After the affair was disclosed in late 1986, some cabinet members and their staffs took the practice to a different level by intentionally withholding their notes and diaries from presidentially appointed, congressional, and criminal investigators. From the evidence it is inconceivable they did not understand the requirement to turn over these records, contrary to the claims of several of those accused.

What emerges from the instances of deception and post hoc rationalizations sanctioned by Reagan and top levels of his administration is that U.S. officials routinely prioritized their narrow policy and political interests over legal and even constitutional responsibilities. Too often, the president and his aides took action first, then worried about whether it was proper later. Only after complaints or alarms were raised did Reagan's advisors tend to seek the necessary justifications. Shultz's warning in June 1984 (noted above) about the impropriety of third-country aid—which precipitated an opinion from the attorney general (subsequently ignored)—and CIA Deputy Director John McMahon's angry demand for a presidential finding after the 1985 HAWK shipment are pertinent examples. Even if officials did not conceive of their actions as deliberate challenges to the constitutional role of Congress, the administration's shoot-from-the-hip approach showed a pattern of disregard for the constitutional implications.

None of the fundamental decisions or operations in Iran-Contra constituted trivial errors in judgment. Rather they gave expression to a widely shared belief of senior officials that the power of the presidency trumped any congressional interests in foreign affairs. This was a viewpoint the president himself brought to Washington in 1981—intensified by his reaction to the congressional reform campaign of the mid-1970s that addressed earlier abuses of power by the executive branch. Reagan grew more enamored of the idea of expansive presidential power, telling National Security Advisor John Poindexter in 1986 he wanted to pursue certain Contra funding options "unilaterally" without regard for the legislature (see Chapter 11). At the same time, the Justice Department under both Edwin Meese and his successor, Richard Thornburgh, explored ideas relating to the "unitary executive." Thornburgh argued in court filings during the North trial the president held exclusive authority in foreign policy (relegating Congress and the judiciary to virtually no role; see Chapter 15). Advocates for President Reagan trivialized the implications, but administration actions—from the president's interventions with the Honduran leadership, to Abrams's bungled solicitation of Brunei government funds, to North's "one-two punch" with wealthy donors, to the diversion itself—were of a piece: none were reported, and all had the ultimate effect of undercutting Congress's power of the purse and its long-standing oversight responsibility. Although virtually no one in the administration saw it this way, their behavior amounted to nothing less than an abuse of presidential power.

How did this all come about? Why did widely respected, lifelong public servants resort to such extensive deceptions, including obstructing official investigations—conduct no one would condone from ordinary citizens? Part of the explanation is that political partisanship had intensified during the Reagan years. Democrats and Republicans were in an almost constant state of conflict and, as Abrams noted, treated each other as the enemy. For the administration, defending the president from a parochial opposition justified almost any tactic in response. Considerations of propriety or lawfulness often simply did not enter into the equation. Much the same can be said about Reagan, who bears significant responsibility for disregarding the potential collateral damage of importuning his aides to fulfill objectives unattainable without placing themselves and the administration in political and legal jeopardy. Unfortunately, the popular credo of his supporters to "let Reagan be Reagan" was wholly unsuited to the circumstances in this case.

After the scandal erupted, another familiar phenomenon of Washington politics took effect—self-protection. Robert McFarlane grasped this right away during the period of damage control that followed the Iran revelation in November 1986. Recalling President Richard Nixon's last crisis, he warned Poindexter: "I lived through Watergate, John. Well-meaning people . . . didn't intend to lie but ultimately came around to it."[3] Egil "Bud" Krogh, who headed the White House "plumbers" unit assigned to plug press leaks for Nixon, was one of those well-intentioned people. (Former White House counsel John Dean was another.) Years afterward, Krogh described the irresistible pull to carry out the president's bidding, especially when the national interest is invoked. "In my zeal to help the president's national security imperative, I never considered the constitutional limits on his power and my own duty to the rule of law and underlying ethical values."[4] U.S. House Select Committee Chair Lee Hamilton identified the same pattern in Iran-Contra—both during and after the affair. "I learned that people in the White House will do anything to protect the president. It is the mantra. It is the reason for their being there: protect the president at all costs. Fall on your sword. . . . That was very apparent with Poindexter and North, but it's true with any aide to the president at any time. . . . It was very strong with Shultz and [Caspar] Weinberger."[5] North and his secretary, Fawn Hall, were especially unabashed in describing their loyalties to superiors as superseding any legal or congressional obligations.

The participants' claims to have acted purely out of good intentions surfaced repeatedly during the aftermath. Their aim was to downplay the import of White House staff activities. Indeed, Reagan's impulsive, emotionally charged decision to pursue the hostages' release by trading weapons was looked upon with a certain indulgence if not full absolution by much of the public. (Again, Bush issued pardons to six individuals on those grounds.) But the bottom line was responsible officials deliberately impeded formal, legitimate inquiries, with potentially significant consequences for informing the public and ensuring government accountability.

Consequences

Part of reaching a judgment about the nature and seriousness of Iran-Contra involves consideration of its impact. A generation after its exposure, many of its effects, internationally and domestically, are in evidence to assess.

Beyond the toll on the individuals directly involved, the affair resulted in substantial short-term harm. On the international front, U.S. standing abroad suffered. The State Department was forced to dispatch teams of diplomats to repair ties with the Persian Gulf states whose leaders supported Iraq in its war with Iran and were incensed at the arms deals and what they implied about Washington's unreliability as an ally. For U.S. diplomats, called upon to apologize for their government, it was a humiliating experience.[6]

The Iran arms deals did indeed appear to sway developments on the battlefield. U.S. Ambassador to Baghdad David Newton recalled the Iraqis believed the arms sales to Iran had "negated their two most critical advantages, that is their overwhelming superiority in armor through the TOW missiles and their overwhelming superiority in the air through the HAWK missiles." A prominent Iranian scholar and war veteran who studied the conflict concluded the U.S. missiles were "very important" in at least one major battle—Karbala-5, one of Iran's main offensives, in January–February 1987—where they contributed to antitank operations and reportedly shot down MIG aircraft providing cover for Iraqi forces.[7]

There is considerable evidence the Reagan administration's perceived need to patch the rift with Arab allies was a factor in the president's decision in late June 1987 to order the U.S. Navy to escort oil tankers through the gulf, despite congressional warnings it could widen the conflict Washington had sought to avoid. Two U.S. warships were subsequently damaged by Iranian mines, which drew the navy into direct combat operations against Iran in fall 1987 and spring 1988. The resulting rise in tensions in turn led to the tragic shooting down of a civilian Iran Air passenger jet in July 1988 by the guided missile cruiser U.S.S. *Vincennes*, which cost the lives of all 290 people on board.

Iran experts have concluded these events—the mishandled secret negotiations (including North's deliberate deceptions the Iranians discovered) and the consequences of a widened U.S. involvement in the war—significantly reinforced Iranian distrust and antagonism toward the United States. It begs the question whether a more sophisticated approach might have better prepared the ground for future attempts by U.S. and Iranian leaders to restore greater stability to the relationship.[8]

The effects of the U.S.-backed covert war in Nicaragua are in some ways easier to judge. The administration's goal was to keep its proxy army functional until congressional funding for direct aid could be restored. Although shortages of weapons and supplies were the norm, the Enterprise's arms sales, the NSC-coordinated private fund-raising, the third-government support, and the Iran arms profit diversion evidently succeeded. This was the case despite the slapdash management of the operation and the number of casualties on both sides. The larger consequences of the secret program and the war effort are more debatable. Exposure of the Contra resupply operation doomed congressional support for further aid. When Bush took office, his administration acted quickly to detach itself from the rebels, whose cause the president had never embraced to the extent Reagan had. Meanwhile, Nicaraguan internal political developments—including exhaustion from years of war and U.S. sanctions—contributed to Sandinista leader Daniel Ortega's decision to participate in revived regional peace talks. He even took part in free national elections in 1990, which unexpectedly produced a victory for his opponent, Violetta Chamorro. The outcome prompted widespread second-guessing about the ultimate benefit of the war to U.S. interests, about the extent to which aid to the Contras pressured the Sandinistas into permitting elections, and whether signing on to the peace process earlier might have produced similar results sooner and at lower human and material costs.

Iran-Contra also had an impact on U.S.-Soviet relations, critical for understanding Reagan's foreign policy thinking.[9] Soviet leader Mikhail Gorbachev, himself weakened by domestic resistance to glasnost and perestroika, believed the scandal had sapped Reagan's ability to pursue a sweeping arms-control agreement, which Gorbachev urgently wanted. Indeed, former ambassador to Moscow Jack Matlock, then on the NSC staff, recalled that as soon as the uproar occurred "everything on START [Strategic Arms Reduction Talks] ground to a halt." In Matlock's view, "probably we could have gotten a START agreement and other things [as early as] 1988 if it had not been for the Iran-Contra affair." CIA senior Soviet analyst Douglas MacEachin went further. "The Iran-Contra affair disrupted the efficient functioning of the foreign policy network, because the key players in it were all fighting for their lives in a major scandal."[10]

Similar considerations were on the minds of congressional select committee members, who acknowledged toning down their investigation of Reagan in order to minimize the damage to ongoing arms talks (see Chapter 14). Ironically, their fears were misplaced in one crucial respect: whereas they assumed Reagan's vulnerability would trigger an aggressive move by Moscow to seize a strategic advantage, Russian historical records and recent scholarship show the crisis actually prompted Gorbachev to work in the opposite direction and ensure the scandal did not derail a major nuclear accord. Shultz and many administration colleagues were delighted with the opportunity to deflect attention from the burgeoning affair.[11]

The President versus Congress

The most pernicious outcome of the Iran-Contra scandal was—paradoxically—its lack of impact on the public and on government accountability. This becomes clearer when comparing the aftermath of Iran-Contra with the Watergate hearings and the intelligence inquiries of the Church and Pike Committees in the mid-1970s. The cold war era national security system, which made it possible for the Iran and Contra operations to occur, emerged essentially unchanged after the congressional and legal procedures had run their course and was therefore in no better position to prevent future abuses along comparable lines.

In fact, the U.S. political and judicial oversight systems failed to prevent, uncover, or ultimately address the consequences of the scandal. Despite legislation and presidential orders prohibiting the sale of weapons to terrorists, negotiating with terrorists, or funneling military aid to the Contras, the Reagan administration managed to pull off each of those activities. The operations went undiscovered for more than a year in the case of Iran and for almost two years on the Contra side. Both disclosures happened only because of events beyond U.S. control—the bubbling over of a political feud in Iran resulting in the leak of the McFarlane mission to a Lebanese news outlet, and the shooting down of an Enterprise cargo plane by a young Sandinista soldier. If not for these two chance occurrences, there is no telling how long the operations might have continued or whether U.S. law enforcement, enterprising journalists, or other means would ever have exposed them.

After the operations became public knowledge, the stage was set for the U.S. political and legal systems to try to fulfill their missions. Insofar as introducing mechanisms needed to avert a similar scandal, it is clear they failed. After holding full-blown televised hearings, uncovering thousands of documents, and interviewing hundreds of witnesses, the presidential commission and congressional select committees could not produce a strong enough case for remedial action to obtain a consensus among the membership and translate the recommendations into meaningful legislation. Although some minority members, conspicuously Richard Cheney, categorically opposed granting Congress any measure of influence over policy at the expense of the executive branch, partisan politics—prioritizing short-term political interests over the risks of an institutional imbalance vis-à-vis the White House—were an important factor.

The U.S. judicial system was also mostly ineffectual. Independent Counsel Lawrence Walsh doggedly pursued a string of prosecutions but faced near-crippling obstacles. One was the courts granting extensive leeway to the intelligence community to block the use of classified evidence at trial. Another was the Reagan administration's persistent opposition to Walsh's efforts, an effective limitation despite his supposed independence. A third was the incompatibility of Walsh's office's mandate with that of Congress, resulting in vacated convictions in his two most important cases. (The appeals panel ruling broke down along party lines.) Finally, Walsh was unable to compete with President Bush's pardons to half a dozen prominent defendants, which he asserted brought the criminal investigations to a sudden halt.

These impediments had several negative effects. They allowed senior Reagan officials essentially to receive a pass for their actions. The president and vice president escaped with little more than a temporary dent in their poll numbers (and Bush was elected president in 1988). Most others of higher rank who paid a more substantial price recouped much or all of their standing. Abrams, Poindexter, and several others whose roles were widely criticized landed appointments in subsequent presidential administrations. North won the Republican nomination for a Senate seat from Virginia in 1994 before being defeated by the Democratic incumbent. He established a lucrative second career as an on-air personality for Fox News, author, and speaker. These developments raise the question of whether the affair further degraded public confidence in the ability of the political system to hold high-level officials accountable.

More disconcertingly, the congressional and independent counsel processes failed to create a disincentive for future administrations against ill-conceived exercises of presidential power. Iran-Contra was, after all, largely a competition for control among the branches. Subsequent presidents have already taken significant steps to enhance their clout. In the George W. Bush administration, Vice President Cheney took the lead in expanding the reach of the executive branch, in particular after the September 11, 2001, terrorist attacks. In early 2002, he lamented that ever since the Nixon administration, congressional demands on the White House to "compromise on important principles" of executive authority had caused "erosion of the powers and the ability of the president of the United States to do his job."[12] Cheney subscribed to the notion of the "unitary executive"—first raised by the Justice Department in the mid-1980s—which posited that the president had virtually exclusive authority to act in the national security area. A 2001 Justice Department memo to the White House embraced the concept: "It is clear that the Constitution secures all federal executive power in the President to ensure a unity in purpose and energy in action." Citing the *Federalist Papers*, the memo noted the "centralization of authority in the President alone is particularly crucial in matters of national defense, war, and foreign policy."[13]

Cheney's experience with Iran-Contra and attempts by Congress to assert meaningful oversight over Reagan administration conduct contributed to his later thinking about presidential authority. In 2005, he pointed reporters to the select committees' minority report as a road map to the subject (see Chapter 14). In effect following that blueprint, senior officials boosted executive power in a variety of controversial ways: rationalizing "enhanced interrogation" of terrorism suspects, approving warrantless wiretaps on U.S. citizens, justifying deceptive administration pronouncements in the lead-up to the U.S. war on Iraq, and engaging in a broad pattern of secrecy in matters ranging from counterterrorism to economics. Along the way, Congress was reluctant to assert its own prerogatives, passing a raft of legislation, notably the USA PATRIOT Act, authorizing vastly expanded federal authority in the name of the war on terror. Likewise, the courts, especially initially, provided extraordinary latitude to the executive branch, including sanctioning the conduct of intrusive domestic activities beyond the scope of public scrutiny. Over time, these developments have prompted increased uneasiness from very different political constituencies on the left and right.

The unsettling facts of Iran-Contra and its consequences make clear the affair was not the aberration it might have seemed. Some of the main characters and circumstances were unusual, to be sure, but they were neither unique nor impossible to replicate. There will always be the prospect that the necessary conditions will recur: a climate of international crisis requiring extreme measures in defense of the nation's security, a charismatic president willing to trade on his approval ratings to push the limits of the office, a crop of loyal aides who see it as their mission to carry out the president's wishes no matter what, a political opposition unwilling to challenge openly a popular president, and a media corps unable to pierce executive branch secrecy. For now, the bureaucratic structures—the CIA, the Defense Department, and the president's NSC staff—put in place after World War II to bolster the chief executive's freedom of action abroad remain fully intact and are far more robust than in the past. The related instruments of choice—covert operations and expansive White House secrecy—favored by Reagan and every other president since the 1940s will continue to provide deniability and minimize unwanted outside interference. Finally, the inability of Congress and the courts to check the abuses of Iran-Contra leaves the way open for future presidents—and their staffs—to press their advantage as far as politics will allow, posing predictable hazards to the broader public interest.

Notes

Preface: Settings for the Scandal

1. John Prados, *Keepers of the Keys: A History of the National Security Council from Truman to Bush* (New York: William and Morrow, 1991), pp. 33–34.

2. Leslie Groves, letter to Richard Groves, June 27, 1958, cited in Thomas S. Blanton, "National Security and Open Government in the United States: Beyond the Balancing Test," in *National Security and Open Government: Striking the Right Balance* (Syracuse, N.Y.: Campbell Public Affairs Institute, Maxwell School of Syracuse University, 2003), p. 40.

3. See generally John Prados, *Safe for Democracy: The Secret Wars of the CIA* (Chicago: Ivan R. Dee, 2006); David M. Barrett, *The CIA and Congress: The Untold Story from Truman to Kennedy* (Lawrence: University Press of Kansas, 2005).

4. James Baker, handwritten notes, November 19, 1980; see also the *Washington Post* website, ca. June 24, 2007, http://blog.washingtonpost.com/cheney/sidebars/cheneys_advice_to _baker/comments.html.

5. Quoted in Frederick A. O. Schwarz Jr. and Aziz Z. Huq, *Unchecked and Unbalanced: Presidential Power in a Time of Terror* (New York: New Press, 2007), p. 156.

6. At a conference with former U.S. and Soviet officials in 1995, President Carter's ex-NSC staff Iran expert Gary Sick and former CIA director Stansfield Turner recalled having to explain to senior White House officials in fall 1978 what an ayatollah was. A former Soviet Central Committee official at the conference acknowledged Kremlin leaders were equally ignorant on the subject. See transcript of the conference "The Intervention in Afghanistan and the Fall of Détente," Lysebu, Norway, September 17–20, 1995, hosted by the Norwegian Nobel Institute, co-organized with the Thomas J. Watson Jr. Institute for International Studies at Brown University and the National Security Archive at George Washington University, pp. 50, 96. (Conference materials are available on the Carter-Brezhnev Project page of the National Security Archive website.)

7. The State Department's Marshall Shulman was a notable exception. See, for example, his letter to Secretary of State Cyrus Vance, February 15, 1980, in the briefing book for the conference. Ibid.

8. Reagan explicitly referred to this theory of Soviet motivations in his November 13, 1986, televised address explaining the rationale for the Iran arms deals.

Acknowledgments

1. For one example, see James G. Blight, Janet M. Lang, Hussein Banai, Malcolm Byrne, and John Tirman, *Becoming Enemies: U.S.-Iran Relations and the Iran-Iraq War, 1979–1988* (Lanham, Md.: Rowman and Littlefield, 2012).

Introduction

1. Rafsanjani's account had several inaccuracies, including the timing of the visit and the gift of the bible, which the United States had provided several months after the McFarlane trip. *New York Times*, November 5, 1986.

2. Although UN Ambassador Jeane Kirkpatrick is sometimes credited with coining the term "Contras" (from *contrarevolucionarios*), it came into use in Nicaragua shortly after the 1979 revolution and referred originally to those who opposed the revolution, then later to those who took up arms to fight the Sandinistas (see Armony, *Argentina*, p. 94). According to another version by a former U.S. official who served in Nicaragua, the term was a "propaganda pejorative" invented by enemies of the "real Contras," who called themselves "Comandos." See Brown, *The Real Contra War*, p. 4.

3. *Washington Post*, November 5, 1986.

4. "Address to the Nation on the Iran Arms and Contra Aid Controversy," November 13, 1986, http://www.reagan.utexas.edu/archives/speeches/1986/111386c.htm.

5. "Remarks Announcing the Review of the National Security Council's Role in the Iran Arms and Contra Aid Controversy," November 25, 1986, http://www.reagan.utexas.edu/archives/speeches/1986/112586a.htm.

6. Transcript of Edwin Meese remarks, *New York Times*, November 26, 1986.

7. Eleanor Clift, quoted in *Washington Post*, November 26, 1986.

8. Transcript of Edwin Meese remarks, *Washington Post*, November 26, 1986.

9. Oliver L. North, *Under Fire: An American Story* (New York: HarperCollins, 1991), p. 7.

10. Robert Squier, quoted in *New York Times*, November 26, 1986.

11. Peter J. Wallison, *Ronald Reagan: The Power of Conviction and the Success of His Presidency* (Boulder, Colo.: Westview Press, 2004), p. 127.

12. The National Security Archive and Public Citizen Litigation Group obtained a declassified set of North's handwritten notebooks from late 1984 to late 1986, albeit with excisions, through a Freedom of Information Act (FOIA) lawsuit filed in 1989.

13. Theodore Draper, *A Very Thin Line: The Iran-Contra Affairs* (New York: Hill and Wang, 1991). Draper addressed some of the withheld evidence in subsequent articles in the *New York Review of Books*.

14. See, in particular, Draper's important two-part review of the memoirs of George Shultz, Elliott Abrams, and Edwin Meese, along with Lawrence Walsh's fourth interim report to Congress, in the *New York Review of Books*, May 27 and June 10, 1993. The final article, "Iran-Contra: The Mystery Solved," concludes: "There is no longer a mystery about who was responsible for the arms-for-hostage deals. It was the President of the United States."

15. Lawrence E. Walsh, *Firewall: The Iran-Contra Conspiracy and Cover-Up* (New York: W. W. Norton, 1997).

Chapter 1: Raising the Contras

1. Ronald Reagan, *An American Life: The Autobiography* (New York: Simon and Schuster, 1990), p. 471.

2. Kiron K. Skinner, Annelise Anderson, and Martin Anderson, eds., *Reagan in His Own Hand: The Writings of Ronald Reagan That Reveal His Revolutionary Vision for America* (New York: Free Press, 2001), p. 158. Reagan borrowed the quote from remarks by then Rep. Steve Symms (R-Idaho).

3. See Reagan, *An American Life*, p. 474.

4. See, for example, the statement by the former head of the Soviet Central Committee department responsible for the third world: "It was not a question of seeking to establish ourselves on the continent to secure some kind of bridgehead [in Latin America], but rather of undertaking diversionary maneuvers, attempting to neutralize or to offset the activities of the United States in other regions." Karen Brutents, "A New Soviet Perspective," in Wayne S. Smith, ed., *The Russians Aren't Coming: New Soviet Policy in Latin America* (Boulder, Colo.: Lynne Rienner Publishers, 1992), pp. 66–80, esp. pp. 72–73.

5. See Karl E. Meyer, "The Elusive Lenin," *New York Times*, October 8, 1985; "Toward the Summit: Excerpts from Reagan Interview by Soviet Journalists on Summit Hopes," *New York Times*, May 29, 1988; Christopher Andrew and Vasili Mitrokhin, *The World Was Going Our Way: The KGB and the Battle for the Third World* (New York: BasicBooks, 2005), p. 27.

6. U.S. National Security Council minutes, "Caribbean Basin; Poland," February 6, 1981.

7. *Washington Post*, January 10, 1981; *New York Times*, January 29, 1981.

8. Quoted in Walter Lafeber, *Inevitable Revolutions: The United States in Central America* (New York: W. W. Norton, 1983), p. 271.

9. U.S. National Security Council minutes, "Caribbean Basin; Poland," February 6, 1981.

10. U.S. Department of State, "Communist Interference in El Salvador," Special Report no. 80, February 23, 1981.

11. But hard-liners in the administration were convinced stronger methods would soon be needed because "the Sandinistas are committed revolutionaries and in the thrall of Cuba." U.S. Department of State, memorandum for the file, "ARA/CIA Meeting, February 2, 1981," notes from a regular meeting of Latin America experts from the State Department and the CIA Division of Operations.

12. See, for example, "Einführungsreferat des Genossen Generalmajor Jänicke auf der Beratung vor Vertretern des KfS der UdSSR, des MdI der CSSR, des MdI der VR Bulgarien, des MdI der SR Kuba und des MfS der DDR zu NIKARAGUA (Berlin 12 and 13 May 1980)," [Introductory Presentation of Comrade Maj. Gen. Jänicke at the Meeting of Representatives of the KGB of the USSR, MI [Ministry of Interior] of the CSSR, MI of the PR of Bulgaria, MI of the SR of Cuba, and MfS [Ministry for State Security] of the GDR about Nicaragua (Berlin 12 and 13 May 1980)], in Federal Commissioner for Stasi Records [BStU], Archiv der Zentralstelle, MfS—Abt. X/327, pp. 53–71. (Obtained with assistance of Bernd Schaefer, translated by Carolina Dahl.)

13. See Roy Gutman, *Banana Diplomacy: The Making of American Policy in Nicaragua, 1981–1987* (New York: Simon and Schuster, 1988), p. 29.

14. Lou Cannon, *President Reagan: The Role of a Lifetime* (New York: Simon and Schuster, 1991), p. 344.

15. Harry W. Shlaudeman was an assistant secretary of state during the Ford administration and served as ambassador to several Latin American capitals during his career. See interview with the Association for Diplomatic Studies and Training, Frontline Diplomacy: The Foreign Affairs Oral History Collection (hereafter Frontline Diplomacy), initial interview date May 24, 1993, http://memory.loc.gov/cgi-bin/query/D?mfdip:1:./temp/~ammem_UljJ::.

16. Ronald Reagan, interview, *Fortune*, September 15, 1986.

17. Anthony Quainton, interview with the Association for Diplomatic Studies and Training, Frontline Diplomacy, November 6, 1997, http://memory.loc.gov/service/mss/mssmisc/mfdip/2005%20txt%20files/2004qua01.txt; Shlaudeman interview.

18. Shlaudeman interview.

19. Central Intelligence Agency, draft presidential finding, "Scope: Central America," ca. February 27, 1981. See also Robert McFarlane, memorandum to Alexander Haig, "Covert Action Proposal for Central America," February 27, 1981.

20. Reagan, *An American Life*, p. 475.

21. Bruce Cameron, *My Life in the Time of the Contras* (Albuquerque: University of New Mexico Press, 2007), p. 51. This view of the political reality of the Contra issue did not prevent more ideologically inclined administration officials from trying to press their cause throughout the Reagan presidency.

22. *Washington Post*, May 8, 1983.

23. Presidential finding, "Scope: Central America," March 9, 1981.

24. The amendment (to the Foreign Assistance Act of 1961) stated the president must "find" a proposed covert action "important to the national security of the United States." Whether the Reagan administration made proper use of findings became a major controversy during the Iran-Contra affair.

25. The administration played up allegations of, in Haig's words, a "massive" arms pipeline, but the story was progressively discredited over time. See the related discussion in Cynthia Arnson, *Crossroads: Congress, the Reagan Administration, and Central America* (New York: Pantheon, 1989), pp. 72–73.

26. Charles Fried, *Order and Law* (New York: Simon and Schuster, 1991), p. 16, cited in Charlie Savage, *Takeover: The Return of the Imperial Presidency and the Subversion of American Democracy* (New York: Little, Brown, 2007), p. 44.

27. U.S. National Security Council minutes, "Caribbean Basin; Poland," February 6, 1981.

28. Anthony Quainton, interview with the author, July 14, 2006. (Quainton mentioned only one bridge, although two were blown up on March 14.) See also Quainton interview with Frontline Diplomacy.

29. U.S. National Security Council minutes, "Strategy toward Cuba and Central America," November 10, 1981, the Reagan Files website, http://jasonebin.com/nsc24.html.

30. The *Washington Post* obtained documents from the NSC meeting and printed excerpts in its March 10, 1982, and May 8, 1983, editions. See also Peter Kornbluh and Malcolm Byrne, *The Iran-Contra Scandal: The Declassified History* (New York: New Press, 1993), p. 1.

31. Presidential finding on Central America, December 1, 1981. See also Kornbluh and Byrne, *The Iran-Contra Scandal*, p. 11. As released to the public, the approximately forty-word paragraph on "purpose" is almost entirely excised.

32. Glenn Garvin, *Everybody Had His Own Gringo: The CIA and the Contras* (McLean, Va: Brassey's, 1992), p. 21. In addition to Garvin's account, this section draws on Peter Kornbluh, *Nicaragua: The Price of Intervention—Reagan's Wars against the Sandinistas* (Washington, D.C.: Institute for Policy Studies, 1987); Timothy C. Brown, *The Real Contra War: Highlander Peasant Resistance in Nicaragua* (Norman: University of Oklahoma Press, 2001); Ariel C. Armony, *Argentina, the United States, and the Anti-Communist Crusade in Central America, 1977–1984* (Athens: Ohio University Center for International Studies, 1997); Sam Dillon, *Comandos: The CIA and Nicaragua's Contra Rebels* (New York: Henry Holt, 1991); Gutman, *Banana Diplomacy*; Duane R. Clarridge with Digby Diehl, *A Spy for All Seasons: My Life in the CIA* (New York: Scribner's, 1997); and Christopher Dickey, *With the Contras: A Reporter in the Wilds of Nicaragua* (New York: Simon and Schuster, 1985).

33. Gutman, *Banana Diplomacy*, pp. 46–49; Armony, *Argentina*, p. 95.

34. See Enrique Bermúdez quote in Gutman, *Banana Diplomacy*, p. 57. For a slightly different description, see Clarridge, *A Spy for All Seasons*, p. 201. See also U.S. Department of State, memorandum for the files, "ARA/CIA Meeting, April 28, 1981," which reports "the Hondurans are thinking of ways to support counterrevolutionary groups in Nicaragua to slow down or stall FSLN consolidation." At this stage, Álvarez and his partners "see this support as a Latin American initiative for which they would seek our nod but not our intervention." However, Álvarez,

who was in Washington, D.C., at that very time, according to this memo, was already beginning to press for a more active U.S. role.

35. See Dickey, *With the Contras*, pp. 107–108.

36. Garvin, *Everybody Had His Own Gringo*, p. 54; Dickey, *With the Contras*, p. 108.

37. See Clarridge, *A Spy for All Seasons*, pp. 190–203, esp. p. 197.

38. Secretary of State Haig, among other officials, said the plan had not been approved by the administration. See Gutman, *Banana Diplomacy*, pp. 55–57, 66–78; Gutman cites Álvarez as the source for Clarridge's quote (p. 57). See also William M. LeoGrande, *Our Own Backyard: The United States in Central America, 1977–1992* (Chapel Hill: University of North Carolina Press, 2000), p. 118.

39. Dickey, *With the Contras*, pp. 109–112, 210; see also Quainton interview with Frontline Diplomacy.

40. Garvin, *Everybody Had His Own Gringo*, p. 111.

41. The act bars private groups from engaging in hostile acts against governments at peace with the United States.

42. Kornbluh, *Nicaragua*, p. 20.

43. Anthony Quainton, cable to Department of State, "One Bridge Destroyed, Another Damaged Near Nicaragua's Border with Honduras," March 16, 1982; Defense Intelligence Agency, "Weekly Intelligence Summary: Insurgent Activity Increases in Nicaragua," July 16, 1982; Kornbluh, *Nicaragua*, pp. 23–24.

44. Arnson, *Crossroads*, p. 80.

45. Kornbluh, *Nicaragua*, p. 55.

46. "A Secret War for Nicaragua," *Newsweek*, November 8, 1982, pp. 42ff.

47. Gutman, *Banana Diplomacy*, pp. 116–117. Boland, whose name would become synonymous with congressional opposition to the covert war, apparently believed continuing allegations of Sandinista gunrunning justified maintaining the program.

48. Defense Appropriations Act for FY 1983, § 793, Public Law 97-377 (1982).

49. Gutman, *Banana Diplomacy*, pp. 153–154.

50. See Kornbluh and Byrne, *The Iran-Contra Scandal*, pp. 1–9, plus associated documents, for a more detailed discussion of the administration's image-building offensive. Clarridge asserts that "circumstances on the ground, not the myth of U.S. government pressure," forced the alliance of the September 15 Legion and the anti-Guardia Nicaraguan Democratic Union. See Clarridge, *A Spy for All Seasons*, p. 200.

51. Reagan, *An American Life*, pp. 478–479.

52. Ibid. The "Geneva" reference is to ongoing Intermediate-Range Nuclear Forces (INF) talks between Washington and Moscow.

53. William Clark (signed by Robert McFarlane), memorandum for Special Policy Group principals, "Public Diplomacy (Central America)," July 1, 1983.

54. Kornbluh and Byrne, *The Iran-Contra Scandal*, p. 4. This quote comes from a chapter drafted for the committees' final report but ultimately cut by Senate Republicans; see Robert Parry and Peter Kornbluh, "Iran-Contra's Untold Story," *Foreign Policy* 72 (Fall 1988): 3–29, for the fullest treatment of the topic.

55. Woody Kepner, letter to Edgar Chamorro, January 24, 1983.

56. This passage relies largely on Kornbluh, *Nicaragua*, Chapter 3.

57. *Chicago Tribune*, June 15, 1993; Armony, *Argentina*, p. 97.

58. "The negotiations spent a great deal of time talking about security issues, particularly, in their case, about military maneuvers in Central America. They regarded these maneuvers . . . as threatening. This was a particular preoccupation of theirs." Shlaudeman interview.

59. Quainton interview with Frontline Diplomacy. The Grenada invasion also was apparently the first occasion on which the U.S. military used civilians to front for their operations. Richard Gadd, who became a central figure in the "Enterprise," which armed the Contras outside of government channels, and Wallace "Buzz" Sawyer, one of the Enterprise pilots, reportedly participated as clandestine operatives during the invasion. See Steven Emerson, *Secret Warriors: Inside the Covert Military Operations of the Reagan Era* (New York: G. P. Putnam's, 1988), pp. 145–146. North, who helped plan the operation, may well have seen the value of this sort of false-front tactic during the invasion for his own future activities.

60. U.S. Department of Defense, "Background" (top-secret/sensitive paper), July 13, 1983.

61. Emerson, *Secret Warriors*, pp. 87–93.

62. On October 30, 1984, North received a call, apparently from an intelligence officer, mentioning the army's Seaspray program and an operation code-named "Quiet Falcon I," part of an activity Emerson (*Secret Warriors*, pp. 89–94, 150) describes as outfitting Beechcraft airplanes with high-technology electronic and aerial surveillance equipment to allow the army's covert units to carry out the signals intelligence operations. This entry appears in a set of secret transcriptions of North's notes created by congressional Iran-Contra committee staff and obtained by the author (hereafter North notebooks [Select Committee extracts]).

63. See Emerson, *Secret Warriors*, pp. 152–154, 216–217.

64. U.S. District Court, D.C. Circuit, stipulation of facts presented in the trial of Oliver North (hereafter North trial stipulation), April 6, 1989, p. 1.

65. U.S. Senate, *Report of the Congressional Committees Investigating the Iran-Contra Affair, with Supplemental, Minority, and Additional Views*, 100th Congress, 1st sess. (1987), S. Rep. 100-216 (Washington, D.C.: Government Printing Office, 1987; hereafter *Select Committees' Report*), pp. 34–35. The CIA "wish list" included $28 million worth of equipment. After the Pentagon's general counsel determined the arrangement violated the Economy Act, which required reimbursements for interagency transfers of equipment, the program ended in February 1985. By then, the agency had received three Cessna aircraft at no cost as well as other equipment at cost.

66. See, for example, Arnson, *Crossroads*, pp. 111–112.

67. *Washington Post*, July 29, 1983.

68. Former Senate committee associate counsel, interview with the author, September 13, 1992.

69. U.S. Department of State, "Legislative Strategy," ca. September 10, 1983. See also Arnson, *Crossroads*, pp. 136–138, for details about this period.

70. Presidential finding, "Scope: Nicaragua," September 19, 1983.

71. Arnson, *Crossroads*, p. 137; Kornbluh and Byrne, *The Iran-Contra Scandal*, p. 3.

72. Bob Woodward described Casey's admiration for Motley in *Veil: The Secret Wars of the CIA, 1981–1987* (New York: Simon and Schuster, 1987), pp. 255–256.

73. Robert McFarlane, memorandum to the president, "Support for the Nicaraguan Democratic Opposition," November 7, 1983. Reagan initialed his approval of the actions McFarlane recommended.

74. Quoted in Woodward, *Veil*, p. 282.

75. See Peter Kornbluh, *The Pinochet File: A Declassified Dossier on Atrocity and Accountability—A National Security Archive Book* (New York: New Press, 2013), Document 1, p. 36.

76. Oliver North and Constantine Menges, memorandum to Robert McFarlane, "Targeting Guerrilla Command and Control Centers in Nicaragua," January 23, 1984; Oliver North, memorandum to Robert McFarlane, "Attack on Guerrilla Command and Control Centers in Nicaragua," February 3, 1984.

77. *Select Committees' Report*, p. 36; Kornbluh, *Nicaragua*, pp. 47–48.

78. *New Republic*, August 5, 1985.

79. Oliver North and Constantine Menges, memorandum to McFarlane, "Special Activities in Nicaragua," March 2, 1984. A handwritten notation on the first page of the document reads: "Briefed to RR, 3/5, RCM," referring to Ronald Reagan and Robert McFarlane.

80. U.S. Office of the Independent Counsel, C. J. Mixter memorandum to Judge Walsh, *Criminal Liability of President Bush*, March 21, 1991, first published in National Security Archive Electronic Briefing Book No. 365, November 25, 2011 (hereafter *Bush Criminal Liability*); U.S. National Security Council minutes, "Strategy toward Cuba and Central America."

81. Barry Goldwater, letter to William Casey, April 9, 1984.

82. Kornbluh, *Nicaragua*, pp. 51–52.

83. The CIA insisted the subject of mining had come up 11 times in congressional briefings. The SSCI countered Casey's testimony had been neither complete nor timely, and had initially left the impression the rebels had acted alone. See *New York Times*, April 17, 1984.

84. Robert McFarlane, testimony at *Joint Hearings before the U.S. House Select Committee to Investigate Covert Arms Transactions with Iran and Senate Select Committee on Secret Military Assistance to Iran and the Nicaraguan Opposition*, vol. 100-2, 100th Congress, 1st sess. (Washington, D.C.: Government Printing Office, 1987; hereafter *Joint Hearings*), p. 10.

Chapter 2: Coping with Iran

1. Skinner, Anderson, and Anderson, *Reagan in His Own Hand*, p. 114.

2. See Eric Hooglund, "The Policy of the Reagan Administration toward Iran," in Nikki R. Keddie and Mark J. Gasiorowski, eds., *Neither East nor West: Iran, the Soviet Union, and the United States* (New Haven, Conn.: Yale University Press, 1990), pp. 180–197.

3. David C. Martin and John Walcott, *Best Laid Plans: The Inside Story of America's War on Terror* (New York: Touchstone, 1989), pp. 210–212.

4. Geoffrey Kemp, memorandum to Robert McFarlane, January 13, 1984, cited in *Report of the President's Special Review Board* (Washington, D.C.: U.S. Government Printing Office, 1987; hereafter *Tower Report*), p. B-2.

5. Ibid., p. B-3.

6. Central Intelligence Agency, cable, Director 023056, "Fabricator Notice—Manuchehr [*sic*] ((Gorbanifar [*sic*]))," July 25, 1984.

7. Saddam Hussein, letter to UN Secretary General, September 26, 1980.

8. Of the many books on the war, the best exposition of the Iraqi viewpoint appears in Kevin M. Woods, Williamson Murray, and Thomas Holaday, with Mounir Elkhamri, *Saddam's War: An Iraqi Military Perspective of the Iran-Iraq War* (Fort Lesley J. McNair, D.C.: National Defense University, 2009); for the U.S. role, see Blight et al., *Becoming Enemies*.

9. Robin Wright, *In the Name of God: The Khomeini Decade* (New York: Simon and Schuster, 1989), p. 114.

10. See, for example, Houchang Chehabi, ed., *Distant Relations: Iran and Lebanon in the Last 500 Years* (London: I. B. Tauris, 2005).

11. Richard Murphy quoted in Blight et al., *Becoming Enemies*, p. 108.

12. See the account in Howard Teicher and Gayle Radley Teicher, *Twin Pillars to Desert Storm: America's Flawed Vision in the Middle East from Nixon to Bush* (New York: William Morrow, 1993), pp. 206–207.

13. See remarks by former U.S. ambassador to Iran William H. Sullivan in late 1980, confirming the hazards of "Soviet mischief" in Iran. James G. Hershberg, "Sullivan Cites Soviet 'Agitation' in Iran," *Harvard Crimson*, December 6, 1980.

14. "Discussion Paper for SIG on Policy Options for Dealing with Iran-Iraq War," undated (ca. late June or early July 1982), Ronald Reagan Library, Geoffrey Kemp files, Box 90492, Folder: Iran/Iraq, July 1982.

15. Thomas Twetten's story appears in Blight et al., *Becoming Enemies*, pp. 114–116; see also Twetten, interview with the author, December 13, 2008.

16. Explicit accounts of U.S. attitudes and conduct during the war appear in Blight et al., *Becoming Enemies,* and in the declassified documents prepared in connection with that volume. See also Patrick Lang (retired Defense Intelligence Agency officer), interview with the author and John Tirman, June 24, 2009. Former Air Force Col. Rick Francona, who served in Baghdad as a military attaché in the 1980s, has also described U.S. awareness of Iraq's chemical use and actions, such as the provision of "targeting packages" for use against Iranian objectives. See, for example, Shane Harris and Matthew M. Aid, "Exclusive: CIA Files Prove America Helped Saddam as He Gassed Iran," *Foreign Policy* online (August 26, 2013).

17. See, for example, U.S. Department of State, cable to various posts, "Kittani Call on Under Secretary Eagleburger," secret, March 18, 1984.

18. See the reporting cable on the encounter, U.S. Embassy in London to the Secretary of State, Cable 27572, "Rumsfeld Mission: December 20 Meeting with Iraqi President Saddam Hussein," December 21, 1983, in Joyce Battle, ed., *Shaking Hands with Saddam Hussein: The U.S. Tilts toward Iraq, 1980–1984*, National Security Archive Electronic Briefing Book No. 82, February 25, 2003, Document 31, http://www2.gwu.edu/~nsarchiv/NSAEBB/NSAEBB82/index.htm.

19. For a major collection of declassified documents detailing U.S. collaborative ties with Iraq during the late 1980s and early 1990s, see Joyce Battle, ed., *Iraqgate: Saddam Hussein, U.S. Policy, and the Prelude to the Persian Gulf War (1980–1994)* (Alexandria, Va.: Chadwyck-Healey, 1995).

20. The T-72s were also on North's wish list, according to his notebooks. The advanced Soviet tank reportedly far outperformed Iran's British-made Chieftains. According to a former IRGC commander, on one occasion the 10th Iraqi Armored Brigade handily defeated the 16th Iranian Armored Division. "It is hard for an armored brigade to destroy a division in 12 hours but it happened; it was a disaster for the Iranians." See Kevin M. Woods, Williamson Murray, Elizabeth A. Nathan, Laila Sabara, and Ana M. Venegas, eds., *Saddam's Generals: Perspectives of the Iran-Iraq War* (Alexandria, Va.: Institute for Defense Analyses, 2011), p. 85.

21. See William French Smith, letter to William Casey, "CIA Exchange of U.S. Weaponry for [word excised]," October 5, 1981. A congressional investigator confirmed to the author the country involved was Iraq. See also *Joint Report of the Task Force to Investigate Certain Allegations Concerning the Holding of American Hostages by Iran in 1980* (Washington, D.C.: Government Printing Office, 1993; hereafter, *October Surprise Task Force Report*), p. 211; Emerson, *Secret Warriors*, pp. 185–186. Emerson identifies the T-72 tank and says Iraq offered at various points to add a Hind-D helicopter and MiG-25 fighter plane to the list. He also reports negotiations for the hostages were conducted by the U.S. Army's highly secretive Intelligence Support Activity.

22. L. Paul Bremer III, memorandum to Richard Allen, "Iran SIG Meeting of July 21, 1981," quoted in *Select Committees' Report*, p. 159.

23. Ibid., p. 159. The *October Surprise Task Force Report*, p. 215, discusses the draft NSDD, which the author's interviews confirm appeared around the time of the SIG meeting.

24. The question of providing military supplies to Iran arose again in 1983 (and possibly

earlier, in 1982), although the circumstances are still classified. See W. George Jameson, memorandum to Stanley Sporkin, "Restrictions on Exports to Iran," January 7, 1983. The document, from the CIA assistant general counsel to the general counsel, deals with a proposal to send military equipment to Iran and for purposes of comparison mentions an occasion in 1982 when the State Department's legal advisor "addressed CIA's authority to transfer arms"—presumably to Iran, although the next line of the memo is excised.

25. Estimates of casualties during the war range from 200,000 or more Iranians to 250,000–500,000 Iraqis killed.

26. See *October Surprise Task Force Report*, Chapter 10, p. 225; p. 228, fn. 109. This footnote lists twenty-nine countries but omits Vietnam, which is mentioned in fn. 105.

27. Serious allegations and official inquiries began in 1986 in France and Italy, both of which had embargoes of Iran in place. The European Parliament passed a resolution condemning shipments to either belligerent in December 1986. See cites to official documents and press reports in Claudia Castiglioni, "Through Thick and Thin: West Europe and Iran from the Golden Rush of the Seventies to the War with Iraq," unpublished paper, November 2012.

28. *Christian Science Monitor*, July 23, 1984.

29. The ambassador was Richard Helms, who served from 1973–1976 before becoming director of the CIA. Quoted in *Washington Post*, August 16, 1987.

30. According to former CIA operative George Cave, Israel had an intelligence arrangement with Iran and Turkey called "Trident" and a nuclear agreement with Iran and South Africa. Transcript of "Towards an International History of the Iran-Iraq War, 1980–1988: A Critical Oral History Workshop," organized by the Woodrow Wilson International Center for Scholars and the National Security Archive, July 19, 2004 (hereafter Iran-Iraq War Workshop—2004), p. 45.

31. George Cave, Select Committees' deposition, vol. B-3, p. 586.

32. Gen. Rafael Vardi, interview with the author, November, 19, 2007.

33. In 1980, Israel earned $1.25 billion from arms deals abroad. See *Financial Times*, August 18, 1981. The figure for how many Jews were in Iran appears in the *New York Times*, August 22, 1981. Oliver North, memorandum to John Poindexter, "Special Project Re Iran," December 5, 1985.

34. Thomas Pickering, quoted in Blight et al., *Becoming Enemies*, Chapter 4.

35. *October Surprise Task Force Report*, pp. 200–201, 226, fn. 17.

36. Vardi interview.

37. *Philadelphia Inquirer*, August 10, 1987.

38. U.S. Department of State to the U.S. Embassy in Tel Aviv, Cable 28467, February 4, 1981. Quoted in *October Surprise Task Force Report*, p. 206.

39. Israeli government report on October surprise allegations, quoted in *October Surprise Task Force Report*, p. 207.

40. Central Intelligence Agency, "USSR-Iran-Israel: Aircraft Forced Down," July 23, 1981.

41. For a more detailed discussion of these events, see the *October Surprise Task Force Report*, pp. 209–214.

42. Former U.S. officials give conflicting estimates of how much equipment Israel provided to Iran in the early 1980s. Some say the amounts were minimal. Assistant Secretary of State Nicholas Veliotes recalled the list of materiel the U.S. compiled totaled "about 40 pages." Iran-Iraq War Workshop—2004, p. 43.

43. Central Intelligence Agency, "Arms Transfers to the Persian Gulf: Trends and Implications," Appendix C (Washington, D.C.: National Archives and Records Administration CREST database, August 1982), pp. 18–19.

44. U.S. Department of State, Cable Baghdad 2745, "Iraqi Views on Iran-Iraq War and Leb-

anon," November 9, 1983. This confidential cable reports on a conversation between U.S. diplomat Robin Raphel and a senior Iraqi Foreign Ministry official, in which Raphel insisted the United States had "strongly urged the Israelis, to the extent that they [are] selling arms to Iran, to cease such activities." Raphel told the Iraqi, "We had given this message to the Israelis on many occasions in the past," including on Lawrence Eagleburger's "recent" visit to Israel.

45. A marine contingent first landed in Beirut in August as part of an international force to oversee the evacuation of Palestine Liberation Organization (PLO) forces from the city, departed on September 10, then returned at the end of the month in the wake of the Sabra and Shatila massacre.

46. For a detailed description of Hezbollah and its origins, see Magnus Ranstorp, *Hizb'Allah in Lebanon: The Politics of the Western Hostage Crisis* (New York: St. Martin's Press, 1997).

47. Hezbollah leaders later acknowledged the use of Islamic Jihad and other cover names to disguise their identity. See ibid., pp. 62–63.

48. For one report on the bombing, see Defense Intelligence Agency cable to the Secretary of Defense, "DIA Spot Report," October 23, 1983, 8:02 a.m. Zulu, Reagan Files website, www.thereaganfiles.com.

49. In addition to various outside observers, one insider who held this view was McFarlane. See his interview with PBS's *Frontline* at www.pbs.org/wgbh/pages/frontline/shows/target/interviews/mcfarlane.html.

50. For the defense secretary's elaboration of what became known as the Weinberger Doctrine, see Caspar Weinberger, "The Uses of Military Power," remarks to the National Press Club, November 28, 1984.

51. The first post-1979 U.S. hostage taken was David Dodge, acting president of the American University of Beirut, whose kidnapping on July 19, 1982, came two weeks after four Iranians (three from their embassy) disappeared at a Christian-controlled checkpoint in East Beirut. Dodge was freed a year later, several months before the abductions that led to the arms-for-hostages deals in 1985.

52. Iraq's population is mostly Shiite, but the Baghdad regime historically kept them under tight control, especially after the Iranian revolution.

53. "National Security Planning Group Meeting Wednesday, October 3, 1984: 2:00 p.m.–3:00 p.m.; White House Situation Room—Subject: Response to Terrorist Activity in Lebanon," October 3, 1984.

54. Minutes of National Security Planning Group meeting, "Response to Threat to Lebanon Hostages," January 18, 1985.

55. See Robert C. McFarlane with Zofia Smardz, *Special Trust* (New York: Cadell and Davies, 1994), pp. 21–23; Martin and Walcott, *Best Laid Plans*, p. 197.

56. Charles Allen, interview with the author, January 9, 2013. Former CIA Iran analyst Bruce Riedel also used the term "obsessed" to describe the president's attitude. Interview with the author, October 23, 2007.

57. William Casey, memorandum to John McMahon, untitled, December 10, 1985.

58. Thomas Twetten, quoted in *Tower Report*, p. B-83.

59. Brent Scowcroft, interview with the author, February 13, 2013.

60. For the results of an official investigation into the controversy, see *October Surprise Task Force Report*, esp. pp. 109–118. For the most comprehensive independent analysis, see Gary Sick, *October Surprise: America's Hostages in Iran and the Election of Ronald Reagan* (New York: Times Books, 1991), esp. pp. 116ff.

61. For a convincing portrait of McFarlane, see Draper, *A Very Thin Line*, pp. 28–30. The full citation to McFarlane's article in the journal *The Presidency and National Security Policy* appears

on p. 616, fn. 8. If the second Reagan term was going to accomplish anything in foreign policy, McFarlane wrote later, "Much of the work was going to fall to me." McFarlane, *Special Trust*, p. 289.

62. Cannon, *President Reagan*, p. 599.

Chapter 3: Taking over the Covert War

1. Public Law 98-473, Section 8066(A), 1984.

2. Text of Executive Order 12333, December 4, 1981; Draper, *A Very Thin Line*, pp. 24–25.

3. Bretton Sciaroni, *Joint Hearings*, vol. 100-5, June 8, 1987, p. 399. Lawrence E. Walsh, *Final Report of the Independent Counsel for Iran/Contra Matters* (Washington, D.C.: Government Printing Office, 1993; hereafter *OIC Final Report*), vol. I, p. 144.

4. See Robert McFarlane, testimony at Oliver North trial, March 10, 1989, p. 3975, and March 13, 1989, pp. 4138–4140.

5. Edwin Meese, *Joint Hearings*, vol. 100-9, July 29, 1987, p. 424.

6. Meese testified to this effect in ibid., p. 377.

7. Donald Regan, *Joint Hearings*, vol. 100-10, July 31, 1987, p. 101.

8. George Will, *Washington Post*, May 24, 1987.

9. John Norton Moore, cited and quoted in the *Dallas Morning News*, July 16, 1987.

10. Draper, *A Very Thin Line*, p. 25.

11. Deputy Director for Intelligence to Director of Central Intelligence, "Nicaragua," December 14, 1984.

12. North used the term "gofer" in his memoir. He claimed to have "groused like hell" about being assigned to the NSC staff. "I made clear to everybody that I wasn't interested. I didn't want another desk job, and I *certainly* didn't want one in Washington." Emphasis in original. North, *Under Fire*, p. 151.

13. Charles E. Allen, Select Committees' deposition, vol. B-1, p. 249.

14. James Steele, Select Committees' deposition, vol. B-26, p. 364.

15. Quoted in Ben Bradlee Jr., *Guts and Glory: The Rise and Fall of Oliver North* (New York: Donald I. Fine, 1988), p. 541.

16. See, for example, ibid., pp. 544–547; Robert Timberg, *The Nightingale's Song* (New York: Touchstone Books, 1996), p. 275.

17. Constantine Menges and Oliver North to Robert McFarlane, undated NSDD attached to memorandum, "Central America—Draft NSDD to Implement NSPG Decisions of January 6, 1984," January 13, 1984.

18. John Poindexter, Select Committees' deposition, vol. B-20, p. 1059.

19. Although Clarridge never faced formal discipline over the so-called assassination manual, it earned him deeper antagonism from critics on Capitol Hill. See *New York Times*, January 21, 1987; see also United Press International, February 9, 1987, reporting Clarridge had acknowledged his responsibility to the CIA inspector general. See also, generally, Clarridge, *A Spy for All Seasons*.

20. Bruce Riedel, interview with the author, December 20, 2012.

21. Edgar Chamorro (a member of the FDN political directorate and a CIA source who attended the meeting), quoted in *New York Times*, January 21, 1987.

22. *OIC Final Report*, vol. I, p. 203.

23. North, *Under Fire*, p. 180.

24. Ibid.

25. Oliver North, memorandum to Robert McFarlane, "Official Travel to Honduras on August 31, 1984," August 28, 1984. (The words "to Honduras" were excised from the title in the public version of the document but appear in the *Select Committees' Report*, p. 55, fn. 175.)

26. These and other examples are cited in Draper, *A Very Thin Line*, pp. 114–116.

27. Richard Secord, *Honored and Betrayed: Irangate, Covert Affairs, and the Secret War in Laos* (New York: John Wiley, 1992), esp. pp. 29–43, 46–51, 52–73. See also biographical sketch of Secord issued by secretary of the U.S. Air Force, Office of Public Affairs, February 1982.

28. In 1983, Edwin Wilson's firm, Egyptian American Transportation and Services Corporation (EATSCO), was found guilty of overcharging the Egyptian government for weapons. Wilson later implicated Secord as a silent partner. At the time, Secord had overseen U.S.-Egyptian arms sales from his post at the Defense Security Assistance Agency. Wilson was later sentenced to a long prison term for conspiring to sell arms to Libya and for conspiring to kill the prosecutor and several witnesses at his trial. See Secord, *Honored and Betrayed*, pp. 185–197. See also Peter Maas, *Manhunt: The Incredible Pursuit of a CIA Agent Turned Terrorist* (New York: Random House, 1986), pp. 140, 247, 279, 285, and 288; *Wall Street Journal*, January 17, 1987.

29. This was Oliver North's testimony regarding William Casey's recommendation of Richard Secord. See North, *Joint Hearings*, vol. 100-7, Part I, July 8, 1987, p. 119.

30. Ibid., pp. 317–318.

31. Secord, *Honored and Betrayed*, p. 206.

32. North memorandum, "FDN Expenditures and Outlays: July 1984 through February 1985," April 9, 1985; *OIC Final Report*, vol. I, p. 161.

33. *OIC Final Report*, vol. I, p. 161. Thomas Green resurfaced as Richard Secord's lawyer during the Iran-Contra proceedings.

34. See Theodore Shackley, memorandum for the record, "Mr. Albert Hakim, Iranian National and Import/Exporter," August 16, 1976; Shackley, cable to excised destination, August 17, 1976; Central Intelligence Agency, cable to headquarters, August 18, 1976. See also *Select Committees' Report*, p. 329, fn. 23; *OIC Final Report*, vol. I, p. 158, fn. 5.

35. Albert Hakim, Select Committees' deposition, vol. B-13, pp. 66–67, 72–74, 869–872; Hakim, *Joint Hearings*, vol. 100-5, June 3, 1987, pp. 197–198.

36. North notebooks (FOIA release), December 4, 1984, AMX000215.

37. Oliver North, memorandum to Robert McFarlane, "Assistance for the Nicaraguan Resistance," December 4, 1984.

38. North notebooks (FOIA release), December 4, 1984, AMX000215.

39. Ibid.

40. FBI memorandum, "Thomas Gregory Clines," August 28, 1984; *OIC Final Report*, vol. I, p. 158, fn. 5.

41. Quintero, too, had ties to Wilson, having once gone along with a plot to assassinate a political opponent of Libyan leader Muammar Qaddafi. Quintero said he believed the operation, which never took place, had official CIA sanction. See Maas, *Manhunt*, pp. 65–66, 279, 285.

42. North notebooks (FOIA release), January 29, 1985, AMX000406-7. See also *Select Committees' Report*, p. 43.

43. North notebooks (FOIA release), January 30, 1985, AMX000408.

44. Ibid., February 5, 1985, AMX000432. Emphasis in original.

45. See North memorandum to McFarlane, "Guatemalan Aid to the Nicaraguan Resistance," March 5, 1985, attaching nine Guatemalan EUCs.

46. The official's name was excised in versions of the document that were made public, but the letterhead and official stamp are from the Guatemalan Ministry of Defense. See North notebooks (FOIA release), March 7, 1985, AMX000507.

47. Oliver North, memorandum to Robert McFarlane, "Guatemalan Aid to the Nicaraguan Resistance," March 5, 1985.

48. Secord, *Joint Hearings*, vol. 100-1, May 7, 1987, p. 196.

49. Secord, *Honored and Betrayed*, p. 206; Secord, *Joint Hearings*, vol. 100-1, May 5, 1987, p. 66.

50. Secord, *Honored and Betrayed*, pp. 206–208.

51. Albert Hakim, Select Committees' deposition, vol. B-13, pp. 80–81, 389.

52. North, *Joint Hearings*, vol. 100-7, Part I, July 8, 1987, p. 119.

53. *OIC Final Report*, vol. I, pp. 172–173.

54. Information in this paragraph comes from Sam Dillon, *Comandos: The CIA and Nicaragua's Contra Rebels* (New York: Henry Holt, 1991), pp. 143–145; Oliver North memorandum to Robert McFarlane, "FDN Air Attack of 1 September," September 2, 1984; Peter Kornbluh and Malcolm Byrne, eds., *The Iran-Contra Affair: The Making of a Scandal, 1983–1988* (Alexandria, Va.: Chadwyck-Healey, 1990), Guide/Index vol. I, p. 113.

55. See North memorandum to McFarlane, "FDN Air Attack of 1 September," September 2, 1984; Dillon, *Comandos*, p. 144.

56. Gerald S. Greenberg, ed., *Historical Encyclopedia of U.S. Independent Counsel Investigations* (Westport, Conn.: Greenwood, 2000), pp. 8–9.

57. See North memorandum to McFarlane, "FDN Air Attack of 1 September," September 2, 1984; Dillon, *Comandos*, p. 144.

58. North, memorandum to McFarlane, "FDN Air Attack of 1 September," September 2, 1984; *Washington Post*, May 22, 1987; *New York Times*, May 22, 1987.

59. Robert Owen, testimony at Oliver North trial, quoted in Associated Press, "Witness Says North Suggested Suicide Mission," February 24, 1989.

60. Ibid.

61. North, memorandum to McFarlane, "Assistance for the Nicaraguan Resistance," December 4, 1984. This apparently was not David Walker's introduction to the Contras. North told McFarlane, "Walker had been approached several months ago, prior to initiating the current financial arrangement for the FDN." This time, North claimed he met Walker "at the request of [Navy] Sec. John Lehman." Nonetheless, North was careful to have the CIA check out Walker. Duane Clarridge, he reported, gave the Briton a "clean bill of health."

62. The British had sold blowpipes to Chile in 1982. See British National Archives, FCO 7/4106, Chile, "Sale of Arms and Military Equipment to Chile (including HMS *Norfolk*)," January 1, 1982–December 31, 1982.

63. North notebooks (FOIA release), December 17, 1984, AMX000257. Emphasis in original. Peter Kornbluh published the first report of this incident in the *Nation*, May 14, 1988.

64. See Oliver North memorandum to Robert McFarlane, "Follow-up with [words excised] re: Terrorism and Central America," December 20, 1984. Every copy of the memo publicly released has been heavily excised, mainly to disguise the name of the country in question. But one version of the document inadvertently leaves in Thatcher's name and refers to the Chilean requirement to "obtain British permission for the transfer" of the Blowpipes. See North trial, Defendant's Exhibit 58.

65. See discussion in *Select Committees' Report*, p. 43.

66. Oliver North, memorandum to Robert McFarlane, "Nicaraguan Arms Shipments," February 6, 1985.

67. Ibid.

68. See North, *Joint Hearings*, July 9, 1987, vol. 100-7, Part I, p. 269; John Poindexter, *Joint Hearings*, vol. 100-8, July 16, 1987, p. 98; *Tower Report*, p. C-4. (The *Tower Report* says only that

the "friendly government" involved pulled out; it does not name South Korea. However, North's memo to McFarlane, "Nicaraguan Arms Shipments," February 6, 1985, does.) It is not clear whether North's statement was accurate.

69. Kornbluh and Byrne, *The Iran-Contra Scandal*, p. 388. News accounts noted conflicting reports of either a string of explosions or a fire. There appear to have been no serious casualties, although the Red Cross reported 100 patients had to be evacuated. *Los Angeles Times*, March 7 and 8, 1985.

70. Alan Fiers, testimony at Clair George trial, October 28, 1992, pp. 1254–1257.

71. North pounded out a lengthy memo to McFarlane insisting he had held back a great deal from the CATF head. See North memorandum to Robert McFarlane, "Clarifying Who Said What to Whom," November 7, 1984.

72. Fiers testimony at Clair George trial, pp. 1263–1264.

73. This is Fiers's account. See ibid., p. 1264.

74. *OIC Final Report*, vol. I, p. 263.

75. See Fiers's cross-examination at George trial, July 31, 1992. Fiers and George's attorney do not mention the Nicaraguan church, only "the project"; however, the *Washington Post* and the *New York Times*, in their editions of August 1, 1992, report the details of the covert operation.

Chapter 4: TOW Missiles to Tehran

1. National security decision directive (NSDD) 99, "United States Security Strategy for the Near East and South Asia," July 12, 1983.

2. Minutes of National Security Planning Group, "Pakistan and NSDD-99 Work Program," September 7, 1984, www.thereaganfiles.com.

3. Graham Fuller, memorandum to William Casey, "Toward a Policy on Iran," May 17, 1985.

4. For a discussion of this concept, see generally Keddie and Gasiorowski: *Neither East nor West*.

5. Analysis by the U.S. Department of State Bureau of Intelligence and Research, forwarded as a cable to regional embassies, "The Iranian Succession," March 16, 1985, released by WikiLeaks.

6. Fuller, memorandum to Casey, "Toward a Policy on Iran," May 17, 1985.

7. Special National Intelligence Estimate 34-84, "Iran: The Post-Khomeini Era," quoted in *Tower Report*, pp. B-7, B-8.

8. Ibid.

9. Ibid. Robert Gates, who figured in other ways in Iran-Contra, admitted persuading the State Department Bureau of Intelligence and Research not to include a contrary footnote in the document. See Gates's testimony in "Nomination of Robert M. Gates," *Hearings before the Select Committee on Intelligence of the United States Senate*, vol. I, 102nd Congress, 1st sess., September 17, 1991, pp. 573–574.

10. *Tower Report*, pp. B-7, B-8; Donald Fortier and Howard R. Teicher, draft NSDD, "U.S. Policy toward Iran," ca. June 11, 1985 (which Robert McFarlane forwarded to members of the cabinet for review).

11. Fortier and Teicher, draft NSDD, "U.S. Policy toward Iran."

12. Sandra L. Charles, then director of Near East and South Asia affairs in the Office of International Security Affairs of the Office of the Secretary of Defense, recalled the meeting in an interview with the author, October 21, 2011.

13. Robert McFarlane, memorandum, "U.S. Policy toward Iran," June 17, 1985.

14. William Casey, memorandum to Robert McFarlane, "Draft NSDD re U.S. Policy toward Iran," July 18, 1985. According to author Bob Woodward, Casey took a more active role in the process, pressing Graham Fuller for months to come up with some new ideas on Iran. See *Veil*, p. 407.

15. Caspar Weinberger, handwritten note to Colin Powell, June 18, 1985.

16. Caspar Weinberger, memorandum to Robert McFarlane, "U.S. Policy toward Iran," July 16, 1985.

17. Ibid.

18. George Shultz, memorandum to Robert McFarlane, "U.S. Policy toward Iran: Comment on Draft NSDD," June 29, 1985.

19. For various accounts of the subject, see Draper, *A Very Thin Line*, pp. 129–134.

20. "The Iranian Transactions: A Historical Chronology," July 29, 1987 (hereafter Israeli Historical Chronology), Part I, pp. 4–5. The Israeli government prepared this classified, two-part chronology of the Iran initiative, along with a second chronology of the financial side of the operations, as part of a deal with the U.S. Congress to avoid submitting Israeli officials to questioning.

21. Ali Bahramani, interview with *Shahrvand Emrooz*, trans. Hussein Banai, June 19, 2008. Bahramani, a nephew of then Speaker of the Majles Akbar Hashemi Rafsanjani, became an intermediary in the U.S.-Iran arms deals in summer 1986 (see Chapter 12).

22. Martin Anderson, *Revolution: The Reagan Legacy* (Stanford, Calif.: Hoover Institution Press, 1990), pp. 344, 376–377. The United States learned later William Buckley's captors had extracted enough information to fill 400 pages. Buckley died in captivity in June 1985.

23. Michael Ledeen, Select Committees' deposition, vol. B-15, pp. 944–958. At the beginning of 1985, Robert McFarlane had sent Ledeen to Europe, where Ledeen had intelligence contacts, to begin to try to improve U.S. knowledge of Iran. McFarlane's enthusiasm may have cooled during spring 1985 after at least three of his aides balked at using Ledeen as the administration's "primary channel for working the Iran issue with foreign governments." Donald Fortier, PROFS note to Robert McFarlane, April 9, 1985, quoted in *Tower Report*, p. B-4. IBM's Professional Office System, or PROFS, was an early intranet (email) platform.

24. Israeli Historical Chronology, Part I, pp. 6–7.

25. It is unclear why the Israelis would have felt the need to ask Robert McFarlane's permission for routine artillery pieces after they had already reportedly worked out a deal with Manucher Ghorbanifar in April for $40 million worth of weapons—which the Iranian had then called off, asking for TOW missiles instead. Theodore Draper has pointed out Peres must have known about the TOW request, which *would* have required U.S. approval to sell legally to Iran, and either Peres was concealing this from Ledeen or Ledeen misunderstood the message. See Draper, *A Very Thin Line*, pp. 139–141. The issue is further clouded by Ledeen's testimony that about a week after he reported on his discussion with Peres, McFarlane instructed him to tell the Israelis a single shipment of artillery shells "was okay, but just that one shipment and nothing else." See Ledeen deposition, *Congressional Final Report*, Appendix B, vol. 15, pp. 960–961.

26. David Kimche, interview with the author, November 16, 2007.

27. See Robert McFarlane, op-ed, *Washington Post*, November 13, 1986.

28. See George Shultz, *Joint Hearings*, vol. 100-9, July 23, 1987, pp. 14, 59. Even though Shultz acknowledged in testimony McFarlane's Middle East trip was on behalf of the president and not on McFarlane's personal initiative, the 1983 incident prompted Shultz to tender his resignation; he seems not to have considered the Ledeen visit as important.

29. George Shultz, cable to Robert McFarlane, "Michael Ledeen in Israel," June 6, 1985; McFarlane, cable to Shultz, title excised, June 7, 1985.

30. Shlomo Gazit, interview with the author, November 14, 2007.

31. Nimrod Novik, interview with the author, November 15, 2007.

32. Ibid. Peres later reportedly sent a letter to Ronald Reagan endorsing the idea and urging he take advantage of the opportunity. CIA Iran expert George Cave, who read the letter when Oliver North showed it to him in spring 1986, was told it had been an important impetus for the president. Cave, interview with the author, September 4, 2007.

33. Kimche interview.

34. Gazit interview; Shimon Peres's advisors, interviews with the author, November 2007.

35. Asked why he did not explicitly mention this point to McFarlane, Kimche insisted McFarlane already knew "that our intelligence was not happy with Ghorbanifar." He theorized Ledeen must have persuaded McFarlane that Ghorbanifar was a "tremendous asset." Kimche interview.

36. See Israeli Historical Chronology, Part I, pp. 6–8. According to this version of events, the Israelis first raised the idea of including all the hostages in one package. This account also indicates the Israelis first received word, via Schwimmer, that McFarlane had approved the TOW deal as early as May 30. There is no other available evidence this happened so soon.

37. Robert McFarlane, *Joint Hearings*, vol. 100-2, May 11, 1987, p. 43; Israeli Historical Chronology, Part I, pp. 11–12. McFarlane told the Tower Commission hostages were discussed along with weapons, although not in the form of a request for deliveries to Iran (see *Tower Report*, pp. III-5, III-6). But McFarlane's account seems to telescope the July 3 meeting with information that came in over the next several days from Ledeen. Kimche says hostages did not come up at the July 3 session.

38. Among the other extremists he named, in addition to Mir-Hossein Mousavi and Ali Khamenei, was Chief of Intelligence Operations Mohsen Kangarlou, who would emerge as one of Ghorbanifar's closest contacts inside Iran. He listed Hassan Karoubi, Ghorbanifar's other early colleague in the arms initiative, among the moderates. See Adnan Khashoggi, letter and attached memorandum to Robert McFarlane, July 1, 1985; see also Raviv and Melman, *Every Spy a Prince*, p. 345.

39. Michael Ledeen, quoted in *Tower Report*, p. B-13. McFarlane testified he could not remember reading Khashoggi's memo, although he acknowledged getting other "think pieces" from him. He was also able to describe in some detail the political breakdown the Iranian intermediaries had given the Israelis and the existence of a lengthy list of political and military officials said to be open to closer ties with the West. See *Tower Report*, pp. B-20–B-21.

40. Ghorbanifar's history with Hassan Karoubi extended back a number of years. He claimed to have once saved Karoubi's life. Official reports on the Iran initiative concealed Karoubi's identity, referring to him only as the "first Iranian." See Israeli Historical Chronology, Part I, p. 13; CIA memorandum, author and subject excised, June 19, 1984.

41. Wilma Hall, note to Robert McFarlane, quoting a message from Michael Ledeen, July 11, 1985.

42. Gazit interview.

43. Thomas Twetten, quoted in Blight et al., *Becoming Enemies*, p. 133.

44. See Theodore Shackley, "American Hostages in Lebanon," November 22, 1984, quoted in the *Tower Report*, p. B-3. As early as May, Shackley reportedly passed his memo to Ledeen, who claimed he did not read it but instead gave it to North.

45. Among many studies of the period, see Shaul Bakhash, *The Reign of the Ayatollahs: Iran and the Islamic Revolution* (New York: BasicBooks, 1984); and Mehdi Moslemi, *Factional Politics in Post-Khomeini Iran* (Syracuse, N.Y.: Syracuse University Press, 2002), esp. Chapter 2.

46. Colin Powell, Select Committees' deposition, vol. B-21, pp. 228–231.

47. Robert McFarlane, cable to George Shultz, "Israeli-Iranian Contact," July 13, 1985.

48. Ibid.

49. Ibid.

50. George Shultz, cable to Robert McFarlane, "Reply to Backchannel No. 3 from Bud," July 14, 1985.

51. Ibid.

52. Cannon, *President Reagan*, p. 538.

53. Other administration officials went further, telling journalists Rafsanjani had personally interceded to find a solution. *Washington Post*, July 5, 1985.

54. Shultz, *Joint Hearings*, vol. 100-9, July 23, 1987, pp. 26–27.

55. Reagan, *An American Life*, p. 506. In the wake of the scandal, administration officials played up the strategic aspects of the deals and minimized the hostage element. But Reagan's priorities show through regularly in his own accounts and in numerous declassified documents.

56. *Fourth Interim Report to Congress* by Lawrence E. Walsh, Independent Counsel for Iran/ Contra Matters, February 8, 1993, Appendix: "Weinberger's Handwritten Notes Regarding the Iran Initiative July 1985–November 1986," p. 2, fn. 2. No information is available about the July 23 meeting except that President Reagan talked about the initiative with senior advisors.

57. Robert McFarlane, testimony to the Tower Commission. *Tower Report*, p. B-20. Although White House logs place Vice President Bush at the session, *Washington Post* reporters Bob Woodward and Walter Pincus have expressed doubts he was there. *Washington Post*, January 7, 1988.

58. Shultz, *Joint Hearings*, vol. 100-9, July 23, 1987, p. 27; Donald Regan, Select Committees' deposition, vol. B-22, p. 578.

59. *Washington Post,* December 7, 1986; *New York Times*, December 25, 1986.

60. Donald Regan gave contradictory testimony on the subject, first telling a House committee the president initially rejected the plan, then informing the Iran-Contra committees he had in fact approved it. See Regan testimony before the House Permanent Select Committee on Intelligence as reported in the *Wall Street Journal*, December 19, 1986; *Los Angeles Times,* December 19 and 21, 1986; Regan, Select Committees' deposition, vol. B-22, p. 578. The president did not commit his authorization to writing, but the Tower Commission concluded he most likely provided it beforehand, and the congressional committees agreed. Moreover, the committees noted, "McFarlane had no motive to approve a sale of missiles to Iran if the President had not authorized it." *Select Committees' Report*, p. 168.

61. The Israeli Historical Chronology confirms this. See also Novik interview; Kimche interview; Efraim Halevy, interview with the author, November 18, 2007; and Rafael Vardi, interview with the author, November 19, 2007.

62. Israeli Historical Chronology, Part I, pp. 19–20.

63. Ibid., pp. 21–23. In a discrepancy with McFarlane's account, the Israeli chronology says Peres reached his decision "in light of the results of the [Kimche] meeting with McFarlane" of August 2, at which it says McFarlane assured Kimche that Reagan had already approved the deal.

64. "A Financial Chronology of the Iranian Transactions," April 26, 1987, submitted by the Israeli government to the congressional Iran-Contra committees (hereafter Israeli Financial Chronology), p. 5.

65. Israeli Historical Chronology, Part I, p. 25. The Ministry of Defense did not get paid until March 1986, receiving $3 million for 504 missiles. See *Select Committees' Report*, p. 168.

66. The Israeli Historical Chronology says the company was named Surinternational Airlines (Part I, pp. 25–26). Other sources indicate it was St. Lucia Airlines, the same company that would transport sophisticated HAWK missiles to Tehran in November 1985. See, for example,

the (partially excised) deposition of the Central Intelligence Agency Air Branch chief in Select Committees' deposition, vol. B-4, p. 799.

67. TOW missiles were packaged in pallets of twelve.

68. Israeli Historical Chronology, Part I, p. 26.

69. Ibid., pp. 28–29.

70. Ibid., p. 30. In describing McFarlane's August 2 meeting with Kimche, in which he purportedly gave Israel the go-ahead, the chronology adds that McFarlane said he understood "it may become necessary to sell additional quantities of arms in order to obtain the release of the hostages," and if the hostages could be freed "it would be a very fine accomplishment." But even that falls well short of the explicit presidential permission Yitzhak Rabin and others had been demanding for the initial 100 missiles.

71. Khashoggi noted later he did not charge any commission for himself because he counted on being able to profit from future transactions with Iran using contacts established during this operation. Israeli Historical Chronology, Part I, p. 30.

72. Iranian Foreign Ministry official who took part in an internal review of the secret operation, interview with the author, September 26, 1999. Also, Hassan Rouhani, who headed the Iranian Air Defense Force, revealed in a published interview years later that by 1985 all such purchases had become the responsibility of the IRGC Khatam-ul Anbiya garrison. Hassan Rouhani interview in *Hamshahri*, September 24, 2008.

73. Caspar Weinberger notes, September 11, 1985, ALZ 0039648.

74. Ibid., September 15, 1985, ALZ 0039653E; the latter quote is from an excerpt of Caspar Weinberger's notes transcribed in Walsh, *Fourth Interim Report*, p. 7.

75. *Tower Report*, p. B-27. It is worth noting that according to ex-CIA official George Cave, "One of the things we found out after the fact was that in order to get some motion in the release of hostages, to get the first one that was released, Ghorbanifar paid $375,000 to Hizballah as a bribe." Iran-Iraq War Workshop—2004, p. 68.

76. McFarlane, *Joint Hearings*, vol. 100-7, Part II, July 14, 1987, p. 224.

Chapter 5: Quid Pro Quos

1. "National Security Planning Group Meeting June 25, 1984: 2:00–3:00 p.m.; Situation Room—Subject: Central America."

2. All quotations from this meeting are taken from detailed minutes prepared by the National Security Council staff at the time. Ibid.

3. The quote is from James Dobbins, then a deputy assistant secretary of state in the Bureau of European and Eurasian Affairs. Interview with the Association for Diplomatic Studies and Training, Foreign Affairs Oral History Collection, July 21, 2003, available at Library of Congress website, http://memory.loc.gov/cgi-bin/query/r?ammem/mfdip:@field(DOCID+mfdip2007 dob01. Shultz and Weinberger's careers had overlapped to an unusual degree, with Weinberger perpetually the subordinate: at the Office of Management and Budget in the early 1970s, in the Nixon cabinet, at the Bechtel Corporation (Shultz was president, Weinberger general counsel), and finally in the Reagan cabinet. Their rivalry was widely reported.

4. Adding to the tensions, Casey and Baker also had a history—each had essentially accused the other of lying in the "Debategate" scandal that had erupted just the year before. The episode involved the 1980 Reagan presidential campaign's mysterious acquisition of Carter's confidential briefing materials just prior to the lone debate between the candidates one week before the

election. In 1983 Baker testified under oath he received the materials from Casey, who flatly denied it. See, for example, *Christian Science Monitor*, May 24, 1984.

5. Although some commentators thought Reagan's remark was an acknowledgment of the illicit nature of third-country funding, it was more likely a tongue-in-cheek reference to finding out the identity of the imagined leaker.

6. Meese, *With Reagan*, p. 277. Meese's justification blurs distinctions between periods of time when different levels of restriction applied. He also does not mention the opinion of his predecessor as attorney general, William French Smith, that Congress would at least have to be notified of any such solicitations.

7. See William Casey, memorandum to Robert McFarlane, "Supplemental Assistance to Nicaragua Program," March 27, 1984.

8. McFarlane, *Special Trust*, pp. 68–69.

9. Robert McFarlane, memorandum to Howard Teicher, April 20, 1984. The first part of the memo details talking points for Teicher to use in connection with an effort by Ghorbanifar to encourage contacts with Iran. This appears to be the earliest example of mixing the Iran and Contra projects. (McFarlane's final—unheeded—instruction to Teicher was, "Destroy this memo.")

10. Casey memorandum to McFarlane, "Supplemental Assistance to Nicaragua Program," March 27, 1984.

11. North trial stipulation, April 6, 1989, paragraphs 1–2.

12. Central Intelligence Agency, cable, Director 904514, "[Deleted] Discussions with [Deleted]," April 10, 1984.

13. Duane Clarridge, cable to [Deleted], Director 928788, "Discussions with [Deleted]," May 1, 1984. Other opportunities involving South Africa appear to have occurred. In late June 1984, North spoke with his lieutenant, Owen, about an offer by a former registered agent of Pretoria to "broker S/A [South African] RPG deal 60 K lbs . . . pay only to ship—need U.S.G. verifications & that it's OK." See North notebooks, June 27, 1984, AMX002355. Then, on January 5, 1985, Clarridge called North to let him know 200 tons of weapons were on their way to Costa Rica, a portion of which was due to be off-loaded that night. North's notation reads: "200 T of arms enroute from South Africa to C.R. David Duncan—off loading 70 t/night." North notebooks (Select Committee extracts), January 5, 1985. On January 17, 1985, North made another cryptic entry in his notes, this time from a conversation with the CIA station chief in Costa Rica, indicating a need to "Move S/A delivery from ARDE," the Contra organization, January 17, 1985.

14. This description of the conversation comes from McFarlane, *Special Trust*, pp. 69–70.

15. Robert McFarlane, *Joint Hearings*, vol. 100-2, May 11, 1987, p. 17; Esther Morales/Nicaraguan Democratic Force bank statements (available at the National Security Archive); *New York Times*, March 6, 1987; *Wall Street Journal*, March 6, 1987; *Los Angeles Times*, March 6, 1987; Woodward, *Veil*, pp. 352–355.

16. Robert McFarlane, testimony before the U.S. House Foreign Affairs Committee, December 8, 1986, pp. 58, 66; McFarlane, *Joint Hearings*, vol. 100-2, May 11, 1987, pp. 16–17; McFarlane, *Joint Hearings*, vol. 100-2, May 12, 1987, p. 86.

17. Robert McFarlane, testimony at Oliver North trial, March 13, 1989, pp. 4201–4206.

18. Ibid.; also cited in U.S. Office of the Independent Counsel, C. J. Mixter memorandum to Judge Walsh, "Criminal Liability of Former President Reagan," March 21, 1991, first published in National Security Archive Electronic Briefing Book No. 365, November 25, 2011 (hereafter *Reagan Criminal Liability*), p. 59.

19. McFarlane, *Joint Hearings*, vol. 100-2, May 11, 1987, p. 18.

20. McFarlane, *Special Trust*, p. 71; McFarlane, *Joint Hearings*, vol. 100-2, May 11, 1987, p. 18.

21. The independent counsel cites John Vessey's recollection, contemporaneous records (including Weinberger's diaries), and "other evidence" to place Bandar's offer and McFarlane's subsequent conversations in late May. See *OIC Final Report*, vol. I, pp. 424–425, text and fn. 170, 172. Walsh's chronicle of his Iran-Contra investigation, *Firewall*, p. 392, indicates the arms deal involved AWACS aircraft.

22. Quoted in *OIC Final Report*, vol. I, p. 423. Emphasis in original.

23. "National Security Planning Group Meeting June 25, 1984: 2:00–3:00 p.m.; Situation Room—Subject: Central America," June 25, 1984.

24. Stanley Sporkin, memorandum for the record, "Nicaragua," June 26, 1984.

25. "National Security Planning Group Meeting June 25, 1984: 2:00–3:00 p.m.; Situation Room—Subject: Central America," June 25, 1984

26. See, for example, notes of the July 27, 1984, National Security Council meeting, quoted in Mixter, *Reagan Criminal Liability*, p. 58.

27. Ibid., p. 60.

28. See Robert Kagan, *A Twilight Struggle: American Power and Nicaragua, 1977–1990* (New York: Free Press, 1996), pp. 345–347.

29. Oliver North, memorandum to Robert McFarlane, "Cable to President Suazo of Honduras," February 6, 1985.

30. Oliver North and Raymond Burghardt, memorandum to Robert McFarlane, "Approach to the Hondurans Regarding the Nicaraguan Resistance," February 11, 1985.

31. Ibid.; see also Robert McFarlane, memorandum to George Shultz, Caspar Weinberger, William Casey, and John Vessey (drafted by Oliver North and Raymond Burghardt), "Approach to the Hondurans Regarding Nicaraguan Military Build-up," February 12, 1985.

32. Oliver North and Raymond Burghardt, memorandum to Robert McFarlane, "Presidential Letter to President Suazo of Honduras," February 15, 1985, and attached draft memo to Reagan, "Approach to the Hondurans Regarding the Nicaraguan Resistance," undated.

33. Robert McFarlane, memorandum to Ronald Reagan, "Approach to the Hondurans Regarding the Nicaraguan Resistance," February 19, 1985, with the president's initials approving McFarlane's recommendations.

34. Ronald Reagan, letter to President Roberto Suazo, ca. February 19, 1985.

35. *New York Times*, January 26, 1985. The article names Sen. Richard Lugar (R-Ind.) and Rep. Lee Hamilton (D-Ind.), the incoming chairs of the Senate and House Intelligence Committees (respectively), as among those in discussions with the administration.

36. North and Burghardt, memorandum to McFarlane, "Presidential Letter to President Suazo of Honduras," February 20, 1985.

37. Ibid.

38. North trial stipulation, April 6, 1989, paragraphs 58–61. Top administration officials later denied any quid pro quo ever took place. In 1989, George Bush told reporters, "The word of the president of the United States, George Bush, is there was no quid pro quo . . . no implication, no quid pro quo, direct or indirect, from me to the president of Honduras on that visit." *Washington Post*, May 5, 1989. George Shultz and other State Department officials also initially made similar claims. See, for example, several instances cited in the *Washington Post*, May 2, 1989. However, the sheer number of officials on the Central Intelligence Agency distribution list for information about the Central America deals gives an idea of how widely informed the Reagan administration was about the provision of aid to the Contras. See North trial stipulation, April 6, 1989, paragraph 60.

39. "We cannot turn away from them," Reagan continued, "for the struggle here is not right

versus left, but right versus wrong." Speech to "Conservative Political Action Conference," March 1, 1985, quoted in *New York Times*, March 2, 1985.

40. Robert McFarlane, memorandum to Ronald Reagan, "Recommended Telephone Call," April 25, 1985, including Reagan's handwritten notes of the conversation with Roberto Suazo.

41. Robert McFarlane, memorandum to Ronald Reagan, "Meeting with Honduran President Suazo," ca. May 20, 1985. In his deposition at the John Poindexter trial in 1990, Reagan confirmed his expectation that "in return for our help in the form of security assurances as well as aid that we do expect cooperation. That we feel that there is an obligation on their part, too." Reagan, trial deposition, February 16, 1990, pp. 109–110.

42. Oliver North, memorandum to Robert McFarlane, "Guatemalan Aid to the Nicaraguan Resistance," March 5, 1985, with attached draft memo to George Shultz et al., a Guatemalan wish list for military equipment, and copies of Guatemalan EUCs.

43. General descriptions of all three programs appear in a court document the U.S. Office of the Independent Counsel prepared as part of its appeal of the dismissal of Joseph Fernandez's 1989 criminal trial. See "Opening Brief of Independent Counsel," July 27, 1989, in appeal of *United States of America v. Joseph F. Fernandez* before the U.S. Court of Appeals for the Fourth Circuit.

44. See North trial stipulation, April 6, 1989, paragraphs 67 and 88.

45. In February 1985, North reported on a major fund-raising success to Adolfo Calero—"Next week, a sum in excess of $20 million will be deposited in the usual account." But he pleaded, "Please do *not* in any way make *anyone* aware. . . . The Congress must believe that there continues to be an urgent need for funding." Letter from "Steelhammer" to "My Friend," February 20, 1985.

46. John Singlaub, *Joint Hearings*, vol. 100-3, May 20, 1987, p. 71.

47. See Oliver North, memorandum to Robert McFarlane, "Cable to President Suazo of Honduras," February 6, 1985; Robert McFarlane, *Joint Hearings*, vol. 100-2 , May 13, 1987, pp. 165–166.

48. John Singlaub, *Joint Hearings*, vol. 100-3, May 20, 1987, pp. 73–74. The names of the two officials and the final quote appear in the Iran-Contra committee's transcription of North's notes for November 28, 1984.

49. North notebooks (FOIA release), November 28, 1984, AMX000196. Emphasis in original. See also North memo to McFarlane, "Assistance for the Nicaraguan Resistance," December 4, 1984.

50. John Singlaub, *Joint Hearings*, vol. 100-3, May 20, 1987, pp. 75–76.

51. Singlaub told the Taiwanese they could either deposit funds directly into a Contra bank account (he offered a three-by-five-inch index card with the account number on it), give the funds to him and have him deposit them, or arrange to split the commission with an arms dealer and donate their portion to the rebels. Singlaub, *Joint Hearings*, vol. 100-3, May 20, 1987, pp. 74–77. See also Maj. Gen. John K. Singlaub, U.S. Army (Ret.), with Malcolm McConnell, *Hazardous Duty: An American Soldier in the Twentieth Century* (New York: Summit Books, 1991), pp. 465–466.

52. North notebooks (FOIA release), February 1, 1985, AMX000419.

53. North memorandum to McFarlane, "Assistance for the Nicaraguan Resistance," December 4, 1984. The Chinese government eventually consented to sell antiaircraft missiles to the Contras.

54. North notebooks (FOIA release), November 28, 1984, AMX000196.

55. Gaston Sigur disagreed with North's assertion he had stayed for the entire lunch with the first official. See Sigur, *Joint Hearings*, vol. 100-2, May 14, 1987, pp. 294–295.

Chapter 6: HAWKS

1. Central Intelligence Agency, cable, Director 023056, "Fabricator Notice—Manuchehr ((Gorbanifar [sic]))," July 25, 1984; Michael A. Ledeen, *Perilous Statecraft: An Insider's Account of the Iran-Contra Affair* (New York: Scribner's, 1988), pp. 136–137.

2. Hassan Rouhani, interview in *Hamshahri*, September 24, 2008. Rouhani went on to become Iran's president in 2013.

3. McFarlane, *Special Trust*, p. 40.

4. Ibid.

5. Meeting in Washington, D.C., especially in a government building, also made it easier for the Central Intelligence Agency to put the visitors under surveillance. See memorandum from Charles E. Allen to [Deleted], "Background on U.S. Initiative to Secure Release of American Hostages," October 7, 1985. Allen told North at the time he believed Buckley had already died, but North continued to hold out hope he was still alive. Allen, Select Committees' deposition, vol. B-1, pp. 349–351. Ledeen later disputed the notion the meeting was connected with Buckley's situation or that any hostage releases were expected at that time. See *Select Committees' Report*, p. 173, fn. 120.

6. Charles Allen, interview with the author, January 9, 2013.

7. Michael Ledeen, Select Committees' deposition, vol. B-15, p. 1014.

8. Israeli Historical Chronology, Part I, pp. 34–35. This was Ledeen's first face-to-face encounter with Hassan Karoubi. His testimony to congressional investigators about the meeting differs widely from the official Israeli version, mainly by giving the impression Karoubi was "vociferously opposed" to the TOW shipments, saying they were a "terrible thing" because they had only strengthened the Khomeini regime. Ledeen, Select Committees' deposition, vol. B-15, pp. 1022–1023. Oliver North's notes of his debriefing of Ledeen within days of the Geneva meeting, however, back up the Israeli description in this instance. North notebooks (FOIA release), October 30, 1985, AMX001836.

9. North notebooks (FOIA release), October 30, 1985, AMX001837.

10. Caspar Weinberger notes, November 10, 1985, ALZ 0039775.

11. Israeli Historical Chronology, Part I, p. 39; Robert McFarlane, *Joint Hearings*, vol. 100-2, May 11–12, 1987, pp. 51–52, 97–98; *Tower Report*, p. B-30.

12. Caspar Weinberger notes, November 9, 1985, ALZ 0039774.

13. Ibid., November 10, 1985, ALZ 0039775.

14. Charles Hill, notes, November 14, 1985, cited in *OIC Final Report*, vol. I, p. 91. Weinberger's notes from November 10 indicate in fact McFarlane had already decided not to send Phoenix missiles to Iran (see n. 9).

15. John McMahon, memorandum for the record, "DCI/DDCI Meeting with Assistant to the President for National Security Affairs, 14 November 1985," November 15, 1985. The final phrase about overthrowing the Iranian government was excised when a copy of the memorandum was released to the public, but the congressional final report quoted the passage. See *Select Committees' Report*, p. 176. According to McMahon, McFarlane mentioned the deals almost in passing as the meeting was breaking up. When the two CIA men rode back to headquarters, Casey relayed the details. McMahon, Select Committees' deposition, vol. B-17, p. 92.

16. See *OIC Final Report*, vol. I, p. 14. Donald Regan also recalls a "momentary conversation" about an arrangement between Israel and Iran "that might possibly lead to our getting some of our hostages out." Regan, *Joint Hearings*, vol. 100-10, July 30, 1987, p. 12.

17. Weinberger notes, November 9, 1985, ALZ 0039774; Charles Hill, notes, November 14, 1985, ANS0001187.

18. *Tower Report*, p. B-31; Regan, *Joint Hearings*, vol. 100-10, July 30, 1987, p. 12.

19. For details of this meeting see Donald Regan, *For the Record: From Wall Street to Washington* (New York: Harcourt Brace Jovanovich, 1988), pp. 319–321; McFarlane, *Special Trust*, p. 43. These descriptions differ from each other, sometimes widely, making it difficult to determine the details of what happened. Regan's is the fuller account, but it has certain discrepancies, such as placing George Shultz in the room when other evidence indicates he was not there. In trying to downplay the Iran deals after the fact, the chief of staff and others pointed to the swirl of events regularly competing for the president's attention. Yet, for Reagan to have interrupted the critical first day of this historic summit for even twenty minutes (Regan's own recollection) is a sign of the importance he attached to the hostage deals.

20. See Charles Hill, notes, November 22, 1986, ALW021273, reflecting a conversation with Attorney General Edwin Meese in which George Shultz recalls the briefing at the summit in November 1985. The independent counsel's final report quotes another selection from Hill's notes of a McFarlane-Shultz secure telephone call at the summit where they discussed some of the same late-breaking details. The text places the call on November 19, although the citation to the document indicates November 18. See *OIC Final Report*, vol. I, p. 92; McFarlane, *Special Trust*, p. 43.

21. Weinberger notes, November 19, 1985, ALZ 0039795.

22. Ibid.

23. Ibid., ALZ 0039797.

24. Henry Gaffney, *Joint Hearings*, vol. 100-6, June 23, 1987, pp. 111–112. McFarlane may have told Weinberger he was considering splitting up the shipments because two days earlier he had instructed North to get in touch with Israel's purchasing agent in New York "to keep orders under $14M." North notebooks (FOIA release), November 17, 1985, AMX001805.

25. Weinberger notes, November 19, 1985, ALZ 0039797. Reagan biographer Lou Cannon wrote, "Weinberger made no effort to conceal his low opinion of McFarlane, and the national security adviser reciprocated." Cannon, *President Reagan*, p. 597.

26. Weinberger notes, November 20, 1985, ALZ 0039799.

27. North, *Under Fire*, p. 26.

28. It is not entirely clear where Schwimmer was at this time. Theodore Draper writes that he was in Tel Aviv (Draper, *A Very Thin Line*, p. 184), but North's notes indicate a telephone number at the Paris Hilton. North notebooks (FOIA release), November 18, 1985, AMX001868.

29. North notebooks (FOIA release), November 18, 1985, AMX001868.

30. Israeli Historical Chronology, Part I, pp. 37–38, 40.

31. North notebooks (FOIA release), November 18, 1985, AMX001870.

32. North, *Joint Hearings*, vol. 100-7, Part I, July 7, 1986, p. 55.

33. North notebooks (FOIA release), November 18, 1985, AMX001869-70, and November 19, 1985, AMX001877.

34. Ibid., November 20, 1985, AMX001878.

35. North notebooks (Select Committee extracts), November 6, 1985.

36. See Samuel Segev, *The Iranian Triangle: The Untold Story of Israel's Role in the Iran-Contra Affair* (New York: Free Press, 1988), pp. 196–197. Segev's account is based largely on the perspective of Schwimmer and other Israelis. Schwimmer told Segev he could find only three charter companies in the world with the right kind of front-loading 747s that could handle the eighteen-foot HAWKs; each demanded $50 million to do the job, he said.

37. Schwimmer's version in the Israeli Historical Chronology is he told North he should deal with the situation, and North said a man named "Copp" (Secord's code name) would be responsible. The date of the conversation appears to be November 18 (p. 40).

38. North, *Joint Hearings*, vol. 100-7, Part I, July 7, 1986, p. 52.

39. Secord, *Honored and Betrayed*, pp. 218–219; North, *Under Fire*, p. 30.

40. Robert McFarlane/Oliver North letter to Secord, November 19, 1985. *Joint Hearings*, Exhibit OLN-42. North signed the letter in McFarlane's name; McFarlane claims he never gave permission to do so. The location of the transshipment point (Lisbon) is frequently blacked out in documents such as this because U.S. government censors considered it a secret, even after George Shultz, Edwin Meese, and others named it repeatedly during televised congressional testimony. As late as 1993, the independent counsel was still unable to print the location in his final report. See *OIC Final Report*, vol. I, p. 14, fn. 41.

41. Secord, *Honored and Betrayed*, p. 219.

42. Central Intelligence Agency, cable IN 9103070, "NSC Mission," November 23, 1985. The congressional final report on Iran-Contra puts the airport incident on November 21 (p. 180).

43. Central Intelligence Agency, cable, "[Deleted] Support to NSC Mission, 22–27 Nov 85," December 4, 1986.

44. Central Intelligence Agency, cable IN 9084924, "NSC Instructions," November 22, 1985; Central Intelligence Agency, cable IN 9088770, "NSC Mission," November 22, 1985; Central Intelligence Agency, cable IN 9092094, "NSC Mission," November 22, 1985.

45. Central Intelligence Agency, cable IN 9091206, "NSC Mission," November 22, 1985; Central Intelligence Agency, cable IN 9103070, "NSC Mission," November 23, 1985; Central Intelligence Agency, cable IN 9102427, "NSC Mission," November 23, 1985.

46. Yaacov Nimrodi, interview with the author, November 16, 2007.

47. Most official U.S. accounts of the episode as well as North's congressional testimony gloss over the question of who authorized the El Al plane to take off. Schwimmer told Israeli investigators that at 7:00 p.m. Tel Aviv time North called from Washington, D.C., and gave an "okay" for the flight. At 10:30 the same night, he got another "urgent" call from North asking him to recall the plane because there was no landing permit. See Israeli Historical Chronology, Part I, p. 45.

48. Oliver North, PROFS message to John Poindexter, "Private Blank Check," November 22, 1985, 17:27:15.

49. North, *Joint Hearings*, vol. 100-7, Part I, July 7, 1986, p. 53.

50. Israeli Financial Chronology, Part I, pp. 14–15.

51. Airline proprietary project officer, Select Committees' deposition, vol. B-1, pp. 18–19. The name of the airline is blacked out in all official documents but came out in press accounts and later was confirmed in, among other places, Clarridge, *A Spy for All Seasons*, pp. 309–318.

52. For details on the Keystone Kops quality of the events of November 23–25, see airline proprietary project officer, Select Committees' deposition, vol. B-1, pp. 1–160, plus attached exhibits, esp. Exhibit 3—memorandum, "Mission TLV/THR," November 30, 1985. See also Clarridge, *A Spy for All Seasons*, pp. 313–315.

53. Most official accounts say the Iranians test-launched one missile. Richard Secord writes that it was disassembled to check for differences in high-altitude flight capability compared with HAWKs already in their inventory. In his version, this was how the Iranians discovered the Star of David stamped on certain interior components (see also nn. 51 and 54). Secord, *Honored and Betrayed*, p. 253.

54. Nimrodi interview. Other reports indicated there had simply been a miscommunication on the Israeli side about what Iran had ordered. See, for example, *Haaretz*, "Someone to Watch Over Them," May 28, 2004.

55. Menachem Meron, former director general of the Israeli Defense Ministry, interview with the author, November 15, 2007; see also Secord, *Honored and Betrayed*, pp. 220–222.

56. Former Iranian deputy foreign minister, interview with the author, September 5, 2007.

57. Nimrodi provided this version of the fiasco in Segev, *The Iranian Triangle*, p. 205; see also Israeli Historical Chronology, Part I, pp. 47–48.

58. Edward S. Juchniewicz, Select Committees' deposition, vol. B-14, pp. 618, 624.

59. John McMahon and Edward Juchniewicz differ slightly in their depiction of these encounters. McMahon says he "went through the overhead" when he heard what had happened. Juchniewicz recalled his boss "stopped, paused, became very contemplative and left . . . my office." They also gave different dates for when McMahon learned of the plans to use St. Lucia Airways. Juchniewicz says it was on Saturday, November 23; McMahon places it the following Monday. The main point of agreement is McMahon pressed for a finding. See McMahon, Select Committees' deposition, vol. B-17, pp. 96–99; Juchniewicz, Select Committees' deposition, vol. B-14, pp. 627–629.

60. The briefers came from either the Near East division or Air Branch of the Directorate of Operations. See Juchniewicz, Select Committees' deposition, vol. B-14, p. 629, and joint congressional committee statement, June 24, 1987.

61. "Finding Pursuant to Section 662 . . . , Scope: Hostage Rescue—Middle East," undated.

62. Ibid.

63. "CYA" stands for "cover your ass." Poindexter, *Joint Hearings*, vol. 100-8, July 15, 1987, p. 17.

64. Ibid., p. 26.

65. See George Shultz, *Joint Hearings*, vol. 100-9, July 23, 1987, pp. 31–32; "Talking Points for Shultz," December 7, 1985. See also Poindexter, *Joint Hearings*, vol. 100-8, July 15, 1987, pp. 24–25; Caspar Weinberger, *Joint Hearings*, vol. 100-10, July 31, 1987, pp. 139–141.

66. Quoted in *Tower Report*, p. B-45.

67. Weinberger notes, December 7, 1985, ALZ 0039831. See also Weinberger, *Joint Hearings*, vol. 100-10, July 31, 1987, p. 140.

68. Weinberger notes, December 7, 1985, ALZ 0039831.

69. Excerpts from Hill's notes, as given to the Federal Bureau of Investigation. See *OIC Final Report*, vol. I, p. 329, fn. 35. Shultz relates this account only slightly differently in his congressional testimony. Shultz, *Joint Hearings*, vol. 100-9, July 23, 1987, p. 32.

70. Donald Regan, quoted in *Tower Report*, p. B-52.

71. Allen interview.

72. Shultz, *Joint Hearings*, vol. 100-9, July 23, 1987, p. 32; *Tower Report*, p. B-44.

73. Ronald Reagan, diary entry for December 7, as reprinted in *An American Life*, p. 510.

74. There is disagreement about McFarlane's position. He states in his memoir, "I urged the President to shut the whole Iran initiative down" (*Special Trust*, p. 50). But Casey wrote in a memo following the meeting: "He recommended that we pursue the relationship . . . on a purely intelligence basis but being alert to any action that might influence events in Iran." He added that McFarlane suggested the United States "let the Israelis go ahead doing what they would probably do anyway, and hope that we get some benefit." Casey, untitled memorandum to deputy director of central intelligence [John McMahon], December 10, 1985. The version released by the joint congressional committees blacks out parts of the quote, but it appears unexcised in *Tower Report*, p. B-50.

75. Ronald Reagan, *The Reagan Diaries: Unabridged*, edited by Douglas Brinkley (New York: HarperCollins, 2009), entry for December 9, 1985, p. 550.

76. Casey, memorandum to deputy director of central intelligence, untitled, December 10, 1985.

Chapter 7: Tightening the Reins on the Contras

1. See, among other accounts, Michael K. Deaver with Mickey Herskowitz, *Behind the Scenes* (New York: William Morrow, 1987), pp. 129–130; Peggy Noonan, *What I Saw at the Revolution* (New York: Random House, 1990), pp. 203–204.

2. *New York Times*, May 26, 1985.

3. McFarlane, *Special Trust*, p. 288.

4. As biographer Lou Cannon described the scene: "Uncharacteristically, Baker asked Reagan why he hadn't cracked the briefing book. 'Well, Jim, *The Sound of Music* was on last night,' Reagan said calmly." Cannon, *President Reagan*, p. 57.

5. *New York Times*, May 26, 1985.

6. Oliver North, *Joint Hearings*, vol. 100-7, Part I, July 8, 1987, p. 126.

7. This paragraph is based substantially on the *OIC Final Report*, vol. I, Chapter 21.

8. The reference in North's notebooks to the supermarket appears on May 1, 1985, AMX000638. Werner Glatt is mentioned only as a "European arms dealer" in the *Select Committees' Report*, p. 43, but his name appears several times (as "Glott") in the committee's secret transcription of North's notes for the month of May 1985. John Singlaub's quotation of North is cited in the *Select Committees' Report*, p. 51. In his autobiography, Singlaub describes his foray into Contra weapons supply with the participation of Glatt, to whom he refers only as "Sam," and with a business associate, Barbara Studley, a former radio talk show host who ran an arms sales company called GeoMiliTech Consultants. Singlaub, *Hazardous Duty*, pp. 471–477.

9. When asked, "Were you surprised to learn that General Secord testified a couple of weeks ago that he was charging a 20 to 30 percent markup on the weapons?" Calero responded, "Well, it was a revelation." Calero, *Joint Hearings*, vol. 100-3, May 20, 1987, p. 14.

10. North notebooks (FOIA release), May 17, 1985, AMX000679.

11. Ibid., May 23, 1985, AMX000706.

12. Oliver North's congressional testimony is quoted in the *Select Committees' Report*, p. 51. The report acknowledges North did not mention Werner Glatt by name as the person William Casey apparently had in mind, but implies the circumstantial connection is close. Singlaub insisted later he had asked Casey to run a background check on Glatt, and Casey had declared him, in Singlaub's words, a "man of high integrity with no shady dealings on his record." Singlaub, *Hazardous Duty*, p. 472.

13. See North notebooks (FOIA release), May 17, 1985, AMX000681; May 20, 1985, AMX000685.

14. Tom Clines used the Portuguese firm Defex to make the purchases, the same company he and Secord would turn to when the HAWK deliveries ran into problems in Portugal in November 1985 (see Chapter 6). Secord, *Joint Hearings*, vol. 100-1, May 5, 1987, pp. 52–53; Oliver North, "FDN Expenditures and Outlays: July 1984 through February 1985," April 9, 1985.

15. For a portrait of Monzer al-Kassar, see Patrick Radden Keefe, "The Trafficker: The Decades-Long Battle to Capture an International Arms Broker," *New Yorker*, February 8, 2010, including quotes from Tom Clines about his connection to the Syrian dealer. Albert Hakim's ledgers show a $1 million payment to al-Kassar on August 30, 1985, and a $500,000 payment on June 20, 1986. See *Joint Hearings*, Exhibit OLN-17. John Poindexter's remark is in *Joint Hearings*, vol. 100-8, July 20, 1987, p. 295.

16. Central Intelligence Agency cable of June 5, 1985, cited in *OIC Final Report*, vol. I, p. 298.

17. *OIC Final Report*, vol. I, pp. 296–297, citing Federal Bureau of Investigation and grand jury statements by Ronald Martin, Tom Clines, and Rafael Quintero.

18. Secord, *Joint Hearings*, vol. 100-1, May 5, 1987, p. 58.

19. Secord, *Honored and Betrayed*, pp. 211–212.

20. See Robert Owen ("TC"—"The Courier"), memorandum to Oliver North ("The Hammer"), "Southern Front," dated April 1, 1985, but with an update of April 9, 1985; for a general discussion of corruption on the part of Bermúdez, among other Contra leaders, see Dillon, *Comandos*, esp. pp. 126–131.

21. Secord, *Joint Hearings*, vol. 100-1, May 5, 1987, p. 59; Secord, *Honored and Betrayed*, p. 212.

22. Rafael Quintero testified the estimated casualty rate ran between 15–20 percent on average. North trial transcript, p. 2902.

23. See Dillon, *Comandos*, pp. 156–158.

24. See *OIC Final Report*, vol. I, p. 298.

25. See generally *Select Committees' Report*, Chapter 3.

26. See the description of Edén Pastora in the testimony of Central Intelligence Agency Costa Rica Station Chief Joseph Fernandez (alias Tomas Castíllo), *Joint Hearings*, vol. 100-5, May 29, 1987, pp. 9–10.

27. Oliver North, memorandum to Robert McFarlane, "FDN Military Operations," May 1, 1985.

28. Lewis Tambs, quoted in *Tower Report*, p. C-12.

29. The details are still classified but are referred to in the North trial stipulation, April 6, 1989, paragraph 66. See also the discussion of Costa Rica's involvement in quid pro quo arrangements in Chapter 5 of this book.

30. Cole Black and George Jameson (CIA investigators), "Interview with Joe Fernandez," January 24, 1986, pp. 3–4.

31. Robert Olmsted, letter to Benjamin Piza Carranza, December 19, 1985; North notebooks (FOIA release), November 15, 1985.

32. For more detail on the airstrip, see Kornbluh and Byrne, *The Iran-Contra Scandal*, pp. 128–130. Joseph Fernandez and the two men's wives also had their pictures taken with the president at the White House on March 19, 1986. Fernandez, interview with inspector general, January 24, 1986, p. 7; see also C. J. Mixter, *Reagan Criminal Liability*, p. 69, fn. 35.

33. Secord, *Joint Hearings*, vol. 100-1, May 5, 1987, p. 61.

34. On September 10, North wrote: "1630—Mtg w/Jim Steele/Don Gregg," an apparent reference to a session in which the three discussed a range of topics directly relating to the Contra resupply operation. Mention was made of arms dealer Dellamico, the existence of problems with radar for flights from Honduras, and a visit by Contra leaders Calero and Bermúdez "to Ilopango to estab. log support/maint." North notebooks, September 10, 1985. Less than a week later, on September 16, North added to his notes: "Call from Jim Steele . . . What about Felix—help for A/C [aircraft] maint." See also North notebooks (FOIA release), December 21, 1984, referring to a call from a State Department official named William R. Bode. At this point, Rodriguez was embarking on his El Salvador activities. Cited in *OIC Final Report*, vol. I, p. 486. Steele discusses Rodriguez at some length in his Iran-Contra deposition. Select Committees' deposition, vol. B-26, pp. 341ff. Unfortunately, the deposition has unusually heavy excisions.

35. Richard Gadd, Select Committees' deposition, vol. B-11, p. 209; North intended, at least, to call Abrams for help and did contact Vince Cannistraro of the CIA, who had been tasked to the NSC staff, but to no avail. See *Select Committees' Report*, pp. 62–63.

36. Secord, *Honored and Betrayed*, p. 215.

37. Southern Air Transport is identified as a proprietary in the congressional *Select Committees' Report*, p. 287. See also Gadd, Select Committees' deposition, vol. B-11, p. 209.

38. Gadd, Select Committees' deposition, vol. B-11, p. 206.

39. Frederick P. Hitz, *Report of Investigation Concerning Allegations between CIA and the Con-*

tras in Trafficking Cocaine to the United States, Central Intelligence Agency Office of Inspector General, 96-0143-IG (hereafter Hitz report), vol. 2, "The Contra Story," citing a September 1981 CIA cable to headquarters. The report is accessible on the CIA website, https://www.cia.gov /library/reports/general-reports-1/cocaine/contra-story/contents.html. It is divided into sections but does not contain page numbers; therefore subsequent cites are only to the report and volume number.

40. North notebooks (FOIA release), March 26, 1985, AMX000554.

41. Hitz report, vol. 2.

42. Chief, Central America Task Force, Select Committees' deposition, vol. B-3, p. 1121.

43. *Washington Post*, October 31, 1996.

44. Hitz report, vol. 2.

45. Cited in *New York Times,* July 17, 1998.

46. Owen, memorandum to North, "Southern Front," April 1, 1985; Hitz report, vol. 2.

47. North notebooks (FOIA release), August 9, 1985, AMX001318. In early 1986, Owen reported to North on another potentially embarrassing narcotics connection: "No doubt you know the DC-4 Foley got was used at one time to run drugs, and part of the crew had criminal records. Nice group the Boys choose." Robert Owen, memorandum to Oliver North, "Update," February 10, 1986.

48. Fernandez described Hull as "one of my station's assets." See Central Intelligence Agency Office of Inspector General, "Interview with Joe Fernandez," January 24, 1986. Fiers's quote is in a description of his Select Senate Intelligence Committee briefing, from Hitz report, vol. 2.

49. Hitz report, vol. 2, section "Findings: The Contra Story," citing an officer who was Central America Task Force chief from 1989–1991; *Washington Post*, October 31, 1996.

50. Hitz report, vol. 2.

51. Ibid.

52. For an account of this phenomenon early in the U.S. war on drugs, see Jefferson Morley and Malcolm Byrne, "The Drug War and 'National Security': The Making of a Quagmire, 1969–1973," *Dissent* (Winter 1989): 39–46.

53. Hitz report, vol. 2, citing Edmund Cohen, an attorney in the Office of General Counsel and chief of the Administrative Law Division in 1982.

54. Hitz report, vol. 2. For a lengthy presentation on how the memorandum of understanding was prepared, see the section "Reporting Potential Crimes to Department of Justice." See also Executive Order 12333, "United States Intelligence Activities," December 4, 1981.

55. William Casey, letter to William French Smith, March 2, 1982, Exhibit 1 attached to Hitz report, vol. 2, "The Contra Story."

56. William Walker, Select Committees' deposition, vol. B-27, p. 330.

57. Ibid.

58. According to Duemling's superior, Abrams, "Duemling was opposed to [hiring Owen] for reasons which I cannot articulate, and which I think were essentially because he and Colonel North did not get along." See Abrams, *Joint Hearings*, vol. 100-5, June 2, 1987 a.m., p. 37.

59. North trial stipulation, April 6, 1989, pp. 28–29, paragraphs 69–70; see also *Washington Post*, January 22, 1986.

60. *OIC Final Report*, vol. I, pp. 300–301.

61. Restricted Interagency Group (RIG) representatives came from the State, Defense, and Justice Departments as well as the Central Intelligence Agency, Joint Chiefs of Staff, and National Security Council staff. From 1985 North, Abrams, and Fiers were the group's key members.

62. See *OIC Final Report*, vol. I, pp. 264–265.

63. Oliver North, memorandum to Robert McFarlane, "FDN Military Operations," May 1, 1985.

64. Richard Miller estimated he spent $270,000 shepherding Zadeh around, with North's approval. See *OIC Final Report*, vol. I, p. 188, fn. 5; see also *Select Committees' Report*, pp. 90–91, 110–112. Further details are in Miller's Select Committee deposition, vol. B-19, pp. 369–411.

65. *Select Committees' Report*, p. 90.

66. Ibid., pp. 85, 94.

67. Ibid., p. 85.

68. William O'Boyle, *Joint Hearings*, vol. 100-3, May 21, 1987, p. 121.

69. These figures come from *OIC Final Report*, vol. I, p. 191. The *Select Committees' Report* (Chapter 4) arrived at somewhat different totals, but the congressional investigation took place at an earlier time and did not include access to important Swiss records made available, at least in part, to the independent counsel.

70. Ibid.

71. "National Security Planning Group Meeting, Tuesday September 11, 1984, 2:00–3:00 p.m.—Subject: Review of the [Excised] and Central America Special Activities," September 11, 1984.

72. Oliver North, memorandum to Robert McFarlane, "Reconnaissance Overflights," October 30, 1985. Poindexter wrote on the document, "President approved 10/30/85, JMP."

73. See *OIC Final Report*, vol. I, p. 452.

74. John Poindexter, *Joint Hearings*, vol. 100-8, July 15, 1987, p. 39.

75. John Poindexter, Select Committees' deposition, vol. B-20, pp. 1060–1062. Poindexter says he does not recall whether he mentioned Richard Secord by name to the president at that point.

76. Ibid., p. 1059.

77. John Poindexter, interview with the author, January 14, 2013.

78. See the discussion in *OIC Final Report*, vol. I, p. 449.

79. Mixter, *Bush Criminal Liability*, March 21, 1991, pp. 23–27, 28ff., 53–56.

80. John Poindexter, handwritten note on routing sheet from White House Situation Room, August 17, 1985.

81. Brenda Reger, memorandum to John Poindexter, "Barnes Request," August 20, 1985.

82. See *Select Committees' Report*, pp. 123–124, and *OIC Final Report*, vol. I, p. 84.

83. The document in this example was "FDN Military Operations," April 11, 1985. See the discussion in the *Select Committees' Report*, p. 126.

84. McFarlane later acknowledged North's proposed changes to the April 1985 document (see n. 83) were "grossly at variance with the original text." McFarlane congressional testimony quoted in *Select Committees' Report*, p. 126. North's remark to Fiers is recorded in the *OIC Final Report*, vol. I, pp. 5–6. (As noted on page 6, fn. 18, of that report, other administration officials, including Casey and Abrams, also evaded questions about North.)

85. Robert McFarlane, letter to Lee Hamilton, September 5, 1985.

86. Ibid.

87. Michael Barnes, letters to Robert McFarlane, September 30, 1985, and October 29, 1985; Barnes, interview with the author, June 26, 2006.

88. Lee Hamilton, unpublished interview with Christian Ostermann, May 22, 2013.

89. Robert McFarlane, testimony at the North trial, quoted in *OIC Final Report*, vol. I, p. 87.

Chapter 8: A Neat Idea

1. John Poindexter, interview with the author, January 14, 2013; White House, "Appointment of John M. Poindexter as Assistant to the President for National Security Affairs," December 4, 1985. For a revealing portrait of Poindexter, McFarlane, and North see Timberg, *The Nightingale's Song*.

2. Poindexter interview, January 14, 2013.

3. See Jane Mayer and Doyle McManus, *Landslide: The Unmaking of the President, 1984–1988* (Boston: Houghton Mifflin, 1988), pp. 61–62; also Bruce Riedel, interview with the author, October 23, 2007.

4. Poindexter interview, January 14, 2013.

5. Oliver North, PROFS note to John Poindexter, "Current Status of Operation Recovery," December 4, 1985, 02:02:55.

6. Ibid.

7. Oliver North, memorandum, "Special Project Re Iran," December 5, 1985. See also *OIC Final Report*, vol. I, p. 435.

8. North memorandum, "Special Project Re Iran," December 5, 1985. North also took note of the importance of the political dimension of the hostage situation, humanitarian concerns aside, when he wrote that the return of the hostages "will relieve a major *domestic* and international liability." Emphasis added.

9. Ibid.

10. Even then, Poindexter was not entirely forthcoming, neglecting to mention Reagan had just that day signed the CIA retroactive finding to cover the HAWK shipment. See *Select Committees' Report*, p. 197.

11. *OIC Final Report*, vol. I, p. 328, fn. 22.

12. Charles Hill, notes, December 6, 1985, quoted in *OIC Final Report*, vol. I, p. 435, fn. 253. Emphasis in original. "Night Owl" was another term occasionally used to describe North and the arms deals. See also ibid., vol. I, p. 328, fn. 22.

13. Secord's account seems credible because he was generally free with his criticism of McFarlane. See *Honored and Betrayed,* p. 233.

14. These quotes are from McFarlane, *Special Trust*, pp. 48–50.

15. David Kimche, quoted in Israeli Historical Chronology, Part I, p. 67.

16. McFarlane, *Special Trust*, p. 49.

17. Draper, *A Very Thin Line*, p. 232.

18. Oliver North, memorandum to Robert McFarlane and John Poindexter, "Next Steps," December 9, 1985.

19. Draper makes this point in *A Very Thin Line*, p. 234.

20. The rescue option and its ramifications were blacked out in the joint congressional committees' version, but the Tower Commission reproduced that portion of the document entirely. See *Tower Report*, p. B-49.

21. David Kimche, interview with the author, November 16, 2007.

22. North notebooks (FOIA release), June 29, 1985, AMX00823.

23. See North, *Under Fire*, p. 212. Some aspects of Nir's background and his acquaintance with North also appear in Martin and Walcott, *Best Laid Plans*, p. 231.

24. Israeli Historical Chronology, Part II, pp. 2–3.

25. Nir noted, "What Druze need most is $" and named the figure, "$1M/month near term." He later claimed the arms deals did not come up during these talks, but some of the same operational concepts did, including whether Israel should make the approach directly and whether

to "have Israelis do all work with U.S. pay?" See North notebooks (FOIA release), November 14, 1985, AMX001857, and November 19, 1985, AMX001872. For uncensored excerpts, see, in part, *Select Committees' Report*, p. 176, and author's copy of the committees' internal transcriptions of the notes.

26. For a look at the underreported and controversial collaboration between Waite and North, see Gavin Hewitt, *Terry Waite and Ollie North: The Untold Story of the Kidnapping—and the Release* (Boston: Little, Brown, 1991), pp. 24–28. Many of the references to Waite in the declassified U.S. record are excised, but for example the version of North's notes transcribed by the congressional select committees reveals information about their contacts. The *Tower Report* also published a passage about Waite's value as a source (p. B-48). Documents obtained much later, in 1998, under an FOIA lawsuit filed on behalf of former hostage Terry Anderson, give more firsthand details. See, for example, Oliver North, memorandum to Robert McFarlane, "Further Actions re AMCIT Hostages," May 20, 1985, reporting on his first meeting with "Terry Wade."

27. Hewitt, *Terry Waite and Ollie North*, pp. 39–40.

28. See Israeli Historical Chronology, Part I, p. 59; Part II, p. 3.

29. Israeli Historical Chronology, Part II, pp. 7–8; *Wall Street Journal*, December 22, 1986; *New York Times*, January 12, 1987.

30. John Poindexter, *Joint Hearings*, vol. 100-8, July 16, 1987, p. 128.

31. *Los Angeles Times*, December 28, 1985.

32. See Israeli Historical Chronology, Part II, pp. 10–13; John Poindexter, handwritten notes, January 2, 1986, written after the session during a flight to California to meet with the president. Nir, North, Poindexter, and the latter's deputy, Fortier, attended the meeting.

33. See Israeli Historical Chronology, Part II, pp. 12–13. Already, Ghorbanifar's status was being checked—and boosted—at Casey's behest.

34. Poindexter interview, January 14, 2013.

35. Draft presidential finding, "Iran," undated (ca. January 3, 1986).

36. Ibid.

37. Stanley Sporkin saw findings as an opportunity to "make a document that contains everything because it's sort of an insurance policy" that lets participants in a covert activity "know that they are protected." Sporkin, *Joint Hearings*, June 24, 1987, p. 143.

38. See John Poindexter, draft memorandum to the president, "Covert Action Finding Regarding Iran," ca. January 4, 1986.

39. See Caspar Weinberger notes, January 7, 1986: "Met with President, Shultz, Poindexter, Bill Casey, Ed Meese, in Oval Office—President decided to go with Israeli-Iranian offer to release our 5 hostages in return for sale of 4000 TOWs to Iran by Israel." Office of the Independent Council transcription, ALZ 0039883.

40. Poindexter corroborated this. Poindexter interview, January 14, 2013.

41. William French Smith, memorandum to William Casey, "CIA Exchange of U.S. Weaponry for [Deleted]," October 5, 1981.

42. Caspar Weinberger, *Joint Hearings*, vol. 100-10, July 31, 1987, p. 142.

43. At the televised Iran-Contra hearings, Meese defended his recommendations but acknowledged under questioning he had not studied the issue in detail until after the fact. See Meese's testimony and U.S. House counsel John Nields's questioning, *Joint Hearings*, vol. 100-9, July 28, 1987, pp. 205–206. According to participants, the Iran operation was expected to be short-lived; Meese said he thought it would take thirty to sixty days. There was no explanation for why the administration failed to review the decision as the initiative continued for months afterward. For more on the January 7 meeting and related topics, see inter alia the testimony in

Joint Hearings: Meese, vol. 100-9, July 28, 1987, pp. 196–197, 205–209; Caspar Weinberger, vol. 100-10, July 31, 1987, pp. 142–144; Donald Regan, vol. 100-10, July 30, 1987, pp. 14–17; George Shultz, vol. 100-9, July 23, 1987, pp. 7–8, 33; John Poindexter, vol. 100-8, July 15, 1987, pp. 30–35; see also *Tower Report*, pp. B-61–B-65.

44. Bush retained this concern throughout 1986, commenting at an administration meeting in November shortly after the McFarlane mission was exposed that the "Israelis may squeeze us." Donald Regan, notes, November 10, 1986. Nevertheless, by most accounts Bush favored going ahead with the operation. See John Poindexter deposition, vol. B-20, p. 1131. The deposition volume reproduces an excised copy of the passage on Israel, but the government later declassified it; extracts were first obtained and reported by James Hershberg in the *Boston Phoenix*, March 4–10, 1988, pp. 1–2, 10–11.

45. See North notebooks (FOIA release), January 7, 1986, AMX000868-9. During questioning, House counsel John Nields incorrectly dates these pages as January 15 but remarks the pages were given to the committees out of order. See North, *Joint Hearings*, vol. 100-7, Part I, July 8, 1987, pp. 99–100.

46. Two other methods mentioned in North's notes were "replenishment by pre-positioning" of TOWs in Israel from U.S. stocks prior to any shipments by Israel to Iran and an unexplained "exchange w/Iranians." See North notebooks (FOIA release), January 6, 1986, AMX000856, and an undated page listing various code words released as part of congressional Exhibit North-69A, *Joint Hearings*, vol. 100-7, Part III, p. 420. Method one, according to the committees' internal transcription of the notes of January 6, envisioned a release of the hostages to Terry Waite "based on religious grounds" and involving a letter from the pope to Antoine Lahad supporting the latter's release of captured Shiites.

47. The *Select Committees' Report* guesses "Albert" is a code name for the operation itself (p. 204).

48. See North, *Joint Hearings*, vol. 100-7, Part I, July 8, 1987, p. 103.

49. See Nir's version of his contacts with Oliver North in the Israeli Historical Chronology, Part II, pp. 15–16, 20.

50. See *Select Committees' Report*, p. 535.

51. Oliver North, PROFS note to John Poindexter, January 15, 1986, 12:04:22.

52. John McMahon, untitled memorandum to the director of Central Intelligence, January 13, 1986; George W. Clarke memorandum, "Telephone Call from General Counsel Regarding Authority to Provide Weapons to Third Parties Pursuant to Presidential Findings," January 15, 1986. Clarke added, "At one point [during the phone call with Sporkin], Mr. North came on the line to 'clarify' the hypothetical facts for me and then put Stan Sporkin back on the line."

53. Clair George, *Joint Hearings*, vol. 100-11, August 6, 1987, pp. 190, 257; see also William S. Cohen and George J. Mitchell, *Men of Zeal: A Candid Inside Story of the Iran-Contra Hearings* (New York: Viking, 1988), pp. 261–262.

54. Noel Koch, at the time a principal deputy assistant secretary of defense, recalled a discussion with Weinberger about the Iran operation in January 1986. Koch's sense was the secretary of defense did not think the legal issues were serious. "I said to him—and I did not say it in a very serious way—. . . do we have a legal problem with this, is somebody going to go to jail, and his response was in the affirmative. But I didn't take that seriously." Asked why not, Koch responded, "I assumed if there was any prospect of it being illegal, that he would have stopped it. I mean, you know, he became Secretary, put his hand on a Bible, and swore to uphold the laws of the land, and I thought that was an ironclad guarantee, so I think, since he didn't leave, I assumed it was legal." Koch, *Joint Hearings*, vol. 100-6, June 23, 1987, p. 76.

55. "Finding Pursuant to Section 662 . . . , Scope: Iran," January 17, 1986.

56. Poindexter memorandum, "Covert Action Finding Regarding Iran," January 17, 1986; Reagan, *The Reagan Diaries*, entry for Friday, January 17, 1986, p. 563.

57. Quoted in Timberg, *The Nightingale's Song*, p. 448.

58. Ron Reagan, *My Father at 100: A Memoir* (New York: Viking, 2011), pp. 205, 218.

59. Twetten's name was excised from the *Tower Report* and all congressional documentation, including his own deposition. He is referred to as "C/NE"—Chief/Near East—although he was not promoted to chief until April 1986. Press accounts later reported his identity, and the *OIC Final Report* refers to him by name throughout. Clair George's name appears uncensored throughout the Iran-Contra investigation.

60. As noted in Chapter 3, Richard Secord was widely mistrusted for his alleged involvement with disgraced CIA operative Ed Wilson. For his part, Secord disparaged agency officials as "shoe salesmen." See Clair George, *Joint Hearings*, vol. 100-11, August 6, 1987, p. 267.

61. Colin Powell, interview with James Brosnahan, November 5, 1992. U.S. National Archives and Records Administration, RG 449: "Records of Independent Counsels," "Records of IC Lawrence Walsh," Folder: "Powell, Colin (1)," p. 8.

62. Central Intelligence Agency, author and subject censored, memorandum to chief of Near East division (likely Bert Dunn), January 13, 1986. See also *OIC Final Report*, vol. I, p. 209, fn. 59.

63. Central Intelligence Agency, routing and record sheet, "Ghorbanifar Polygraph Examination," January 13, 1986.

64. Thomas M. Barksdale, memorandum to deputy director for intelligence, "The Iranian Imbroglio: Implications for the Intelligence Process," December 2, 1986.

65. Charles Allen, Select Committees' deposition, vol. B-1, pp. 547, 575; *Select Committees' Report*, pp. 201, 205.

66. Israeli Historical Chronology, Part II, pp. 22–23.

67. John McMahon, cable to William Casey, "Present Status in Saga Regarding the Movement of TOW Missiles," January 25, 1986.

68. Thomas Twetten, quoted in Blight et al., *Becoming Enemies*, p. 146.

69. North notebooks (FOIA release), January 22, 1986. For an excellent analysis of connections between the Iran arms deals and the Soviet occupation of Afghanistan, see James G. Hershberg, "The War in Afghanistan and the Iran-Contra Affair: Missing Links?" *Cold War History* 3, no. 3 (April 2003): 23–48.

70. The congressional select committees found no proof U.S. Army officials intentionally lowered the price. *Select Committees' Report*, p. 215.

71. Ibid., pp. 213–217.

72. Secord credits North with the remark. See *Honored and Betrayed*, p. 229.

73. North, *Joint Hearings*, vol. 100-7, Part I, July 8, 1987, p. 116.

74. Israeli Historical Chronology, Part I, pp. 55–56, citing notes taken by one of the Israelis present; see also Secord, *Joint Hearings*, vol. 100-2, July 8, 1987, pp. 95–96. Whether the Israelis actually made such a generous offer to the U.S. participants is an open question. Secord's account in his memoir differs from his congressional testimony. He writes that Nir, not North, personally told him at the January 22 meeting (i.e., not in December) before the session with Ghorbanifar, "Those are your funds. Keep them. That was a commercial undertaking." Secord, *Honored and Betrayed*, pp. 242–243. The secret Israeli government chronology reports that on December 3, 1985, Secord told an Israeli Ministry of Defense official "he had already paid the $1 million he had received from Nimrodi," apparently referring to the transfer made to Lake Resources on November 20. Israeli Historical Chronology, Part I, p. 55.

75. North, *Joint Hearings*, vol. 100-7, Part I, July 8, 1987, p. 109.

76. Ibid.

77. Oliver North, tape recording of meeting, January 22, 1986, quoted in *Select Committees' Report*, p. 216. Hassan Karoubi's name is consistently censored from official reports of the scandal; as noted elsewhere, the congressional committees identified him as the "first Iranian."

78. Ibid.

79. Ibid., pp. 108–109; North notebooks (FOIA release), January 27, 1986, AMX000934, among other entries, refers to one of the code-named projects, "TH-1." It is also mentioned in a later context in the *Select Committees' Report*, p. 226.

80. Charles Allen, Select Committees' deposition, vol. B-1, p. 603. The other CIA official's name is excised in the deposition, but it was probably Tom Twetten, mentioned earlier by his title, deputy chief of the Near East division.

81. Twetten later called the notion "ludicrous" and "just Ghorbanifar nonsense." "C/NE," Select Committees' deposition, vol. B-5, p. 909.

82. Israeli Historical Chronology, Part II, p. 26; *Select Committees' Report*, p. 217.

83. The Israeli Historical Chronology says the unmarked Israeli aircraft picked up the HAWKs in Tehran after dropping off the TOWs (p. 27).

84. North notebooks (FOIA release), January 13, 1986, AMX000896 (misdated 1985), list as one of the requirements for the operation that "1st plane must deliver 'flashy' intelligence." See also Israeli Historical Chronology, Part II, pp. 24–25.

85. See Chapters 4 and 6 of this book.

86. Israeli Historical Chronology, Part II, pp. 29–30; Hakim, *Joint Hearings*, vol. 100-5, June 3, 1987, p. 225; Secord, *Joint Hearings*, vol. 100-1, May 6, 1987, p. 90; North notebooks (FOIA release), December 1, 1985, AMX 001914.

87. Quoted in *Select Committees' Report*, p. 219.

88. See Richard Secord, coded message to Oliver North, reproduced (with slight differences) in both the *Tower Report*, pp. B-77–B-78, and *Select Committees' Report*, pp. 219–220. See also Oliver North, PROFS message to Robert McFarlane, "How Are Things?" February 27, 1986, 08:54 a.m., also quoted at length in the *Select Committees' Report*, p. 220.

89. See Chapter 4, n. 40, of this book.

90. George Cave, Select Committees' deposition, vol. B-3, pp. 886–888.

Chapter 9: Air Contra

1. John Poindexter, *Joint Hearings*, vol. 100-8, July 20, 1987, pp. 226–227.

2. See the discussion in *OIC Final Report*, vol. I, p. 449.

3. Ronald Reagan, testimony at John Poindexter trial, February 16, 1990, p. 122.

4. The congressional Iran-Contra report dates the finding January 17, but a declassified version of the document signed by President Reagan bears the January 9 date. See *Select Committees' Report*, p. 64; see also the report's Appendix A, vol. 2, pp. 1161–1162.

5. National Security Council meeting, "Review of US Policy in Central America," January 10, 1986.

6. Ibid.

7. Ibid. The congressional report suggested Casey manipulated intelligence on the Contras' precarious position to push for a particular policy. The report cites a January 8 CIA Special Analysis that included contradictory views and a set of notes taken by an agency official at an "NSC Pre-Brief" the day before the NSC meeting that indicate "DCI wants to make the insurgency choice stark—either we go all out to support them or they'll go down the drain." *Select Committees' Report*, p. 382, and Appendix A, vol. 2, pp. 1058 and 1064.

8. National Security Council meeting, "Review of US Policy in Central America," January 10, 1986.

9. Ibid.

10. Ibid.

11. Ibid.

12. Ibid.

13. Ibid.

14. Ibid.

15. Central Intelligence Agency, "Team Interview of Alan Fiers," December 2, 1986, p. 20.

16. Ibid.

17. Robert Owen, memorandum to Oliver North, "Political and Military Report from Trip," November 26, 1985.

18. National Security Council meeting, "Review of US Policy in Central America," January 10, 1986.

19. U.S. Department of State, memorandum to Donald Gregg, cited in North trial stipulation, April 6, 1989, paragraph 79.

20. George Bush told investigators he did not remember the talking points but added, "I can't deny I received the card." Asked if he recalled whether the subject came up with Azcona at any point, he replied, "I don't specifically but it might well have." See Bush deposition, North trial, January 11, 1988, pp. 105–107.

21. "For years we've been begging you for surface-to-air missiles," North quoted the Hondurans as saying earlier in 1985. "Now you're sending them to the contras. Why don't you have any for us?" North, *Under Fire*, p. 260.

22. North trial stipulation, April 6, 1989, paragraph 95.

23. Robert Owen, memorandum to UNO/NHAO, December 20, 1985.

24. Central Intelligence Agency, Special Analysis, "Nicaragua: Resupply Problems for Insurgents," January 8, 1986.

25. *Washington Post*, January 22, 1986.

26. *OIC Final Report*, vol. I, p. 490.

27. Robert Owen, memorandum to Oliver North, "Update," February 10, 1986.

28. North, *Under Fire*, p. 256.

29. *OIC Final Report*, vol. I, p. 6.

30. Felix Rodriguez, testimony at Clair George trial, August 4, 1992, p. 1912.

31. Lewis Tambs, *Joint Hearings*, vol. 100-3, May 28, 1987, p. 409.

32. See Central Intelligence Agency Office of Inspector General views in Joseph Fernandez, interview, April 24, 1987, p. 12.

33. Robert Owen, memorandum to Oliver North (TC to BG), "Trip Report," March 28, 1986.

34. Afterward, Calero called the session "very profitable and very encouraging towards unity," and the *New York Times* described it as "especially significant because the two groups had been divided by factional differences and have now promised to work together in the fight against the Nicaraguan Government." Elliott Abrams testified later he disagreed with the CIA's and North's "extremely shortsighted view" of Pastora. *New York Times*, March 8, 1986; Abrams, *Joint Hearings*, vol. 100-5, June 2, 1987, pp. 27, 29.

35. The text of the agreement is in an untitled one-page document dated March 26, 1986. It also appears in a CIA cable sent on the same date from the San José station, entitled "Pastora/Singlaub Agreement." Lewis Tambs ordered the CIA deputy station chief to send the cable instead of going through normal State Department channels, apparently his standard practice when reporting on sensitive Contra issues. See Tambs, *Joint Hearings*, vol. 100-3, May 28, 1987,

pp. 386–387, 388, 390. John Singlaub testified to discussing Pastora with Abrams prior to his trip to Costa Rica to meet the ARDE leader. Singlaub, *Joint Hearings*, vol. 100-3, May 20, 1987, p. 92. He also wrote about the subject in his memoir. *Hazardous Duty*, p. 486. Abrams testified he did not meet with Singlaub until late April. *Joint Hearings*, vol. 100-5, June 2, 1987, p. 27.

36. Cable traffic between Fiers and the U.S. Embassy in Costa Rica dated March 27 and 28, 1986, quoted in *OIC Final Report*, vol. I, p. 273.

37. The first quote is from "Remarks at a White House Meeting for Supporters of United States Assistance for the Nicaraguan Democratic Resistance," March 3, 1986, public papers of Ronald Reagan, available on the University of Texas website, http://www.reagan.utexas.edu /archives/speeches/1986/30386a.htm. The second quote is from "Remarks to Jewish Leaders during a White House Briefing on United States Assistance for the Nicaraguan Democratic Resistance," March 5, 1986. Available on Gerhard Peters and John T. Woolley, American Presidency Project website, http://www.presidency.ucsb.edu/ws/?pid=36953.

38. Ronald Reagan: "Address to the Nation on the Situation in Nicaragua," March 16, 1986. Available on Gerhard Peters and John T. Woolley, American Presidency Project website, http:// www.presidency.ucsb.edu/ws/?pid=36999.

39. Reagan, *The Reagan Diaries*, entry for Tuesday, April 8, 1986, p. 587.

40. National Security Council meeting, "Subject: Aid to the Nicaraguan Democratic Resistance," March 20, 1986.

41. *New York Times*, March 21, 1986.

42. National Security Council meeting, "Subject: Aid to the Nicaraguan Democratic Resistance," March 20, 1986.

43. Alan Fiers's and investigators' quotes are in the *OIC Final Report*, vol. I, p. 6.

44. See Thomas R. Johnson, National Security Agency Center for Cryptologic History, "The NSA Period, 1952–Present," *United States Cryptologic History, Series VI*, vol. 5, "American Cryptology during the Cold War, 1945–1989," Book IV, "Cryptologic Rebirth, 1981–1989" (CCH-S54-99-01, 1999), Chapter 25. (A redacted version of this top-secret code-word history was obtained by Bill Burr of the National Security Archive under the Freedom of Information Act.)

45. See Rafael Quintero, testimony at Oliver North trial, March 2, 1989, pp. 2930–2934.

46. Oliver North, KL-43 message to Richard Secord, early April 1986 (less excised versions quoted in *OIC Final Report*, vol. I, p. 274; *Select Committees' Report*, p. 66 [see Chapter 1, note 66]).

47. Richard Secord, KL-43 message to Oliver North, ca. April 10, 1986, 14:50.

48. Richard Secord, *Joint Hearings*, vol. 100-1, May 5, 1987, p. 64.

49. Central Intelligence Agency, cable, January 25, 1986, quoted in *OIC Final Report*, vol. I, p. 265.

50. North notes (Select Committee extracts), January 6, 1986; *OIC Final Report*, vol. I, p. 265.

51. Central Intelligence Agency, cable traffic from February 6–7, 1986, quoted in *OIC Final Report*, vol. I, p. 266.

52. Central Intelligence Agency, cable, February 14, 1986; Oliver North, KL-43 message to Richard Secord, both cited in *OIC Final Report*, vol. I, pp. 302–303.

53. Richard Secord, grand jury testimony; KL-43 message; Federal Bureau of Investigation 302 report, quoted in *OIC Final Report*, vol. I, pp. 395, 397; Richard Gadd, Select Committees' deposition, vol. B-11, May 1, 1987, pp. 36–39; Felix I. Rodriguez and John Weisman, *Shadow Warrior* (New York: Pocket Books, 1989), p. 296.

54. Steele's comment as recalled by the U.S. embassy's deputy chief of mission, David B. Dlouhy, in *OIC Final Report*, vol. I, p. 400.

55. Edwin Corr's notes as early as February 1986 reflect his awareness of the involvement of

North and others in Nicaragua in violation of the second Boland Amendment restrictions, and more specifically his interest in becoming "in effect . . . 'desk officer' [on the] Contra question." Corr notes, quoted in ibid., vol. I, p. 395. For his part, Steele claimed to be unaware of the Boland II terms. During Steele's Iran-Contra deposition, a congressional lawyer asked: "With regard to the Boland question, so to speak—at some point somebody at the Defense Department must have informed you in some way, shape or form" about the limits on U.S. aid to the Contras. Steele replied, "Nobody, the simple fact is nobody did." The incredulous attorney responded, "If that's a fact, say it. That's alright. But, it's all hard for me to appreciate that." Steele, Select Committees' deposition, vol. B-26, p. 422.

56. Felix Rodriquez, *Joint Hearings*, vol. 100-3, May 27, 1987, p. 298.

57. See Donald Gregg to Debbie Hutton, Schedule Proposal, "Purpose: To brief the Vice President on the status of the war in El Salavador [*sic*] and resupply of the Contras," April 16, 1986. For a comparison of various versions of events, see *OIC Final Report*, vol. I, pp. 491–493. Office of the Independent Council investigators determined Gregg's secretary got the phrase from Samuel Watson, who denied it but whose truthfulness on this and other matters investigators believed suspect. For Gregg's and Watson's replies to the allegations against them, see ibid., vol. III, pp. 309–318, 943–950.

58. Mixter, *Bush Criminal Liability*, March 21, 1991, pp. 40–41. See also Elliott Abrams, grand jury testimony, referred to in *OIC Final Report*, vol. I, p. 497.

Chapter 10: Road to Tehran

1. Shimon Peres, letter to Ronald Reagan, February 28, 1986; Israeli Historical Chronology, Part II, p. 34.

2. Israeli Historical Chronology, Part II, p. 36; Thomas Twetten on Oliver North, quoted in Blight et al., *Becoming Enemies*, p. 133. See also North, PROFS note to Robert McFarlane, "How's It Going?" March 11, 1986, 07:23: "We wd do well to explore other contacts if they can be opened [passage excised]." Apparently referring to existing Central Intelligence Agency channels, North continues, "George [Cave] is going to see what we have on this so that we can assess whether or not it wd be useful to make such an approach."

3. George Cave, interview with the author, September 4, 2007.

4. Israeli Historical Chronology, Part II, pp. 35–36. In fact, Iran's inventory of HAWK missiles and spare parts had almost run out, forcing the head of the country's air defense operations to order HAWK systems defending the capital to be temporarily shut down. Hassan Rouhani, interview in *Hamshahri*, "Untold Stories of the Eight-Year Sacred Defense," trans. Hussein Banai, September 24, 2008.

5. George Cave, memorandum, undated, *Joint Hearings*, Exhibit OLN-289. Other released versions of this memo have the reference to Afghanistan excised.

6. Ghorbanifar specifically referred to two Iranian officials in addition to Mousavi—Karoubi and Farassi. Both appear in North's notes under "Line 2," the "moderate" faction in Khashoggi's analysis. Karoubi, therefore, was probably Hassan Karoubi, already known to the U.S. and Israeli team, who appears under Khashoggi's second category. Hassan's brother, Mehdi, then deputy speaker of the Majles and head of the powerful and virtually independent Martyr's Fund, is listed by Khashoggi under the third line, neither moderate nor radical. (In 2009, Mehdi Karoubi and Mousavi would run unsuccessfully for president of Iran as reform candidates.) Farassi, North's notes read, was a leading cleric in the revolution. See North notebooks (FOIA

release), April 3, 1986, AMX001052, and the less excised version transcribed by the joint congressional committees, which reveals Karoubi's and Farassi's names. Cave's notes of the Paris meeting of March 7 also refer to an Ayatollah Farassi. *Joint Hearings*, Exhibit OLN-289.

7. See the discussion in *Select Committees' Report*, p. 225; see also George Cave, "Eyewitness to 'Irangate': Why Secret 1986 U.S.-Iran 'Arms for Hostages' Negotiations Failed," *Washington Report on Middle East Affairs* 13, no. 3 (September–October 1994): 8, 89.

8. For detailed rundowns of the accounting from different perspectives, see *OIC Final Report*, vol. I, p. 169; Israeli Financial Chronology, pp. 9–11; Israeli Historical Chronology, Part II, pp. 38–39.

9. Oliver North, memorandum, "Release of American Hostages in Beirut," undated, ca. April 4, 1986; see also North, *Joint Hearings*, vol. 100-7, Part I, July 8, 1987, pp. 107–110.

10. For a forceful argument on the issue, see generally Louis Fisher, *Presidential War Power* (Lawrence: University Press of Kansas, 2004).

11. Oliver North, *Joint Hearings*, vol. 100-7, Part I, July 8, 1987, p. 109.

12. Ibid., p. 124.

13. John Poindexter, PROFS note to Oliver North, "Iran," April 3, 1986, 12:57.

14. Charles Hill, notes, quoted in *OIC Final Report*, vol. I, p. 339. As before, Hill referred to North and the Iran operation by the derisive term "Polecat"; at some point he began to number the Polecat entries in his notes with Roman numerals.

15. Nicholas Platt, notes, May 8, 1986, quoted in ibid., vol. I, p. 340. The *OIC Final Report* cites several other examples from Platt and Charles Hill's notes that indicate Shultz heard repeatedly about the unfolding events leading to the Tehran trip.

16. John Poindexter, interview with the author, January 14, 2013.

17. During the 1987 congressional hearings, Shultz described his knowledge of the initiative as minimal, but the independent counsel's report lists several examples based on contemporaneous evidence and later testimony of access by Shultz or his assistants to information derived from intercepts. See *OIC Final Report*, vol. I, p. 341, fn. 123.

18. Robert B. Oakley, memorandum to Nicholas Platt, "Efforts to Free US Hostages in Lebanon," June 2, 1986.

19. Robert B. Oakley, interview with Charles Stuart Kennedy and Thomas Stern, Association for Diplomatic Studies and Training Foreign Affairs Oral History Project, http://memory.loc .gov/cgi-bin/query/D?mfdip:4:./temp/~ammem_rhFT::. Shultz was equivocal in testimony about his recollections of Oakley's memo, but the document's forceful language and Oakley's stature as well as that of Michael Armacost, the undersecretary for political affairs, and Arnold Raphel, deputy assistant secretary for the Near East, make it improbable their warnings would have failed to reach the secretary. Oakley never received a response.

20. Colin L. Powell with Joseph E. Persico, *My American Journey* (New York: Random House, 2003), p. 297.

21. Caspar Weinberger, notes, May 13, 1986; intercepts cited in *OIC Final Report*, vol. I, pp. 340–341.

22. North notebooks (FOIA release), March 28, 1986, AMX001039.

23. John Poindexter, PROFS note to Oliver North, "Private Blank Check," April 16, 1986, 19:02.

24. See court papers from the so-called Evans-Bar-Am case, U.S. District Court for the Southern District of New York, cited in Scott Armstrong, Malcolm Byrne, and Tom Blanton, *The Chronology: The Documented Day-by-Day Account of the Secret Military Assistance to Iran and the Contras* (New York: Warner Books, 1987), pp. 347–349. See also Charles Hill, notes from

April 24, 1986, cited in *OIC Final Report*, vol. I, p. 340; Charles Allen deposition, cited in *Select Committees' Report*, p. 226.

25. The Libya raid threw another wrench into the plans for Tehran. Shortly after the attack, North received orders to report back to full-time duty with the U.S. Marine Corps. This followed a death threat he said he received from the notorious terrorist Abu Nidal following the Libya raid. Rather than accept a permanent change of station (PCS) off the NSC staff, North asked John Poindexter to "please call either SecDef or SecNav or [Marine Corps Commandant] Gen. [P.X.] Kelley to advise them that North will not be detached from the NSC." North went on, "The incredible answer to the current Abu Nidal threat is to immediately PCS North to Camp Lejeune, N.C. . . . It wd be best for you or the President to do this—if it is indeed what you want." North received his wish. See North, PROFS note to Poindexter, "Private Blank Check," May 6, 1986, 00:19.

26. North notebooks (FOIA release), May 6, 1986, AMX001096, AMX001100.

27. See George Cave, Select Committees' deposition, vol. B-3, pp. 628–629. The *Select Committees' Report* describes the supposed Cave-Kangarlou agreement in more precise terms, saying that after the first load of spares arrived, "an Iranian delegation would be dispatched to Lebanon to barter for the release of the hostages." The only source for the paragraph in which this appears is the Israeli Historical Chronology, but the relevant passages there (pp. 40–41) make no reference to this part of the agreement.

28. Oliver North, PROFS note to John Poindexter, "Iran," May 8, 1986, 08:07.

29. The Tiny Rowlands affair caused some further ripples for the operation after the Briton contacted the U.S. embassy in London to verify what he had been told by Amiram Nir and the others. Shultz soon got wind of the story and angrily confronted Poindexter, who told him there was only a "smidgen" of truth to it. Poindexter later testily wrote to North: "What in the hell is Nir doing? We really can't trust those SOB's." Poindexter, PROFS note to North, "Iran," May 3, 1986, 06:59. See also Israeli Financial Chronology, pp. 25–27.

30. This aspect of the financing also generated confusion and problems. Later in the year, after delays in getting repaid, the two Canadians reportedly threatened Casey through a mutual acquaintance, Roy Furmark, to expose the operation if they did not receive their due. Later still, Khashoggi claimed he had invented the loan by the Canadians to put pressure on Washington, a claim accepted by some observers afterward. However, the independent counsel's report eventually confirmed Vertex International, among other corporate entities, had indeed been involved. (Various details of the transaction, and the alleged deception by Khashoggi, appear in the depositions of Furmark and Donald Fraser; in Draper, *A Very Thin Line*, pp. 449–450; in the *New York Times*, March 10, 1987; and in the *OIC Final Report*, vol. I, p. 169.)

31. Howard Teicher, who was "volunteered" for the trip, understood his role to be providing analytical expertise, taking notes, and other "substantive staff" support to McFarlane, for whom he had worked in the past. Teicher and Teicher, *Twin Pillars*, pp. 363–366.

32. Ibid., p. 365; Secord, *Honored and Betrayed*, p. 3; McFarlane, *Special Trust*, p. 55; North, *Under Fire*, p. 36; Draper, *A Very Thin Line*, pp. 313–314 (including the statement, without citation, McFarlane "was prevailed on to carry a poison pill to be used if he was tortured"); *Select Committees' Report*, p. 243, fn. 11.

33. Former Iranian deputy foreign minister, interview with the author, September 5, 2007. In North's retelling, a brass key from one of the pistol presentation boxes fell into the cake's chocolate icing during the flight to Tehran and made such a deep indentation he decided to leave it there in hopes Ghorbanifar's mother would think it was part of the decoration. McFarlane saw the cake as nothing more than the "sort of sophomoric prank Ollie would enjoy . . .

but I told him that I wanted no part of it." See North, *Under Fire*, pp. 41–42; McFarlane, *Special Trust*, p. 56.

34. Ghordatollah Rahmani, *Direct with Hashemi Rafsanjani*, trans. Mahsa Rouhi (Tehran: Keyhan, 2003).

35. U.S. officials believed Mehdinejad ran intelligence for the Islamic Revolutionary Guard Corps (IRGC); Mohsen Rezaie, the IRGC former commander, identified him later as the deputy chief. Rezaie, interview with Fars News Agency, trans. Hussein Banai, September 22, 2008. The director general of the European and North American affairs section of the Iranian Foreign Ministry also reportedly met with the group at one point, although he is not identified in official U.S. accounts. Former Iranian deputy foreign minister, interview with the author, September 5, 2007.

36. The Israeli Historical Chronology identifies Mustafavi. However, the known deputy prime ministers at the time were Hadi Manafi, Hamid Mirzadeh, and Ali Reza Mo'ayeri. See also George Cave, Select Committees' deposition, vol. B-3, p. 884; Albert Hakim, *Joint Hearings*, vol. 100-5, June 3, 1987, pp. 288–289. North's notes for late July 1986, relating to the release of Father Lawrence Jenco, contain several references to the name "Vahaidi," including the following: "Vahaidi = Mustavavi-Najavi," which seems to indicate Vahaidi may have been Mustafavi's (or Mustafavi-Najafi's) real name. North notebooks (FOIA release), July 27, 1986, AMX001357.

37. The principal contemporaneous sources on the May 25 meeting are Howard Teicher, National Security Council, "U.S.-Iran Dialogue," May 25, 1986, 5:15 p.m. (the first in Teicher's series of memoranda of conversation covering talks in Tehran); George Cave, untitled and undated memo, ca. May 30, 1986 (the version reprinted as fn. 24 in Chapter 13 of the *Select Committees' Report* is less excised than Cave's Select Committees' deposition exhibit, which appears in vol. B-3, pp. 999–1003); North's notebooks (FOIA release), AMX001128–1134. See also Israeli Historical Chronology, Part II, p. 44.

38. Akbar Hashemi Rafsanjani, memoir excerpt, trans. Hussein Banai, reprinted in *Jomhouriyat* (Tehran) 1, no. 20 (April 19, 2009).

39. Ibid.

40. George Cave, untitled and undated "account of the U.S. mission to Tehran," ca. May 30, 1986. See also Malcolm Byrne, "Mixed Messages: U.S. Intelligence Support to Both Sides during the Iran-Iraq War," paper delivered at the conference "The Iran-Iraq War: The View from Baghdad," Woodrow Wilson International Center for Scholars, October 27, 2011.

41. Quotations are taken from the next in Teicher's series of memoranda, National Security Council, memorandum of conversation, "U.S.-Iran Dialogue," May 26, 1986, 3:30 p.m.

42. See Israeli Historical Chronology, Part II, p. 47. Official U.S. accounts of the initiative refer to Najafabadi as the "Adviser."

43. Rafsanjani, memoir excerpt, reprinted in *Jomhouriyat*. After Hassan Rouhani's election to the presidency in 2013, some U.S. press accounts erred in reporting he had met with the McFarlane delegation. See, for example, *New York Times*, July 27, 2013. After this author questioned the assertion, the *Times* rechecked its sources and attributed the statement to unnamed Iranian officials, adding Rouhani's presence "could not be confirmed independently." See *New York Times* "Corrections," December 21, 2013. However, Rafsanjani's memoirs, the Israeli Historical Chronology, North and Weinberger's notes, and interviews with Cave and Iranian ex-officials (all predating Rouhani's election by several years) consistently indicate the official in question was Najafabadi, not Rouhani. Howard Teicher, who is quoted in one account (www.foreignpolicy .com, September 26, 2013) as confirming Rouhani had been there, later clarified there was no firm evidence placing him at meetings with the group. Teicher, interview with the author, October 8, 2013.

44. The same concerns apparently applied to relations with the Soviets. Later in the conversation, Najafabadi told the group: "After [the] death of Brezhnev, Iran sent a delegation. The leadership was attacked by the nation for this act. No one went out to Chernenko's funeral."

45. For accounts of this meeting, see primarily Teicher, National Security Council, memorandum of conversation, "U.S.-Iran Dialogue," May 26, 1986, 9:30 p.m.; George Cave, untitled and undated notes, ca. May 30, 1986.

46. Rafsanjani, memoir excerpt, reprinted in *Jomhouriyat*; Rouhani interview in *Hamshahri*, "Untold Stories of the Eight-Year Sacred Defense"; Ghordatollah Rahmani, *Direct with Hashemi Rafsanjani*.

47. Robert McFarlane, message to John Poindexter, untitled May 27, 1986, early morning Tehran time. Reproduced in *Select Committees' Report*, Appendix A, vol. 1, pp. 1252–1254. Certain words are indistinct in the document, and someone has attempted to clarify (or perhaps alter) the original by inserting text by hand. In the *Tower Report* the description of the "surviving . . . vice president" is given as "Tatar" (p. B-101). However, in the narrative of the *Select Committees' Report* it is "tailor" (p. 238), and in McFarlane's memoir, he has substituted "cobbler." See *Special Trust*, p. 58.

48. Robert McFarlane, message to John Poindexter, untitled, May 27, 1986.

49. Teicher, National Security Council, memorandum of conversation, "U.S.-Iran Dialogue," May 27, 1986, 10:00 a.m.

50. Ibid.

51. Robert McFarlane, message to John Poindexter, untitled, May 27, 1986, afternoon.

52. Ibid.

53. Ibid.

54. Cave interview, September 4, 2007.

55. Teicher, National Security Council, Memorandum of Conversation, "U.S.-Iran Dialogue," May 27, 1986, 5:00 p.m.

56. Ibid.

57. Ibid.

58. Untitled draft agreement, see *Select Committees' Report*, pp. 240–241; Teicher, National Security Council, memorandum of conversation, "U.S.-Iran Dialogue," May 27, 1986, 9:30 p.m.

59. Teicher notes, reprinted in *OIC Final Report*, vol. I, p. 96, fn. 155.

60. The aircraft eventually did take off from Tel Aviv (Nir puts the time at 6:00 a.m.), but it was ordered to return well before reaching Iranian air space. See Israeli Historical Chronology, Part II, p. 56. In their congressional testimony, McFarlane and North gave differing accounts of the decision to launch the plane. Both contended North gave the order to Secord; North said he was following the original plan, but McFarlane claimed not to have learned about North's actions until afterward. See *OIC Final Report*, vol. I, p. 96, fn. 155. Neither mentioned McFarlane's communications with the White House in the early morning hours of May 28.

61. Cave, interview with the author September 4, 2007. Cave added, "I'll go to my grave before I tell anyone how I got them to refuel it." Charles Allen, Cave's colleague at the CIA, later expressed doubt about the mob story. Allen, interview with the author, January 9, 2013.

62. Robert McFarlane's quotes are from Teicher, National Security Council, memorandum of conversation, "U.S.-Iran Dialogue," May 28, 1986, 7:50 a.m. Cave described the approaching mob and the ride to the airport in interviews with the author; see also the story in the *Independent* from Nicosia, Cyprus, as reported by the Associated Press, November 7, 1986; Cave, "Eyewitness to 'Irangate,'" pp. 8, 89.

63. Ali Bahramani, interview with *Shahrvand Emrooz*, trans. Hussein Banai, June 19, 2008.

64. George Cave, untitled memorandum describing Tehran mission, ca. May 30, 1986,

65. Robert McFarlane, message to John Poindexter, untitled, May 27, 1986, afternoon.

66. McFarlane, *Special Trust*, p. 63.

67. George Cave, Select Committees' deposition, vol. B-3, p. 834.

68. Cave, interview with the author, June 23, 2009.

69. Charles Allen, memorandum to William Casey, "Comments on the Ghorbanifar Operation," May 5, 1986.

70. Giandomenico Picco, a former UN assistant secretary general who negotiated the freedom of several Western hostages from Lebanon in the 1990s and later became a hostage himself, was once scolded by one of his captors: "Would you stop talking to me as if we were Iranians? We are Lebanese!" Picco comments at Iran-Iraq War Workshop—2004, July 19, 2004, pp. 70–71.

71. For a detailed discussion of the Hezbollah-Iranian relationship, based in part on accounts by members of Hezbollah, see Ranstorp, *Hizb'Allah in Lebanon*, esp. Chapter 3.

72. In early 1987, a CIA witness at a House Select Iran-Contra Committee briefing testified: "Hezbollah clearly has contacts with Iran but . . . there is no information that Iran controls the organization, and moreover their agendas do not always run in tandem." The witness also added, "There was some disagreement over the degree of Iranian control/influence over Hezbollah." Memorandum for the record, "HSCICATI Briefing on Iran/Iraq War and Iranian Political Developments," February 10, 1987, p. 2. Differences on this question persist among U.S. intelligence experts. See, for example, Daniel Benjamin and Steven Simon, *The Age of Sacred Terror: Radical Islam's War against America* (New York: Random House, 2003), pp. 223–224.

73. Cave interview, September 4, 2007.

74. George Cave, comments at Iran-Iraq War Workshop—2004, July 19, 2004, pp. 70–71.

75. Israeli Historical Chronology, Part II, p. 55.

76. Oliver North, *Joint Hearings*, vol. 100-7, Part I, July 10, 1987, p. 295.

77. McFarlane, *Special Trust*, p. 58.

78. Robert McFarlane, message to John Poindexter, untitled, May 27, 1986, early morning Tehran time; Cave, untitled and undated memo, ca. May 30, 1986.

79. Reagan, *The Reagan Diaries*, entries for May 27 and 28, 1986, p. 603; Reagan, *An American Life*, pp. 520–521.

80. Teicher, National Security Council, memorandum of conversation, "U.S.-Iran Dialogue," May 29, 1986, 9:30 a.m. Cave agreed, insisting afterward several of the key officials with whom he had spoken favored better ties with Washington, even proposing in September the creation of a joint commission on ending the war and improving relations. Cave, "Eyewitness to 'Irangate,'" p. 8.

81. Reagan, *The Reagan Diaries*, entry for May 28, 1986, p. 603; Teicher, National Security Council, memorandum of conversation, "U.S.-Iran Dialogue," May 29, 1986, 9:30 a.m.; Robert McFarlane, quoted in *Tower Report*, p. B-127.

Chapter 11: Meltdown

1. Minutes of National Security Planning Group, "Subject: Central America," May 16, 1986. This document was kept classified in its entirety when the congressional Iran-Contra select committees released their final report. It was declassified in major part in 2006 through the Freedom of Information Act (FOIA), with further portions released in April 2009.

2. Shultz persisted, though he did not name anyone at the table: "I was assaulted by Jack Kemp in the Cabinet Room." Ibid. At the time, Kemp was a conservative Republican U.S. representative from New York.

3. Ibid.

4. Ibid.

5. Ibid.

6. Alan Fiers, testimony at Clair George trial, July 28, 1992, p. 1197.

7. Figures cited in *OIC Final Report*, vol. I, p. 169.

8. Oliver North, PROFS note to John Poindexter, "Iran and Terrorism," May 16, 1986, 19:29.

9. Robert Dutton, Select Committees' deposition, vol. B-9, p. 471.

10. An entry in North's notebooks a month after Dutton came on board suggests not all of these questions were resolved: "Call from Steele re: Dutton visit—Questions of Neutrality Act and probs. w/looking for official sanction." North notebooks (Select Committee extracts), June 5, 1986.

11. Robert Dutton, *Joint Hearings*, vol. 100-3, May 27, 1987, p. 209.

12. Ibid., p. 205.

13. Rafael Quintero, testimony at North trial, pp. 2957–2959.

14. *OIC Final Report*, vol. I, p. 164; *Select Committees' Report*, p. 68.

15. Robert Dutton, memorandum to Richard Secord, "How to Present the Reorganization to ACE," June 4, 1986.

16. Dutton, *Joint Hearings*, vol. 100-3, May 27, 1987, p. 212.

17. Francisco J. Alvarez, Select Committees' deposition, vol. B-1, p. 215.

18. Rafael Quintero, testimony at North trial, pp. 2916–2918, 2994–2995; also Dutton, *Joint Hearings*, vol. 100-3, May 27, 1987, p. 215.

19. Oliver North, PROFS note to John Poindexter, "Private Blank Check," June 10, 1986, 23:21:54.

20. Richard Secord, KL-43 message to Oliver North, June 12, 1986, 10:30.

21. Joseph Fernandez, interview with Central Intelligence Agency inspector general, January 24, 1986, p. 8. In the same interview, Fernandez recalled being shocked in fall 1985 when Abrams asked him about Point West. "I flipped out," he said, telling Abrams "only five people in this country" knew about the strip. Abrams replied, "We all know about it in Washington" (p. 4).

22. Ibid., p. 6.

23. North recorded the incident in his notes for August 6, 1986: "Wing fell off Maule last week." North notebooks (FOIA release), AMX001398.

24. Dutton, *Joint Hearings*, vol. 100-3, May 27, 1987, pp. 215–216; Dutton and North, KL-43 messages, June 17 and June 18, 1986.

25. Dutton, *Joint Hearings*, vol. 100-3, May 27, 1987, p. 217.

26. Quintero, testimony at North trial, pp. 2938–2939, 2943; Dutton, *Joint Hearings*, vol. 100-3, May 27, 1987, p. 216; Alvarez, Select Committees' deposition, vol. B-1, pp. 187ff., 194–195, 212.

27. James Steele, KL-43 message to Robert Dutton, untitled, August 18, 1986, *Joint Hearings*, Exhibit RCD-4; Dutton, *Joint Hearings*, vol. 100-3, May 27, 1987, pp. 226–227.

28. Brian Barger and Robert Parry, "FBI Reportedly Probes Contras on Drugs, Guns," Associated Press, April 10, 1986.

29. *Washington Post*, April 17, 1986.

30. John Poindexter, PROFS note to Oliver North, May 15, 1986; North, PROFS note to Poindexter, May 15, 1986.

31. North learned about the upcoming CBS broadcast from an NSC media liaison officer. The program was accurate in its essentials, exposing White House involvement in covert Contra aid, but after viewing it, North, without denying the basic facts, disparaged it to his colleague as "the single most distorted piece of reporting I have ever seen." Karna Small, PROFS note to North, date indistinct; North, PROFS note to Small, June 27, 1986, 12:52:41.

32. See *Select Committees' Report*, pp. 106–109.

33. John Poindexter, *Joint Hearings*, vol. 100-8, July 17, 1987, pp. 152–153.

34. Oliver North, PROFS note to John Poindexter, "President Azcona," September 17, 1986, 19:28:55; Peter Kornbluh, ed., *The Contras, Cocaine, and Covert Operations*, National Security Archive Electronic Briefing Book No. 2 (November 1996); *Washington Post*, May 29, 1994; *New York Times*, February 23, 1987; *Select Committees' Report*, pp. 109–110.

35. North, PROFS note to Poindexter, "President Azcona," September 18, 1986, 19:40:49. In the publicly released version of this document the entire section dealing with José Bueso Rosa is excised. North's quote appears in *Select Committees' Report*, p. 110.

36. Robert Owen, memorandum to Oliver North, "Recent Trip," April 7, 1986.

37. Glenn Robinette, Select Committees' deposition, vol. B-23, pp. 624–625.

38. Robert Owen, memorandum to Oliver North (TC to William), "Recent Trip," April 7, 1986.

39. Oliver B. Revell, Select Committees' deposition, vol. B-22, p. 968.

40. The judge said there was insufficient evidence to prove the existence of a criminal racketeering enterprise or a tie to the La Penca bombing. Avirgan called the ruling absurd. *Sun Sentinel* (Ft. Lauderdale, Fla.), June 24, 1988.

41. Robert Dutton, handwritten note, ca. June 8–10, 1986.

42. Dutton, *Joint Hearings*, vol. 100-3, May 27, 1987, p. 220.

43. North, *Under Fire*, p. 249.

44. Luis Posada Cariles (alias Ramon Medina) was an ex-CIA asset linked to several bombings in Cuba and the 1976 downing of a Cuban passenger airliner. See Peter Kornbluh and Erin Maskell, "The CIA File on Luis Posada Cariles," National Security Archive Electronic Briefing Book No. 334, January 11, 2011, http://www2.gwu.edu/~nsarchiv/NSAEBB/NSAEBB334/

45. Dutton, handwritten note, ca. June 8–10, 1986.

46. *Select Committees' Report*, p. 72.

47. Dutton, *Joint Hearings*, vol. 100-3, May 27, 1987, p. 220.

48. Ibid., p. 217.

49. "PRT-250 Conversation," August 6, 1986, quoted in *OIC Final Report*, vol. I, p. 267.

50. Donald Gregg, Select Committees' deposition, vol. B-12, p. 1058.

51. Felix Rodriguez, Select Committees' deposition, vol. B-23, pp. 793–803.

52. Fiers had always considered that prospect a vain hope at best. His superior, George, told Congress he would not have considered buying Secord's aircraft "if they were the last three planes in Central America." *OIC Final Report*, vol. I, pp. 267–268, fn. 23; *Select Committees' Report*, p. 73.

53. North notebooks (FOIA release), September 30, 1986, AMX001536.

54. Donald Gregg, Select Committees' deposition, vol. B-12, pp. 1077, 1082. A serious question also surfaced as to whether Gregg knew about the Contra-related operation well before August 1986. Almost a year earlier, on September 10, 1985, North wrote in detail about a meeting on the resupply operation that apparently included both a key U.S. military operative in El Salvador and the vice president's close aide: "1630—Mtg w/Jim Steele/Don Gregg." All three participants either claimed no memory of the session or disputed the accuracy of the notes. The independent counsel thought Steele's belief that the three did not discuss the resupply "seemed credible." But prosecutors also pointed out Steele failed a polygraph question "that squarely addressed Gregg's attendance" at the meeting. See North notebooks (FOIA release), September 10, 1985, AMX001726; *OIC Final Report*, vol. I, pp. 488–489, including fn. 42.

55. Rodriguez, *Joint Hearings*, vol. 100-3, May 27, 1987, p. 306. North said he did not recall the conversation. *Joint Hearings*, vol. 100-7, Part I, July 7, 1987, p. 48.

56. Robert McFarlane, PROFs note to John Pointdexter, "Odds and Ends," June 10, 1986.

57. Responding to a *Miami Herald* reporter about the hospitalization story, which sourced "several of North's fellow officers," North said, "I'm not going to confirm. I'm not going to deny. I'm not going to comment." His attorney said only, "I cannot talk to you about it." *Miami Herald*, December 23, 1986.

58. Robert McFarlane, PROFs note to John Poindexter, "Odds and Ends," June 10, 1986.

59. *Newsweek*, July 13, 1987.

60. John Poindexter, PROFS note to Robert McFarlane, "Odds and Ends," ca. June 11, 1986.

61. North, PROFS note to Poindexter, "Private Blank Check," June 10, 1986, 23:21:54.

62. *Washington Times*, July 15, 1986.

63. Oliver North, PROFS note to John Poindexter, "Private Blank Check," July 15, 1986, 12:21:30.

64. John Poindexter, PROFS note to Oliver North, "Private Blank Check," July 15, 1986.

65. The figures presented here are from *OIC Final Report*, vol. I, pp. 193–197.

66. Ibid.

67. Ibid.; Select Committees' chart displayed for television audience; see also North, *Under Fire*, pp. 272–273.

68. Robinette, *Joint Hearings*, vol. 100-6, June 23, 1987, pp. 5ff.; *OIC Final Report*, vol. I, pp. 175–176. Robinette disputed the independent counsel's description of the job as installing a full "security fence." Response to independent counsel, November 26, 1993, *OIC Final Report*, vol. III, p. 795.

69. Revell, Select Committees' deposition, vol. B-22, p. 972.

70. The congressional committees confirmed through a document expert that the ball had been filed to make it look like letters had worn away over time. See Robinette, *Joint Hearings*, vol. 100-6, June 23, 1987, pp. 18–19; *Joint Hearings*, Exhibits 9A–B; North, *Joint Hearings*, vol. 100-7, Part I, July 8, 1987, pp. 131–134.

71. North, testimony at his trial, pp. 7145, 7149.

72. See *OIC Final Report,* vol. I, Chapter 9, for details.

73. Albert Hakim, *Joint Hearings*, vol. 100-5, June 3, 1987, pp. 271–272.

74. Minutes of National Security Planning Group, "Subject: Central America," May 16, 1986.

75. The change came in the form of an amendment to the December 1985 Intelligence Authorization Act.

76. North, PROFS note to Poindexter, June 10, 1986, 23:21:54.

77. Poindexter, PROFS note to North, "Private Blank Check," June 11, 1986.

78. Elliott Abrams, *Joint Hearings*, vol. 100-5, June 2, 1987, p. 49.

79. Instead of 386.430.22.1, Lake Resources' account at Credit Suisse bank, the funds went into an account numbered 368.430.22.1. A news report cited John Singlaub and two senior Swiss officials as saying the account belonged to Swiss businessman Bruce Rappaport, an associate of E. Robert Wallach, in turn a friend of Edwin Meese. The sources contended the deposit was "no accident." Rappaport denied to the independent counsel the account was his; prosecutors reported they were unable to identify the account holder. *Newsweek*, August 7, 1989; *OIC Final Report*, vol. I, p. 197.

80. George Shultz, cable to U.S. Embassy (Brunei), State 372184, "[Excised] Project," December 1, 1986.

81. Fiers reportedly thought Clair George meant only the Iran arms deals, not the Contra diversion. See generally *OIC Final Report,* vol. 1, Chapter 15.

82. John Poindexter, PROFS note to Donald Fortier, "Contra Project," May 2, 1986, 23:01:50.

83. This was most likely Benjamin Netanyahu, *Terrorism: How the West Can Win* (New York:

Farrar, Straus, and Giroux, 1986). Another inspiration, Poindexter reported, was a recent op-ed by conservative academic Daniel Pipes on the same subject.

84. Poindexter, PROFS note to Fortier, "Contra Project," May 2, 1986, 23:01:50.

85. The president did not follow all of Netanyahu's advice. In an interview at around the same time, the future Israeli leader declared: "Terrorists are bullies, they are cowards. When you are dealing with bullies, there is no substitute to standing up to the bully." "Benjamin Netanyahu: Standing Up to Terrorists," *Maclean's*, July 28, 1986.

86. See, for example, Stephen J. Markman, memorandum to Edwin Meese III, "Separation of Powers," April 30, 1986. National Archives and Records Administration, Record Group 60, General Records of the Department of Justice, Box 86, Component Correspondent Files of Attorney General Edwin Meese III, Folder: OLP (April–May 1986). Interestingly, Appendix A, "Summary of Reagan Administration Conflicts with Congress," lists twenty-one controversies, but only two deal with foreign affairs—the War Powers Resolution and the SALT treaties. The Boland Amendments are not mentioned. Nicaragua appears in a brief reference on p. 27, but in relation to the War Powers Resolution. The main body of the Markman memo is discussed in Charlie Savage, *Takeover: The Return of the Imperial Presidency and the Subversion of American Democracy* (New York: Little, Brown, 2007), p. 342, fn. 16.

87. North, PROFS note to Poindexter, "Contra Project," May 6, 1986, 00:04:05.

88. Ibid.

89. Ibid. North discusses the idea briefly in his memoir, noting "Militarily, it could have worked." *Under Fire*, pp. 275–276.

90. See, for example, Rodney B. McDaniel, PROFS note to Oliver North, "Contra Project," undated, forwarding note from Raymond Burghardt, "Contra Project," May 6, 1986, 12:15.

91. National Security Planning Group minutes, May 16, 1986, pp. 10–11.

92. See Kornbluh and Byrne, *The Iran-Contra Scandal*, pp. 63–64; North trial stipulation, April 6, 1989, paragraphs 97–99, 101.

93. Oliver North, PROFS note to John Poindexter, "Iran," August 23, 1986, 15:52:52. The entire section on Noriega was excised when Congress first released its report to the public. The virtually unexpurgated Panama passage appears in Tom Blanton, ed., *White House E-Mail: The Top Secret Computer Messages the Reagan/Bush White House Tried to Destroy* (New York: New Press, 1995), p. 24.

94. As for why Manual Noriega would approach Oliver North, the NSC staff aide reminded his superior Noriega typically refused to deal with the CIA, and the two of them had "developed a fairly good relationship" over the years.

95. Ibid.

96. Ibid.

97. John Poindexter, PROFS note to Oliver North, "Iran," August 23, 1986, 17:45:02. For the unexpurgated version, see Blanton, *White House E-Mail*, p. 25.

98. North notebooks (FOIA release), August 24, 1986. This section was also initially denied in its entirety. It was revealed in response to the National Security Archive's FOIA lawsuit for North's notebooks.

99. Fiers, testimony at George trial, July 29, 1992, pp. 1236, 1237; quoted in Kornbluh and Byrne, *The Iran-Contra Scandal*, p. 64.

100. Charles Hill, notes, September 20, 1986, quoted in *OIC Final Report*, vol. I, p. 380.

101. Ten days earlier, North had met with Rabin, and the two discussed an offer by the Israelis to provide the Contras Soviet-made weaponry captured from the Palestine Liberation Organization (PLO)—apparently in addition to the Noriega sabotage school. See North-Poin-

dexter PROFS exchange, both messages entitled "Iran," September 13, 1986. The Rabin-North conversation is also mentioned in the *Select Committees' Report*, pp. 75–76.

102. North notebooks (FOIA release), September 22, 1986, AMX001511.

103. Ibid., September 30, 1986, AMX001529. Emphasis in original.

104. Ibid., September 6, 1986, AMX001458. In a PROFS note to Poindexter, North put the phone call at "2330 hours" on September 5. North, PROFS note to Poindexter, "Iran," September 6, 1986, 15:31:36.

105. See *Select Committees' Report*, p. 76. According to Tambs's deputy at the embassy in San José, Arias told Tambs he had not known about the planned press conference. See James L. Tull, Select Committees' deposition, vol. B-27, p. 205.

106. North, PROFS note to Poindexter, "Iran," September 6, 1986, 15:31:36.

107. Alan Fiers ("C/CATF"), *Joint Hearings*, vol. 100-11, August 5, 1987, pp. 135, 171, quoted in Draper, *A Very Thin Line*, p. 350.

108. Quintero, KL-43 message to Secord, September 10, 1986, 17:30.

109. Associated Press, September 25, 1986.

110. Oliver North, PROFS note to John Poindexter, "Public Affairs Campaign on Central America," September 25, 1986, 11:23:45. This text was originally excised but was released in response to a National Security Archive FOIA lawsuit. First published in Blanton, *White House E-Mail*, p. 99.

111. North, PROFS note to Poindexter, "Public Affairs Campaign on Central America," September 25, 1986, 16:06. First published in Blanton, *White House E-Mail*, p. 100.

112. North, PROFS note to Poindexter, "Public Affairs Campaign on Central America," September 25, 1986, 11:23:45.

113. The Central Intelligence Agency inspector general noted, for example, that North exaggerated the period of time the strip was in use: North dated it from July 1985, when "construction could not have begun before August 1985." Office of Inspector General, "Special Investigation into Certain Activities of the Former COS San Jose," April, 24, 1987.

114. Oliver North, memorandum to John Poindexter, "Press Guidance re Costa Rican Airstrip," September 30, 1986, with guidance attached.

115. *Select Committees' Report*, pp. 74–75. See also Dutton's discussion in *Joint Hearings*, vol. 100-3, May 27, 1987, p. 231.

116. Rodriguez, *Joint Hearings*, vol. 100-3, May 27, 1987, p. 293; Dutton, KL-43 message to North, September 11, 1986, 1700Z.

117. Dutton, *Joint Hearings*, vol. 100-3, May 27, 1987, p. 233.

118. Ibid., pp. 234–235.

119. Ibid., p. 236.

120. Robert Dutton, KL-43 message to "Goode's Office," October 6, 1986, 1930Z.

121. Dutton, Select Committees' deposition, vol. B-9, p. 508.

122. According to the Nicaraguan government, quoted in Associated Press, "Nicaragua Claims It Captured U.S. Military Adviser," October 7, 1986.

123. Associated Press, "Relatives Say Downed U.S. Crewmember from Wisconsin," October 7, 1986.

124. Dutton, KL-43 message to "Goode's Office," October 6, 1986, 1930Z.

125. Vince Cannistraro, PROFS note to John Poindexter, "Downed Plane," October 8, 1986, 16:08. An earlier release of this note excised the paragraph about El Salvador's role.

126. North, *Under Fire*, p. 272.

Chapter 12: Blowback

1. John Poindexter, PROFS note to Oliver North, May 31, 1986, cited in *Tower Report*, pp. B-127, B-128; see also Draper, *A Very Thin Line*, pp. 374–375.

2. Oliver North, PROFS note to John Poindexter, June 3, 1986. The transcription provided in the *Tower Report* (p. B-128) is more complete than the heavily excised version in the *Select Committees' Report*, Appendix A, vol. 2, p. 950.

3. See the *Wall Street Journal*, December 26, 1986, and the *New York Times*, March 2, 1987. According to a document in the archives of East Germany's secret police (Stasi), Nicaragua's interior minister, Tomás Borge, met with Muammar Qaddafi, who told Borge he intended to kidnap and kill U.S. citizens in the mid-1980s—following the Iranian model—to show that the U.S. government could not protect its own. Borge related Qaddafi's remarks to his East German counterpart, Stasi Chief Erich Mielke. See "On a Conversation of Comrade Minister Mielke with Comrade Interior Minister Borge," September 20, 1984, in Federal Commissioner for Stasi Records [BStU], Archiv der Zentralstelle, MfS—Abt. X/327, p. 321.

4. Clair George, *Joint Hearings*, vol. 100-II, August 6, 1987, p. 235.

5. For a summary of the DEA operation, see the *Select Committees' Report*, pp. 361–365. The quote is from Clair George's testimony in *Joint Hearings*, vol. 100-II, August 6, 1987, p. 235.

6. See Oliver North, memorandum to Robert McFarlane, "Status of Hostage Recovery Efforts," June 7, 1985; North, memorandum to Edwin Meese, "DEA Support for Recovery of American Hostages Seized in Beirut," ca. June 10, 1985. The DEA operation was one of several incidents that landed Meese in hot water after the Iran initiative was exposed. In his televised congressional testimony, he denied knowing the DEA agents would have any operational role—which they were not authorized by law to undertake—beyond gathering intelligence. As the *Select Committees' Report* found, however, the "memo he received from North stated that the agents would rent a safehouse and open a bank account. . . . The Attorney General did not consider such activities to be operational, although the head of the DEA, John Lawn, does" (p. 370, fn. 47).

7. See *Select Committees' Report*, p. 365; also Ronald Reagan, letter to H. Ross Perot, June II, 1986, thanking him for his "discreet assistance" on behalf of "our Americans abducted in Beirut." Appendix A, vol. 2, p. 944.

8. North, PROFS note to Poindexter, June 3, 1986, transcribed in *Tower Report*, p. B-128.

9. Israeli Historical Chronology, Part II, p. 57.

10. George Cave, interview with the author, September 4, 2007.

11. See Israeli Historical Chronology, Part II, pp. 58–59; Secord, *Honored and Betrayed*, p. 283.

12. North, *Joint Hearings*, vol. 100-7, Part I, July 7, 1987, p. 8.

13. A few days later, Ghorbanifar reminded Kangarlou about the idea in a letter, lamenting, "As usual, nobody paid any attention to my suggestions." Cave obtained the letter, dated either July 8 or 9, 1986, from an unidentified source later that month. Although the Tower Commission could not verify the letter's authenticity, the report reproduced it in its entirety (pp. B-131–B-135).

14. Nir's account of this episode appears in the Israeli Historical Chronology, Part II, p. 60. Allen reported on Nir's alarm; cited in *Tower Report*, p. B-135, fn. 78.

15. North notebooks (Select Committee extracts), August 8, 1986. The transcription for July 29 reflects a call from Nir to North (at 1745 hours) identifying an Iranian official named "Vahaidi" as the source of the order to release Jenco and to pay Ghorbanifar. This was probably Gen. Ahmad Vahidi, who later became head of the al Qods force of the Islamic Revolution-

ary Guard Corps and was a key liaison for Tehran with Hezbollah. From 2009–2013, he was Iran's minister of defense. For information on Vahidi, see Ranstorp, *Hizb'allah in Lebanon*, pp. 84–85.

16. William Casey, draft memorandum to John Poindexter, "American Hostages," July 27, 1986.

17. Oliver North and George Cave, untitled message to John Poindexter, July 27, 1986 (misdated as June).

18. This is according to Nir. See Israeli Historical Chronology, Part II, p. 62.

19. Craig L. Fuller, "The Vice President's Meeting with Mr. Nir—7/29/86 0735-0805," July 29, 1986, reproduced in *Tower Report*, p. B-146.

20. Ibid. See also Nir's account in Israeli Historical Chronology, Part II, pp. 63–64.

21. Secord, *Honored and Betrayed*, pp. 280–281.

22. Ibid., p. 279.

23. See Secord's version in ibid., pp. 278–279; for Nir's version, see Israeli Historical Chronology, Part II, p. 57.

24. See Mohammad Javad Larijani, quoted in Toronto *Globe and Mail*, June 27, 1986.

25. U.S. Department of State, "Summary Chronology of Dealings with Iran" (hereafter "Summary Chronology"), ca. late December 1986, pp. 31, 34–35; see also generally *Tower Report*, pp. B-127–B-138.

26. Farnejad is referred to as the "First Contact" and Darwish the "Second Contact" in the *Select Committees' Report*, p. 249. Their names are revealed in State Department, "Summary Chronology," p. 33. Draper incorrectly identifies the first contact as Sadeqh Tabatabai in *A Very Thin Line*, pp. 398–399. Although Tabatabai's name comes up occasionally in connection with the NSC-run operation, he denies having been involved. Sadeqh Tabatabai, interview with the author, September 4, 2012.

27. State Department, "Summary Chronology." The cites for Bahramani's background are Charles Allen, "Memorandum on Evaluation of U.S.-Iranian Contacts," November 25, 1986, and "[Excised] Biographic Summaries of Iranian Principals Involved in NSC's Iranian Program," undated. See also Bahramani interview with *Shahrvand Emrooz*, trans. Hussein Banai, June 19, 2008.

28. North notes (FOIA release), August 20, 1986, AMX001414. "Nephew" is excised in this version but appears in the congressional committees' transcription.

29. Richard Secord ("Copp") to Oliver North, August 26, 1986, quoted in *Tower Report*, p. B-147.

30. Bahramani interview.

31. Ibid. Parts of Bahramani's account were supported by an Iranian Foreign Ministry official who took part in an internal review of the secret operation. Interview with the author, September 26, 1999. See also "Mohsen Rezaie Interview with Fars News Agency," trans. Hussein Banai, September 22, 2008.

32. Oliver North, "Nonpaper" to John Poindexter, "Next Steps with Iran," September 2, 1986.

33. Oliver North, PROFS note to Robert McFarlane, "Anything Going On??" September 3, 1986, 20:12:50.

34. *Select Committees' Report*, p. 250.

35. North, PROFS note to McFarlane, "Anything Going On??" September 3, 1986, 20:12:50.

36. North, memorandum to Poindexter, "Next Steps with Iran," September 8, 1986, with attached "Supplement: Next Steps with Iran." The quote is from the attachment.

37. Ibid.

38. Charles Allen, memorandum to John Poindexter, "Mughniyah Threatens to Kill US and

French Hostages," September 8, 1986. Mughniyah's name is excised throughout the document but appears in *Tower Report* excerpts, p. B-153.

39. Oliver North, memorandum to John Poindexter, "Next Steps with Iran," October 2, 1986. This concern applied on different levels. Israel had policy goals with respect to Iran, including wanting to free two Israeli hostages. Shimon Peres also took a personal interest in the deals. Furthermore, North had a stake in keeping Nir involved with other hostage-related activities.

40. Oliver North, memorandum to John Poindexter, "Meeting with Amiram Nir," September 9, 1986. Kennedy's and Haig's names are excised in the publicly released version of the document, but not in the *Tower Report*, p. B-154.

41. Oliver North memorandum, "Possible Peres Discussion Items with the President," September 15, 1986, attached to memo from North to John Poindexter, "Follow-on Meeting with Amiram Nir," September 15, 1986.

42. Ibid.

43. Israeli Historical Chronology, Part II, p. 69.

44. Oliver North, PROFS note to John Poindexter, "Iran," September 17, 1986, 12:59:11.

45. George Cave, Select Committees' deposition, vol. B-3, pp. 694–702; see also Secord, *Honored and Betrayed*, pp. 290–291.

46. Cave interview, September 4, 2007.

47. Quoted in *Select Committees' Report*, p. 252.

48. Later in his career, Mehdinejad also came to be referred to as Verdinejad. Under the Mohammad Khatami administration (1997–2005), he served as head of Iran's government news agency, IRNA, and ambassador to China.

49. Secord, *Honored and Betrayed*, pp. 295–296.

50. Quoted in *Select Committees' Report*, p. 255. This section of the transcript does not appear in the report's source documents (Appendix A, vol. 1) under Chapter 14, fn. 190. George Bush reportedly witnessed Ronald Reagan's inscription. *Washington Post*, January 7, 1988.

51. Verbatim transcription of taped Frankfurt discussion, *Select Committees' Report*, Appendix A, vol. 1, p. 1538.

52. This is a footnote to Hakim's original text: "The Letter of Credit will be opened in favor of Mr. [Excised] and he will make the money for the 500 TOWs available by using 80% of the Letter of Credit."

53. This is a footnote to Hakim's original text: "After discussion between Mr. Secord and Mr. [Excised], it was agreed regarding the Moslem prisoners that the sentence (text) will be written in the following manner: [end of text]."

54. Library of Congress, translation of Hakim's Farsi original, quoted verbatim from *Select Committees' Report*, p. 257.

55. Oliver North, PROFS note to John Poindexter, "Iran," October 10, 1986, 21:55:31.

56. Verbatim transcription of taped Frankfurt discussion, "Tape A17," *Select Committees' Report*, Appendix A, vol. 1, p. 1636.

57. Verbatim transcription of taped Frankfurt discussion, "Minitape," *Select Committees' Report*, Appendix A, vol. 1, p. 1658–1659.

58. Cave interview, September 4, 2007. The State Department "Summary Chronology" also names "Air Defense CINC Hasan Rouhani" as the fourth member along with Mehdinejad, Najafabadi, and Kangarlou (p. 38).

59. *Select Committees' Report*, p. 260.

60. North notebooks (FOIA release), October 29, 1986, AMX001637. Mehdinejad's alias, Samii, is excised in the declassified version of North's notes but is given in the Select Committees' transcribed version.

61. See Gary Sick, "Iran's Quest for Superpower Status," *Foreign Affairs* (Spring 1987), http://www.foreignaffairs.com/articles/42020/gary-g-sick/irans-quest-for-superpower-status?page=5; see also Robin Wright, "Iranian Power Plays Reflected in Terrorist Moves?" *Christian Science Monitor*, November 5, 1986.

62. Former Iranian Foreign Ministry official, interview with the author, September 5, 2007.

63. Allen, untitled overview of the Iran initiative, October 14, 1986; State Department, "Summary Chronology," p. 39; Cave interview, September 4, 2007.

64. State Department, "Summary Chronology," p. 43.

Chapter 13: The Early Cover-Up

1. Joseph Fernandez, KL-43 message to Robert Dutton, October 5, 1986, partial transcription in *Select Committees' Report*, p. 144.

2. North, *Under Fire*, p. 272.

3. Ibid., p. 249.

4. Associated Press, October 7, 1986.

5. Ibid., October 8, 1986.

6. *Washington Post*, October 8, 1986.

7. Elliott Abrams, on *Evans & Novak* program, October 11, 1986, quoted in Kornbluh and Byrne, *The Iran-Contra Scandal*, pp. 186–187.

8. Elliott Abrams, Senate Foreign Relations Committee transcript, October 10, 1986, quoted in *OIC Final Report*, vol. I, p. 384.

9. Elliott Abrams, House Permanent Select Committee on Intelligence testimony, October 14, 1986, quoted in ibid., pp. 384–385.

10. Abrams, Senate Foreign Relations Committee and House Foreign Affairs Committee testimony quoted in ibid., pp. 386 and 387, fn. 82.

11. Ibid., pp. 390–391.

12. Quotes provided in *Select Committees' Report*, p. 147.

13. Ibid.

14. *New York Times*, April 15, 1988.

15. Reuters, November 6, 1986; *New York Times*, December 4, 1986.

16. Bush diary, November 5, 1986. The vice president's notes reveal numerous sharply negative reactions to the daily news coverage.

17. Howard Teicher, PROFS note to John Poindexter, November 4, 1986, 09:35, quoted in *Tower Report*, p. B-171.

18. Robert McFarlane, PROFs note to Oliver North, "Audit Trail," November 8, 1986. The National Security Agency (NSA) is excised in the *OIC Final Report*, Chapter 1, but Walsh includes it in *Firewall* (pp. 8 and 177), albeit in slightly different form in each instance. On the latter page, Walsh makes clear McFarlane meant the NSA, not the national security advisor. The former independent counsel goes on to berate that agency for misleading his criminal investigation and "forcing us to support silly redactions" such as this one.

19. Quoted in Walsh, *Firewall*, p. 8.

20. L. Paul Bremer ("amateur hour"); George Shultz, quoted in Charles Hill, notes, November 4, 1986, ALW021115, and November 6, 1986, ALW021122.

21. Ibid., November 9, 1986, ALW021143.

22. Ibid., November 10, 1986, ALW021153. Emphasis in original. Gearing up for his 1988 presidential bid, Bush sharply downplayed his role in the Iran operation. In his preelection autobi-

ography, he made it appear he had been unaware of Shultz's and Weinberger's "serious doubts" about the initiative. "If I had known that and asked the President to call a meeting of the NSC, he might have seen the project in a different light, as a gamble doomed to fail." George Bush with Victor Gold, *Looking Forward: An Autobiography* (New York: Doubleday, 1987), p. 242.

23. Charles Hill, notes, November 10, 1986, ALW021153.

24. Bush diary, November 9, 1986.

25. Donald Regan, notes, November 10, 1986.

26. Ibid.

27. Charles Hill, notes, November 22, 1986, ALW021279.

28. Regan, notes, November 10, 1986; Charles Hill, notes, November 10, 1986, ALW021159, ALW021165-6.

29. Regan, notes, November 10, 1986.

30. Mixter, *Bush Criminal Liability*, March 21, 1991, p. 129. During a telephone discussion after the meeting, Shultz repeatedly admonished Poindexter the original statement was "misleading if not inaccurate." Charles Hill, notes, November 10, 1986, ALW021165.

31. Bush diary, November 10, 1986.

32. See Walsh, *Firewall*, pp. 322–326.

33. Charles Hill, notes, January 7, 1986, reproduced in *OIC Final Report*, vol. I, p. 338.

34. Nicholas Platt, notes, May 8, 1986; Charles Hill, notes, February 21, 1986, reproduced in *OIC Final Report*, vol. I, pp. 339–340.

35. Walsh, *Firewall*, pp. 325–326.

36. Ibid., p. 326.

37. Note by Christopher W. S. Ross, principal deputy to Undersecretary of State Richard Armitage, January 23, 1986, reproduced in *OIC Final Report*, vol. I, p. 338.

38. During one "combative" deposition (Independent Counsel Walsh's phrase) in early 1992, Shultz insisted his HAWK statements had been accurate because the Iranians had returned the missiles, which meant technically the deal had not been "consummated." *OIC Final Report*, vol. I, p. 352. Abrams made similar, highly specific denials in October 1986 about his knowledge of the Contra support network and his own solicitations of foreign funds.

39. George Shultz, *Joint Hearings*, vol. 100-9, July 23, 1987, pp. 40–41.

40. *New York Times*, December 4, 1986.

41. Ibid.; *Washington Post*, December 28, 1986.

42. Wallison, *Ronald Reagan*, p. 185; Wallison diary, November 14, 1986, quoted in *OIC Final Report*, vol. I, p. 528.

43. See Sofaer's discussion of the legalities with Shultz in Charles Hill, notes, November 10, 1986, ALW021154-6.

44. *OIC Final Report*, vol. I, p. 529.

45. Walsh, *Firewall*, p. 373.

46. Bush diary, November 12, 1986. The attendees were Sen. Robert Dole (R-Kans.), the outgoing majority leader; Rep. Dick Cheney (R-Wyo.), who would figure centrally in the congressional Iran-Contra hearings; Sen. Robert Byrd (D-W.Va.), the incoming majority leader; and Rep. Jim Wright (D-Tex.), the incoming speaker of the House.

47. Reagan, *The Reagan Diaries*, p. 656.

48. Bush diary, November 13, 1986.

49. *Tower Report*, pp. D-11, D-12.

50. Ronald Reagan, address to the nation, November 13, 1986, http://www.reagan.utexas .edu/archives/speeches/1986/111386c.htm.

51. *New York Times*, December 4, 1986; *Washington Post*, December 18, December 27, 1986, and December 28, 1986; *Los Angeles Times*, December 19, 1986.

52. Charles Hill, notes, dated November 13, 1986, ALW021193. The excerpts of Hill's notes released by the OIC include handwritten dates on each page that appear to have been supplied after the fact and are not always reliable. Shultz met with Reagan on Friday, November 14, as he indicates in his memoir (*Turmoil and Triumph*, p. 820).

53. George Shultz testified to three occasions: mid-1983 after learning Robert McFarlane had made a secret trip to the Middle East; December 1985 in connection with an administration-ordered lie detector test over leaks; and August 1986 over White House refusal to authorize his use of aircraft for foreign travel. *Joint Hearings*, vol. 100-9, July 23, 1987, pp. 58–60.

54. Bush diary, November 15, 1986.

55. *Washington Post*, November 17, 1986; Shultz, *Turmoil and Triumph*, pp. 822–823.

56. Bush diary, November 16, 1986; Caspar Weinberger, notes, November 16, 1986, ALZ0040539.

57. Within days, both the president and vice president began to sour on Shultz. Bush recorded in his diary on November 25 he "went in and told the President that I really felt that Regan should go [and] Shultz should go. . . . The President is very unhappy. He keeps worrying about the people at the State Department. And, he also thinks that George is not backing him." Bush diary, November 25, 1986.

58. National Security Council draft chronology, November 17, 1986, *Joint Hearings*, Exhibit CJC-3.

59. Ibid.; Charles Cooper, *Joint Hearings*, June 25, 1987, pp. 234–236.

60. Abraham Sofaer, Select Committees' deposition, vol. B-26, pp. 235–243, 246–247; Charles Hill, notes, November 18, 1986, ALW021220-1.

61. North notebooks (FOIA release), November 18, 1986, AMX001695-6.

62. Robert McFarlane, PROFS note to John Poindexter, "Chronology," November 18, 1986, 23:06.

63. Richard Secord, *Joint Hearings*, vol. 100-1, May 6, 1987, pp. 125–126.

64. Robert McFarlane, PROFS note to John Poindexter, "Chronology," November 18, 1986, 23:06.

65. Bush diary, November 19, 1986.

66. Ronald Reagan, news conference, November 19, 1986, http://www.reagan.utexas.edu /archives/speeches/1986/111986a.htm.

67. *Washington Post*, November 20, 1986.

68. Despite expressing sympathy for the president, Bush hesitated to defend him in public. "My gut instinct is to rise to Reagan's defense and jump into the fray. But, you don't want to shout into a hurricane. You want to say something that can be effective." Bush diary, November 19, 1986.

69. Charles Hill, notes, November 20, 1986, ALW021253.

70. The *OIC Final Report* indicates there is no direct evidence Clair George "independently recalled" the 1985 shipment.

71. Robert Gates, quoted in Draper, *A Very Thin Line*, p. 495.

72. David Doherty, notes; Federal Bureau of Investigation 302 interview, cited in *OIC Final Report*, vol. I, pp. 320–322.

73. Central Intelligence Agency, "Subject: CIA Airline Involvement," ca. November 20, 1985. One version of the relevant page has North's handwritten edits. *Joint Hearings*, Exhibit OLN-31A. Another version shows the same essential change in Meese's handwriting. *Joint Hearings*, Exhibit EM-33. See also Oliver North, *Joint Hearings*, vol. 100-7, Part I, July 7, 1987, pp. 39–40;

Edwin Meese, *Joint Hearings*, vol. 100-9, July 28, 1987, pp. 216–220, esp. pp. 218–219. See also the discussion in Draper, *A Very Thin Line*, pp. 486–489.

74. North, *Joint Hearings*, vol. 100-7, Part I, July 7, 1987, p. 70. North also rewrote the reason for Iran's return of the HAWKs—claiming the United States had "jawboned" Tehran into giving them back after allegedly being disturbed to discover the shipment had taken place. Charles Cooper, grand jury testimony, cited in *OIC Final Report*, vol. I, p. 531.

75. Meese, *Joint Hearings*, vol. 100-9, July 28, 1987, pp. 219–220.

76. Sofaer, Select Committees' deposition, vol. B-26, p. 270.

77. Draper, *A Very Thin Line*, pp. 490–491.

78. Cooper, *Joint Hearings*, vol. 100-6, June 25, 1987, p. 250; Sofaer, Select Committees' deposition, vol. B-26, p. 276. In the meantime, CIA officials were already trying to correct the false testimony. During the evening of November 20, David Doherty had a sentence removed from Casey's draft statement that claimed no CIA contemporaneous knowledge of the true cargo. See *OIC Final Report*, vol. I, p. 323.

79. William Weld, Select Committees' deposition, vol. B-27, pp. 592–594.

80. Charles Cooper, notes, November 21, 1986, quoted in *OIC Final Report*, vol. I, p. 535.

81. *OIC Final Report*, vol. I, pp. 535–536, fn. 108.

82. Edwin Meese, Select Committees' deposition, vol. B-18, p. 83.

83. John Poindexter, Select Committees' deposition, vol. B-20, pp. 1109–1110.

84. Ibid., pp. 1106–1107.

85. Cooper notes, November 21, 1986, quoted in *OIC Final Report*, vol. I, p. 537.

86. McFarlane, *Joint Hearings*, vol. 100-2, May 14, 1987, pp. 261–262.

87. Robert McFarlane, PROFS note to John Poindexter, November 21, 1986, 14:56; North notebooks (FOIA release), November 21, 1986, AMX001707.

88. Robert McFarlane, Select Committees' deposition, vol. B-16, pp. 620, 655.

89. Charles Hill, notes, November 22, 1986, ALW021272.

90. Ibid., ALW021274.

91. Ibid., ALW021280.

92. Ibid., ALW021279.

93. Charles Hill, quotes from unpublished interviews and grand jury testimony, reprinted in *OIC Final Report*, vol. I, p. 544.

94. William Reynolds, Select Committees' deposition, vol. B-22, p. 1258.

95. Robert Earl, Select Committees' deposition, vol. B-9, p. 627.

96. Oliver North, memorandum, "Release of American Hostages in Beirut," ca. April 4, 1986.

97. Reynolds, Select Committees' deposition, vol. B-22, pp. 1129–1130.

98. The expletive is deleted in most sources, except Cohen and Mitchell, *Men of Zeal*, p. 126. See also Richardson, Select Committees' deposition, vol. B-23, p. 293.

99. Observation by Draper, *A Very Thin Line*, pp. 509–510.

100. Richardson, notes of North interview, November 23, 1986, p. 1.

101. Ibid., p. 13. Emphasis in original.

102. Ibid.

103. Ibid. Meese told Congress he based this comment on public and private remarks he had heard Reagan make in the past. See Meese, *Joint Hearings*, vol. 100-9, July 29, 1987, p. 414.

104. Richardson, Select Committees' deposition, vol. B-23, pp. 320–322.

105. Cohen and Mitchell, *Men of Zeal*, p. 191. Members of Congress criticized Reynolds for missing an opportunity to draw out North on whether a cover memo might have existed.

106. Richardson, Select Committees' deposition, vol. B-23, pp. 324–325; Richardson, notes, p. 15; Meese, *Joint Hearings*, vol. 100-9, July 29, 1987, pp. 338–339.

107. Richardson, notes of North interview, November 23, 1986, p. 19.

108. Cooper, *Joint Hearings*, vol. 100-6, June 25, 1987, p. 295.

109. Meese, testimony at North trial, March 28, 1989, p. 5749.

110. Cooper, *Joint Hearings*, vol. 100-6, June 25, 1987, pp. 264–265.

111. Meese, *Joint Hearings*, vol. 100-9, July 29, 1987, pp. 337–338.

112. Ibid., p. 337.

113. Ibid., p. 338.

114. North, *Joint Hearings*, vol. 100-7, Part I, July 7, 1987, pp. 15–16; Fawn Hall, *Joint Hearings*, vol. 100-5, June 8, 1987, pp. 484–500, esp. p. 497. Among the ways investigators identified altered memoranda was the fact the NSC had changed its stationery earlier in 1986, so the letterhead on the revised records did not match the originals prepared in 1985. Hall, *Joint Hearings*, vol. 100-5, June 8, 1987, p. 488.

115. Hall, *Joint Hearings*, vol. 100-5, June 8, 1987, pp. 504–506.

116. Weinberger notes, November 24, 1986, ALZ0040669II.

117. Charles Hill, notes, November 24, 1986, pp. ALW02191-3. Emphasis in original.

118. Weinberger notes, November 24, 1986, ALZ0040669KK, ALZ0040669LL.

119. Ibid., ALZ0040669MM.

120. *OIC Final Report*, vol. I, p. 542.

121. Donald Regan, grand jury testimony, cited in ibid., vol. I, p. 545; Charles Hill, notes, November 24, 1986, ALW021292. Theodore Draper has disputed Walsh's conclusion the team's behavior constituted a "conspiracy" Meese "spearheaded." Draper, "Walsh's Last Stand," *New York Review of Books*, March 3, 1994. Draper contends in part that at the time Meese knew "little more than North had told him two days earlier." In fact, Meese had also heard from Shultz and McFarlane that Reagan had been informed. Furthermore, in his memoir, published in 1992, Meese took the opposite view: "As for the HAWK shipments . . . we have good evidence that the President approved the initiative in question." The apparent explanation is by then Meese had decided the president's actions in November 1985 were fully legal because the "mental finding" could now be argued sufficient "under the law as it then stood." (In 1991, legislation had passed that specifically required written findings, which Meese asserted "obviously acknowledges" this was not the case in 1985.) In late November 1986, however, that question was by no means resolved, and Meese instead took the position the president had been in the dark about the operation. See Meese, *With Reagan*, p. 267. Attorneys for President Reagan also sharply rejected the independent counsel's theory, but their case was undermined by a number of mischaracterizations of the independent counsel's account and reliance on public statements by administration officials made well after the fact rather than on contemporaneous documentation. For the president's rebuttal of the independent counsel's assertions, see *OIC Final Report*, vol. III, pp. 701–727.

122. Weinberger notes, November 24, 1986, ALZ0040669SS.

123. "NSC Matter: Plan of Action—Donald T. Regan," ca. November 24, 1986.

124. Meese, *Joint Hearings*, vol. 100-9, July 29, 1987, pp. 333–334; Cohen and Mitchell, *Men of Zeal*, p. 127.

125. Regan, Select Committees' deposition, vol. B-22, p. 656.

126. Secord, *Honored and Betrayed*, pp. 330–331.

Chapter 14: Congress Steps In

1. Associated Press, January 5, 1987; *New York Times*, January 6, 1987.

2. Democratic staff member, interview with the author, August 12, 1992.

3. Warren B. Rudman, *Combat: Twelve Years in the U.S. Senate* (New York: Random House, 1996), p. 111.

4. Dennis Teti, "The Coup That Failed: An Insider's Account of the Iran/Contra Hearings," *Policy Review* 42 (Fall 1987): 27; *New York Times*, December 18, 1986; *Washington Post*, December 18, 1986.

5. Democratic staff member interview; Senate Democratic member's designated liaison, interview with the author, August 10, 1992.

6. John Nields, interview with the author, March 29, 2012.

7. Cohen and Mitchell, *Men of Zeal*, p. 22; Rudman, *Combat*, p. 126.

8. Rudman, *Combat*, p. 114.

9. At one point Liman's deputy, Mark Belnick, dictated a cable to State Department typists for transmittal to the government of Brunei, but could not have the same text read back to him because he did not yet have clearance. Arthur L. Liman with Peter Israel, *Lawyer: A Life of Counsel and Controversy* (New York: PublicAffairs, 1998), p. 309.

10. Democratic staff member interview.

11. *Select Committees' Report*, p. 639.

12. U.S. Senate, Select Committee on Intelligence, *Were Relevant Documents Withheld from the Congressional Committees Investigating the Iran-Contra Affair?* 101st Congress, 1st sess., S. Rep. 101-44, June 1989. The "exhausting" quote is on p. 7; the "chaos" quote is in the headline of an Associated Press story of June 24, 1989, and is based on a comment by SSCI member Cohen; Hamilton's quote appears in *Washington Post*, April 21, 1989.

13. For example, Democratic majority staff attorney, interview with the author, December 30, 2012; Democratic staff member interview.

14. "The Cannon Centenary Conference: The Changing Nature of the Speakership," November 12, 2003, H. Doc. No. 108-204 (Washington, D.C.: Government Printing Office, 2004).

15. Liman, *Lawyer*, p. 310.

16. Ibid.

17. Nields interview.

18. *New York Times*, May 24, 1987.

19. Seymour Hersh, *New York Times Magazine*, April 29, 1990.

20. James G. Hershberg, *Boston Phoenix*, February 3–9, 1989; Liman, *Lawyer*, p. 313. In an aside, Liman recalls Independent Counsel Walsh also had the cold war on his mind, expressing the concern at his first meeting with Liman that Poindexter might be a Soviet agent—another Alger Hiss. Otherwise, Walsh reportedly said, Poindexter could not possibly have caused more harm to the U.S. government. *Lawyer*, p. 312.

21. Daniel Inouye, speech at Tufts University, October 1988, cited in Hershberg, *Boston Phoenix*, February 3–9, 1989.

22. Hersh, *New York Times Magazine*, April 29, 1990.

23. "Cannon Centenary Conference."

24. *New York Times*, December 14, 1986.

25. Hersh, *New York Times Magazine*, April 29, 1990.

26. Executive Order No. 12575; *Tower Report*, Appendix A.

27. Brent Scowcroft, interview with the author, February 13, 2013.

28. *Tower Report*, p. IV-11.

29. Ibid., p. IV-10.

30. Scowcroft interview.

31. Ibid.

32. Abshire, *Saving the Reagan Presidency*, pp. 118–124; *Tower Report*, pp. B-19–B-20.

33. Abshire, *Saving the Reagan Presidency*, p. 119.

34. John Poindexter, interview with the author, January 14, 2013.

35. Ibid.

36. Cannon quotes and description appear in Mayer and McManus, *Landslide*, pp. vii–xi.

37. Ibid., p. xi; Abshire, *Saving the Reagan Presidency*, pp. 124–125.

38. Liman, *Lawyer*, p. 305.

39. Nancy Reagan reportedly urged the president to make a public acknowledgment the Iran initiative had been problematic. On March 4, he declared: "A few months ago I told the American people I did not trade arms for hostages. My heart and my best intentions still tell me that's true, but the facts and the evidence tell me it is not." Ronald Reagan, address to the nation, http://millercenter.org/president/speeches/detail/3414; Bush diary, March 4, 1987.

40. Ibid.; Rudman, *Combat*, pp. 115, 129.

41. Nields, interview.

42. Cohen and Mitchell, *Men of Zeal*, p. 37.

43. Liman, *Lawyer*, p. 310; Rudman, *Combat*, p. 127; Walsh, *Firewall*, p. 67; Cohen and Mitchell, *Men of Zeal*, pp. 40–42.

44. Cohen and Mitchell, *Men of Zeal*, p. 39; Liman, *Lawyer*, p. 313. Only U.S. Rep. Jack Brooks objected publicly to the immunity decision.

45. Liman, *Lawyer*, p. 319.

46. Ibid.

47. Ibid., pp. 318–320.

48. Ibid., p. 336.

49. *Time*, September 23, 2010.

50. An early proposal to start with a panel of foreign policy, intelligence, and covert operations experts to provide historical and legal context to the complicated story foundered, like so many others in this politicized setting, on disagreements over who the panelists would be and where their sympathies would lie.

51. Cohen and Mitchell, *Men of Zeal*, pp. 65–66.

52. Nields interview.

53. Liman, *Lawyer,* p. 323.

54. Gaston Sigur Jr., *Joint Hearings*, vol. 100-2, May 14, 1987, p. 303.

55. Robert Owen, *Joint Hearings*, vol. 100-2, May 19, 1987, p. 440.

56. North said he used $4,300 in travelers checks to reimburse himself for out-of-pocket expenses in the course of the affair. North testimony at his trial, April 10, 1989, pp. 7141–7145.

57. *Washington Post*, May 21, 1987.

58. Ellen Garwood, *Joint Hearings*, vol. 100-3, May 21, 1987, pp. 131–132.

59. Robert Dutton, KL-43 message to Richard Secord, September 13, 1986 (1330Z).

60. Bush diary, May 11, 1987.

61. Ibid., May 27, 1987.

62. Felix Rodriguez, *Joint Hearings*, vol. 100-3, May 27, 1987, p. 306.

63. Jack Brooks, *Joint Hearings*, vol. 100-5, June 3, 1987, p. 163.

64. Lee Hamilton, *Joint Hearings*, vol. 100-5, June 3, 1987, p. 186.

65. Fawn Hall, *Joint Hearings*, vol. 100-5, June 9, 1987, p. 552.

66. Liman, *Lawyer,* p. 326.

67. Cohen and Mitchell, *Men of Zeal*, pp. 147–149. The concessions included a sharply curtailed focus for North's deposition and limiting access to the full set of North's revelatory notebooks to a single committee representative (John Nields).

68. North, *Under Fire*, p. 351.

69. Oliver North, *Joint Hearings*, vol. 100-7, Part I, July 7, 1987, pp. 4–5.

70. *New York Times*, July 8, 1987.

71. Liman, *Lawyer*, p. 338.

72. North, *Joint Hearings*, vol. 100-7, Part I, July 9, 1987, p. 245.

73. Mary McGrory, *Washington Post*, July 9, 1987.

74. North, *Joint Hearings*, vol. 100-7, Part I, July 9, 1987, pp. 245–246.

75. *New York Times*, July 8, 1987; North, *Under Fire*, p. 362.

76. Rudman, *Combat*, p. 139.

77. Liman, *Lawyer*, p. 340; U.S. Senate Historical Office, "Richard A. Arenberg: Staff to Senators Paul Tsongas, George Mitchell, and Carl Levin, 1975–2009," Oral History Interviews, Interview 4, June 8–10, 2010, p. 135.

78. *New York Times*, July 11, 1987.

79. Andrew Laperriere, guest column, *St. Petersburg Times*, August 1, 1987.

80. Craig Keller, interview with the author, August 11, 1992.

81. Steven F. Hayward, *The Age of Reagan: The Conservative Counterrevolution, 1980–1989* (New York: Three Rivers Press, 2009), p. 547; Teti, "The Coup That Failed," p. 26.

82. Sullivan, during North testimony, *Joint Hearings*, vol. 100-7, Part I, July 9, 1987, pp. 238, 239, 240, 263.

83. By comparison, a former assistant chief counsel to the Senate Watergate committee commented that the legendary chair of the committee, Sen. Sam Ervin (D-N.C.), would never have allowed an accompanying attorney such leeway. Interview with the author, June 16, 2006.

84. Democratic majority staff attorney, December 29, 2012.

85. Beatrice Chestnut, dissertation, "The Narrative Construction of Iran-Contra: The Failure of Congress and the Press to Hold Reagan Accountable," Northwestern University, December 1996, pp. 391–392 (available at ProQuest Dissertations and Theses). For a discussion of the polls showing aversion to North's conduct, see Eric Alterman, *When Presidents Lie: A History of Official Deception and Its Consequences* (New York: Viking, 2004), pp. 289–290.

86. Hersh, *New York Times Magazine*, April 29, 1990.

87. Malcolm Byrne, "Ronald Reagan and the Iran-Contra Affairs," paper presented at "Reconsidering the Reagan Presidency" conference, University of California–Santa Barbara, March 28–30, 2002; Liman, *Lawyer*, pp. 328–332; Rudman, *Combat*, p. 128.

88. John Poindexter, *Joint Hearings*, vol. 100-8, July 15, 1987, pp. 36, 37, 40.

89. Ibid., pp. 37, 38.

90. Ibid., July 17, 1987, p. 158.

91. Liman, *Lawyer*, p. 331. Liman also wondered how a national security advisor could presume to tear up a presidential finding on his own authority. What if the president needed it at some later date? What would Poindexter tell him? (pp. 333–335).

92. Rudman, *Combat*, p. 130.

93. (Toronto) *Globe and Mail*, July 18, 1987.

94. Cohen and Mitchell, *Men of Zeal*, p. 201.

95. Teti, "The Coup That Failed," p. 31.

96. *Washington Post*, July 22, 1987.

97. *New York Times*, August 9, 1987.

98. George Shultz, *Joint Hearings*, vol. 100-9, July 23, 1987, p. 31; July 24, 1987, p. 140.

99. Ibid., July 23, 1987, p. 32.

100. *New York Times*, August 9, 1987.

101. Rudman, *Combat*, p. 109.

102. *New York Times*, July 29, 1987; Edwin Meese, *Joint Hearings*, vol. 100-9, July 29, 1987, p. 380.

103. *Washington Post*, July 31, 1987.

104. Ibid., August 1, 1987.

105. Caspar Weinberger, *Joint Hearings*, vol. 100-10, July 31, 1987, p. 140.

106. *Select Committees' Report*, pp. 11–22.

107. Ibid., p. 437.

108. Michael Malbin, principal drafter of the Minority Report, email to the author, December 21, 2012.

109. *Select Committees' Report* (Minority Report), p. 449.

110. Ibid., pp. 444–445.

111. Rudman, *Combat*, p. 148.

112. Federal News Service, "Remarks by Vice President Richard Cheney to the Traveling Press (as Released by the White House)," December 20, 2005.

113. *Select Committees' Report*, Preface, p. xvi.

114. Four CIA officials would testify in closed session in the following days to wrap up the hearings.

115. *New York Times*, November 20, 1987.

116. *Washington Post,* editorial, July 15, 1987.

117. Rudman, *Combat*, p. 131.

118. Dick Cheney, with Liz Cheney, *In My Time: A Personal and Political Memoir* (New York: Threshold Editions, 2011), p. 147.

119. U.S. Senate Historical Office, "Richard A. Arenberg," p. 141. 120. Nields interview.

121. Arthur Liman, "Contra Indications," *Boston Phoenix*, April 14, 1989, p. 4.

122. *Select Committees' Report*, p. 21.

123. Statements on last day of hearings, *Joint Hearings*, vol. 100-10, August 3, 1987, pp. 262, 273–274.

Chapter 15: The Independent Counsel

1. Philip Shenon, "Walsh Makes His Move," *New York Times Magazine*, October 25, 1987, p. 46ff.

2. Walsh, *Firewall*, pp. 27–29.

3. *Newsweek*, December 26, 1988; Walsh, *Firewall*, pp. 28–29.

4. Walsh, *Firewall*, p. 34.

5. *New York Times Magazine*, July 4, 1993.

6. Walsh, *Firewall*, p. 65.

7. 18 U.S.C. § 371, "Conspiracy to Commit Offense or to Defraud the United States." (Prosecutors must prove an illegal agreement, criminal intent, and the commission of at least one overt act.)

8. U.S. Department of Justice, *United States Attorneys' Manual*, Title 9, Criminal Resource Manual 923. See also *OIC Final Report*, vol. I, pp. 55–75.

9. Walsh, *Firewall*, pp. 65–66.

10. Ibid., p. 61.

11. Kate Rix, "War Stories: In Pursuit of Oliver North." Interview with John Keker, *Recorder*, November 25, 1998.

12. David Zornow, interview with the author, February 5, 2007.

13. *United States of America v. John M. Poindexter, Oliver L. North, Richard V. Secord, and Albert Hakim*, Criminal no. 88-0080, March 16, 1988.

14. Walsh, *Firewall*, p. 31.

15. The legal precedent regarding immunity was *Kastigar v. United States*, 406 U.S. 441 (1972).

16. *OIC Final Report*, vol. I, p. 32. Walsh himself conferred immunity on several individuals later in order to persuade them to cooperate in other trials, but the committees agreed not to immunize Secord's associate, Clines.

17. Walsh, *Firewall*, p. 54.

18. Ibid., p. 170.

19. Walsh and Thornburgh did reach an agreement—the Justice Department would not raise further objections to the introduction of evidence regarding North's remaining counts. This left "only one intelligence agency [that] persisted in abusing its classification powers." *OIC Final Report*, p. 111. Although the report does not provide a name in its public version, it was likely the National Security Agency (NSA).

20. Greenberg, *Historical Encyclopedia of U.S. Independent Counsel Investigations*, pp. 58–59.

21. Richard Thornburgh, quoted in the *Washington Post*, February 16, 1989; Walsh, *Firewall*, p. 180.

22. Zornow interview; *New York Times*, February 12, 1989.

23. Quoted in *Washington Post Magazine*, April 11, 1993.

24. *OIC Final Report*, vol. I, pp. 27–28; U.S. Senate, "Were Relevant Documents Withheld from the Congressional Committees Investigating the Iran-Contra Affair?" Report of the Select Committee on Intelligence, 101st Congress, 1st Sess., S. Rep. 101-44, June 1989, p. 30; Walsh, *Firewall*, pp. 55, 69, 170.

25. David M. Abshire, *Saving the Reagan Presidency*, p. 110. Abshire is careful to state Walsh's criticisms came after his White House tour had ended.

26. Ibid., p. 93.

27. Lawrence E. Walsh, *Second Interim Report to Congress by Independent Counsel for Iran/Contra Matters*, December 11, 1989, p. 60. Walsh also credited Abshire's efforts to cooperate in the first months of 1987. Abshire, *Saving the Reagan Presidency*, p. 110; Walsh, *Firewall*, pp. 56, 69.

28. Walsh, *Second Interim Report*, p. 53.

29. Jeffrey Toobin, *Opening Arguments: A Young Lawyer's First Case—United States v. Oliver North* (New York: Viking, 1991), pp. 172–173.

30. *Washington Post*, March 1, 1989; see also *New York Times*, February 28, 1989.

31. Toobin, *Opening Arguments*, p. 173.

32. "Memorandum of Law of the United States Department of Justice, as *Amicus Curiae* with Respect to the Independent Counsel's Opposition to the Defendant's Motions to Dismiss or Limit Count One," *United States v. North*, 708 F. Supp. 375 (D.D.C. 1988) (No. 88-0080-02), quoted in Harold Hongju Koh, *The National Security Constitution: Sharing Power after the Iran-Contra Affair* (New Haven, Conn.: Yale University Press, 1990), p. 28.

33. Gesell, cited in Walsh, *Firewall*, pp. 173–174.

34. Robert Dole, press release, "Walsh Investigation," August 11, 1992; *Washington Post*, November 11, 1992, April 11, 1993, and October 16, 1996.

35. Associated Press, June 16, 1992; *USA Today*, June 17, 1992.

36. The Abrams and Ledeen quotes are in the *New York Times Magazine*, July 4, 1993; Burton's remarks appear in *Congressional Record*, October 22, 1991, p. E3497.

37. *Washington Times*, September 23, 1992; Walsh, *Firewall*, p. 440; *Washington Post*, November 11, 1992.

38. *OIC Final Report*, vol. I, p. 113.

39. North, *Under Fire*, p. 390.

40. North, trial testimony, April 7, 1989, p. 6928.

41. *Washington Post*, April 8, 1989.

42. Rix, "War Stories."

43. See North, *Under Fire*, p. 393, for example.

44. Judge Gerhard Gesell, sentencing hearing for Oliver North, quoted in *New York Times*, July 6, 1989.

45. OIC attorney, interview with the author, February 5, 2007.

46. *OIC Final Report*, vol. I, p. 120.

47. Ibid., p. 121.

48. "I, to this day, do not recall ever hearing that there was a diversion. No one has proven to me that there was a diversion." Ronald Reagan, Poindexter trial transcript, February 17, 1990, p. 240.

49. *Chicago Tribune*, February 23, 1990.

50. Some observers found it peculiar Reagan would feel the need to give that instruction to his staff, "as if he could not take it for granted that they would do so as a matter of course." Draper, *A Very Thin Line*, p. 571.

51. See *OIC Final Report*, vol. I, pp. 131–134.

52. *New York Times*, June 12, 1990.

53. *Washington Post*, November 16, 1991; *New York Times*, November 16, 1991.

54. *New York Times*, November 25, 1989; Walsh, *Second Interim Report*, pp. 28–36; *OIC Final Report*, vol. I, pp. 288–292. After the dismissal, Fernandez did not hesitate to point fingers at his superiors in the CIA. He maintained several senior administration officials knew about his activities in Costa Rica but chose to let him take the blame. The officials included Fiers and George at the CIA and Abrams at the State Department. *New York Times*, November 26, 1989.

55. Walsh, *Second Interim Report*, pp. 40–45, 53–54.

56. Charles Hill, note, August 7, 1987, ALW0056370.

57. The independent counsel underscored the following quote from the book Donald Regan eventually produced: "All my life I have kept detailed notes of my workaday actions and conversations, and I did the same while I worked for the President." See *For the Record*, p. xiii, quoted in *OIC Final Report*, vol. I, p. 506, fn. 1.

58. *USA Today*, November 2, 1992.

59. Malcolm S. Forbes Jr., "Fact and Comment," *Forbes*, November 23, 1992; James J. Kilpatrick, Universal Press Syndicate, December 31, 1992.

60. According to Walsh, court schedules, the judge's decision not to grant a prosecution request for postponement, and the insistence of Weinberger's attorney on a speedy submission were among the factors behind the timing of the superseding indictment. He acknowledges telling his staff he had no objection to including the relevant excerpt from Weinberger's notes—recording Bush's support of the Iran initiative on January 7, 1986—and recalls thinking it would not be "newsworthy" because the substance of it had been in the public domain since Poindexter's July 1987 congressional testimony. Although "chagrined . . . that I had been oblivious to the dramatic effect of the quotation," he maintains he still "would not have modified an indictment for political reasons." Walsh, *Firewall*, pp. 447–449.

61. Walsh made the first statement on ABC's *Nightline* on December 24, 1992; the second is the name of a chapter in *Firewall*, p. 490.

62. *OIC Final Report*, vol. I, p. 445.

63. Mixter, *Reagan Criminal Liability*, pp. 5–7, 23.

64. Ibid., pp. 22, 34–35.

65. Ibid., pp. 36, 39, 46.

66. Ibid., pp. 36, 38, 42.

67. Ibid., p. 54.

68. Ibid., pp. 82, 84; John Poindexter, Select Committees' deposition, vol. B-20, p. 1311.

69. See *OIC Final Report*, vol. I, p. 446. For the response on Reagan's behalf, see ibid., vol. III, pp. 633–760.

70. Mixter, *Reagan Criminal Liability*, p. 160.

71. See *OIC Final Report*, vol. I, p. 465.

72. Lawrence Walsh, interview with National Public Radio, "All Things Considered," June 9, 1997.

73. Mixter, *Bush Criminal Liability*. Mixter points out that like his memo on Reagan, this one covers strictly potential criminal liability. It "is not focused on the wisdom of any Vice Presidential policies during the relevant period, or the candor or lack thereof that has been exhibited in Mr. Bush's public statements concerning Iran/Contra" (pp. 2–3).

74. See the Bush chapter in *OIC Final Report*, vol. I, pp. 473–483, esp. pp. 474–475.

75. Griffin B. Bell and J. Sedwick Sollers III, "Report to the President," January 15, 1993, p. 10.

76. Ibid., p. 12.

77. Liberman told the OIC and FBI the comment came from Gray's attorney, Richard Willard, in early December 1992, but that it might have come originally from Gray himself. (A second explanation related to OIC's deferral of the request until after the election.) See U.S. National Archives and Records Administration, RG 449, "Records of Independent Counsels," "Records of IC Lawrence Walsh," Folder: "Bush, George—Discovery and production of his transcribed diaries in 1992," "Record of Interview" with Lee S. Liberman, March 17, 1993, p. 11; see also Peter Kornbluh, "The Iran-Contra Scandal, 25 Years Later," *Salon*, November 25, 2011.

78. Bush diary, July 20, 1987.

79. See *OIC Final Report*, vol. I, p. 474. For the response on Bush's behalf, see ibid., vol. III, pp. 19–50. See also Lawrence E. Walsh, "Prepared Statement before the Senate Judiciary Committee Subcommittee on the Constitution, Federalism, and Property Rights," August 26, 1998.

80. *New York Times*, December 4, 1988.

81. Ibid., December 25, 1992.

82. Lawrence E. Walsh, *Fourth Interim Report to Congress by Independent Counsel for Iran/Contra Matters*, February 8, 1993, pp. 3, 76.

83. Lawrence E. Walsh, "Political Oversight, the Rule of Law, and Iran-Contra," speech first delivered at the Cleveland-Marshall College of Law on September 22, 1994, reprinted in *Cleveland State Law Review* 42 (1994): 587–597.

84. Walsh, *Fourth Interim Report*, p. 77.

85. *Newsweek*, January 4, 1993.

86. Walsh, *Firewall*, p. 495.

87. See *OIC Final Report*, vol. I, Chapter 24. For a fascinating analysis of Charles Hill's perspective, see Molly Worthen, *The Man on Whom Nothing Was Lost: The Grand Strategy of Charles Hill* (New York: Houghton Mifflin, 2005). The author, a former-student-turned-biographer of Hill, does not reject the allegation he deliberately withheld some of his notes. Instead, she details Hill's argument that partial records of isolated conversations, distilled and assembled without context, could give an impression of coherence and a level of understanding of events

Shultz and his advisors did not have at the time. In Worthen's words, "For purposes of piecing together Iran-Contra, Hill's notebooks were as capable of distorting as clarifying" (pp. 234–235).

88. Much was made of how often Meese failed to recall important events during his testimony before Congress and at the North trial. See, for example, John B. Oakes, op-ed, *New York Times*, February 4, 1985; also Maureen Dowd, *New York Times*, July 29, 1987. His longtime personal secretary, Florence Randolph, offered a revealing perspective: "He has a fantastic memory. I have never seen anybody with a memory like Mr. Meese's. . . . He is remarkable, absolutely." Quoted in Haynes Johnson, *Sleepwalking through History: America in the Reagan Years* (New York: Anchor Books), p. 89.

89. See *OIC Final Report*, vol. I, Chapter 31. For Edwin Meese's response, see ibid., vol. III, pp. 403–480; see also Meese, *With Reagan,* esp. pp. 294–301, 322–327.

90. See *OIC Final Report*, vol. I, Chapter 30. For Regan's response, see ibid., vol. III, pp. 761–794.

91. See ibid., vol. I, Chapter 15, esp. p. 221.

92. See ibid., Chapter 16, esp. pp. 226, 232.

93. *New York Times Magazine*, July 4, 1993.

94. Draper, "Walsh's Last Stand."

95. Samuel Dash, "Saturday Night Massacre II—Final Report of the Independent Counsel for Iran/Contra Matters (3 Volumes) by Lawrence E. Walsh," *Foreign Policy* 96 (Fall 1994): 173.

96. Quoted in Marjorie Williams, *Washington Post Magazine*, April 11, 1993.

97. Walsh, *Firewall*, p. 386.

98. This point was made by, among others, a majority staff attorney. Interview with the author, December 29, 2012.

99. Koh, *The National Security Constitution*, p. 29. See also Harold Hongju Koh, "Why the President (Almost) Always Wins in Foreign Affairs: Lessons of the Iran-Contra Affair," Yale Law School Faculty Scholarship Series paper 2071, 1988. http://digitalcommons.law.yale.edu/fss _papers/2071?utm_source=digitalcommons.law.yale.edu%2Ffss_papers%2F2071&utm_medi um=PDF&utm_campaign=PDFCoverPages.

100. Zornow interview.

101. Ibid.; Jeffrey Toobin, interview with the author, February 5, 2007.

102. See, for example, Liman, *Lawyer*, pp. 312–314, 352–353. A select committee majority staff attorney, who attended Walsh's first meeting with congressional committee leaders, corroborates published accounts he gave a "very poor performance" that hurt his case on Capitol Hill. Interview with the author, December 29, 2012.

103. *Washington Post Magazine*, April 11, 1993; Dole press release, August 11, 1992.

Conclusion

1. Marjorie Williams, *Washington Post*, September 19, 1991.

2. Abrams, *Undue Process*, p. 171.

3. Robert McFarlane, PROFS note to John Poindexter, "Perspective," November 15, 1986.

4. Egil Krogh, *New York Times*, June 13, 2012. See also, Egil "Bud" Krogh, with Matthew Krogh, *Integrity: Good People, Bad Choices, and Life Lessons from the White House* (New York: PublicAffairs, 2007).

5. Lee Hamilton, unpublished interview with Christian Ostermann, May 22, 2013.

6. See, for example, the recollections of former U.S. officials in Blight et al., *Becoming Enemies*, Chapter 4.

7. Hadi Semati, Iran-Iraq War Conference, p. 78. This view presumes these were TOWs acquired through the arms-for-hostages arrangement and not from a different source.

8. Former ambassador David Newton asked years later, "What if Iran-Contra hadn't happened? Would Saddam still have invaded Kuwait [in 1990]?" Furthermore, "If he hadn't invaded Kuwait, would the U.S. have later invaded Iraq? If we hadn't invaded Iraq in 2003, what then?" Blight et al., *Becoming Enemies*, p. 145. Another hypothetical question is whether a more positive outcome of the Iran initiative might have mitigated pressures within Iran to pursue a nuclear deterrent.

9. I am grateful to James G. Hershberg for his insights into this topic.

10. Quoted in Svetlana Savranskaya, Thomas Blanton, and Vladislav Zubok, *Masterpieces of History: The Peaceful End of the Cold War in Europe, 1989* (Budapest: Central European University Press, 2010), pp. 186–187; also, Jack Matlock, interview with the author, November 12, 2011.

11. See Elizabeth Charles, doctoral dissertation, "The Game Changer: Reassessing the Impact of SDI on Gorbachev's Foreign Policy, Arms Control, and US-Soviet Relations," George Washington University, August 31, 2010, pp. 250–252, 278, 281, 297, 306.

12. ABC, *This Week*, January 28, 2002.

13. Memorandum of Opinion for the Deputy Counsel to the President, "The President's Constitutional Authority to Conduct Military Operations against Terrorists and Nations Supporting Them," September 25, 2001.

Selected Bibliography

Note on Sources

The most important materials used to prepare this book were the declassified records released by the various official investigations into the Iran-Contra scandal, principally by the joint select congressional committees and the U.S. Office of the Independent Counsel (OIC). The President's Special Review Board (Tower Commission) contributed by reproducing dozens of important documents government censors later excised heavily before allowing their release to the public. A substantial body of additional documentation came from Freedom of Information Act (FOIA) and Mandatory Declassification Review (MDR) requests filed with federal agencies or the U.S. National Archives and Records Administration (NARA), particularly the "Records of Independent Counsel Lawrence Walsh Relating to Iran/Contra," part of Record Group 449.9.

In addition to NARA's facility in College Park, Maryland, the main government repository of relevance is the Ronald Reagan Presidential Library in Simi Valley, California. The materials gathered for this book from those locales and through the FOIA are also available at the National Security Archive, a nongovernmental research organization, library, and publisher based at George Washington University in Washington, D.C. The archive began collecting these records systematically in the 1980s, and its staff has worked steadily over the years to break loose additional documentation through research and use of the FOIA.

A mountain of public source material exists on the Iran-Contra affair that cannot be reflected adequately here. From 1986–1992, the scandal generated thousands of print and television news stories as well as opinion pieces. Hundreds more articles appeared in scholarly and legal journals. Among all these sources, and despite some notable gaps and flaws in U.S. media treatment of the scandal, the work of several journalists and authors deserves recognition. At the risk of omitting some excellent reporting, the best daily coverage generally came from Walter Pincus, Joe Pichirallo, Patrick Tyler, Haynes Johnson (commentary), and others at the *Washington Post*; Stephen Engelberg, Jeff Gerth, Philip Shenon, Joel Brinkley, James LeMoyne, Seymour Hersh, Stephen Kinzer, David Johnston, and others from the *New York Times*; Doyle McManus, Jane Mayer, and their colleagues at the *Los Angeles Times*; Alfonso Chardy, Sam Dillon, and the staff of the *Miami Herald*; Roy Gutman and Knute Royce of *Newsday*; Jonathan Kwitny at the *Wall Street Journal*; and Robert Parry, Brian Barger, and Pete Yost of the Associated Press. (Parry and Barger broke some of the earliest stories about Oliver North's secret Contra activities.) Jefferson Morley of the *New Republic* and the *Nation*, and David Corn of the *Nation* provided a steady flow of news and analysis. The *New York Review of Books* printed several important assessments by Theodore Draper, Mark Danner, and others. On television, the ABC program *Nightline* with Ted Koppel, the PBS program *Frontline*, Bill Moyers, and certain network reporters (for example, David Martin of CBS and Brian Ross of NBC) often stood out for their coverage.

A surprising amount of material is available from other countries. For example, the Iranian, Nicaraguan, and Israeli media covered many stories accessible either in English or through translations provided by the BBC and the U.S. Foreign Broadcast Information Service (FBIS). Iranian media in recent years have published fascinating interviews with leading figures including Ayatollah Montazeri, Akbar Hashemi Rafsanjani, Mohsen Rezaie, Ali Akbar Velayati, and others directly involved in the arms-for-hostages initiative, such as Rafsanjani's nephew, Ali Bahramani. Numerous memoirs also cover relevant issues.

Beyond these sources, I conducted several dozen interviews with people who took part in the clandestine operations, members of the National Security Council staff, Central Intelligence Agency officials, members of Congress and their staff, attorneys at the OIC, and other investigators. (Many of those directly involved declined to be interviewed or did not respond to requests.) I also spoke with Iranian officials and experts based in Tehran, former Contras and Sandinistas, Israeli military and civilian officials, and ex-diplomats and party officials from the Soviet Union and its former allies.

For all the valuable materials available, it should be little surprise the accessible record represents only a small percentage of the total record, most of which remains out of the public eye. U.S. government archives, for example, hold millions of pages of classified documentation on foreign, military, and intelligence policy toward the Middle East and Central America from the 1980s. Other governments have been far less open with their records, and there is little expectation they will be forthcoming in the future.

Books, Document Compilations, and Government Sources

Abrams, Elliott. *Undue Process: A Story of How Political Differences Are Turned into Crimes*. New York: Free Press, 1993.

Abshire, David M. *Saving the Reagan Presidency: Trust Is the Coin of the Realm*. College Station: Texas A&M University Press, 2005.

Alterman, Eric. *Why Presidents Lie: A History of Official Deception and Its Consequences*. New York: Viking, 2005.

Anderson, Martin. *Revolution: The Reagan Legacy*. Stanford, Calif.: Hoover Institution Press, 1990.

Armony, Ariel C. *Argentina, the United States, and the Anti-Communist Crusade in Central America, 1977–1984*. Athens: Ohio University Press, 1997.

Arnson, Cynthia J. *Crossroads: Congress, the President, and Central America, 1976–1993*, 2nd ed. University Park: Pennsylvania State University Press, 1993.

Association for Diplomatic Studies and Training. *Frontline Diplomacy: The Foreign Affairs Oral History Collection of the Association for Diplomatic Studies and Training*. Library of Congress website, http://memory.loc.gov/ammem/collections/diplomacy.

Barrett, David M. *The CIA and Congress: The Untold Story from Truman to Kennedy*. Lawrence: University Press of Kansas, 2005.

Battle, Joyce. *Iraqgate: Saddam Hussein, U.S. Policy, and the Prelude to the Persian Gulf War, 1980–1994*. Alexandria, Va.: Chadwyck-Healey, 1995.

Benjamin, Daniel, and Steven Simon. *The Age of Sacred Terror: Radical Islam's War against America*. New York: Random House, 2003.

Bergman, Ronen. *The Secret War with Iran: The 30-Year Clandestine Struggle against the World's Most Dangerous Terrorist Power*. New York: Free Press, 2008.

Blanton, Tom, ed. *White House E-Mail: The Top Secret Computer Messages the Reagan/Bush White House Tried to Destroy*. New York: New Press, 1995.

Blight, James G., janet Lang, Hussein Banai, Malcolm Byrne, and John Tirman. *Becoming Enemies: U.S.-Iran Relations and the Iran-Iraq War, 1979–1988*. Lanham, Md.: Rowman and Littlefield, 2012.

Bok, Sissela. *Lying: Moral Choice in Public and Private Life*. New York: Vintage, 1999.

Bradlee, Ben, Jr. *Guts and Glory: The Rise and Fall of Oliver North*. New York: Donald I. Fine, 1988.

Brown, Timothy C. *The Real Contra War: Highlander Peasant Resistance in Nicaragua*. Norman: University of Oklahoma Press, 2001.

Byrne, Malcolm, Scott Armstrong, Tom Blanton, and the staff of the National Security Archive, eds. *The Chronology: The Documented Day-by-Day Account of Secret Military Assistance to Iran and the Contras*. New York: Warner Books, 1987.

Byrne, Malcolm, and Peter Kornbluh. *The Iran-Contra Affair: The Making of a Scandal, 1983–1988*. Alexandria, Va.: Chadwyck-Healey, 1990.

Byrne, Malcolm, and Jeffrey T. Richelson. *Terrorism and U.S. Policy, 1968–2002*. Alexandria, Va.: Chadwyck-Healey, 2003.

Cameron, Bruce P. *My Life in the Time of the Contras*. Albuquerque: University of New Mexico Press, 2007.

Cannon, Lou. *President Reagan: The Role of a Lifetime*. New York: Simon and Schuster, 1991.

Central Intelligence Agency Inspector General. *Report of Investigation Concerning Allegations of Connections between CIA and the Contras in Cocaine Trafficking to the United States*. Vol. I: *The California Story*, January 29, 1998; Vol. II: *The Contra Story*, October 8, 1998.

Clarridge, Duane R., with Digby Diehl. *A Spy for All Seasons: My Life in the CIA*. New York: Scribner's, 1997.

Cohen, William S., and George J. Mitchell. *Men of Zeal: A Candid Inside Story of the Iran-Contra Hearings*. New York: Viking, 1988.

Crist, David. *The Twilight War: The Secret History of America's Thirty-Year Conflict with Iran*. New York: Penguin Books, 2012.

Cruz, Arturo, Jr. *Memoirs of a Counterrevolutionary: Life with the Contras, the Sandinistas, and the CIA*. New York: Doubleday, 1989.

Deaver, Michael K., with Mickey Herskowitz. *Behind the Scenes*. New York: William Morrow, 1987.

Dickey, Christopher. *With the Contras: A Reporter in the Wilds of Nicaragua*. New York: Simon and Schuster, 1987.

Dillon, Sam. *Comandos: The CIA and Nicaragua's Contra Rebels*. New York: Henry Holt, 1991.

Doyle, Kate. *El Salvador: War, Peace, and Human Rights, 1980–1994*. Alexandria, Va.: Chadwyck-Healey, 1996.

Draper, Theodore. *A Very Thin Line: The Iran-Contra Affairs*. New York: Hill and Wang, 1991.

Emerson, Steven. *Secret Warriors: Inside the Covert Military Operations of the Reagan Era*. New York: Putnam's, 1988.

Fisher, Louis. *Presidential War Power*. Lawrence: University Press of Kansas, 2004.

Galster, Steven R. *Afghanistan: The Making of U.S. Policy, 1973–1990*. Alexandria, Va.: Chadwyck-Healey, 1991.

Garvin, Glenn. *Everybody Had His Own Gringo: The CIA and the Contras*. New York: Brassey's, 1992.

Gates, Robert M. *From the Shadows: The Ultimate Insider's Story of Five Presidents and How They Won the Cold War*. New York: Simon and Schuster, 1996.

Glennon, Michael J. *Constitutional Diplomacy*. Princeton, N.J.: Princeton University Press, 1990.

Greenberg, Gerald S., ed. *Historical Encyclopedia of U.S. Independent Counsel Investigations*. Westport, Conn.: Greenwood Press, 2000.

Gutman, Roy. *Banana Diplomacy: The Making of American Policy in Nicaragua, 1981–1987*. New York: Simon and Schuster, 1988.

Haig, Alexander M. Jr. *Caveat: Realism, Reagan, and Foreign Policy*. New York: Macmillan, 1984.

Hayward, Steven F. *The Age of Reagan: The Conservative Counterrevolution, 1980–1989*. New York: Crown Forum, 2009.

Henkin, Louis. *Constitutionalism, Democracy, and Foreign Affairs*. New York: Columbia University Press, 1990.

———. *Foreign Affairs and the U.S. Constitution*. New York: Oxford University Press, 1996.

Hewitt, Gavin. *Terry Waite and Ollie North: The Untold Story of the Kidnapping—and the Release*. Boston: Little, Brown, 1991.

Johnson, Haynes. *Sleepwalking through History: America in the Reagan Years*. New York: W. W. Norton and Company, 1991.

Johnson, Loch K. *America's Secret Power: The CIA in a Democratic Society*. New York: Oxford University Press, 1991.

Kagan, Robert. *A Twilight Struggle: American Power and Nicaragua, 1977–1990*. New York: Free Press, 1996.

Kinzer, Stephen. *Blood of Brothers: Life and War in Nicaragua*. New York: Putnam's, 1991.

Koh, Harold Hongju. *The National Security Constitution: Sharing Power after the Iran-Contra Affair*. New Haven, Conn.: Yale University Press, 1990.

Kornbluh, Peter. *Nicaragua: The Making of U.S. Policy, 1978–1990*. Alexandria, Va.: Chadwyck-Healey, 1991.

———. *Nicaragua: The Price of Intervention*. Washington, D.C.: Institute for Policy Studies.

Kornbluh, Peter, and Malcolm Byrne, eds. *The Iran-Contra Scandal: The Declassified History*. New York: New Press, 1993.

Lafeber, Walter. *Inevitable Revolutions: The United States in Central America*. New York: W. W. Norton, 1983.

Ledeen, Michael A. *Perilous Statecraft: An Insider's Account of the Iran-Contra Affair*. New York: Scribner's, 1988.

Liman, Arthur L., with Peter Israel. *Lawyer: A Life of Counsel and Controversy*. New York: Public Affairs, 1998.

MacKenzie, John P. *Absolute Power: How the Unitary Executive Theory Is Undermining the Constitution*. New York: Century Foundation Press, 2008.

Mann, James. *Rise of the Vulcans: The History of Bush's War Cabinet*. New York: Penguin Books, 2004.

Martin, David C., and John Walcott. *Best Laid Plans: The Inside Story of America's War against Terrorism*. New York: HarperCollins, 1988.

May, Christopher. *Presidential Defiance of "Unconstitutional" Laws: Reviving the Royal Prerogative*. New York: Praeger, 1998.

Mayer, Jane, and Doyle McManus. *Landslide: The Unmaking of the President, 1984–1988*. Boston: Houghton Mifflin, 1988.

McFarlane, Robert C., with Zofia Smardz. *Special Trust*. New York: Cadell and Davies, 1994.

Meese, Edwin, III. *With Reagan: The Inside Story*. Washington, D.C.: Regnery Gateway, 1992.

Menges, Constantine C. *Inside the National Security Council: The True Story of the Making and Unmaking of Reagan's Foreign Policy*. New York: Simon and Schuster, 1988.

Morris, Edmund. *Dutch: A Memoir of Ronald Reagan*. New York: Modern Library, 1999.

Moyers, Bill. *The Secret Government: The Constitution in Crisis.* Washington, D.C.: Seven Locks Press, 1988.

Naftali, Timothy. *Blind Spot: The Secret History of American Counterterrorism.* New York: Basic-Books, 2006.

Neustadt, Richard E. *Presidential Power and the Modern Presidents: The Politics of Leadership from Roosevelt to Reagan.* New York: Free Press, 1991.

Noonan, Peggy. *What I Saw at the Revolution: A Political Life in the Reagan Era.* New York: Random House, 1990.

North, Oliver L., with William Novak. *Under Fire: An American Story.* New York: HarperCollins, 1991.

Pardo-Maurer, R. *The Contras, 1980–1989: A Special Kind of Politics.* New York: Praeger, 1990.

Parsi, Trita. *Treacherous Alliance: The Secret Dealings of Israel, Iran, and the U.S.* New Haven, Conn.: Yale University Press, 2007.

Pastor, Robert A. <u>Not</u> *Condemned to Repetition: The United States and Nicaragua.* Rev. ed. Boulder, Colo.: Westview Press, 2002.

Persico, Joseph E. *Casey: From the OSS to the CIA.* New York: Viking, 1990.

Picco, Giandomenico. *Man without a Gun: One Diplomat's Secret Struggle to Free the Hostages, Fight Terrorism, and End a War.* New York: Times Books, 1999.

Powell, Colin L., with Joseph E. Persico. *My American Journey.* New York: Random House, 2003.

Prados, John. *CIA Covert Operations: From Carter to Obama, 1977–2010.* Alexandria, Va.: Chadwyck-Healey, 2013.

————. *Keepers of the Keys: A History of the National Security Council from Truman to Bush.* New York: William Morrow, 1991.

————. *Presidents' Secret Wars: CIA and Pentagon Covert Operations from World War II through the Persian Gulf War.* Chicago: Ivan R. Dee, 1996.

————. *Safe for Democracy: The Secret Wars of the CIA.* Chicago: Ivan R. Dee, 2006.

Ranstorp, Magnus. *Hizb'allah in Lebanon: The Politics of the Western Hostage Crisis.* London: Macmillan, 1997.

Raviv, Dan, and Yossi Melman, *Every Spy a Prince: The Complete History of Israel's Intelligence Community.* (New York: Houghton Mifflin, 1991).

Reagan, Ron. *My Father at 100: A Memoir.* New York: Viking, 2011.

Reagan, Ronald. *An American Life.* New York: Simon and Schuster, 1990.

————. *The Reagan Diaries: Unabridged.* Edited by Douglas Brinkley. 2 vols. New York: Harper-Collins, 2009.

Reeves, Richard. *President Reagan: The Triumph of Imagination.* New York: Simon and Schuster, 2005.

Regan, Donald T. *For the Record: From Wall Street to Washington.* New York: Harcourt Brace Jovanovich, 1988.

Richelson, Jeffrey T. *Presidential Directives on National Security from Truman to Clinton.* Alexandria, Va.: Chadwyck-Healey, 1994.

————. *Presidential Directives on National Security, Part II: From Harry Truman to George W. Bush.* Alexandria, Va.: Chadwyck-Healey, 2003.

————. *U.S. Espionage and Intelligence: Organization, Operations, and Management, 1947–1996.* Alexandria, Va.: Chadwyck-Healey, 1997.

————. *The U.S. Intelligence Community: Organization, Operations, and Management, 1947–1989.* Alexandria, Va.: Chadwyck-Healey, 1990.

Rodriguez, Felix I., and John Weisman. *Shadow Warrior.* New York: Pocket Books, 1989.

Rothkopf, David. *Running the World: The Inside Story of the National Security Council and the Architects of American Power.* New York: PublicAffairs, 2006.

Rudman, Warren B. *Combat: Twelve Years in the U.S. Senate.* New York: Random House, 1996.

Savage, Charlie. *Takeover: The Return of the Imperial Presidency and the Subversion of American Democracy.* Boston: Little, Brown, 2007.

Savranskaya, Svetlana, Thomas Blanton, and Vladislav Zubok. *Masterpieces of History: The Peaceful End of the Cold War in Europe, 1989.* Budapest: Central European University Press, 2010.

Schieffer, Bob, and Gary Paul Gates. *The Acting President.* New York: Dutton, 1990.

Secord, Richard, with Jay Wurts. *Honored and Betrayed: Irangate, Covert Affairs, and the Secret War in Laos.* New York: Wiley, 1992.

Segev, Samuel. *The Iranian Triangle: The Untold Story of Israel's Role in the Iran-Contra Affair.* Translated by Haim Watzman. New York: Free Press, 1988.

Shultz, George P. *Turmoil and Triumph: My Years as Secretary of State.* New York: Scribner's, 1993.

Singlaub, John K., with Malcolm McConnell. *Hazardous Duty: An American Soldier in the Twentieth Century.* New York: Summit Books, 1991.

Skinner, Kiron K., Annelise Anderson, and Martin Anderson, eds. *Reagan: A Life in Letters.* New York: Free Press, 2003.

———. *Reagan in His Own Hand: The Writings of Ronald Reagan That Reveal His Revolutionary Vision for America.* New York: Free Press, 2001.

Smist, Frank J., Jr. *Congress Oversees the United States Intelligence Community, 1947–1989.* Knoxville: University of Tennessee Press, 1990.

Taheri, Amir. *Nest of Spies: America's Journey to Disaster in Iran.* New York: Pantheon Books, 1988.

Tanter, Raymond. *Who's at the Helm? Lessons of Lebanon.* Boulder, Colo.: Westview Press, 1990.

Teicher, Howard, and Gayle Radley Teicher. *Twin Pillars to Desert Storm: America's Flawed Vision in the Middle East from Nixon to Bush.* New York: William Morrow, 1993.

Timberg, Robert. *The Nightingale's Song.* New York: Simon and Schuster, 1995.

Toobin, Jeffrey. *Opening Arguments: A Young Lawyer's First Case—United States v. Oliver North.* New York: Viking, 1991.

Tower, John, Edmund S. Muskie, and Brent Scowcroft. *Report of the President's Special Review Board.* Washington, D.C.: U.S. Government Printing Office, February 26, 1987.

Treverton, Gregory F. *Covert Action: The Limits of Intervention in the Postwar World.* New York: BasicBooks, 1987.

U.S. House Committee on Foreign Affairs. *The Foreign Policy Implications of Arms Sales to Iran and the Contra Connection: Hearings before the House Committee on Foreign Affairs.* 99th Congress, 2nd Sess., 1986.

U.S. House of Representatives. *Joint Report of the Task Force to Investigate Certain Allegations Concerning the Holding of American Hostages by Iran in 1980.* 102nd Congress, 2nd Sess., 1993. House Report no. 102-11-2, January 3.

U.S. Senate Committee on Foreign Relations, Subcommittee on Terrorism, Narcotics, and International Operations. *Drugs, Law Enforcement, and Foreign Policy.* 100th Congress, 2nd Sess., 1988. Senate Report 100-165.

U.S. Senate Select Committee on Intelligence. *Nomination of Robert M. Gates To Be Director of Central Intelligence.* 3 vols. 102nd Congress, 1st Sess., 1991. Senate Hearing 102-799.

———. *Preliminary Inquiry into the Sale of Arms to Iran and Possible Diversion of Funds to the Nicaraguan Resistance.* 100th Congress, 1st Sess., 1987. Senate Report 7, February 2.

———. *Were Relevant Documents Withheld from the Congressional Committees Investigating the Iran-Contra Affair?* 101st Congress, 1st Sess., 1989. Senate Report 101-44. Washington, D.C.: U.S. Government Printing Office, June.

U.S. Senate Select Committee on Secret Military Assistance to Iran and the Nicaraguan Opposition, and House Select Committee to Investigate Covert Arms Transactions with Iran. *Iran-Contra Investigation: Joint Hearings.* Vols. 100-1–100-11. 100th Congress, 1st Sess., 1987. Senate Report 100-216.

———. *Report of the Congressional Committees Investigating the Iran-Contra Affair, with Supplemental, Minority, and Additional Views.* 100th Congress, 1st Sess., 1987. Senate Report 100-216, November.

———. *Report of the Congressional Committees Investigating the Iran-Contra Affair.* Appendix A: Exhibits, vols. 1–2.

———. *Report of the Congressional Committees Investigating the Iran-Contra Affair.* Appendix B: Depositions, vols. 1–27.

———. *Report of the Congressional Committees Investigating the Iran-Contra Affair.* Appendix C: Chronology of Events.

———. *Report of the Congressional Committees Investigating the Iran-Contra Affair.* Appendix D: Testimonial Chronology, vols. 1–5.

Walker, Thomas W., ed. *Revolution and Counterrevolution in Nicaragua.* Boulder, Colo.: Westview Press, 1991.

Wallison, Peter. *Ronald Reagan: The Power of Conviction and the Success of His Presidency.* New York: Westview Press, 2004.

Walsh, Lawrence E. *Final Report of the Independent Counsel for Iran/Contra Matters.* U.S. Court of Appeals for the District of Columbia Circuit, August 4, 1993. Vol. I: *Investigations and Prosecutions*; vol. II: *Indictments, Plea Agreements, Interim Reports to the Congress, and Administrative Matters*; vol. III: *Comments and Materials Submitted by Individuals and Their Attorneys Responding to Volume I of the Final Report.*

———. *Firewall: The Iran-Contra Conspiracy and Cover-Up.* New York: W.W. Norton, 1997.

Weinberger, Caspar. *Fighting for Peace: Seven Critical Years in the Pentagon.* New York: Warner Books, 1990.

Westad, Odd Arne. *Global Cold War: Third World Interventions and the Making of Our Times.* Cambridge: Cambridge University Press, 2007.

Wills, Gary. *Reagan's America.* New York: Penguin Books, 1988.

Wise, David. *The Politics of Lying: Government Deception, Secrecy, and Power.* New York: Random House, 1973.

Woodward, Bob. *Veil: The Secret Wars of the CIA, 1981–1987.* New York: Simon and Schuster, 1987.

Wright, Robin. *Sacred Rage: The Wrath of Militant Islam.* New York: Simon and Schuster, 1985.

Wroe, Ann. *Lives, Lies, and the Iran-Contra Affair.* New York: I. B. Tauris, 1991.

Index

and Israel's role in Iran arms deals, 157, 371n44
and Nicaraguan harbor mining, 26–27
and Nir briefing, 241–242
notes of, 320, 324–325
pardons of Iran-Contra participants, 321, 325–326, 331
and Reagan's press conference (November 19, 1986), 265–266, 270, 275, 393n68
and Rodriguez, 183, 184, 218, 220, 234–235, 293
Bush, George W., 304, 338–339
Bustillo, Juan Rafael, 52, 136, 175, 183, 218, 219–220, 228
Byrd, Robert C., 280

Calero, Adolfo, 110 (photo)
and arms purchases, 52, 125–126
and Avirgan-Honey lawsuit, 216
congressional testimony of, 292–293
and Contra aid, 81, 89, 90, 361n45
and Contra resupply operations, 214
and humanitarian aid, 135
and Monimbó, 56
and North, 47, 55, 57, 127, 177, 292, 314
and North's, traveler's check of, 222, 292–293
and Pastora, 177, 375n34
and private fundraising, 136–138
and Santa Clara helicopter crash (1984), 54
and Secord, 49–50, 366n9
Calero, Mario, 127
Cannistraro, Vincent M., 48, 367n35
Cannon, James, 287
Caribbean Basin Initiative, 20
Carmon, Chaim, 103
Carter, Jimmy, 10, 14, 16, 17, 35, 40
Casey, William J., 13, 22, 26, 112 (photo)
background of, 13, 358n4
and Boland Amendments, 22, 56, 58
and Central America policy, 11, 15, 45
and Clarridge, 18–19, 47
Cold War views of, 11, 61, 169, 178–179
congressional testimony of, 266–267, 295, 394n74, 394n78
and Contra aid, 49, 78, 79, 169, 374n7

and Contra aid, request for legal opinion on, 83–84
and Contra aid from Guatemala, 88
and covert operations, 13, 29, 286
and Ghorbanifar, 160–161
and HAWK-missile shipments, 365n74
and independent counsel investigation, 327–328
and Iran policy, 59–62, 355n14
Nicaragua harbor mining, 347n83
and North, 42, 46–47, 57
and NSC-led Contra operations, 57–58
Presidential Finding on covert operations, 25
and Secord, 49
See also Central Intelligence Agency
Castillo Tomás. See Fernandez, Joseph
Catholic Church (Nicaragua), 58
Cavaco Silva, Aníbal, 99
Cave, George, 188, 192, 249, 252, 276
background of, 187
and Bahramani, 244, 247
and Ghorbanifar, 388n13
and Israel, 34, 349n30, 377n2
and Kangarlou, 193, 239, 379n27
and McFarlane mission to Tehran, 194, 196–198, 200, 201, 381nn61–62
and McFarlane mission to Tehran, assessment of, 203–205, 382n80
and "second channel," 251
Central American Task Force (CATF), 57, 129, 133
Central Intelligence Agency, 14
and Boland Amendment II, 42, 68, 292, 294
and Central America, 14
and Contra drug trade, 132–134
and Contra operations, 16, 18, 21, 25–26, 42, 46–47, 57–58, 293, 294 (see also Clarridge, Duane "Dewey"; Fernandez, Joseph; Rodriguez, Felix I.)
and Costa Rica, 88
and Defense Department cooperation, 20, 23–24
documents, withholding of, 14, 312
and domestic lobbying, 22